西安 XI'AN STATISTICAL YEARBOOK

2012

统计年鉴

中国统计出版社
China Statistics Press

西安市统计局
XI'AN MUNICIPAL BUREAU OF STATISTICS
国家统计局西安调查队
NBS SURVEY OFFICE IN XI'AN

（京）新登字 041 号

图书在版编目（CIP）数据

西安统计年鉴.2012 / 西安市统计局，国家统计局西安调查队 编.
—北京：中国统计出版社，2012.9
ISBN 978-7-5037-6652-7/C.2723

Ⅰ.①西…
Ⅱ.①西… ②国…
Ⅲ.①统计资料-西安市-2012-年鉴
Ⅳ.①C832.411-54

中国版本图书馆CIP数据核字（2012）第193585号

西安统计年鉴—2012

作　　者/ 西安市统计局　国家统计局西安调查队
责任编辑/ 陈越月
责任校对/ 赵群洁
封面设计/ 优尼布雷广告有限公司
出版发行/ 中国统计出版社
通信地址/ 北京市西城区月坛南街57号　邮编 100826
办公地址/ 北京市丰台区西三环南路甲6号
电　　话/（010）63376907
网　　址/ http://csp.stats.gov.cn
印　　刷/ 中煤地西安地图制印有限公司
经　　销/ 新华书店
开　　本/ 890×1240毫米　1/16
字　　数/ 1358千字
印　　张/ 42.5
版　　别/ 2012年9月第1版
版　　次/ 2012年9月第1次印刷
书　　号/ ISBN 978-7-5037-6652-7/C·2723
定　　价/ 260.00元

《西安统计年鉴—2012》编辑部

XI'AN STATISTICAL YEARBOOK-2012
EDITORLAL STAFF

编者说明

一、《西安统计年鉴2012》系统收录了全市、区县及开发区2011年经济、社会各方面统计数据，以及重要历史年份主要统计数据，是一部全面记载西安市国民经济和社会发展情况的大型连续性统计文献资料和重要工具书。

二、本年鉴正文内容分为二十个篇章：（一）综合；（二）国民经济核算；（三）人口、从业人员与职工工资；（四）固定资产投资；（五）财政；（六）物价指数；（七）人民生活；（八）城市公用事业；（九）环境保护；（十）农业；（十一）工业；（十二）能源；（十三）建筑业；（十四）运输和邮电；（十五）国内贸易；（十六）对外经济贸易和旅游；（十七）金融业；（十八）教育和科技；（十九）文化、体育、卫生、社会福利和其他；（二十）企业调查。同时，为方便读者使用，各篇章前设有简要说明和2011年主要统计指标，对本篇章的主要内容、资料来源、以及历史变动情况予以简要概述，篇末附有主要统计指标解释。

三、为便于国内外读者查阅，本年鉴全部内容均采用中英文对照编辑。

四、本年鉴各篇资料均为正式年报数，因此，凡与本年鉴有出入的均以本年鉴为准。

五、本年鉴中的部分指标合计数或相对数由于单位取舍不同产生的计算误差均未作机械调整。

六、本年鉴所使用的计量单位均依据2011年统计报表制度。

七、本年鉴使用的符号说明：“空白”表示该项统计指标无数据或数据不详；“#”表示其中项。

感谢社会各界长期以来对《西安统计年鉴》的广泛关注和大力支持。为进一步做好工作，更好地为广大读者服务，希望社会各界提出宝贵意见。

PREFACE

I. Xi'an Statistical Yearbook 2012 is a periodical statistic yearbook which record economic and social development of Xi'an all-around, with its features of comprehensive and intensive information, which pratically provides data covering the situation of social and economic developments and changes of 2011 in Xi'an. The book is an excellent publicity material to introduce Xi'an City to the different people from the home and abroad.

II.The yearbook covers the Xi'an's various aspects of economic and social developments in 2011 and some selected data series in historical important years and since 'reform and opening'. The book contains 20 parts, 1.General Survey; 2.National Economic Account; 3.Population, Employment and Wages; 4.Investment in Fixed Assets; 5. Government Finance; 6.Price Indices; 7.People's Livelihood; 8.Urban Public Utilities; 9.Environmental Protection; 10.Agriculture; 11.Industry; 12.Energy; 13.Construction; 14.Transportation, Post and Telecommunication Service; 15.Domestic Trade; 16.Foreign Trade; 17.Banking and Insurance; 18.Education, Science and Technology; 19.Culture, Sports, Public Health, Social Welfare Institutions and Other Social Activities; 20.Enterprises Investigation. As insert pages including statistical graphs and charts.

III. For the convenience of being consulted by foreigners, the book is Chinese-English bilingual edition, while providing brief introduction and explanatory notes on main indicators at end of each part. Also, the Yearbook has the foundation of processing data,drawing data-map and inquiring data quickly.

IV. All the data in this yearbook are from formal annual report. If there are some differences between the historic information and the data of this yearbook, we should take the data in this book as the standard.

V. Statistical discrepancies due to rounding are not adjusted automatically in this yearbook.

VI. The units of measurement used in the Yearbook are based on 2011 statistical reporting system.

VII. Explanations on symbols used in this yearbook:

(blank) indicates the data not available;

\# indicates the items of the total.

Here we would like to express our sincere thanks to the people for their concerning and support to the Xi'an Statistical Yearbook. In order to do better and provide better service to readers, we hope that the whole society fields can propose constructive advices.

生产总值（亿元）

Gross Domestic Product(100 million yuan)

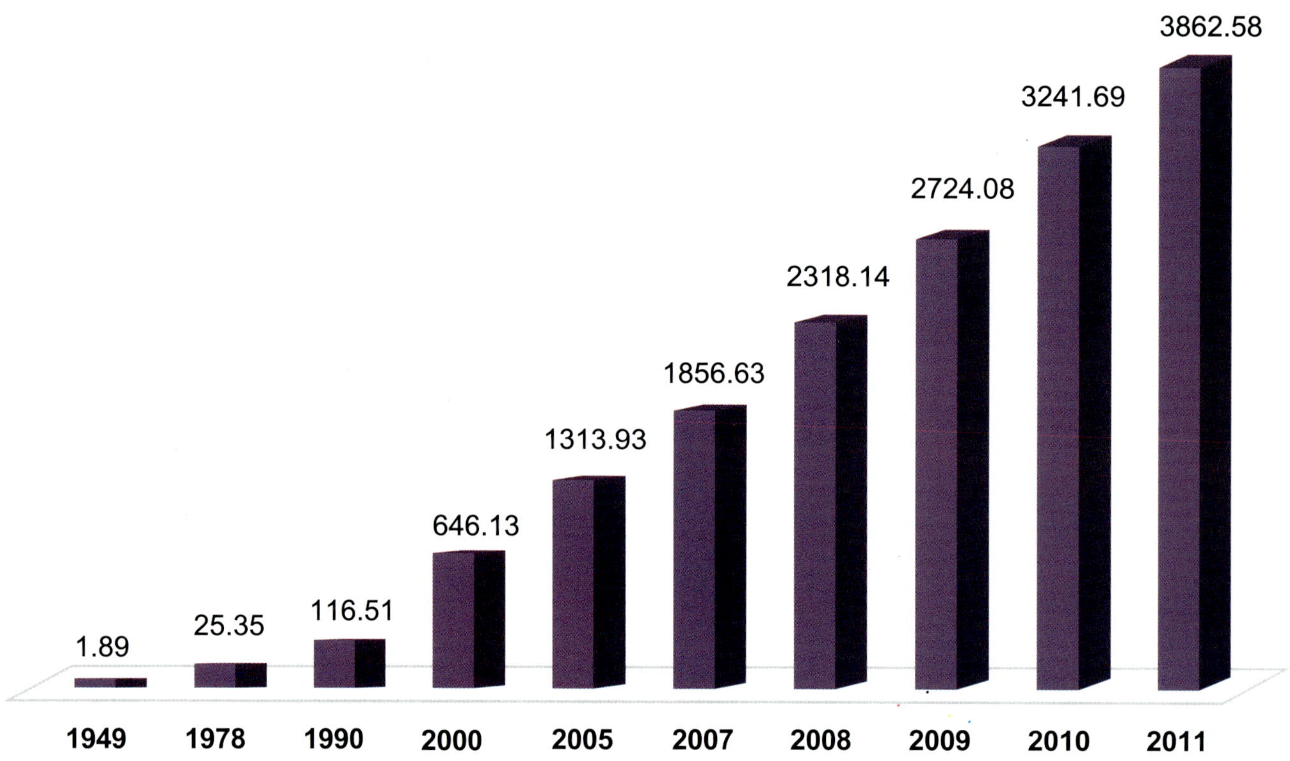

生产总值指数（以上年为100）

Indices of Gross Domestic Product(preceding year=100)

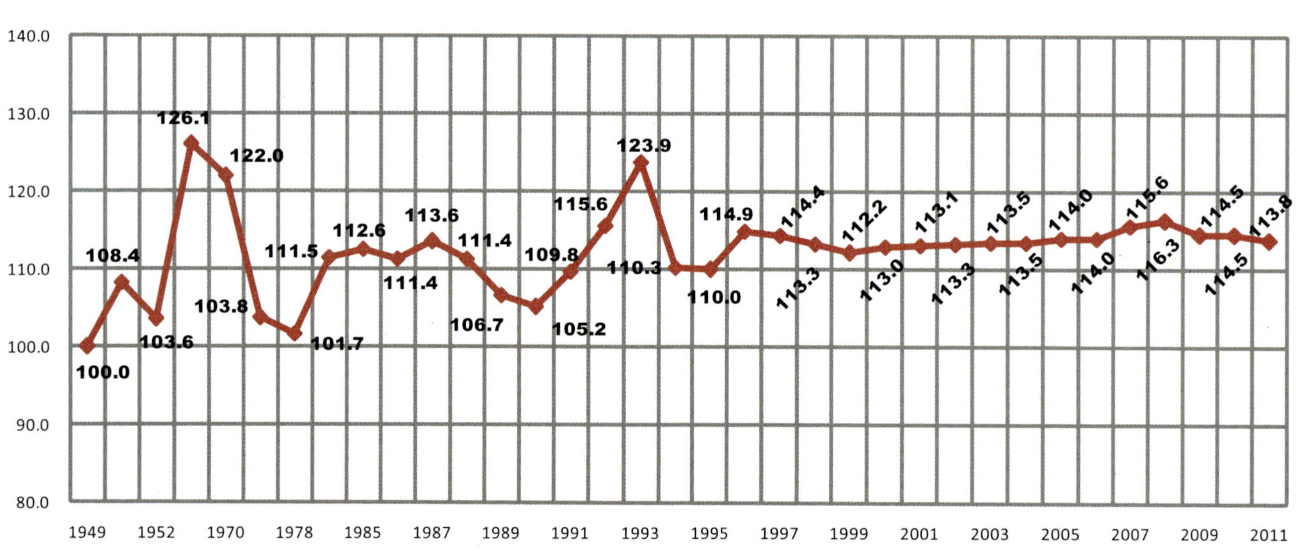

生产总值构成（%）

Composition of Gross Domestic Product(%)

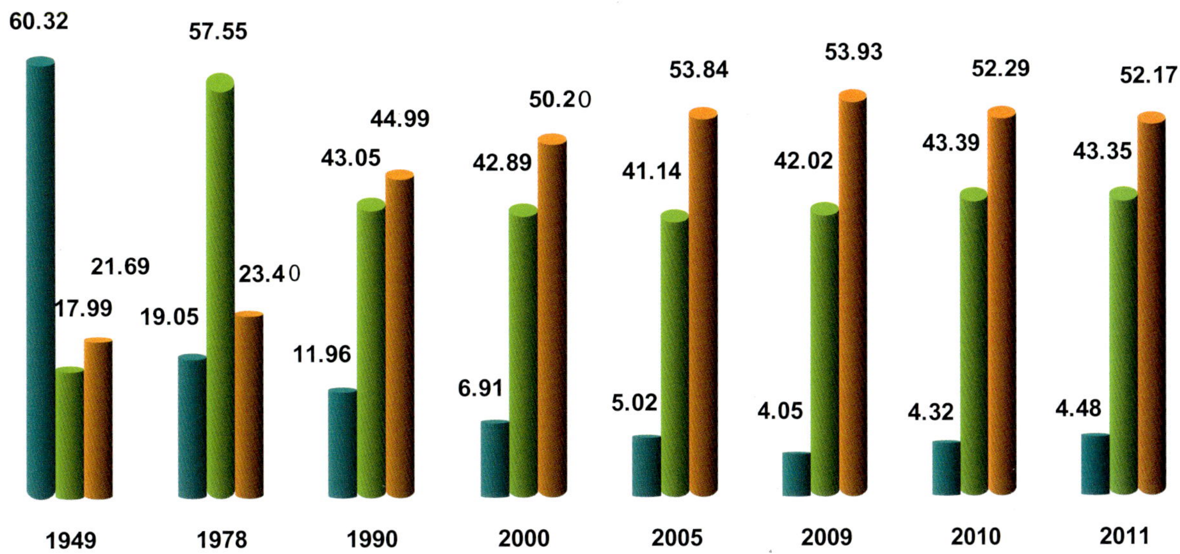

人均GDP(元/人)

Per Capita GDP(yuan/person)

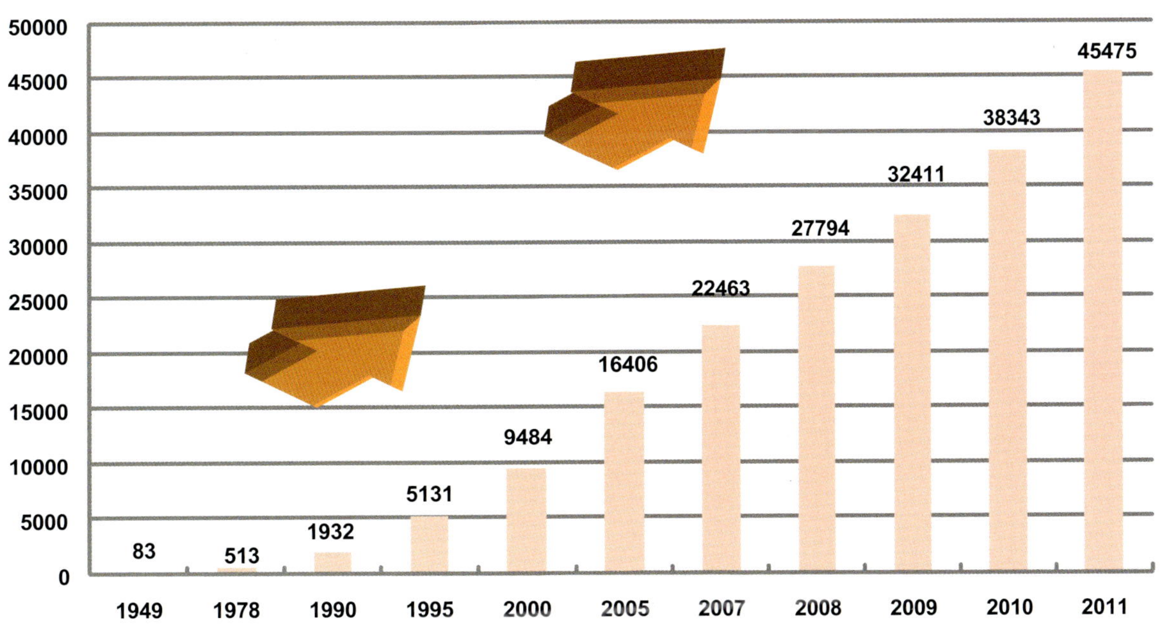

年末常住人口（万人）

Year-end Permanent population (10000 persons)

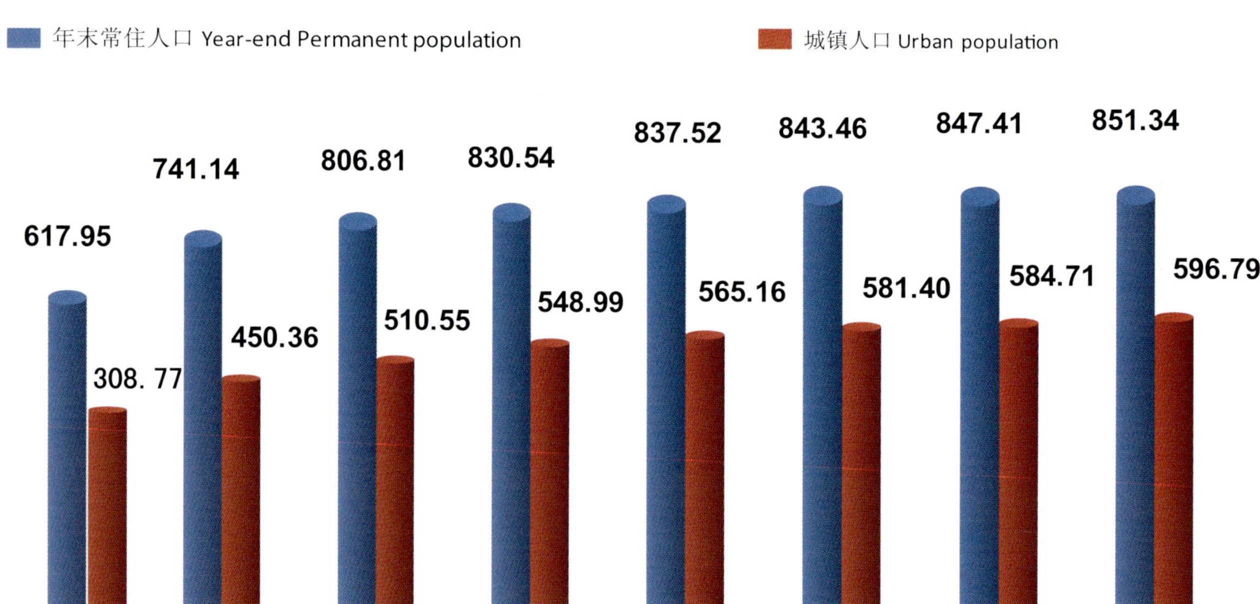

社会从业人数（万人）

Social Workers(10000 persons)

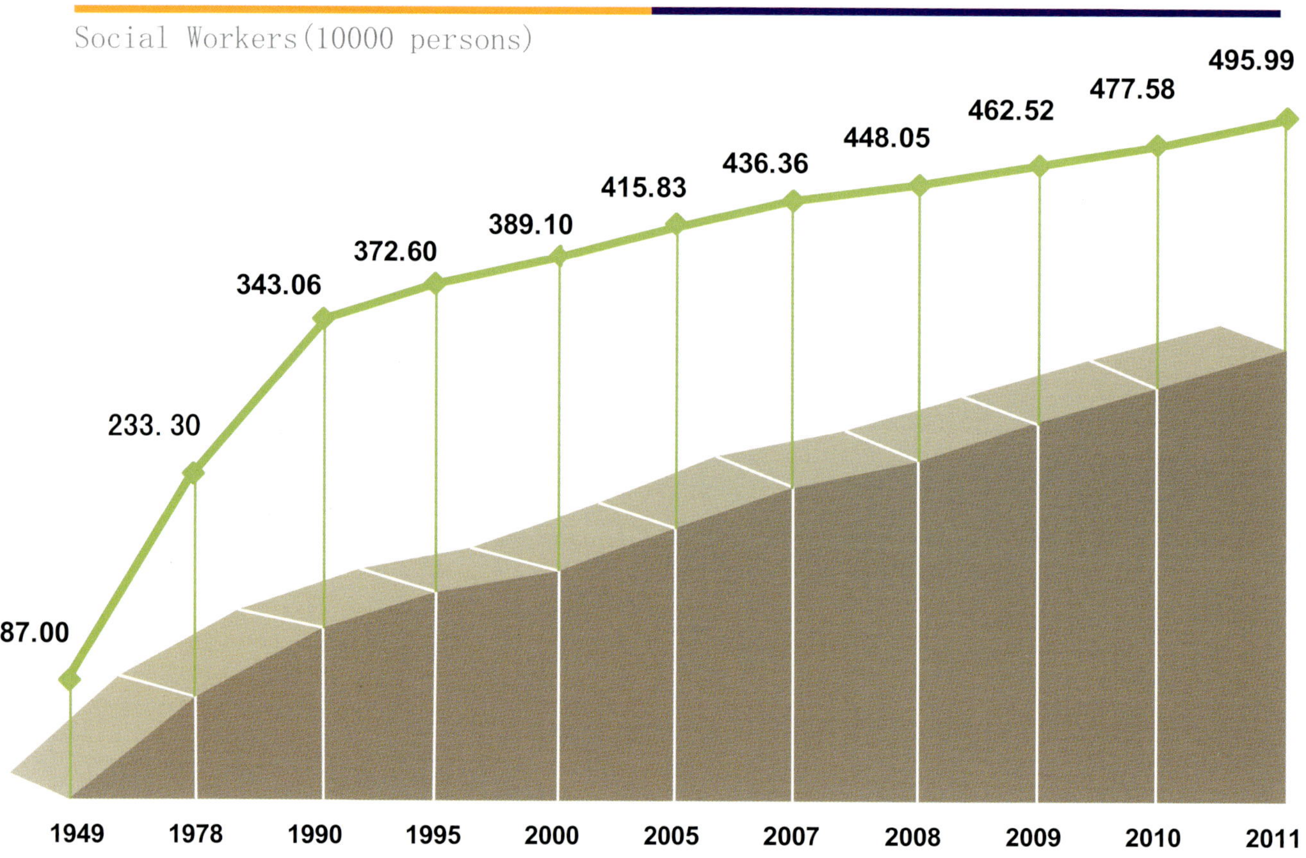

固定资产投资（亿元）

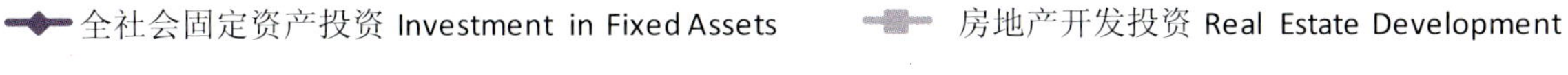

Investment in Fixed Assets (100 million yuan)

全社会固定资产投资 Investment in Fixed Assets　　房地产开发投资 Real Estate Development

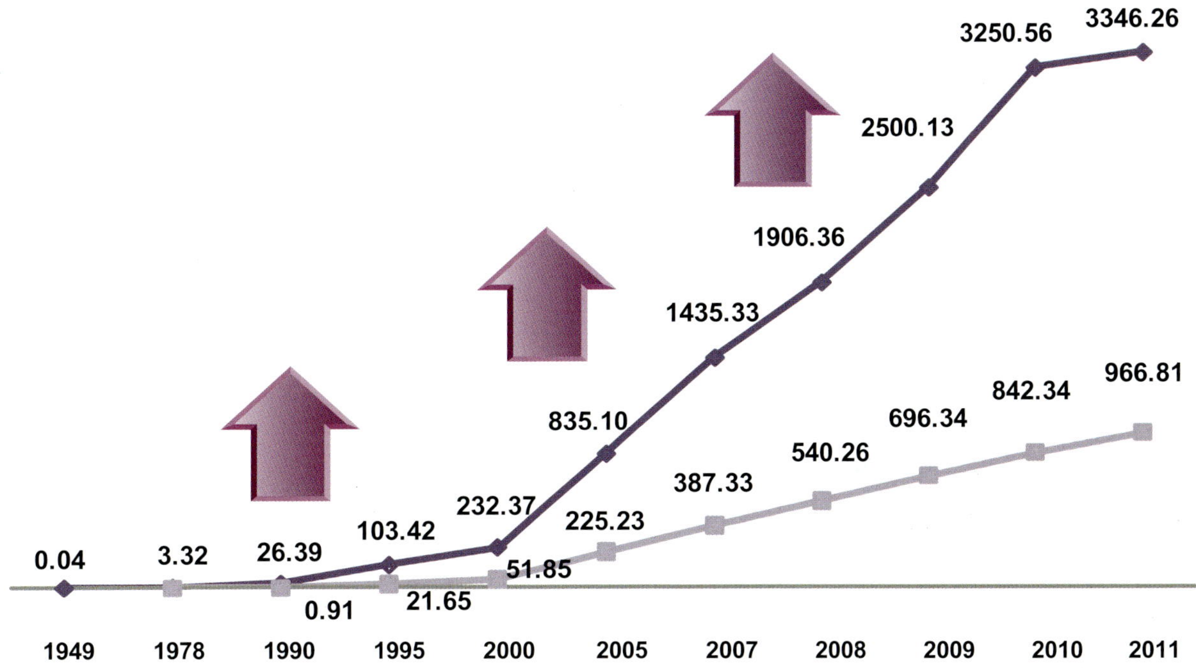

新增固定资产及住宅竣工面积

Newly Increased Fixed Assets and Residenctial Area of Completion

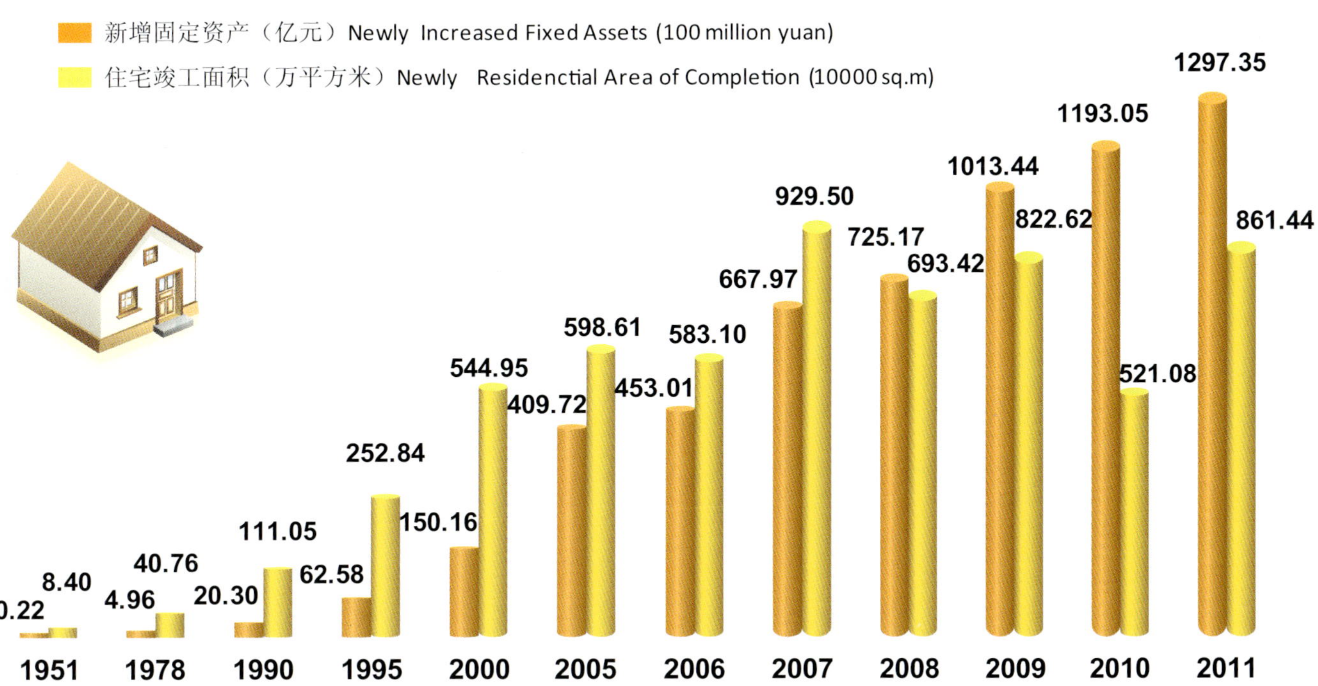

农林牧渔及服务业总产值(亿元)

Gross Output Value of Farming, Forestry, Animal Husbandry, Fishery and Service(100 million yuan)

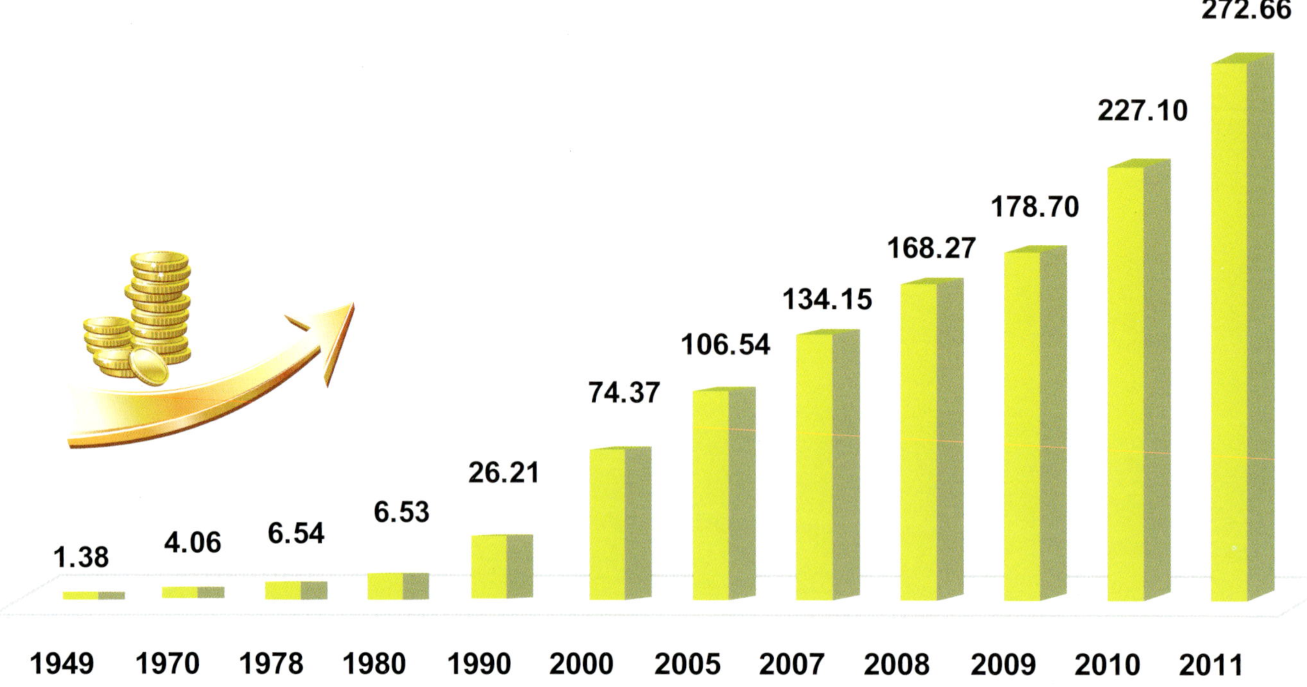

粮食、蔬菜产量（万吨）

Grain ,Vegetables Product(10000 ton)

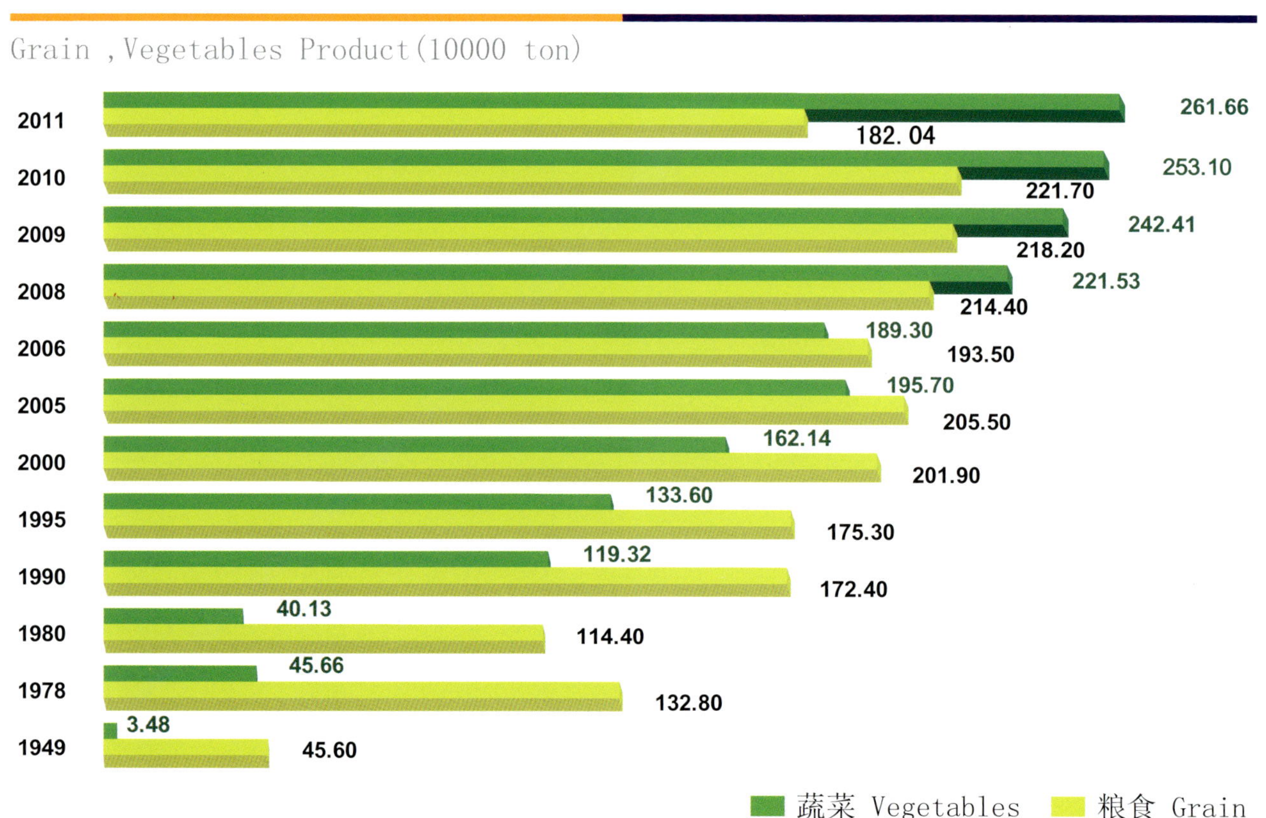

全部工业总产值及指数

Total Industrial Output Value and Indices

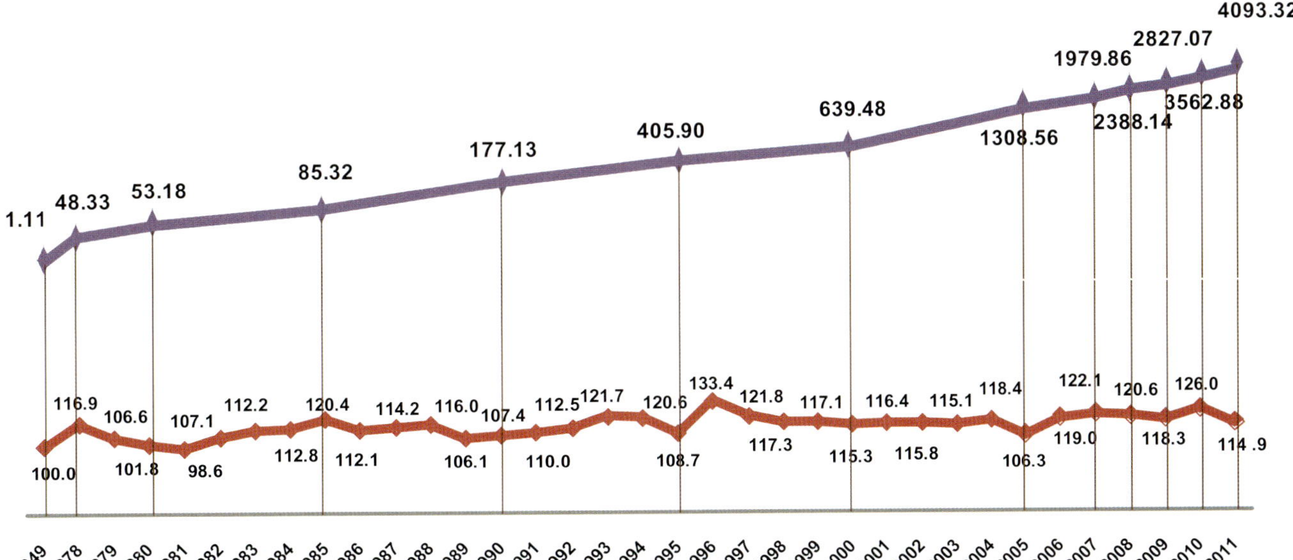

规模以上工业企业主要产品产量

Output of Major Industrial Products Of EnterprisesAbove Designated Size

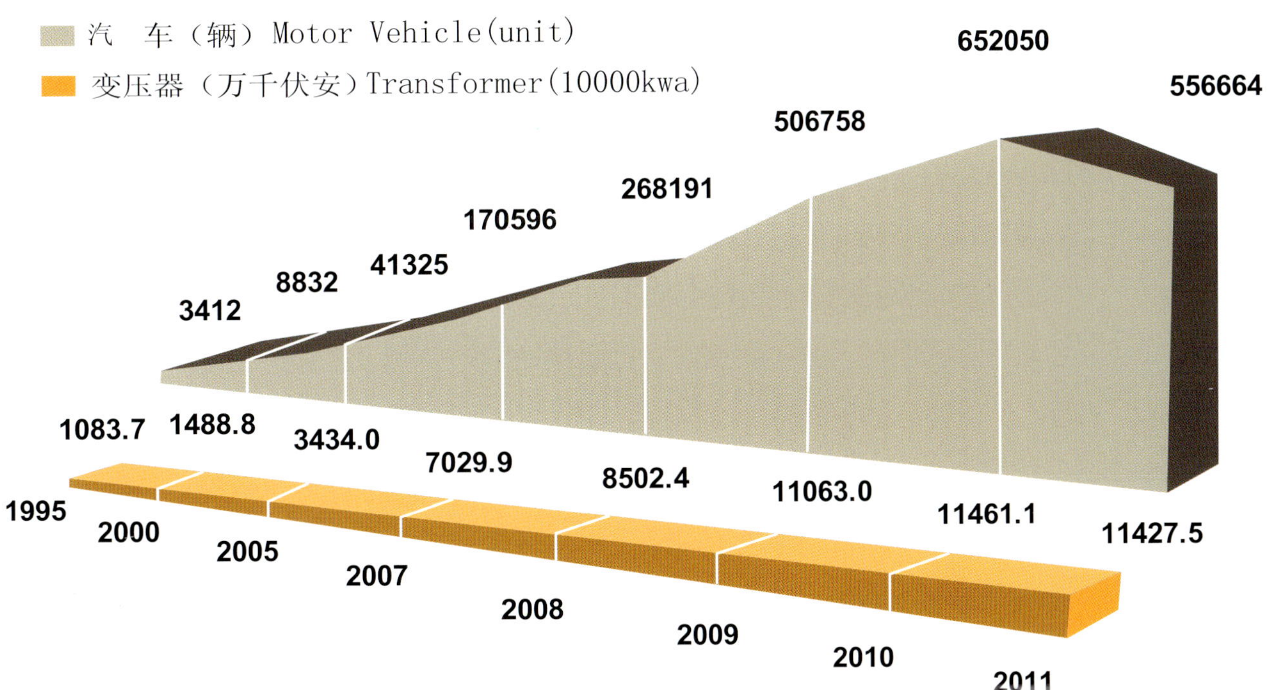

交通

等级公路（公里） Expressways and Clas Ⅰ to Ⅳ Highways

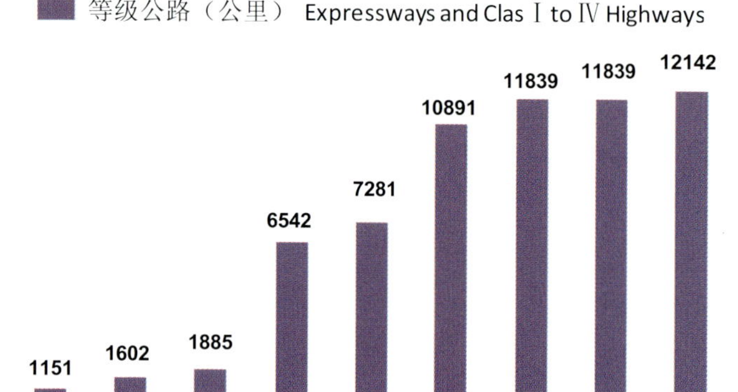

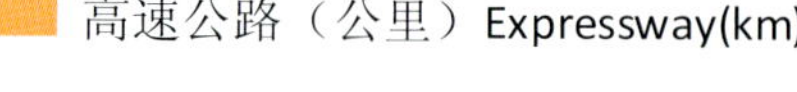

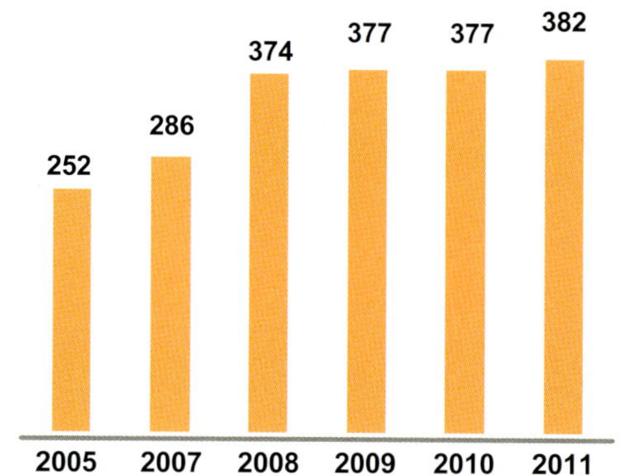

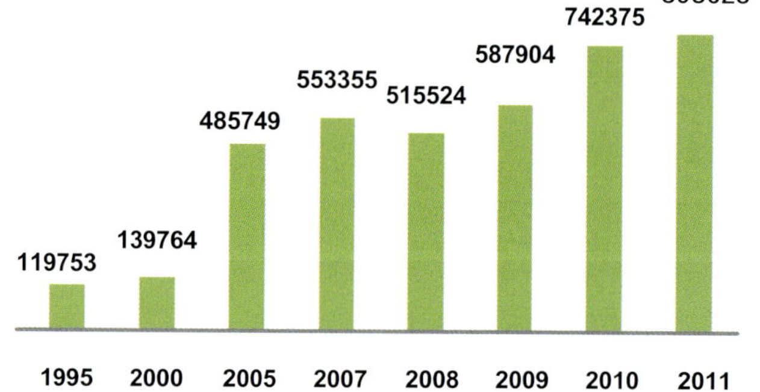

全社会车辆数（万辆）

Possession of Civil Vehicles(10000 unit)

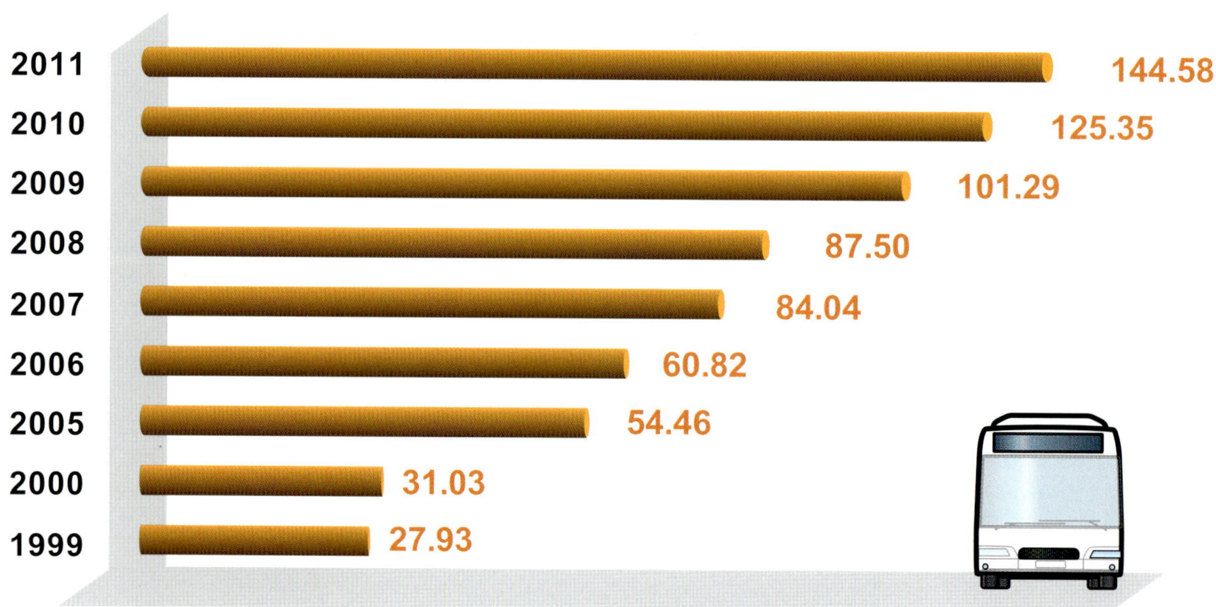

社会消费品零售总额(亿元)

Total Retail Sales of Consumer Goods (100 million yuan)

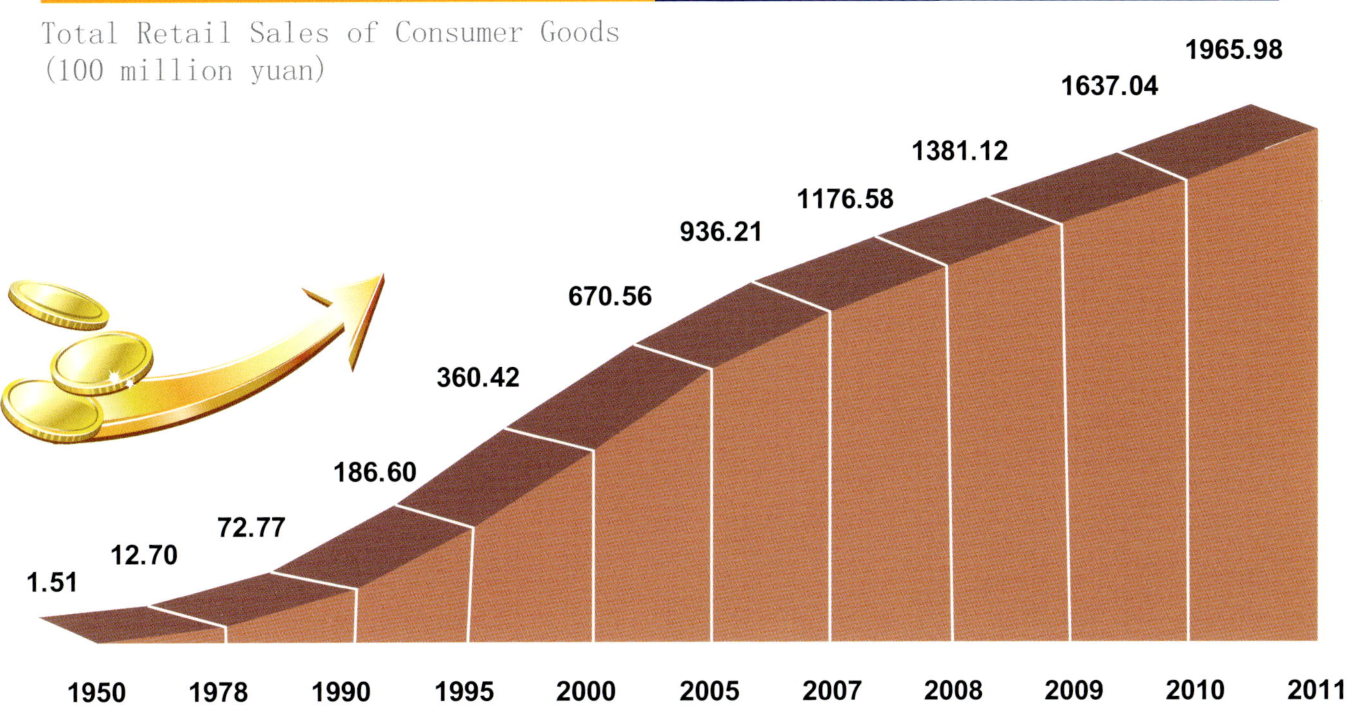

经营网点（个）

Bussiness Net work(unit)

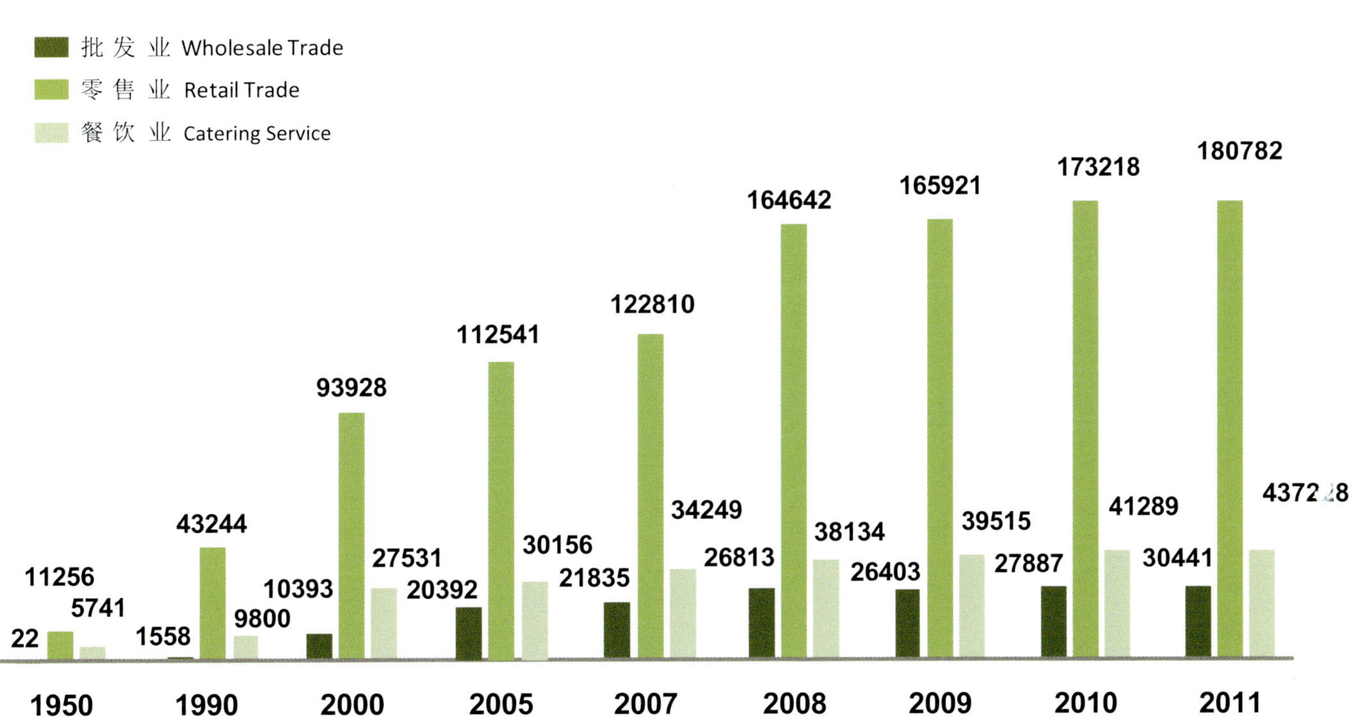

实际利用外商直接投资额（亿美元）

Value of Foreign Direct Investment(USD 100 million)

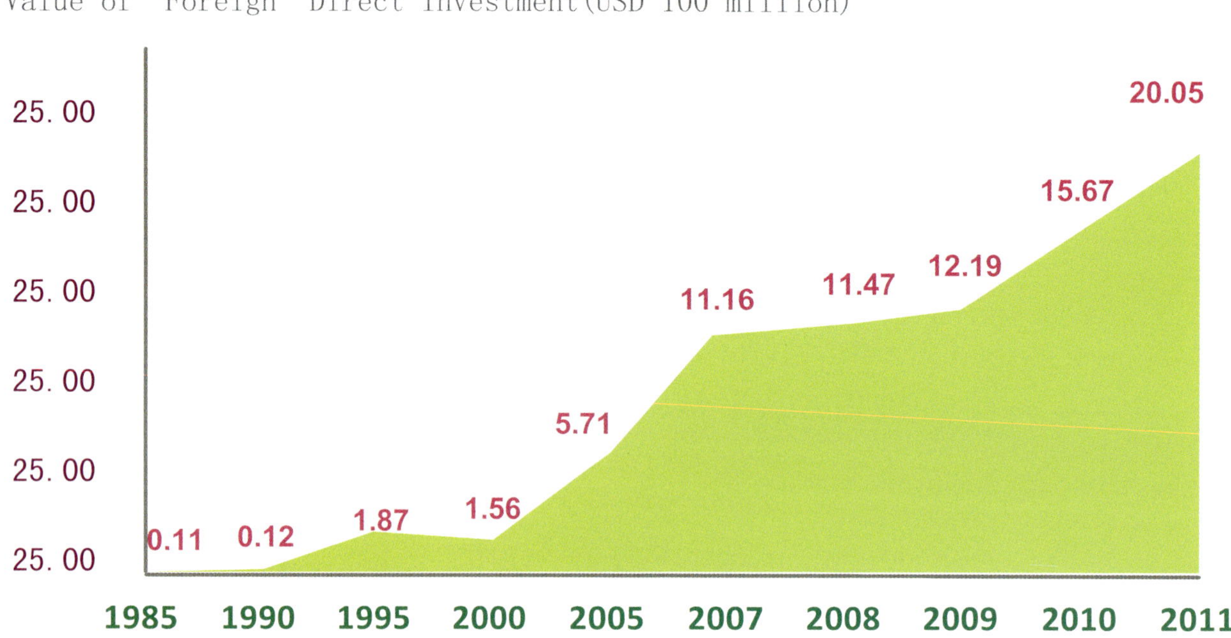

进出口总额(亿美元)

Total Value of Imports and Exports(USD 100 million)

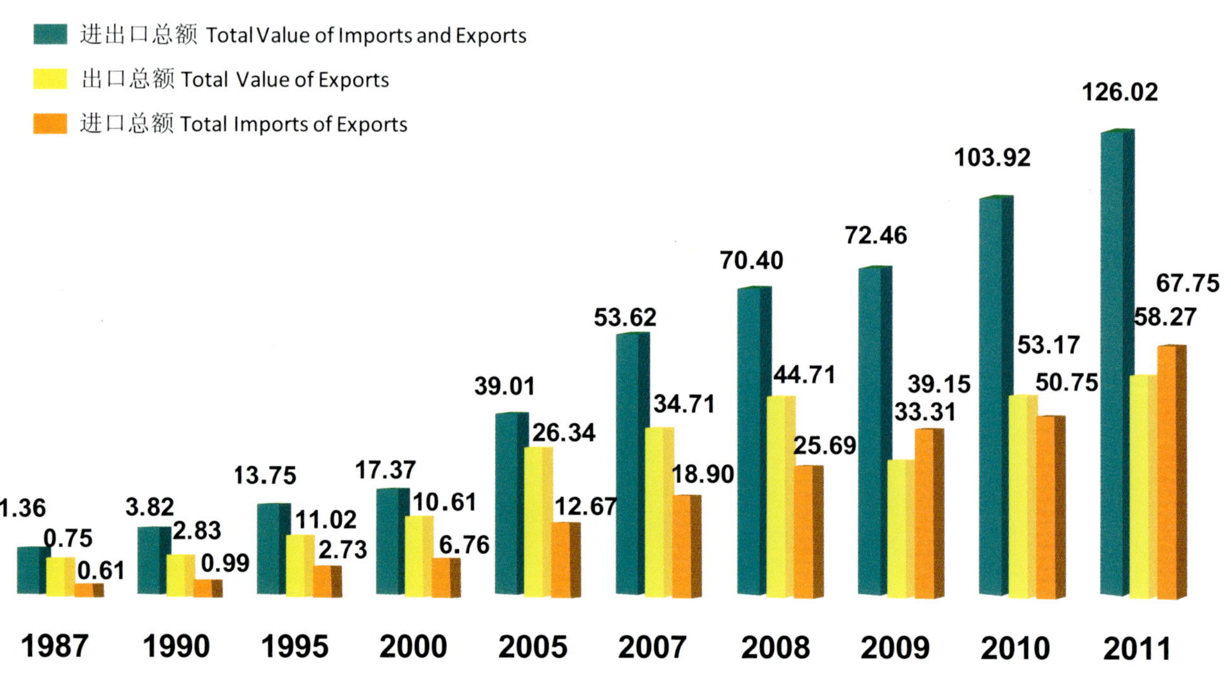

旅游人数及收入

Number of Tourists and Tourism Income

国际旅游人数及收入

Number of International Tourists and Tourism Income

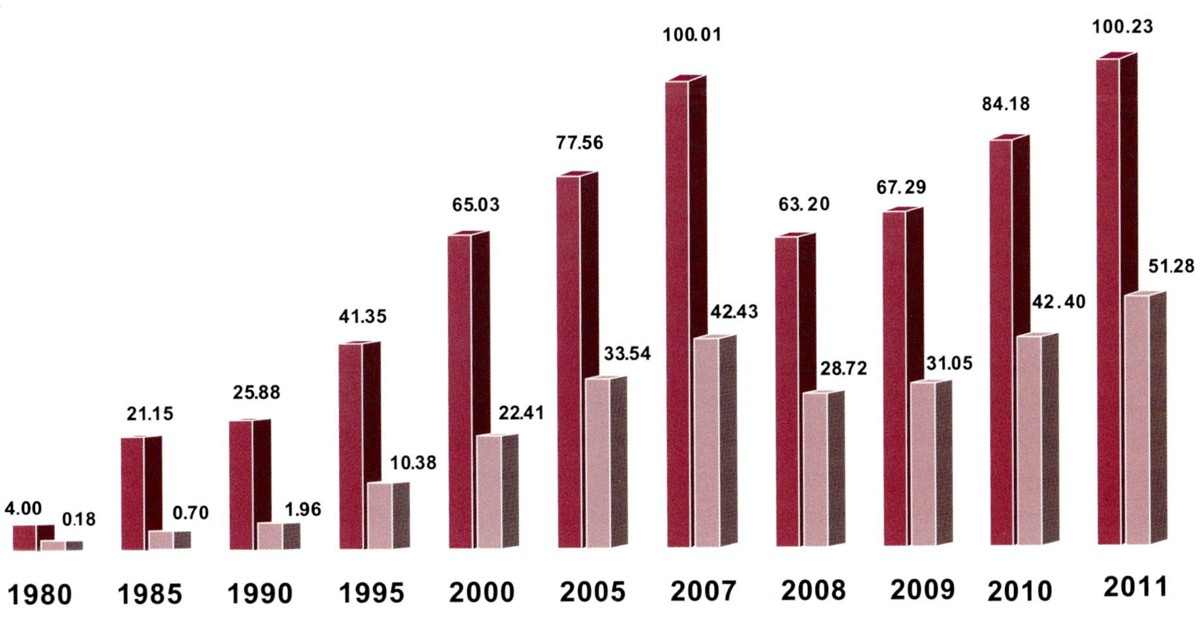

财政收支（亿元）

Govement Revenue and Expenditure(100 million yuan)

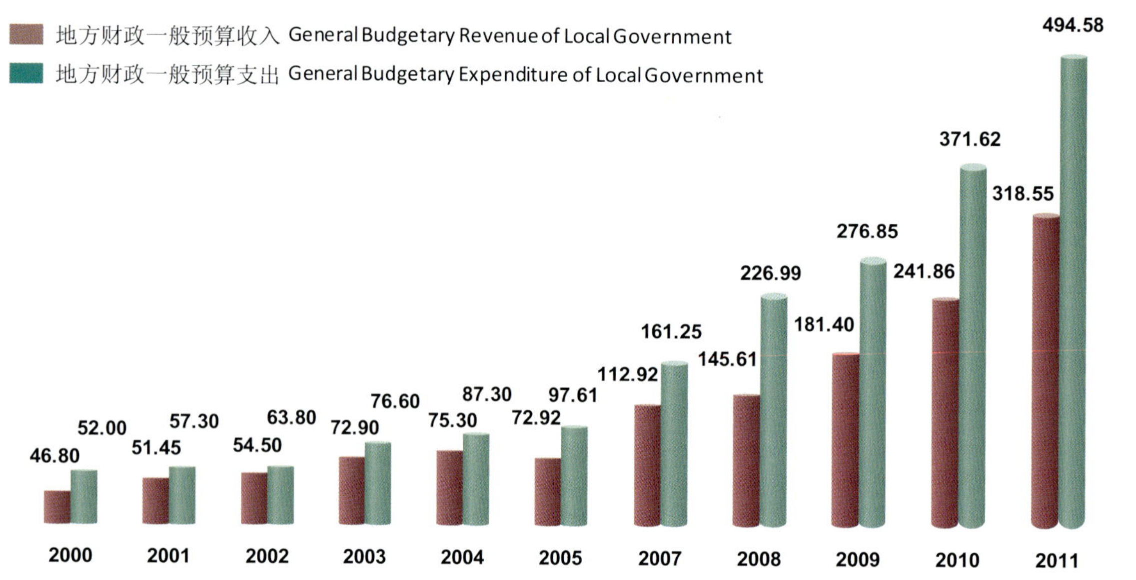

金融机构人民币存贷款年末余额（亿元）

Year-end Deposit in Financial Institutions(100 million yuan)

建成区面积（平方公里）

Area of Regions Constructed (sq.km)

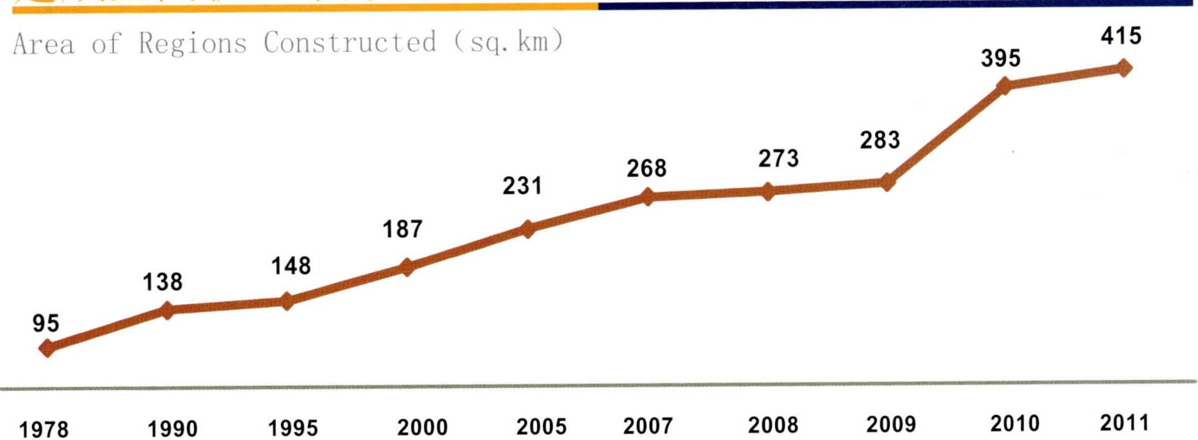

城市公共营运车辆（辆）

City Operating Vehicles(unit)

园林绿地总面积(公顷)

Total Area of Park, Gardens and Green Area(hectane)

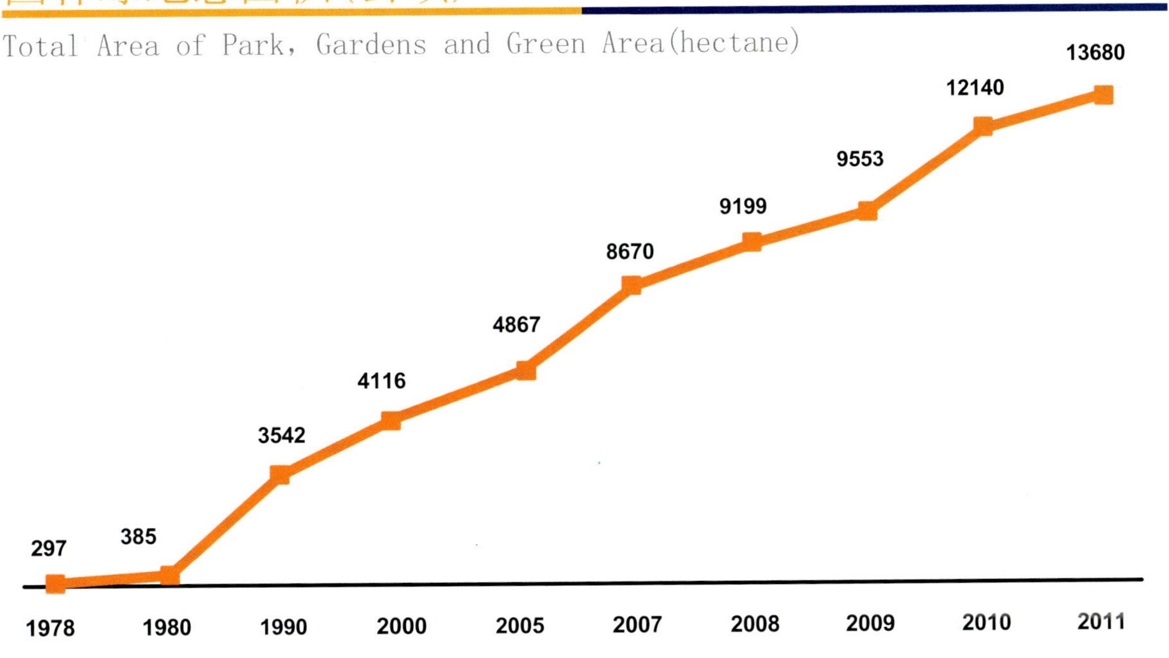

普通教育在校学生（万人）

Total Enrollment of Regular Education (10000 persons)

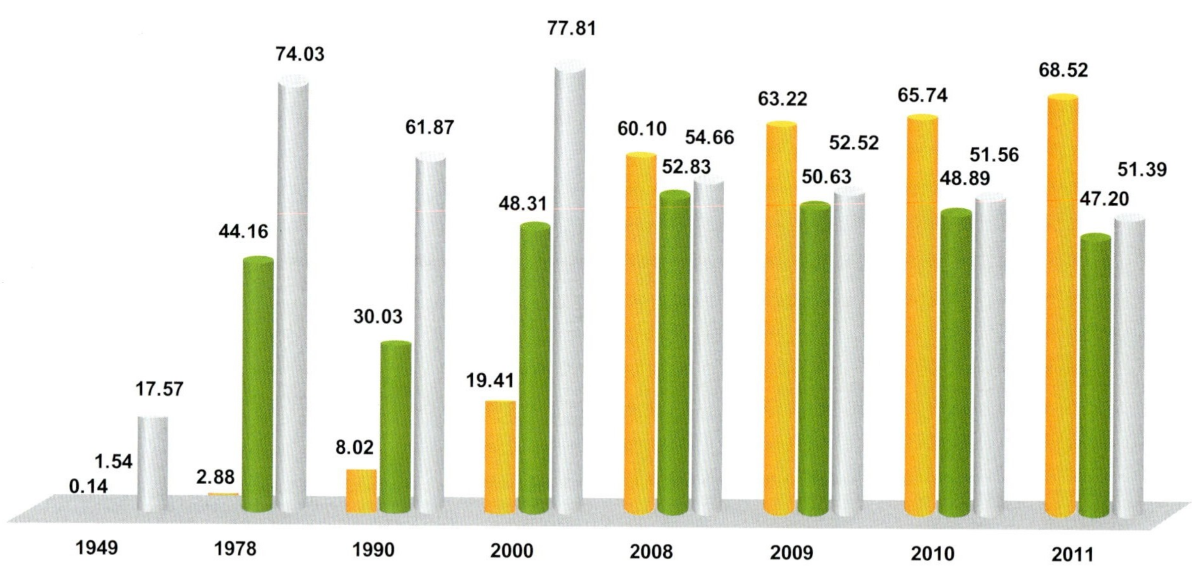

专任教师(万人)

Full-time Teachers (10000 persons)

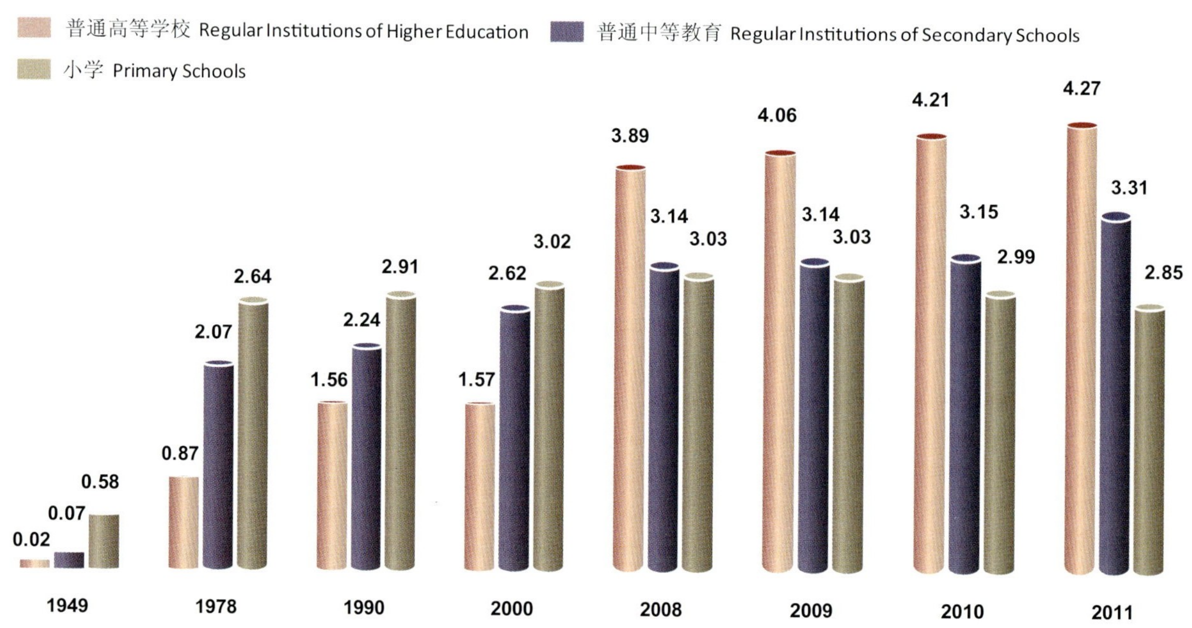

城乡居民收入（元）

The Income of Urban and Rural residents (yuan)

农村居民家庭人均纯收入 Per Capita Annual Net Income of Rural Households
城镇居民家庭人均可支配收入 Per Capita Annual Disposable Income of Urban Households

价格指数（以上年价格为100）

Price Indices(Price of Preceding year=100)

居民消费价格指数 Consumer price index
商品零售价格指数 Retail Price Index

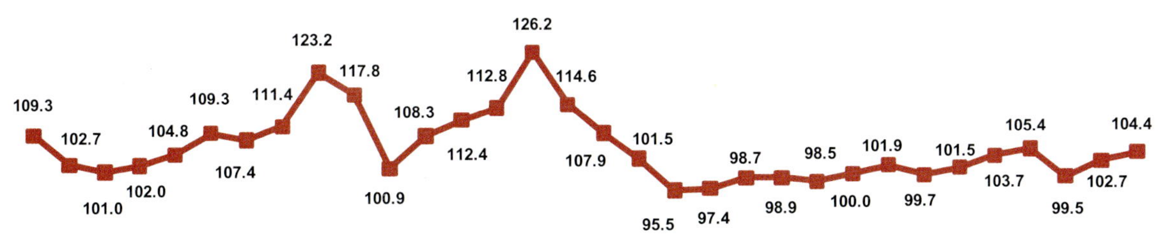

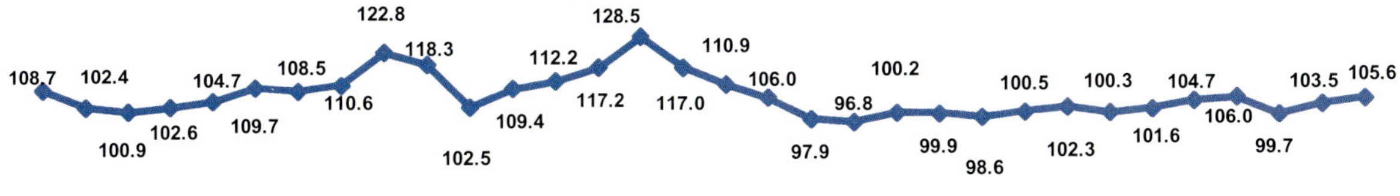

1980 1981 1982 1983 1984 1985 1986 1987 1988 1989 1990 1991 1992 1993 1994 1995 1996 1997 1998 1999 2000 2001 2002 2003 2004 2005 2006 2007 2008 2009 2010 2011

2012
西安统计年鉴

XI' AN STATISTICAL YEARBOOK

目　录

一、综　　合

二、国民经济核算

三、人口、从业人员与职工工资

四、固定资产投资

五、财　　政

六、物价指数

七、人民生活

八、城市公用事业

九、环境保护

十、农　业

十一、工　业

十二、能　源

十三、建筑业

十四、运输和邮电

十五、国内贸易

十六、对外经济贸易和旅游

十七、金融业

十八、教育和科技

十九、文化、体育、卫生、社会福利和其他

二十、企业调查

CONTENTS

CHAPTER 1 GENERAL SURVEY

CHAPTER 2 NATIONAL ECONOMIC ACCOUNTS

CHAPTER 3 POPULATION, EMPLOYMENT AND WAGES

CHAPTER 4 INVESTMENT IN FIXED ASSETS

CHAPTER 5 GOVERNMENT FINANCE

CHAPTER 6 PRICE INDICES

CHAPTER 7 PEOPLE'S LIVELIHOOD

CHAPTER 8 URBAN PUBLIC UTLITIES

CHAPTER 9 ENVIRONMENT PROTECTION

CHAPTER 10 AGRICULTURE

CHAPTER 11 INDUSTRY

CHAPTER 12 ENERGY

CHAPTER 13 CONSTRUCTION

CHAPTER 14 TRANSPORT, POSTAL AND TELECOMMUNICATION SERVICES

CHAPTER 15 DOMESTIC TRADE

CHAPTER 16 FOREIGN TRADE AND ECONOMIC COOPERATION, TOURISM

CHAPTER 17 Financial Intermediation

CHAPTER 18 EDUCATION, SCIENCE AND TECHNOLOGY

CHAPTER 19 CULTURES, SPORTS, PUBLIC HEALTH, SOCIAL WELFARE INSTITUTIONS AND OTHER SOCIAL ACTIVITIES

CHAPTER 20 ENTERPRISES INVESTIGATION

西安市2011年国民经济和社会发展统计公报

西安市统计局　国家统计局西安调查队

2012年3月15日

2011年，市委、市政府牢牢把握科学发展这个主题，紧紧围绕加快转变经济发展方式这条主线，贯彻落实中央各项宏观调控政策，积极应对国际环境新变化和国内经济运行新情况，全年经济保持平稳较快增长，实现了“十二五”开局良好、起步稳健。

一、综合

初步核算，全年实现生产总值（GDP）3864.21亿元，比上年增长13.8%，分产业看，第一产业增加值173.14亿元，增长6.7%；第二产业增加值1697.16亿元，增长16.4%；第三产业增加值1993.91亿元，增长12.1%。第一产业增加值占地区生产总值的比重为4.5%，第二产业增加值比重为43.9%，第三产业增加值比重为51.6%。

图1 2006-2011年地区生产总值及其增长速度

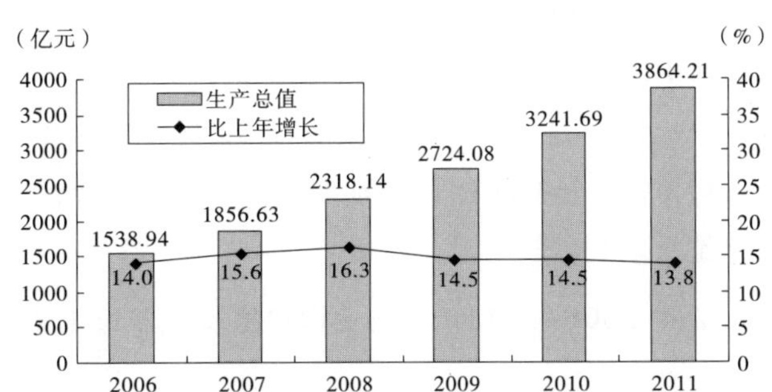

全年居民消费价格比上年上涨5.6%，其中食品价格上涨11.3%。商品零售价格上涨4.4%，工业生产者出厂价格上涨2.5%，工业生产者购进价格上涨8.8%。

图2 2011年居民消费价格月度涨跌幅度

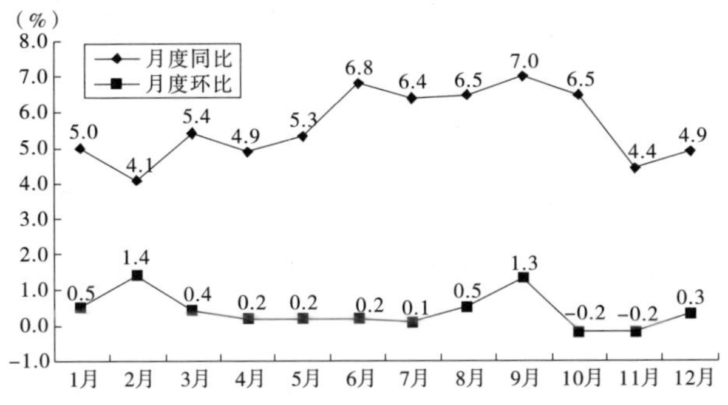

2011年全市居民消费价格比上年涨跌幅度

指　　标	2011年（%）
居民消费价格总水平	5.6
食品	11.3
#粮食	11.0
烟酒及用品	3.0
衣着	4.0
家庭设备用品及维修服务	1.8
医疗保健和个人用品	5.3
交通和通讯	0.3
娱乐教育文化用品及服务	1.0
居住	5.1

全市城镇新增就业人数11.94万人，下岗失业人员再就业4.32万人，就业困难人员实现再就业1.24万人。城镇登记失业率3.9%。全市农村劳动力实现转移就业人员66.64万人。

全年财政总收入649.88亿元，比上年增长27.3%。地方财政一般预算收入318.55亿元，增长31.7%，其中，营业税、增值税、企业所得税和个人所得税分别增长25.9%、19.8%、32.4%和20.2%。全年地方财政一般预算支出494.58亿元，比上年增长33.1%，其中，医疗卫生支出增长24.1%；农林水事务支出增长54.3%；教育支出增长40.4%；社会保障和就业支出增长17.7%；一般公共服务支出增长20.2%；节能环保支出增长19.6%。

二、农业

全年粮食播种面积573.13万亩，比上年下降1.3%；油料播种面积8.82万亩，下降1.8%；蔬菜播种面积96.93万亩，增长1.1%；棉花5.97万亩，下降4.6%。全年粮食产量182.04万吨，比上年下降1.0%，其中，夏粮产量90.54万吨，增长3.5%，秋粮91.50万吨，下降5.0%。

2011年全市农业主要产品产量

产品名称	计量单位	绝对数	比上年增长（%）
油　料	万吨	1.17	0.2
蔬　菜	万吨	261.52	3.1
园林水果	万吨	91.14	7.5
肉　类	万吨	14.46	6.0
奶　类	万吨	64.80	2.3
禽　蛋	万吨	12.56	1.5
大牲畜年末存栏数	万头	21.24	-1.7
猪年末存栏数	万头	94.40	0.1
羊年末存栏数	万只	29.60	0.5
家禽年末存栏数	万只	1154.00	11.6

全市农用机械总动力289.02万千瓦，比上年增长8.0%；农田有效灌溉面积262.32万亩，下降6.7%；全年农用化肥施用量（实物量）78.59万吨，增长0.6%。

三、工业和建筑业

全年全部工业增加值1189.61亿元，比上年增长16.2%。规模以上工业增加值1012.58亿元，增长17.2%。其中，轻工业增加值212.26亿元，增长14.6%，重工业增加值800.32亿元，增长18.0%。

图3 2006-2011年全部工业增加值及其增长速度

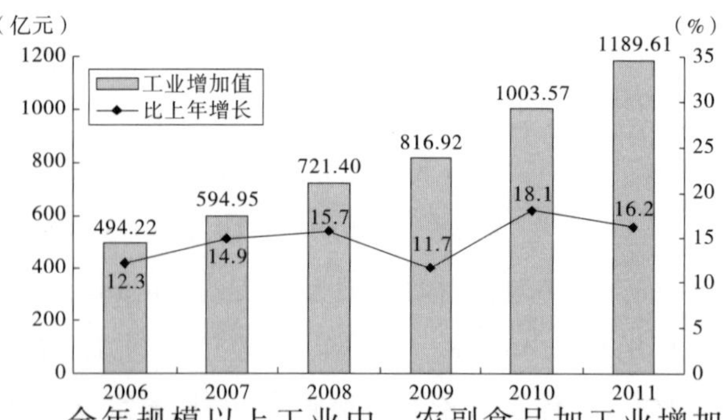

全年规模以上工业中，农副食品加工业增加值比上年增长10.5%；通用设备制造业增长19.5%；专用设备制造业增长26.0%；交通运输设备制造业增长13.4%；通信设备、计算机及其他电子设备制造业增长65.4%。六大高耗能行业比上年增长19.8%，其中，非金属矿物制品业增长24.1%；化学原料及化学制品制造业增长25.1%；有色金属冶炼及压延加工业增长43.2%；黑色金属冶炼及压延加工业增长3.2%；电力、热力的生产和供应业增长19.6%；石油加工、炼焦及核燃料加工业增长8.4%。

2011年全市规模以上工业主要产品产量

产品名称	计量单位	产量	比上年增长（%）
发电量	亿千瓦小时	95.01	-0.1
原油加工量	万吨	153.17	-12.1
乳制品	万吨	114.68	12.3
液体乳	万吨	107.25	12.5
商品混凝土	万立方米	1781.17	87.5
机制纸及纸板	万吨	49.79	0.7
交流电动机	万千瓦	564.69	24.4
饲料	万吨	65.73	25.9
合成洗涤剂	万吨	8.69	4.2
水泥	万吨	409.99	-19.8
风机	台	1174	-29.1
汽车	万辆	55.67	-14.6
其中：轿车	万辆	38.68	-25.3
高压开关板	面	10840	236.9
变压器	万千伏安	11427.51	0.0
电力电缆	千米	7489	84.0
气体压缩机	万台	712.36	32.3
电子元件	亿只	3.27	-76.2

全市规模以上工业企业经济效益综合指数为231.6，比上年提高7.2个百分点。规模以上工业企业主营业务收入3380.15亿元，增长16.8%。实现利税总额332.36亿元，同比增长6.3%，其中，利润总额216.14亿元，同比增长2.9%。

全年建筑业实现增加值507.55亿元，比上年增长17.0%。全年具有资质等级的总承包和专业承包建筑企业332家。

图4 2006-2011年建筑业增加值及其增长速度

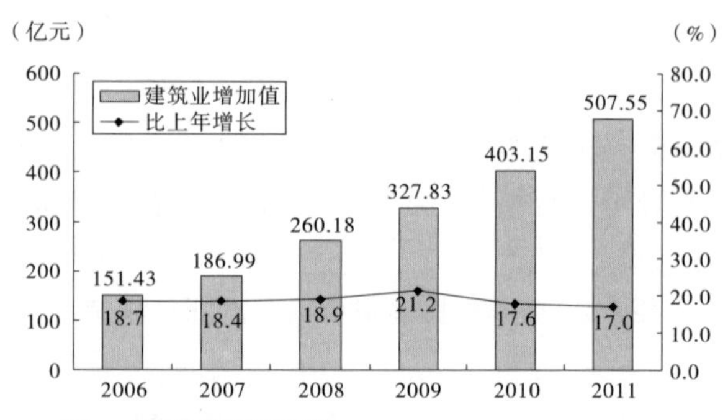

四、固定资产投资

全年全社会固定资产投资3352.12亿元，比上年增长30.2%，扣除价格因素，实际增长23.5%。其中，全市固定资产投资（不含农户）3279.61亿元，增长29.9%。

图5 2006-2011年全社会固定资产投资及其增长速度

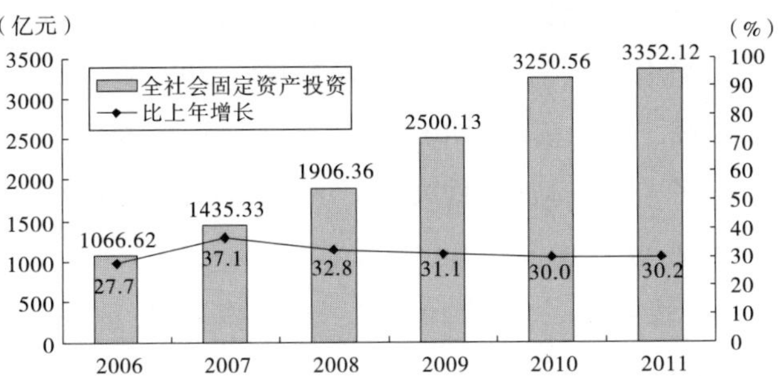

在全市固定资产投资中，第一产业投资72.23亿元，增长22.2%；第二产业投资483.67亿元，增长21.3%，其中，工业投资398.99亿元，增长18.5%；第三产业投资2723.71亿元，增长31.8%。

2011年重点行业固定资产投资及其增长速度

指　标	投资额（亿元）	比上年增长（%）
农林牧渔业	72.23	22.2
制造业	366.15	33.5
交通运输、仓储及邮政业	205.37	67.2
信息传输、计算机服务和软件业	33.43	-4.1
批发和零售业	111.47	132.3
住宿和餐饮业	59.89	56.8
水利、环境和公共设施管理业	490.55	34.4
教　育	75.43	41.5
卫生、社会保障和社会福利业	28.97	109.3
公共管理和社会组织	166.41	8.2

全年房地产开发投资1002.67亿元，增长19.0%；商品房销售面积1796.03万平方米，增长13.1%。

2011年房地产开发和销售主要指标

指　标	计量单位	绝对数	比上年增长（%）
房地产开发投资	亿元	1002.67	19.0
#住宅	亿元	833.37	24.3
商品房施工面积	万平方米	8215.57	22.7
#住宅	万平方米	7074.47	22.4
新开工面积	万平方米	2280.07	11.6
#住宅	万平方米	2004.25	13.2
商品房竣工面积	万平方米	633.97	36.7
#住宅	万平方米	558.55	35.4
商品房销售面积	万平方米	1796.03	13.1
#住宅	万平方米	1687.08	10.8

全年新增固定资产1370.06亿元，固定资产交付使用率41.8%。各类房屋竣工面积1257.59万平方米，竣工率10.2%。共有1430个城镇建设项目建成投产，项目建成投产率60.3%。

五、国内贸易

全年社会消费品零售总额1935.18亿元，比上年增长20.1%，扣除价格因素，实际增长15.0%。按经营单位所在地统计，城镇消费品零售额1877.84亿元，增长20.5%；乡村消费品零售额57.34亿元，增长9.8%。按消费形态统计，商品零售额1732.43亿元，增长20.5%；餐饮收入额202.75亿元，增长16.7%。

图6 2006-2011年社会消费品零售总额及其增长速度

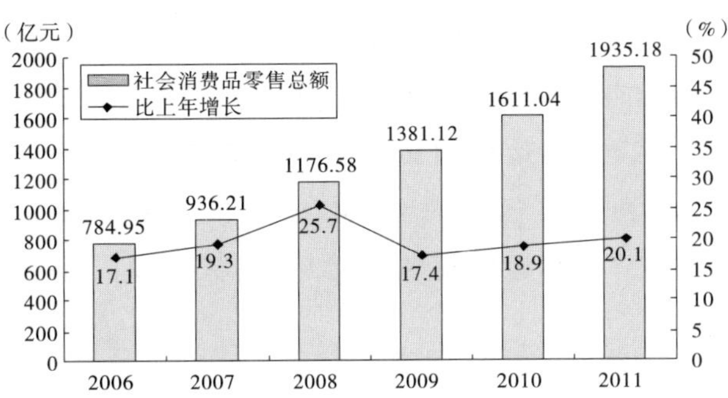

在限额以上企业商品零售额中，食品、饮料、烟酒类零售额比上年增长27.3%，服装鞋帽、针纺织品类增长34.8%，体育娱乐用品类增长14.7%，书报杂志类增长0.6%，日用品类增长23.4%，家用电器和音像器材类增长29.2%，通讯器材类增长19.1%，文化办公用品类增长28.9%，金银珠宝类增长47.3%，汽车类增长19.3%。

六、对外经济

全年进出口总额125.79亿美元，比上年增长21.0%。其中，出口58.04亿美元，增长9.2%；进口67.75亿美元，增长33.5%。

图7 2006-2011年进出口总额及其增长速度

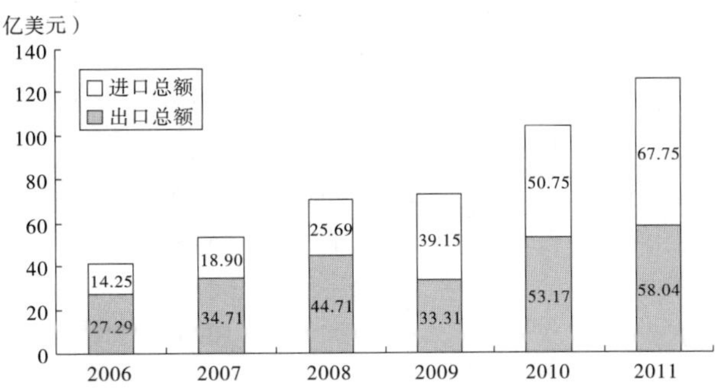

在进出口总额中，一般贸易进出口75.30亿美元，增长36.9%，占同期西安地区进出口总值的59.9%；加工贸易进出口36.71亿美元，下降7.7%，占同期西安地区进出口总值的29.2%。

主要进出口商品中，机电产品出口38.42亿美元，下降0.3%，进口42.03亿美元，增长21.6%；农产品出口4.80亿美元，增长57.8%，进口1.41亿美元，增长38.5%；矿产品出口3.58亿美元，增长0.1%，进口9.73亿美元，增长58.5%；纺织服装出口1.78亿美元，下降4.6%，进口373万美元，下降22.6%。

全年批准外商直接投资项目99个，合同利用外商直接投资12.01亿美元，比上年增长0.3%；实际利用外商直接投资20.05亿美元，增长28.0%。

七、交通、邮电和旅游

全年货物运输总量3.92亿吨，比上年增长14.3%，货物运输周转量521.20亿吨公里，增长21.4%。旅客运输总量3.43亿人，比上年增长10.3%，旅客运输周转量322.36亿人公里，增长9.8%。

2011年各种运输方式完成货物运输量及其增长速度

指　标	计量单位	绝对数	比上年增长（%）
货物运输总量	万吨	39239.26	14.3
公路	万吨	38399.00	14.2
铁路	万吨	823.00	16.5
民航（吞吐量）	万吨	17.26	11.3
货物运输周转量	亿吨公里	521.20	21.4
公路	亿吨公里	311.09	25.1
铁路	亿吨公里	208.96	16.5
民航	亿吨公里	1.15	-17.0

2011年各种运输方式完成旅客运输量及其增长速度

指　标	计量单位	绝对数	比上年增长（%）
旅客运输总量	万人	34335.20	10.3
公路	万人	29358.00	10.6
铁路	万人	2860.90	2.6
民航（吞吐量）	万人	2116.30	17.5
旅客运输周转量	亿人公里	322.36	9.8
公路	亿人公里	160.33	19.1
铁路	亿人公里	59.54	9.2
民航	亿人公里	102.49	-1.9

年末全市民用汽车保有量达到117.49万辆，比上年末增长22.4%，其中私人汽车保有量97.67万辆，增长24.8%。全市轿车保有量61.89万辆，增长25.8%，其中私人轿车54.71万辆，增长27.6%。

全年邮政业务总收入8.16亿元，增长15.5%；电信业务总收入100.47亿元，增长13.3%。全市固定电话年末用户270.36万户。移动电话用户1614.15万户，其中，3G移动电话用户177.37万户。电信互联网用户184.10万户。

全年共接待国内游客6553万人次，比上年增长26.0%；海外游客100.23万人次，增长19.1%。全年实现旅游总收入530.15亿元，增长30.8%，其中，外汇收入6.41亿美元，增长20.9%。

八、金融

年末全市金融机构本外币各项存款余额10526.32亿元，比上年末增长16.4%。人民币存款余额10430.27亿元，增长16.8%，其中，城乡居民储蓄存款余额4155.65亿元，增长14.1%。金融机构本外币贷款余额7700.19亿元，比上年末增长16.8%。人民币贷款余额7564.93亿元，增长16.7%，其中，短期贷款1431.29亿元，增长30.4%；中长期贷款5776.48亿元，增长13.8%。

全年证券市场各类证券成交额9851.43亿元，比上年下降18.6%。年末全市拥有上市股份公司28家，上市总股本193.70亿股，总市值1592.65亿元。年末股票市场累计开户数165万户，比上年末增长8.4%。

截止2011年底，全市共有保险公司45家，其中，财产险21家，人寿险24家。保险专业中介机构110家。全年保费收入162.57亿元，比上年增长25.7%。其中，财产险保费收入44.96亿元，增32.8%；人身险保费收入117.61亿元，增长23.1%。全年支付各类保险赔款及给付37.14亿元，比上年增长40.7%。其中财产险、人身险分别为20.33亿元和16.81亿元，分别比上年增长38.8%和43.2%。

九、教育和科学技术

全市研究生培养单位44个，招收研究生2.67万人，在学研究生8.17万人；普通高校50所，在校学生68.52万人，毕业生17.68万人；普通中学423

所，在校学生47.20万人，毕业生16.44万人；小学1424所，在校学生51.39万人，毕业生8.92万人。小学、初中学龄人口入学率分别为99.97%和99.65%。

全年实施市级科技计划项目236项，其中高新技术专项27项，科技创新和成果转化项目116项。重点扶持高新技术企业163家，支持建设农业科技示范园11家，科技示范乡镇6个，实施区县工业科技引导项目14个。全年争取国家、省资金4.6亿元。技术市场交易额204.59亿元。申请专利量27717件。

十、文化、体育和卫生

全市艺术表演团体14个，公共图书馆15个，文化馆15个，文化站181个，博物馆20个。全年组织开展各类群众文化活动7497场次。全市拥有电视台2座、广播电台2座、广播电视台6座，电视人口覆盖率和广播人口覆盖率分别达98.60%、99.42%。

全年举办各类群众体育展示表演和竞赛活动共计260项次，体育社团举办和承办体育赛事300项次，其中国际性和全国性赛事1项次，累计参与群众200万人次。新建城市社区全民健身器材配送工程45个、乡镇农民体育健身工程5个、社区全民健身路径104个，其中更新30个。全市已有社会体育指导员7376名，晨晚练点1800个，健身气功站点125个、在册练功人数5625人。

在第七届全国城市运动会上，我市代表团取得了2金、7银、6铜，团体总分362分的好成绩，并荣获“体育道德风尚奖”称号。

年末全市共有各类卫生机构5554个，其中医院、卫生院368个；各类卫生技术人员6.13万人，其中执业（助理）医师2.16万人；卫生机构床位4.10万张。

十一、人口、人民生活和社会保障

年末常住人口851.34万人，其中男性人口437.30万人，占51.4%；女性人口414.04万人，占48.6%，性别比为105.62（以女性为100，男性对女性的比例）。全年出生人口8.25万人，出生率为9.71‰；死亡人口4.57万人，死亡率为5.38‰；全年净增人口3.93万人，自然增长率为4.33‰。城镇人口596.79万人，占70.1%；乡村人口254.55万人，占29.9%。年末全市户籍总人口791.83万人，比上年增长1.2%。

全市城镇居民人均可支配收入25981元，扣除价格因素，比上年实际增长10.6%；农民人均纯收入9788元，实际增长19.6%。城镇居民家庭食品消费支出占家庭消费总支出的比重为31.3%，农村为31.9%。城镇居民人均住房建筑面积28.9平方米，农村居民人均住房面积67平方米。

图8 2006-2011年城乡居民收入

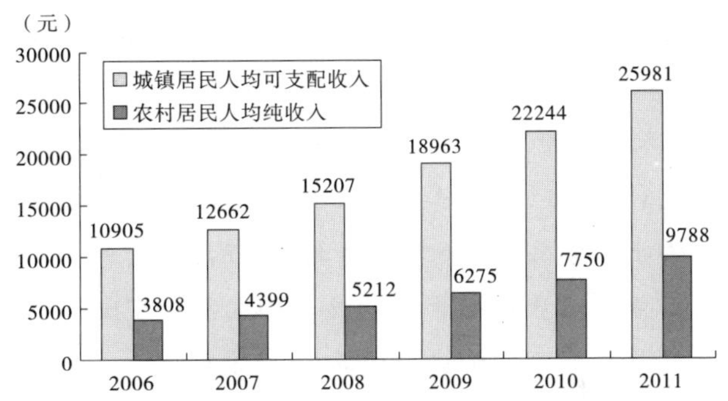

全市城镇基本医疗保险参保人数404.27万人；城镇职工养老保险参保人数215.80万人；失业保险参保人数134.82万人；工伤保险参保人数123.07万人，职工生育保险参保人数95.45万人。参加农村新型合作医疗的农民人数达394.85万人，实际参合率97.79%，覆盖率100%。

十二、城市建设、环境和安全生产

全年完成市政公用设施投资236.80亿元，新增人行天桥20座，建设公交港湾6处，新增城区集中供热面积119万平方米，新建改造绿地广场92个，新建道路面积160万平方米。

城市环境空气质量全年好于国家二级标准（良好）以上的天数305天，比上年增加1天。二氧化硫、二氧化氮和可吸入颗粒物的年平均浓度分别为0.042毫克/标立方米、0.041毫克/标立方米和0.118毫克/标立方米，比上年分别下降2.3%、8.9%和6.3%。全市集中式饮用水源地的水质达标率为100%。区域环境噪声等效声级均值为55.3分贝，道路交通噪声等效声级均值为68.6分贝。

全年共发生各类安全生产事故4199起，比上年增加26起；死亡566人，比上年减少2人；受伤2271人，比上年减少258人；经济损失2780.53万元，比上年减少886.27万元。

注释：

1.本公报数据为初步统计数，部分数据因四舍五入的原因，存在着分项与合计不等的情况。

2.地区生产总值、各产业增加值绝对数按现价计算，增长速度按不变价格计算。

3.从2011年开始，纳入规模以上工业统计范围的工业企业起点标准从年主营业务收入500万元提高到2000万元。

4.六大高耗能行业分别为：化学原料及化学制品制造业、非金属矿物制品业、黑色金属冶炼及压延加工业、有色金属冶炼及压延加工业、石油加工炼焦及核燃料加工业、电力热力的生产和供应业。

5.从2011年开始，固定资产投资统计的起点标准从计划总投资50万元提高到500万元，因此2011年全社会固定资产投资绝对数与2010年不可比，但比上年增速是按可比口径计算的。与此同时，月度投资统计制度将统计范围从城镇扩大到城镇和农村企事业组织，并定义为“固定资产投资（不含农户）”。

6.从2010年起，社会消费品零售总额统计采用新的分组，即将经营单位所在地分组由“市”、“县”、“县以下”改为“城镇”、“乡村”；取消按行业分组，新设按“商品零售额”和“餐饮收入额”两种消费形态的分组。

资料来源：本公报中物价数据来自国家统计局西安调查队；城镇新增就业、登记失业率、社会保障数据来自西安市人力资源和社会保障局；财政数据来自市财政局；进出口数据来自西安海关；利用外资数据来自市商务局；铁路运输数据来自西安铁路局；公路运输数据来自市交通运输局；民航运输数据来自西安咸阳国际机场；民用汽车数据来自市车管所；邮政业务数据来自市邮政局；电信数据来自中国移动西安分公司、中国电信西安分公司、中国联通西安分公司、陕西铁通西安分公司；旅游数据来自市旅游局；货币金融数据来自中国人民银行西安分行营业管理部；证券数据、保险业数据来自市金融办；教育数据来自市教育局；科技数据来自市科技局；艺术表演团体、公共图书馆、文化馆、广播、电视数据来自市文化广电新闻出版局；博物馆数据来自市文物局；体育数据来自市体育局；卫生、新农合数据来自市卫生局；集中供热面积、建成区绿化面积来自市城乡建设委员会；城市污水处理、环境监测数据来自市环境保护局；安全生产数据来自市安全生产监督管理局；其他数据均来自市统计局。

Statistical Communique of Xi'an on the 2011 Economic and Social Development

Xi'an Municipal Bureau of Statistics and NBS Survey Office in xi'an

Mar.15th, 2012

In 2011, the municipal party committee and municipal government of Xi'an seized the theme of 'Scientific Outlook on Development', closely center on the main line of transformation of economic development way, implement various macro-control policies from Chinese Communist Party Central Committee, actively responded to the new domestic and international economic environment. Above of all, the economy of the whole city maintained steady and rapid development, the steady start opened a 'Twelfth Five-Year' new and bright age.

I. General Outlook

In 2011, the gross domestic product (GDP) preliminarily estimated was 386.421 billion Yuan, up by 13.8 percent against the previous year. Analyzed by different industries, the value added of the primary industry was 17.314 billion Yuan, up by 6.7 percent; the value added of the secondary industry was 169.716 billion Yuan, a rise of 16.4 percent; and the value added of the tertiary industry was 199.391 billion Yuan, up by 12.1 percent. The value added of the primary industry accounted for 4.5 percent of the GDP, that of the secondary industry accounted for 43.9 percent, and that of the tertiary industry accounted for 51.6 percent.

Table 1 The GDP and growth rate in 2006-2011

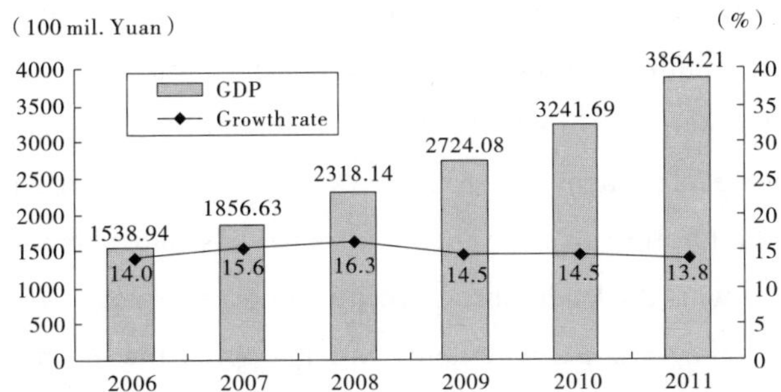

The general level of consumer prices in Xi'an was up by 5.6 percent against the previous year. Of this total, the prices for food went up by 11.3 percent; the retail prices for commodities up by 4.4 percent; the producer prices for manufactured goods were up by 2.5 percent; The purchasing prices for manufactured goods went up by 8.8 percent.

Table 2 The rate of increase and decrease of CPI in 2011

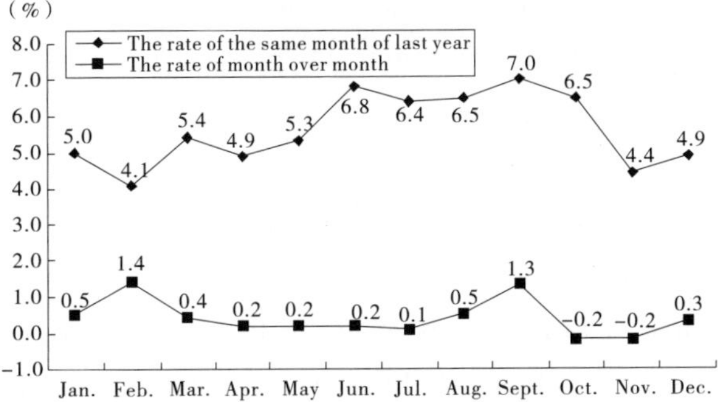

Up and fall extent of Residents Consumer Price Indices with previous year (2011)

unit:%

Item	2011
General Level of Residents Consumer Price	5.6
Food	11.3
#Grain	11.0
Tobaccos and Alcohols	3.0
Clothing	4.0
Household facilities and maintaining services	1.8
Medical, Health and Personal Articles	5.3
Transportation and Communication	0.3
Recreation, Education and Cultural articles and Services	1.0
Residence	5.1

In 2011, the newly increased employed people in urban areas in Xi'an numbered 119.4 thousand. The number of reemployment of laid-off workers was 43.2 thousand, and the number of reemployment of people who were difficult to find job was 12.4 thousand. The urban unemployment rate through unemployment registration was 3.9 percent at the end of 2011. The transfer of surplus agricultural labor force employment in Xi'an numbered 666.4 thousand.

The financial revenue totaled 64.988 billion Yuan, an increase of 27.3 percent as compared with the previous year. The General Budget Revenue of Regional Finance reached 31.855 billion Yuan, up by 31.7 percent. Of this, business tax, value added tax, income tax of enterprises and individual income tax were up by 25.9 percent, 19.8 percent, 32.4 percent and 20.2 percent respectively. The General Budget Expenditure of Regional Finance totaled 49.458 billion Yuan, up by 33.1 percent. Of this total expenditure, the expenditure on health care was up by 24.1 percent; that on agriculture, forestry and water affairs was up by 54.3 percent; that on education was up by 40.4 percent; that on social security and employment was up by 17.7 percent; that on general public service was up by 20.2 percent; that on environmental protection was up by 19.6 percent.

II. Agriculture

In 2011, the sown area of grain was 573.13 thousand hectares, a decrease of 1.3 percent as compared with the previous year; the sown area of oil-bearing crops was 8.82 thousand hectares, a decrease of 1.8 percent; the sown area of vegetables was 96.93 thousand hectares, up by 1.1 percent; the sown area of cotton was 5.97 thousand hectares, a decrease of 4.6 percent. The total output of grain in 2011 was 1.8204 million tons, a decrease of 1.0 percent. Of this, the output of summer crops was 0.9054 million tons, up by 3.5 percent, and that of the autumn grain was 0.9150 million tons, a decrease of 5.0 percent.

Mail Product of Agriculture Production in 2011

Name of Products	Unit	Output	Increase over the last year（%）
Edible	10,000 ton	1.17	0.2
Vegetable	10,000 ton	261.52	3.1
Fruit	10,000 ton	91.14	7.5
Meat	10,000 ton	14.46	6
Milk	10,000 ton	64.80	2.3
Egg	10,000 ton	12.56	1.5
Year-end Cattle on hand	10,000 head	21.24	-1.7
Year-end Pig on hand	10,000 head	94.40	0.1
Year-end Sheep on hang	10,000 head	29.60	0.5
Year-end Fowl on hand	10,000 head	1154.00	11.6

The total power of agricultural machinery was 2.8902 million kilowatts, up by 8.0 percent against the previous year; over 262.32 thousand hectares of farmland was with effective irrigation systems, a decrease of 6.7 percent; the total of fertilizer utilized (physical quantity) was 785.9 thousand tons, up by 0.6 percent.

III. Industry and Construction

In 2011, the value added by the industrial sector was 118.916 billion Yuan, up by 16.2 percent over the previous year. The value added of industrial enterprises above the designated size was 101.258 billion Yuan, up by 17.2 percent. Of this, the value added of the light industry was 21.226 billion Yuan, up by 14.1 percent; that of the heavy industry was 80.032 billion Yuan, up by 18.0 percent.

Table 3 The whole value added of Industry and growth rate in 2006-2011

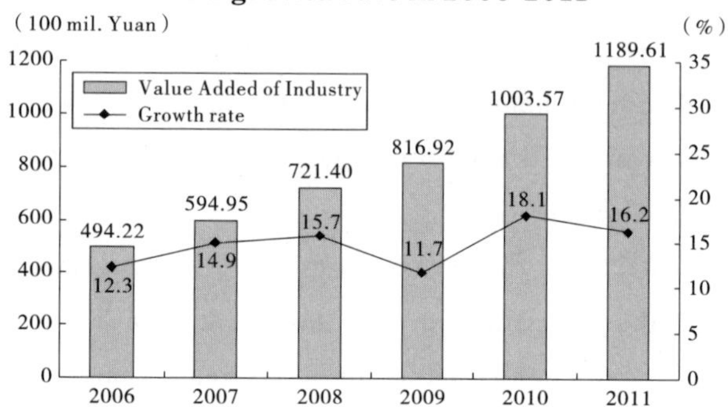

In 2011, of the industrial enterprises above designated size, the growth of value added for processing of food from agricultural products was up by 10.5 percent over the previous year; for manufacture of general machinery up by 19.5 percent; for manufacture of special purpose machinery up by 26.0 percent; for manufacture of transport equipment up by 13.4 percent; for manufacture of communication equipment, computers and other electronic equipment up by 65.4 percent; The growth of the value added for the major six high energy consuming industries were 19.8 percent, of which, that of the manufacture of non-metallic mineral products was 24.1 percent, manufacture of raw chemical materials and chemical products 25.1 percent, smelting and pressing of ferrous metals 43.2 percent, smelting and pressing of non-ferrous metals 3.2 percent, production and supply of electric power and heat power19.6 percent and 8.4 percent for processing of petroleum, coking, processing of nuclear fuel.

Output of Major Industrial Products above designated size in Xi'an(2011)

Name of Products	Unit	Output	Increase over the last year（%）
Electricity	100 million kilowatt-hour	95.01	-0.1
Crude Oil Processing	10,000 tons	153.17	-12.1
Dairy	10,000 tons	114.68	12.3
Liquid milk	10,000 tons	107.25	12.5
Commercial Concrete	10,000 cubic meter	1781.17	87.5
Machine-made paper and Cardboard	10,000 tons	49.79	0.7
AC motors	10,000 tons	564.69	24.4
Feed	10,000 tons	65.73	25.9
Synthetic detergent	10,000 tons	8.69	4.2
Cement	10,000 tons	409.99	-19.8
Draught fan	unit	1174	-29.1
Motor vehicle	10,000 units	55.67	-14.6
#Car	10,000 units	38.68	-25.3
High voltage switch board	unit	10840	236.9
Transformer	10,000 kilovolt amperes	11427.5	0.0
Electric cable	Km	7489	84.0
Gas compressor	10,000 units	712.36	32.3
Electronic component	100 million units	3.27	-76.2

The composite index on economic benefits of the industrial enterprises above the designated size in 2011 was 231.6, an increase of 7.2 percent over the previous year. The main business income of the industrial enterprises above designated size is 338.015 billion Yuan, up by 16.8 percent over the previous year. The profit and tax from the industrial enterprises above the designated size in 2011 was 33.236 billion Yuan, up by 6.3 percent. Of this, the profit was 21.614 billion Yuan, up by 2.9 percent.

In 2011, the value added by the construction enterprises in Xi'an was 50.755 billion Yuan, up by 17.0 percent over the previous year, and 332 construction enterprises qualified for general contracts and specialized contracts.

Table 4 The value added of construction and growth rate in 2006-2011

IV. Investment in Fixed Assets

The completed investment in fixed assets of the city in 2011 was 335.212 billion Yuan, up by 30.2 percent over the previous year. The real growth was 23.5 percent after deducting the price factors. Of the total investment in fixed assets(Not include farm-household investment) was 327.961 billon Yuan, up by 29.9 percent.

Table 5 The total fixed asset investment and growth rate in 2006-2011

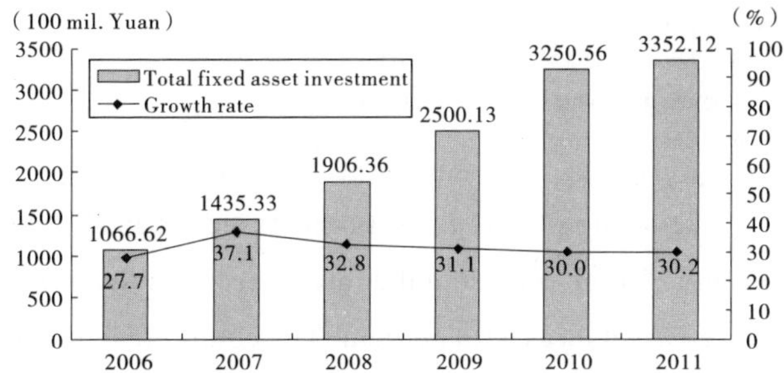

In whole investment, the investment in the primary industry was 7.223 billion Yuan, up by 22.2 percent against the previous year; in the secondary industry, it was 48.367 billion Yuan, up by 21.3 percent, of which industrial investment was 39.899 billion Yuan, up by 18.5 percent; in the tertiary industry, it was 272.371billion Yuan, up by 31.8 percent.

The investment in fixed assets and growth rate in Key industries in 2011

Item	Investment（100 mil. Yuan）	Increase over the last year（%）
Farming ,Forestry,Animal Husbandry and Fishery	72.23	22.2
Manufacturing	366.15	33.5
Transport,Storage and Postal Service	205.37	67.2
Information Transmission,Computer Service and Software Service	33.43	-4.1
Wholesale and Retail Trade	111.47	132.3
Accommodation and Catering Trade	59.89	56.8
Water conservancy,environment and public facilities administration industry	490.55	34.4
Education	75.43	41.5
Sanition,social insurance and social welfare industry	28.97	109.3
Public administration	166.41	8.2

In 2011, the investment in real estate development was 100.267 billion Yuan, up by 19.0 percent; the sold area of commercial housing was 17.9603 million square meters, up by 13.1 percent.

Mail Indicators of Real estate development and sales in 2011

Item	Unit	Absolute Number	Increase over the last year (%)
Investment in Real Estate Development	100 million yuan	1002.67	19.0
#Residential Building	100 million yuan	833.37	24.3
Floor Spaces of Commercial Houses Construction	10,000 sq.m	8215.57	22.7
#Residential Building	10,000 sq.m	7074.47	22.4
Floor Spaces of Newly Construction	10,000 sq.m	2280.07	11.6
#Residential Building	10,000 sq.m	2004.25	13.2
Floor Spaces of Commercial Houses Completed	10,000 sq.m	633.97	36.7
#Residential Building	10,000 sq.m	558.55	35.4
Floor Spaces of Commercial Houses Sold	10,000 sq.m	1796.03	13.1
#Residential Building	10,000 sq.m	1687.08	10.8

The value of fixed assets increased in 2011, was 137.006 billion Yuan, and the rate of projects delivered of fixed assets was 41.8 percent. The completed area of various kinds of buildings was 12.5759 million square meters, and the rate of completed area was 10.2 percent. 1430 projects of urban construction were completed and put into use this year, and the rate of construction projects completed and put into use was 60.3 percent.

V. Domestic Trade

In 2011, the total retail sales of consumer goods reached 193.518 billion Yuan, a growth of 20.1 percent over the previous year or a real growth of 15.0 percent after deducting price factors. An analysis on different areas showed that the retail sales of consumer goods in urban areas stood at 187.784 billion Yuan, up by 20.5 percent, and that in rural areas reached 5.734 billion Yuan, up by 9.8 percent. Grouped by consumption patterns, the income of retail sales of commodities was 173.243 billion Yuan, up by 20.5 percent; that of catering industry was 20.275 billion Yuan, up by 16.7 percent.

Table 6 The total retail sales of social consumer goods and growth rate in 2006-2011

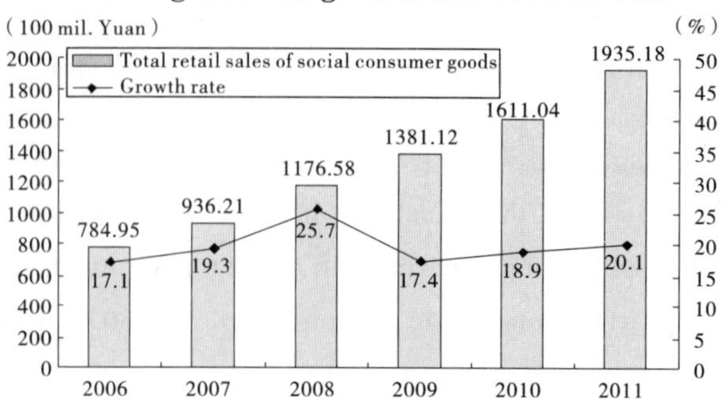

Of the total retail sales by wholesale and retail enterprises above designated size, the sales of food, beverage, wine and cigarette was up by 27.3 percent; clothing ,shoes, hats, and needle textiles up by 34.8 percent; sports-recreation up by 14.7 percent; books, newspapers and magazines up by 0.6 percent; daily necessities up by 23.4 percent; electric and electronic appliances for household use and audio-video equipment up by 29.2 percent; telecommunication equipment down by 19.1 percent; cultural and office goods up by 28.9 percent; gold, silver and jewelry up by 47.3 percent and motor vehicles up by 19.3 percent.

VI. Foreign Economic Relations

In 2011, the total value of imports and exports reached 12.579 billion US Dollars, up by 21.0 percent over the previous year. Of this, the value of exports was 5.804 billion US Dollars, up by 9.2 percent, and that of imports was 6.775 billion US Dollars, up by 33.5 percent.

Table 7 The total imports and exports and growth rate in 2006-2011

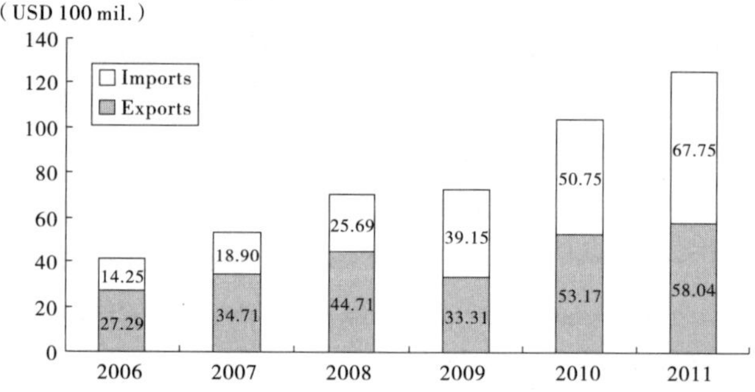

In total imports and exports, the value of imports and exports of general trade was 7.530 billion US Dollars, up by 36.9 percent, accounted for 29.2 percent of import and export whole value of Xi'an region. The value of processing trade was 3.671 billion US Dollars, up by 7.7 percent, accounted for 29.2 percent of import and export whole value of Xi'an region.

Of the main import and export commodities, the value of exports of electromechanical products was 3.824 billion US Dollars, a decrease of 0.3 percent; that of imports of electromechanical products was 4.203 billion US Dollars, up by 21.6 percent. The value of exports of agricultural product was 0.480 billion US Dollars, up by 57.8 percent; that of imports of agricultural products was 0.141 billion US Dollars, up by 38.5 percent. The value of exports of mineral products was 0.358 billion US Dollars, up by 0.1percent; that of imports of mineral products was 0.973 billion US Dollars, up by 58.5 percent. The value of exports of textile products was 0.178 billion US Dollars, a decrease of 4.6 percent; that of imports of textile products was 3.73 million US Dollars, a decrease of 22.6 percent.

In 2011, there were 99 Foreign Direct Investment projects approved in Xi'an; the contracted Foreign Direct Investment was 1.201 billion US dollars, up by 0.3 percent over the pervious year; the realized Foreign Direct Investment was 2.005 billion US dollars, up by 28.0 percent.

VII. Transportation, Post, Telecommunications and Tourism

In 2011, the total freight traffic reached 0.392 billion tons, up by 14.3 percent over the previous year. The total goods transportation turnover reached 52.120 billion ton-kilometers, up by 21.4 percent over the previous year. The Total passenger transport reached 0.343 billion persons, up by 10.3 percent over the previous year. The passenger transport turnover reached 32.236 billion person-kilometers, up by 9.8 percent over the previous year.

The Total Freight Traffic and growth rate created by Kinds of transport Mode in 2011

Item	Unit	Amount	Growth rate (%)
The Total Freight Traffic	10,000 tons	39239.26	14.3
Highway	10,000 tons	38399.00	14.2
Railway	10,000 tons	823.00	16.5
Airway	10,000 tons	17.26	11.3
Goods Transportation Turnover	100 million ton-kilometers	521.20	21.4
Highway	100 million ton-kilometers	311.09	25.1
Railway	100 million ton-kilometers	208.96	16.5
Airway	100 million ton-kilometers	1.15	-17.0

The Total Passenger Traffic and growth rate created by Kinds of transport Mode in 2011

Item	Unit	Amount	Growth rate (%)
The Total Passenger Transport	10,000 person	34335.20	10.3
Highway	10,000 person	29358.00	10.6
Railway	10,000 person	2860.90	2.6
Airway	10,000 person	2116.30	17.5
The Passenger Transport Turnover	billion person-kilometers	32.24	9.8
Highway	billion person-kilometers	16.03	19.1
Railway	billion person-kilometers	5.95	9.2
Airway	billion person-kilometers	10.25	-1.9

The total number of motor vehicles for civilian use reached 1174.9 thousand by the end of 2011, up by 22.4 percent, of which private-owned vehicles numbered 976.7 thousand, up 24.8 percent. The total number of cars for civilian use stood at 618.9 thousand, up by 25.8 percent, of which private-owned cars numbered 547.1thousand, up by 27.6 percent.

The revenue of post services totaled 0.816 billion Yuan, up by 15.5 percent over the previous year; that of telecommunication services was 10.047 billion Yuan, up by 13.3 percent. At the end of 2011, there were 2.7063 million fixed telephone users; there were 16.1415 million mobile phone users, of which the number of telecom and China Unicom 3G mobile phone was 1773.7 thousand, and that of Telecom Internet was 1.841 million.

The total of domestic tourists was 65.53 million person-times, up by 26.0 percent; that of oversea tourists was 1002.3 thousand person-times, up by 19.1 percent. The revenue from tourism totaled 53.015 billion Yuan, up by 30.8 percent. Of this, the revenue from foreign exchange was 0.641 billion US Dollars, up by 20.9 percent.

VIII. Financial Intermediation

Savings deposit in Renminbi and foreign currencies in all items of financial institutions totaled 1052.632 billion Yuan at the end of 2011, an increase of 16.4 percent as compared with the end of the previous year. The savings deposit in Renminbi stood at 1043.027 billion Yan, an increase of 16.8 percent, of which the savings deposit of urban and rural residents was 415.565 billion Yuan, up by 14.1 percent. Loans in all items of financial institutions in Renminbi and foreign currencies reached 770.019 billion Yuan, an increase of 16.8 percent as compared with the end of the previous year. The loans in Renminbi stood at 756.493 billion Yuan, an increase of 16.7 percent, of which the short-term loans totaled 143.129 billion Yuan, down by 30.4 percent, and medium-and-long term loans reached 577.648 billion Yuan, up by 13.8 percent.

The trading volume of stock exchange market was 985.143 billion Yuan in 2011, a decrease of 18.6 percent as compared with the previous year. There were

28 listed companies in Xi'an at the end of 2011 of which the total capital stock was 19.370 billion shares, and the total market value was 159.265 billion Yuan. The were 1.65 million accounts in stock market at the end of 2011, an increase of 8.4 percent as compared with the end of the previous year.

By the end of 2011, there were 45 insurance institutions, of which the number of property insurance was 21, and that of life insurance was 24. There were 110 intermediary organs of insurance. The received by the insurance companies totaled 16.257 billion Yuan in 2011, up by 25.7 percent. Of this, the revenue from property insurance was 4.496 billion Yuan, up by 32.8 percent; that from life insurance was 11.761 billion Yuan, up by 23.1 percent. In total, insurance companies paid an indemnity worth of 3.714 billion Yuan, up by 40.7 percent over the previous year, of which the worth of property insurance and life insurance were 2.033 billion Yuan and 1.681 billion Yuan respectively, up by 38.8 percent and 43.2 percent respectively.

IX. Education and Science and Technology

There were 44 post-graduate training units, with 81.7 thousand post-graduate education enrollments, including 26.7 thousand new students; there were 50 general universities and colleges, with 685.2 thousand general tertiary education enrollments, including 176.8 thousand graduates; there were 423 general middle schools and high schools, with 472 thousand junior high education enrollments and 164.4 thousand graduates; there were 1424 primary schools, with 513.9 thousand primary education enrollments and 89.2 thousand graduates. The enrollment rates for school-age population of primary school and junior high school were 99.97 percent and 99.65 percent respectively.

236 science and technology projects were carried out in 2011 (including 27 projects of high technology). Of this, there were 116 projects carried out for technology innovation and achievements transfer. There were 163 high-tech enterprises major supported, 11 demonstration gardens of agricultural science and technology supported for construction, 6 technology demonstration towns and 14 important direction projects of industry science and technology in districts and counties implemented. 0.46 Billion Yuan was strived from the national and the province. The turnover in technology market reached 20.459 billion Yuan. 27717 patents were applied in 2011.

X. Culture, Sports and Public Health

By the end of 2011, there were 14 art-performing groups, 15 public libraries, 181 culture stations, 20 museums. 7497 various kinds of mass cultural activities were organized in 2011. There were 2 television stations, 2 radio broadcasting stations, and 6 radio broadcasting and television stations. The coverage rate of television broadcasting and radio broadcasting were 98.6 percent and 99.42 percent respectively.

260 mass sports performances and competition activities were organized in 2011, and 300 sports competition were organized and host by sports associations, including 1 international and national sports competition, with more than 2 million persons per time taking part in these sports above. In 2011, there were 45 fitness equipment delivery projects of urban communities, 5 fitness projects for township farmers, 30 sports demonstration stations of villages and towns, and 104 public national fitness paths of community built, and 30 were updated. There were 7,376 social sport instructors, 1,800 sites for morning and evening exercise and 125 sites for fitness Qigong, with 5,625 taking part in fitness Qigong.

In 2011, the delegation of Xi'an won 2 gold medals, 7 silver medals and 6 bronze medals in the Seventh National City Games, and obtained 362 group total scores finally. The team from Xi'an city won Sportsmanship Award in this sports competition.

At the end of 2011, there were 5,554 health institutions in Xi'an, including 368 general hospitals and health centers. There were all 61.3 thousand health care workers, including 21.6 thousand practicing (assistant) doctors. General health centers in Xi'an possessed 41.0 thousand beds.

XI. Population, Living Conditions and Social Security

The resident population of Xi'an city at the end of

2011 was 8.5134 million, 4.373 million male and 4.1404 million female, accounted for 51.4 percent and 48.6 percent respectively. The sex ratio was 105.62(granted the female was 100).The born population in the whole year was 82.5 thousand, and the birth rate was 9.71‰.The death population in the whole year was 45.7 thousand, and the death rate was 5.38‰. The net growth of population was 39.3 thousand and the natural growth rate was 4.33‰. The urban population was 5.9679 million, accounted for 70.1 percent; the rural population was 2.5455 million, accounted for 29.9 percent. The total household population was 7.9183 million, up by 1.2 percent by previous year.

In 2011, the annual per capita disposable income of urban households was 25,981 Yuan, or a real increase of 10.6 percent over the previous year when the factors of price increase were deducted, and the annual per capital net income of rural households was 9,788 Yuan, or a real increase of 19.6 percent. The proportion of expenditure on food to the total expenditure of households was 31.3 percent for urban households and 31.9 percent for rural households. The annual per capita building area of urban households was 28.9 square meters, and annual per capita living space of rural households was 67 square meters.

Table 8 Urban and rural resident's income in 2006-2008

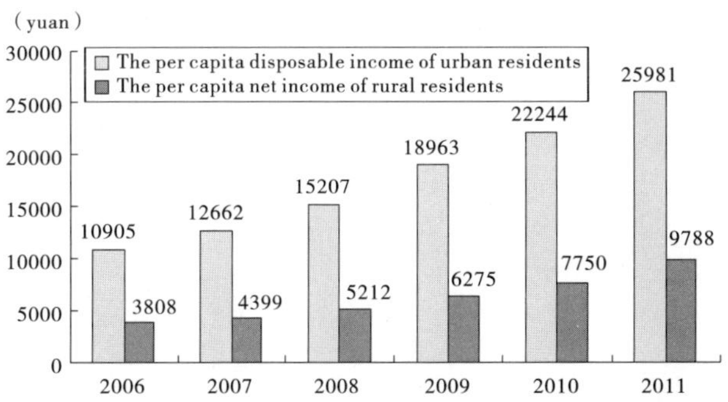

By the end of 2011, a total of 4.0427 million people participated in urban basic health insurance program; a total of 2.158 million people participated in basic pension program for staff and workers of enterprises; a total of 1.3482 million people participated in unemployment insurance programs; a total of 1.2307 million people participated in work accident insurance; a total of 954.5 thousand people participated in maternity insurance programs for staff and workers. The number of farmers taking part in the new cooperative medical care system in rural areas reached 3.9485 million, with a participation rate of 97.79 percent, 100 percent covered.

XII. Urban Construction, Environment and Work Safety

The total investment of municipal utilities was 23.68 billion Yuan.20 pedestrian bridges and 6 bus harbors were newly built. 1.19 million square meters area for centralized heating in urban areas was newly added,92 green squares were reformed and newly built. 1.6 million square meters area for landscaping in urban was newly added.

In 2011, there were 305 days with air quality better than standard Grade II, 1 day more than last year. The annual mean concentration of Sulfur dioxide, Nitrogen dioxide and Respirable particulate matter was 0.042 Mg / cu.m, 0.041 Mg / cu.m and 0.118 Mg / cu.m, a decrease by 2.3 percent, 8.9 percent and 6.3 percent. All of water quality of reference water source reached the state standard. The average value of sound level equivalent of regional environmental noises was 55.3 decibel, and the average value of sound level equivalent of transportation noises was 68.6 decibel.

In 2011, various kinds of work accidents amounted to 4,199, an increase of 26 as compared with the previous year. Of this, there were 566 people dead, a decrease of 2 person; there were 2,271 people injured, a decrease of 258; the property losses was 27.8053 million Yuan, a decrease of 8.8627 million Yuan.

Notes:

1. All figures in this Communiqué are preliminary statistics.

2. Gross domestic product (GDP) and value added as quoted in this Communiqué are calculated at current prices, whereas their growth rates are at constant prices.

3. From 2011, the count level of Industrial enterprises Above Designated Size of the index that of annual main business income is raised from 5 million to 20 million.

4. Six highly energy-consuming industries are: manufacture of raw chemical materials and chemical products, manufacture of non-metallic mineral products, smelting and pressing of ferrous metals, smelting and pressing of non-ferrous metals, oil processing, coking and nuclear fuel processing, and production and supply of electricity and heat.

5. From 2011, the count level of Investment in Fixed Assets of the index that of the total planned investment is raised from 500 Thousand Yuan to 5 million, then the investment of 2011 can not compared with that of 2010. Corresponding to the investment, the growth rate can be compared for the rate is calculated in the same statistical coverage. From 2011, the index was redefined of " Investment in Fixed Assets (not include farm-household investment)" for the statistical coverage of the index expand to rural enterprises and organization.

6. From 2010, new grouping method is adopted for the statistics on the total retail sales of consumer goods: grouping according to operation location changes from city, county and below county level to urban and rural areas; grouping according to industries is cancelled and new grouping according to retail sales of commodities and earnings of catering is added.

Data Sources:

In this communiqu é , data of price are from NBS Survey Office in Xi'an ;data of newly increased employed people, unemployment rate through unemployment registration and social security are from the Xi'an Municipal Bureau of Human Resources and Social Security; financial data are from the Xi'an Municipal Bureau of Finance; data of imports and exports are from the Xi'an Customs; data of utilizing foreign capital are from the Xi'an Municipal Bureau of Business; data of railway transportation are from the Xi'an Municipal Bureau of Railways; data of highway transportation are from the Xi'an Municipal Bureau of Transport; data of air transport are from the Xi'an-Xian yang International Airport; data of motor vehicles for civilian use are from the Xi'an vehicle administration; data of post services are from the Xi'an Municipal Bureau of post; data of telecommunications are from Xi'an branch of China Mobile、China Unicom、 China Telecom, and Shaanxi CTT; data of tourism are from the Xi'an Tourism Administration; data of monetary and financial are from business management department for Xi'an branch of the People's Bank of China; data of listed companies and insurance are from Xi'an Municipal Finance Office; data of education are from the Xi'an Municipal Bureau of Education; data of technology are from Xi'an Municipal Bureau of Technology; data of art-performing groups, public libraries, culture centers, radio and television are from the Xi'an Municipal Bureau of Culture, Radio, Press and Publication; data of museum are from Xi'an Municipal Bureau of Heritage; data of sports are from the Xi'an Municipal Bureau of Sport; data of health and new cooperative medical care system in rural areas are from the Xi'an Municipal Bureau of Health; data of central heating area and green area are from Xi'an Municipal Urban and Rural Construction Committee; data of sewage treatment in urban and environment monitoring are from the Xi'an Municipal Bureau of Environmental Protection; data of work safety are from the State Administration of Work Safety; all the other data are from Xi'an Municipal Bureau of Statistics.

1 综　合

GENERAL SURVEY

资料整理：张小文　刘　婷　张利民　张　奇
Data management:Zhang Xiaowen　Liu Ting　Zhang Limin　Zhang Qi

第一部分　综合

一、简要说明

本章资料主要包括西安市行政区划、自然地理、自然资源、气象、法人单位、产业活动单位、国民经济和社会发展等综合资料，法人单位和产业活动单位由西安市统计局普查中心提供，其他由综合处根据局内各专业处及有关部门统计资料进行整理和编辑。

二、主要指标

法人单位数（个）	87493	比上年增长	24.5%
产业活动单位数（个）	96146	比上年增长	22.2%
生产总值（亿元）	3862.58	比上年增长	13.8%
农林牧渔业总产值（亿元）	272.66	比上年增长	6.6%
工业增加值（亿元）	1189.61	比上年增长	16.2%
全社会固定资产投资额（亿元）	3346.26	比上年增长	30.0%
社会消费品零售总额（亿元）	1965.98	比上年增长	20.1%
地方财政一般预算收入（亿元）	318.55	比上年增长	31.7%
地方财政一般预算支出（亿元）	494.58	比上年增长	33.1%
出口总额（亿美元）	58.27	比上年增长	9.6%
城镇居民人均可支配收入（元）	25981	比上年增长	16.8%
农村居民人均纯收入（元）	9788	比上年增长	26.3%

1 GENERAL SURVEY

Ⅰ.Brief Introduction

This chapter consists of mainly unified data of administrative divisions, natural geography, natural resources, meteorology, Number of Enterprises,Number of Industrial Active Units,national economy and social development of Xi'an city. Corporate units and industrial activity units were provided by the Xi'an Bureau of Statistics census.It is compiled by Integration Division according to the reported data from other divisions of the Xi'an Bureau of Statistics and other departments of the municipal government.

Ⅱ.Major Indicators

		Increase over Preceding Year
Number of Enterprises(unit)	87493	24.5%
Number of Industrial Active Units(unit)	96146	22.2%
Gross Domestic Product(100 mil. Yuan)	3862.58	13.8%
Gross Output Value of Farming, Forestry, Animal Husbandry and Fishery(100 mil. Yuan)	272.66	6.6%
Gross Industrial Added Value(100 mil. yuan)	1189.61	16.2%
Investment Fulfilled In Fixed Assets(100 mil. yuan)	3346.26	30.0%
Total Retail Sales of Consumer Goods(100 mil. yuan)	1965.98	20.1%
Local Government Revenue(100 mil. yuan)	318.55	31.7%
Local Government Expenditures(100 mil. yuan)	494.58	33.1%
Total Value of Exports(USD 100 mil.)	58.27	9.6%
Per Capita Annual Disposable Income of Urban Households (yuan)	25981	16.8%
Per Capita Net Income of Rural Residents(yuan)	9788	26.3%

1-1 行政区划（2011年底）

Administrative Division （End of 2011）

单位:个 (unit)

区县名称	Name of District and County	乡镇及街道办 Township and Urban Subdistrict Office	镇数 Town	乡数 Township	街道办事处 Urban Subdistrict Office	村民委员会 Villagers' Committee	社区居委会 Neighbourhood Committee
西安市	**Xi'an**	**176**	**69**	**1**	**106**	**3025**	**721**
(一)市区	**Urban Districts**	**108**	**2**		**106**	**1524**	**673**
新城区	Xincheng	9			9	1	104
碑林区	Beilin	8			8	0	103
莲湖区	Lianhu	9			9	5	127
灞桥区	Baqiao	9			9	223	37
未央区	Weiyang	8			8	103	78
雁塔区	Yanta	8			8	92	117
阎良区	Yanliang	7	2		5	80	23
临潼区	Lintong	23			23	284	38
长安区	Chang'an	22			22	603	29
沣东新城	Fengdongxincheng	5			5	133	17
(二)四县	**Four Counties**	**68**	**67**	**1**		**1501**	**48**
蓝田县	Lantian	22	22			519	9
周至县	Zhouzhi	22	22			376	14
户　县	Huxian	16	16			518	21
高陵县	Gaoling	8	7	1		88	4

注：本表数据来自2011年市民政部门报表。

Note:Figures in the table are from the 2011 report of civil administration department.

1-2 土地面积和常住人口密度（2011年）

Statistics on Land Area and Density of Permanent Population （2011）

区县名称	Name of District and County	土地面积 Area 绝对数（平方公里）Absolute Value (sq.km)	比重(%) Proportion (%)	常住人口（万人）Total of Permanent Population (10 000 persons)	常住人口密度(人/平方公里) Density of Permanent Population (person/ sq.km)
西安市	**Xi 'an**	**10108**	**100.0**	**851.34**	**842**
(一)市区	**Urban Districts**	**3582**	**35.4**	**653.72**	**1825**
新城区	Xincheng	30	0.3	59.23	19743
碑林区	Beilin	24	0.2	61.87	25779
莲湖区	Lianhu	43	0.4	70.13	16309
灞桥区	Baqiao	325	3.2	59.87	1842
未央区	Weiyang	262	2.6	81.14	3097
雁塔区	Yanta	149	1.5	118.48	7952
阎良区	Yanliang	244	2.4	28.01	1148
临潼区	Lintong	915	9.1	65.98	721
长安区	Chang'an	1590	15.7	109.01	686
(二)四县	**Four Counties**	**6526**	**64.6**	**197.62**	**303**
蓝田县	Lantian	2008	19.9	51.65	257
周至县	Zhouzhi	2949	29.2	56.59	192
户　县	Huxian	1282	12.7	55.85	436
高陵县	Gaoling	287	2.8	33.53	1168

注：本表土地面积数据来自2011年市土地部门报表。

Note: Figures in the table are from the 2011 report of department in charge of land.

1-3　自然状况和资源（2011年）

Nature Conditions and Resources（2011）

指　　标	Item	2011
一、自然状况	**Nature Conditions**	
土地总面积(平方公里)	Total Land Area (sq.km)	10108
# 市区面积	Urban Area	3582
气候（市区）	Climate (Urban Area)	
平均气温(℃)	Average Annual Temperature (℃)	14.5
年降水量(毫米)	Total Annual Precipitation (mm)	723.6
日照时数(小时)	Total Sunshine Time (hour)	1594.1
平均风速(米/秒)	Average Wind-speed (m/sec.)	1.2
二、自然资源	**Natural Resources**	
年末实有耕地面积（万亩）	Cultivated Area Year-end (10 000 mu)	377.10
林业用地面积（千公顷）	Area of Forestry (1 000 hectare)	508.39
全市水面面积 (万亩)	Whole Water Area (10 000 mu)	4.50
# 可养殖面积	Area for Aquatics Breeding	3.00
水资源总量(亿立方米)	Total Water Resource (0.1 billion cu.m)	30.74
# 天然地表水资源总量	Total Savageness Surface Water Resource	25.84
地下水资源总量(亿立方米)	Total Ground Water Resource (0.1 billion cu.m)	18.76

注：1.本表数据来自2011年气象、林业、水务等部门报表。

2.全市水面面积包括湖泊、水库、鱼塘、城市段河流面积等。

Note:1.Figures in the table are from the 2011 reports of departments in charge of meteorology, forestry and water affairs.

2.The whole water area of Xi'an includes the water area of lakes,reservoirs,fish ponds city sections of river,etc.

1-4　气 象 情 况（2011年）

Climate Condition （2011）

区县名称	Name of District and County	平均气温 (℃) Average Temperature (℃)	日照时数 (小时) Sunshine Time (hour)	降水天数 (天) Raining days (day)	年降水量 (毫米) Total Annual Precipitation (mm)	平均风速 (米/秒) Average Wind-speed (m/second)
市　区	Urban Districts	14.5	1594.1	101	723.6	1.2
临潼区	Lintong	13.9	1537.5	99	769.0	1.6
长安区	Chang'an	13.3	1717.5	121	656.0	1.5
蓝田县	Lantian	13.0	2069.3	118	872.8	1.4
周至县	Zhouzhi	13.2	1719.9	131	948.0	1.1
户　县	Huxian	14.3	2023.5	107	878.2	0.8
高陵县	Gaoling	14.1	2039.2	111	670.0	1.4

注：本表数据来自2011年市气象部门报表。

Note:Figures in the table are from the 2011 report of meteorological department.

1-5　市区各月主要气象指标（2011年）

Main Climate Condition Every Month in Urban Districts（2011）

月 份	Month	平均气温 (℃) Average Temperature (℃)	日照时数 (小时) Sunshine Time (hour)	降水天数 (天) Raining days (day)	年降水量 (毫米) Total Annual Precipitation (mm)	平均风速 (米/秒) Average Wind-speed (m/second)
一月	January	-0.2	108.9	5	2.1	1.1
二月	February	4.2	77.0	3	12.9	1.2
三月	March	8.8	184.2	5	11.9	1.2
四月	April	18.0	222.6	4	18.3	1.3
五月	May	21.0	175.6	8	77.6	1.4
六月	June	26.3	186.4	9	39.3	1.4
七月	July	27.4	175.7	9	72.4	1.4
八月	August	24.9	141.8	9	75.9	1.2
九月	September	19.0	51.0	18	298.9	1.2
十月	October	15.0	115.4	12	51.5	1.1
十一月	November	9.8	64.6	15	54.3	1.1
十二月	December	2.0	90.9	4	8.5	1.0

1-6　国有土地使用权出让、划拨情况

Basic Statistics on Lease and Administrative Allocation of Use Right of State-Owned Land

项　　目	Item	2000	2005	2006	2007	2008	2009	2010	2011
国有土地使用权出让	**Lease of the Use Right of State-owned Land**								
出让地块(宗)	Land leased (item)	202	312	316	333	278	297	386	474
协议	Agreement	200	241	225	171	119	100	173	133
招标	Invitation for Bid				1	3		3	
拍卖	Auction	2	8	7	3	5	1	11	
挂牌交易	Listed Transaction		63	84	158	149	196	199	341
出让面积（公顷）	Area of Totally Leased Land (hectare)	3115	986	1208	843	809	1047	1364	1386
土地使用权出让总收入（万元）	**Total Revenue from Leasing of the Use Right(10 000 yuan)**	**38428**	**89039**	**156231**	**267666**	**309181**	**284405**	**358098**	**334069**
国有土地使用权划拨	**Administrative Allocation of the Use Right of State-owned Land**								
划拨地块（宗）	Land Allocated (item)	113	100	90	100	102	79	108	253
划拨面积（公顷）	Area of Land Allocated(hectare)	12543	835	259	388	455	1721	1027	1426

注：本表数据来自2011年市土地部门报表。

Note:Figures in the table are from the 2011 report of meteorological department.

1-7 按登记注册类型分法人单位（2011年）

Impersonal Entities Grouped by Status of Registion （2011）

单位：个 （unit）

分组	Item	法人单位数 Number of Enterprises	企业 Enterprises
总计	**Total**	**87493**	**74673**
按登记注册类型分	**Grouped by Status of Registion**		
（一）内资企业	Domestic Funded Enterprises	86690	73876
国有企业	State-owned Enterprises	6901	1912
集体企业	Collective-owned Enterprises	2798	1652
股份合作企业	Cooperative Enterprises	398	366
联营企业	Joint Ownership Enterprises	240	213
国有联营企业	State Joint Ownership Enterprises	34	26
集体联营企业	Collective Joint Ownership Enterprises	79	71
国有与集体联营企业	Joint State-collective Ownership Enterprises	20	16
其他联营企业	Other Joint Ownership Enterprises	107	100
有限责任公司	Limited Liability Corporations	26365	26322
国有独资公司	State Sole Funded Corporations	170	169
其他有限责任公司	Other Limited Liability Corporations	26195	26153
股份有限公司	Share-holding Corporations Limited	1068	1059
私营企业	Private Enterprises	39511	38910
私营独资企业	Private-funded Enterprises	10765	10312
私营合伙企业	Private Partnership Enterprises	2156	2074
私营有限责任公司	Private Limited Liability Corporations	23748	23692
私营股份有限公司	Private Share-holding Corporations Ltd.	2842	2832
其他内资企业	Other Domestic Funded Enterprises	9409	3442
（二）港、澳、台商投资企业	Enterprises with Funds from Hong Kong, Macao and Taiwan	266	264
与港澳台商合资经营	Joint-venture with Funds from Hong Kong,Macao and Taiwan	98	98
与港澳台商合作经营	Cooperative Enterprises with Funds from Hong Kong Macau and Taiwan	14	14
港澳台商独资	Enterprises with Sole Investment from Hong Kong Macau and Taiwan	132	130
港澳台商投资股份有限公司	Share-holding Corporations Ltd. with funds from Hong Kong, Macao & Taiwan	20	20
其他港、澳、台商投资企业	Other Enterprises with Funds from Hong Kong, Macao and Taiwan	2	2
（三）外商投资企业	Foreign Funded Enterprises	537	533
中外合资营企业	Sino-foreign Joint Ventures	207	207
中外合作企业	Sino-Foreign Cooperation Enterprises	19	17
法人外资企业	Foreign Owned Enterprises	275	273
外商投资股份有限公司	Limited Company Funded by Foreign Investment	34	34
其他外商投资	Other Foreign Funded Enterprises	2	2
在总计中企业按控股情况分	**Grouped by Controlling Share Hold**		
国有控股	Controlling Share Hold by the State	2945	2945
集体控股	Controlling Share Hold by the Collective	3033	3033
私人控股	Controlling Share Hold by the Private	54688	54688
港澳台控股	Controlling Share Hold by the Hong Kong,Macao and Taiwan	271	271
外商控股	Controlling Share Hold by the Foreign Investment	537	537
其他	Others	13199	13199

1-8 按行业分法人单位（2011年）

Impersonal Entities by Sector（2011）

单位：个 （unit)

分组	Item	法人单位数 Number of Enterprises	企业 Enterprises
总　计	**Total**	**87493**	**74673**
（一）农、林、牧、渔业	Agriculture,Forestry,Animal Husbandry and Fishery	1579	1258
农　业	Farming	706	599
林　业	Forestry	199	180
畜牧业	Animal Husbandry	370	302
渔　业	Fishery	27	24
农、林、牧、渔服务业	Services in Support of Agriculture	277	153
（二）采矿业	Mining	215	215
煤炭开采和洗选业	Mining and Washing of Coal	16	16
石油和天然气开采业	Extraction of Petroleum and Natural Gas	65	65
黑色金属矿采选业	Mining of Ferrous Metal Ores	9	9
有色金属矿采选业	Mining of Non-ferrous Metal Ores	26	26
非金属矿采选业	Mining and Processing of Nonmetal Ores	63	63
其他采矿业	Mining of Other Ores	36	36
（三）制造业	Manufacturing	12262	12262
农副食品加工业	Processing of Food from Agricultural Products	346	346
食品制造业	Manufacture of Foods	350	350
饮料制造业	Manufacture of Beverages	111	111
烟草制品业	Manufacture of Tobacco	4	4
纺织业	Manufacture of Textile	149	149
纺织服装、鞋、帽制造业	Manufacture of Textile Wearing Apparel, Footware and Caps	157	157
皮革、毛皮、羽毛（绒）及其制品业	Manufacture of Leather, Fur, Feather and Related Products	24	24
木材加工及木、竹、藤、棕、草制品业	Processing of Timber,Manufacture of Wood,Bamboo,Rattan, Plam and Straw Products	139	139
家具制造业	Manufacture of Furniture	339	339
造纸及纸制品业	Manufacture of Paper and Paper Products	307	307
印刷业和记录媒介的复制	Printing,Reproduction of Recording Media	488	488
文教体育用品制造业	Manufacture of Articles For Culture,Education and Sport Activities	49	49
石油加工、炼焦及核燃料加工业	Processing of Petroleum, Coking, Processing of Nuclear Fuel	50	50
化学原料及化学制品制造业	Manufacture of Raw Chemical Materials and Chemical Products	639	639

1-8　续表1 continued 1

单位：个 (unit)

分　组	Item	法人单位数 Number of Enterprises	企 业 Enterprises
医药制造业	Manufacture of Medicines	325	325
化学纤维制造业	Manufacture of Chemical Fibers	20	20
橡胶制品业	Manufacture of Rubber	99	99
塑料制品业	Manufacture of Plastics	301	301
非金属矿物制品业	Manufacture of Non-metallic Mineral Products	986	986
黑色金属冶炼及压延加工业	Smelting and Pressing of Ferrous Metals	133	133
有色金属冶炼及压延加工业	Smelting and Pressing of Non-ferrous Metals	148	148
金属制品业	Manufacture of Metal Products	851	851
通用设备制造业	Manufacture of General Purpose Machinery	1655	1655
专用设备制造业	Manufacture of Special Equipment	1366	1366
交通运输设备制造业	Manufacture of Transport Equipment	448	448
电气机械及器材制造业	Manufacture of Electric Equipment and Machinery	1251	1251
通信设备、计算机及其他电子设备制造业	Manufacture of Communication Equipment, Computers and other Electronic Equipment	772	772
仪器仪表及文化办公用	Manufacture of Measuring Instruments and Machinery for Cultural Activity and Office Work	469	469
工艺品及其他制造业	Manufacture of Artwork and Other Manufacturing	231	231
废弃资源和废旧材料回收加工业	Recycling and Disposal of Waste	55	55
（四）电力、燃气及水的生产和供应业	Production and Distribution of Electricity,Gas and Water	218	218
电力、热力的生产和供应业	Production and Supply of Electric Power and Heat Power	120	120
燃气生产和供应业	Gas mining and supplying industry	38	38
水的生产和供应业	Production and Supply of Water	60	60
（五）建筑业	Construction	5777	5777
房屋和土木工程建筑业	Construction of Building & Civil Engineering	1658	1658
建筑安装业	Architectural Installation	1191	1191
建筑装饰业	Architectural Decoration	2153	2153
其他建筑业	Other Construction	775	775
（六）交通运输、仓储和邮政业	Traffic, Transport, Storage and Post	1505	1476
铁路运输业	Transport Via Railway	28	28
道路运输业	Transport Via Road	764	743
城市公共交通业	Urban Public Traffic	101	99

1-8 续表2 continued 2

单位：个 (unit)

分　组	Item	法人单位数 Number of Enterprises	企业 Enterprises
水上运输业	Water Transport	3	3
航空运输业	Air Transport	40	39
管道运输业	Transport Via Pipeline	7	7
装卸搬运和其他运输服务业	Loading, Unloading, Portage and Other Transport Services	321	320
仓储业	Storage	195	191
邮政业	Post	46	46
（七）信息传输、计算机服务和软件业	Information Transmission, Computer Services and Software	2872	2856
电信和其他信息传输服务业	Telecom & Other Information Transmission Services	468	466
计算机服务业	Computer Services	1311	1300
软件业	Software Industry	1093	1090
（八）批发和零售业	Wholesale and Retail Trades	28073	28073
批发业	Wholesale Trade	15449	15449
零售业	Retail Trade	12624	12624
（九）住宿和餐饮业	Hotels and Catering Services	2439	2439
住宿业	Hotels	934	934
餐饮业	Catering Services	1505	1505
（十）金融业	Financial Intermediation	480	458
银行业	Bank	71	68
证券业	Security Activities	59	59
保险业	Insurance	120	118
其他金融活动	Other Financial Intermediation	230	213
（十一）房地产业	Real Estate	5060	5045
房地产业	Real Estate	5060	5045
（十二）租赁和商务服务业	Leasing and Business Services	7773	7567
租赁业	Leasing	667	665
商务服务业	Business Services	7106	6902
（十三）科学研究、技术服务和地质勘查业	Scientific Research, Technical Sevice and Geologic Prospecting	3443	2923
研究与试验发展	Research and Experimental Development	306	211
专业技术服务业	Professional Technical Services	1747	1580
科技交流和推广服务业	Services of Science and Technology Exchanges and Promotion	1264	1036
地质勘查业	Geologic Prospecting	126	96

1–8 续表3 continued 3

单位：个 (unit)

分 组	Item	法人单位数 Number of Enterprises	企 业 Enterprises
（十四）水利、环境和公共设施管理业	Management of Water Conservancy, Environment and Public Facilities	614	449
水利管理业	Management of Water Conservancy	106	34
环境管理业	Environmental Management	138	101
公共设施管理业	Management of Public Facilities	370	314
（十五）居民服务和其他服务业	Services to Households and Other Services	2563	2493
居民服务业	Services to Households	865	812
其他服务业	Other Services	1698	1681
（十六）教育	Education	3212	245
教 育	Education	3212	245
（十七）卫生、社会保障和社会福利业	Health, Social Security and Social Welfare	2270	80
卫 生	Health	2130	71
社会保障业	Social Security	34	2
社会福利业	Social Welfare	106	7
（十八）文化、体育和娱乐业	Culture, Sports and Entertainment	1093	839
新闻出版业	Journalism and Publishing Activities	135	87
广播、电视、电影和音像业	Broadcasting, Movies, Television and Audiovisual Activities	202	176
文化艺术业	Cultural and Art Activities	448	299
体 育	Sports Activities	50	23
娱乐业	Entertainment	258	254
（十九）公共管理和社会组织	Public Management and Social Organizaion	6045	
中国共产党机关	Organs of Communist Party of China	176	
国家机构	Government Agencies	1599	
人民政协和民主党派	People's Political Consultative Conference and Democratic Parties	27	
群众团体、社会团体和宗教组织	Non-Government Organizations, Social Organizations and Religion Organizations	771	
基层群众自治组织	Grass-roots Mass Self-Government Organizations	3472	
（二十）国际组织	International Organizations		
国际组织	International Organizations		

1-9 各区县法人单位（2011年）

Impersonal Entities by Region（2011）

单位：个　　　　(unit)

分　组	Item	法人单位数 Number of Enterprises	企　业 Enterprises
合　计	**Total**	**87493**	**74673**
新城区	Xincheng	6004	5247
碑林区	Beilin	10530	9758
莲湖区	Lianhu	10136	9351
灞桥区	Baqiao	3957	3242
未央区	Weiyang	14471	13945
雁塔区	Yanta	23818	22821
阎良区	Yanliang	1437	1097
临潼区	Lintong	2114	1105
长安区	Chang'an	4694	3222
蓝田县	Lantian	2538	702
周至县	Zhouzhi	2700	1118
户　县	Huxian	3315	1803
高陵县	Gaoling	1779	1262

1-10 按登记注册类型分产业活动单位（2011年）

Industrial Active Units by Status of Registion （2011）

单位：个 （unit）

分 组	Item	产业活动单位数 Number of Industrial Active Units	企 业 Enterprises
总 计	**Total**	**96146**	**80533**
按登记注册类型分	Grouped by Status of Registion		
内资企业	Domestic Funded Enterprises	94924	79318
国有企业	State-owned Enterprises	9805	2739
集体企业	Collective-owned Enterprises	3370	1952
股份合作企业	Cooperative Enterprises	733	698
联营企业	Joint Ownership Enterprises	281	250
国有联营企业	State Joint Ownership Enterprises	41	32
集体联营企业	Collective Joint Ownership Enterprises	89	79
国有与集体联营企业	Joint State-collective Ownership Enterprises	23	18
其他联营企业	Other Joint Ownership Enterprises	128	121
有限责任公司	Limited Liability Corporations	27911	27865
国有独资公司	State Sole Funded Corporations	188	187
其他有限责任公司	Other Limited Liability Corporations	27723	27678
股份有限公司	Share-holding Corporations Limited	2135	2125
私营企业	Private Enterprises	40657	40049
私营独资企业	Private-funded Enterprises	10916	10458
私营合伙企业	Private Partnership Enterprises	2204	2122
私营有限责任公司	Private Limited Liability Corporations	24600	24542
私营股份有限公司	Private Share-holding Corporations Ltd.	2937	2927
其他企业	Other Enterprises	10032	3640

1-10 续表 continued

单位：个 (unit)

分　组	Item	产业活动单位数 Number of Industrial Active Units	企业 Enterprises
港、澳、台商投资企业	Enterprises with Funds from Hong Kong,Macao and Taiwan	421	419
与港澳台商合资经营	Joint-venture with Funds from Hong Kong,Macao and Taiwan	113	113
与港澳台商合作经营	Cooperative Enterprises with Funds from Hong Kong Macau and Taiwan	34	34
港澳台商独资	Enterprises with Sole Investment from Hong Kong Macau and Taiwan	249	247
港澳台商投资股份有限公司	Share-holding Corporations Ltd. with funds from Hong Kong, Macao & Taiwan	23	23
其他港、澳、台商投资企业	Other Enterprises with Funds from Hong Kong,Macao and Taiwan	2	2
外商投资企业	Foreign Funded Enterprises	801	796
中外合资营企业	Sino-foreign Joint Ventures	241	241
中外合作企业	Sino-Foreign Cooperation Enterprises	21	19
外资企业	Foreign Owned Enterprises	487	484
外商投资股份有限公司	Limited Company Funded by Foreign Investment	47	47
其他外商投资企业	Other Foreign Funded Enterprises	5	5

1-11 按行业分产业活动单位（2011年）

Industrial Active Units by Sector（2011）

单位：个 （unit）

分　组	Item	产业活动单位数 Number of Industrial Active Units	企业 Enterprises
总　计	**Total**	**96146**	**80533**
（一）农、林、牧、渔业	Agriculture,Forestry,Animal Husbandry and Fishery	1606	1265
农　业	Farming	707	600
林　业	Forestry	201	182
畜牧业	Animal Husbandry	374	306
渔　业	Fishery	27	24
农、林、牧、渔服务业	Services in Support of Agriculture	297	153
（二）采矿业	Mining	228	228
煤炭开采和洗选业	Mining and Washing of Coal	16	16
石油和天然气开采业	Extraction of Petroleum and Natural Gas	78	78
黑色金属矿采选业	Mining of Ferrous Metal Ores	9	9
有色金属矿采选业	Mining of Non-ferrous Metal Ores	26	26
非金属矿采选业	Mining and Processing of Nonmetal Ores	63	63
其他采矿业	Mining of Other Ores	36	36
（三）制造业	Manufacturing	12522	12522
农副食品加工业	Processing of Food from Agricultural Products	362	362
食品制造业	Manufacture of Foods	353	353
饮料制造业	Manufacture of Beverages	116	116
烟草制品业	Manufacture of Tobacco	4	4
纺织业	Manufacture of Textile	152	152
纺织服装、鞋、帽制造业	Manufacture of Textile Wearing Apparel, Footware and Caps	157	157
皮革、毛皮、羽毛（绒）及其制品业	Manufacture of Leather, Fur, Feather and Related Products	25	25
木材加工及木、竹、藤、棕、草制品业	Processing of Timber,Manufacture of Wood,Bamboo,Rattan, Plam and Straw Products	145	145
家具制造业	Manufacture of Furniture	347	347
造纸及纸制品业	Manufacture of Paper and Paper Products	311	311
印刷业和记录媒介的复制	Printing,Reproduction of Recording Media	497	497
文教体育用品制造业	Manufacture of Articles For Culture,Education and Sport Activities	50	50
石油加工、炼焦及核燃料加工业	Processing of Petroleum, Coking, Processing of Nuclear Fuel	50	50
化学原料及化学制品制造业	Manufacture of Raw Chemical Materials and Chemical Products	653	653

1-11 续表1 continued 1

单位：个 (unit)

分　组	Item	产业活动单位数 Number of Industrial Active Units	企业 Enterprises
医药制造业	Manufacture of Medicines	329	329
化学纤维制造业	Manufacture of Chemical Fibers	22	22
橡胶制品业	Manufacture of Rubber	99	99
塑料制品业	Manufacture of Plastics	304	304
非金属矿物制品业	Manufacture of Non-metallic Mineral Products	1001	1001
黑色金属冶炼及压延加工业	Smelting and Pressing of Ferrous Metals	133	133
有色金属冶炼及压延加工业	Smelting and Pressing of Non-ferrous Metals	150	150
金属制品业	Manufacture of Metal Products	863	863
通用设备制造业	Manufacture of General Purpose Machinery	1680	1680
专用设备制造业	Manufacture of Special Equipment	1404	1404
交通运输设备制造业	Manufacture of Transport Equipment	479	479
电气机械及器材制造业	Manufacture of Electric Equipment and Machinery	1267	1267
通信设备、计算机及其他电子设备制造业	Manufacture of Communication Equipment, Computers and other Electronic Equipment	792	792
仪器仪表及文化办公用	Manufacture of Measuring Instruments and Machinery for Cultural Activity and Office Work	486	486
工艺品及其他制造业	Manufacture of Artwork and Other Manufacturing	235	235
废弃资源和废旧材料回收加工业	Recycling and Disposal of Waste	56	56
（四）电力、燃气及水的生产和供应业	Production and Distribution of Electricity,Gas and Water	231	229
电力、热力的生产和供应业	Production and Supply of Electric Power and Heat Power	126	124
燃气生产和供应业	Gas mining and supplying industry	42	42
水的生产和供应业	Production and Supply of Water	63	63
（五）建筑业	Construction	6013	6013
房屋和土木工程建筑业	Construction of Building & Civil Engineering	1814	1814
建筑安装业	Architectural Installation	1216	1216
建筑装饰业	Architectural Decoration	2188	2188
其他建筑业	Other Construction	795	795
（六）交通运输、仓储和邮政业	Traffic, Transport, Storage and Post	1895	1844
铁路运输业	Transport Via Railway	31	31
道路运输业	Transport Via Road	876	837
城市公共交通业	Urban Public Traffic	111	109

1-11 续表2 continued 2

单位：个 （unit）

分 组	Item	产业活动单位数 Number of Industrial Active Units	企 业 Enterprises
水上运输业	Water Transport	5	4
航空运输业	Air Transport	40	39
管道运输业	Transport Via Pipeline	8	8
装卸搬运和其他运输服务业	Loading, Unloading, Portage and Other Transport Services	346	345
仓储业	Storage	211	206
邮政业	Post	267	265
（七）信息传输、计算机服务和软件业	Information Transmission, Computer Services and Software	3027	3005
电信和其他信息传输服务业	Telecom & Other Information Transmission Services	568	562
计算机服务业	Computer Services	1336	1324
软件业	Software Industry	1123	1119
（八）批发和零售业	Wholesale and Retail Trades	30098	30098
批发业	Wholesale Trade	15794	15794
零售业	Retail Trade	14304	14304
（九）住宿和餐饮业	Hotels and Catering Services	2834	2831
住宿业	Hotels	1014	1013
餐饮业	Catering Services	1820	1818
（十）金融业	Financial Intermediation	2084	2044
银行业	Bank	1373	1358
证券业	Security Activities	94	94
保险业	Insurance	375	368
其他金融活动	Other Financial Intermediation	242	224
（十一）房地产业	Real Estate	5216	5190
房地产业	Real Estate	5216	5190
（十二）租赁和商务服务业	Leasing and Business Services	8091	7778
租赁业	Leasing	684	682
商务服务业	Business Services	7407	7096
（十三）科学研究、技术服务和地质勘查业	Scientific Research, Technical Sevice and Geologic Prospecting	3566	2969
研究与试验发展	Research and Experimental Development	313	216
专业技术服务业	Professional Technical Services	1790	1610
科技交流和推广服务业	Services of Science and Technology Exchanges and Promotion	1335	1045
地质勘查业	Geologic Prospecting	128	98

1-11 续表3 continued 3

单位：个 （unit）

分组	Item	产业活动单位数 Number of Industrial Active Units	企业 Enterprises
（十四）水利、环境和公共设施管理业	Management of Water Conservancy, Environment and Public Facilities	726	463
水利管理业	Management of Water Conservancy	145	34
环境管理业	Environmental Management	186	102
公共设施管理业	Management of Public Facilities	395	327
（十五）居民服务和其他服务业	Services to Households and Other Services	2923	2827
居民服务业	Services to Households	1167	1100
其他服务业	Other Services	1756	1727
（十六）教育	Education	3531	259
教 育	Education	3531	259
（十七）卫生、社会保障和社会福利业	Health, Social Security and Social Welfare	2621	95
卫 生	Health	2460	86
社会保障业	Social Security	48	2
社会福利业	Social Welfare	113	7
（十八）文化、体育和娱乐业	Culture, Sports and Entertainment	1168	873
新闻出版业	Journalism and Publishing Activities	152	96
广播、电视、电影和音像业	Broadcasting, Movies, Television and Audiovisual Activities	207	179
文化艺术业	Cultural and Art Activities	477	300
体 育	Sports Activities	56	28
娱乐业	Entertainment	276	270
（十九）公共管理和社会组织	Public Management and Social Organizaion	7766	
中国共产党机关	Organs of Communist Party of China	187	
国家机构	Government Agencies	2847	
人民政协和民主党派	People's Political Consultative Conference and Democratic Parties	27	
群众团体、社会团体和宗教组织	Non-Government Organizations, Social Organizations and Religion Organizations	1225	
基层群众自治组织	Grass-roots Mass Self-Government Organizations	3480	
（二十）国际组织	International Organizations		
国际组织	International Organizations		

1-12 各区县产业活动单位（2011年）

Industrial Active Units by Region（2011）

单位：个 （unit）

分　组	Item	产业活动单位数 Number of Industrial Active Units	企　业 Enterprises
合　计	**Total**	**96146**	**80533**
新城区	Xincheng	6916	5962
碑林区	Beilin	11841	10938
莲湖区	Lianhu	11093	10200
灞桥区	Baqiao	4335	3574
未央区	Weiyang	15076	14517
雁塔区	Yanta	25226	23878
阎良区	Yanliang	1642	1247
临潼区	Lintong	2691	1269
长安区	Chang'an	5016	3408
蓝田县	Lantian	2929	833
周至县	Zhouzhi	3451	1215
户　县	Huxian	3837	2129
高陵县	Gaoling	2093	1363

1-13 国民经济和社会发展总量与速度指标

指　　标	Item	总量指标				
		1995	2000	2005	2007	2008
人口与就业	**Population and Employment**					
人口	**Population**					
年底总人口(万人)	Population at the Year-end (10 000 persons)	648.21	688.01	741.73	764.25	772.30
非农业人口	Non-agricultural Population	255.71	285.79	333.14	353.85	363.87
农业人口	Agriculturral Population	392.50	402.22	408.59	410.40	408.43
男性人口	Male	334.75	355.18	382.02	392.41	395.54
女性人口	Female	313.46	332.83	359.71	371.84	376.76
就业	**Employment**					
全社会就业人员数(万人)	Employment(10 000 persons)	372.60	389.10	415.83	436.36	448.05
#全部单位在岗职工人数	Number of Employed Staff and Workers	141.17	109.62	119.73	125.56	126.89
城镇登记失业人数(万人)	Registered Unemployed in Urban Areas(10 000 persons)	5.92	3.85	8.45	8.77	9.40
宏观经济	**Macroeconomic Indicator**					
国民经济核算	**National Accounts**					
生产总值(亿元)	Gross Domestic Product(100 mil. yuan)	330.35	646.13	1313.93	1856.63	2318.14
第一产业	Primary Industry	41.40	44.65	66.01	82.51	103.45
第二产业	Secondary Industry	135.33	277.13	540.50	781.94	981.58
工业	Industry	112.50	218.44	420.00	594.95	721.40
第三产业	Tertiary Industry	153.62	324.35	707.42	992.18	1233.11
#最终消费	Total Consumption	239.64	413.43	766.62	995.22	1182.61
资本形成总额	Total Investment	151.55	287.82	839.01	1451.47	1837.86
固定资产投资	**Investment in Fixed Assets**					
全社会固定资产投资总额(亿元)	Total Investment in Fixed Assets(100 mil. yuan)	103.42	232.37	835.10	1435.33	1906.36
城镇	Urban Area	88.50	203.01	776.33	1340.59	1786.60
#房地产	Real Estate	21.65	51.85	225.23	387.33	540.26
农村	Rural Area	14.92	29.36	58.77	94.74	119.76
国有经济	State-Owned	69.08	159.60	373.70	476.78	694.89
集体经济	Collective-Owned	9.78	14.65	59.23	207.08	246.89
个体经济	Self-employed Individual	11.13	24.40	79.04	183.09	50.43
其他经济	Other	13.43	33.72	323.13	568.38	914.15
财政	**Public Finance**					
地方财政一般预算收入(亿元)	General Budgetary Revenue of Local Government (100 mil. yuan)	18.21	46.80	72.92	112.92	145.61
地方财政一般预算支出(亿元)	General Budgetary Expenditure of Local Government (100 mil. yuan)	18.42	52.00	97.61	161.25	226.99
物价指数(上年=100)	**Price Indices(preceding year=100)**					
商品零售价格指数	Retail Price Index	114.6	98.7	99.7	103.7	105.4
居民消费价格指数	Consumer Price Index	117.0	100.2	100.3	104.7	106.0
工业生产者出厂价格指数	Producer Price Indices（PPI） for Manufactured Goods	110.8	99.4	103.9	101.9	103.7
利用外资签订协议金额	**Utilization of Foreign Capital**					
利用外资签定协议额(万美元)	Amount of Foreign Capital for Utilization Through Signed Contracts or Agreements(USD 10 000)	28956	54123	121499	143978	118230
外商实际直接投资额(万美元)	Amount of Foreign Capital Actually Utilized (USD 10 000)	18653	15633	57113	111567	114738

注：1.国民经济核算2004-2008年为全国第二次经济普查修订数据。
　　2.2009年及以前年份财政收支为一般预算收支与基金预算收支之和。

Principal Aggregate Indicators on National Economic and Social Development and Their Related Indices and Growth Rates

Aggregate Data			速度指标(%) Indices and Growth Rates						
			指数 Index (2011比以下各年) (2011 as percentage of the following years)			平均增长速度 Average Annual Growth Rate			
2009	2010	2011	2000	2005	2010	1996-2000	2001-2005	2006-2010	2002-2011
781.67	782.73	791.83	115.1	106.8	101.2	1.2	1.5	1.1	1.3
370.66	374.64	391.31	136.9	117.5	104.4	2.2	3.1	2.4	2.9
411.01	408.09	400.52	99.6	98.0	98.1	0.5	0.3	-0.02	-0.04
399.28	398.80	402.52	113.3	105.4	100.9	1.2	1.5	0.9	1.2
382.39	383.93	389.31	117.0	108.2	101.4	1.2	1.6	1.3	1.5
462.52	477.58	495.99	127.5	119.3	103.9	0.9	1.3	2.8	2.5
129.62	130.70	154.33	140.8	128.9	118.1	-4.9	1.8	1.8	3.4
10.02	10.46	10.37	269.4	122.7	99.1	-8.2	17.0	4.4	10.9
2724.08	3241.69	3862.58	430.3	228.7	113.8	13.5	13.5	15.0	14.3
110.38	140.06	173.14	180.2	146.0	106.7	4.6	4.3	6.5	5.8
1144.75	1406.72	1674.31	479.9	236.7	114.9	16.8	15.2	15.5	15.3
816.92	1003.57	1189.61	456.6	228.8	116.2	15.5	14.3	14.5	14.7
1468.95	1694.91	2015.13	424.6	230.4	113.4	10.9	13.0	15.2	14.2
1403.10	1598.51	1856.91	309.8	202.3	110.4	9.9	8.9	12.9	11.1
2281.91	2835.42	3264.83	816.3	307.9	108.4	11.8	21.5	23.2	22.1
2500.13	3250.56	3346.26	1440.1	400.7	130.0	15.6	28.0	31.3	29.8
2367.58	3104.92	3207.97	1580.2	413.2	132.1	16.0	30.2	31.8	30.8
696.34	842.34	996.81	1922.5	442.6	118.3	18.2	33.3	31.4	32.7
132.55	145.64	138.29	471.0	235.3	94.9	13.0	8.3	24.1	18.6
932.91	1348.76	1204.80	754.9	322.4	124.8	17.0	17.9	25.2	22.2
289.91	326.44	258.15	1762.1	435.8	110.4	4.0	24.9	50.3	41.7
97.86	54.73	74.64	305.9	94.4	189.7	11.8	29.7	7.5	13.2
1179.45	1520.63	1808.67	5363.8	559.7	135.4	18.4	57.8	37.4	44.0
181.40	241.86	318.55	680.7	436.8	131.7	20.8	9.3	27.1	20.0
276.85	371.62	494.58	951.1	506.7	133.1	23.1	13.4	30.7	24.1
99.5	102.7	104.4							
99.7	103.5	105.6							
99.9	102.3	102.5							
60027	119689	120083	221.9	98.8	100.3	13.3	17.6	-0.3	7.1
121872	156653	200522	1282.7	351.1	128.0	-3.5	29.6	22.4	27.5

Note: 1.The data of national account between 2004 and 2008 was from the second national economic census.

2.Government revenue and expenditure in 2009 and before 2009 was the sum of ordinary budgetary revenue and expenditure plus fund budgetary revenue and expenditure.

1-13 续表1

指　标	Item	总量指标				
		1995	2000	2005	2007	2008
产　业	**Industry**					
农业	**Agriculture**					
耕地面积(万亩)	Cultivated Areas(10 000 hectares)	463.97	443.37	400.17	391.77	390.77
乡村劳动力资源总数（万人）	Total Number of Rural Labor Source (10 000 persons)	213.80	240.76	255.93	254.06	256.17
农林牧渔及服务业总产值(亿元)	Gross Output Value of Farming Forestry, Animal Husbandry and Fishery(100 mil yuan)	75.46	74.37	106.54	134.15	168.27
主要农产品产量(万吨)	Output of Major Farm Products(10 000 tons)					
粮　食	Grain	175.37	201.92	205.53	189.06	214.40
奶　类	Milk	13.29	24.59	42.22	52.80	58.97
油　料	Oil-bearing Crops	2.17	1.34	1.16	0.96	1.15
蔬　菜	Vegetables	133.60	162.14	195.70	204.30	221.53
水　果	Fruits	24.10	34.35	51.28	60.51	71.69
肉　类	Meat	12.78	14.75	18.20	10.22	11.54
水产品	Aquatic Products	0.85	1.14	0.94	1.24	1.25
工业	**Industry**					
全部工业总产值（亿元）	Gross industrial Output Value(100 mil. yuan)	405.90	639.48	1308.56	1979.86	2388.14
规模以上工业企业主要经济指标（亿元）	Principal Indicators of Industrial Enterprises of State Ownership and Non-state-owned Above Designated Size(100 mil. yuan)					
工业增加值	Value Added of Industrial		130.18	314.01	499.96	605.25
资产总计	Total Assets		958.05	1503.85	1940.52	2426.13
主营业务收入	Revenue from Principal Business		420.42	980.97	1561.25	1928.05
利润总额	Profits		16.11	28.72	106.22	84.89
从业人员年平均人数（万人）	Annual Average Employers(10 000 persons)		43.25	37.92	38.55	40.17
主要工业产品产量	Output of Major Industrial Products					
布(万米)	Cloth(10 000 m)	30332	24818	27012	27995	22721
机制纸及纸板(吨)	Machine-Made Paper(tons)	364400	54711	221865	426520	442758
家用电冰箱(台)	Household Refrigerators(unit)	13000	5860	25407	94090	100854
发电量(亿千瓦小时)	Electricity(100 million kwh)	22.00	19.00	48.00	71.00	71.69
钢材(吨)	Steel Products(ton)	314400	100000	240182	787274	478819
汽车(万辆)	Motor Vehicle (10 000 units)	0.3	0.9	4.1	17.1	26.8
建筑业	**Construction**					
建筑业企业从业人数(人)	Number of Employed Persons(person)		136718	158311	296538	400740
建筑业总产值(亿元)	Gross Output Value(100 mil. yuan)	42.55	105.93	326.65	604.75	915.19
房屋建筑施工面积(万平方米)	Floor Space of Buildings under Construction (10 000 sq.m)	601.70	793.30	1801.20	2802.00	3133.90
房屋建筑竣工面积(万平方米)	Floor Space of Buildings Completed (10 000 sq.m)	177.15	336.80	569.01	835.95	1056.53

continued 1

Aggregate Data			速度指标(%) Indices and Growth Rates						
			指数 Index (2011比以下各年) (2011 as percentage of the following years)			平均增长速度 Average Annual Growth Rate			
2009	2010	2011	2000	2005	2010	1996-2000	2001-2005	2006-2010	2002-2011
387.89	383.32	377.10	85.1	94.2	98.4	-0.9	-2.0	-9.0	-1.3
255.00	256.36	260.97	108.4	102.0	101.8	2.4	1.2	0.04	0.7
178.70	227.10	272.66	186.2	148.4	106.6	4.9	5.1	6.8	6.1
218.20	221.65	182.04	90.2	88.6	99.0	2.9	0.4	1.5	-0.8
61.82	63.37	64.80	263.5	153.5	102.3	13.1	11.4	8.5	9.8
1.12	1.20	1.17	87.3	100.9	97.5	-10.0	-1.6		-0.5
242.41	253.10	261.66	161.4	133.7	103.4	3.9	3.8	5.3	5.5
78.96	84.78	91.14	265.3	177.7	107.5	7.4	8.3	10.6	10.4
12.62	13.65	14.46	98.0	79.5	105.9	2.9	4.2	-5.6	-0.8
1.30	1.19	1.18	103.5	125.5	99.2	4.1	-3.9	5.7	-0.6
2827.07	3562.88	4093.32	586.0	300.1	114.9	16.4	14.3	21.2	17.5
700.13	862.28	1012.58			117.2				
2913.56	3592.13	3975.38	414.9	264.3	110.7		9.4	19.0	14.2
2384.52	3011.09	3381.27	804.3	344.7	112.3		18.5	25.1	22.3
177.20	245.37	172.94	1073.5	602.2	70.5		12.3	53.6	25.4
43.42	47.11	50.42	116.6	133.0	107.0		-2.6	4.4	2.3
22202	23810	16344	65.9	60.5	102.7	-3.9	1.7	-2.5	-4.6
476258	495966	497882	910.0	224.4	100.7	-31.6	32.3	17.5	22.4
92146	107571	72218	1232.4	284.2	67.1	-14.7	34.1	33.5	4.2
83.21	96.94	95.01	500.1	197.9	99.9	-2.9	20.4	15.1	18.1
1105074	1107663	184753	184.8	76.9	56.1	-57.6	123.4	35.8	45.7
50.7	65.2	55.7	6185.6	1357.8	85.4	24.6	35.4	73.9	49.5
461080	539000	372088	272.2	235.0	69.0		3.0	27.8	9.8
1296.58	1820.35	1619.09	1528.5	495.7	88.9	20.0	25.3	41.0	30.3
3947.01	4592.57	6218.70	783.9	345.3	135.4	5.7	17.8	20.6	21.8
1209.88	1391.91	2392.39	710.3	420.4	171.9	13.7	11.1	19.6	19.7

1-13 续表2

指　标	Item	总量指标				
		1995	2000	2005	2007	2008
交通运输	**Transportation**					
货运量(万吨)	Freight Traffic(10 000 tons)	9590	6999	12051	15124	27560
铁 路	Railways	3317	3101	540	589	605
公 路	Highways	6268	3890	11505	14530	26949
民用航空	Civil Aviation	5	8	6	5	6
客运量(万人次)	Passenger Traffic(10 000 persons-times)	9069	8068	10479	12466	26501
铁 路	Railways	2678	2130	1796	2380	2680
公 路	Highways	6128	5578	8294	9466	23175
民用航空	Civil Aviation	263	360	389	620	646
邮电通信业	**Post and Telecommunication Services**					
邮电业务总量(亿元)	Total Business Revenue(100 mil. yuan)	7.65	46.16	132.04	226.76	264.67
函 件(万件)	Number of Letters Delivered(10 000 pieces)	14647	8230	9526	5544	5638
本地电话局用交换机容量(万门)	Capacity of Local Office Telephone Exchanges (10 000 line)	58.3	204.8	457.3	479.7	462.5
本地电话年末用户(万户)	Number of Subscribers of Local Telephone at Year-end(10 000 subscribers)	30.79	141.28	321.48	314.58	306.88
城市电话用户	Urban Telephone Subscribers	29.95	124.26	271.40	272.64	268.49
乡村电话用户	Rural Telephone Subscribers	0.84	17.02	50.08	41.94	38.39
移动电话用户(万户)	Number of Mobile Telephone Subscribers (10 000 subscribers)		73.10	419.96	664.59	737.76
互联网年末宽带用户(万户)	Number of Subscribers of Internet Services (10 000 subscribers)			33.93	58.62	81.40
国内商业	**Domestic Trade**					
社会消费品零售总额(亿元)	Total Retail Sales of Consumer Goods (100 mil. yuan)	186.60	360.42	670.56	936.21	1176.58
对外经济贸易	**Foreign Trade**					
进出口总额(万美元)	Total Exports and Imports(USD 10 000)	137510	173696	390146	536162	704029
出口额	Exports	110163	106062	263441	347133	447113
进口额	Imports	27347	67634	126705	189029	256916
国际旅游	**International Tourism**					
国际旅游者人数(万人次)	Number of International Tourists(10 000 persons)	41.35	65.03	77.56	100.01	63.20
国际旅游收入(亿元)	Foreign Exchange Earnings from Tourism (10 000 yuan)	10.38	22.41	33.54	42.43	28.72
金融业	**Financial Intermediation**					
金融机构（不含外资）人民币存款余额(亿元)	Balance of Deposits in Domestic Funded Financial Institutions (100 mil. yuan)	359.51	1335.63	3599.70	4582.71	5788.43
金融机构（不含外资）人民币贷款余额 (亿元)	Balance of Loans in Domestic Funded Financial Institutions (100 mil. yuan)	334.50	972.52	2158.10	2683.77	3267.89

注：1.2006年铁路数据按新口径统计；

2.2006年国际互联网络用户改为互联网宽带用户。

continued 2

Aggregate Data			速度指标(%)			Indices and Growth Rates			
2009	2010	2011	指数 Index (2011比以下各年) (2011 as percentage of the following years)			平均增长速度 Average Annual Growth Rate			
			2000	2005	2010	1996-2000	2001-2005	2006-2010	2002-2011
30606	34323	39231	560.5	325.5	114.3	-6.1	11.5	23.3	17.6
614	706	823	26.5	152.4	116.6	-1.3	-29.5	5.5	-13.4
29986	33610	38399	987.1	333.8	114.2	-9.1	24.2	23.9	24.7
6	7	9	112.5	150.0	128.6	9.9	-5.6	3.1	4.1
28693	30294	33375	413.7	318.5	110.2	-2.3	5.4	23.7	13.9
2585	2781	2861	134.3	159.3	102.9	-4.5	-3.4	9.1	3.3
25271	26536	29358	526.3	354.0	110.6	-1.9	8.3	26.2	16.0
837	977	1156	321.1	297.2	118.3	6.5	1.6	20.2	11.7
298.92	323.11	200.50				43.3	23.4	19.6	
6128	8176	3061	37.2	32.1	37.4	-10.9	3.0	-3.0	-9.9
441.1	449.0	441.5	215.6	96.5	98.3	28.6	17.4	-0.4	6.1
289.10	261.77	270.36	191.4	84.1	103.3	32.9	20.9	-4.0	3.2
253.28	228.27	238.34	191.8	87.8	104.4	29.8	20.4	-3.4	3.4
35.82	33.50	32.02	188.1	63.9	95.6	82.5	24.1	-7.7	2.1
1120.06	1423.08	1614.15	2208.1	384.4	113.4		41.9	27.6	28.9
116.79	146.18	184.10		542.6	125.9			33.9	59.7
1381.12	1637.04	1965.98	545.5	293.2	120.1	14.1	13.2	19.5	17.1
724618	1039273	1260179	725.5	323.0	121.3	4.8	17.6	21.6	22.2
333114	531729	582662	549.4	221.2	109.6	-0.8	20.0	15.1	20.8
391504	507544	677517	1001.7	534.7	133.5	19.9	13.4	32.0	23.5
67.29	84.18	100.23	154.1	129.2	119.1	9.5	3.6	1.7	4.1
31.05	42.40	51.28	228.8	152.9	120.9	16.6	8.4	4.8	7.9
7457.71	8863.36	10350.80	775.0	287.5	116.8	30.0	21.9	19.7	20.3
4436.50	6420.72	7496.25	770.8	347.4	116.8	23.8	17.3	24.4	20.2

Note:1. The railway data is added up according to new aperture in 2006.

2. The number of broadband internet subscribers changed from Internet subscribers in 2006.

1-13 续表3

指标	Item	总量指标 1995	2000	2005	2007
保险公司保费收入(亿元)	Insurance Premium of Insurance Companies (100 mil. yuan)	4.70	13.58	44.94	72.33
保险公司赔款及付给金额(亿元)	Indemnity Expenditure and Payment of Insurance Companies (100 mil. yuan)	1.70	1.39	9.50	19.91
教育、科技、文化	**Education, Science and Technology and Culture**				
教育	**Education**				
专任教师数(人)	Full-time Teachers(person)				
#普通高等学校	Institutions of Higher Education	15914	15679	29498	36717
普通中等专业教育学校	Regular Specialized Secondary Schools		3172	2130	2011
普通中等教育学校	Regular Secondary Education Schools		26230	31094	31373
小学	Primary Schools	30270	30215	29647	30533
在校学生数(万人)	Students Enrollment(10 000 person)				
#普通高等学校	Institutions of Higher Education	11.67	19.41	53.06	62.31
普通中等专业教育学校	Regular Specialized Secondary Schools	3.74	6.02	6.16	8.06
普通中等教育学校	Regular Secondary Education Schools	32.32	48.31	55.74	54.68
小学	Primary Schools	79.36	77.81	60.47	56.83
科技	**Science and Technology**				
高新技术企业(个)	Hi-tech Enterprises (unit)		632	1029	1311
企事业单位累计授权专利数（件）	Accumulated patents awarded(unit)	3164	6139	11670	15971
文化	**Culture**				
图书馆总藏量(千册件)	Total Collections in Library (1000 Volume-time)	2830	3214	3671	3893
文化馆、站（个)	Cultural Centers or Stations (unit)	201	251	192	197
电视节目制作时间(小时)	Time for TV Programs Production(hours)	5738	11871	27377	25883
家庭、生活、环境	**Family, People's Livelihood and Environment**				
家庭	**Family**				
家庭总户数 (万户)	Total Number of Households(10 000 households)	171.25	187.08	203.04	211.12
城镇居民平均每户家庭人口(人)	Average Household Size in Urban Areas(person)	3.88	2.99	2.93	2.91
农村居民平均每户家庭人口(人)	Average Household Size in Rural Areas(person)	4.60	4.30	4.22	4.48
婚姻	**Marriages and Divorces**				
结婚对数(对)	Register Number of Marriages(couples)	47236	46415	49962	67637
离婚对数(对)	Number of Divorces(couples)	4296	5161	12747	15536
居住	**Housing**				
城镇居民人均现住房总建筑面积(平方米)	Per Capita Total Building Area of Urban Residents' Houses(sq.m)	13.05	14.82	16.38	23.63
农村居民人均居住面积(平方米)	Per Capita Net Floor Space of Rural Residents(sq.m)	21.77	28.31	36.73	42.92

注：1.2008年及以前图书馆总藏量为图书馆藏书量。
2.2005年以前城镇居民人均现住房总建筑面积为城镇人均住房使用面积。

continued 3

Aggregate Data				速度指标(%)		Indices and Growth Rates				
				指数 Index (2011比以下各年) (2011 as percentage of the following years)			平均增长速度 Average Annual Growth Rate			
2008	2009	2010	2011	2000	2005	2010	1996-2000	2001-2005	2006-2010	2002-2011
101.45	122.11	129.37	162.57	1197.1	361.7	125.7	23.6	27.0	29.3	24.4
25.92	25.16	26.39	37.14	2671.9	390.9	140.7	-3.9	46.9	24.8	22.2
38926	40605	42098	42734	272.6	144.9	101.5	-0.3	13.5	7.4	9.3
1904	1720	1845	1723	54.3	80.9	93.4	4.6	-7.7	-2.8	-3.5
31425	31415	31506	33122	126.3	106.5	105.1	3.6	3.5	0.3	2.0
30382	30334	29944	28453	94.2	96.0	95.0	-0.04	-0.4	0.2	-0.3
66.68	70.31	73.30	76.60	394.6	144.4	104.5	10.7	22.3	6.7	11.6
8.06	7.44	6.75	6.16	101.8	98.5	89.9	9.9	0.7	1.9	0.8
52.88	50.63	48.89	47.20	97.7	84.7	96.5	8.4	2.9	-2.6	-1.1
54.66	52.52	51.56	51.39	66.0	85.0	99.6	-0.4	-4.9	-3.1	-3.6
1324	592	672	774	122.5	75.2	115.2		10.2	-8.2	0.8
19256	23962	31999	41273	672.3	353.7	129.0	14.2	13.7	22.4	19.5
4040	4324	4465	4907	152.7	133.7	109.9	2.6	2.7	4.0	4.0
197	197	197	194	77.3	101.0	98.5	4.5	-5.4	0.6	-2.3
26897	27131	29626	43925	370.0	160.4	148.3	15.6	18.2	1.6	4.6
216.52	221.51	226.71	234.34	125.3	115.4	103.4	1.8	1.7	2.2	2.2
2.82	2.84	2.81	2.83	94.6	96.6	100.7	-5.1	-0.4	-0.8	-0.7
4.03	4.07	3.94	3.97	92.3	94.1	100.8	-1.3	-0.4	-1.6	-0.6
77912	88138	83645	94398	203.4	188.9	112.9	-0.4	1.5	10.9	8.3
15722	15796	19060	19421	376.3	152.4	101.9	3.7	19.8	8.4	13.7
26.32	28.4	28.70	28.9	195.0	176.4	100.7	2.6	2.0	11.9	6.8
54.97	56.73	66.73	67.00	236.7	182.4	100.4	5.4	5.3	12.7	8.5

Note:1.'Total collections in libraries' was the 'number of collections in libraries' in 2008 and before.

2.The per capital total building area of urban residents' houses was replaced as the per Capital dwelling area of urban residents before 2005.

1-13 续表4

指　标	Item	总量指标			
		1995	2000	2005	2007
生活	**People's Livelihood**				
城镇居民人均可支配收入(元)	Per Capita Annual Disposable Income of Urban Households (yuan)	4153	6364	9628	12662
农村居民人均纯收入(元)	Per Capita Net Income of Rural Residents(yuan)	1353	2344	3460	4399
城乡居民人民币储蓄存款余额(亿元)	Savings Deposit of Urban and Rural Households (100 mil yuan)	230.63	675.83	1716.76	2002.38
工资	**Wages and Welfare**				
在岗职工工资总额(亿元)	The Gross Salary of Workers (100 mil yuan)	67.23	101.68	211.14	313.40
城镇非私营单位在岗职工年平均工资(元)	Aunual Average Wage of Stuff and Workers in Urban Non-privite Enterprises(yuan)	4763	9179	17728	25012
卫生	**Health Care**				
医院、卫生院(个)	Number of Hospitals(unit)	368	426	479	459
执业（助理）医师（人）	Licensed（Assistant） Doctors (person)	18846	18750	17730	17266
医院、卫生院床位数(张)	Number of Hospital Beds(unit)	28265	28697	30087	30823
市政建设	**City Construction**				
自来水供应量(万立方米)	Volume of Tap Water Supply(10 000 cu.m)	35885	30273	35776	32959
自来水供水管道长度(公里)	Length of Water Supply Pipelines(km)	1066	2237	2315	2424
城市天然气供气量(万立方米)	Volume of Natural Gas Supply in Urban Areas (10 000 cu.m)	8419	11513	53202	72253
公交运营汽(电)车总数(辆)	Total Number of Public Buses and Trolley Buses(unit)	977	2573	4762	5836
道路长度(公里)	Length of Paved Roads(km)	835	975	1382	1842
绿地面积(公顷)	Areas of Green Land(hectare)	5603	4116	4867	8670
环境、灾害	**Environment and Disaster**				
工业废水排放量(万吨)	Volume of Waste Water up to the Standard for Discharge(10 000 tons)	12479	9145	16969	19069
火灾发生数(起)	Number of Fire Disasters(case)	426	1040	2664	2009
火灾事故损失额（万元）	Fire Loss(10 000 yuan)	742.1	472.4	1565.5	773.9
交通事故发生数（起）	Number of Traffic Accidents(case)	3065	4099	4903	3647
交通事故损失额（万元）	Loss of Traffic Accidents(10 000 yuan)	1103.2	1116.1	2024.4	1038.0

continued 4

Aggregate Data				速度指标(%) Indices and Growth Rates						
				指数 Index (2011比以下各年) (2011 as percentage of the following years)			平均增长速度 Average Annual Growth Rate			
2008	2009	2010	2011	2000	2005	2010	1996-2000	2001-2005	2006-2010	2002-2011
15207	18963	22244	25981	408.2	269.8	116.8	8.9	8.6	18.2	14.5
5212	6275	7750	9788	417.6	282.9	126.3	11.6	8.1	17.5	14.7
2513.70	3084.20	3641.09	4155.65	614.9	242.1	114.1	24.0	20.5	16.2	17.9
373.24	439.74	501.76	629.35	619.0	298.1	125.4	8.6	15.7	18.9	18.0
29749	34032	37870	41679	454.1	235.1	110.1	14.0	14.1	16.4	14.5
432	415	412	368	86.4	76.8	89.3	3.0	2.4	-3.0	-1.5
18066	19284	18763	21551	114.9	121.6	114.9	-0.1	-1.1	1.1	1.5
32998	34904	36796	37264	129.9	123.9	101.3	0.3	1.0	4.1	2.7
36471	38307	41089	38934	128.6	108.8	94.8	-3.3	3.4	2.8	2.0
2385	1985	2416	2721	121.6	117.5	112.6	16.0	0.7	0.9	1.4
84874	95885	109052	120330	1045.2	226.2	110.3	6.5	35.8	15.4	21.8
6123	7039	7107	7462	290.0	156.7	105.0	21.4	13.1	8.3	10.5
2115	2296	2662	2755	282.6	199.3	103.5	3.1	7.2	14.0	10.8
9199	9553	12140	13680	332.4	281.1	112.7	-6.0	3.4	20.1	12.4
18304	13168	13840	13148				-6.0	13.2	-4.0	
1537	1485	1825	1920	184.6	72.1	105.2	19.5	20.7	-7.3	5.4
1907.7	1850.6	2224.2	1587.2	336.0	101.4	71.4	-8.6	27.1	7.3	18.2
2576	2702	2323	2264	55.2	46.2	97.5	6.0	3.6	-13.9	-6.0
522.8	851.7	736.6	611.9	54.8	30.2	83.1	0.2	12.6	-18.3	-6.1

1-14 国民经济和社会发展结构指标

Structural Indicators on National Economic and Social Development

单位: %　　　　(%)

指　　标	Item	1995	2000	2005	2007	2008	2009	2010	2011
人口与就业	**Population and Employment**								
人口	**Population**								
农业与非农业结构	Structure								
农业	Agriculture	60.55	58.46	55.09	53.70	52.88	52.58	52.14	49.42
非农业	Non-Agriculture	39.45	41.54	44.91	46.30	47.12	47.42	47.86	50.58
性别结构	Sexual Structure								
男	Male	51.64	51.62	51.50	51.35	51.22	51.08	50.95	50.83
女	Female	48.36	48.38	48.50	48.65	48.78	48.92	49.05	49.17
就业	**Employment**								
产业结构	Industrial Structure								
第一产业	Primary Industry	41.17	37.78	32.78	30.55	28.50	26.40	25.65	24.41
第二产业	Secondary Industry	29.43	27.57	27.46	28.66	29.10	28.45	29.65	30.51
第三产业	Tertiary Industry	29.40	34.65	39.76	40.79	42.40	45.15	44.70	45.08
宏观经济	**Macro Economy**								
国民经济核算	**National Accounting**								
生产总值产业结构	Industrial Structure								
第一产业	Primary Industry	12.53	6.91	5.02	4.44	4.46	4.05	4.32	4.48
第二产业	Secondary Industry	40.97	42.89	41.14	42.12	42.34	42.02	43.39	43.35
第三产业	Tertiary Industry	46.50	50.20	53.84	53.44	53.20	53.93	52.29	52.17
生产总值支出结构	Structure of Gross Domestic by Expenditures								
最终消费	Total Consumption	72.54	63.99	58.35	53.60	51.02	51.51	49.31	48.07
资本形成总额	Total Investment	45.88	44.55	63.85	78.18	79.28	83.77	87.47	84.52
货物和服务净出口	Net Export of Goods and Services	-18.42	-8.54	-22.20	-31.78	-30.30	-35.28	-36.78	-32.60
投　资	**Investment**								
全社会固定资产投资结构	Structure of Total Investment in Fixed Assets								
城乡结构	Urban and Rural Composition								
城镇	Urban Area	85.57	87.36	92.96	93.40	93.72	94.70	95.52	95.87
#房地产	Real Estate	20.93	22.31	27.00	26.09	28.34	27.85	25.91	31.07
农村	Rural Area	14.43	12.64	7.04	6.60	6.28	5.30	4.48	4.13
经济类型结构	Registion Status Composition								
国有单位	State-owned Enterprises Investment	66.79	68.68	44.75	33.22	36.45	37.31	41.49	36.00
集体单位	Collective-owned Enterprises Investment	9.46	6.30	7.09	14.43	12.95	11.60	10.04	7.71
个体经济	Self-employed Individual	10.76	10.50	9.46	12.75	2.65	3.91	1.68	2.23
其他经济	Other	12.99	14.51	38.69	39.60	47.95	47.18	46.78	54.05

1-14 续表1 continued 1

单位:% (%)

指标	Item	1995	2000	2005	2007	2008	2009	2010	2011
财 政	**Government Finance**								
财政收入结构	Structure of Government Revenue								
#中 央	Central Government		31.94	58.30	60.40	39.49	39.68	37.28	35.78
地 方	Local Governments		68.06	41.70	39.60	44.87	45.32	47.36	49.02
产 业	**Industrial**								
农 业	**Agriculture**								
农林牧渔及服务业总产值结构	Structure of Gross Output Value of Farming,Forestry,Animal Husbandry, Fishery and Service								
农 业	Farming	68.03	69.23	61.69	59.50	56.85	59.42	63.36	63.42
林 业	Forestry	0.96	1.14	1.23	1.18	1.13	1.27	1.18	1.26
牧 业	Animal Husbandry	30.29	28.58	30.96	30.58	33.52	30.56	27.72	27.68
渔 业	Fishery	0.72	1.05	0.69	0.68	0.66	0.66	0.56	0.55
农林牧渔服务业	Farming,Forestry,Animal Husbandry and Fishery			5.43	8.06	7.84	8.09	7.18	7.09
工 业	**Industry**								
工业总产值经济类型结构	Structure of Gross Output Value of Industry by Registion Status								
国有经济	State-owned Enterprises	51.04	43.00	45.21	51.41	52.26	51.07	51.52	50.46
集体经济	Collective-owned Enterprises	40.98	32.76	5.16	1.85	1.85	1.38	1.22	0.92
其他经济类型	Others	7.98	24.24	49.63	46.74	45.89	47.55	47.26	48.62
工业总产值轻重结构	Structure of Gross Output Value of Industry by Ligth Industry and Heavy Industry								
轻工业	Light Industry	40.31	48.81	31.17	37.03	25.17	23.47	22.01	21.97
重工业	Heavy Industry	59.69	51.19	68.83	62.97	74.83	76.53	77.99	78.03
工业总产值规模结构	Structure of Gross Output Value of Industry by Size of Enterprises								
大型企业	Large Enterprises	38.80	36.29	35.46	42.18	43.85	43.54	42.11	41.15
中型企业	Medium-sized Enterprises	9.14	5.14	24.67	21.07	20.96	21.88	23.96	15.17
小型企业	Small Enterprises	52.06	58.57	39.87	36.75	35.19	34.58	33.93	43.68

注：本表2008年以后财政收入结构中地方指地方财政一般预算收入。

Note:Composition of government revenue after 2008 in this table refers to local government ordinary bugdetaty revenue.

1-14 续表2 continued 2

单位: % (%)

指 标	Item	1995	2000	2005	2007	2008	2009	2010	2011
建筑业	**Construction**								
建筑业总产值结构	Structure of Gross Output Value of Construction Industry								
土木工程建筑业	Civil Engineering Construction	86.27	88.50	56.59	57.78	59.14	67.14	68.61	53.75
房屋工程建筑	Building Construction	12.84	9.28	34.05	32.44	29.80	25.50	24.63	36.81
建筑安装业	Installation of Construction							4.39	6.70
装修装饰业	Decoration	0.89	2.21	1.08	1.74	1.67	1.50	0.82	0.90
其 他	Others		0.01	8.28	8.04	9.39	5.86	1.55	1.15
交通运输业	**Transportation**								
客运量结构	Structure of Freight Traffic								
铁 路	Railways	29.13	26.40	17.14	19.09	10.11	9.01	9.18	8.57
公 路	Highways	67.57	69.14	79.15	75.93	87.45	88.07	87.59	87.96
民用航空	Civil Aviation	2.90	4.46	3.71	4.97	2.44	2.92	3.23	3.46
货运量结构	Structure of Freight Traffic								
铁 路	Railways	34.59	44.30	26.92	3.90	2.20	2.01	2.06	2.10
公 路	Highways	65.36	55.58	73.04	96.07	97.78	97.97	97.92	97.88
民用航空	Civil Aviation	0.05	0.12	0.04	0.03	0.02	0.02	0.02	0.02
国内商业	**Domestic Trade**								
社会消费品零售总额结构	Composition of Retail Sales of Consumer Goods								
城镇	Urban Area	88.95	87.99	90.17	90.32	90.43	90.49	95.91	97.08
农村	Rural Area	11.05	12.01	9.83	9.68	9.57	9.51	4.09	2.92
国际旅游	**International Tourism**								
国际旅游人数结构	Structure of Tourists								
外国人	Foreigners	89.76	84.03	84.91	85.09	84.78	87.81	86.97	88.42
华侨及港澳台同胞	Overseas Chinese and Compatriots form Hong Kong, Macao and Taiwan	10.24	15.97	15.09	14.91	15.22	12.19	13.03	11.58
教育文化、卫生、人民生活	**Education and Culture，Health Care，People's Livelihood**								
教 育	**Education**								
在校学生结构	Structure of Student Enrollment								
#普通高等学校	Institutions of Higher Education	8.81	12.44	28.48	31.74	33.38	34.55	36.14	29.74
普通中等专业教育学校	Regular Specialized Secondary Schools	2.84	3.84	3.33	4.07	4.06	3.64	3.35	2.37
普通中等教育学校	Regular Secondary Education Schools	24.55	30.93	29.89	27.86	26.44	24.87	24.11	18.32
小学	Primary Schools	59.91	49.89	32.45	28.94	27.37	25.81	25.44	19.95

1-14 续表3 continued 3

单位: % (%)

指　　标	Item	1995	2000	2005	2007	2008	2009	2010	2011
专任教师结构	Full-time Teachers by Type								
#普通高等学校	Institutions of Higher Education	21.25	19.89	29.93	34.68	35.19	35.29	36.33	34.82
普通中等专业教育学校	Regular Specialized Secondary Schools	3.38	4.02	2.16	1.90	1.72	1.49	1.59	1.40
普通中等教育学校	Regular Secondary Education Schools	29.37	33.21	31.55	29.64	28.41	27.30	27.19	27.00
小学	Primary Schools	40.41	38.34	30.08	28.84	27.46	26.36	25.85	23.18
人民生活	**People's Livelihood**								
城镇居民消费结构	Consumption Structure of Urban Residents								
食　品	Food	44.68	36.46	37.04	36.61	36.40	32.43	31.29	31.29
衣　着	Clothing	12.67	8.13	9.03	9.41	10.25	10.98	11.11	12.27
家庭设备用品及服务	Household facilities,Articles and Services	13.75	11.33	4.73	5.91	6.33	7.28	7.56	8.11
医疗保健	Health Care	3.27	7.23	9.45	8.40	9.67	9.65	9.50	9.00
交通和通信	Transportation and Communication	5.58	6.93	9.67	11.35	10.37	11.33	12.06	12.81
教育文化娱乐服务	Recreation,Education and Culture Articles	9.05	13.74	17.18	14.52	14.35	14.34	14.66	14.26
居　住	Residence	6.49	11.23	9.10	10.18	8.81	8.86	9.33	8.26
杂项商品和服务	Articles for Daily Use and Others	4.51	4.95	3.80	3.62	3.82	5.13	4.49	4.00
农村居民消费结构	Consumption Structure of Rural Residents								
食品消费支出	Food	50.31	36.63	36.34	38.15	36.95	35.81	32.54	31.89
衣　着	Clothing	8.39	6.65	6.11	6.09	6.52	6.40	6.55	7.20
居　住	Residence	5.92	21.41	17.76	22.72	19.39	19.47	24.41	23.92
家庭设备用品及服务	Household facilities,Articles and Services	5.17	5.47	5.11	5.66	7.02	6.97	6.53	7.10
医疗保健	Health Care	1.78	6.93	8.19	7.61	8.05	8.50	8.54	8.65
交通和通讯	Transportation and Communication	8.09	4.21	8.19	7.58	7.84	9.83	8.45	9.01
文化娱乐用品及服务	Recreation,Education and Culture Articles	18.53	14.49	16.15	10.44	12.43	11.13	11.20	10.43
其它商品及服务	Articles for Daily Use and Others	1.81	4.21	2.15	1.75	1.80	1.89	1.78	1.80
卫　生	**Health Care**								
卫生技术人员结构	Medical Technical Personnel by Types								
执业（助理）医师	Licensed（Assistant） Doctors	45.42	44.82	41.96	39.51	38.09	37.34	33.16	35.17
注册护士	Registered Nurses	32.68	34.29	33.14	35.09	36.23	39.05	40.01	40.87
药　师	Junior Paramedics	8.78	8.31	7.30	6.19	5.74	5.45	5.36	5.10
技　师	Technicians	5.21	5.21	5.33	6.97	6.68	6.49	8.11	5.91
其　他	Others	7.91	7.37	12.27	12.24	13.26	11.67	13.36	12.95

1-15 国民经济和社会发展比例和效益指标

指　　标	Item	1995
人口与就业	**Population and Employment**	
人口	**Population**	
出生率(‰)	Birth Rate(‰)	11.95
死亡率(‰)	Death Rate(‰)	4.98
自然增长率(‰)	Natural Growth Rate(‰)	6.97
就业	**Employment**	
就业者负担人口	Dependency Ratio	1.7
三次产业就业者比例	Employment Ratio by Type of Industry	
(以第一产业为100)	(Employment in primary industry=100)	
第一产业	Primary Industry	100.0
第二产业	Secondary Industry	71.5
第三产业	Tertiary Industry	71.4
城镇登记失业率(%)	Unemployment Rate in Urban Areas(%)	3.1
宏观经济	**Macro Economy**	
国民核算	**National Accounting**	
三次产业增加值比例	Ratio of Value-added by Type of Industry	
(以第一产业为100)	(Employment in primary industry=100)	
第一产业	Primary Industry	100.0
第二产业	Secondary Industry	326.9
第三产业	Tertiary Industry	371.1
全社会劳动生产率(元／人)	Overall Labor Productivity(yuan/person)	8963
第一产业	Primary Industry	2698
第二产业	Secondary Industry	12404
第三产业	Tertiary Industry	14488
人均生产总值(元)	Per Capita GDP(yuan)	5131
固定资产投资	**Investment in Fixed Assets**	
全社会固定资产投资相当于生产总值比例(%)	Proportion of Investment in fixed Assets to GDP(%)	31.3
房屋建筑面积竣工率(%)	Rate of Floor Space of Buildings Completed in Construction(%)	33.4
固定资产交付使用率(%)	Rate of Fixed Assets Completed in Capital Construction and Put into Use(%)	70.7
建设项目建成投产率(%)	Rate of Projects Completed in Capital Construction and Put into Use(%)	43.7
财政	**Finance**	
财政总收入相当于生产总值比例(%)	Proportion of Local Government Revenue to GDP(%)	5.5
一般预算支出相当于生产总值比例(%)	Proportion of Local Government Expenditures to GDP(%)	5.6
利用外资	**Utilization of Foreign Capital**	
外商实际直接投资额相当于利用外资协议金额比例(%)	Proportion of Foreign Capital Actually Used to Total Amount of Foreign Capital for Utilization by Signed Contracts or Agreements (%)	64.42

注：本表财政收入数据2009年及以前为一般预算财政收入和基金收入之和。

Indicators on Proportions and Efficiency in National Economic and Social Development

2000	2003	2004	2005	2006	2007	2008	2009	2010	2011
13.07	8.48	9.19	9.58	9.98	10.00	10.15	10.08	9.73	9.71
5.96	4.68	5.87	5.16	5.46	5.48	5.57	5.63	5.34	5.38
7.11	3.80	3.32	4.42	4.52	4.52	4.58	4.45	4.39	4.33
1.8	1.8	1.8	1.8	1.8	1.9	1.9	1.9	1.8	1.7
100.0	100.0	100.0	100.0	100.0	100.0	100.0	100.0	100.0	100.0
73.0	74.4	78.8	83.8	85.9	93.8	101.9	107.7	124.0	125.0
91.7	101.7	110.1	121.3	126.5	133.5	148.6	171.0	183.3	184.7
3.4	4.5	4.3	4.3	4.3	4.3	4.2	4.3	4.2	3.9
100.0	100.0	100.0	100.0	100.0	100.0	100.0	100.0	100.0	100.0
620.7	803.2	792.1	818.8	916.6	947.7	948.8	1037.1	1004.4	967.0
726.4	963.3	938.8	1071.7	1168.2	1202.5	1192.0	1330.8	1210.1	1163.9
16367	23605	27069	31837	36730	43252	52422	59832	68965	79349
2960	3501	4174	4747	5191	6148	7921	8830	11452	14530
25443	36914	43199	47853	56073	64851	76899	87452	102992	112851
24024	33502	37040	44024	48938	56870	67031	73674	80267	91908
9484	13341	15294	16406	18890	22463	27794	32411	38343	45475
36.0	50.5	58.7	65.8	72.4	81.4	82.2	91.8	100.3	86.6
42.0	33.8	24.4	28.1	26.1	29.0	16.9	16.0	6.9	10.0
74.0	62.7	42.8	52.8	46.6	49.8	40.5	42.8	38.4	40.4
44.2	39.9	41.5	54.2	47.0	40.6	53.3	72.5	53.9	54.9
7.3	7.7	7.8	6.6	6.5	7.1	10.9	12.2	15.8	16.8
8.0	8.2	8.1	8.1	9.1	9.9	14.5	15.4	11.5	12.8
28.88	26.52	35.24	47.01	45.18	77.49	97.05	203.03	130.9	167.0

Note:Figures of government revenue for 2009 and before are sum of general budgetary revenue and fund revenue.

1–15 续表1

指　　标	Item	1995
能　源	**Energy**	
单位生产总值能耗降低率（%）	Decreasing Rate of Energy Consumption per Unit GDP(%)	
规模以上工业单位工业增加值能耗降低率（%）	Decreasing Rate of Energy Consumption per Unit Industrial value-added of Industry Above Designated Size(%)	
单位生产总值电耗降低率（%）	Decreasing Rate of Electricity Consumption per Unit GDP(%)	
产　业	**Industries**	
农业	**Agriculture**	
人均耕地面积(公顷)	Per Capita Cultivated Land(hectare)	0.08
农业从业者人均耕地面积(公顷)	Cultivated Land per Agricultural Laborer(hectare)	0.20
每公顷耕地农业机械总动力(千瓦)	Total Power of Agricultural Machinery per Hectare of Cultivated Land(kw)	5.23
每公顷耕地化肥施用量(公斤)	Chemical Fertilizer Consumption per Hectare of Cultivated Land(kg)	536
每公顷耕地生产的农业总产值(元)	Agricultural Output Value per Hectare of Cultivated Land(yuan)	24396
每个农林牧渔及服务业劳动力农产品生产量(公斤)	Output of Farm Products per Farming,Forestry,Animal Husbandry,Fishery and Service Husbandry and Fishery Laborer (kg)	
粮食	Grain	1150
蔬菜	Vegetables	877
禽蛋	Poultry Eggs	93
肉类	Meat	84
水产品	Aquatic Products	6
每公顷播种面积农产品产量(公斤)	Output of Farm Crops per Hectare of Sown Area(kg)	
粮食	Grain	3806
油料	Oil-bearing Crops	1753
蔬菜	Vegetables	34800
规模以上工业企业经济效益	**Economic Benefit of Industrial Enterprises above Designated Size**	
总资产贡献率（%）	Ratio of Total Assets to Industrial Output Value (%)	
资产负债率（%）	Assets-Liability Ratio (%)	
流动资产周转次数（次/年）	Rate of Annual Turnover Working Capitals(times/year)	
成本费用利润率（%）	Ratio of Profits to Cost (%)	
产品销售率（%）	Proportion of Industrial Products Sold(%)	
全员劳动生产率（元/人）	Overall Labor Productivity (yuan/person)	
建筑业	**Construction**	
机械装备率(元／人)	Value of Machinery per Laborer(yuan/person)	5990
产值利税率(%)	Ratio of Per-tax Profits to Gross Output Value (%)	3.5
全员劳动生产率(元／人)(按总产值计算)	Overall Labor Productivity(yuan/person) (in terms of gross output value per employee)	37689
邮电通信业	**Post and Communication Services**	
电话普及率(含移动电话）(部/百人)	Access to Telephones, National(include mobilphone) (set/100 persons)	7.9
移动电话普及率(部/百人)	Access to Mobilphones (set/100 persons)	0.48
国内商业	**Domestic Trade**	
人均批发零售和住宿餐饮业消费品零售额(元)	Per Capita Retail Sales of Wholesale,Retail Trade and Accommodation Catering Trade (yuan)	1979

continued 1

2000	2003	2004	2005	2006	2007	2008	2009	2010	2011
				4.15	5.75	6.65	5.56	2.06	3.56
				3.04	12.56	13.43	10.48	12.18	15.44
				4.48	6.94	6.93	5.33	1.00	4.43
0.07	0.07	0.07	0.07	0.06	0.06	0.06	0.06	0.06	0.06
0.20	0.19	0.19	0.22	0.23	0.25	0.21	0.21	0.22	0.22
6.78	7.54	7.93	8.39	8.63	8.99	10.41	10.12	10.48	11.50
664	725	780	794	819	843	867	891	922	953
25161	30357	35862	39937	43261	51361	64593	69106	88869	108457
1382	1213	1392	1493	1569	1433	1695	1792	1901	1567
1110	1167	1287	1421	1536	1549	1752	1990	2171	2253
95	89	84	86	92	74	86	96	106	108
101	114	122	132	145	77	91	104	117	124
8	7	7	7	7	9	10	11	10	10
4342	4182	4656	4796	5025	4452	5102	5206	5349	4764
1526	1532	1758	1821	1880	1934	2008	1956	2004	1988
37797	36657	35002	35231	35916	33677	35723	38344	39667	40475
	7.0	6.9	8.4	7.8	10.2	8.6	11.3	12.2	8.6
65.0	61.3	65.2	65.0	64.3	64.6	62.6	61.1	57.6	57.7
1.0	1.1	1.2	1.3	1.4	1.6	1.5	1.7	1.7	1.5
4.2	5.7	5.0	3.1	5.5	7.3	4.6	8.1	8.8	5.2
97.1	96.3	97.9	97.5	98.2	96.8	96.1	97.6	97.1	97.4
29496	58801	66752	82815	97561	129706	150641	161289	188483	194105
6805	9453	13240	13332	13502	9079	12026	11928	9461	28669
3.4	4.1	4.4	4.8	4.5	5.2	6.0	6.3	4.4	8.3
74347	132981	163414	206337	241887	203994	226669	285854	321340	334172
31.2	69.1	88.8	100.0	111.1	117.9	124.7	167.1	199.0	221.3
10.62	33.67	48.29	56.62	66.99	80.02	88.09	132.79	168	189.58
4027	6956	7859	8795	9437	10932	13840	16432	19363	23145

1-15 续表2

指　　标	Item	1995
对外经济贸易	**Foreign Trade**	
进出口总额相当于生产总值比例(%)	Proportion of Total Imports & Exports to GDP(%)	34.76
国际旅游	**International Tourism**	
每一来华游客花费(元)	Expenditure per International Tourist in China(yuan)	2511
金融	**Finance and Insurance**	
金融机构存款相当于生产总值比例(%)	Bank Deposits as Percentage of GDP(%)	108.83
金融机构贷款相当于生产总值比例(%)	Bank Loans as Percentage of GDP(%)	101.26
教育、科技、文化	**Education, Science and Technology and Culture**	
教育	**Education**	
入学率(%)	Enrollment Rate(%)	
小学	Primary Schools	
初中	Junior Schools	
毕业率(%)	Graduation Rate(%)	
小学	Primary Schools	
初中	Junior Schools	
学校教师负担系数	Student-teacher Ratio(in percentage)	
高等学校	Colleges and Universities	6.83
中等学校	Secondary Schools	14.42
小学	Primary Schools	26.22
文化(个)	**Culture (unit)**	
每百万人有艺术表演团体	Number of Troupes per Million Persons	3.39
每百万人有公共图书馆	Number of Public Libraries per Million Persons	2.31
家庭、生活、环境	**Family, People's Livelihood and Environment**	
家庭	**Family**	
城市居民家庭	Urban Households	
平均每户就业面（%）	Percentage of Employees Per Household (%)	55.90
每一就业者负担人数(人)	Persons Supported by Each Laborer (person)	1.79
农村居民家庭	Rural Households	
平均每一劳动力负担人口（人）	Persons Supported by Each Laborer(person)	1.58
卫生	**Health Care**	
每千人医院数(个)	Number of Hospitals per 1000 Persons(unit)	0.06
每千人医生数(人)	Number of Doctors per 1000 Persons(person)	2.91
每千人医院床位数(张)	Number of Hospital Beds per 1000 Persons(unit)	4.36
市政建设	**City Construction**	
城市自来水普及率(%)	Percentage of Households with Access to Tap Water(%)	
城市用气普及率(%)	Percentage of Households with Access to Tap Gas (%)	
人均公园绿地面积(平方米)	Public Green Areas per 10 000 Persons(hectare)	3.80

continued 2

2000	2003	2004	2005	2006	2007	2008	2009	2010	2011
22.25	20.19	23.29	24.79	22.01	22.21	21.97	18.17	21.20	21.07
3445	3584	4212	4324	4353	4242	4544	4614	5037	5116
206.71	281.61	277.73	283.41	275.92	259.80	264.31	279.84	278.99	267.98
150.51	206.43	186.17	169.91	159.11	152.16	149.22	166.65	203.30	194.07
								100.0	100.0
								99.6	99.6
								100.4	100.2
								99.7	100.6
12.38	19.87	16.69	17.99	17.36	16.97	17.13	17.32	17.41	17.92
17.84	18.52	18.78	18.47	20.51	19.99	18.97	18.27	17.78	16.77
25.75	22.69	21.71	20.38	19.78	18.61	17.99	17.32	17.22	18.06
3.20	3.07	3.03	2.56	2.31	2.16	2.15	2.13	1.53	3.52
2.18	1.95	2.07	2.02	1.82	1.81	1.79	1.78	1.77	1.76
45.73	48.00	48.80	47.44	48.30	47.77	47.87	53.20	53.70	54.80
2.19	2.08	2.05	2.11	2.07	2.09	2.09	1.88	1.86	1.83
1.57	1.56	1.56	1.60	1.59	1.57	1.50	1.50	1.50	1.50
0.03	0.04	0.04	0.04	0.04	0.04	0.03	0.03	0.03	0.03
2.35	2.02	2.04	2.39	2.19	2.08	2.16	2.29	2.21	2.53
3.83	3.94	3.91	3.75	3.46	3.42	3.65	3.84	4.04	4.23
98.95	99.04	99.09	99.00	99.09	100.01	111.22	100.00	98.77	99.95
81.51	91.23	91.20	91.30	92.62	98.60	97.66	98.15	97.02	97.46
5.12	5.35	5.03	5.63	7.59	7.61	7.80	7.90	9.11	9.89

1-16 平均每天主要社会经济活动

指　　标	Item	1995	2000
一、每天创造的财富	**Daily Production**		
生产总值(万元)	Gross Domestic Product(10 000 yuan)	9050.7	17702.2
第一产业	Primary Industry	1134.3	1223.3
第二产业	Secondary Industry	3707.7	7592.6
工业	Industry	3082.2	5984.7
建筑业	Construction	625.5	1608.0
第三产业	Tertiary Industry	4208.8	8886.3
#交通运输、仓储及邮政业	Transport, Storage, Post & Telecommunication Services	674.0	1709.3
批发和零售业	Wholesale and Retail Trade		
住宿和餐饮业	Hotels and Catering Services		
财政总收入(万元)	Total Government Revenue(10 000 yuan)	498.8	1304.0
财政一般预算支出(万元)	Government General Budgetary Expenditures(10 000 yuan)	504.7	1274.1
粮食(吨)	Grain(ton)	4801	5532
奶类(吨)	Milk(ton)	364	674
蔬菜(吨)	Vegetables(ton)	3660	4442
肉类(吨)	Meat(ton)	350	404
水产品(吨)	Aquatic Products(ton)	23	31
布(万米)	Cloth(10 000 m)	83.0	77.0
发电量(万千瓦小时)	Electricity(10 000 kwh)	610.0	534.0
钢材(吨)	Steel(ton)	861	274
汽车(辆)	Motor Vehicle(unit)	8	25
二、每天消费量	**Daily National Consumption**		
最终消费(万元)	Final Consumption Expenditure(10 000 yuan)	6565.5	11326.9
社会消费品零售总额(万元)	Total Retail Sales of Consumer Goods (10 000 yuan)	5112.3	9874.5
三、每天其他经济活动	**Other Daily Economic Activities**		
资本形成总额(万元)	Gross Capital Formation(10 000 yuan)	4152.1	7885.5
固定资本形成	Fixed Capital Formation		
存货增加	Changes in Stock		
竣工住宅面积(平方米)	Floor Space of Buildings Completed (sq.m)	6927	14930
货运量(万吨)	Freight Traffic(10 000 tons)	26.3	19.2
客运量(万人次)	Passenger Traffic(10 000 person-times)	24.8	22.1
邮电业务总量(万元)	Business Volume of Postal and Telecommunications Services(10 000 yuan)	209.6	1264.7
进出口总额(万美元)	Total Value of Imports and Exports (USD 10 000)	110.2	475.9
出口额	Exports	82.5	290.6
进口额	Imports	27.7	185.3
外商实际直接投资额(万美元)	Foreign Capital Actually Used(USD 10 000)	51.1	42.8
国际旅游人数(人次)	Number of Tourists from Abroad(person-time)	1134	1782
城乡居民人民币储蓄额(万元)	Savings Deposit of Urban and Rural Households(10 000 yuan)	1546.3	2450.3
四、每天人口变动和婚姻	**Daily Population Changes and Marriages**		
出　生(人)	Births(person)	211	247
死　亡(人)	Deaths(person)	88	113
结　婚(对)	Marriages(couple)	129	129
离　婚(对)	Divorces(couple)	12	14

注：本表财政收入数据2009年及以前为一般预算财政收入和基金收入之和。

Selected Indicators on Average Daily Social and Economic Activities

2005	2006	2007	2008	2009	2010	2011
35998.1	42162.7	50866.6	63510.7	74632.3	88813.4	105824.1
1808.5	1929.9	2260.6	2834.3	3024.1	3837.3	4743.6
14808.2	17689.0	21423.0	26892.6	31363.0	38540.3	45871.5
11506.9	13540.3	16300.0	19764.4	22381.4	27495.1	32592.1
3301.4	4148.8	5123.0	7128.2	8981.6	11045.2	13279.5
19381.4	22543.8	27183.0	33783.8	40245.2	46435.9	55209.0
1816.4	2029.6	2307.1	2716.7	3030.1	3416.2	4044.9
4032.9	4567.7	5356.4	6655.1	8028.8	9256.4	11477.8
1381.9	1431.0	1920.3	2346.6	2576.7	2837.8	3405.2
2300.6	2638.6	3433.6	6517.8	9080.0	13991.5	17805.0
2819.6	3689.0	4771.4	8679.2	11509.0	10181.4	13550.0
5631	5831	5180	5874	5978	6074	4987
1157	1292	1447	1616	1694	1736	1775
5362	5709	5601	6069	6641	6934	7169
499	538	280	316	346	374	396
26	27	34	34	36	33	32
74.0	72.6	76.7	62.3	60.8	65.2	44.8
1316.3	1830.1	1946.3	1964.1	2279.7	2655.9	2603.0
658	1960	2157	1312	3028	3035	506
112	282	468	734	1389	1787	1525
21003.3	23861.1	27266.3	32400.3	38441.1	43794.8	50874.2
18371.5	21505.5	25649.6	32235.1	37838.9	44850.4	53862.5
22986.6	28637.5	39766.3	50352.3	62518.1	77682.7	89447.4
20918.4	26404.9	34795.6	45315.3	58878.9	72237.8	83395.6
2068.2	2232.6	4970.7	5037.0	3639.2	5444.9	6051.8
16400	15975	25466	18998	22537	12287	23601
33.0	32.4	41.4	75.5	83.9	94.0	107.5
28.7	30.8	34.2	72.6	78.6	83.0	91.4
3617.7	5116.7	6212.7	7256.4	8189.6	8852.3	5494.8
1068.9	1138.1	1468.9	1928.9	1985.3	2847.3	3452.5
721.8	747.6	951.0	1225.0	912.6	1456.8	1596.3
347.1	390.5	517.9	703.9	1072.6	1390.5	1856.2
156.5	225.9	305.7	314.4	333.9	429.2	549.4
2125	2376	2740	1732	1844	2306	2746
47034.5	53439.1	54727.7	68614.0	84175.6	99318.4	113853.4
210	223	226	232	232	225	226
63	122	124	127	130	124	125
137	184	185	213	241	229	259
35	35	43	43	43	52	53

Note: Figures of government revenue for 2009 and before are sum of general budgetary revenue and fund revenue.

1-17 各区县国民经济和社会发展主要指标（2011年）

指　　标	Item	新城区 Xincheng	碑林区 Beilin	莲湖区 Lianhu
一、年底总人口（常住人口）（万人）	Population at the Year-end Permanent population(10 000 persons)	59.23	61.87	70.13
二、生产总值(亿元)	Gross Domestic Product(100 mil. yuan)	379.89	436.71	437.18
第一产业	Primary Industry			
第二产业	Secondary Industry	152.99	110.42	199.48
工　业	Industry	90.35	43.47	137.62
第三产业	Tertiary Industry	226.90	326.29	237.70
三、全社会固定资产投资总额(亿元)	Total Investment in Fixed Assets(100 mil. yuan)	288.48	291.13	326.40
#城镇	Urban Area	211.83	133.06	287.40
#房地产	Real Estate	76.65	158.07	89.00
四、财政一般预算收入(亿元)	Local Financial Revenue(100 mil. yuan)	20.57	26.76	28.13
财政一般预算支出(亿元)	Local Financial Expenditure(100 mil. yuan)	17.06	14.46	19.48
五、农林牧渔及服务业总产值(亿元)	Gross Output Value of Farming Forestry, Animal Husbandry and Fishery(100 mil yuan)			
主要农产品产量(万吨)	Output of Major Farm Products(10 000 tons)			
粮　食	Grain			
蔬　菜	Vegetables			
水　果	Fruits			
肉　类	Meat			
奶　类	Milk			
六、规模以上工业总产值(亿元)	Gross industrial Output Value(100 mil. yuan)	83.85	39.75	128.72
七、建筑业总产值(亿元)	Gross Output Value(100 mil. yuan)	225.55	375.40	172.77
建筑业房屋建筑施工面积 (万平方米)	Floor Space of Buildings under Construction (10 000 sq.m)	985.21	1983.92	1048.10
建筑业房屋建筑竣工面积(万平方米)	Floor Space of Buildings Completed(10 000 sq.m)	246.90	1135.18	218.12
八、社会消费品零售总额(亿元)	Total Retail Sales of Consumer Goods (100 mil. yuan)	341.82	342.07	281.61
九、城镇居民人均可支配收入(元)	Per Capita Annual Disposable Income of Urban Households (yuan)	26498	27025	26962
农村居民人均纯收入(元)	Per Capita Net Income of Rural Residents(yuan)			
十、医疗机构数(个)	Number of Health Care Institutions(unit)	302	338	337
卫生技术人员(人)	Number of Medical Technical Personnel（person）	9930	9883	7883
床位数(张)	Number of Beds(unit)	6236	6250	4994

Principal Indicators of National Economy and Social Development by Region（2011）

灞桥区 Baqiao	未央区 Weiyang	雁塔区 Yanta	阎良区 Yanliang	临潼区 Lintong	长安区 Chang'an	蓝田县 Lantian	周至县 Zhouzhi	户 县 Huxian	高陵县 Gaoling
59.87	81.14	118.48	28.01	65.98	109.01	51.65	56.59	55.85	33.53
207.07	469.00	726.78	119.77	184.75	324.92	81.94	66.27	129.13	188.30
14.41	2.31	2.61	17.61	28.27	28.97	20.49	20.30	21.24	16.93
120.53	244.40	255.65	59.79	102.03	160.06	29.46	17.53	70.84	150.99
102.89	174.79	137.95	48.82	93.33	128.47	18.35	13.42	61.81	138.20
72.13	222.29	468.52	42.37	54.45	135.89	31.99	28.44	37.05	20.38
186.51	449.83	767.74	120.92	117.89	314.35	77.09	68.46	109.81	177.65
128.51	259.22	445.09	100.01	97.81	216.31	45.68	48.15	80.28	157.80
50.17	186.68	318.84	11.01	8.38	66.87	6.30	3.50	7.44	13.89
13.15	17.46	26.45	6.50	6.26	18.02	2.12	1.55	4.48	7.00
14.41	14.30	16.40	10.97	19.43	30.42	15.54	18.18	17.78	12.38
21.97	3.75	3.69	25.94	44.76	43.85	33.75	33.00	34.00	27.95
5.71	2.05	0.03	8.11	32.03	34.62	26.58	22.60	30.27	20.03
26.47	5.13	0.37	57.44	36.77	52.78	16.88	17.43	27.50	20.89
8.97	1.09	0.58	6.27	4.42	7.37	11.84	36.42	9.05	5.13
0.72	0.37	0.24	0.55	3.75	1.94	1.76	2.66	1.80	0.69
6.21	2.53	0.13	8.50	33.81	2.21	3.77	1.30	3.40	2.92
82.98	151.49	112.47	40.96	84.67	105.37	10.78	4.52	34.53	132.49
30.31	333.76	327.10	18.17	9.74	36.25	13.11	4.93	12.04	59.96
97.10	578.69	490.22	95.33	110.10	250.05	137.79	37.94	109.05	295.20
24.29	73.89	200.66	26.66	71.27	91.80	46.70	15.52	41.13	201.62
46.40	278.26	380.19	23.21	48.54	109.97	35.45	23.72	38.85	15.89
26041	27601	24817	26839	21271	22918	17309	17353	19532	20313
12383	12585	11291	11426	9109	9421	6704	6615	8265	9053
550	274	461	155	463	771	632	488	575	208
3773	4117	11076	1559	2336	3690	1356	1837	2610	1231
2157	2718	7542	1265	1756	2772	1225	1026	2035	1034

主要统计指标解释

行政区划 指国家对行政区域的划分。根据有关法规规定，我国的行政区域划分如下：（1）全国分为省、自治区、直辖市；（2）省、自治区分为自治州、县、自治县、市；（3）自治州分为县、自治县、市；（4）县、自治县分为乡、民族乡、镇；（5）直辖市和较大的市分为区、县；（6）国家在必要时设立的特别行政区。

气候 指地球与大气之间长期能量交换与质量交换所形成的一种自然环境状态，它是多种因素综合作用的结果。气候既是人类生活和生产的环境要素之一，又是供给人类生活和生产的重要资源。气温、降水、湿度等气象要素的多年平均值是用来描述一个地区气候状况的主要参数，而各种气象要素某年、某月的平均值（或总量）则可以反映出该时期天气气候状况的重要特征。

自然资源 指人类可以直接从自然界获得，并用于生产和生活的物质资源。自然资源一般可以分成可再生资源和非再生资源两大类。可再生资源指在较短时间内可以再生、可以循环利用的资源，包括土地资源、水资源、气候资源、生物资源和海洋资源等。非再生资源指在使用后不能再生的资源，包括矿产资源和地热能源。

土地资源 土地指陆地的表层部分，它主要由岩石、岩石的风化物和土壤构成。土地资源按利用类型可以分为农用地、建筑用地和未利用地。农用地包括耕地、园地、林地、牧草地和水面。建筑用地包括居民点及工矿用地、交通用地和水利设施用地。未利用地指农用地和建筑用地以外的土地，包括滩涂、荒漠、戈壁、冰川和石山等。

耕地面积 指经过开垦用以种植农作物并经常进行耕耘的土地面积。包括种有作物的土地面积、休闲地、新开荒地和抛荒未满三年的土地面积。

森林面积 指由乔木树种构成，郁闭度0.2以上（含0.2）的林地或冠幅宽度10米以上的林带的面积，即有林地面积。森林面积包括天然起源和人工起源的针叶林面积、阔叶林面积、针阔混交林面积和竹林面积，不包括灌木林地面积和疏林地面积。

林业用地面积 指生长乔木、竹类、灌木、沿海红树林等林木的土地面积，包括有林地、灌木林、疏林地、未成林造林地、迹地、苗圃等。

水资源总量 指评价区内降水形成的地表和地下产水总量，即地表产流量与降水入渗补给地下水量之和，不包括过境水量。

地表水资源量 指评价区内河流、湖泊、冰川等地表水体中可以逐年更新的动态水量，即当地天然河川径流量。

地下水资源量 指评价区内降水和地表水对饱水岩土层的补给量，包括降水入渗补给量和河道、湖库、渠系、渠灌田间等地表水体的入渗补给量。

气温 指空气的温度，我国一般以摄氏度（℃）为单位表示。气象观测的温度表是放在离地面约1.5米处通风良好的百叶箱里测量的，因此，通常说的气温指的是离地面1.5米处百叶箱中的温度。其统计计算方法为：

月平均气温是将全月各日的平均气温相加，除以该月的天数而得。

年平均气温 是将12个月的月平均气温累加后除以12而得。

降水量 指从天空降落到地面的液态或固态（经融化后）水，未经蒸发、渗透、流失而在地面上积聚的深度。其统计计算方法为：

月降水量是将全月各日的降水量累加而得。

年降水量是将12个月的月降水量累加而得。

日照时数 指太阳实际照射地面的时间。其统计方法与降水量相同。

平均增长速度 平均增长速度表明社会经济现象在一个较长的时期内逐期平均增长变化的程度，它不能根据各个环比增长速度直接求得，但与平均发展速度之间存在着一定的数量关系：平均增长速度 = 平均发展速度 - 1。

平均发展速度 是一种根据环比发展速度计算的序时平均数,由于各时期对比的基础不同，所以计算平均发展速度不能采用一般的序时平均数的计算方法，计算方法分为水平法和累计法。水平法，又称几何平均法，即将环比发展速度按连乘法用几何平均数公式计算。累计法，也称方程法，根据一段时期内各年发展水平总和与基期水平的关系，列出方程式计算平均发展速度。水平法着重考虑最后一年所达到的发展水平；累计法着重考虑整个时期累计发展水平的总量。

本《年鉴》内所列的平均增长速度，除固定资产投资用“累计法”计算外，其余均用“水平法”计算。从某年到某年平均增长速度的年份，均不包括基期年在内。如建国六十年以来的平均增长速度是以1949年为基期计算的，则写为1950-2009年平均增长速度，其余类推。

企业（单位）登记注册类型 是以在工商行政管理机关登记注册的各类企业为划分对象，以工商行政管理部门对企业登记注册的类型为依据，将企业登记注册类型分为内资企业、港澳台商投资企业和外商投资企业三大类。内资企业包括国有企业、集体企业、股份合作企业、联营企业、有限责任公司、股份有限公司、私营公司和其他企业；港澳台商投资企业和外商投资企业分别包括合资经营企业、合作经营企业、独资经营企业和股份有限公司。对不在工商行政管理部门进行登记注册的行政机关、事业单位和社会团体，主要按其经费来源和管理方式进行划分。

国有企业 指企业全部资产归国家所有，并按《中华人民共和国企业法人登记管理条例》规定登记注册的非公司制的经济组织。不包括有限责任公司中的国有独资公司。

集体企业 指企业资产归集体所有，并按《中华人民共和国企业法人登记管理条例》规定登记注册的经济组织。

股份合作企业 指以合作制为基础，由企业职工共同出资入股，吸收一定比例的社会资产投资组建，实行自主经营，自负盈亏，共同劳动，民主管理，按劳分配与按股分红相结合的一种集体经济组织。

联营企业 指两个及两个以上相同或不同所有制性质的企业法人或事业单位法人，按自愿、平等、互利的原则，共同投资组成的经济组织。联营企业包括国有联营企业、集体联营企业、国有与集体联营企业和其他联营企业。

有限责任公司 指根据《中华人民共和国公司登记管理条例》规定登记注册，由两个以上、五十个以下的股东共同出资，每个股东以其所认缴的出资额对公司承担有限责任，公司以其全部资产对其债务承担责任的经济组织。有限责任公司包括国有独资公司以及其他有限责任公司。

股份有限公司 指根据《中华人民共和国公司登记管理条例》规定登记注册，其全部注册资本由等额股份构成并通过发行股票筹集资本，股东以其认购的股份对公司承担有限责任，公司以其全部资产对其债务承担责任的经济组织。

私营企业 指由自然人投资设立或由自然人控股，以雇佣劳动为基础的营利性经济组织。包括按照《公司法》、《合伙企业法》、《私营企业暂行条例》规定登记注册的私营有限责任公司、私营股份有限公司、私营合伙企业和私营独资企业。

其他企业 指上述企业之外的其他内资经济组织。

与港澳台商合资经营企业 指港澳台地区投资者与内地企业依照《中华人民共和国中外合资经营企业法》及有关法律的规定，按合同规定的比例投资设立、分享利润和分担风险的企业。

与港澳台商合作经营企业 指港澳台地区投资者与内地企业依照《中华人民共和国中外合作经营企业法》及有关法律的规定，依照合作合同的约定进行投资或提供条件设立、分配利润和分担风险的企业。

港澳台商独资经营企业 指依照《中华人民共和国外资企业法》及有关法律的规定，在内地由港澳台地区投资者全额投资设立的企业。

港澳台商投资股份有限公司 指根据国家有关规定，经原外经贸部依法批准设立，其中港、澳、台商的股本占公司注册资本的比例达25% 以上的股份有限公司。凡其中港、澳、台商的股本占公司注册资本的比例小于25%的，属于内资企业中的股份有限公司。

中外合资经营企业 指外国企业或外国人与中国内地企业依照《中华人民共和国中外合资经营企业法》及有关法律的规定，按合同规定的比例投资设立、分享利润和分担风险的企业。

中外合作经营企业 指外国企业或外国人与中国内地企业依照《中华人民共和国中外合作经营企业法》及有关法律的规定，依照合作合同的约定进行投资或提供条件设立、分配利润和分担风险的企业。

外资企业 指依照《中华人民共和国外资企业法》及有关法律的规定，在中国内地由外国投资者全额投资设立的企业。

外商投资股份有限公司 指根据国家有关规定，经原外经贸部依法批准设立，其中外资的股本占公司注册资本的比例达25% 以上的股份有限公司。凡其中外资股本占公司注册资本的比例小于25%的，属于内资企业中的股份有限公司。

行政机关、事业单位和社会团体 参照企业登记注册类型，主要按其经费来源和管理方式划分。具体规定如下：

（1）行政机关：包括国家机关和政党机关，原则上均列为“国有”。但有特殊规定的，如供销社等，则列为“集体”。

（2）事业单位：包括经国家机构编制部门和有关业务主管部门批准成立的各类事业单位，不包括实行企业化管理的事业单位。事业单位的划分办法如下：

①由国家财政预算拨款或列入财政预算外资金管理以及经费主要来源于国有主管部门或国有上级单位的事业单位，列为“国有”。

②经费主要来源于集体单位的事业单位，列为“集

体”。

③公民个人（或个人合伙）开办的事业单位，列为“私营”。

④上述以外的其他事业单位，如果其经费来源不明确，按管理方式进行归类。

（3）社会团体：包括经民政部门批准成立以及未纳入社会团体管理条例范围的工会、妇联等各类社会团体。社会团体的划分办法如下：

①未纳入民政部社会团体管理条例范围的工会、妇联、共青团、青联、工商联、科协、侨联等社会团体，国家拨款设立的基金会或基金管理组织以及经费主要来源于国有业务主管部门或国有上级单位的社会团体，列为“国有”。

②经费主要来源于集体单位的社会团体，列为“集体”。

③公民个人（或个人合伙）开办的社会团体，划为“私营”。

④上述以外的其他社会团体，如果其经费来源不明确，改按管理方式进行归类。

Explanatory Notes on Main Statistical Indicators

Divisions of Administrative Areas refers to the division of administrative areas by the State. The relative laws stipulate that (1)the whole country is divided into provinces, autonomous regions and municipalities directly under the Central Government;(2)provinces and autonomous regions are further divided into autonomous prefectures, counties, autonomous counties and cities; (3)autonomous prefectures are further divided into counties, autonomous counties and cities; (4)counties and autonomous counties are further divided into townships, ethnic townships and towns; (5)municipalities directly under the Central Government and large cities are divided into districts and counties, (6)the State shall, when necessary, establish special administrative regions.

Climate refers to the natural environmental status formed by the long-term exchange of energy and mass between the earth and the atmosphere, and is the result of interaction of many factors. Climate is both one of the environment factors and also the important resources for living and production activities of the human being. The average values across several years of meteorological factors such as temperature, rainfall and humidity are used as important parameters to describe the climate of a region, while the average values (or total values)of a given year or month of meteorological factors reflect the key characteristics of climate for that period of time.

Natural Resources refer to material resources that could be obtained from the nature by human being and used for production and living. Natural resources in general can be classified as renewable resources and non-renewable resources. Renewable resources refer to resources that could be renewed and recycled during a relatively short period of time, including land resource, water resource, climate resource, biology resource and marine resource. Non-renewable resources include resources that could not be renewed, such as minerals and geothermal resource.

Land Resource Land refers to the surface of the earth, consisting of mainly rocks and its whethering and earth. Land resource can be classified, by its utilization, as land for agriculture, land for construction and unused land. Land for agriculture includes cultivated land, plantation land, forestland, grassland and waters. Land for construction includes land for residential purpose, for manufacturing and mining, for transportation and for water-conservancy projects. Unused land refers to land other than land for agriculture and construction, including beaches, deserts, Gobi, glaciers and rock mountains.

Area of Cultivated Land refers to area of land reclaimed for the regular cultivation of various farm crops, including crop-cover land, fallow, newly reclaimed land and land laid idle for less than 3 years.

Forest Area refers to the area of trees and bamboo grow with canopy density above 0.2, the area of shrubby tree according to regulations of the government, the area of forest land inside farm land and the area of trees planted by the side of villages, farm houses and along roads and rivers.

Area of Afforested Land refers to area for land for trees bamboo, bushes and mangrove, including forest-covered land, bush-covered land, sparse forest land, land planned for afforestation and nurseries of young trees.

Total Water Resources refers to total volume of water resources measured as run-off for surface water from rainfall and recharge for groundwater in a given area, excluding transit water.

Surface Water Resources refers to total renewable resources which exist in rivers, lakes, glaciers and other collectors from rainfall and are measured as run-off of rivers.

Groundwater Resources refers to replenishment of aquifers with rainfall and surface water.

Temperature refers to the air temperature. China uses centigrade as the unit. The thermometry used for weather observation is put in a breezy shutter, which is 1.5 meters high from the ground. Therefore, the commonly used temperature refers to the temperature in the breezy shutter 1.5 meters away from the ground. The calculation method is as follows:

Monthly average temperature is the summation of average daily temperature of one month divided by the actual days of that particular month.

Annual average temperature is the summation of monthly average of a year divided by 12 months.

Volume of Precipitation refers to the deepness of liquid state or solid state (thawed)water falling from the sky to the ground that has not been evaporated, infiltrated or run off. The calculation method is as follows:

Monthly precipitation is the summation of daily precipitation of a month.

Annual precipitation is the summation of 12 months precipitation of a year.

Sunshine Hours refer to the actual hours of sun irradiating the earth. The calculation method is the same as that of the precipitation.

Average Annual Growth Rate shows the average growth rate of social and economic development during a longer period. It can not be directly calculated by chain based growth rate. The relation is:

Average Annual Growth Rate=Average Speed of Development 1

Average speed of development is the time series average of speed which calculated by chain based. Because the reference bases during the different periods are not same, average speed of development can not be calculated by the general method. Level approach and accumulative approach for calculating average speed of development rate are applied. The "level approach", or the method of calculating the geometric average, is derived by the formula of geometric average of the chain-based speeds of development, or comparing the level of the last year of the interval with that of the beginning year; the other is called the "accumulative approach" or the "algebraic average", "equation" method, which is derived by the summation of the actual figure of each year in the interval divided by the figure in the base year. The level approach focuses on the level of the last year, while the accumulative approach emphasizes the aggregate development in the duration.

The average annual growth rates listed in the Yearbook are calculated by the level approach except for the growth rate of investment in fixed assets. The base year is not listed in the duration for which average annual growth rates are computed. For instance, the average annual growth rate of the 60 years since 1949 is shown as the average annual growth rate of 1950-2009 without showing the base year 1949.

Registration Status of Enterprises Enterprises are classified into 3 categories, namely domestic-funded enterprises, enterprises with investment from Hong Kong, Macau and Taiwan, and enterprises with foreign investment, according to the registration status of an enterprise in industrial and commercial administration agencies. Domestic-funded enterprises include State-owned enterprises, collective-owned enterprises, cooperative enterprises, joint ownership enterprises, limited liability corporations, share-holding corporations Ltd., private enterprises and other enterprises. Included in the enterprises with investment from Hong Kong, Macau and Taiwan and enterprises with foreign investment are joint-venture enterprises, cooperative enterprises, sole investment enterprises and share-holding corporations Ltd. For government agencies, institutions and social organizations which are not registered in industrial and commercial administration agencies, they are classified mainly by their sources of funding and manner of management.

State-owned Enterprises refer to non-corporation economic units where the entire assets are owned by the State and which have been registered in accordance with the Regulation of the People's Republic of China on the Management of Registration of Corporate Enterprises. Not included from this category are solely State-funded corporations in the limited liability corporations.

Collective-owned Enterprises refer to economic units where the assets are owned collectively and which have been registered in accordance with the Regulation of the People's Republic of China on the Management of Registration of Corporate Enterprises.

Cooperative Enterprises refer to a form of collective economic units (enterprises)where capitals come mainly from employees as their shares, with certain proportion of capital from the outside, where production is organized on the basis of independent operation, independent accounting for profits and losses, joint work, democratic management, and a distribution system that integrates remuneration according to work with dividend according to capital share.

Joint Ownership Enterprises refer to economic units established by two or more corporate enterprises or corporate institutions of the same or different ownership, through joint investment on the basis of voluntary participation, equality, and mutual benefits. They include State joint ownership enterprises; collective joint ownership enterprises; joint State-collective enterprises; and other joint ownership enterprises.

Limited Liability Corporations refer to economic units established with investment from 2-50 investors and registered in accordance with the Regulation of the People's Republic of China on the Management of Registration of Corporations, each investor bearing limited liability to the corporation depending on its share of investment, and the corporation bearing liability to its debt to the maximum of its total assets. Limited liability corporations include solely State-funded limited liability corporations and other limited liability corporations.

Share-holding Corporations Ltd. refer to economic units registered in accordance with the Regulation of the People's Republic of China on the Management of Registration of Corporations, with total registered capital divided into equal shares and raised through issuing stocks. Each investor bears limited liability to the corporation depending on the holding of shares, and the corporation bears liability to its debt to the maximum of its total assets.

Private Enterprises refer to profit-making economic units invested and established by natural persons, or controlled by natural persons using employed labour. Included in this category are private limited liability corporations, private share-holding corporations Ltd., private partnership enterprises and private-funded enterprises registered in accordance with the Company Law, the Law on Partnership Business and Interim Regulations on Private Enterprises .

Other Domestic-funded Enterprises refer to domestic-funded economic units other than those mentioned above.

Joint Venture Enterprises with Funds from Hong Kong, Macau and Taiwan are enterprises established by investors from Hong Kong, Macau and Taiwan with enterprises in the mainland of China in accordance with the Law of the People's Republic of China on Sino-foreign Equity Joint Ventures and other relevant laws, where the establishment of the investment and the sharing of profits and risks are stipulated under joint venture contracts.

Cooperative Enterprises with Funds from Hong Kong, Macau and Taiwan established by investors from Hong Kong, Macau and Taiwan with enterprises in the mainland of China in accordance with the Law of the People's Republic of China on Sino-foreign Contractual Joint Venture and other relevant laws, where the investment or provision of facilities and the sharing of profits and risks are stipulated under cooperative contracts.

Enterprises with Sole (exclusive)Investment from Hong Kong, Macau and Taiwan refer to enterprises established in the mainland of China with exclusive investment from investors from Hong Kong, Macau and Taiwan in accordance with the Law of the People's Republic of China on Wholly Foreign-owned Enterprises and other relevant laws.

Share-holding Corporations Ltd. with Investment from Hong Kong, Macau and Taiwan refer to share-holding corporations Ltd. established with the approval from the former Ministry of Foreign Trade and Economic Relations in line with relevant State regulations, where the share of investment from Hong Kong, Macau or Taiwan businessmen exceeds 25% of the total registered capital of the corporation. In case the share of investment from Hong Kong, Macau or Taiwan is less than 25% of the total registered capital, the enterprise is to be classified as domestic-funded share-holding corporation Ltd.

Joint Venture Enterprises with Foreign Investment refer to enterprises jointly established by foreign enterprises or foreigners with enterprises in the mainland of China in accordance with the Law of the People's Republic of China on Sino-foreign Equity Joint Ventures and other relevant laws, where the sharing of investment, profits and risks is stipulated under contract.

Cooperative Enterprises with Foreign Investment refer to enterprises jointly established by foreign enterprises or foreigners with enterprises in the mainland of China in accordance with the Law of the People's Republic of China on Sino-foreign Contractual Joint Venture and other relevant laws, where the investment or provision of facilities and the sharing of profits and risks are stipulated under cooperative contracts.

Enterprises with Sole (exclusive)Foreign Investment refer to enterprises established in the mainland of China with exclusive investment from foreign investors in accordance with the Law of the People's Republic of China on Wholly Foreign-owned Enterprises and other relevant laws.

Share-holding Corporations Ltd. with Foreign Investment refer to share-holding corporations Ltd. established with the approval from the former Ministry of Foreign Trade and Economic Relations in line with relevant State regulations, where the share of investment from foreign investors exceeds 25% of the total registered capital of the corporation. In case the share of foreign investment is less than 25% of the total registered capital, the enterprise is to be classified as domestic-funded share-holding corporation Ltd.

Government Agencies, Institutions and Social Organizations are classified into the following categories by source of funds and manner of management taking reference of the registration status of enterprises:

(1)Government agencies: include State and party agencies, classified in principle as State-owned. There are exceptions, such as supply and marketing cooperatives which are classified as collective-owned.

(2)Institutions: include institutions of various types established with the approval by organization and staffing departments of the government, but exclude institutions where enterprise management system is introduced. Institutions are further classified as follows:

(a)Institutions for which their main budgets are from government budget appropriations or extra-budget funds, or allocated from the budget of their competent government agencies. Such institutions are classified as state-owned.

(b)Institutions for which their budget mainly come from collective units. Such institutions are classified as collective-owned.

(c)Social institutions established by individual or a group of citizens, which are classified as private.

(d)Institutions other than those mentioned above for which their sources of budget are not clear. Such institutions are classified by the manner of management.

(3)Social organizations: include social organizations established with the approval from the Ministry of Civil Affairs, and organizations that are not covered by social organization management regulations such as trade unions, women's federations etc.. Social organizations are further classified as follows:

(a)Social organizations that are not covered by social organization management regulations of the Ministry of Civil Affairs such as trade unions, women federations, communist youth leagues, youth associations, industrial and commerce associations, scientist associations, overseas Chinese associations, etc., foundations and fund management organizations established with funds from the state, and social organizations whose funds mainly come from the budget of their competent government agencies. Such institutions are classified as State-owned.

(b)Social organizations for which their budget mainly come from collective units. Such institutions are classified as collective-owned.

(c)Social organizations established by individual or a group of citizens, which are classified as private.

(d)Social organizations other than those mentioned above for which their sources of budget are not clear. Such organizations are classified by the manner of management.

2 国民经济核算

NATIONAL ECONOMIC ACCOUNTS

资料整理：吴 羽 徐 枫
Data management: Wu Yu Xu Feng

第二部分　国民经济核算

一、简要说明

本章资料包括西安生产总值、构成和指数，分区县生产总值等。根据国家统计局的统一要求，为保持GDP数据的历史可比性，根据国家统计局和陕西省统计局《年度GDP历史数据修订办法》，对2005—2007年度GDP历史数据进行了修订；人均GDP按户籍人口计算，2005年以后按常住人口计算。资料由西安市统计局国民经济核算处提供。

二、主要指标

生产总值（亿元）	3862.58	比上年增长	13.8%
第一产业	173.14	比上年增长	6.7%
第二产业	1674.31	比上年增长	14.9%
第三产业	2015.13	比上年增长	13.4%
人均生产总值（元/人）	45475	比上年增长	13.2%

2 NATIONAL ECONOMIC ACCOUNTS

Ⅰ.Brief Introduction

The data in this chapter consists of composition and indices of the GDP in Xi'an and GDP by region, etc. According to the request of National Bureau of Statistic, in order to keep the history GDP data comparable, the GDP of 2005 - 2007 had been adjusted based on Adjusting Method of yearly GDP released by National Bureau of Statistic and Shaan'xi Provincial Bureau of Statistic. Per capital GDP had been calculated on register population, and after 2005 was calculated on permanent population. Data in this chapter is provided by National Economic Accounting Division of the Xi'an Bureau of Statistics.

Ⅱ.Major Indicators

		Increase over Preceding Year
Gross Domestic Product(100 mil. yuan)	3862.58	13.8%
Primary Industry	173.14	6.7%
Secondary Industry	1674.31	14.9%
Tertiary Industry	2015.13	13.4%
Per Capita Gross Domestic Product（yuan/person)	45475	13.2%

2-1 主要年份生产总值

Gross Domestic Product in Representative Years

（本表按当年价格计算） (Data in the table are calculated at current prices)

单位：亿元 (100 million yuan)

年 份 Year	生产总值 Gross Domestic Product	第一产业 Primary Industry	第二产业 Secondary Industry	第三产业 Tertiary Industry	人均GDP（元/人） Per Capita Gross Domestic Product (yuan/person)
1952	3.37	1.59	0.88	0.90	135
1965	12.76	2.62	7.22	2.92	323
1970	17.76	3.13	10.96	3.67	412
1975	21.33	4.14	12.63	4.56	448
1978	25.35	4.83	14.59	5.93	513
1980	31.66	4.73	18.69	8.24	623
1983	35.89	5.22	20.14	10.53	674
1984	44.14	7.45	24.17	12.52	817
1985	57.58	8.76	30.83	17.99	1049
1986	65.78	9.59	33.86	22.33	1178
1987	80.16	10.73	37.69	31.74	1409
1988	99.22	11.47	46.58	41.17	1711
1989	109.38	12.78	48.91	47.69	1861
1990	116.51	13.94	50.15	52.42	1932
1991	136.14	17.17	57.06	61.91	2224
1992	164.85	18.78	69.22	76.85	2662
1993	229.56	22.58	110.88	96.10	3661
1994	289.82	31.68	128.27	129.87	4563
1995	330.35	41.40	135.33	153.62	5131
1996	406.95	46.94	161.63	198.38	6246
1997	488.82	51.33	197.97	239.52	7424
1998	525.85	51.91	216.32	257.62	7906
1999	577.29	45.53	243.35	288.41	8599
2000	646.13	44.65	277.13	324.35	9484
2001	734.86	45.87	312.90	376.09	10628
2002	826.68	47.77	353.58	425.33	11831
2003	946.66	50.72	407.38	488.56	13341
2004	1102.39	60.21	476.92	565.26	15294
2005	1313.93	66.01	540.50	707.42	16406
2006	1538.94	70.44	645.65	822.85	18890
2007	1856.63	82.51	781.94	992.18	22463
2008	2318.14	103.45	981.58	1233.11	27794
2009	2724.08	110.38	1144.75	1468.95	32411
2010	3241.69	140.06	1406.72	1694.91	38343
2011	3862.58	173.14	1674.31	2015.13	45475

注：2005年以后人均GDP按平均常住人口计算。根据全国第二次经济普查结果，对2005-2007年生产总值及人均GDP进行了修订。

Note:Per capital GDP after 2005 was calculated on permanent population,according to the second national census,we made adjustments to the GDP , the value-added of the primary industry and per capital local GDP of 2005-2007.

2-2 主要年份生产总值指数（上年=100）

Indices of Gross Domestic Product in Representative Years(preceding year = 100)

（本表按可比价格计算） (Data in the table are calculated at constant prices)

年 份	Year	生产总值 Gross Domestic Product	第一产业 Primary Industry	第二产业 Secondary Industry	第三产业 Tertiary Industry	人均生产总值 Per Capita Gross Domestic Product
1952		103.6	92.2	137.5	123.7	
1965		126.1	134.1	133.0	106.7	
1970		122.0	109.4	140.0	100.1	
1975		103.8	92.6	107.1	107.5	
1978		101.7	101.6	99.4	108.2	
1980		111.5	83.3	119.7	116.5	
1985		112.6	107.5	111.8	116.9	
1986		111.4	107.7	108.4	118.8	
1987		113.6	100.8	109.1	126.6	
1988		111.4	81.2	115.5	114.7	
1989		106.7	103.0	104.5	110.8	
1990		105.2	103.0	102.5	109.6	
1991		109.8	118.6	108.6	108.6	108.2
1992		115.6	109.4	118.1	115.0	114.3
1993		123.9	112.5	142.7	108.4	122.3
1994		110.3	98.4	110.6	113.2	108.8
1995		110.0	104.5	112.1	108.6	108.5
1996		114.9	106.8	118.8	111.7	113.5
1997		114.4	109.1	116.7	112.4	113.2
1998		113.3	106.5	117.5	108.8	112.1
1999		112.2	97.4	115.7	110.1	111.2
2000		113.0	103.5	115.1	111.5	111.4
2001		113.1	102.5	115.3	112.6	111.4
2002		113.3	103.1	115.0	113.0	112.1
2003		113.5	101.8	117.5	111.2	111.7
2004		113.5	106.7	115.9	112.0	111.7
2005		114.0	107.5	112.3	116.3	112.2
2006		114.0	107.1	113.7	114.9	112.9
2007		115.6	104.5	115.7	116.4	113.9
2008		116.3	107.6	116.4	116.9	115.3
2009		114.5	106.3	114.0	115.5	113.7
2010		114.5	106.9	118.0	112.5	113.8
2011		113.8	106.7	114.9	113.4	113.2
平均每年增长	**Yearly Average Growth Rates**					
"一五"时期	**The First Five-Year Plan Period**	**15.8**	**5.9**	**37.7**	**16.9**	
"二五"时期	**The Second Five-Year Plan Period**	**2.0**	**-3.7**	**2.4**	**8.4**	
1963--1965年	**Readjust Period**	**14.2**	**16.2**	**23.3**	**0.3**	
"三五"时期	**The Third Five-Year Plan Period**	**7.1**	**0.1**	**11.7**	**5.4**	
"四五"时期	**The Fourth Five-Year Plan Period**	**5.0**	**4.0**	**5.3**	**5.0**	
"五五"时期	**The Fifth Five-Year Plan Period**	**6.0**	**-0.7**	**6.5**	**10.1**	
"六五"时期	**The Sixth Five-Year Plan Period**	**10.7**	**7.9**	**10.4**	**12.9**	
"七五"时期	**The Seventh Five-Year Plan Period**	**9.6**	**-1.3**	**7.9**	**16.0**	
"八五"时期	**The Eighth Five-Year Plan Period**	**13.8**	**8.5**	**17.8**	**10.7**	**12.3**
"九五"时期	**The Ninth Five-Year Plan Period**	**13.5**	**4.6**	**16.8**	**10.9**	**12.3**
"十五"时期	**The Tenth Five-Year Plan Period**	**13.5**	**4.3**	**15.2**	**13.0**	**11.8**
"十一五"时期	**The Eleventh Five-Year Plan Period**	**15.0**	**6.5**	**15.5**	**15.2**	**13.9**

注：根据全国第二次经济普查结果，对2005-2007年生产总值指数进行了修订。

Note:according to the second national census,we made the Indices to the GDP , the value-added of the primary industry and per capital local GDP of 2005-2007.

2-3 主要年份生产总值指数（1952年=100）

Indices of Gross Domestic Product in Representative Years(1952=100)

（本表按可比价格计算） (Data in the table are calculated at constant prices)

年　份 Year	生产总值 Gross Domestic Product	第一产业 Primary Industry	第二产业 Secondary Industry	第三产业 Tertiary Industry
1952	100.0	100.0	100.0	100.0
1965	341.6	173.3	1048.3	329.2
1970	481.6	174.3	1821.0	428.6
1975	614.2	211.9	2362.5	547.9
1978	678.7	231.3	2560.8	643.8
1980	821.4	204.2	3237.2	885.2
1983	988.4	222.5	3846.2	1154.4
1984	1213.6	278.2	4748.8	1388.7
1985	1366.8	299.1	5310.6	1632.4
1986	1523.1	322.3	5756.7	1928.9
1987	1730.0	324.9	6280.6	2441.6
1988	1926.3	263.7	7256.6	2801.2
1989	2054.8	271.6	7583.1	3104.6
1990	2162.5	279.7	7772.7	3403.6
1991	2374.4	331.7	8441.2	3696.3
1992	2744.8	362.9	9969.1	4250.7
1993	3400.8	408.2	14225.9	4607.8
1994	3751.1	401.8	15733.8	5216.0
1995	4126.2	419.9	17637.6	5664.6
1996	4741.0	448.5	20953.5	6327.4
1997	5423.7	489.3	24452.7	7112.0
1998	6145.1	521.1	28731.9	7737.9
1999	6894.8	507.6	33242.8	8519.4
2000	7791.1	525.4	38262.5	9499.1
2001	8811.7	538.5	44116.7	10696.0
2002	9983.7	555.2	50734.2	12086.5
2003	11331.5	265.2	59612.7	13440.2
2004	12861.3	603.1	69091.1	15053.0
2005	14661.9	648.3	77589.3	17506.6
2006	16714.6	694.3	88219.0	20115.1
2007	19322.1	725.5	102069.4	23414.0
2008	22471.6	780.6	118808.8	27371.0
2009	25730.0	829.8	135442.0	31613.5
2010	29460.9	950.1	155081.1	36197.5
2011	33513.2	1013.8	178177.0	41045.6

2-4 主要年份生产总值构成

Composition of Gross Domestic Product in Representative Years

（本表按当年价格计算） (Data in the table are calculated at current prices)

单位：% (%)

年 份	Year	生产总值 Gross Domestic Product	第一产业 Primary Industry	第二产业 Secondary Industry	第三产业 Tertiary Industry
1952		100	47.18	26.11	26.71
1965		100	20.53	56.58	22.89
1970		100	17.62	61.71	20.67
1975		100	19.41	59.21	21.38
1978		100	19.05	57.55	23.40
1980		100	14.94	59.03	26.03
1985		100	15.22	53.54	31.24
1986		100	14.58	51.47	33.95
1987		100	13.38	47.02	39.60
1988		100	11.56	46.95	41.49
1989		100	11.68	44.72	43.60
1990		100	11.96	43.05	44.99
1991		100	12.61	41.91	45.48
1992		100	11.39	41.99	46.62
1993		100	9.84	48.30	41.86
1994		100	10.93	44.26	44.81
1995		100	12.53	40.97	46.50
1996		100	11.53	39.72	48.75
1997		100	10.50	40.50	49.00
1998		100	9.87	41.14	48.99
1999		100	7.89	42.15	49.96
2000		100	6.91	42.89	50.20
2001		100	6.24	42.58	51.18
2002		100	5.78	42.77	51.45
2003		100	5.36	43.03	51.61
2004		100	5.46	43.26	51.28
2005		100	5.02	41.14	53.84
2006		100	4.58	41.95	53.47
2007		100	4.44	42.12	53.44
2008		100	4.46	42.34	53.20
2009		100	4.05	42.02	53.93
2010		100	4.32	43.39	52.29
2011		100	4.48	43.35	52.17
"一五"时期	**The First Five-Year Plan Period**	**100**	**32.88**	**43.92**	**23.20**
"二五"时期	**The Second Five-Year Plan Period**	**100**	**18.08**	**58.63**	**23.29**
1963-1965年	**Readjust Period**	**100**	**19.36**	**55.37**	**25.27**
"三五"时期	**The Third Five-Year Plan Period**	**100**	**18.60**	**57.33**	**24.07**
"四五"时期	**The Fourth Five-Year Plan Period**	**100**	**20.46**	**59.59**	**19.95**
"五五"时期	**The Fifth Five-Year Plan Period**	**100**	**18.40**	**57.69**	**23.91**
"六五"时期	**The Sixth Five-Year Plan Period**	**100**	**16.03**	**55.01**	**28.96**
"七五"时期	**The Seventh Five-Year Plan Period**	**100**	**12.42**	**46.11**	**41.47**
"八五"时期	**The Eighth Five-Year Plan Period**	**100**	**11.44**	**43.52**	**45.04**
"九五"时期	**The Ninth Five-Year Plan Period**	**100**	**9.09**	**41.45**	**49.46**
"十五"时期	**The Tenth Five-Year Plan Period**	**100**	**5.49**	**42.47**	**52.04**
"十一五"时期	**The Eleventh Five-Year Plan Period**	**100**	**4.34**	**42.47**	**53.19**

2-5 全市各区县生产总值（2011年）

Gross Domestic Product by Region（2011）

单位：亿元 (100 million yuan)

区县名称	Name of District and County	生产总值 Gross Domestic Product	第一产业 Primary Industry	第二产业 Secondary Industry	工业 Industry	第三产业 Tertiary Industry
新城区	Xincheng	379.89		152.99	90.35	226.90
碑林区	Beilin	436.71		110.42	43.47	326.29
莲湖区	Lianhu	437.18		199.48	137.62	237.70
灞桥区	Baqiao	207.07	14.41	120.53	102.89	72.13
未央区	Weiyang	469.00	2.31	244.40	174.79	222.29
雁塔区	Yanta	726.78	2.61	255.65	137.95	468.52
阎良区	Yanliang	119.77	17.61	59.79	48.82	42.37
临潼区	Lintong	184.75	28.27	102.03	93.33	54.45
长安区	Chang'an	324.92	28.97	160.06	128.47	135.89
蓝田县	Lantian	81.94	20.49	29.46	18.35	31.99
周至县	Zhouzhi	66.27	20.30	17.53	13.42	28.44
户　县	Huxian	129.13	21.24	70.84	61.81	37.05
高陵县	Gaoling	188.30	16.93	150.99	138.20	20.38

2-6 全市各区县生产总值指数（2011年）（上年=100）

Indices of Gross Domestic Product by Region（2011）（preceding year = 100）

区县名称	Name of District and County	生产总值 Gross Domestic Product	第一产业 Primary Industry	第二产业 Secondary Industry	工业 Industry	第三产业 Tertiary Industry
新城区	Xincheng	113.0		113.9	113.3	112.4
碑林区	Beilin	115.5		123.3	127.8	113.1
莲湖区	Lianhu	113.4		114.6	113.2	112.3
灞桥区	Baqiao	116.3	108.2	120.9	121.8	110.5
未央区	Weiyang	113.0	90.0	111.0	113.7	115.8
雁塔区	Yanta	113.4	95.9	110.1	116.7	115.2
阎良区	Yanliang	113.8	108.0	115.8	115.7	113.2
临潼区	Lintong	113.6	104.2	117.1	117.3	112.7
长安区	Chang'an	114.0	107.2	115.0	114.6	114.3
蓝田县	Lantian	110.5	107.8	110.8	108.1	111.9
周至县	Zhouzhi	111.1	108.3	112.3	110.7	112.3
户　县	Huxian	111.0	108.2	111.3	111.7	111.7
高陵县	Gaoling	120.0	108.1	122.2	121.5	112.9

2-7 全市各区县生产总值构成（2011年）

Composition of Gross Domestic Product by Region（2011）

单位：% (%)

区县名称	Name of District and County	生产总值 Gross Domestic Product	第一产业 Primary Industry	第二产业 Secondary Industry	第三产业 Tertiary Industry
新城区	Xincheng	100.0		40.3	59.7
碑林区	Beilin	100.0		25.3	74.7
莲湖区	Lianhu	100.0		45.6	54.4
灞桥区	Baqiao	100.0	7.0	58.2	34.8
未央区	Weiyang	100.0	0.5	52.1	47.4
雁塔区	Yanta	100.0	0.4	35.2	64.4
阎良区	Yanliang	100.0	14.7	49.9	35.4
临潼区	Lintong	100.0	15.3	55.2	29.5
长安区	Chang'an	100.0	8.9	49.3	41.8
蓝田县	Lantian	100.0	25.0	36.0	39.0
周至县	Zhouzhi	100.0	30.6	26.5	42.9
户　县	Huxian	100.0	16.4	54.9	28.7
高陵县	Gaoling	100.0	9.0	80.2	10.8

2–8 主要年份分行业增加值

Value-added by Sector in Representative Years

单位：亿元 (100 million yuan)

指标	Item	2004	2005	2006	2007	2008	2009	2010	2011
生产总值	**Gross Domestic Product**	**1102.39**	**1313.93**	**1538.94**	**1856.63**	**2318.14**	**2724.08**	**3241.69**	**3862.58**
第一产业	Primary Industry	60.21	66.01	70.44	82.51	103.45	110.38	140.06	173.14
第二产业	Secondary Industry	476.92	540.50	645.65	781.94	981.58	1144.75	1406.72	1674.31
工业	Industry	383.46	420.00	494.22	594.95	721.40	816.92	1003.57	1189.61
建筑业	Construction	93.46	120.50	151.43	186.99	260.18	327.83	403.15	484.70
第三产业	Tertiary Industry	565.26	707.42	822.85	992.18	1233.11	1468.95	1694.91	2015.13
交通运输、仓储及邮政业	Transportation,Storage,Post and Telecommunications	55.10	66.30	74.08	84.21	99.16	110.60	124.69	147.64
批发和零售业	Wholesale and Retail Trades	125.12	147.20	166.72	195.51	242.91	293.05	337.86	418.94
住宿和餐饮业	Accommodation and Catering Trade	35.89	50.44	52.23	70.09	85.65	94.05	103.58	124.29
金融保险业	Banking and Insurance	61.49	75.00	96.50	128.50	160.84	198.47	226.42	256.57
房地产业	Real Estate	39.05	52.48	62.32	75.26	92.97	124.98	158.86	187.99
其他服务业	Others Services	248.61	316.00	371.00	438.61	551.58	647.80	743.50	879.70

2–9 主要年份分行业增加值指数（上年=100）

Indices of Value -added by Sector in Representative Years(preceding year=100)

（本表按可比价格计算） (Data in the table are calculated at constant prices)

指标	Item	2005	2006	2007	2008	2009	2010	2011
生产总值	**Gross Domestic Product**	**114.0**	**114.0**	**115.6**	**116.3**	**114.5**	**114.5**	**113.8**
第一产业	Primary Industry	107.5	107.1	104.5	107.6	106.3	106.9	106.7
第二产业	Secondary Industry	112.3	113.7	115.7	116.4	114.0	118.0	114.9
工业	Industry	110.3	112.3	114.9	115.7	111.7	118.1	116.2
建筑业	Construction	120.0	118.7	118.4	118.9	121.2	117.6	111.7
第三产业	Tertiary Industry	116.3	114.9	116.4	116.9	115.5	112.5	113.4
交通运输、仓储及邮政业	Transportation,Storage,Post and Telecommunications	113.2	112.3	110.3	108.4	105.0	111.5	112.5
批发和零售业	Wholesale and Retail Trades	112.7	112.5	112.9	115.0	119.7	112.3	118.8
住宿和餐饮业	Hotels and Catering Services	136.1	116.6	117.3	111.6	106.6	107.2	113.4
金融保险业	Banking and Insurance	109.3	107.3	126.7	113.6	121.4	110.7	107.2
房地产业	Real Estate	112.9	117.5	119.7	107.6	131.6	118.6	111.5
其他服务业	Others Services	117.7	117.7	116.3	122.5	113.2	112.7	113.4

2-10　主要年份支出法生产总值

Gross Domestic Product by Expenditure Approach in Representative Years

（本表按当年价格计算）　　(Data in the table are calculated at current prices)

单位：亿元　　(100 million yuan)

年　份 Year	生产总值 Gross Domestic Product	最终消费支出 Final Consumption Expenditures	资本形成总额 Total Investment	货物和服务净出口 Net Export of Goods and Services
1992	164.85	148.09	68.61	-51.85
1993	229.56	172.60	113.48	-56.52
1994	289.82	200.88	131.97	-43.03
1995	330.35	239.64	151.55	-60.84
1996	406.95	272.46	170.35	-35.86
1997	488.82	317.61	182.30	-11.09
1998	525.85	343.15	200.96	-18.26
1999	577.29	377.89	257.65	-58.25
2000	646.13	413.43	287.82	-55.12
2001	734.86	456.78	328.59	-50.51
2002	826.68	505.57	385.45	-64.34
2003	946.66	541.73	507.87	-102.94
2004	1102.39	689.24	649.93	-236.78
2005	1313.93	766.62	839.01	-291.70
2006	1538.94	870.93	1045.27	-377.26
2007	1856.63	995.22	1451.47	-590.06
2008	2318.14	1182.61	1837.86	-702.33
2009	2724.08	1403.10	2281.91	-960.93
2010	3241.69	1598.51	2835.42	-1192.24
2011	3862.58	1856.91	3264.83	-1259.16

2–11 主要年份支出法生产总值指数（上年=100）

Indices of Gross Domestic Product by Expenditure Approach in Representative Years（preceding year = 100）

年 份 Year	生产总值 Gross Domestic Product	最终消费 Final Consumption Expenditures	资本形成总额 Total Investment
1992	115.6	114.4	116.0
1993	123.9	103.1	124.9
1994	110.3	104.9	116.4
1995	110.0	110.0	114.6
1996	114.9	102.1	105.8
1997	114.4	108.2	106.6
1998	113.3	114.9	108.1
1999	112.2	114.8	123.6
2000	113.0	109.9	116.2
2001	113.1	108.5	111.2
2002	113.3	109.7	117.1
2003	113.5	108.8	129.6
2004	113.5	109.8	123.7
2005	114.0	107.7	127.0
2006	114.0	109.4	120.1
2007	115.6	109.5	135.2
2008	116.3	116.9	120.2
2009	114.5	118.4	122.6
2010	114.5	110.5	118.7
2011	113.8	110.4	108.4

2-12 按支出法计算的生产总值及指数（2011年）

Gross Domestic Product and Indices by Expenditure Approach（2011）

单位：亿元 (100 million yuan)

指　　标	Item	2011	指数（以上年为100）Indices (preceding year=100)
生产总值	**Gross Domestic Product**	**3862.58**	**113.8**
（一）最终消费支出	Final Consumption Expenditures	1856.91	110.4
1.居民消费支出	Resident Consumption Expenditures	1388.05	111.4
农村居民	Village Residents	176.88	109.5
城镇居民	Urban Residents	1211.17	111.7
2.政府消费支出	Government Consumption Expenditures	468.86	107.6
（二）资本形成总额	Gross Total Capital Formation	3264.83	108.4
1.固定资本形成总额	Fixed Capital	3043.94	108.5
2.存货增加	Change of Goods in Stock	220.89	107.1
（三）货物和服务净出口	Net Export of Goods and Services	-1259.16	96.5

2-13 分行业资本形成总额（2011年）

Gross Capital Formation by Sector（2011）

单位：亿元 (100 million yuan)

指　　标	Item	2011
资本形成总额	**Total Investment**	**3264.83**
一、固定资本形成总额	**Gross Fixed Capital Formation**	**3043.94**
1.住宅	Residential Buildings	1195.60
2.非住宅建筑物	Non-residential Buildings	1408.21
3.机器和设备	Machinery and Equipment	197.55
4.土地改良支出	Land Reform Expenditure	3.46
5.矿藏勘探费	Cost of Mineral Deposits Prospecting	0.30
6.计算机软件	Computer Softwares	75.36
7、其他	Others	163.46
二、存货增加	**Change of Goods in Stock**	**220.89**
1.农林牧渔业	Agriculture, Forestry, Animal Husbandry and Fishery	1.54
2.工业	Industry	94.49
3.建筑业	Construction	20.70
4.交通运输、仓储及邮政业	Transportation, Storage and Post	4.41
5.批发和零售业	Wholesale and Retail Trades	19.45
6.住宿和餐饮业	Hotels and Catering Services	-0.39
7.房地产	Real Estate	79.02
8.其他	Others	1.67

2–14 最 终 消 费 支 出（2011年）

Final Consumption Expenditures（2011）

单位：亿元 (100 million yuan)

指　　标	Item	2011
最终消费支出	**Final Consumption Expenditures**	**1856.91**
一、居民消费支出	**Resident Consumption Expenditures**	**1388.05**
（一）农村居民	Rural Residents	176.88
1.食品类支出	Food Expenditures	55.29
2.衣着类支出	Clothing Expenditures	12.49
3.居住类支出	Residence Expenditures	17.90
4.家庭设备、用品及服务类支出	Household Facilities、Articles and Services Expenditures	12.31
5.医疗保健类支出	Medical Care Expenditures	15.00
6.交通和通信类支出	Transportion and Communication Expenditures	15.62
7.文教娱乐用品及服务类支出	Culture、Education and Entertainment Expenditures	18.08
8.银行中介服务支出	Indirect Calculated Expenditures of Financial Intermediation Services	7.23
9.保险服务消费支出	Insurance Services Consumption Expenditures	0.39
10.自有住房服务虚拟类支出	Virtual Expenditures of Private Housing Services	19.44
11.其它商品和服务类支出	Other goods and services Expenditures	3.13
（二）城镇居民	Urban Residents	1211.17
1.食品类支出	Food Expenditures	356.88
2.衣着类支出	Clothing Expenditures	139.93
3.居住类支出	Residence Expenditures	94.20
4.家庭设备、用品及服务类支出	Household Facilities、Articles and Services Expenditures	92.50
5.医疗保健类支出	Medical Care Expenditures	102.63
6.交通和通信类支出	Transportion and Communication Expenditures	146.07
7.文教娱乐用品及服务类支出	Culture、Education and Entertainment Expenditures	162.68
8.银行中介服务支出	Indirect Calculated Expenditures of Financial Intermediation Services	31.84
9.保险服务消费支出	Insurance Services Consumption Expenditures	3.82
10.自有住房服务虚拟类支出	Virtual Expenditures of Private Housing Services	27.06
11.实物收入消费支出	Physical goods Consumption Expenditures	7.96
12.其它商品和服务类支出	Other goods and services Expenditures	45.60
二、政府消费支出	**Government Consumption Expenditures**	**468.86**

2-15 居民总消费水平（2011年）

Consumption of Residents （2011）

指　　标	Item	2011	指数（%）(上年=100) Indices (preceding year=100)
一、按当年价格计算 (元/人)	**Calculated at Current Prices (yuan/person)**		
全体居民消费水平	Per Capita Consumption of All Residents	16342	116.5
农村居民	Farmer	6839	117.3
城镇居民	Non-Farmer	20502	115.7
二、按可比价格计算 (元/人)	**Calculated at Comparable Prices (yuan/person)**		
全体居民消费水平	Per Capita Consumption of All Residents	15553	110.9
农村居民	Farmer	6473	111.0
城镇居民	Non-Farmer	19529	110.2
三、常住居民年平均人口(万人)	**Average Annual Population of Residents (10 000 persons)**	**849.38**	**100.5**

2-16 主要年份非公有制经济增加值

The Added Value of Non-public-owned Economic in Representative Years

单位：亿元　　(100 million yuan)

年份 Year	非公有制经济增加值 the Added Value of Non-public-owned Economic	第一产业 Primary Industry	第二产业 Secondary Industry	第三产业 Tertiary Industry	非公有制经济增加值占GDP比重(%) the Added Value of Non-public-owned Economic Percentage to GDP	第一产业 Primary Industry	第二产业 Secondary Industry	第三产业 Tertiary Industry
2005	**568.45**	**20.86**	**232.66**	**314.93**	**43.26**	**31.60**	**43.05**	**44.52**
2006	684.66	26.27	279.06	379.33	44.46	37.29	43.22	46.04
2007	854.26	25.25	365.24	463.77	46.01	30.60	46.71	46.74
2008	1103.96	36.42	468.58	598.96	47.62	35.21	47.74	48.57
2009	1327.49	36.32	542.37	748.80	48.73	32.90	47.38	50.98
2010	1611.28	42.66	665.90	902.72	49.70	30.46	47.34	53.26
2011	1952.78	52.93	814.44	1085.41	50.56	30.57	48.64	53.86

2-17 主要年份五大主导产业增加值

Value-added of the Five Leading Industries in Representative Years

单位：亿元 (100 million yuan)

产 业 Industries	五大主导产业增加值(剔除重复） Value-added of Five Leading Industries	高新技术产业增加值 High-Tech Industry	装备制造业增加值 Manufacture of Equipment	旅游业增加值 Tourism	文化产业增加值 Culture Industry	现代服务业增加值 Modern Services
2004	429.37	78.70	154.28	83.14	46.01	209.23
2005	536.08	100.46	179.88	99.90	60.46	272.51
2006	654.05	119.37	218.10	120.37	77.93	332.65
2007	839.20	142.45	280.12	148.53	99.98	416.26
2008	1084.89	199.23	344.61	189.86	127.44	734.95
2009	1324.33	296.68	392.27	226.82	151.02	881.20
2010	1622.99	361.92	485.53	275.35	190.62	1056.73
2011	1963.85	432.43	566.78	329.02	250.70	1270.12

注：五大主导产业增加值为剔除产业间重复计算部分；
各产业增加值为包含产业间重复计算部分。

Note: 'Value-added of Five Leading Industries' excludes the overlaps between different industries.
Value-added of each industry includes the overlaps.

2-18 主要年份五大主导产业增加值占GDP比重

Proportions of Value-added of the Five Leading Industries to GDP in Representative Years

单位：% (%)

产 业 Industries	五大主导产业增加值(剔除重复） Value-added of Five Leading Industries	高新技术产业增加值 High-Tech Industry	装备制造业增加值 Manufacture of Equipment	旅游业增加值 Tourism	文化产业增加值 Culture Industry	现代服务业增加值 Modern Services
2004	38.9	7.1	14.0	7.5	4.2	19.0
2005	40.8	7.6	13.7	7.6	4.6	20.7
2006	42.5	7.8	14.2	7.8	5.1	21.6
2007	45.2	7.7	15.1	8.0	5.4	22.4
2008	46.8	8.6	14.9	8.2	5.5	31.7
2009	48.6	10.9	14.4	8.3	5.5	32.3
2010	50.1	11.2	15.0	8.5	5.9	32.6
2011	50.8	11.2	14.7	8.5	6.5	32.9

注：五大主导产业增加值为剔除产业间重复计算部分，各产业增加值为包含产业间重复计算部分。根据全国第二次经济普查结果，对2005-2008年各产业增加值数据进行了修订。

Note: 'Value-added of Five Leading Industries' excludes the overlaps between different industries,Value-added of each industry includes the overlaps.According to the second national census,Data of value-added of each industry from 2005 to 2008 was revided.

主要统计指标解释

生产总值（GDP） 是按市场价格计算的一个地区（或国家）所有常住单位在一定时期内生产活动的最终成果。生产总值有三种表现形态，即价值形态、收入形态和产品形态。从价值形态看，它是所有常住单位在一定时期内生产的全部货物和服务价值超过同期中间投入的全部非固定资产货物和服务价值的差额，即所有常住单位的增加值之和;从收入形态看，它是所有常住单位在一定时期内创造并分配给常住单位和非常住单位的初次收入分配之和;从产品形态看，它是所有常住单位在一定时期内最终使用的货物和服务价值与货物和服务净出口价值之和。在实际核算中，生产总值有三种计算方法，即生产法、收入法和支出法。三种方法分别从不同的方面反映生产总值及其构成。

三次产业 是根据社会生产活动历史发展的顺序对产业结构的划分，产品直接取自自然界的部门称为第一产业，对初级产品进行再加工的部门称为第二产业，为生产和消费提供各种服务的部门称为第三产业。它是世界上较为通用的产业结构分类，但各国的划分不尽一致。

三产业的划分是世界上较为常用的产业结构分类，但各国的划分不尽一致。我国的三次产业划分是：

第一产业:农业（包括农业、林业、畜牧业、渔业和农林牧渔服务业）。

第二产业:工业（包括采矿业，制造业，电力、燃气及水的生产和供应业）和建筑业。

第三产业:除第一、第二产业以外的其他各业。

劳动者报酬 指劳动者因从事生产活动所获得的全部报酬。包括劳动者获得的各种形式的工资、奖金和津贴，既包括货币形式的，也包括实物形式的，还包括劳动者所享受的公费医疗和医药卫生费、上下班交通补贴、单位支付的社会保险费、住房公积金等。

生产税净额 指生产税减生产补贴后的余额。生产税指政府对生产单位从事生产、销售和经营活动以及因从事生产活动使用某些生产要素(如固定资产、土地、劳动力)所征收的各种税、附加费和规费。生产补贴与生产税相反，指政府对生产单位的单方面转移支出，因此视为负生产税，包括政策亏损补贴、价格补贴等。

固定资产折旧 指一定时期内为弥补固定资产损耗按照规定的固定资产折旧率提取的固定资产折旧，或按国民经济核算统一规定的折旧率虚拟计算的固定资产折旧。它反映了固定资产在当期生产中的转移价值。各类企业和企业化管理的事业单位的固定资产折旧是指实际计提的折旧费；不计提折旧的政府机关、非企业化管理的事业单位和居民住房的固定资产折旧是按照统一规定的折旧率和固定资产原值计算的虚拟折旧。原则上，固定资产折旧应按固定资产当期的重置价值计算，但是目前我国尚不具备对全社会固定资产进行重估价的基础，所以暂时只能采用上述办法。

营业盈余 指常住单位创造的增加值扣除劳动者报酬、生产税净额和固定资产折旧后的余额。它相当于企业的营业利润加上生产补贴，但要扣除从利润中开支的工资和福利等。

支出法国内生产总值 是从最终使用的角度反映一个国家(或地区)一定时期内生产活动最终成果的一种方法，包括最终消费支出、资本形成总额及货物和服务净出口三部分。计算公式为：

支出法国内生产总值=最终消费支出+资本形成总额+货物和服务净出口

最终消费支出 指常住单位为满足物质、文化和精神生活的需要，从本国经济领土和国外购买的货物和服务的支出。它不包括非常住单位在本国经济领土内的消费支出。最终消费支出分为居民消费支出和政府消费支出。

居民消费支出 指常住住户在一定时期内对于货物和服务的全部最终消费支出。居民消费支出除了直接以货币形式购买的货物和服务的消费支出外，还包括以其他方式获得的货物和服务的消费支出，即所谓的虚拟消费支出。居民虚拟消费支出包括如下几种类型：单位以实物报酬及实物转移的形式提供给劳动者的货物和服务；住户生产并由本住户消费了的货物和服务，其中的服务仅指住户的自有住房服务和付酬的家庭雇员提供的家庭和个人服务；金融机构提供的金融媒介服务。

政府消费支出 指政府部门为全社会提供的公共服务的消费支出和免费或以较低的价格向居民住户提供的货物和服务的净支出，前者等于政府服务的产出价值减去政府单位所获得的经营收入的价值，后者等于政府部门免费或以较低价格向居民住户提供的货物和服务的市场价值减去向住户收取的价值。

资本形成总额 指常住单位在一定时期内获得减去处置的固定资产和存货的净额，包括固定资本形成总额和存货增加两部分。

固定资本形成总额 指常住单位在一定时期内获得的固定资产减处置的固定资产的价值总额。固定资产是通过生产活动生产出来的，且其使用年限在一年以上、单位价值在规定标准以上的资产，不包括自然资产。可分为有形固定资本形成总额和无形固定资本形成总额。有形固定资本形成总额包括一定时期内完成的建筑工程、安装工程和设备工器具购置（减处置）价值，以及土地改良、新增役、种、奶、毛、娱乐用牲畜和新增经济林木价值。无形固定资本形成总额包括矿藏的勘探、计算机软件等获得减处置。

存货增加 指常住单位在一定时期内存货实物量变动的市场价值，即期末价值减期初价值的差额，再扣除当期由于价格变动而产生的持有收益。存货增加可以是正值，也可以是负值，正值表示存货上升，负值表示存货下降。存货包括生产单位购进的原材料、燃料和储备物资等存货，以及生产单位生产的产成品、在制品和半成品等存货。

货物和服务净出口 指货物和服务出口减货物和服务进口的差额。出口包括常住单位向非常住单位出售或无偿转让的各种货物和服务的价值；进口包括常住单位从非常住单位购买或无偿得到的各种货物和服务的价值。由于服务活动的提供与使用同时发生，一般把常住单位从非常住单位得到的服务作为进口，非常住单位从常住单位得到的服务作为出口。货物的出口和进口都按离岸价格计算。

Explanatory Notes on Main Statistical Indicators

Gross Domestic Product (GDP) refers to the final products at market prices produced by all resident units in a country (or a region) during a certain period of time. Gross domestic product is expressed in three different perspectives, namely value, income, and products respectively. GDP in its value perspective refers to the total value of all goods and services produced by all resident units during a certain period of time, minus the total value of input of goods and services of the nature of non-fixed assets; in other words, it is the sum of the value-added of all resident units. GDP from the perspective of income includes the primary income created by all resident units and distributed to resident and non-resident units. GDP from the perspective of products refers to the value of all goods and services for final demand by all resident units plus the net exports of goods and services during a given period of time. In the practice of national accounting, gross domestic product is calculated from three approaches, namely production approach, income approach and expenditure approach, which reflect gross domestic product and its composition from different angles.

For a region, it is called as Gross Regional Product(GRP) or regional GDP.

Three Strata of Industry Classification of economic activities into three strata of industry is a common practice in the world, although the grouping varies to some extent from country to country. In China economic activities are categorized into the following three strata of industry:

Primary industry refers to agriculture, forestry, animal husbandry and fishery and services in support of these industries.

Secondary industry refers to mining and quarrying, manufacturing, production and supply of electricity, water and gas, and construction.

Tertiary industry refers to all other economic activities not included in the primary or secondary industries.

Compensation of Employees refers to the total payment of various forms to employees for the productive activities they are engaged in. It includes wages, bonuses and allowances, which the employees earn in cash or in kind. It also includes the free medical services provided to the employees and the medicine expenses, transport subsidies and social insurance, and housing fund paid by the employers.

Net Taxes on Production refers to taxes on production less subsidies on production. The taxes on production refers to the various taxes, extra charges and fees levied on the production units on their production, sale and business activities as well as on the use of some factors of production, such as fixed assets, land and labour in the production activities they are engaged in. In contrast to taxes on production, subsidies on production refer to the unilateral government transfer to the production units and are therefore regarded as negative taxes on production. They include subsidies on the loss due to implementation of government policies, price subsidies, etc.

Depreciation of Fixed Assets refers to the depreciation of fixed assets in a given period, drawn in accordance with the stipulated depreciation rate for the purpose of compensating the wear-and-tear loss of the fixed assets or the depreciation of fixed assets imputed in accordance with the stipulated unified depreciation rate in the national economic accounting system. It reflects the value of transfer of the fixed assets in the production of the current period. The depreciation of fixed assets in various enterprises and institutions managed as enterprises refers to the depreciation expenses actually drawn. In government agencies and institutions not managed as enterprises which do not draw the depreciation expenses, as well as for the houses of residents, the depreciation of fixed assets is the imputed depreciation, which is calculated in accordance with the stipulated unified depreciation rate. In principle, the depreciation of fixed assets should be calculated on the basis of the re-purchased value of the fixed assets. However, currently the conditions in China do not facilitate the revaluation of all the fixed assets. Therefore, only the above-mentioned methods can be adopted at present.

Operating Surplus refers to the balance of the value added created by the resident units after deducting the labourers remuneration, net taxes on production and the depreciation of fixed assets. It is equivalent to the business profit of the enterprises plus subsidies to production, but the wages and welfare expenses paid from the profits should be deducted.

GDP by Expenditure Approach refers to the method of measuring the final results of production activities of a country (region) during a given period from the perspective of final uses. It includes final consumption expenditure, gross capital formation and net export of goods and services. The formula for computation is.:

GDP by expenditure approach = final consumption expenditure + gross capital formation + net export of goods and services

Final Consumption Expenditure refers to the total expenditure of resident units for purchases of goods and services from both the domestic economic territory and abroad to meet the needs of material, cultural and spiritual life. It does not include the expenditure of non-resident units on consumption in the economic territory of the country. The final consumption expenditure is broken down into household consumption expenditure and government consumption expenditure.

Household Consumption Expenditure refers to the total expenditure of resident households on the final consumption of goods and services. In addition to the consumption of goods and services bought by the households directly with money, the household consumption expenditure also includes expenditure on goods and services obtained by the households in other ways, i.e. the so-called imputed consumption expenditure, which includes the following: (a) the goods and services provided to households by employers in the form of payment in kind and transfer in kind; (b) goods and services produced and consumed by the households themselves, in which the services refer to the owner-occupied housing and services offered by payed family employees; (c) financial intermediate services provided by financial institution.

Government Consumption Expenditure refers to the consumption expenditure spent for the provision of public services provided by the government to the whole country and the net expenditure on the goods and services provided by the government to households free of charge or at reduced prices. The former equals to the output value of the government services minus the value of operating income obtained by the government departments. The latter equals to the market value of the goods and services provided by the government free of charge or at reduced prices to the households minus the value received by the government from the households.

Gross Capital Formation refers to the fixed assets acquired less disposals and the net value of inventory, thus including gross fixed capital formation and changes in inventories.

Gross Fixed Capital Formation refers to the value of acquisitions less those disposals of fixed assets during a given period. Fixed assets are the assets produced through production activities with unit value above a specified amount and which could be used for over one year. Natural assets are not included. Gross fixed capital formation can be categorized into total tangible fixed capital formation and total intangible fixed capital formation. Total tangible fixed capital formation includes the value of the construction projects and installation projects completed and the equipment, apparatus and instruments purchased (less those disposed) as well as the value of land improved, the value of draught animals, breeding stock and animals for milk, for wool and for recreational purposes and the newly increased forest with economic value. Total intangible fixed capital formation includes the prospecting of minerals and the acquisition of computer software minus the disposal of them.

Changes in Inventories refers to the market value of the change in the physical volume of inventory of resident units during a given period, i.e. the difference between the values at the beginning and at the end of the period minus the gains due to the change in prices. The changes in inventories can have a positive or a negative value. A positive value indicates an increase in inventory while a negative value indicates a decrease in inventory. The inventory includes raw materials, fuels and reserve materials purchased by the production units as well as the inventory of finished products, semi-finished products and work-in-progress.

Net Export of Goods and Services refers to the exports of goods and services subtracting the imports of goods and services. Exports include the value of various goods and services sold or gratuitously transferred by resident units to non-resident units. Imports include the value of various goods and services purchased or gratuitously acquired resident units from non-resident units. Because the provision of services and the use of them happen simultaneously, the acquisition of services by resident units from abroad is usually treated as import while the acquisition of services by non-resident units in this country is usually treated as export. The exports and imports of goods are calculated at FOB.

3 人口、从业人员与职工工资

POPULATION，EMPLOYMENT AND WAGES

资料整理：王义龙　张　静
Data management:Wang Yilong　Zhang Jing

第三部分　人口、从业人员与职工工资

一、简要说明

本章资料包括主要年份人口、分区县户籍和常住人口及变动、从业人员及劳动报酬等。户籍人口数为公安年报数，1991年以前年份市区数未包括临潼、长安。主要数据由西安市统计局人口就业处提供。

二、主要指标

年末户籍人口（万人）	791.83	比上年增长	1.2%
人口自然增长率（‰）	4.33	比上年下降	0.06个千分点
常住人口（万人）	851.34	比上年增长	0.5%
男女性别比（以女性为100）	105.62	比上年增加	0.44个百分点
户籍人口密度（人/平方公里）	783	比上年增加	9人/平方公里
城镇非私营单位在岗职工年平均工资（元）	41679	比上年增长	10.1%

3 POPULATION,EMPLOYMENT AND WAGES

Ⅰ.Brief Introduction

This chapter consists of the data about the population of consequent years, population of all the districts and counties and the correspondent changes, the employed and their wages. The population data are from the annual report of the Xi'an Bureau of Public Security, with Lintong, Chang'an not included before 1991. The population data is provided primarily by Population & Employment Division of the Xi'an Bureau of Statistics.

Ⅱ.Major Indicators

		Increase over Preceding Year
Total Population of Year-end(10 000 persons)	791.83	1.2%
Natural Gorwth Rate(‰)	4.33	-0.06thousands of points
Permanent Population(10 000 persons)	851.34	0.5%
Sex Ratio (female = 100)	105.62	0.44percentage points
Density of Population (person/sq.km)	783	9
Aunual Average Wage of Stuff and Workers in Urban Non-privite Enterprises(yuan)	41679	10.1%

3-1 主要年份人口、人口密度和人口发展情况

Population, Population Density and Population Development in Representative years

单位：万人 (10 000 persons)

年份 Year	总人口 Total population	市区 Urban Area	女性人口数 Number of Female	非农业人口数 Non-Agricultural Population	人口密度 (人/平方公里) Density of Population (person/sq.km)	总人口指数(上年为100) Total Population Index (100 for preceding year) 全市 Whole City	市区 Urban Area
1952	252.92	92.42	118.81	57.61	254	102.6	103.1
1965	400.05	179.88	190.72	136.39	401	102.5	103.4
1970	435.12	188.12	210.47	139.12	436	101.9	101.4
1978	498.10	210.15	241.82	159.98	499	101.7	102.7
1980	511.91	221.19	249.26	172.85	513	101.4	102.6
1985	553.11	245.76	268.40	201.90	554	101.6	102.2
1986	563.97	251.80	273.30	205.92	565	102.0	102.5
1987	574.46	257.69	278.12	210.25	575	101.9	102.3
1988	585.85	264.94	283.68	216.99	587	102.0	102.8
1989	597.36	270.80	289.44	222.54	598	102.0	102.2
1990	608.89	275.69	295.29	226.98	610	101.9	101.8
1991	615.48	419.29	298.13	230.85	617	101.1	152.1
1992	623.20	429.54	301.92	236.45	624	101.3	102.4
1993	630.91	435.41	305.30	240.85	632	101.2	101.4
1994	639.45	442.30	309.17	248.35	641	101.4	101.6
1995	648.21	448.65	313.46	255.71	645	101.4	101.4
1996	654.87	454.68	316.60	261.28	653	101.0	101.3
1997	662.06	461.17	320.18	267.52	663	101.1	101.4
1998	668.22	466.31	323.20	271.75	669	100.9	101.1
1999	674.50	463.56	326.12	276.14	676	100.9	99.4
2000	688.01	483.10	332.83	285.79	689	102.0	104.2
2001	694.84	489.88	336.04	292.62	696	101.0	101.4
2002	702.59	497.38	339.51	300.05	704	101.1	101.5
2003	716.58	510.26	346.26	312.88	718	102.0	102.6
2004	725.01	516.30	350.85	318.50	717	101.2	101.2
2005	741.73	533.21	359.71	333.14	734	102.3	103.3
2006	753.11	540.97	365.74	343.78	745	101.5	101.5
2007	764.25	549.19	371.84	353.85	756	101.5	101.5
2008	772.30	554.73	376.76	363.87	764	101.1	101.0
2009	781.67	561.58	382.39	370.66	773	101.2	101.2
2010	782.73	562.65	383.93	374.64	774	100.1	100.2
2011	791.83	568.77	389.31	391.31	783	101.2	101.1

注:人口部分均为公安年报数据，系户籍人口。1991年以前年份，市区数未包括临潼、长安。

Note: The population data are taken from annual reports of pulic recurity, namely the registered household population..The population of urban area before 1991 doesn't include Lintong and Chang'an.

3-2 主要年份人口变动情况

Population Changes in Representative Years

单位：万人 （10 000 persons）

年份 Year	出生 Birth 人数 Population	出生率(‰) Birth Rate (‰)	死亡 Death 人数 Population	死亡率(‰) Death Rate (‰)	自然增长率(‰) Natural Gorwth Rate (‰)	迁入人口 Immigrant population	迁出人口 Emigrant population
1952	7.68	30.74	2.21	8.86	21.88		
1965	11.53	29.19	3.36	8.50	20.69	13.11	10.83
1970	12.05	27.96	2.34	5.44	22.52	6.88	8.39
1978	7.81	19.04	3.17	6.66	12.38	8.98	9.16
1980	6.59	12.96	3.19	6.28	6.68	13.36	9.64
1985	8.95	16.30	3.01	5.48	10.82	11.60	8.74
1986	10.14	18.15	2.78	4.97	13.18	11.79	8.39
1987	9.76	17.14	2.83	4.97	12.17	12.58	9.26
1988	9.42	16.24	2.89	4.98	11.26	13.54	8.97
1989	11.78	19.92	3.04	5.13	14.79	12.73	10.15
1990	12.40	20.55	3.45	5.72	14.83	11.82	9.86
1991	8.73	14.25	3.26	5.33	8.92	8.98	6.09
1992	8.98	14.49	3.39	5.48	9.01	13.94	9.54
1993	9.25	14.75	3.37	5.38	9.37	11.50	8.33
1994	8.08	12.71	3.16	4.97	7.74	13.40	8.59
1995	7.69	11.95	3.21	4.98	6.97	14.41	8.85
1996	7.26	11.15	3.41	5.24	5.91	11.94	8.88
1997	6.84	10.38	3.12	4.75	5.63	12.58	8.62
1998	6.40	9.62	3.10	4.66	4.96	10.89	8.36
1999	6.19	9.22	3.88	5.78	3.44	12.58	9.23
2000	8.90	13.07	4.06	5.96	7.11	17.12	9.23
2001	5.11	7.39	2.89	4.19	3.20	15.16	10.83
2002	5.34	7.64	3.08	4.41	3.23	13.90	9.41
2003	6.02	8.48	3.32	4.68	3.80	20.60	9.15
2004	6.63	9.19	4.23	5.87	3.32	15.56	10.19
2005	7.67	9.58	4.13	5.16	4.42	22.61	9.46
2006	8.13	9.98	4.45	5.46	4.52	17.23	11.75
2007	8.27	10.00	4.53	5.48	4.52	19.90	14.01
2008	8.47	10.15	4.65	5.57	4.58	18.49	15.04
2009	8.47	10.08	4.73	5.63	4.45	16.84	13.14
2010	8.23	9.73	4.51	5.34	4.39	14.09	13.50
2011	8.25	9.71	4.57	5.38	4.33	14.21	11.74

注：2004年以前为公安年报数据。迁入人口和迁出人口为公安年报数据。2010年出生、死亡、自然增长率根据第六次人口普查数据推算得出。2005-2009、2011年出生、死亡、自然增长率为人口变动抽样调查数据。

Note:Before 2004, the data were taken from annual reports of public security. Immigrant population and Emigrant population were taken from annual reports of public security.The data of rate for birth、death and naturally increase in 2010 is inferred according to the data of the sixth national population.The data of birthrate, death rate and the natural population growth rate in 2005-2009 and 2011 were taken from the statistics from spot check on population changes.

3-3 全市及各区县人口和户数（2011年）

Population and Households by Region（2011）

单位：万人　(10 000 person)

区县 District and County	总户数(万户) Number of Households (10 000 households)	总人口 Total Population	非农业人口 Non-agriculture	按性别分 Grouped by Sex 男 Male	女 Female	迁入人口（人） Immigrant population (person)	迁出人口（人） Emigrant population (person)
合　计 Total	**234.34**	**791.83**	**391.31**	**402.52**	**389.31**	**142070**	**117422**
新城区 Xincheng	16.86	50.47	50.47	25.63	24.84	3917	2255
碑林区 Beilin	20.62	72.47	72.47	37.56	34.91	23467	28232
莲湖区 Lianhu	21.86	64.46	64.46	32.60	31.86	7538	5657
灞桥区 Baqiao	17.00	51.62	24.64	25.53	26.09	8033	4164
未央区 Weiyang	16.71	53.73	38.16	26.77	26.96	16053	7197
雁塔区 Yanta	23.05	80.21	68.95	40.24	39.97	32136	39570
阎良区 Yanliang	7.44	25.49	8.83	12.86	12.63	2856	1738
临潼区 Lintong	19.44	70.40	11.95	35.60	34.80	3340	2281
长安区 Chang'an	27.94	99.92	16.46	50.06	49.86	14956	7876
蓝田县 Lantian	18.31	64.74	5.90	33.55	31.19	4840	5403
周至县 Zhouzhi	17.41	67.39	6.38	35.54	31.85	5689	4597
户　县 Huxian	18.32	60.07	11.38	31.14	28.93	5823	6062
高陵县 Gaoling	9.38	30.86	11.26	15.44	15.42	13422	2390

注：以上均为公安年报数据。

Note:The data were taken from annual reports of public security.

3-4 全市及各区县常住人口及人口变动情况（2011年）

Permanent Population and Population Changes by Region（2011）

单位：万人 (10 000 person)

区县 District and County		常住人口 Permanent Population 2007	2008	2009	2010	2011	2011年末城镇常住人口 Urban Permanent Population of 2011 year-end	出生率(‰) Birth Rate (‰)	死亡率(‰) Death Rate (‰)	自然增长率(□) Natural Gorwth Rate (‰)
合 计	**Total**	**830.54**	**837.52**	**843.46**	**847.41**	**851.34**	**596.79**	**9.71**	**5.38**	**4.33**
新城区	Xincheng	62.85	62.49	60.91	59.01	59.23	59.23	6.57	3.36	3.21
碑林区	Beilin	70.23	68.74	64.94	61.62	61.87	61.87	7.52	4.32	3.20
莲湖区	Lianhu	71.31	71.27	70.56	69.86	70.13	70.13	8.56	5.18	3.38
灞桥区	Baqiao	54.49	55.29	57.49	59.56	59.87	53.73	10.53	6.19	4.34
未央区	Weiyang	73.71	76.42	78.59	80.72	81.14	71.74	10.62	5.46	5.16
雁塔区	Yanta	113.63	114.77	115.53	117.98	118.48	118.48	8.42	4.15	4.27
阎良区	Yanliang	25.28	25.76	26.27	27.87	28.01	14.90	9.04	4.98	4.06
临潼区	Lintong	67.29	67.90	68.62	65.60	65.98	19.96	10.25	4.94	5.31
长安区	Chang'an	102.59	103.59	104.37	108.48	109.01	58.44	10.85	6.47	4.38
蓝田县	Lantian	52.00	52.00	52.89	51.42	51.65	12.91	11.46	6.91	4.55
周至县	Zhouzhi	54.60	54.78	55.72	56.29	56.59	14.89	12.98	7.59	5.39
户 县	Huxian	55.56	55.88	56.77	55.65	55.85	20.61	9.97	5.54	4.43
高陵县	Gaoling	27.00	28.63	30.80	33.35	33.53	19.90	9.87	5.39	4.48

注：2007-2009年分区县常住人口为依据2010年人口普查修正后数据。2010年年末常住人口根据第六次人口普查数据推算得出。其余数据均为人口变动抽样调查数据。

Note:2007-2009 resident population of districts and counties in Xi'an was based on the correction of the 2010 census data.Resident population at the end of 2010 is extrapolated by the sixth census data . The remaining data are from the sample surveys of population changes data.

3-5 主要年份常住人口

Permanent population in Representative Years

单位：万人 (10 000 persons)

年份 Year	年末常住人口 Permanent population (year-end)	城镇 Urban	农村 Rural
2000	741.14	450.36	290.78
2005	806.81	510.55	296.26
2006	822.52	530.94	291.58
2007	830.54	548.99	281.55
2008	837.52	565.16	272.36
2009	843.46	581.40	262.06
2010	847.41	584.71	262.70
2011	851.34	596.79	254.55

注：2000年常住人口为人口普查数据。2010年常住人口为年末常住人口数，根据第六次人口普查数据推算得出。2005-2009、2011年常住人口为人口变动抽样调查数据。

Note:Data in 2000 were taken from population census, The data of inhabitant in 2010 is the data for the end of 2010, and that is inferred according to the data of the sixth national population.The permanent population in 2005-2009 and 2011 were taken from sample survey on population changing.

3-6 主要年份社会从业人数

Number of Social Laborers in Representative Years

单位：万人 (10 000 persons)

年份 Year	合计 Total	一、按城乡分 Grouped by Urban area and Rural area					二、按三次产业分 Grouped by Industry		
		1.城镇 Urban	国有经济 State-owned Enterprises	集体经济 Collective-owned Enterprises	其他经济 Others	2.乡村 Village	第一产业 Primary Industry	第二产业 Secondary Indusyry	第三产业 Tertiary Industry
1985	296.80	129.07	96.80	29.07	3.20	167.73	135.89	98.61	62.30
1986	299.45	132.82	101.28	28.43	3.11	166.63	127.46	100.61	71.38
1987	312.16	138.56	104.58	30.72	3.26	173.60	130.36	107.75	74.05
1988	327.76	142.24	106.46	30.73	5.05	185.52	138.87	108.12	80.77
1989	332.65	145.65	108.80	30.44	6.41	187.00	142.21	106.40	84.04
1990	343.06	147.93	110.95	29.78	7.20	195.13	149.64	106.74	86.68
1991	347.65	149.48	111.87	29.80	7.81	198.17	152.24	108.19	87.22
1992	357.51	151.67	113.19	29.97	8.51	205.84	154.75	110.22	92.54
1993	363.70	155.72	112.98	29.77	12.97	207.98	154.02	114.02	95.66
1994	364.56	154.88	113.39	27.97	13.52	209.68	153.51	108.53	102.52
1995	372.60	158.80	113.79	25.58	19.43	213.80	153.39	109.67	109.54
1996	379.29	164.54	113.29	24.82	26.43	214.75	153.43	109.17	116.69
1997	385.14	169.52	112.44	23.52	33.56	215.62	153.23	109.46	122.45
1998	393.95	177.20	106.06	21.50	49.64	216.75	153.00	110.45	130.50
1999	400.43	180.27	105.08	20.50	54.69	220.16	154.64	110.58	135.21
2000	389.10	176.45	103.46	18.40	54.59	212.65	147.03	107.26	134.81
2001	389.30	177.94	100.47	17.10	60.37	211.36	145.09	108.96	135.25
2002	397.16	181.85	100.54	16.90	64.41	215.31	143.04	111.62	142.50
2003	404.92	183.23	94.51	16.78	71.94	221.69	146.67	109.09	149.16
2004	409.57	187.53	93.43	15.41	78.69	222.04	141.81	111.70	156.06
2005	415.83	192.53	93.27	14.47	84.79	223.30	136.31	114.20	165.32
2006	422.15	196.16	84.46	14.41	97.29	225.99	135.10	116.09	170.96
2007	436.36	214.27	90.58	11.88	111.81	222.09	133.33	125.06	177.97
2008	448.05	224.20	90.17	10.60	123.43	223.85	127.87	130.23	189.95
2009	462.52	239.39	90.83	7.63	140.93	223.13	122.13	131.57	208.82
2010	477.58	252.54	94.01	5.48	153.05	225.04	117.27	145.40	214.91
2011	495.99	265.43	91.62	5.33	168.48	230.56	121.05	151.33	223.61

3-7 分行业从业人数（2011年）

单位：万人

行　业	Sector	合计 Total
总　计	**Total**	**495.99**
一、按国民经济行业分组	**Grouped by Sector**	
（一）农、林、牧、渔业	Agriculture ,Forestry,Animal Husbandry and Fishery	121.05
（二）采矿业	Mining	0.32
（三）制造业	Manufacturing	94.95
（四）电力、燃气及水的生产和供应业	Production and Distribution of Electricity,Gas and Water	1.50
（五）建筑业	Construction	54.55
（六）交通运输、仓储和邮政业	Traffic,Transport,Storage and Post	32.01
（七）信息传输、计算机服务和软件业	Information Transmission,Computer Service and Software	8.32
（八）批发和零售业	Wholesale and Retail Trades	50.62
（九）住宿和餐饮业	Hotels and Catering Services	27.49
（十）金融业	Financial Intermediation	6.21
（十一）房地产业	Real Estate	4.53
（十二）租赁和商务服务业	Leasing and Business Services	11.10
（十三）科学研究、技术服务和地质勘察业	Scientific Research,Technical Service and Geologic Prospecting	14.08
（十四）水利、环境和公共设施管理业	Management of Water Conservancy, Environment and Public Facilities	2.30
（十五）居民服务和其他服务业	Services to Households and Other Services	14.06
（十六）教育	Education	24.89
（十七）卫生、社会保障和社会福利业	Health,Social Security and Social Welfare	13.42
（十八）文化、体育和娱乐业	Culture, Sports and Entertainment	3.39
（十九）公共管理和社会组织	Public Management and Social Organization	11.21
二、按三次产业分	**Guroped by Industry**	
第一产业	Primary Industry	121.05
第二产业	Secondary Industry	151.33
第三产业	Tertiary Industry	223.61

Number of Employed Persons by Sector（2011）

(10 000 persons)

国有经济 State-owned Enterprises	集体经济 Collective-owned Enterprises	城镇其他经济 Urban Other Enterprises	城镇私营经济及个体劳动者 Urban Private Enterprises and Individual Labors	乡镇劳动者 Rural and Urban Labourer
91.62	**5.33**	**57.38**	**111.10**	**230.56**
0.37		0.01	4.52	116.15
0.05		0.28		
20.07	0.89	23.42	24.21	26.36
0.69	0.01	0.80		
9.06	2.36	6.37	6.98	29.78
8.50	0.08	2.32	8.55	12.56
2.48	0.03	2.61	1.43	1.77
1.95	0.26	5.52	31.74	11.15
1.24	0.07	3.71	13.10	9.37
1.30	0.16	3.91		0.84
0.66	0.28	3.59		
1.00	0.60	0.69	5.31	3.49
9.16	0.04	1.19	2.21	1.47
2.14	0.04	0.13		
0.34	0.38	0.40	6.35	6.59
15.93	0.02	0.89	4.23	3.82
5.81	0.11	0.22	1.69	5.59
1.30		1.31	0.78	
9.59				1.62
0.37		0.01	4.52	116.15
29.87	3.26	30.87	31.19	56.14
61.38	2.07	26.50	75.39	58.27

3-8　全部单位从业人员情况（2011年）

单位：人

分　组	Classify	单位从业人员 Employed Persons	女性 Female
总　计	**Total**	**1543300**	**558133**
一、按机构类型分组	**Groped by Organization Type**		
#企业	Enterprises	1161809	389441
事业	Institutions	281148	137340
机关	Agencies and Organizations	97318	29971
二、按国民经济行业分组	**Grouped by Sector**		
（一）农、林、牧、渔业	Agriculture ,Forestry,Animal Husbandry and Fishery	3767	1146
（二）采矿业	Mining	3237	248
（三）制造业	Manufacturing	443830	140721
（四）电力、燃气及水的生产和供应业	Production and Distribution of Electricity,Gas and Water	14980	4887
（五）建筑业	Construction	177929	26753
（六）交通运输、仓储和邮政业	Traffic,Transport,Storage and Post	108955	30733
（七）信息传输、计算机服务和软件业	Information Transmission,Computer Service and Software	51167	22192
（八）批发和零售业	Wholesale and Retail Trades	77332	37940
（九）住宿和餐饮业	Hotels and Catering Services	50196	28451
（十）金融业	Financial Intermediation	53711	29213
（十一）房地产业	Real Estate	45279	16320
（十二）租赁和商务服务业	Leasing and Business Services	22958	7606
（十三）科学研究、技术服务和地质勘察业	Scientific Research,Technical Services and Geological Prospecting	103950	32807
（十四）水利、环境和公共设施管理业	Management of Water Conservancy, Environment and Public Facilities	23010	11537
（十五）居民服务和其他服务业	Services to Households and Other Services	11150	4663
（十六）教育	Education	168445	84532
（十七）卫生、社会保障和社会福利业	Health,Social Security and Social Welfare	61398	37771
（十八）文化、体育和娱乐业	Culture, Sports and Entertainment	26139	11234
（十九）公共管理和社会组织	Public Management and Social Organization	95867	29379

Basic Facts on All Employed Persons（2011）

(person)

在岗职工合计 Total Fully Employed Staff and Workers	其他从业人员 Other Employed Persons	单位从业人员平均人数 Average Employment	在岗职工 Fully Employed Staff and Workers	其他从业人员 Other Employed Persons
1437981	**105319**	**1617598**	**1510001**	**107597**
1078559	83250	1242634	1156442	86192
269458	11690	271611	260312	11299
87327	9991	99868	90175	9693
3662	105	4121	4016	105
3218	19	3226	3206	20
430758	13072	500254	485042	15212
14563	417	16723	16321	402
136713	41216	198793	156400	42393
106180	2775	107468	104970	2498
49656	1511	50105	48598	1507
75860	1472	80876	79380	1496
49292	904	49634	48820	814
45449	8262	53787	45623	8164
40700	4579	46075	41415	4660
20513	2445	23103	20235	2868
99910	4040	101222	97555	3667
21385	1625	25109	23507	1602
10872	278	11016	10740	276
161179	7266	161187	154080	7107
56799	4599	60479	56102	4377
25321	818	26006	25196	810
85951	9916	98414	88795	9619

3-9 国有单位从业人员情况（2011年）

单位：人

分 组	Classify	单位从业人员 Employed Persons	女性 Female
合 计	**Total**	**916160**	**333118**
一、按机构类型分组	**Groped by Organization Type**		
#企业	Enterprises	538976	166409
事业	Institutions	279866	136738
机关	Agencies and Organizations	97318	29971
二、按国民经济行业分组	**Grouped by Economic Sector**		
(一)农、林、牧、渔业	Agriculture ,Forestry,Animal Husbandry and Fishery	3685	1111
(二)采矿业	Mining	481	39
(三)制造业	Manufacturing	200698	59237
(四)电力、燃气及水的生产和供应业	Production and Distribution of Electricity,Gas and Water	6870	2297
(五)建筑业	Construction	90617	14826
(六)交通运输、仓储和邮政业	Traffic,Transport,Storage and Post	84980	23198
(七)信息传输、计算机服务和软件业	Information Transmission,Computer Service and Software	24770	13181
(八)批发和零售业	Wholesale and Retail Trades	19490	8219
(九)住宿和餐饮业	Hotels and Catering Services	12412	7184
(十)金融业	Financial Intermediation	12977	6029
(十一)房地产业	Real Estate	6563	2078
(十二)租赁和商务服务业	Leasing and Business Services	9995	3738
(十三)科学研究、技术服务和地质勘察业	Scientific Research,Technical Service and Geologic Prospecting	91585	29684
(十四)水利、环境和公共设施管理业	Management of Water Conservancy, Environment and Public Facilities	21373	10765
(十五)居民服务和其他服务业	Services to Households and Other Services	3364	1335
(十六)教育	Education	159346	79790
(十七)卫生、社会保障和社会福利业	Health,Social Security and Social Welfare	58103	35687
(十八)文化、体育和娱乐业	Culture, Sports and Entertainment	12984	5341
(十九)公共管理和社会组织	Public Management and Social Organization	95867	29379

Basic Facts on Persons Employed by State-owned Units （2011）

(person)

在岗职工合计 Total Fully Employed Staff and Workers	其他从业人员 Other Employed Persons	单位从业人员平均人数 Average Employment	在岗职工 Fully Employed Staff and Workers	其他从业人员 Other Employed Persons
856832	**59328**	**958497**	**901346**	**57151**
501303	37673	588321	552137	36184
268202	11664	270308	259034	11274
87327	9991	99868	90175	9693
3580	105	4021	3916	105
481		481	481	
193329	7369	233561	226724	6837
6616	254	7486	7232	254
70647	19970	107094	87461	19633
82885	2095	83917	82091	1826
24709	61	23240	23179	61
19044	446	20965	20518	447
12215	197	12345	12174	171
12834	143	12948	12808	140
5386	1177	6610	5426	1184
8928	1067	10067	8971	1096
87758	3827	89048	85567	3481
19751	1622	23467	21868	1599
3253	111	3368	3257	111
153392	5954	151156	145354	5802
53605	4498	57259	52982	4277
12468	516	13050	12542	508
85951	9916	98414	88795	9619

3-10 城镇集体单位从业人员情况（2011年）

单位：人

分 组	Classify	单位从业人员 Employed Persons	女性 Female
总 计	**Total**	**53315**	**13247**
一、按机构类型分组	**Groped by Organization Type**		
#企业	Enterprises	53182	13173
事业	Institutions	133	74
机关	Agencies and Organizations		
二、按国民经济行业分组	**Grouped by Sector**		
(一)农、林、牧、渔业	Agriculture ,Forestry,Animal Husbandry and Fishery		
(二)采矿业	Mining		
(三)制造业	Manufacturing	8886	3592
(四)电力、燃气及水的生产和供应业	Production and Distribution of Electricity,Gas and Water	108	15
(五)建筑业	Construction	23584	3156
(六)交通运输、仓储和邮政业	Traffic,Transport,Storage and Post	792	146
(七)信息传输、计算机服务和软件业	Information Transmission,Computer Service and Software	316	36
(八)批发和零售业	Wholesale and Retail Trades	2598	961
(九)住宿和餐饮业	Hotels and Catering Services	687	435
(十)金融业	Financial Intermediation	1625	762
(十一)房地产业	Real Estate	2775	930
(十二)租赁和商务服务业	Leasing and Business Services	6041	569
(十三)科学研究、技术服务和地质勘察业	Scientific Research,Technical Service and Geologic Prospecting	441	113
(十四)水利、环境和公共设施管理业	Management of Water Conservancy, Environment and Public Facilities	360	161
(十五)居民服务和其他服务业	Services to Households and Other Services	3781	1697
(十六)教育	Education	164	111
(十七)卫生、社会保障和社会福利业	Health,Social Security and Social Welfare	1122	553
(十八)文化、体育和娱乐业	Culture, Sports and Entertainment	35	10
(十九)公共管理和社会组织	Public Management and Social Organization		

Basic Facts on Persons Employed by Urban Collective-owned Units（2011）

(person)

在岗职工合计 Total Fully Employed Staff and Workers	其他从业人员 Other Employed Persons	单位从业人员平均人数 Average Employment	在岗职工 Fully Employed Staff and Workers	其他从业人员 Other Employed Persons
50223	**3092**	**55223**	**50891**	**4332**
50090	3092	55090	50763	4327
133		133	128	5
8517	369	8251	7888	363
108		107	107	
22652	932	25350	23582	1768
786	6	781	775	6
316		376	376	
2268	330	2989	2659	330
671	16	674	658	16
1505	120	1620	1491	129
2734	41	2653	2613	40
4798	1243	6527	4887	1640
441		441	441	
360		360	360	
3780	1	3773	3772	1
164		164	164	
1088	34	1122	1083	39
35		35	35	

3-11 其他经济类型单位从业人员情况（2011年）

单位：人

分　组	Classify	单位从业人员 Employed Persons	女性 Female
合　计	**Total**	**573825**	**211768**
一、按机构类型分组	**Groped by Organization Type**		
#企业	Enterprises	569651	209859
事业	Institutions	1149	528
机关	Agencies and Organizations		
二、按国民经济行业分组	**Grouped by Sector**		
（一）农、林、牧、渔业	Agriculture,Forestry,Animal Husbandry and Fishery	82	35
（二）采矿业	Mining	2756	209
（三）制造业	Manufacturing	234246	77892
（四）电力、燃气及水的生产和供应业	Production and Distribution of Electricity,Gas and Water	8002	2575
（五）建筑业	Construction	63728	8771
（六）交通运输、仓储和邮政业	Traffic,Transport,Storage and Post	23183	7389
（七）信息传输、计算机服务和软件业	Information Transmission,Computer Service and Software	26081	8975
（八）批发和零售业	Wholesale and Retail Trades	55244	28760
（九）住宿和餐饮业	Hotels and Catering Services	37097	20832
（十）金融业	Financial Intermediation	39109	22422
（十一）房地产业	Real Estate	35941	13312
（十二）租赁和商务服务业	Leasing and Business Services	6922	3299
（十三）科学研究、技术服务和地质勘察业	Scientific Research,Technical Service and Geologic Prospecting	11924	3010
（十四）水利、环境和公共设施管理业	Management of Water Conservancy, Environment and Public Facilities	1277	611
（十五）居民服务和其他服务业	Services to Households and Other Services	4005	1631
（十六）教育	Education	8935	4631
（十七）卫生、社会保障和社会福利业	Health,Social Security and Social Welfare	2173	1531
（十八）文化、体育和娱乐业	Culture, Sports and Entertainment	13120	5883
（十九）公共管理和社会组织	Public Management and Social Organization		

Basic Facts on Persons Employed by Other Units（2011）

(person)

在岗职工合计 Fully Employed Staff and Workers	其他从业人员 Other Employed Persons	单位从业人员平均人数 Average Employment	在岗职工 Fully Employed Staff and Workers	其他从业人员 Other Employed Persons
530926	**42899**	**603878**	**557764**	**46114**
527166	42485	599223	553542	45681
1123	26	1170	1150	20
82		100	100	
2737	19	2745	2725	20
228912	5334	258442	250430	8012
7839	163	9130	8982	148
43414	20314	66349	45357	20992
22509	674	22770	22104	666
24631	1450	26489	25043	1446
54548	696	56922	56203	719
36406	691	36615	35988	627
31110	7999	39219	31324	7895
32580	3361	36812	33376	3436
6787	135	6509	6377	132
11711	213	11733	11547	186
1274	3	1282	1279	3
3839	166	3875	3711	164
7623	1312	9867	8562	1305
2106	67	2098	2037	61
12818	302	12921	12619	302

3-12 主要年份单位从业人员数及劳动报酬

Number of Employed Persons and Remuneration in Representative Years

年 份 Year	单位从业人员（万人） Number of Employed Persons (10 000 persons)	从业人员劳动报酬（万元） Remuneration of Employed Persons (10 000 yuan)	城镇非私营单位在岗职工平均工资（元） Aunual Average Wage of Stuff and Workers in Urban Non-privite Enterprises (yuan)
1978	67.19	47063	713
1980	91.76	73072	859
1985	127.04	141720	1148
1986	132.78	168662	1311
1987	135.48	191340	1446
1988	137.56	228142	1702
1989	139.86	256371	1873
1990	141.55	294784	2133
1991	142.86	268773	2276
1992	144.51	307995	2545
1993	146.03	432460	2999
1994	142.37	588678	4172
1995	141.17	672268	4763
1996	140.60	756364	5407
1997	138.89	808250	5785
1998	138.78	828495	6900
1999	115.88	901300	7764
2000	112.45	1038045	9179
2001	113.93	1231202	10786
2002	115.77	1388794	12138
2003	116.68	1559517	13504
2004	118.15	1846339	15473
2005	123.66	2156676	17728
2006	125.10	2508689	20475
2007	129.40	3192288	25012
2008	130.85	3792890	29749
2009	135.64	4504836	34032
2010	140.38	5208781	37870
2011	154.33	6587290	41679

3-13 全部单位从业人员工资总额（2011年）

Total Wages of All Employed Persons（2011）

单位: 万元 (1 0000yuan)

分组	Classify	单位从业人员工资总额 Total Wages of Employment	在岗职工工资总额 Total Wages of Employed Staff and Workers
总计	**Total**	**6587290**	**6293468**
一、按机构类型分组	**Groped by Organization Type**		
#企业	Enterprises	4764498	4510046
事业	Institutions	1388109	1364528
机关	Agencies and Organizations	421089	405746
二、按国民经济行业分组	**Grouped by Sector**		
（一）农、林、牧、渔业	Agriculture,Forestry,Animal Husbandry and Fishery	9712	9667
（二）采矿业	Mining	12437	12397
（三）制造业	Manufacturing	1735796	1695669
（四）电力、燃气及水的生产和供应业	Production and Distribution of Electricity, Gas and Water	79777	79016
（五）建筑业	Construction	591857	455642
（六）交通运输、仓储和邮政业	Traffic,Transport,Storage and Post	518330	512048
（七）信息传输、计算机服务和软件业	Information Transmission,Computer Service and Software	256213	241142
（八）批发和零售业	Wholesale and Retail Trades	226419	224137
（九）住宿和餐饮业	Hotels and Catering Services	113785	112696
（十）金融业	Financial Intermediation	388315	364077
（十一）房地产业	Real Estate	159540	151433
（十二）租赁和商务服务业	Leasing and Business Services	72887	69049
（十三）科学研究、技术服务和地质勘察业	Scientific Research,Technical Service and Geologic Prospecting	652360	640701
（十四）水利、环境和公共设施管理业	Management of Water Conservancy, Environment and Public Facilities	65306	63776
（十五）居民服务和其他服务业	Services to Households and Other Services	26431	25921
（十六）教育	Education	877538	865962
（十七）卫生、社会保障和社会福利业	Health,Social Security and Social Welfare	295357	282066
（十八）文化、体育和娱乐业	Culture, Sports and Entertainment	90285	88413
（十九）公共管理和社会组织	Public Management and Social Organization	414947	399656

3–13 续表 continued

单位: 万元 (1 0000yuan)

分组	Classify	其他从业人员劳动报酬 Remuneration of Other Employed Persons	城镇非私营单位在岗职工平均工资（元） Aunual Average Wage of Stuff and Workers in Urban Non-privite Enterprises (yuan)
总　计	**Total**	**293823**	**41679**
一、按机构类型分组	**Groped by Organization Type**		
#企业	Enterprises	254452	38999
事业	Institutions	23580	52419
机关	Agencies and Organizations	15343	44995
二、按国民经济行业分组	**Grouped by Sector**		
（一）农、林、牧、渔业	Agriculture,Forestry,Animal Husbandry and Fishery	45	24072
（二）采矿业	Mining	40	38668
（三）制造业	Manufacturing	40127	34959
（四）电力、燃气及水的生产和供应业	Production and Distribution of Electricity, Gas and Water	761	48414
（五）建筑业	Construction	136214	29133
（六）交通运输、仓储和邮政业	Traffic,Transport,Storage and Post	6283	48780
（七）信息传输、计算机服务和软件业	Information Transmission,Computer Service and Software	15072	49620
（八）批发和零售业	Wholesale and Retail Trades	2282	28236
（九）住宿和餐饮业	Hotels and Catering Services	1089	23084
（十）金融业	Financial Intermediation	24237	79801
（十一）房地产业	Real Estate	8107	36565
（十二）租赁和商务服务业	Leasing and Business Services	3839	34123
（十三）科学研究、技术服务和地质勘察业	Scientific Research,Technical Service and Geologic Prospecting	11659	65676
（十四）水利、环境和公共设施管理业	Management of Water Conservancy, Environment and Public Facilities	1530	27131
（十五）居民服务和其他服务业	Services to Households and Other Services	510	24135
（十六）教育	Education	11576	56202
（十七）卫生、社会保障和社会福利业	Health,Social Security and Social Welfare	13291	50277
（十八）文化、体育和娱乐业	Culture, Sports and Entertainment	1872	35090
（十九）公共管理和社会组织	Public Management and Social Organization	15291	45009

3-14 国有单位从业人员工资总额（2011年）

Total Wages of Persons Employed by State-owned Units（2011）

单位: 万元　　　　(1 0000yuan)

分　　组	Classify	单　位从业人员工资总额 Total Wages of Employment	在岗职工工资总额 Total Wages of Employed Staff and Workers
总　计	**Total**	**4225719**	**4075601**
一、按机构类型分组	**Groped by Organization Type**		
#企业	Enterprises	2422277	2311049
事业	Institutions	1382352	1358806
机关	Agencies and Organizations	421089	405746
二、按国民经济行业分组	**Grouped by Sector**		
（一）农、林、牧、渔业	Agriculture,Forestry,Animal Husbandry and Fishery	9533	9489
（二）采矿业	Mining	832	832
（三）制造业	Manufacturing	847310	828749
（四）电力、燃气及水的生产和供应业	Production and Distribution of Electricity, Gas and Water	30947	30451
（五）建筑业	Construction	338756	267498
（六）交通运输、仓储和邮政业	Traffic,Transport,Storage and Post	433483	429397
（七）信息传输、计算机服务和软件业	Information Transmission,Computer Service and Software	113888	113754
（八）批发和零售业	Wholesale and Retail Trades	44841	44003
（九）住宿和餐饮业	Hotels and Catering Services	28858	28579
（十）金融业	Financial Intermediation	93928	93658
（十一）房地产业	Real Estate	18962	18083
（十二）租赁和商务服务业	Leasing and Business Services	39265	37219
（十三）科学研究、技术服务和地质勘察业	Scientific Research,Technical Service and Geologic Prospecting	584629	573649
（十四）水利、环境和公共设施管理业	Management of Water Conservancy, Environment and Public Facilities	60092	58571
（十五）居民服务和其他服务业	Services to Households and Other Services	9173	8968
（十六）教育	Education	819484	810325
（十七）卫生、社会保障和社会福利业	Health,Social Security and Social Welfare	284501	271390
（十八）文化、体育和娱乐业	Culture, Sports and Entertainment	52291	51330
（十九）公共管理和社会组织	Public Management and Social Organization	414947	399656

3-14 续表 continued

单位: 万元 (1 0000yuan)

分　组	Classify	其他从业人员劳动报酬 Remuneration of Other Employed Persons	城镇非私营单位在岗职工平均工资（元） Aunual Average Wage of Stuff and Workers in Urban Non-privite Enterprises (yuan)
总　计	**Total**	**150118**	**45217**
一、按机构类型分组	**Groped by Organization Type**		
#企业	Enterprises	111229	41856
事业	Institutions	23547	52457
机关	Agencies and Organizations	15343	44995
二、按国民经济行业分组	**Grouped by Sector**		
（一）农、林、牧、渔业	Agriculture,Forestry,Animal Husbandry and Fishery	45	24231
（二）采矿业	Mining		17289
（三）制造业	Manufacturing	18561	36553
（四）电力、燃气及水的生产和供应业	Production and Distribution of Electricity, Gas and Water	497	42106
（五）建筑业	Construction	71258	30585
（六）交通运输、仓储和邮政业	Traffic,Transport,Storage and Post	4086	52307
（七）信息传输、计算机服务和软件业	Information Transmission,Computer Service and Software	133	49076
（八）批发和零售业	Wholesale and Retail Trades	837	21446
（九）住宿和餐饮业	Hotels and Catering Services	279	23476
（十）金融业	Financial Intermediation	271	73124
（十一）房地产业	Real Estate	879	33326
（十二）租赁和商务服务业	Leasing and Business Services	2046	41488
（十三）科学研究、技术服务和地质勘察业	Scientific Research,Technical Service and Geologic Prospecting	10980	67041
（十四）水利、环境和公共设施管理业	Management of Water Conservancy, Environment and Public Facilities	1521	26784
（十五）居民服务和其他服务业	Services to Households and Other Services	205	27533
（十六）教育	Education	9159	55748
（十七）卫生、社会保障和社会福利业	Health,Social Security and Social Welfare	13111	51223
（十八）文化、体育和娱乐业	Culture, Sports and Entertainment	960	40927
（十九）公共管理和社会组织	Public Management and Social Organization	15291	45009

3-15 城镇集体单位从业人员工资总额（2011年）

Total Wages of Persons Employed by Urban Collective-owned Units in Towns and Cities（2011）

单位: 万元 (1 0000yuan)

分　组	Classify	单　位 从业人员 工资总额 Total Wages of Employment	在岗职工 工资总额 Total Wages of Employed Staff and Workers
总　计	**Total**	**126364**	**118274**
一、按机构类型分组	**Groped by Organization Type**		
#企业	Enterprises	125865	117781
事业	Institutions	499	493
机关	Agencies and Organizations		
二、按国民经济行业分组	**Grouped by Sector**		
（一）农、林、牧、渔业	Agriculture,Forestry,Animal Husbandry and Fishery		
（二）采矿业	Mining		
（三）制造业	Manufacturing	22150	21593
（四）电力、燃气及水的生产和供应业	Production and Distribution of Electricity, Gas and Water	233	233
（五）建筑业	Construction	52779	47771
（六）交通运输、仓储和邮政业	Traffic,Transport,Storage and Post	2175	2163
（七）信息传输、计算机服务和软件业	Information Transmission,Computer Service and Software	1882	1882
（八）批发和零售业	Wholesale and Retail Trades	4842	4464
（九）住宿和餐饮业	Hotels and Catering Services	1534	1498
（十）金融业	Financial Intermediation	7866	7558
（十一）房地产业	Real Estate	8045	7950
（十二）租赁和商务服务业	Leasing and Business Services	11523	9897
（十三）科学研究、技术服务和地质勘察业	Scientific Research,Technical Service and Geologic Prospecting	1502	1502
（十四）水利、环境和公共设施管理业	Management of Water Conservancy, Environment and Public Facilities	446	446
（十五）居民服务和其他服务业	Services to Households and Other Services	6239	6238
（十六）教育	Education	565	565
（十七）卫生、社会保障和社会福利业	Health,Social Security and Social Welfare	4490	4422
（十八）文化、体育和娱乐业	Culture, Sports and Entertainment	93	93
（十九）公共管理和社会组织	Public Management and Social Organization		

3–15 续表 continued

单位: 万元 (1 0000yuan)

分 组	Classify	其他从业人员劳动报酬 Remuneration of Other Employed Persons	城镇非私营单位在岗职工平均工资（元） Aunual Average Wage of Stuff and Workers in Urban Non-privite Enterprises (yuan)
总 计	**Total**	**8090**	**23241**
一、按机构类型分组	**Groped by Organization Type**		
#企业	Enterprises	8084	23202
事业	Institutions	6	38531
机关	Agencies and Organizations		
二、按国民经济行业分组	**Grouped by Sector**		
（一）农、林、牧、渔业	Agriculture,Forestry,Animal Husbandry and Fishery		
（二）采矿业	Mining		
（三）制造业	Manufacturing	558	27374
（四）电力、燃气及水的生产和供应业	Production and Distribution of Electricity, Gas and Water		21757
（五）建筑业	Construction	5009	20257
（六）交通运输、仓储和邮政业	Traffic,Transport,Storage and Post	12	27911
（七）信息传输、计算机服务和软件业	Information Transmission,Computer Service and Software		50064
（八）批发和零售业	Wholesale and Retail Trades	377	16789
（九）住宿和餐饮业	Hotels and Catering Services	37	22763
（十）金融业	Financial Intermediation	308	50688
（十一）房地产业	Real Estate	95	30423
（十二）租赁和商务服务业	Leasing and Business Services	1626	20252
（十三）科学研究、技术服务和地质勘察业	Scientific Research,Technical Service and Geologic Prospecting		34059
（十四）水利、环境和公共设施管理业	Management of Water Conservancy, Environment and Public Facilities		12381
（十五）居民服务和其他服务业	Services to Households and Other Services	1	16537
（十六）教育	Education		34463
（十七）卫生、社会保障和社会福利业	Health,Social Security and Social Welfare	67	40834
（十八）文化、体育和娱乐业	Culture, Sports and Entertainment		26686
（十九）公共管理和社会组织	Public Management and Social Organization		

3-16 其他经济类型单位从业人员工资总额（2011年）

Total Wages of Persons Employed by Other Units（2011）

单位: 万元　　(1 0000yuan)

分　组	Classify	单位从业人员工资总额 Total Wages of Employment	在岗职工工资总额 Total Wages of Employed Staff and Workers
总　计	**Total**	**2235207**	**2099592**
一、按机构类型分组	**Groped by Organization Type**		
#企业	Enterprises	2216356	2081216
事业	Institutions	5258	5229
机关	Agencies and Organizations		
二、按国民经济行业分组	**Grouped by Sector**		
（一）农、林、牧、渔业	Agriculture,Forestry,Animal Husbandry and Fishery	179	179
（二）采矿业	Mining	11605	11565
（三）制造业	Manufacturing	866336	845328
（四）电力、燃气及水的生产和供应业	Production and Distribution of Electricity, Gas and Water	48597	48332
（五）建筑业	Construction	200322	140374
（六）交通运输、仓储和邮政业	Traffic,Transport,Storage and Post	82672	80488
（七）信息传输、计算机服务和软件业	Information Transmission,Computer Service and Software	140443	125505
（八）批发和零售业	Wholesale and Retail Trades	176736	175669
（九）住宿和餐饮业	Hotels and Catering Services	83392	82619
（十）金融业	Financial Intermediation	286521	262862
（十一）房地产业	Real Estate	132533	125400
（十二）租赁和商务服务业	Leasing and Business Services	22099	21933
（十三）科学研究、技术服务和地质勘察业	Scientific Research,Technical Service and Geologic Prospecting	66227	65549
（十四）水利、环境和公共设施管理业	Management of Water Conservancy, Environment and Public Facilities	4768	4760
（十五）居民服务和其他服务业	Services to Households and Other Services	11019	10716
（十六）教育	Education	57489	55072
（十七）卫生、社会保障和社会福利业	Health,Social Security and Social Welfare	6367	6253
（十八）文化、体育和娱乐业	Culture, Sports and Entertainment	37901	36989
（十九）公共管理和社会组织	Public Management and Social Organization		

3–16 续表 continued

单位: 万元 (1 0000yuan)

分组	Classify	其他从业人员劳动报酬 Remuneration of Other Employed Persons	城镇非私营单位在岗职工平均工资（元） Aunual Average Wage of Stuff and Workers in Urban Non-privite Enterprises (yuan)
总　计	**Total**	**135615**	**37643**
一、按机构类型分组	**Groped by Organization Type**		
#企业	Enterprises	135140	37598
事业	Institutions	28	45473
机关	Agencies and Organizations		
二、按国民经济行业分组	**Grouped by Sector**		
（一）农、林、牧、渔业	Agriculture,Forestry,Animal Husbandry and Fishery		17870
（二）采矿业	Mining	40	42441
（三）制造业	Manufacturing	21008	33755
（四）电力、燃气及水的生产和供应业	Production and Distribution of Electricity, Gas and Water	265	53810
（五）建筑业	Construction	59948	30949
（六）交通运输、仓储和邮政业	Traffic,Transport,Storage and Post	2185	36413
（七）信息传输、计算机服务和软件业	Information Transmission,Computer Service and Software	14938	50116
（八）批发和零售业	Wholesale and Retail Trades	1067	31256
（九）住宿和餐饮业	Hotels and Catering Services	773	22957
（十）金融业	Financial Intermediation	23659	83917
（十一）房地产业	Real Estate	7133	37572
（十二）租赁和商务服务业	Leasing and Business Services	167	34393
（十三）科学研究、技术服务和地质勘察业	Scientific Research,Technical Service and Geologic Prospecting	678	56767
（十四）水利、环境和公共设施管理业	Management of Water Conservancy, Environment and Public Facilities	9	37213
（十五）居民服务和其他服务业	Services to Households and Other Services	303	28877
（十六）教育	Education	2417	64321
（十七）卫生、社会保障和社会福利业	Health,Social Security and Social Welfare	114	30698
（十八）文化、体育和娱乐业	Culture, Sports and Entertainment	912	29312
（十九）公共管理和社会组织	Public Management and Social Organization		

3-17 主要年份城镇登记失业人数及失业率

Registered Unemployed Persons and Unemployment Rate in Urban Area in Representative Years

年　　份 Year	城镇登记失业人数（万人） Real Number of Registered Unemployed Persons (10 000 persons)	城镇登记失业率 (%) Registered Unemployment in Urban Area (%)
2002		3.7
2003		4.5
2004	8.29	4.3
2005	8.45	4.3
2006	8.74	4.3
2007	8.77	4.3
2008	9.40	4.2
2009	10.02	4.3
2010	10.46	4.2
2011	10.37	3.9

主 要 统 计 指 标 解 释

人口数 指一定时点、一定地区范围内的有生命的个人的总和。年度统计的年末人口数，指每年12月31日24时的人口数。

常住人口 指实际经常居住在某地区一定时间（半年以上，含半年）的人口。常住人口包括户口在本辖区人也在本辖区居住的人，户口在本辖区之外但在户口登记地半年以上的人，户口待定（无户口和口袋户口）的人，户口在本辖区但离开本辖区半年以下的人。

城镇人口和乡村人口 城镇人口是指居住在城镇范围内的全部常住人口；乡村人口是除上述人口以外的全部人口。

出生率（又称粗出生率） 指在一定时期内（通常为一年）平均每千人所出生的人数的比率，一般用千分率表示。其计算公式为:

出生率=年出生人数/年平均人数*1000‰

式中:出生人数指活产婴儿，即胎儿脱离母体时（不管怀孕月数），有过呼吸或其他生命现象。年平均人数指年初、年底人口数的平均数，也可用年中人口数代替。

死亡率（又称粗死亡率） 指在一定时期内（通常为一年）一定地区的死亡人数与同期内平均人数（或期中人数）之比，一般用千分率表示。本资料中的死亡率指年死亡率，其计算公式为:

死亡率=年死亡人数/年平均人数*1000‰

人口自然增长率 指在一定时期内（通常为一年）人口自然增加数（出生人数减死亡人数）与该时期内平均人数（或期中人数）之比，一般用千分率表示。计算公式为:

人口自然增长率=（本年出生人数-本年死亡人数）/年平均人数*1000‰

从业人员 指在16周岁及以上，从事一定社会劳动并取得劳动报酬或经营收入的人员。这一指标反映了一定时期内全部劳动力资源的实际利用情况，是研究我国基本国情国力的重要指标。

单位从业人员 指在各级国家机关、政党机关、社会团体及企业、事业单位中工作，取得工资或其他形式的劳动报酬的全部人员。包括在岗职工、再就业的离退休人员、民办教师以及在各单位中工作的外方人员和港澳台方人员、兼职人员、借用的外单位人员和第二职业者。不包括离开本单位仍保留劳动关系的职工。各单位的就业人员反映了各单位实际参加生产或工作的全部劳动力。

城镇私营和个体就业人员 城镇私营就业人员指在工商管理部门注册登记，其经营地址设在县城关镇（含城关镇）以上的私营企业就业人员；包括私营企业投资者和雇工。城镇个体就业人员指在工商管理部门注册登记，并持有城镇户口或在城镇长期居住，经批准从事个体工商经营的就业人员；包括个体经营者和在个体工商户劳动的家庭帮工和雇工。

国有单位 指资产归国家所有的经济组织。包括按《中华人民共和国企业法人登记管理条例》规定登记注册的非公司制的经济组织，以及中央、地方各级国家机关、事业单位和社会团体。

集体单位 指生产资料归集体所有，并按《中华人民共和国企业法人登记管理条例》规定登记注册的经济组织。

其他单位 包括股份合作单位、联营单位、有限责任公司、股份有限公司、港澳台商投资单位以及外商投资单位等其他登记注册类型单位。

在岗职工 指在本单位工作并由单位支付工资的人员，以及有工作岗位，但由于学习、病伤产假等原因暂未工作，仍由单位支付工资的人员。

职工工资总额 指各单位在一定时期内直接支付给本单位全部职工的劳动报酬总额。工资总额的计算原则应以直接支付给职工的全部劳动报酬为根据。各单位支付给职工的劳动报酬以及其他根据有关规定支付的工资，不论是计入成本的还是不计入成本的，不论是按国家规定列入计征奖金税项目的，还是未列入计征奖金税项目的，不论是以货币形式支付的还是以实物形式支付的，均包括在工资总额内。

职工平均工资 指企业、事业、机关单位的职工在一定时期内平均每人所得的货币工资额。它表明一定时期职工工资收入的高低程度，是反映职工工资水平的主要指标。计算公式为:

职工平均工资=报告期实际支付的全部职工工资总额/报告期全部职工平均人数

城镇登记失业人员 指有非农业户口，在一定的劳动年龄内，有劳动能力，无业而要求就业，并在当地就业服务机构进行求职登记的人员。

城镇登记失业率 指城镇登记失业人数同城镇从业人数与城镇从业人数与城镇登记失业人数之和的比。计算公式为:

$$\text{城镇登记失业率}=\frac{\text{城镇登记失业人数}}{\begin{array}{l}\text{(城镇单位就业人员－使用的农村劳动力－聘用的离退休人员－聘用}\\\text{的港澳台及外方人员)＋不在岗职工＋城镇私营业主＋城镇个体户主＋}\\\text{城镇私营企业及个体就业人员＋城镇登记失业人数}\end{array}}\times 100\%$$

Explanatory Notes on Main Statistical Indicators

The annual statistics on total population is taken at midnight, the 3lst of December, not including residents in Taiwan province, Hong Kong SAR and Macao SAR and Chinese national residing abroad.

Permanent population refers to the population of actual habitual residence in a certain area in a certain period of more than six months time, including six months. Permanent population include the accounts in this area which are also living in this area, accounts outside this area but with more than half a year of household registration, accounts to be determined including people without accounts or pockets of accounts, and accounts in the area but leaving this area less than six months.

Urban Population and Rural Population Urban population refers to all people residing in cities and towns, while rural population refers to population other than urban population.

Birth Rate (or Crude Birth Rate) refers to the ratio of the number of births to the average population (or mid-period population) during a certain period of time (usually a year), expressed in ‰. Birth rate in the chapter refers to annual birth rate. The following formula is used:

$$\text{Birth Rate}=\frac{\text{Number of Births}}{\text{Annual Average Population}}\times 1000‰$$

Number of births in the formula refers to live births, i.e. when a baby has breathed or showed any vital phenomena regardless of the length of pregnancy.

Annual average population is the average of the number of population at the beginning of the year and that at the end of the year. Sometimes it is substituted by the mid-year population.

Death Rate (or Crude Death Rate) refers to the ratio of the number of deaths to the average population (or mid-period population) during a certain period of time (usually a year), expressed in ‰. Death rate in the chapter refers to annual death rate. The following formula is used:

$$\text{Death Rate}=\frac{\text{Number of Deaths}}{\text{Annual Average Population}}\times 1000‰$$

Natural Growth Rate of Population refers to the ratio of natural increase in population (number of births minus number of deaths) in a certain period of time (usually a year) to the average population (or mid-period population) of the same period, expressed in ‰ . The following formula is applied:

Natural Growth Rate of Population =(Number of Births-Number of Deaths)/Annual Average Population× 1000‰

Employed Persons refer to persons aged 16 and over who are engaged in gainful employment and thus receive remuneration payment or earn business income. This indicator reflects the actual utilization of total labour force during a certain period of time and is often used for the research on China's economic situation and national power.

Persons Employed in Various Units refer to all the persons working in government agencies of various levels, political and party organizations, social organizations, enterprises and institutions, and receiving wages or other forms of payment. They include fully-employed staff and workers, re-employed retirees, teachers in the schools run by the local people, foreigners and Chinese compatriots from Hong Kong, Macao, and Taiwan working in various units, part-time employees, employees of other units working temporarily at current posts, and employees holding the second job, but do not include persons who have left their working units while keeping their labour contract (employment relation) unchanged. This indicator reflects the total number of laborers actually engaged in production or other operations in various units.

Persons Employed in Private Enterprises and Self-Employed Individuals in Urban Areas Persons employed in private enterprises refer to the persons employed in the private enterprises which have been registered at the departments of industrial and commercial administration for which the business operation are situated at a county town (i.e. a town where the county government is located), or at urban areas with administrative hierarchy higher than a county town. The self-employed individuals in urban areas refer to persons who hold the certificates of residence in urban areas or have resided in the urban areas for a long time and have been registered at the departments of industrial and commercial administration and approved to be engaged in individual industrial or commercial business, including self-employed persons as well as helpers and hired labourers who work in individual households.

State-owned Units refer to economic units whose assets are owned by the state, including non-corporation units registered according to Regulation of the People's Republic of China on the Registration of Enterprises and

Corporations, state organs, institutions and social organizations at the central-level and local levels.

Collective-owned Units refer to economic units registered according to Regulation of the People's Republic of China on the Registration of Enterprises and Corporations where the means of production are collectively owned.

Units of Other Types of Ownership refer to units registered with other types of ownership, including cooperative units, joint ownership units, limited liability corporations, share holding corporations, units funded by entrepreneurs from Hong Kong, Macao, and Taiwan, and foreign- funded units.

Employed Staff and Workers refer to persons who work in, and receive wages from their working units, including persons who have their work posts but are temporarily absent from work for reasons of study or on sick, injury or maternal leave and still receive wages from their working units.

Total Wage Bill refers to the total remuneration payment to employed persons in various units during a certain period of time. The calculation of total wage bill is based on the total remuneration payment to employed persons . Therefore, all the wages and salaries and other payments to employed persons are included in the total wage bill regardless of sources, reckoning the cost of production or not, category, listing as items of premium taxation or not, and forms, paying in cash or in kind.

Average Wage refers to the average wage in money terms per person during a certain period of time for employed persons in enterprises, institutions, and government agencies, which reflects the general level of wage income during a certain period of time and is calculated as follows:

$$\text{Average Wage} = \frac{\text{Total Wage Bill of Employed Persons at Reference Time}}{\text{Average Number of Persons Employed at Reference Time}}$$

Registered Unemployed Persons in Urban Areas refer to the persons with non-agricultural household registration at certain working ages (16 years old to retirement age), who are capable of working, unemployed and willing to work, and have been registered at the local employment service agencies to apply for a job.

Registered Unemployment Rate in Urban Areas refers to the ratio of the number of the registered unemployed persons to the sum of the number of persons employed in various units (minus the employed rural labour force, re-employed retirees, and Hong Kong, Macao, Taiwan or foreign employees), laid-off staff and workers in urban units, owners of private enterprises in urban areas, owners of self-employed individuals in urban areas, employees of private enterprises in urban areas, employee of self-employed individuals in urban areas, and the registered unemployed persons in urban areas. The formula is as follows:

$$\text{Registered Unemployment rate in urban areas} = \frac{\text{number of registered urban unemployed persons}}{\begin{array}{c}\text{number of persons employed in urban units - employed rural labour force}\\ \text{- re-employed retirees - Hong Kong, Macao, Taiwan or foreign employees}\\ \text{+ laid-off staff and workers + owners of urban private Enterprises + owners of}\\ \text{urban self-employed Individuals + employees of urban private Enterprises}\\ \text{+ employees of urban self-employed Individuals + registered unemployed persons in urban areas}\end{array}} \times 100\%$$

4 固定资产投资

INVESTMENT IN FIXED ASSETS

资料整理：赵　晖　令润翠　王　峰　康　敏
Data management:Zhao Hui Ling Runcui Wang Feng Kang Min

第四部分　固定资产投资

一、简要说明

本章资料主要包括全社会固定资产投资、城镇投资、房地产开发投资、城乡集体固定资产投资和城乡私人建房投资以及分区县情况，由西安市统计局固定资产投资处提供。2011年固定资产投资增速基数为按2011年统计制度中投资项目新标准调整的2010年固定资产投资。

二、主要指标

全社会固定资产投资（亿元）	3346.26	比上年增长	30.0%
#国有经济单位	1204.80	比上年增长	24.8%
集体经济单位	258.15	比上年增长	10.4%
#城镇投资	3207.97	比上年增长	33.2%
房地产开发	996.81	比上年增长	18.3%
全市新增固定资产（亿元）	1297.35	比上年增长	76.8%
全市竣工住宅面积（万平方米）	861.44	比上年下降	65.3%

4　INVESTMENT IN FIXED ASSETS

Ⅰ.Brief Introduction

This chapter consists of primarily the data on fixed asset investment, Investment of Urban Units, real estate development investment, urban and rural area collective fixed asset investment, urban and rural area private housing investment and the classified Data of the districts and the counties on real estate development investment, provided by Fixed Asset Investment Division of the Xi'an Bureau of Statistics. The base of 2011 growth rate of fixed assets is the 2010 national asset investment by the new standards of the project to invest adjusted by the 2011 statistical system.

Ⅱ.Major Indicators

		Increase over Preceding Year
Investment Fulfilled In Fixed Assets(100 mil. yuan)	3346.26	30.0%
State-owned Enterprises	1204.80	24.8%
Collective-owned Enterprises	258.15	10.4%
Investment of Urban Units	3207.97	33.2%
Real Estate Development	996.81	18.3%
Investment Fulfilled Newly Increased Fixed Assets(100 mil. yuan)	1297.35	76.8%
Total Floor Space of Building Completed(10 000 sq.m)	861.44	65.3%

4-1 主要年份按城乡分全社会固定资产投资

Total Investment in Fixed Assets in the Whole Country by Rural and Urban Areas in Representative Years

单位：亿元 (100 million yuan)

年 份 Year	合 计 Total	城镇 Urban Area	房地产开发 Real Estate	农村 Rural Area
1979	4.08	3.01		1.07
1980	6.12	4.48		1.64
1981	5.59	4.56		1.03
1982	9.49	8.02		1.47
1983	10.46	9.17		1.29
1984	12.89	10.69		2.20
1985	18.44	14.44		4.00
1986	22.15	18.54		3.61
1987	27.05	23.15		3.90
1988	29.14	24.43		4.71
1989	28.30	23.85		4.45
1990	26.39	23.10	0.91	3.29
1991	30.76	25.55	2.01	5.21
1992	38.48	32.85	3.32	5.63
1993	75.06	66.65	7.39	8.41
1994	85.57	73.47	12.02	12.10
1995	103.42	88.50	21.65	14.92
1996	114.38	96.98	24.66	17.40
1997	116.90	95.17	24.68	21.73
1998	154.80	138.68	38.21	16.12
1999	197.31	172.64	44.30	24.67
2000	232.37	203.01	51.85	29.36
2001	287.72	256.95	67.42	30.77
2002	338.15	307.24	79.37	30.91
2003	478.10	445.74	124.82	32.36
2004	646.69	612.03	169.67	34.66
2005	835.10	776.33	225.23	58.77
2006	1066.62	971.84	285.76	94.78
2007	1435.33	1340.59	387.33	94.74
2008	1906.36	1786.60	540.26	119.76
2009	2500.13	2367.58	696.34	132.55
2010	3250.56	3104.92	842.34	145.64
2011	3346.26	3207.97	996.81	138.29

4-2 主要年份按经济类型分全社会固定资产投资

Total Investment in Fixed Assets in the Whole Country by Registion Status in Representative Years

单位：亿元 (100 million yuan)

年 份 Year	合 计 Total	国有经济 State-owned	集体经济 Collective-owned	个体经济 Self-employed Individual	其他经济 Others
1985	18.44	13.96	1.36	3.12	
1986	22.15	18.05	0.97	3.13	
1987	27.05	22.18	1.50	3.37	
1988	29.14	23.72	1.86	3.56	
1989	28.30	23.22	1.46	3.62	
1990	26.39	22.21	1.44	2.74	
1991	30.76	24.42	2.26	4.08	
1992	38.48	32.04	1.45	4.99	
1993	75.06	59.66	3.03	6.55	5.82
1994	85.57	64.71	4.14	10.09	6.63
1995	103.42	69.08	9.78	11.13	13.43
1996	114.38	80.66	8.73	12.50	12.49
1997	116.90	77.46	10.21	15.11	14.12
1998	154.80	113.07	7.89	10.59	23.25
1999	197.31	136.50	13.62	16.22	30.97
2000	232.37	159.60	14.65	24.40	33.72
2001	287.72	175.58	14.67	38.57	58.90
2002	338.15	200.06	13.70	44.68	79.71
2003	478.10	264.83	22.33	73.43	117.51
2004	646.69	329.14	40.06	48.95	228.54
2005	835.10	373.70	59.23	79.04	323.13
2006	1066.62	401.14	110.68	107.33	447.47
2007	1435.33	476.78	207.08	183.09	568.38
2008	1906.36	694.89	246.89	50.43	914.15
2009	2500.13	932.91	289.91	97.86	1179.45
2010	3250.56	1348.76	326.44	54.73	1520.63
2011	3346.26	1204.80	258.15	74.64	1808.67

注：集体经济：包括城镇集体和农村集体。

个体经济：包括私营个体投资及城镇工矿区私人建房和农村私人建房。

Note: Collective-owned: Including Urban Collective-owned and Rural Collective-owned.

Individual: Including Individual Investment, Private Building Construction in Urban Industrial and Mining Regions and Rural Areas.

4-3 主要年份按产业分全市固定资产投资

Total Investment in Fixed Assets in the Whole City by Three Strata of Industry in Representative Years

单位：亿元　　　　(100 million yuan)

年 份 Year	合 计 Total	第一产业 Primary Industry	第二产业 Secondary Industry	工业 Industry	第三产业 Tertiary Industry
1979	3.01	0.06	1.24	1.20	1.71
1980	4.48	0.06	2.09	1.99	2.33
1981	4.56	0.11	2.10	1.83	2.35
1982	8.02	0.04	4.07	3.63	3.91
1983	9.17	0.11	4.97	4.41	4.09
1984	10.69	0.19	4.56	3.99	5.94
1985	14.44	0.18	7.22	6.45	7.04
1986	18.54	0.16	8.98	8.37	9.40
1987	23.15	0.19	11.81	11.26	11.15
1988	24.43	0.15	11.95	11.20	12.33
1989	23.85	0.13	11.94	11.50	11.78
1990	23.10	0.25	11.03	10.59	11.82
1991	25.55	0.27	12.48	11.95	12.80
1992	32.85	0.10	15.60	14.73	17.15
1993	66.65	0.07	24.50	22.44	42.08
1994	73.47	0.03	27.04	25.85	46.40
1995	88.50	0.14	28.80	27.71	59.56
1996	96.98	0.13	25.96	24.24	70.89
1997	95.17	0.24	23.65	21.66	71.28
1998	138.68	0.48	35.33	29.86	102.87
1999	172.64	0.94	39.88	36.40	131.82
2000	203.01	0.76	57.21	54.37	145.04
2001	256.95	0.86	63.31	61.28	192.78
2002	307.24	4.29	74.34	68.45	228.61
2003	445.74	3.34	83.25	78.41	359.15
2004	612.03	3.38	97.69	95.67	510.96
2005	776.33	5.26	144.25	140.44	626.82
2006	971.84	10.04	213.43	206.48	748.37
2007	1340.59	10.20	297.53	286.61	1032.86
2008	1786.60	23.75	369.74	356.12	1393.11
2009	2367.58	24.46	458.44	442.70	1884.68
2010	3104.92	39.83	556.10	498.62	2508.99
2011	3207.97	43.10	474.73	390.30	2690.14

4-4 全市固定资产投资（2011年）

Total Investment in Fixed Assets in the Whole City（2011）

单位：万元 (10 000 yuan)

分组	Classify	合计 Total	房地产开发 Real Estate
一、本年完成投资	**Investment Completed This Year**	**32079666**	**9968097**
#住宅	Residential Buildings	10473886	8343108
按登记注册类型分	**Grouped by Registion Status**		
内资	Domestic Funded	30510196	9001504
国有	State-owned Enterprises	11753754	557727
集体	Collective-owned Enterprises	1632845	139221
股份合作	Share-holding Corperative	272768	72481
国有联营	State Joint Ownership Enterprises	34231	
集体联营	Collective Joint Ownership Enterprises	18035	
国有与集体联营	Joint State-collective Enterprises	23498	3915
其他联营	Other Joint Ownership Enterprises	27604	2425
国有独资公司	State Sole-funded Corporations	260004	32802
其他有限责任公司	Other Limited Liability Corporations	11149667	5686705
股份有限公司	Share-holding Corperation Ltd.	1032132	267541
私营及个体	Private and Individual	3557196	1978292
其他	Others	748462	260395
港澳台商投资	Enterprises with Funds from Hong Kong,Macao and Taiwan	798711	444713
合资经营企业(港或澳、台资)	Joint Venture	326608	107010
合作经营企业(港或澳、台资)	Cooperation	9965	9965
独资企业	Sole-funded	402347	327738
股份有限公司	Share-Holding Corporations Ltd.	59791	
其他企业	Other Enterprises		

4-4 续表1 continued 1

单位：万元 (10 000 yuan)

指　　标	Item	合计 Total	房地产开发 Real Estate
外商投资	Enterprises with Foreign Investment	770759	521880
合资经营企业(港或澳、台资)	Joint Venture	240145	223225
合作经营企业(港或澳、台资)	Cooperation	214743	185173
独资企业	Sole-Funded	252972	113482
股份有限公司	Share-Holding Corporations Ltd.	62899	
其他	Others		
按隶属关系分	**Grouped by Jurisdiction of Management**		
中央	Central	1028899	154997
省属	Provincial	4230738	811147
市属	Municipal	26820029	9001953
按建设性质分	**Grouped by Type of Construction**		
#新建	New Construction	16077747	
扩建	Expansion	1956527	
改建和技术改造	Reconstruction	2155112	
按构成分	**Grouped by Composition**		
1.建筑工程	Construction Projects	22258253	7652228
2.安装工程	Installment Projects	3294908	994157
3.设备、工器具购置	Purchasing of Equipment and Instruments	1911180	97873
4.其他费用	Others	4615325	1223839

4-4 续表2 continued 2

指　　标	Item	合计 Total	房地产开发 Real Estate
二、构成（%）	**Proportion (%)**		
按登记注册类型分	**Grouped by Status**		
#国有经济	State-owned	37.6	5.9
集体经济	Collective-owned	6.0	2.1
按隶属关系分	**Grouped by Jurisdiction of Management**		
中央	Central	3.2	1.6
省属	Provincial	13.2	8.1
市属	Municipal	83.6	90.3
按建设性质分	**Grouped by Type of Construction**		
#新建	New Construction	50.1	
扩建	Expansion	6.1	
改建和技术改造	Reconstruction	6.7	
按构成分	**Grouped by Composition of Funds**		
1.建筑工程	Construction Projects	69.4	76.8
2.安装工程	Installation Projects	10.3	10.0
3.设备工器具购置	Purchasing of the Equipment and Instruments	6.0	1.0
4.其他费用	Others	14.4	12.3
三、本年新增固定资产(万元)	**Newly Increase in Fixed Assets(10 000 yuan)**	**12973505**	**2552861**
四、房屋面积(万平方米)	**Floor Space (10 000 sq.m)**		
本年施工房屋面积	Floor Space of Buildings Under Construction This Year	12353	8248
#住宅	Residential Buildings	8843	7108
本年竣工房屋面积	Floor Space of Buildings Completed This Year	1232	631
#住宅	Residential Buildings	861	565
五、竣工房屋价值(万元)	**Value of the Building Completed (10 000 yuan)**	**3377311**	**2132894**
#住宅	Residential Buildings	2447001	2552861

4–5 主要年份按行业分全市固定资产投资

Total Investment in Fixed Assets in the Whole City by Sector in Representative Years

指　标	Item	2008	2009	2010	2011
本年完成投资（万元）	**Grouped by Sector (10 000 yuan)**	**17865977**	**23675759**	**31049184**	**32079666**
（一）农、林、牧、渔业	Agriculture,Forestry,Animal Husbandry and Fishery	237521	244605	398240	431024
（二）采矿业	Mining	84506	124845	290955	10580
（三）制造业	Manufacturing	3025912	3785001	4069216	3625173
农副食品加工业	Processing of Food from Agricultural Products	57376	75602	128749	59620
食品制造业	Manufacture of Foods	64182	58245	174352	221737
饮料制造业	Manufacture of Beverages				
石油加工、炼焦及核燃料加工业	Processing of Petroleum, Coking,Processing of Nuclear Fuel	22710	23960	20665	42531
化学原料及化学制品制造业	Manufacture of Raw Chemical Materials and Chemical Products	84082	70330	53698	51027
医药制造业	Manufacture of Medicines	99665	88348	106766	94727
金属制品业	Manufacture of Metal Products	134787	139521	111837	71337
通用设备制造业	Manufacture of General Purpose Machinery	639444	574901	258725	297499
专用设备制造业	Manufacture of Special Purpose Machinery	251553	371236	799620	782521
交通运输设备制造业	Manufacture of Transport Equipment	283652	585419	645384	510418
电气机械及器材制造业	Manufacture of Electrical Machinery and Equipment	344276	339615	294786	281853
通信设备、计算机及其他电子设备制造业	Manufacture of Communication Equipment, Computers and Other Electronic Equipment	180453	656228	700801	421230
仪器仪表及文化办公用机械制造业	Manufacture of Measuring Instruments and Machinery for Cultural Activity and Office Work	44965	63071	88993	225119
（四）电力、燃气及水的生产 和供应业	Production & Supply of Electricity,Gas & Water	450773	517149	625986	267291
（五）建筑业	Construction	136161	157365	574873	844204
（六）交通运输、仓储和邮政业	Transport,Storage and Post	1123643	1505375	1769356	2025763
（七）信息传输、计算机服务和软件业	Information Transmission,Computer Service and Software	129092	212287	509902	334295
（八）批发和零售业	Wholesale and Retail Trades	676458	630216	547444	1096207
（九）住宿和餐饮业	Hotels and Catering Services	372528	445102	389667	573638
（十）金融业	Financial Intermediation	44395	10730	12868	8665
（十一）房地产业	Real Estate	5539238	8016677	12543310	14016422
（十二）租赁和商务服务业	Leasing and Business Services	458350	551354	435042	731207
（十三）科学研究、技术服务和地质勘察业	Scientific Research,Technical Service and Geologic Prospecting	203477	305797	370377	484583
（十四）水利、环境和公共设施管理业	Management of Water Conservancy, Environment and Public Facilities	2153599	3616972	5115257	4697878
（十五）居民服务和其他服务业	Services to Households and Other Services	38845	63999	80836	73631
（十六）教育	Education	575968	764845	779341	750084
（十七）卫生、社会保障和社会福利业	Health,Social Security and Social Welfare	148884	165639	197291	288287
（十八）文化、体育和娱乐业	Culture, Sports and Entertainment	273253	326143	156596	160873
（十九）公共管理和社会组织	Public Management and Social Organization	2193374	2231658	2182627	1659861

4–6 主要年份按资金来源及建设性质分全市固定资产投资

指　　标	Item	1995	2000	2001
一、投资总额(万元)	**Total Investment (10 000 yuan)**	**884994**	**2030122**	**2569496**
（一）按资金来源分	Grouped by Funds Source			
1.国家预算内资金	State Budgetary Funds	69185	160982	256403
2.国内贷款	Domestic Loans	216565	432282	672379
3.债券	Bonds	873	32460	6753
4.利用外资	Utilization of Foreign Funds	80792	31622	54907
5.自筹资金	Self-raising Funds	385047	875352	1121502
6.其他资金	Others	132532	497424	457552
（二）按构成分	Grouped by Composition of Funds			
1.建筑安装工程	Construction and Installation Projects	527220	1404184	1698777
2.设备、工器具购置	Purchasing of Equipment and Instruments	233730	382495	452602
3.其它费用	Others	124044	243443	418117
（三）按建设性质分	Grouped by Type of Construction			
#新 建	New Construction	210926	533058	723957
扩 建	Expansion	180210	542510	581138
改 建	Reconstruction	157457	263657	344879
二、房屋施工面积(万平方米)	**Floor Space Under Construction**	**1070.58**	**1702.5783**	**1767.1256**

Total Investment in Fixed Assets in the Whole City
by Sources of Funds and Type of Construction in Representative Years

2002	2003	2004	2005	2006	2007	2008	2009	2010	2011
3072442	**4457381**	**6120324**	**7763283**	**9718418**	**13405920**	**17865977**	**23675759**	**31049184**	**32079666**
355960	365263	436496	728885	677145	670592	1555809	2562756	1649563	1480412
666146	1219234	1565246	1257175	1631689	1619218	2162957	3301919	4288663	3546561
766	3278								
15192	47509	47401	40583	165390	183422	261325	144124	126802	89047
1392915	1733132	2629720	4001700	5538393	8565573	12771844	15776565	18279153	19460468
641463	1088965	1441461	1734940	1705801	2367115	1114042	1890395	6705003	7563178
2119151	3067309	4127677	5086664	6486233	9165668	12864657	16337466	21690205	25553161
552251	577240	708988	1021079	1409589	1858720	2024631	2619783	3094336	1911180
401040	812832	1283659	1655540	1822596	2381532	2976689	4718510	6264643	4615325
874392	1294032	1874116	2907551	3511432	5123975	6356716	8567540	14292899	16077747
868603	1102914	1169537	1208430	1101740	994841	2118013	3054929	2649749	1956527
343184	447944	670229	782953	1099304	1548130	1921664	2738799	2620997	2155112
2396.89	2716.18	3177.36	4030.38	4589.39	5759.28	6570.94	9571.25	11166.19	12353.11

4–7 主要年份国有经济单位固定资产投资

指　　标	Item	1995	2000	2001
一、投资总额(万元)	**Total Investment (10 000 yuan)**	**690806**	**1596002**	**1755787**
1.按资金来源分	Grouped by Funds Source			
国家预算内投资	State Budgetary Funds	67426	165304	255860
国内贷款	Domestic Loans	145108	280585	471506
债 券	Bonds		32886	6865
利用外资	Utilization of Foreign Funds	46811	15276	20815
自筹资金	Self-raising Funds	330333	689732	715351
其它资金	Others	101128	412219	285390
2.按构成分	Grouped by Composition of Funds			
建筑安装工程	Construction and Installation Projects	405057	1102548	1177790
设备、工具、器具购置	Purchasing of Equipment and Instruments	209351	328432	334174
其它费用	Others	76398	165022	243823
3.按建设性质分	Grouped by Type of Construction			
#新　建	New Construction	165793	390119	486585
扩　建	Expansion	162796	460381	436404
改　建	Reconstruction	145783	254860	328685
二、新增固定资产(万元)	**Newly Increased in Fixed Assets (10 000 yuan)**	**509328**	**1220632**	**1120240**
三、房屋建筑面积(万平方米)	**Floor Space of Buildings (10 000 sq.m)**			
施工面积	Floor Space Under Construction	841	1342	1155
竣工面积	Floor Space Completed	304	577	492
#住 宅	Residential Building	214	475	392

Investment in Fixed Assets of State-owned Units in Representative Years

2002	2003	2004	2005	2006	2007	2008	2009	2010	2011
2000636	**2648283**	**3291356**	**3736992**	**4011446**	**4767827**	**6948899**	**9329071**	**13487620**	**12047989**
351540	268537	361654	722673	699765	655259	1034930	1367405	1312512	954708
453958	823374	858396	850554	882295	664703	1175473	1766395	2305605	1531874
	2310								
6617	4846	10851	9900	73830	58711	65209	29033	24222	20299
840082	803648	779205	1405167	1968662	2830256	4055904	5047734	8335268	8609254
348439	745568	1281250	748698	386894	558898	617383	1118504	1510013	931855
1449583	1897323	2197052	2394409	2532743	2925696	4973312	5596104	8591043	9003654
347647	335454	333272	384157	536340	865951	728554	1131474	1522615	663500
203406	415506	761032	958426	942363	976180	1247033	2601493	3373962	2380835
537537	883859	1157470	1740071	1737828	1893488	2881551	4358755	7363825	8155566
672297	726753	965832	907723	884083	658048	1617290	1670225	1685886	1286807
272499	377060	514870	617680	642848	950958	1005897	1484559	1715761	1001685
1134623	**1732895**	**1733550**	**1988546**	**1799515**	**2651549**	**1963274**	**3743856**	**3859619**	**5607068**
1590	1331	1041	1397	1331	1546	1367	2384	2765	2377.21
452	514	255	518	390	552	266	312	189	336.43
311	343	162	234	219	350	151	226	112	177.54

4-8 农村集体固定资产投资（2011年）

Investment in Fixed Assets of Rural Collective Owned Units（2011）

单位：万元 (10 000 yuan)

指　　标	Item	2011
一、本年完成投资	**Investment Completed This Year**	**657825**
建筑工程	Constrution Projects	521706
安装工程	Installment Projects	53431
设备购置	Purchasing of Equipment	28295
其他	Others	54393
二、本年新增固定资产	**Newly Increased Fixed in Assets This Year**	**578177**
三、本年资金来源合计	**Total of Sources of Funds This Year**	**709810**
上年末结余资金	**Balance of Last Year**	**22107**
本年资金来源小计	**Subtotal Funds This Year**	**687703**
国家资金	State Funds	29170
国内贷款	Domestic Loans	10350
利用外资	Utilization of Foreign Funds	
自筹资金	Self-raising Funds	643090
其他资金	Others	5093
四、房屋建筑面积(平方米)	**Floor Space of Buildings(sq.m)**	
施工面积	Floor Space Under Construction	334426
#住宅	Residential Buildings	132190
竣工面积	Floor Space Completed	227437
#住宅	Residential Buildings	132190

4-9 主要年份农村集体固定资产投资

Investment in Fixed Assets of Rural Collective Owned Units in Representative Years

指　　标	Item	1995	2000	2001	2002
一、投资总额(万元)	**Total Investment (10 000 yuan)**	**37892**	**89626**	**82623**	**68610**
1.按资金来源分	Grouped by Funds Source				
国家资金	State Funds	1442	9388	994	2369
国内贷款	Domestic Loans	10925	2977	5596	1818
利用外资	Utilization of Foreign Funds	5021	5394	70	8973
自筹资金	Self-raising Funds	12220	53338	58911	41183
群众集资	Mass Fund-raising	3732	7413	8248	10647
其他资金	Others	4552	11116	8804	3620
2.按行业划分	Grouped by Sector				
农林牧渔业	Ariculture, Forestry, Animal Husbandry, Fishery	170	9075	4452	4358
工业	Industry	20286	32437	21155	16998
建筑业	Construction	2475	12309	8523	5243
交通运输、仓储和邮政业	Transport,Storage,and Post	668	2444	1023	1057
信息传输、计算机服务和软件业	Information Transmission,Computer Service and Software				
批发和零售贸易业	Wholesale and Retail Trade	3749	8444	26611	9273
住宿和餐饮业	Hotels and Catering Services				
金融业	Financial Intermediation		10	700	
房地产业	Real Estate	2338	12519	8260	10286
租赁和商务服务业	Leasing and Business Services				
居民服务和其他服务	Services to Households and Other Services				
卫生体育社会福利业	Health Care,Sports and Social Welfare	3054	126	107	281
教育文化艺术及广播电影电视业	Education,Culture and Arts,Radio, Film and Television	4642	6110	7973	9713
科学研究和综合技术服务业	Scientific Research and Polytechnical Services		500	790	
水利、环境和公共设施管理业	Management of Water Conservancy, Environment and Public Facilities	350	5017	1170	8747
国家机关政党机关和社会团体	Governmental and Party Agencies and Social Organizations	160	635	1859	2654
二、竣工房屋建筑面积(万平方米)	**Floor Space of the Building Completed (10 000 sq.m)**	**16.08**	**83.96**	**41.1**	**43.31**
#住宅	Residential Buildings	0.92	21.33	10.82	8.35
三、本年新增固定资产(万元)	**Newly Increase Fixed Assets This Year (10 000 yuan)**	**32405**	**89626**	**75732**	**55215**

4–9 续表1 continued 1

指　　标	Item	2003	2004	2005	2006
一、投资总额(万元)	**Total Investment (10 000 yuan)**	**79216**	**132614**	**324932**	**704576**
1.按资金来源分	Grouped by Funds Source				
国家资金	State Funds	3198	3388	4295	14889
国内贷款	Domestic Loans	742	981	10994	19415
利用外资	Utilization of Foreign Funds	3887	41		21
自筹资金	Self-raising Funds	52946	95820	212297	576709
群众集资	Mass Fund-raising	6256			
其他资金	Others	12187	32384	97346	93542
2.按行业划分	Grouped by Sector				
农林牧渔业	Ariculture, Forestry, Animal Husbandry, Fishery	3632	3174	17663	11684
工业	Industry	5228	19382	21023	72083
建筑业	Construction	10248	17442	1591	2437
交通运输、仓储和邮政业	Transport,Storage,and Post	220	3188	21479	17576
信息传输、计算机服务和软件业	Information Transmission,Computer Service and Software			390	905
批发和零售贸易业	Wholesale and Retail Trade	2760	6819	12528	33516
住宿和餐饮业	Hotels and Catering Services			15182	15160
金融业	Financial Intermediation	25			
房地产业	Real Estate	19315	1400		70
租赁和商务服务业	Leasing and Business Services			300	
居民服务和其他服务	Services to Households and Other Services			1049	1760
卫生体育社会福利业	Health Care,Sports and Social Welfare	326	150	55	3595
教育文化艺术及广播电影电视业	Education,Culture and Arts,Radio, Film and Television	4831	6160	10054	21602
科学研究和综合技术服务业	Scientific Research and Polytechnical Services			10571	641
水利、环境和公共设施管理业	Management of Water Conservancy, Environment and Public Facilities	20001	62016	212007	61173
国家机关政党机关和社会团体	Governmental and Party Agencies and Social Organizations	12630	12883	1040	462374
二、竣工房屋建筑面积(万平方米)	**Floor Space of the Building Completed (10 000 sq.m)**	**48.26**	**55.62**	**46.04**	**215.98**
#住宅	Residential Buildings	23.2	34.46	25.89	86.45
三、本年新增固定资产(万元)	**Newly Increase Fixed Assets This Year (10 000 yuan)**	**72862**	**87865**	**148210**	**432586**

4–9 续表2 continued 2

指　标	Item	2007	2008	2009	2010	2011
一、投资总额(万元)	**Total Investment (10 000 yuan)**	**666887**	**785921**	**861851**	**949949**	**657825**
1.按资金来源分	Grouped by Funds Source					
国家资金	State Funds	26924	35800	53406	52158	27903
国内贷款	Domestic Loans	42216	79031	31422	54952	9900
利用外资	Utilization of Foreign Funds	2029	3058			
自筹资金	Self-raising Funds	528735	590202	766778	826731	615150
群众集资	Mass Fund-raising					
其他资金	Others	66983	77830	10245	16108	4872
2.按行业划分	Grouped by Sector					
农林牧渔业	Ariculture, Forestry, Animal Husbandry, Fishery	27578	30115	69950	349761	291242
工业	Industry	136203	184342	142060	64821	43407
建筑业	Construction	1200	5400		7705	17372
交通运输、仓储和邮政业	Transport,Storage,and Post	55138	42731	30990	8070	26930
信息传输、计算机服务和软件业	Information Transmission,Computer Service and Software	670	650		800	
批发和零售贸易业	Wholesale and Retail Trade	62206	19691	10740	12060	18895
住宿和餐饮业	Hotels and Catering Services	5631	19178	27580	58330	25218
金融业	Financial Intermediation			1600		
房地产业	Real Estate	900	7256	8330	96900	17004
租赁和商务服务业	Leasing and Business Services	1300	1000	250		
居民服务和其他服务	Services to Households and Other Services	5390	500	3630		200
卫生体育社会福利业	Health Care,Sports and Social Welfare	200	795	7613		1430
教育文化艺术及广播电影电视业	Education,Culture and Arts,Radio, Film and Television	32247	12294	21622		4260
科学研究和综合技术服务业	Scientific Research and Polytechnical Services	930		900		
水利、环境和公共设施管理业	Management of Water Conservancy, Environment and Public Facilities	49418	133369	218661	280703	207594
国家机关政党机关和社会团体	Governmental and Party Agencies and Social Organizations	287876	328600	317925	70799	4273
二、竣工房屋建筑面积(万平方米)	**Floor Space of the Building Completed (10 000 sq.m)**	**192.01**	**46.89**	**207.69**	**54**	**23**
#住宅	Residential Buildings	37.06	11.8	11.08	12.81	13
三、本年新增固定资产(万元)	**Newly Increase Fixed Assets This Year (10 000 yuan)**	**586012**	**376378**	**792448**	**671743**	**578177**

4-10 主要年份市属固定资产投资

单位：万元

指　标	Item	1995	2000	2001	2002	2003
一、投资总额	**Total Investment**	**432451**	**1263023**	**1539717**	**1848833**	**2978747**
1.按经济类型分	Grouped by Type of Enterprises					
国有经济	State-owned Enterprises	258545	890546	894700	1006245	1586057
集体经济	Collective-owned Enterprises	5720	52893	62895	63877	142849
其他经济	Others	168186	319584	582122	778711	1249841
2.按管理渠道分	Grouped by Management					
城镇投资	Investment of Urban Units	432451	1263023	1539717	1848833	2978747
房地产开发	Real Estate	171291	473787	566557	702233	1114809
二、新增固定资产	**Newly Increased Fixed Assets**	**273324**	**953173**	**1159980**	**1295389**	**1812099**
三、房屋竣工面积	**Floor Space of the**	**202.52**	**509.48**	**535.98**	**537.44**	**631.89**
(万平方米)	**Building Completed(10000sq.m)**					
#住 宅	Residential Buildings	143.30	373.51	396.01	331.45	387.82

Investment In Fixed Assets of Municipal Units in Representative Years

(10 000 yuan)

2004	2005	2006	2007	2008	2009	2010	2011
4355271	**5788693**	**7835681**	**10555849**	**14648360**	**19063075**	**25474854**	**26820029**
1884624	2198836	2591184	2972840	4480627	6527566	9306901	8750285
257226	258327	363909	1366567	1646111	1614290	2253851	1897980
2213421	3331530	4880588	6216442	8521622	10921219	13914102	16171764
4355271	5788693	7835681	10555849	14648360	19063075	25474854	26820029
1492693	2062940	2641871	3515719	4938202	6575526	8020893	9001953
1962795	**3011104**	**3495179**	**5279938**	**6488364**	**8380033**	**10423906**	**10663882**
606.23	**767.7**	**914.8**	**1343.88**	**987.05**	**1359.46**	**668.49**	**1002.82**
388.79	436.43	432.43	734.05	602.69	727.41	448.46	531.38

4-11 市属固定资产投资（2011年）

Investment in Fixed Assets of Municipal Units（2011）

单位：万元 (10 000 yuan)

分　　类	Classify	城镇 Urban Area	房地产开发 Real Estate
一、本年完成投资	**Accomplished Investment This Year**	**26820029**	**9001953**
#区县属	District and County	**17529784**	**6598633**
#住宅	Residential Buildings	**9341663**	**7606546**
按登记注册类型分	**Grouped by Registion Status**		
内资	Domestic Funded	25211229	8035360
国有	State-owned Enterprises	8584379	479238
集体	Collective-owned Enterprises	1626616	139221
股份合作	Share-holding Corperative	253329	65607
国有联营	State Joint Ownership Enterprises	31817	
集体联营	Collective Joint Ownership Enterprises	18035	
国有与集体联营	State-owned and Collective-owned Joint Enterprises	19583	
其他联营	Other Joint Ownership Enterprises	27604	2425
国有独资公司	Sole State-funded Corporations	134089	
其他有限责任公司	Other Limited Liability Corporations	9425565	4945797
股份有限公司	Share-holding Corperation Ltd.	968247	236732
私营及个体	Private and Individual	3517866	1978292
其他	Others	604099	188048
港澳台商投资	Enterprises with Investment from Hong Kong, Macao and Taiwan	798711	444713
合资经营企业(港或澳、台资)	Joint Venture	326608	107010
合作经营企业(港或澳、台资)	Cooperation	9965	9965
独资企业	Sole-Funded	402347	327738
股份有限公司	Share-Holding Corporations Ltd.	59791	
外商投资	Enterprises with Foreign Investment	770759	521880
合资经营企业(港或澳、台资)	Joint Venture	240145	223225
合作经营企业(港或澳、台资)	Cooperation	214743	185173
独资企业	Sole-funded	252972	113482
股份有限公司	Share-holding Corporations Ltd.	62899	
按建设性质分	**Grouped by Type of Construction**		
#新建	New Construction	12967161	
扩建	Expansion	1592226	
改建和技术改造	Reconstruction	1945016	
按构成分	**Grouped by Composition**		
1.建筑工程	Construction Projects	18916130	6927685
2.安装工程	Installment Projects	2559229	928020
3.设备工器具购置	Purchasing of Equipment and Instruments	1335493	86004
4.其他费用	Others	4009177	1060244

4-11 续表 continued

指　　标	Item	城镇 Urban Area	房地产开发 Real Estate
二、构成（%）	**Proportion (%)**		
按登记注册类型分	**Grouped by Status**		
#国有经济	State-owned	32.6	5.3
集体经济	Collective-owned	7.1	2.3
按建设性质分	**Grouped by Type of Construction**		
#新建	New Construction	48.3	
扩建	Expansion	5.9	
改建和技术改造	Reconstruction	7.3	
按构成分	**Grouped by Composition of Funds**		
1.建筑工程	Construction Projects	70.5	77.0
2.安装工程	Installation Projects	9.5	10.3
3.设备工器具购置	Purchasing of the Equipment and Instruments	5.0	1.0
4.其他费用	Others	14.9	11.8
三、本年新增固定资产(万元）	**Newly Increase in Fixed Assets(10 000 yuan)**	**10663882**	**2387311**
四、房屋面积(万平方米)	**Floor Space (sq.m)**		
本年施工房屋面积	Floor Space of Buildings Under Construction This Year		
#住宅	Residential Buildings		
本年竣工房屋面积	Floor Space of Buildings Completed This Year		
#住宅	Residential Buildings		
五、竣工房屋价值(万元)	**Value of the Building Completed (10 000 yuan)**		
#住宅	Residential Buildings		

4-12 按行业分市属固定资产投资（2011年）

Investment in Fixed Assets of Municipal Units by Sector（2011）

指　标	Item	2011
本年完成投资（万元）	**Grouped by Sector (10 000 yuan)**	**26820029**
（一）农、林、牧、渔业	Agriculture,Forestry,Animal Husbandry and Fishery	422494
（二）采矿业	Mining	10580
（三）制造业	Manufacturing	2586933
#农副食品加工业	Processing of Food from Agricultural Products	59620
食品制造业	Manufacture of Foods	221737
饮料制造业	Manufacture of Beverages	19371
石油加工、炼焦及核燃料加工业	Processing of Petroleum, Coking,Processing of Nuclear Fuel	
化学原料及化学制品制造业	Manufacture of Raw Chemical Materials and Chemical Products	51027
医药制造业	Manufacture of Medicines	92002
金属制品业	Manufacture of Metal Products	71337
通用设备制造业	Manufacture of General Purpose Machinery	217392
专用设备制造业	Manufacture of Special Purpose Machinery	511040
交通运输设备制造业	Manufacture of Transport Equipment	352150
电气机械及器材制造业	Manufacture of Electrical Machinery and Equipment	241265
通信设备、计算机及其他电子设备制造业	Manufacture of Communication Equipment, Computers and Other Electronic Equipment	251133
仪器仪表及文化办公用机械制造业	Manufacture of Measuring Instruments and Machinery for Cultural Activity and Office Work	35205
（四）电力、燃气及水的生产和供应业	Production & Supply of Electricity,Gas & Water	157880
（五）建筑业	Construction	756656
（六）交通运输、仓储和邮政业	Transport,Storage and Post	1111676
（七）信息传输、计算机服务和软件业	Information Transmission,Computer Service and Software	241018
（八）批发和零售业	Wholesale and Retail Trades	870489
（九）住宿和餐饮业	Hotels and Catering Services	342946
（十）金融业	Financial Intermediation	8665
（十一）房地产业	Real Estate	12909392
（十二）租赁和商务服务业	Leasing and Business Services	691362
（十三）科学研究、技术服务和地质勘察业	Scientific Research,Technical Service and Geologic Prospecting	117579
（十四）水利、环境和公共设施管理业	Management of Water Conservancy, Environment and Public Facilities	4467766
（十五）居民服务和其他服务业	Services to Households and Other Services	64031
（十六）教育	Education	276754
（十七）卫生、社会保障和社会福利业	Health,Social Security and Social Welfare	230684
（十八）文化、体育和娱乐业	Culture, Sports and Entertainment	112949
（十九）公共管理和社会组织	Public Management and Social Organization	1440175

4-13 按资金来源及建设性质分市属固定资产投资（2011年）

Investment in Fixed Assets of Municipal Units by Sources of Funds and Type of Construction（2011）

指　　标	Item	2011
一、投资总额(万元)	**Total Investment (10 000 yuan)**	**26820029**
（一）按资金来源分	Grouped by Funds Sources	
1.国家预算内资金	State Budgetary Funds	1101225
2.国内贷款	Domestic Loans	2465783
3.债 券	Bonds	
4.利用外资	Utilization of Foreign Funds	74788
5.自筹资金	Self-raising Funds	16425313
6.其他资金	Others	6752920
（二）按建设性质分	**Grouped by Type of Construction**	
#新 建	New Construction	12967161
扩 建	Expansion	1592226
改 建	Reconstruction	1945016
（三）按构成分	**Grouped by Composition of Funds**	
1.建筑工程	Construction Project	18916130
2.安装工程	Installation Projects	2559229
3.设备、工器具购置	Purchasing of Equipment and Instruments	1335493
4.其它费用	Others	4009177
二、房屋施工面积(万平方米)	**Floor Space of Buildings Under Construction（10 000 sq.m)**	**415.1**

4-14 按登记注册类型及隶属关系分市区固定资产投资（2011年）

Investments in Fixed Assets of Urban Districts by Registration Status and Jurisdiction of Management（2011）

分　　组	Classify	2011
本年完成投资（万元）	**Investment Completed This Year (10 000yuan)**	**28390963**
#住宅	Residential Buildings	
一、按登记注册类型分	**Grouped by Registion Status**	
内资	Domestic Funded	26827676
国有	State-owned Enterprises	9935089
集体	Collective-owned Enterprises	1425758
股份合作	Share-holding Corperative	265894
国有联营	State Joint Ownership Enterprises	9681
集体联营	Collective Joint Ownership Enterprises	18035
国有与集体联营	Joint State-collective Enterprises	23498
其他联营	Other Joint Ownership Enterprises	27604
国有独资公司	State Sole-funded Corporations	260004
其他有限责任公司	Other Limited Liability Corporations	10340651
股份有限公司	Share-holding Corperation Ltd.	727684
私营及个体	Private and Individual	3084436
其他	Others	709342
港澳台商投资	Enterprises with Funds from Hong Kong,Macao and Taiwan	792528
合资经营企业(港或澳、台资)	Joint Venture	320425
合作经营企业(港或澳、台资)	Cooperation	9965
独资企业	Sole-funded	402347
股份有限公司	Share-Holding Corporations Ltd.	59791
外商投资	Enterprises with Foreign Investment	770759
合资经营企业(港或澳、台资)	Joint Venture	240145
合作经营企业(港或澳、台资)	Cooperation	214743
独资企业	Sole-Funded	252972
股份有限公司	Share-Holding Corporations Ltd.	62899
二、按隶属关系分	**Grouped by Jurisdiction of Management**	
中央	Central	914860
省属	Provincial	4038301
市属	Municipal	23437802

4-15 按行业分市区固定资产投资（2011年）

Investments in Fixed Assets of Urban Districts by Sector（2011）

指 标	Item	2011
本年完成投资（万元）	**Grouped by Sector (10 000 yuan)**	**28390963**
（一）农、林、牧、渔业	Agriculture,Forestry,Animal Husbandry and Fishery	145548
（二）采矿业	Mining	6960
（三）制造业	Manufacturing	2703809
农副食品加工业	Processing of Food from Agricultural Products	25980
食品制造业	Manufacture of Foods	189973
饮料制造业	Manufacture of Beverages	15557
石油加工、炼焦及核燃料加工业	Processing of Petroleum, Coking,Processing of Nuclear Fuel	42531
化学原料及化学制品制造业	Manufacture of Raw Chemical Materials and Chemical Products	21957
医药制造业	Manufacture of Medicines	71331
金属制品业	Manufacture of Metal Products	63287
通用设备制造业	Manufacture of General Purpose Machinery	207661
专用设备制造业	Manufacture of Special Purpose Machinery	514738
交通运输设备制造业	Manufacture of Transport Equipment	346151
电气机械及器材制造业	Manufacture of Electrical Machinery and Equipment	210748
通信设备、计算机及其他电子设备制造业	Manufacture of Communication Equipment, Computers and Other Electronic Equipment	409468
仪器仪表及文化办公用机械制造业	Manufacture of Measuring Instruments and Machinery for Cultural Activity and Office Work	213983
（四）电力、燃气及水的生产 和供应业	Production & Supply of Electricity,Gas & Water	227105
（五）建筑业	Construction	661579
（六）交通运输、仓储和邮政业	Transport,Storage and Post	1768074
（七）信息传输、计算机服务和软件业	Information Transmission,Computer Service and Software	322645
（八）批发和零售业	Wholesale and Retail Trades	1027267
（九）住宿和餐饮业	Hotels and Catering Services	521668
（十）金融业	Financial Intermediation	8665
（十一）房地产业	Real Estate	13419021
（十二）租赁和商务服务业	Leasing and Business Services	726907
（十三）科学研究、技术服务和地质勘察业	Scientific Research,Technical Service and Geologic Prospecting	478228
（十四）水利、环境和公共设施管理业	Management of Water Conservancy, Environment and Public Facilities	3708199
（十五）居民服务和其他服务业	Services to Households and Other Services	54847
（十六）教育	Education	599172
（十七）卫生、社会保障和社会福利业	Health,Social Security and Social Welfare	263071
（十八）文化、体育和娱乐业	Culture, Sports and Entertainment	139543
（十九）公共管理和社会组织	Public Management and Social Organization	1608655

4-16 按资金来源及建设性质分市区固定资产投资（2011年）

Investment in Fixed Assets of Urban Area by Sources of Funds and Type of Construction（2011）

指　　标	Item	2011
投资总额(万元)	**Total Investment (10 000 yuan)**	**28390963**
一、按资金来源分	**Grouped by Funds Sources**	
1.国家预算资金	State Budgetary Funds	1201083
2.国内贷款	Domestic Loans	3411943
3.债 券	Bonds	
4.利用外资	Utilization of Foreign Funds	59321
5.自筹资金	Self-raising Funds	16564723
6.其他资金	Others	7153895
二、按建设性质分	**Grouped by Type of Construction**	
#新 建	New Construction	13424983
扩 建	Expansion	1592515
改 建	Reconstruction	1868876
三、按构成分	**Grouped by Composition of Funds**	
1.建筑工程	Construction Project	19747997
2.安装工程	Installation Projects	2953249
3.设备、工器具购置	Purchasing of Equipment and Instruments	1638376
4.其它费用	Others	4051341
四、房屋施工面积（万平方米）	**Floor Space of Buildings (10 000 sq.m)**	**3270.12**

4-17　全市固定资产投资资金来源（2011年）

Source of Funds for Total Fixed Assets Investment of Whole City（2011）

单位：万元　　(10 000 yuan)

指　　标	Item	城镇 Urban Area	房地产开发 Real Estate
一、本年资金来源合计	**Total of Sources of Funds This Year**	**44437785**	**18048367**
1.上年末结余资金	Balance of Last Year	4873318	3392728
2.本年资金来源小计	Subtotal Funds This Year	39564467	14655639
(1) 国家预算资金	State Budgetary Funds	1825821	
(2) 国内贷款	Domestic Loans	4374042	1871437
(3) 债券	Bonds		
(4) 利用外资	Utilization of Foreign Funds	109823	18
(5) 自筹资金	Self-raising Funds	23926969	4750053
(6) 其他资金	Others	9327812	8034131
二、本年各项应付款合计	**Total Sums of Money to be Paid This Year**	**2585247**	**1303213**

4-18　市属固定资产投资资金来源（2011年）

Source of Funds for Fixed Estate of Municipal Units（2011）

单位：万元　　(10 000 yuan)

指　　标	Item	城镇 Urban Area	房地产开发 Real Estate
一、本年资金来源合计	**Total of Sources of Funds This Year**	**37905816**	**16363445**
1.上年末结余资金	Balance of Last Year	4259504	2912739
2.本年资金来源小计	Subtotal Funds This Year	33646312	13450706
(1) 国家预算资金	State Budgetary Funds	1381511	
(2) 国内贷款	Domestic Loans	3093379	1627382
(3) 债券	Bonds		
(4) 利用外资	Utilization of Foreign Funds	93823	18
(5) 自筹资金	Self-raising Funds	20605914	4410608
(6) 其他资金来源	Others	8471685	7412698
二、本年各项应付款合计	**Total Sums of Money to be Paid This Year**	**2228799**	**1218250**

4-19 全市固定资产投资效果（2011年）

Achievements of Total Assets Investment of Whole City（2011）

指　　标	Item	城镇 Urban Area	房地产开发 Real Estate
一、建设项目投产率(%)	**Rate of Projects Put Into use(%)**	**54.9**	
施工项目个数（个）	Number of Constructing Projects (unit)	1924	
本年投产项目个数（个）	Number of Projects Put into Use (unit)	1057	
二、固定资产交付使用率(%)	**Rate of Fixed Assets Put into Use(%)**	**40.4**	**47.1**
本年新增固定资产（亿元）	Newly Increased Fixed Assets This Year(100 million yuan)	1297.35	1042.06
本年完成投资（亿元）	Investment Completed This Year (100 million yuan)	3207.97	2211.16
三、建设周期(年)	**Construction Period (year)**	**3.5**	**3.0**
计划总投资（亿元）	Total Planned Investment(100 million yuan)	11268.30	6649.70
本年完成投资（亿元）	Investment Completed This Year (100 million yuan)	3207.97	2211.16
四、房屋建筑面积竣工率(%)	**Completion Rate of Buildings (%)**	**10.0**	**14.6**
本年施工房屋面积（万平方米）	Floor Space of the Constructing Buildings This Year (10 000 sq.m)	12353.11	4105.42
本年竣工房屋面积（万平方米）	Floor Space of the Buildings Completed This Year (10 000 sq.m)	1231.90	600.87

4-20 市属固定资产投资效果（2011年）

Achievement of Fixed Assets Investment of Municipal Units（2011）

指　　标	Item	城镇 Urban Area	房地产开发 Real Estate
一、建设项目投产率(%)	**Rate of Projects Put Into use(%)**	**56.0**	
施工项目个数（个）	Number of Constructing Projects (unit)	1724	
本年投产项目个数（个）	Number of Projects Put into Use (unit)	965	
二、固定资产交付使用率(%)	**Rate of Fixed Assets Put into Use(%)**	**39.8**	**46.5**
本年新增固定资产（亿元）	Newly Increased Fixed Assets This Year(100 million yuan)	1066.39	827.66
本年完成投资（亿元）	Investment Completed This Year (100 million yuan)	2682.00	1781.81
三、建设周期(年)	**Construction Period (year)**	**3.6**	**3.1**
计划总投资（亿元）	Total Planned Investment(100 million yuan)	9743.38	5552.20
本年完成投资（亿元）	Investment Completed This Year (100 million yuan)	2682.00	1781.81
四、房屋建筑面积竣工率(%)	**Completion Rate of Buildings (%)**	**9.2**	**12.4**
本年施工房屋面积（万平方米）	Floor Space of the Constructing Buildings This Year (10 000 sq.m)	10954.06	3352.58
本年竣工房屋面积（万平方米）	Floor Space of the Buildings Completed This Year (10 000 sq.m)	1002.82	415.10

4–21 分区县、开发区全社会固定资产投资额（2011年）

Investment Fulfilled In Fixed Assets by Region and Development Zone（2011）

单位：万元 (10 000 yuan)

区县名称	Name of District and County	全社会固定资产投资 Investment Fulfilled In Fixed Assets	城镇 Urban Area	房地产 Real Estate	农村集体 Rural Collective-owned Units	农村私人建房 Private Housing in Country
区　县	**Region**	**33462621**	**22111569**	**9968097**	**657825**	**725130**
新城区	Xincheng	2884809	2118334	766475		
碑林区	Beilin	2911287	1330624	1580663		
莲湖区	Lianhu	3764003	2873959	890044		
灞桥区	Baqiao	1865078	1285075	501683	27321	50999
未央区	Weiyang	4498254	2592237	1866793		39224
雁塔区	Yanta	7677355	4450900	3188440		38015
阎良区	Yanliang	1209231	1000120	110147	64290	34674
临潼区	Lintong	1178946	978016	83831	17002	100098
长安区	Chang'an	3143523	2163136	668725	165029	146633
蓝田县	Lantian	770932	456854	63017	156013	95048
周至县	Zhouzhi	684630	481527	34981	71578	96544
户　县	Huxian	1098101	802752	74404	135242	85703
高陵县	Gaoling	1776472	1578035	138894	21350	38192
开发区	**Development Zones**	**11732045**	**8141485**	**3590560**		
高新区	GaoXin	3327812	2492424	835388		
经开区	JingKai	3016337	2430902	585435		
曲江新区	Qujiang	2682342	1460954	1221388		
浐灞生态区	Chanba Eco-District	959076	314047	645029		
航空基地	Aviation Industry Base	356115	308315	47800		
航天基地	Aerospace Base	473381	252221	221160		
国际港务区	International Trade&Logistic Park	385772	352372	33400		
沣东新城	FengDongXinCheng	531210	530250	960		

4-22 全市分行业房屋建筑面积（2011年）

单位：平方米

行　　业	Item	本年施工房屋面积 Floor Space of Buildings Under Construction This Year	住 宅 Residential Buildings
合　计	**Total**	**123531105**	**88428270**
（一）农、林、牧、渔业	Agriculture, Forestry, Animal Husbandry and Fishery	41250	9000
（二）采矿业	Mining	145900	
（三）制造业	Manufacturing	7547725	634449
（四）电力、燃气及水的生产和供应业	Generation and Supply of Electricity, Production and Supply of Gas and Water	29469	
（五）建筑业	Construction	2186075	301761
（六）交通运输、仓储和邮政业	Transportation, Storage and Post	1318892	
（七）信息传输、计算机服务和软件业	Information Transmission, Computer Service and Software	830191	
（八）批发和零售业	Wholesale and Retail Trades	1432527	109843
（九）住宿和餐饮业	Hotels and Catering Services	581330	105200
（十）金融业	Financial Intermediation		
（十一）房地产业	Real Estate	97336294	82792036
（十二）租赁和商务服务业	Leasing and Business Services	516112	
（十三）科学研究、技术服务和地质勘查业	Scientific Research, Technical Service and Geologic Prospecting	1023539	399869
（十四）水利、环境和公共设施管理业	Management of Water Conservancy, Environment and Public Facilities	1578674	893529
（十五）居民服务和其他服务业	Services to Households and Other Services	40625	
（十六）教育	Education	4095290	661675
（十七）卫生、社会保障和社会福利业	Health,Social Security and Social Welfare	703489	93808
（十八）文化、体育和娱乐业	Culture, Sports and Entertainment	385818	117760
（十九）公共管理和社会组织	Public Management and Social Organization	3737905	2309340

Floor Space of Buildings Construction by Sector（2011）

(sq.m)

本年竣工房屋面积 Floor Space of Buildings Completed This Year	住 宅 Residential Buildings	竣工房屋价值（万元） Value of Buildings Completed(10 000yuan)	住 宅 Residential Buildings
12319069	**8614405**	**3377311**	**2447001**
27060	9000	4305	700
990546	29638	224052	9552
42961	25000	17500	9500
323519		64325	
107903	14603	18656	3000
25853		19250	
8624710	7682018	2654405	2317749
88401		32000	
12560		2806	
22907	7600	7885	1900
726995	30000	91501	3000
48994	13200	12636	4900
57355		24825	
1219305	803346	203165	96700

4-23 市属分行业房屋建筑面积（2011年）

单位：平方米

行　　业	Item	本年施工房屋面积 Floor Space of Buildings Under Construction This Year	住　宅 Residential Residence
合　计	**Total**	**109540639**	**79463962**
（一）农、林、牧、渔业	Agriculture, Forestry, Animal Husbandry and Fishery	41250	9000
（二）采矿业	Mining	145900	
（三）制造业	Manufacturing	6207996	101367
（四）电力、燃气及水的生产和供应业	Generation and Supply of Electricity, Production and Supply of Gas and Water	29469	
（五）建筑业	Construction	1918511	58000
（六）交通运输、仓储和邮政业	Transportation, Storage and Post	931092	
（七）信息传输、计算机服务和软件业	Information Transmission, Computer Service and Software	830191	
（八）批发和零售业	Wholesale and Retail Trades	1411287	88603
（九）住宿和餐饮业	Hotels and Catering Services	247580	5200
（十）金融业	Financial Intermediation		
（十一）房地产业	Real Estate	90180838	76783726
（十二）租赁和商务服务业	Leasing and Business Services	502112	
（十三）科学研究、技术服务和地质勘查业	Scientific Research, Technical Service and Geologic Prospecting	274753	
（十四）水利、环境和公共设施管理业	Management of Water Conservancy, Environment and Public Facilities	1571289	893529
（十五）居民服务和其他服务业	Services to Households and Other Services	40625	
（十六）教育	Education	2045821	11633
（十七）卫生、社会保障和社会福利业	Health,Social Security and Social Welfare	579882	13200
（十八）文化、体育和娱乐业	Culture, Sports and Entertainment	227559	45860
（十九）公共管理和社会组织	Public Management and Social Organization	2354484	1453844

Floors Space of Buildings Construction of Municipal Units by Sector（2011）

(sq.m)

本年竣工房屋面积 Floor Space of Buildings Completed This Year	住　宅 Residential Residence	竣工房屋价值(万元) Value of Buildings Completed (10 000 yuan)	住　宅 Residential Residence
10028229	**7423155**	**2823950**	**2229986**
27060	9000	4305	700
760908		130700	
17961		8000	
57519		18325	
107903	14603	18656	3000
2103		7750	
8191599	7349902	2508955	2207786
88401		32000	
12560		2806	
22907	7600	7885	1900
613986		45351	
33900	13200	8436	4900
35355		10994	
56067	28850	19787	11700

4-24 主要年份全市新增固定资产及房屋竣工面积

Value of Newly Added Fixed Assets and Floor Spaces Completed of Whole City in Representative Years

年 份 Year	新增固定资产(万元) Newly Increased Fixed Assets (10 000 yuan)	房屋竣工面积(平方米) Floor Space of Buildings Completed (sq.m)	住 宅 Residential Residence
1978	49582	990996	407554
1980	46377	1648691	1001544
1985	86174	2224195	1290728
1986	134037	2729528	1559067
1987	167160	2414751	1192115
1988	168152	2118312	1024255
1989	165811	1784546	877691
1990	203000	2118777	1110535
1991	178572	1853384	958364
1992	223270	2047478	1126628
1993	416963	2578987	1448829
1994	553714	2829057	1844859
1995	625803	3576699	2528435
1996	600353	3321838	2495208
1997	628819	3744631	2865398
1998	802337	3828026	2756265
1999	1189176	6810370	5508336
2000	1501585	7148313	5449502
2001	1677665	6925619	5022617
2002	1989689	7732772	4861279
2003	2794439	9179629	5780646
2004	2619467	7765905	4983286
2005	4097225	11314125	5986051
2006	4530136	11994519	5830981
2007	6679699	16721647	9295019
2008	7251721	11133098	6934222
2009	10134370	15291263	8226162
2010	11930457	7751562	5210847
2011	12973505	12319069	8614405

4-25 主要年份市属新增固定资产及房屋竣工面积

Value of Newly Added Fixed Assets and Floor Spaces Completed of Municipal Units in Representative Years

年 份 Year	新增固定资产 (万元) Newly Increased Fixed Assets (10 000 yuan)	房屋竣工面积 (平方米) Floor Space of Buildings Completed (sq.m)	住 宅 Residential Buildings
1978	7529	249793	103060
1980	10664	497472	284022
1985	27872	986197	451128
1986	47827	1077660	690965
1987	56953	937402	417050
1988	50175	717169	351330
1989	69817	713432	315937
1990	69434	950215	501234
1991	67392	788184	377550
1992	108469	981637	417800
1993	181449	1384411	689602
1994	314996	1351075	894704
1995	273324	2025223	1433005
1996	296898	1984330	1487837
1997	374318	2264862	1666509
1998	521350	2383041	1691699
1999	859070	5012547	4074889
2000	953173	5094751	3735111
2001	1159980	5359752	3960060
2002	1295389	5374374	3314467
2003	1812099	6318902	3878178
2004	1962795	6062317	3887867
2005	3011104	7677031	4364275
2006	3495179	9147989	4324291
2007	5279938	13438785	7340515
2008	6488361	9870482	6026891
2009	8380033	13594584	7274105
2010	10423906	6684868	4484575
2011	10663882	10028229	7423155

4-26 各区县、开发区新增固定资产及房屋施工、竣工面积（2011年）

区县名称	Name of District and County	新增固定资产（亿元）Increased Fixed Assets (10 000 yuan)	房屋施工面积（平方米）Floor Space of Buildings Under Construction(sq.m)	住 宅 Residenctial Buildings
区 县	**Region**			
新城区	Xincheng	106.67	6039272	4306512
碑林区	Beilin	63.00	13033035	10901995
莲湖区	Lianhu	188.54	11415411	9178717
灞桥区	Baqiao	46.67	9525802	7199884
未央区	Weiyang	232.00	25274351	19779061
雁塔区	Yanta	197.91	29028697	22042848
阎良区	Yanliang	59.70	5854827	2744159
临潼区	Lintong	44.10	1913226	1519475
长安区	Chang'an	146.38	7923789	5141519
蓝田县	Lantian	47.48	1686513	1357470
周至县	Zhouzhi	17.17	2535959	1325915
户 县	Huxian	53.35	2993443	1539931
高陵县	Gaoling	92.29	6306780	1390784
开发区	**Development Zones**			
高新区	GaoXin	130.45	10889544	6199542
经开区	JingKai	143.82	9590569	5250409
曲江新区	Qujiang	72.93	6667106	5970556
浐灞生态区	Chanba Eco-District	8.70	5600064	5228791
航空基地	Aviation Industry Base	1.17	286921	145619
航天基地	Aerospace Base	7.85	4342120	2994957
国际港务区	International Trade&Logistic Park	0.26	163000	139000
沣东新城	FengDongXinCheng	15.71	600162	597862

Newly Added Fixed Assets and Floor Space of Constructing and Completed Buildings by Region and Development Zone（2011）

竣工房屋面积（平方米）Floor Space of Buildings Completed(sq.m)	住　宅 Residenctial Buildings	竣工房屋价值（万元）Value of Buildings Completed(sq.m)	住　宅 Residenctial Buildings	商品房销售面积（平方米）Floor Space of Houses Sales(sq.m)	商品房销售额（亿元）Sales Income of Commercial Houses(100 million yuan)
187582	185657	51822	51255	990584	61.86
423973	348120	156626	128166	1407732	79.53
1464711	1274820	484058	374575	1866365	108.13
410181	397681	113414	112135	1347192	65.70
3479168	2755983	984594	793516	4054780	221.12
2979990	2276102	887091	649721	4571787	373.68
187229	145791	60855	47095	549456	24.83
547499	281548	123406	65058	156641	6.20
251223	153864	93409	60734	1493428	84.16
126901	115071	35687	31990	474671	25.89
34664	24383	7500	4794	255059	12.79
1694328	459832	284747	94497	286995	13.55
531620	195553	94102	33465	325461	13.88
1235789	1075995	440604	381715	1513956	123.68
1224795	867172	302498	232956	1198163	71.33
1282239	1130243	530829	469089	2006796	191.75
121746	120246	46020	45473	549013	40.67
				16669	0.67
181450	89671	74490	43058	423267	24.74
59500	59500	27500	27500	59430	2.02

4-27 全市分行业施工项目（2011年）

行　业	Item	本年新增固定资产（万元）Increased Fixed Assets This Year(10 000 yuan)
合　计	**Total**	**12973505**
（一）农、林、牧、渔业	Agriculture, Forestry, Animal Husbandry and Fishery	321303
（二）采矿业	Mining	12330
（三）制造业	Manufacturing	1846870
（四）电力、燃气及水的生产和供应业	Generation and Supply of Electricity, Production and Supply of Gas and Water	189213
（五）建筑业	Construction	413329
（六）交通运输、仓储和邮政业	Transportation, Storage and Post	573003
（七）信息传输、计算机服务和软件业	Information Transmission, Computer Service and Software	162461
（八）批发和零售业	Wholesale and Retail Trades	501748
（九）住宿和餐饮业	Hotels and Catering Services	499815
（十）金融业	Financial Intermediation	20665
（十一）房地产业	Real Estate	4162863
（十二）租赁和商务服务业	Leasing and Business Services	145183
（十三）科学研究、技术服务和地质勘查业	Scientific Research, Technical Service and Geologic Prospecting	295526
（十四）水利、环境和公共设施管理业	Management of Water Conservancy, Environment and Public Facilities	1922623
（十五）居民服务和其他服务业	Services to Households and Other Services	98120
（十六）教育	Education	815311
（十七）卫生、社会保障和社会福利业	Health,Social Security and Social Welfare	182378
（十八）文化、体育和娱乐业	Culture, Sports and Entertainment	134080
（十九）公共管理和社会组织	Public Management and Social Organization	676684

Construction Projects of Whole City by Sector（2011）

施工项目个数（个） Number of Constructing Projects（unit）	本年新开工 Newly Started This Year	投产项目个数（个） Projects put into Use (unit)
1924	**1126**	**1057**
93	69	68
4	2	4
466	255	223
34	14	20
130	109	84
91	49	38
28	19	11
130	95	91
67	34	52
1	0	1
234	115	99
40	15	22
45	26	27
293	187	138
16	10	11
94	57	66
37	20	27
32	17	20
89	33	55

4-28 市属分行业施工项目（2011年）

行　业	Item	本年新增固定资产（万元）Increased Fixed Assets This Year(10 000 yuan)
合　计	**Total**	**10663882**
（一）农、林、牧、渔业	Agriculture, Forestry, Animal Husbandry and Fishery	321303
（二）采矿业	Mining	12330
（三）制造业	Manufacturing	1401974
（四）电力、燃气及水的生产和供应业	Generation and Supply of Electricity, Production and Supply of Gas and Water	171186
（五）建筑业	Construction	372128
（六）交通运输、仓储和邮政业	Transportation, Storage and Post	406398
（七）信息传输、计算机服务和软件业	Information Transmission, Computer Service and Software	125792
（八）批发和零售业	Wholesale and Retail Trades	463727
（九）住宿和餐饮业	Hotels and Catering Services	291151
（十）金融业	Financial Intermediation	20665
（十一）房地产业	Real Estate	3965424
（十二）租赁和商务服务业	Leasing and Business Services	141195
（十三）科学研究、技术服务和地质勘查业	Scientific Research, Technical Service and Geologic Prospecting	111517
（十四）水利、环境和公共设施管理业	Management of Water Conservancy, Environment and Public Facilities	1904823
（十五）居民服务和其他服务业	Services to Households and Other Services	88520
（十六）教育	Education	227081
（十七）卫生、社会保障和社会福利业	Health,Social Security and Social Welfare	89184
（十八）文化、体育和娱乐业	Culture, Sports and Entertainment	89249
（十九）公共管理和社会组织	Public Management and Social Organization	460235

Construction Projects of Municipal Units by Sector（2011）

施工项目个数（个） Number of Constructing Projects（unit）	本年新开工 Newly Started This Year	投产项目个数（个） Projects put into Use (unit)
1724	**1044**	**965**
92	68	68
4	2	4
416	232	204
31	11	17
123	106	80
83	48	33
26	18	11
122	92	86
60	34	47
1	0	1
215	106	92
36	14	21
26	18	19
279	177	136
15	9	10
58	44	49
31	18	22
27	15	18
79	32	47

4-29 主要年份房地产开发投资主要指标

单位：亿元、万平方米

指　标	Item	1997	1998	1999	2000	2001
本年完成投资额	Investment Completed This Year	24.68	38.21	44.30	51.85	67.42
本年房屋施工面积	Floor Space of Buildings Under Construction This Year	451.47	678.87	793.46	763.18	743.78
#住宅	Residential Buildings	331.16	552.37	649.53	619.85	580.43
本年房屋竣工面积	Floor Space of Buildings Completed This Year(sq.m)	135.62	156.17	377.79	321.10	316.24
#住宅	Residential Buildings	120.33	133.33	352.28	295.55	269.61
本年房屋竣工价值	Value of Floor Space of Buildings Completed	11.96	14.36	38.22	26.94	37.20
#住宅	Residential Buildings	9.63	11.00	33.02	22.97	28.62
商品房销售面积	Floor Space of Commercialized Buildings sold(sq.m)	78.45	117.11	296.97	212.92	225.35
#住宅	Residential Buildings	72.69	108.61	284.95	200.77	192.20
商品房销售额	Total Sales of Commercialized Buildings	12.81	17.74	35.19	32.52	47.22
#住宅	Residential Buildings	11.39	15.46	32.35	29.46	35.53
商品房预售面积	Floor Space of Commercialized Buildings Presold	26.35	252.02	30.25	253.03	67.44
#住宅	Residential Buildings	23.27	246.77	27.34	253.03	65.20
商品房空置面积	Floor Space of Vacant Commercialized Buildings	58.71	32.52	62.38	36.41	50.82
#住宅	Residential Buildings	50.26	22.81	52.32	24.02	34.18
商品房出租面积	Floor Space of Commercialized Buildings Recenting	25.69	1.04	1.88	1.17	9.19
#住宅	Residential Buildings	22.87	0.01	0.15	0.02	0.10
本年新增固定资产	Newly Increased Fixed Assets This Year	14.36	19.93	43.10	38.38	50.77

Main Indicators of Investment in Real Estate Development in Representative Years

(100 million yuan,10 000 sq.m)

2002	2003	2004	2005	2006	2007	2008	2009	2010	2011
79.37	124.82	169.67	225.23	285.76	387.33	540.26	696.34	842.34	996.81
1172.58	1343.12	1633.68	2174.29	2383.56	2915.95	3632.87	5708.63	6697.39	8247.69
964.68	943.61	1204.01	1783.36	1890.27	2376.82	3079.13	4901.59	5777.71	7108.27
329.71	339.67	380.84	361.62	399.64	483.30	443.96	542.81	463.65	631.03
290.30	289.56	308.06	316.52	342.15	422.47	412.46	453.49	412.44	564.59
36.93	54.73	73.75	80.58	82.02	101.13	106.50	168.08	145.62	213.29
30.46	44.01	55.58	68.11	65.80	77.13	96.02	137.42	128.69	185.31
252.90	252.74	305.47	497.34	621.50	833.92	760.72	1256.02	1587.81	1778.02
237.04	230.28	279.90	476.39	584.06	782.91	715.76	1202.12	1523.24	1674.85
51.35	54.29	81.35	171.29	206.15	281.79	296.44	488.55	707.00	1091.31
45.46	44.25	71.27	158.03	179.47	251.74	268.92	450.71	661.27	973.71
61.02	52.35	17.60	300.07	428.20	491.07	569.22	1125.44	1510.20	3105.76
55.73	49.12	159.10	287.13	408.11	457.54	541.20	1095.17	1452.20	2826.79
57.14	63.85	108.52	123.59	112.49	45.42	55.40	40.68	34.32	59.76
44.70	52.34	72.76	99.17	85.89	38.62	35.40	28.73	26.23	45.41
15.75	10.56	11.18	17.32	8.53	10.84	34.94	38.23	28.60	8.01
1.13	5.43	5.78	4.09	3.74	5.36	4.53	6.55	0.70	3.25
48.43	62.13	83.36	92.78	100.22	143.17	124.02	195.71	168.20	25.53

4-30 各区县、开发区房地产开发主要指标（2011年）

单位：万元

区县名称	Name of District and County	企业（单位）个数（个） Number of Enterprises (Unit)	本年完成投资 Investment Completed This Year	本年新增固定资产 Increased Fixed Assets This Year(10 000 yuan)
区　县	**Region**			
新城区	Xincheng	55	766475	68364
碑林区	Beilin	61	1580663	142626
莲湖区	Lianhu	58	890044	214132
灞桥区	Baqiao	42	501683	119539
未央区	Weiyang	92	1866793	588703
雁塔区	Yanta	121	3188440	1196159
阎良区	Yanliang	28	110147	10600
临潼区	Lintong	6	83831	34882
长安区	Chang'an	40	668725	78502
蓝田县	Lantian	10	63017	40000
周至县	Zhouzhi	11	34981	7500
户　县	Huxian	11	74404	35160
高陵县	Gaoling	19	138894	16694
开发区	**Development Zones**			
高新区	GaoXin	50	835388	572495
经开区	JingKai	35	585435	351897
曲江新区	Qujiang	27	1221388	530829
浐灞生态区	Chanba Eco-District	23	645029	51645
航空基地	Aviation Industry Base	5	47800	
航天基地	Aerospace Base	11	221160	47338
国际港务区	International Trade&Logistic Park	1	33400	19600
沣东新城	FengDongXinCheng	6	960	

Main Indicators of Real Estate Development by Region and Development Zone（2011）

(10 000 yuan)

房屋施工面积（平方米）Floor Space of Buildings Under Construction(sq.m)	住　宅 Residenctial Buildings	房屋竣工面积（平方米）Floor Space of Buildings Completed(sq.m)	住　宅 Residenctial Buildings	竣工房屋价值（万元）Value of Buildings Completed(10 000yuan)	住　宅 Residenctial Buildings
7147835	6155950	123545	123545	32122	32122
9802007	7853153	387912	348120	142626	128166
7701181	6472698	470001	309020	194037	99009
5960193	5500786	410181	397681	113414	112135
17423128	15521607	1506132	1295943	450779	386041
23501831	19842039	2750078	2544981	1019456	937937
1364327	1121789	46906	42661	10600	9500
474260	474260	120998	120998	20882	20882
5889791	5143307	142388	136226	65167	51335
569469	560739	96601	89871	29687	26990
804001	695059	34664	24383	7500	4794
634749	581844	137213	128741	29934	27519
1204130	1159495	83718	83718	16690	16690
8443114	5902258	1147388	1075995	408604	381715
5350488	4677131	858795	757172	248418	218876
6388615	5705251	1282239	1130243	530829	469089
5600064	5228791	121746	120246	46020	45473
226421	145619				
3259469	2810719	66195	60033	47338	33506
106562	106562	43500	43500	18500	18500
4000	4000				

4-31 房地产开发投资主要指标（2011年）

Main Indicators of Investment in Real Estate Development（2011）

单位：万元 (10 000 yuan)

指标	Item	全市合计 Total	国有 State-owned	市区 Urban Area	市属 Municipal
一、企业(单位)个数(个)	**Number of Enterprises(unit)**	**579**	**34**	**528**	**529**
二、本年完成投资	**Investment Completed This Year**	**9968097**	**590529**	**9713556**	**9001953**
按工程用途分	Grouped by Function				
住宅	Residential Buildings	8343108	458342	8107350	7606546
#别墅、高档公寓	Villas and Top-Grade Apartments	368130	18775	368130	368130
办公楼	Office Buildings	300862	12414	299892	269581
商业营业用房	Houses for Business Use	812529	46230	797519	750013
其他	Others	511598	73543	508795	375813
三、本年新增固定资产	**Increased Fixed Assets This Year**	**2552861**	**134622**	**2460507**	**2387311**
四、房屋施工面积(平方米)	**Floor Space of Buildings Under Construction (sq.m)**	**82476902**	**5910200**	**80226015**	**76014815**
#住宅	Residential Buildings	71082726	5384600	68957227	65431389
五、竣工房屋面积(平方米)	**Floor Space of Buildings Completed (sq.m)**	**6310337**	**380998**	**5994221**	**5877226**
#住宅	Residential Buildings	5645888	380998	5352725	5313772
竣工房屋价值	Value of Buildings Completed	2132894	129258	2055717	1987444
#住宅	Residential Buildings	1853120	129258	1783027	1743157
六、商品房销售面积(平方米)	**Floor Space of Commercialized Buildings Sold(sq.m)**	**17780151**	**1292075**	**16912983**	**16245359**
商品房销售额	Sales Income of Commercialized Buildings	10913135	780225	10609101	10148690

4-32 商品房销售情况（2011年）

Sales of Commercial Houses（2011）

指　　标	Item	全市合计 Total	国 有 State Owned	市 区 Urban Area	市 属 municipal
商品房销售面积(平方米)	**Floor Space of Commercialized Buildings Sold(sq.m)**	**17780151**	**1292075**	**16912983**	**16245359**
现房销售面积	**Floor Space of Completed Apartment Sales**	**886941**	**52994**	**863399**	**520421**
期房销售面积	**Floor Space of Forward Delivery Housing Sales**	**16893210**	**1239081**	**16049584**	**15724938**
住宅	Residential Buildings	16748518	1260040	15916087	15309740
#别墅、高档公寓	Villas and High-grade Apartments	511865		511865	511865
办公楼	Office Buildings	303375	9955	302375	291779
商业营业用房	Houses for Business Use	531242	20126	501135	494473
其他	Others	197016	1954	193386	149367
商品房销售额(万元)	**Sales Income of Commercialized Buildings (10 000 yuan)**	**10913135**	**780225**	**10609101**	**10148690**
现房销售额(万元)	**Floor Space of Completed Apartment Sales**	**400695**	**27551**	**394220**	**252410**
期房销售额(万元)	**Floor Space of Forward Delivery Housing Sales**	**10512440**	**752674**	**10214881**	**9896280**
住宅	Residential Buildings	9737148	741238	9448313	9040933
#别墅、高档公寓	Villas and High-grade Apartments	505147		505147	505147
办公楼	Office Buildings	298510	8276	297827	292202
商业营业用房	Houses for Business Use	758123	29904	744649	715422
其他	Others	119354	807	118312	100133
商品房空置面积(平方米)	**Vacancy of Commercialized Buildings(sq.m)**	**597645**	**102332**	**581777**	**562153**
#待售一年以上	Being Idle for One Year	326485	27532	325781	307622
待售三年以上(含三年）	Being Idle for One Year	1176		1176	1176
住宅	Residence	454064	87400	438196	429612
#别墅、高档公寓	Villas and High-grade Apartments				
办公楼	Office Buildings	2901	2666	2901	235
商业营业用房	Houses for Business Use	72719	4864	72719	71747
其他	Others	67961	7402	67961	60559
商品房出租面积(平方米)	**Floor Space of Commercialized Leased Buildings(sq.m)**	**80075**	**6900**	**80075**	**66520**
住宅	Residential Buildings	32533		32533	32533
办公楼	Office Buildings	256		256	256
商业营业用房	Houses for Business Use	47286	6900	47286	33731
其他	Others				

4-33 房地产开发投资资金来源（2011年）

Source of Funds for Investment in Real Estate Development（2011）

单位：万元 (10 000 yuan)

指 标	Item	全市合计 Total	国有 State-owned	市区 Urban Area	市属 Municipal
一、本年资金来源合计	**Total**	**18048367**	**1170106**	**17643500**	**16363445**
1.上年末结余资金	Balance of Last Year	3392728	291777	3344462	2912739
2.本年资金来源小计	Total Funds This Year	14655639	878329	14299038	13450706
(1) 国内贷款	Domestic Loans	1871437	192650	1867807	1627382
#银行贷款	Bank Loan	1646014	174650	1642384	1455959
非银行金融机构贷款	Loans from financial Institutions except Bank	225423	18000	225423	171423
(2) 利用外资	Utilization of Foreign Funds	18		18	18
#外商直接投资	Foreign Direct Investment				
(3) 自筹资金	Self-raising Funds	4750053	205831	4633507	4410608
#自有资金	Funds at the disposal of Enterprises	2248326	54360	2199112	2079618
(4) 其他资金	Others	8034131	479848	7797706	7412698
#定金及预付款	Earnest Money and Advance payment	4894996	293834	4823899	4617783
个人按揭贷款	Personal Mortgage loan	2146003	114872	1999165	2047707
二、本年各项应付款合计	**Total Sums of Money to be Paid This Year**	**1303213**	**87224**	**1157727**	**1218250**
#工程款	Project Fund	726888	54906	655561	675535

4-34 房地产开发经营情况（2011年）

Running of Real Estate Development（2011）

单位：万元 (10 000 yuan)

指 标	Item	全市合计 Total	国有 State-owned	市区 Urban Area	市属 Municipal
一、资产负债情况	**Assets and Liabilities**				
1.资产总计	Total Assets	**28591720**	**2309844**	**28084391**	**26382058**
2.负债总计	Total Liabilities	22834861	2061650	22375648	21195411
3.所有者权益合计	Total Creditor's Equity	5756874	248195	5708742	5186647
#实收资本	Held Capital	4029266	185862	3964533	3738866
二、损益及分配情况	**Profit or Loss and the Distribution**				
1.主营业务收入	Revenue from Principal Business	8353923	440245	8331162	7826753
土地转让收入	Revenue of Land Transferred	11129	8748	10129	11129
商品房屋销售收入	Revenue of Commercial Houses Sold	8218332	417018	8205090	7701684
房屋出租收入	Revenue of Houses Leased	28846	3359	25846	26307
其他收入	Other Revenue	95616	11120	90096	87632
2.主营业务成本	Cost of Principal Business	6160356	325802	5957951	5624025
3.主营业务税金及附加	Taxes and Other Charges on Principal Business	553064	23328	539546	485477
4.其他业务利润	Other Business Profit	6488	94	6488	6394
5.销售费用	Sales Expenditures	246597	13996	237929	232313
6.管理费用	Management Cost	264925	21965	257100	247079
#税金	Tax	19389	1335	19010	17329
差旅费	Travel Expense	10571	336	10144	9976
工会经费	Labor Union Expenditure	1013	116	893	872
7.财务费用	Fiscal Expenditure	52110	2517	50358	48495
#利息支出	Interest Exchange	44362	2310	44030	41446
8.营业利润	Operating Profit	1034604	53816	981511	942967
投资收益	Investment Revenue	8377	2014	8377	4026
营业外收入	Non-business Revenue	1775	139	1748	1704
营业外支出	Non-business Expenditures	15689	920	12951	10370
9.利润总额	Total Profit	945928	50916	891022	852467
10.应付职工薪酬	Salary Payable	153188	16744	129561	110416

主要统计指标解释

全社会固定资产投资 是以货币形式表现的在一定时期内全社会建造和购置固定资产的工作量以及与此有关的费用的总称。该指标是反映固定资产投资规模、结构和发展速度的综合性指标,又是观察工程进度和考核投资效果的重要依据。全社会固定资产投资按登记注册类型可分为国有、集体、联营、股份制、私营和个体、港澳台商、外商、其他等。

城镇固定资产投资 指城镇各种登记注册类型的企业、事业、行政单位及个体户进行的计划总投资50万元及50万元以上的建设项目投资和房地产开发投资。县城及以上区域内发生的投资，县及县以上各级政府及主管部门直接领导、管理的建设项目和企业事业单位的投资均为城镇固定资产投资。

房地产开发投资 指各种登记注册类型的房地产开发公司、商品房建设公司及其他房地产开发法人单位和附属于其他法人单位实际从事房地产开发或经营活动的单位统一开发的包括统代建、拆迁还建的住宅、厂房、仓库、饭店、宾馆、度假村、写字楼、办公楼等房屋建筑物和配套的服务设施，土地开发工程（如道路、给水、排水、供电、供热、通讯、平整场地等基础设施工程）的投资；不包括单纯的土地交易活动。

农村投资 包括在农村区域范围内进行固定资产投资活动的企业、事业、行政单位及农户投资。

固定资产投资的资金来源 根据固定资产投资的资金来源不同，分为国家预算资金、国内贷款、利用外资、自筹资金和其他资金。

（1）国家预算资金：包括一般预算、政府性基金预算、国有资本经营预算和社保基金预算等资金。

（2）国内贷款：指报告期固定资产投资单位向银行及非银行金融机构借入的用于固定资产投资的各种国内借款，包括银行利用自有资金及吸收的存款发放的贷款、上级主管部门拨入的国内贷款、国家专项贷款、地方财政专项资金安排的贷款、国内储备贷款、周转贷款等。

（3）利用外资：指报告期收到的用于固定资产建造和购置的境外资金（包括设备、材料、技术在内）。包括对外借款（外国政府、国际金融组织贷款、出口信贷、外国银行商业贷款、对外发行债券和股票）、外商直接投资及外商其他投资。不包括我国自有外汇资金（国家外汇、地方外汇、留成外汇、调剂外汇和中国银行自有资金发行的外汇贷款等）。计算利用外资时，需要折算成人民币，折算中所使用的外汇汇率按现汇计算，即按使用外汇时的汇率计算。

（4）自筹资金：指固定资产投资单位报告期收到的，由各地区、各部门及企、事业单位筹集用于固定资产投资的预算外资金，包括中央各部门、各级地方和企、事业单位的自筹资金。

（5）其他资金：指在报告期收到的除以上各种资金之外其他用于固定资产投资的资金，包括企业或金融机构通过发行各种债券筹集到的资金、社会集资、个人资金、无偿捐赠的资金及其他单位拨入的资金等。

固定资产投资按国民经济行业分 根据现有企业、事业、行政单位和建设项目建成投产后的主要产品种类或主要用途及社会经济活动性质来确定国民经济行业。一般情况下，一个建设项目或一个企业、事业单位只能属于一种国民经济行业。

固定资产投资按隶属关系分 是按建设单位或企业、事业、行政单位的主管上级机关确定的。

（1）中央：是指中共中央、人大常委会和国务院各部、委、局、总公司以及直属机构直接领导的建设项目和企业、事业、行政单位。这些单位的固定资产投资计划由国务院各部门直接编制和下达，建设中所需物资、主要设备以及建设中的问题都由中央有关部门安排和解决。

（2）地方：是由省（自治区、直辖市）、地区（州、盟、省辖市）、县（旗、县级市）三级政府及业务主管部门直接领导和管理的建设项目、企业、事业、行政单位。地方项目还包括不隶属以上各级政府及主管部门的建设项目和企业、事业单位，如外商投资企业和无主管部门的企业等。

固定资产投资按建设性质分 根据整个建设项目情况来确定。建设项目的性质一般分为新建、扩建、改建和技术改造、单纯建造生活设施、迁建、恢复、单纯购置。房地产开发单位、农户投资不划分建设性质。

（1）新建：一般指从无到有开始建设的企业、事业和行政单位或建设项目。有的单位原有基础很小，经过建设后新增的固定资产价值超过该企、事业、行政单位原有固定资产价值（原值）三倍以上的也应作为新建。

（2）扩建：指在厂内或其他地点，为扩大原有产品的生产能力（或效益）或增加新的产品生产能力，而增建主要的生产车间（或主要工程）、分厂、独立的生产线。行政、事业单位在原单位增建业务用房（如学校增建教学用房、医院增建门诊部、病房等）也作为扩建。

现有企、事业单位为扩大原有主要产品生产能力或增加新的产品生产能力，增建一个或几个主要生产车间（或主要工程）、分厂，同时进行一些更新改造工程的，也应作为扩建。

（3）改建和技术改造：指现有企业、事业单位，对原有设施进行技术改造或更新（包括相应配套的辅助性生产、生活福利设施）的建设项目。现有企业、事业单位为适应市场变化的需要，而改变企业的主要产品种类（如军工企业转产民用品等）的建设项目，应作为改建。原有产品生产作业线由于各工序（车间）之间能力不平衡，为填平补齐充分发挥原有生产能力而增建不增加本企业主要产品设计能力的车间，也应作为改建。技术改造是指企业、事业单位在现有基础上，用先进的技术代替落后的技术，用先进的工艺和装备代替落后的工艺和装备，以改变企业落后的技术经济面貌，实现以内涵为主的扩大再生产，达到提高产品质量、促进产品更新换代、节约能源、降低消耗、扩大生产规模、全面提高社会经济效益的目的。技术改造具体包括以下内容：机器设备和工具的更新改造；生产工艺改革、节约能源和原材料的改造；厂房建筑和公共设施的改造；劳动条件和生产环境的改造等。

固定资产投资按构成分 固定资产投资活动按其工作内容和实现方式分为建筑安装工程，设备工具器具购置和其他费用三个部分。

（1）建筑安装工程（建筑安装工作量）：指各种房屋、建筑物的建造工程和各种设备、装置的安装工程。包括各种房屋建造工程；各种用途设备基础和各种工业窑炉的砌筑工程及金属结构工程；为施工而进行的各种准备工作和临时工程以及完工后的清理工作等；铁路、道路的铺设，矿井的开凿及石油管道的架设等；水利工程；防空地下建筑等特殊工程；列入房屋工程预算内的暖气、卫生、通风、照明、煤气等设备的价值及装设油饰工程；列入建筑工程预算内的各种管道（蒸汽、压缩空气、石油、给排水等管道）、电力、电讯电缆导线等的敷设工程；以及各种机械设备的安装工程；为测定安装工程质量，对设备进行的试运工作；房地产开发单位进行的商品房屋开发建设工程、土地开发工程。

在建筑安装工程中，不包括被安装设备本身的价值。

（2）设备工具器具购置：指建设单位或企、事业单位购置或自制的，达到固定资产标准的设备、工具、器具的价值。新建单位及扩建单位的新建车间，按照设计或计划要求购置或自制的全部设备、工具、器具，不论是否达到固定资产标准均计入“设备工具器具购置”中。

（3）其他费用：指在固定资产建造和购置过程中发生的，除上述几项内容以外的各种应分摊计入固定资产的费用。

施工项目 指报告期内所有施工的建设项目个数，包括本年新开工的项目和以前年度开工在本年继续施工的建设项目。凡是报告期内施过工的建设项目，不论施工时间长短，均作为施工项目统计。施工项目个数可以反映一定时期固定资产投资的实际规模，与同期全部建成投产项目个数相比，可以从建设速度的角度反映固定资产投资的效果。

全部建成投产项目 指报告期内按设计文件规定的全部生产能力（或效益）建成投产，经验收合格交付使用的建设项目。

新增生产能力（或工程效益） 指通过固定资产投资活动而增加的设计能力（或工程效益）。主要指标包括建设规模、本年施工规模、自开始建设累计新增生产能力（或工程效益）、本年新增生产能力（或工程效益）等。

建设规模 指建设项目或工程设计文件中规定的全部设计能力（或工程效益）。包括已经建成投产和尚未建成投产的工程的生产能力（或工程效益）。

本年施工规模 指报告期内施工的单项工程的设计能力（或工程效益），即全部建设规模中在本年正式施工的部分。

自开始建设累计新增生产能力（或工程效益） 指自开始建设至本年底止建成投产的全部单项工程累计的新增生产能力（或工程效益）。

本年新增生产能力（或工程效益） 指在本年度内按照新增生产能力（或工程效益）的计算条件和标准，实际建成投入生产或交付使用的生产能力（或工程效益）。

施工房屋面积 指报告期内施工的全部房屋（包括地下室、半地下室以及配套房屋）建筑面积。包括本期新开工的面积和上期开工跨入本期继续施工的房屋面积，以及上期已停建在本期恢复施工的房屋面积。本期竣工和本期施工后又停缓建的房屋，其建筑面积仍计入本期房屋施工面积中。

竣工房屋面积 指在报告期内房屋建筑按照设计要

求已经全部完工，达到住人和使用条件，经验收鉴定合格（或达到竣工验收标准），可正式移交使用单位的各栋房屋建筑面积的总和。

新增固定资产 指报告期内交付使用的固定资产价值。包括本年内建成投入生产或交付使用的工程投资和达到固定资产标准的设备、工具、器具的投资及有关应摊入的费用。该指标是表示固定资产投资成果的价值指标，也是反映建设进度，计算固定资产投资效果的重要指标。

项目建成投产率 指一定时期内全部建成投产项目个数与同期施工项目个数的比率。该指标是从建设单位建设速度的角度反映投资效果的指标。

固定资产交付使用率 指一定时期新增固定资产与同期完成投资额的比率。该指标是反映固定资产动用速度，衡量建设过程中宏观投资效果的综合指标。由于新增固定资产是较长时期内形成的结果，而投资额则是当年完成的，因此，该指标一般适宜于反映较长时期内固定资产的动用情况。

商品房销售面积 指报告期内出售商品房屋的合同总面积（即双方签署的正式买卖合同中所确定的建筑面积）。由现房销售建筑面积和期房销售建筑面积两部分组成。

商品房销售额 指报告期内出售商品房屋的合同总价款（即双方签署的正式买卖合同中所确定的合同总价）。该指标与商品房销售面积同口径，由现房销售额和期房销售额两部分组成。

经济适用房 指根据经济适用房计划安排建设的政策性住宅。经济是指房屋建筑造价和销售价格低于一般商品住宅；适用是指适合中低收入家庭购买使用。经济适用房主要是由地方政府统一下达投资计划，房地产公司开发，对外销售；用地一般采用行政划拨或招标投标方式，免收土地出让金；对各种经批准的收费减半征收，开发利润不超过3%；销售价格实行政府指导价。该指标可以分析房地产投资结构，反映中低收入家庭商品住宅的供求平衡情况。

Explanatory Notes on Main Statistical Indicators

Total Investment in Fixed Assets in the Whole Country refers to the volume of activities in construction and purchases of fixed assets of the whole country and related fees, expressed in monetary terms during the reference period. It is a comprehensive indicator which shows the size, structure and growth of the investment in fixed assets, providing a basis for observing the progress of construction projects and evaluating results of investment. Total investment in fixed assets in the whole country includes, by type of ownership, the investment by State-owned units, collective-owned units, joint ownership units, share-holding units, private units individuals as well as investments by entrepreneurs from Hong Kong, Macao and Taiwan, foreign investors and others.

Urban Investment in Fixed Assets refers to construction projects involving a total planned investment of 500,000 yuan and over by enterprises of various types of ownership, institutions, administrative units and individuals in urban areas, investment in real estate development. In other words, all investments that take place in county towns and urban areas, investment in construction projects under the direct leadership and management of government agencies at and above county levels and investments by enterprises and institutions at and above county levels are covered in urban investment in fixed assets.

Investment in Real Estate Development refers to investment by real estate development companies, commercialized buildings construction companies and other real estate development units of various types of ownership in the construction of buildings, such as residential buildings, factory buildings, warehouses, hotels, guesthouses, holiday villages, office buildings, and the complementary service facilities and land development projects, such as roads, water supply, water drainage, power supply, heating supply, telecommunications, land leveling and other infrastructural projects. It does not include activities in pure land transactions.

Investment in Rural Areas refers to investment in fixed assets by enterprises, institutions, administrative units and households in rural areas.

Sources of Funds for Investment in Fixed Assets are categorized as funds from the State budget, domestic loans, foreign investment, self-raised funds, and others, depending on the sources of investment.

(1) Fund from the State budget consists of budgetary appropriation and loans from the State budget. More specifically, it includes, from the budget of the central government, capital construction fund (operation fund and non-operational fund), special expenses, loans from repayment, discount fund, expenses on innovation and trial production of new products, expenses on urban construction, expenses on temporary construction from business departments, development fund for less developed areas, as well as local budgetary fund transferred from the central budget.

(2) Domestic loans refer to loans of various forms borrowed by investing units from banks and non-bank financial institutions during the reference period for the purpose of investment in fixed assets, including loans issued by banks from their self-owned funds and deposit, loans appropriated by higher authorities, special loans by government, loans arranged by local government from special funds, domestic reserve loan, and working loan.

(3) Foreign investment refers to overseas funds received during the reference period for the construction and purchase of investment in fixed assets (covering equipment, materials and technology), including foreign borrowings (loans from foreign governments and international financial institutions, export credit, commercial loans from foreign banks, issue of bonds and stocks overseas), foreign direct investment and other foreign investments. Excluded from this category is capital in foreign exchanges owned by China (foreign exchanges owned by the central and local governments, foreign exchanges retained by enterprises, foreign exchanges by enterprises through the regulating mechanism, loans in foreign exchanges issued by the Bank of China with its own fund, etc.). In calculating the utilization of foreign capital, foreign currencies are converted into Chinese Renminbi applying the current exchange rate when the foreign capitals are actually used.

(4) Self-raised funds refer to extra-budgetary funds for investment in fixed assets received during the reference period by investing units from central government ministries, local governments, enterprises and institutions, including their self-raised funds.

(5) Others refer to funds for investment in fixed

assets received from sources other than those listed above, including capital raised through issuing bonds by enterprises or financial institutions, funds raised from individuals and through donations, and funds transferred from other units.

Investment in Fixed Assets by Sector The classification of construction projects by sector is determined by enterprises, institutions, administrative units and the major products or the purpose of the projects of existing enterprises, institutional and administrative units when they are put into production or use, and by the nature of their social economic activities. In general, one project or one enterprise or institution can only be classified into one sector.

Investment in Fixed Assets by Jurisdiction of Management refers to the classification of investment by the competent authorities under which investment is made by construction units, enterprises, institutions or administrative units.

(1) Central investment refers to the investment in projects or by enterprises, institutions or administrative units which are under the direct leadership and management of the State Council and of the national commissions, ministries, agencies and State-owned large corporations. Various ministries and departments of the State Council prepare and implement plans for investment in fixed assets by those departments, and arrange and ensure the supply of materials and key equipment required for the projects.

(2) Local investment refers to the investment in projects or by enterprises, institutions or administrative units which are under the direct leadership and management of departments under the provincial, prefecture and county governments. Also included are projects by foreign-invested enterprises and enterprises without competent managing authorities.

Investment in Fixed Assets by Type of Construction Construction projects in general can be classified, by the type of construction, into new construction, expansion, reconstruction and technical transformation, purely construction of living facilities, moving, restoration and purely purchasing. However, investment by type of construction is not applied to investment by real-estate development units and investment by rural households.

(1) New construction in general refers to construction projects, which start from scratch, of enterprises, institutions, administrative agencies. In case the size of the existing unit is quite small, and the value of newly added fixed assets is more than three times of the original value, the expansion will be considered as new construction.

(2) Expansion refers to construction of new major production workshop, branch factory or independent production line within a factory or in other locations, for the purpose of increasing the production capacity (or improving efficiency) or adding new production capacity. Newly constructed accommodation for the operation of institutions and administrative organizations (such as newly constructed buildings for teaching in schools, buildings for clinics or wards in hospitals, etc.) are also classified as expansion.

Also included in expansion are investments by existing enterprises or institutions in building major production line(s) or branch factory(ies) along with some work on innovation, for the purpose of expanding the production capacity of original products or producing new products.

(3) Reconstruction and technical transformation refers to construction projects by existing enterprises or institutions in innovation or technical transformation of the old facilities (including auxiliary production equipment and welfare facilities). Also considered as reconstruction is the construction of new workshops by the existing enterprises or institutions to change the variety of products to meet the market demand (such as the production of civil products by defence industries), or to bring the designed production capacity into full play through a more balanced production process on production lines. Technical transformation refers to replacement of old technology or equipment by new technology or equipment, in order to expand the reproduction through improvement of technology contents in production, to improve product quality, to promote new products, to save energy, to reduce consumption, to expand the production scale and to improve overall social-economic efficiency. Contents of technical transformation include: updating of machinery, equipment and tools; reforming production process by using energy or materials saving technology; construction of factory workshops and transformation of public facilities; improvement of working conditions and environment, etc.

Investment in Fixed Assets by Structure By their contents and the mode of implementation, investment activities are classified into 3 categories, i.e. construction and installation, purchase of equipment and instrument, and other expenses.

(1) Construction and installation (work volume of construction and installation) refers to the construction of houses and buildings and the installation of various kinds of equipment and instruments. They include construction of houses; equipment foundations, industrial kilns and stoves, and metal structure work; preparation works and temporary works for project construction, and clearing up works post project construction; pavement of railways and roads, drilling of mines and putting up of oil pipes; construction of water conservancy; construction of underground air-raid shelters and construction of other special projects; value of equipment for heating, sanitation, ventilation, lighting, gas, painting, etc. that are covered by the budget of housing projects; laying out of various pipelines (for steam, compressed air, petroleum, tap water and sewage) and wiring and cabling for electric power and for communications; installation of various machinery and equipment; testing operation for pre-testing the quality of installation projects, and land and other development work conducted by real estate developers for commercialized housing.

The value of equipment installed is itself not included in the value of construction and installation projects.

(2) Purchase of equipment and instruments refers to the total value of equipment, tools, and instruments purchased or self-produced which come up to the cut-off point for fixed assets by the construction units or investing enterprises or institutions. Equipment, tools and instruments purchased or self-produced for new workshops by newly established or expanded units are categorized as " purchase of equipment and instruments" no matter whether they come up to the cut-off point for fixed assets.

(3) Other expenses refer to expenses arising during the construction or purchase of fixed assets other than those mentioned above.

Projects under Construction refer to number of all projects with construction activities newly started in current year or left-over from the previous year in the reference period. All projects that have construction activities undertaken during the reference period are reported as projects under construction irrespective of the length of construction work. The number of projects under construction can reflect the actual size of investment in fixed assets during a given period, and when compared with the number of projects completed and put into use during the same period, it demonstrates the results of investment in fixed assets from the angle of the speed of the construction.

Projects Completed and Put into Use refer to projects have been completed in accordance with the design documents, resulting in forming production capacity (efficiency) and have been checked and accepted after relevant tests, and have been formally delivered for use.

Newly Increased Production Capacity (or Project Efficiency) refers to the increase in design capacity (or project efficiency) through investment in fixed assets. The main indicators include: construction scale, scale of projects under construction in current year, the accumulated newly increased production capacity (project efficiency) since the start of the projects and the newly increased production capacity (project efficiency) of current year.

Construction Scale refers to the total designed production capacity (project efficiency) of the construction projects in accordance with the design document, including those have been put into operation and those that have not been completed.

Scale of Projects under Construction in Current Year refers to the designed production capacity (project efficiency) of a single project under construction in the reference period, i.e. the part of the total scale of project which is officially under construction in current year.

The Accumulated Newly Increased Production Capacity (project efficiency) since the Start of the Projects refers to the accumulated newly increased production capacity of all the single projects which have been put into use from the beginning of the projects till the end of current year.

The Newly Increased Production Capacity (project efficiency) of Current Year refers to the production capacity (project efficiency) that has been completed and put into operation in current year according to the calculation conditions and standards on newly increased production capacity (project efficiency).

Floor Space of Buildings under Construction refers to the total floor space of all the buildings (including basement, semi-basement and auxiliary buildings), including the effective area and the area occupied by the structure. This indicator is one of the important indicators in physical terms to reflect the scale and accomplishment of the construction industry and also an important basis for monitoring the progress, calculating the cost, analyzing the efficiency and studying the supply of building materials in relation to the construction projects.

Floor Space Completed refers to the floor space of all buildings completed in the reference period, which have been appraised and accepted (or come up to the designed standards) and have been transferred to owner units.

Newly Increased Fixed Assets refer to the value of fixed that has been put into use, including investment in projects that have been completed and put into operation in current year and the investment in equipment, tools and appliance that meet the standard of fixed assets and fees that should be apportioned. This is an indicator that demonstrates the results of investment in fixed assets in monetary terms, and an important indicator to reflect the speed of construction and to calculate the efficiency of investment.

Rate of Construction Projects Completed and Put into Use refers to the ratio of the number of construction projects completed and put into use in a certain period of time to the number of projects under construction in the same period. This reflects the investment efficiency from the perspective of the speed of projects construction.

Rate of Projects of Fixed Assets Completed and Put into Operation refers to the ratio of the newly increased fixed assets to the total investment made in the same period. This is a comprehensive indicator reflecting the speed of the employment of fixed assets and the investment efficiency at the macro-level. As the newly increase fixed assets is the result of a long period while the investment is completed in the current year, this indicator is expected to be used to reflect the employment of fixed assets over a long period of time.

Area of Commercialized Housing Sold refers to total contracted area of commercialized housing (i.e. area of floor space as designated in the formal contracts signed by both sides) during the reference time. It constitutes floor space of completed housing and floor space of future housing.

Value of Commercialized Housing Sold refers to the total contracted value (i.e. value of sales/purchase for selling/purchase of commercialized housing as designated in the contract signed by both sides) during the reference time. This indicator has the same coverage as the area of commercialized housing sold, which constitutes floor space of completed housing and floor space of housing yet to be completed.

Economically Affordable Housing refers to housing constructed according to the State Plan for economically affordable housing. The features of houses of this category are low cost of construction and low prices, and therefore are affordable to mid-income and low income households. Economically affordable housing projects are developed and saled by real estate companies under the Local Government Investment Plan. Developers are exempted from land utilization fees and enjoy another 50% exemption of all other legitimate fees, while their profits are limited to less than 3%, and the completed houses are sold under government-guided prices. This indicator helps to analyze the investment structure of the real estate industry and the demand and supply of housing for mid-income and low income households.

5 财　政

GOVERNMENT FINANCE

资料整理：刘　婷
Data management:Liu Ting

第五部分　财政

一、简要说明

本章资料主要包括地方财政收入、支出总额构成及分区县情况，由西安市统计局综合处根据西安市财政局提供资料整理。

二、主要指标

财政总收入（亿元）	649.88	比上年增长 27.3%
一般预算收入（亿元）	318.55	比上年增长 31.7%
一般预算支出（亿元）	494.58	比上年增长 33.1%

5　GOVERNMENT FINANCE

Ⅰ.Brief Introduction

This chapter consists primarily of data on regional revenue, expenditure of the municipal government, regional revenue and expenditure of the districts and the counties. The data are provided by the Xi'an Bureau of Finance and are compiled by Integration division of the Xi'an Bureau of Statistics.

Ⅱ.Major Indicators

		Increase over Preceding Year
Total Government Revenue(100 mil. Yuan)	649.88	27.3%
General Budgetary Revenue(100 mil. Yuan)	318.55	31.7%
Ordinary Budgetary Expenditures(100 mil. Yuan)	494.58	33.1%

5-1 主要年份地方财政一般预算收入及支出

General Budgetary Local Government Revenue and Expenditure in Representative Years

单位：亿元 （100 million yuan）

年 份 Year	地方财政一般预算收入 General Budgetary Revenue of Local Government	地方财政一般预算支出 General Budgetary Expenditure of Local Government
2000	46.80	52.00
2001	51.45	57.30
2002	54.50	63.80
2003	72.90	76.60
2004	75.30	87.30
2005	72.92	97.61
2006	85.89	119.22
2007	112.92	161.25
2008	145.61	226.99
2009	181.40	276.85
2010	241.86	371.62
2011	318.55	494.58

5-2 财政收入（2011年）

Government Revenue（2011）

单位：万元　　　　（10 000 yuan）

指　　标	Item	2011
财政总收入	**Total Government Revenue**	**6498826**
#一般预算收入	**General Budgetary Revenue**	**3185486**
一、税收收入	**Total Tax Revenue**	**2615050**
1.增值税	Value Added Tax	253176
2.营业税	Business Tax	1083523
3.企业所得税	Corporate Income Tax	249501
4.企业所得税退税	Return for Corporate Income Tax	
5.个人所得税	Individual Income Tax	97884
6.资源税	Resource Tax	363
7.固定资产投资方向调节税	Tax on Adjustment of the Orientation of Investment in Fixed Assets	
8.城市维护建设税	City Maintenance and Construction Tax	212619
9.房产税	House Property Tax	88231
10.印花税	Stamp Tax	63386
11.城镇土地使用税	Urban Land Use Tax	67394
12.土地增值税	Land Appreciation Tax	155318
13.车船税	Tax on the Use of Vehicles and Ships	38715
14.耕地占用税	Farm Land Occupatian Tax	132792
15.契税	Deed Tax	172148
16.其他税收收入	Other Tax Revenue	
二、非税收入	**Total Non-tax Revenue**	**570436**
1.专项收入	Special Program Receipts	104655
2.行政事业性收费收入	Charge of Adminnistrative and Institutional Units	250679
3.罚没收入	Penalty Receipts	77110
4.国有资本经营收入	State-owned Assets Profit	34114
5.国有资源（资产）有偿使用收入	Revenue for the use of State-owned Assets（Resources）	100048
6.其他收入	Other Revenue	3830
政府性基金收入	**Governmental Fund Revenue**	**2555954**

5-3 财政支出（2011年）

Government Expenditures（2011）

单位:万元 (10 000 yuan)

指 标	Item	2011
一、政府性基金支出	**Governmental Fund Revenue Expenditure**	**2527691**
二、一般预算支出	**General Budgetary Expenditure**	**4945750**
1.一般公共服务支出	Expenditure for General Public Services	544839
2.国防支出	Expenditure for National Defense	8875
3.公共安全支出	Expenditure for Public Security	284056
4.教育支出	Expenditure for Education	745310
5.科学技术支出	Expenditure for Science and Technology	52192
6.文化体育与传媒支出	Expenditure for Cultural, sports and the media	97611
7.社会保障和就业支出	Expenditure for Social Safety Net and Employment Effort	614349
8.医疗卫生支出	Expenditure for Medical and Health Care	336241
9.节能环保支出	Expenditure for Energy Saving and Environment Protection	66108
10.城乡社区事务支出	Expenditure for Urban and Rural Community Affairs	662640
11.农林水事务支出	Expenditure for Agriculture, Forestry and Water Conservancy	387899
12.交通运输支出	Expenditure for Transportation	261474
13.资源勘探电力信息等事务支出	Expenditure for Mining ,Electricity and Information	194948
14.商业服务业等事务支出	Expenditure for Commerce and Services	134479
15.金融监管等事务支出	Expenditure for Financial Supervision	29898
16.地震灾后恢复重建支出	Expenditure for Post-earthquake Recovery and Reconstruction	25
17.国土资源气象等事务支出	Expenditure for Land Recources and Meteorological Affairs	20299
18.住房保障支出	Expenditure for Housing Support	318294
19.粮油物资储备管理等事务支出	Material Reserves Management Affairs Spending	9763
20.储备事务支出	Expenditure for Reserve	12118
21.国债还本付息支出	Expenditure for National Debt and Interest(10 000yuan)	62898
22.其它支出	Other Expenditure	101434

5-4 各区县、开发区一般预算收入（2011年）

General Budgetary Revenue by Region and Development Zone（2011）

单位：万元 （10 000 yuan）

区县	Region	一般预算收入 General Budgetary Revenue	税收收入 Tax Revenue	增值税 Value Added Tax	营业税 Business Revenue	企业所得税 Corporate Income Tax
全市	**Total**	**3185486**	**2615050**	**253176**	**1083523**	**249501**
市本级	**Sum of city level**	**589445**	**378974**	**27766**	**48060**	**48602**
区、县合计	**Region**	**1784426**	**1514649**	**144596**	**729186**	**126935**
新城区	Xincheng	205654	141347	12171	65366	23181
碑林区	Beilin	267590	243862	22240	123558	29709
莲湖区	Lianhu	281296	214430	29768	105111	17977
雁塔区	Yanta	264486	253048	15108	164598	20272
灞桥区	Baqiao	131500	125246	6193	56122	4340
未央区	Weiyang	174578	165230	17722	78973	11781
阎良区	Yanliang	65023	55949	3578	17089	2343
临潼区	Lintong	62604	56802	10973	11888	3170
长安区	Chang'an	180176	129370	10614	57866	8550
蓝田县	Lantian	21224	16186	1504	8429	931
周至县	Zhouzhi	15510	11622	760	7115	97
户县	Huxian	44754	37373	5764	14039	1100
高陵县	Gaoling	70031	64184	8201	19032	3484
开发区合计	**Sum of Development Zones**	**811615**	**721427**	**80814**	**306277**	**73964**
高新区	GaoXin	435663	364119	51403	134493	48695
经开区	JingKai	167203	158799	24240	71372	16065
曲江新区	Qujiang	106345	102592	505	61526	6219
浐灞生态区	Chanba Eco-District	55887	52978	880	20966	1453
航空基地	Aviation Industry Base	3086	2937	206	1321	71
航天基地	Aerospace Base	14575	13388	219	7394	649
国际港务区	International Trade&Logistic Park	5194	4822	42	732	24
沣东新城	FengDongXinCheng	23662	21792	3319	8473	788

5-4 续表1 continued 1

单位：万元 （10 000 yuan）

区　县	Region	税收收入 Tax Revenue					
		个　人 所得税 Individual Income Tax	资源税 Resource Tax	城市维护建设税 City Maintenance and Construction Tax	耕地占用税 Farm Land Occupation Tax	契税 Deed Tax	其他各项税收收入 Other Tax Revenue
全市	**Total**	**97884**	**363**	**212619**	**132792**	**172148**	**413044**
市本级	**Sum of city level**	**15742**		**9952**		**45000**	**183852**
区、县合计	**Region**	**57680**	**362**	**133173**	**130089**	**34722**	**157906**
新城区	Xincheng	8557		13468			18604
碑林区	Beilin	18475		22812			27068
莲湖区	Lianhu	8268		25116	2780		25410
雁塔区	Yanta	9337		21857	3490		18386
灞桥区	Baqiao	1978	1	9153	39059		8400
未央区	Weiyang	3555		17783	19097		16319
阎良区	Yanliang	2134		2277	13749	7983	6796
临潼区	Lintong	1359		5789	13134	4869	5620
长安区	Chang'an	2258	4	6757	15200	11345	16776
蓝田县	Lantian	168	299	868	980	1730	1277
周至县	Zhouzhi	95	38	628	865	935	1089
户　县	Huxian	500	20	2519	7135	2200	4096
高陵县	Gaoling	996		4146	14600	5660	8065
开发区合计	**Sum of Development Zones**	**24462**	**1**	**69494**	**2703**	**92426**	**71286**
高新区	GaoXin	17698		40845		32306	38679
经开区	JingKai	4356	1	16068		9500	17197
曲江新区	Qujiang	1110		5824		21048	6360
浐灞生态区	Chanba Eco-District	669		2471		22531	4008
航空基地	Aviation Industry Base	54		323		495	467
航天基地	Aerospace Base	259		894		2767	1206
国际港务区	International Trade&Logistic Park	37		162		3779	46
沣东新城	FengDongXinCheng	279		2907	2703		3323

5-4 续表2

单位：万元

区　县	Region	非税收入 Non-tax Revenue	专项收入 Special Program Receipts	行政事业性收费收入 Charge of Adiministrative and Institutional Units
全市	**Total**	**570436**	**104655**	**250679**
市本级	**Sum of city level**	**210471**	**15799**	**98674**
区、县合计	**Region**	**269777**	**58749**	**99646**
新城区	Xincheng	64307	6425	5195
碑林区	Beilin	23728	9829	9675
莲湖区	Lianhu	66866	10077	36521
雁塔区	Yanta	11438	9326	
灞桥区	Baqiao	6254	3604	702
未央区	Weiyang	9348	8192	715
阎良区	Yanliang	9074	972	6022
临潼区	Lintong	5802	2285	1416
长安区	Chang'an	50806	2884	31805
蓝田县	Lantian	5038	623	2027
周至县	Zhouzhi	3888	470	2332
户　县	Huxian	7381	1712	1661
高陵县	Gaoling	5847	2350	1575
开发区合计	**Sum of Development Zones**	**90188**	**30107**	**52359**
高新区	GaoXin	71544	17564	49732
经开区	JingKai	8404	6888	571
曲江新区	Qujiang	3753	2668	200
浐灞生态区	Chanba Eco-District	2909	1151	1262
航空基地	Aviation Industry Base	149	139	
航天基地	Aerospace Base	1187	382	479
国际港务区	International Trade&Logistic Park	372	69	8
沣东新城	FengDongXinCheng	1870	1246	107

continued 2

(10 000 yuan)

罚没收入 Penalty Receipts	国有资本经营收入 State-owned Assets Profit	国有资源(资产)有偿使用收入 The Revenues of the Compensation for the Use of State-owned Resoures(Assants)	其他收入 Other Income	基金收入 Fund Revenue
77110	**34114**	**100048**	**3830**	**2555954**
45204	**30110**	**17442**	**3242**	**550992**
28803	**4004**	**77987**	**588**	**384180**
3493	4004	45190		1029
2389		1835		2163
4201		15479	588	42886
1373		739		1017
1497		451		23345
390		51		579
800		1280		6596
1543		558		14124
7022		9095		133093
1594		794		19437
961		125		5017
1708		2300		18243
1832		90		116651
3103		**4619**		**1620782**
729		3519		182758
643		302		120088
608		277		741540
262		234		238765
2		8		72787
141		185		130003
217		78		122587
501		16		12254

5-5 各区县、开发区一般预算支出（2011年）

单位:万元

区 县	Region	一般预算支出 Ordinary Budgetary Expenditures	一般公共服务支出 General Public Services	国防支出 Expenditure for National Defense	公共安全支出 Expenditure for Public Safety
合 计	**Total**	**4945750**	**544839**	**8875**	**284056**
市本级	**Sum of city level**	**2055493**	**174457**	**6227**	**120641**
区、县合计	**Region**	**2208665**	**268943**	**2441**	**145458**
新城区	Xincheng	170555	30138	210	15414
碑林区	Beilin	144602	21700	369	18374
莲湖区	Lianhu	194774	25953	404	16842
雁塔区	Yanta	164006	20121	158	18081
灞桥区	Baqiao	144121	16909	390	9810
未央区	Weiyang	143641	22620	305	13709
阎良区	Yanliang	109707	15298		6538
临潼区	Lintong	194348	18966		7764
长安区	Chang'an	304227	33703	265	13139
蓝田县	Lantian	155355	13753	132	6236
周至县	Zhouzhi	181790	13850	58	5134
户 县	Huxian	177764	16574	81	8265
高陵县	Gaoling	123775	19358	69	6152
开发区合计	**Sum of Development Zones**	**681592**	**101439**	**207**	**17957**
高新区	GaoXin	272886	31730	207	3821
经开区	JingKai	144334	18661		3827
曲江新区	Qujiang	104568	22122		1366
浐灞生态区	Chanba Eco-District	79368	13074		5341
航空基地	Aviation Industry Base	9787	1873		
航天基地	Aerospace Base	23173	3080		1800
国际港务区	International Trade&Logistic Park	12167	2002		
沣东新城	FengDongXinCheng	35309	8897		1802

Ordinary Budgetary Expenditures by Region and Development Zone (2011)

(10 000 yuan)

教育支出 Expenditure for Education	科学技术支出 Expenditure for Science and Technology	文化体育与传媒支出 Expenditure for Culture,Sport and Media	社会保障和就业支出 Expenditure for Social Safety Net and Employment Effort	医疗卫生支出 Expenditure for Medical and Health Care	节能环保支出 Expenditure for Energy Saving and Environment Protection
745310	**52192**	**97611**	**614349**	**336241**	**66108**
165460	**25260**	**49506**	**284023**	**118712**	**42761**
561726	**14126**	**21804**	**324143**	**216364**	**21566**
38553	1431	379	30146	8001	39
36348	1240	1010	33428	9841	476
38035	1625	665	38196	11491	82
40609	1704	999	23740	15582	63
43350	841	859	23810	14628	658
39771	1414	927	15423	12006	625
29043	887	904	13922	12358	549
59371	492	3076	21626	21610	1904
69916	1501	3635	49166	34579	2189
46916	634	2391	17848	21480	7535
46110	308	2082	20785	22014	5354
45778	580	2858	20660	17980	1757
27926	1469	2019	15393	14794	335
18124	**12806**	**26301**	**6183**	**1165**	**1781**
11728	12679	2415	874	500	501
3452	67		489		95
879	60	23654		83	500
1618		200	2793		438
98					5
					72
110					
239		32	2027	582	170

5-5 续表1

单位:万元

区 县	Region	一般预算支出 Ordinary Budgetary Expenditures 城乡社区事务支出 Expenditure for Urban and Rural Community Affairs	农林水事务支出 Expenditure for Agriculture,Foresty Water Conservancy	交通运输支出 Expenditure for Industry,Commerce and Banking	资源勘探电力信息等事务支出 Expenditure for Mining,Electricity and Information
合 计	**Total**	**662640**	**387899**	**261474**	**194948**
市本级	**Sum of city level**	**224862**	**149204**	**198102**	**66320**
区、县合计	**Region**	**226775**	**230813**	**59796**	**10587**
新城区	Xincheng	38973	152	772	225
碑林区	Beilin	19055	72	602	366
莲湖区	Lianhu	46906	204	555	341
雁塔区	Yanta	28540	4103	723	287
灞桥区	Baqiao	4840	13204	3827	393
未央区	Weiyang	24498	5119	1871	595
阎良区	Yanliang	9253	10108	2624	5112
临潼区	Lintong	6708	33616	10567	563
长安区	Chang'an	26966	43396	14337	732
蓝田县	Lantian	4887	23612	4508	261
周至县	Zhouzhi	3590	46636	7002	95
户 县	Huxian	8163	33595	7335	1286
高陵县	Gaoling	4396	16996	5073	331
开发区合计	**Sum of Development Zones**	**211003**	**7882**	**3576**	**118041**
高新区	GaoXin	133841			68063
经开区	JingKai	11173	289		16743
曲江新区	Qujiang	32386	5900	1174	90
浐灞生态区	Chanba Eco-District	14999			25032
航空基地	Aviation Industry Base	3401			2210
航天基地	Aerospace Base	3799			5903
国际港务区	International Park	1281		162	
	Trade&Logistic Park	10123	1693	2240	
沣东新城	FengDongXinCheng				

continued 1

(10 000 yuan)

商业服务业等事务支出 Expenditure for Commerce and Services	金融监管等事务支出 Expenditure for Financial Supervision	地震灾后恢复重建支出 Expenditure for Post-earthquake Reconstruction	国土资源气象等事务支出 Expenditure for Land Recources and Meteorological Affairs	住房保障支出 Expenditure for Housing Support	粮油物资储备管理等事务支出 Material Reserves Management Affairs Spending
134479	**29898**	**25**	**20299**	**318294**	**9763**
97172	**29805**		**3517**	**219734**	**7669**
30429	**93**	**25**	**16645**	**47577**	**2094**
1382			406	4323	10
1063			632		11
4123			665	6322	11
4343			2281	163	8
578			784	9112	80
2292			1475	963	9
933			1100	597	321
3027	13		1458	3205	94
2670			2798	4432	397
1613			737	2285	174
2122	67	25	1449	4464	219
4084			996	6924	318
2199	13		1864	4787	442
6878			**137**	**50983**	
820			47	5081	
453				6889	
1151				10151	
300			90	9483	
				7500	
4154				4375	
				7504	

5-5 续表2 continued 2

单位:万元 (10 000 yuan)

区 县	Region	一般预算支出 Ordinary Budgetary Expenditure			基金支出
		储备事务支出 Expenditure for Reserve	国债还本付息支出 Expenditure for National Debt and Interst	其他支出 Other Expenditure	Fund Expenditure
合 计	**Total**	**12118**	**62898**	**101434**	**2527691**
市本级	**Sum of city level**	**11309**	**56716**	**4036**	**464184**
区、县合计	**Region**	**809**	**898**	**5553**	**455223**
新城区	Xincheng		1		5345
碑林区	Beilin			15	2079
莲湖区	Lianhu		3	2351	39647
雁塔区	Yanta		1	2500	2024
灞桥区	Baqiao		48		51909
未央区	Weiyang		19		4809
阎良区	Yanliang		96	64	8594
临潼区	Lintong	80	113	95	22046
长安区	Chang'an	286	120		148101
蓝田县	Lantian	137	87	129	26751
周至县	Zhouzhi		190	236	9875
户 县	Huxian	296	119	115	14164
高陵县	Gaoling	10	101	48	119879
开发区合计	**Sum of Development Zones**		**5284**	**91845**	**1608284**
高新区	GaoXin		88	491	180231
经开区	JingKai		45	82151	104966
曲江新区	Qujiang		5052		747417
浐灞生态区	Chanba Eco-District			6000	238666
航空基地	Aviation Industry Base			2200	72792
航天基地	Aerospace Base		16	1003	129560
国际港务区	International Trade&Logistic Park		83		122592
沣东新城	FengDongXinCheng				12060

主要统计指标解释

财政收入 指国家财政参与社会产品分配所取得的收入，是实现国家职能的财力保证。主要包括：

（1）各项税收：包括国内增值税、国内消费税、进口货物增值税和消费税、出口货物退增值税和消费税、营业税、企业所得税、个人所得税、资源税、城市维护建设税、房产税、印花税、城镇土地使用税、土地增值税、车船税、船舶吨税、车辆购置税、关税、耕地占用税、契税、烟叶税等。

（2）非税收入：包括专项收入、行政事业性收费、罚没收入和其他收入。

财政支出 指国家财政将筹集起来的资金进行分配使用，以满足经济建设和各项事业的需要。主要包括：

（1）一般公共服务：指政府提供基本公共管理与服务的支出，包括人大事务、政协事务、政府办公厅（室）及相关机构事务、发展与改革事务、统计信息事务、财政事务、税收事务、审计事务、海关事务、人力资源事务、纪检监察事务、人口与计划生育事务、商贸事务、知识产权事务、工商行政管理事务、国土资源事务、海洋管理事务、测绘事务、地震事务、气象事务、民族事务、宗教事务、港澳台侨事务、档案事务、共产党事务、民主党派事务及工商联事务、群众团体事务、彩票事务等。

（2）外交：指政府外交事务支出，包括外交行政管理、驻外机构、对外援助、国际组织、对外合作与交流、边界勘界联检等方面的支出。

（3）国防：指政府用于国防方面的支出，包括用于现役部队、预备役部队、民兵、国防科研事业、专项工程、国防动员等方面的支出。

（4）公共安全：指政府维护社会公共安全方面的支出，包括武装警察、公安、国家安全、检察、法院、司法行政、监狱、劳教、国家保密、缉私警察等。

（5）教育：指政府教育事务支出，包括教育行政管理、学前教育、小学教育、初中教育、普通高中教育、普通高等教育、初等职业教育、中专教育、技校教育、职业高中教育、高等职业教育、广播电视教育、留学生教育、特殊教育、干部继续教育、教育机关服务等。

（6）科学技术：指用于科学技术方面的支出，包括科学技术管理事务、基础研究、应用研究、技术研究与开发、科技条件与服务、社会科学、科学技术普及、科技交流与合作等。

（7）文化教育与传媒：指政府在文化、文物、体育、广播影视、新闻出版等方面的支出。

（8）社会保障和就业：指政府在社会保障与就业方面的支出，包括社会保障和就业管理事务、民政管理事务、财政对社会保险基金的补助、补充全国社会保障基金、行政事业单位离退休、企业改革补助、就业补助、抚恤、退役安置、社会福利、残疾人事业、城市居民最低生活保障、其他城镇社会救济、农村社会救济、自然灾害生活救助、红十字事务等。

（9）医疗卫生：指政府医疗卫生方面的支出，包括医疗卫生管理事务支出、医疗服务支出、医疗保障支出、疾病预防控制支出、卫生监督支出、妇幼保健支出、农村卫生支出等。

（10）环境保护：指政府环境保护支出，包括环境保护管理事务支出、环境监测与监察支出、污染治理支出、自然生态保护支出、天然林保护工程支出、退耕还林支出、风沙荒漠治理支出、退牧还草支出、已垦草原退耕还草、能源节约利用、污染减排、可再生能源和资源综合利用等支出。

（11）城乡社区事务：指政府城乡社区事务支出，包括城乡社区管理事务支出、城乡社区规划与管理支出、城乡社区公共设施支出、城乡社区住宅支出、城乡社区环境卫生支出、建设市场管理与监督支出等。

（12）农林水事务：指政府农林水事务支出，包括农业支出、林业支出、水利支出、扶贫支出、农业综合开发支出等。

（13）交通运输：指政府交通运输和邮政业方面的支出，包括公路运输支出、水路运输支出、铁路运输支出、民用航空运输支出、邮政业支出等。

（14）工业商业金融等事务：指政府对工业、商业及金融等方面的支出，包括采掘业支出、制造业支出、建筑业支出、工业和信息产业监管支出、国有资产监管支出、商业流通事务支出、金融业监管支出、旅游业管理与服务支出等。

中央财政收入和地方财政收入 指按现行分税制财政体制划分的中央本级收入和地方本级收入。属于中央财政的收入包括关税，进口货物增值税和消费税，出口货物退增值税和消费税，消费税，铁道部门、各银行总行、各保险公司总公司等集中交纳的营业税和城市维护建设税，增值税75%部分，纳入共享范围的企业所得税60%部分，未纳入共享范围的中央企业所得税、中央企业上交的利润，个人所得税60%部分，车辆购置税，船舶吨税，证券交易印花税97%部分，海洋石油资源税，中央非税收入等。属于地方财政的收入包括营业税（不含铁道部门、各银行总行、各保险公司总公司集中交纳的营业税），地方企业上交利润，城市维护建设税（不含铁道部门、各银行总行、各保险公司总公司集中交纳的部分），房产税，城镇土地使用税，土地增值税，车船税，耕地占用税，契税，烟叶税，印花税，增值税25%部分，纳入共享范围的企业所得税40%部分，个人所得税40%部分，证券交易印花税3%部分，海洋石油资源税以外的其他资源税，地方非税收入等。

中央财政支出和地方财政支出 指根据政府在经济和社会活动中的不同职责，划分中央和地方政府的责权，按照政府的责权划分确定的支出。中央财政支出包括一般公共服务，外交支出，国防支出，公共安全支出，以及中央政府调整国民经济结构、协调地区发展、实施宏观调控的支出等。地方财政支出包括一般公共服务，公共安全支出，地方统筹的各项社会事业支出等。

Explanatory Notes on Main Statistical Indicators

Government Revenue refers to income for the government finance through participating in the distribution of social products. It is the financial guarantee to ensure government functioning. The contents of government revenue include the following main items:

(1) Various tax revenues, including domestic value added tax (VAT), domestic consumption tax, VAT and consumption tax from imports, VAT and consumption tax rebate for exports, business tax, corporate income tax, individual income tax, resource tax, city maintenance and construct tax, house property tax, stamp tax, urban land use tax, land appreciation tax, tax on vehicles and boat operation, ship tonnage tax, vehicle purchase tax, tariffs, farm land occupation tax, deed tax, and tobacco leaf tax, etc.

(2) Non-tax revenue, including special program receipts, charge of administrative and institutional units, penalty receipts and others non-tax receipts.

Government Expenditure refers to the distribution and use of the funds which the government finance has raised, so as to meet the needs of economic construction and various causes. It includes the following main items:

(1) Expenditure for general public services: It refers to the spending on the basic public management and services which provided by governments, including the expense on affairs of People' s Congress, affairs of People' s Political Consultative Conference, affairs of government general office and relative institutions, affairs of development and reform, affairs of statistics, affairs of finance, affairs of taxation, affairs of audit, affairs of customs, affairs of human resources and social security, affairs of discipline inspection and supervision, affairs of population and family planning, affairs of commerce and trade, affairs of intellectual property, affairs of administration for industry and commerce, affairs of land and resources, affairs of oceanic administration, affairs of surveying and mapping, affairs of earthquake, ethnic affairs, religious affairs, affairs of Hong Kong, Macao, Taiwan, and Overseas Chinese, affairs of archives administration, affairs of Chinese Communist Party, affairs of democratic parties and federation of industry and commerce, affairs of mass organization, and affairs of lottery, etc.

(2) Expenditure for foreign affairs: It refers to the spending of government on foreign affairs, including the expense on administration of foreign affairs, missions overseas, external assistance, international organizations, foreign cooperation and communication, surveying and joint inspection on borderline, etc.

(3) Expenditure for national defence: It refers to the spending of government on national defence, including the expense on active force, reserve force, militia, scientific research on national defence, special projects, mobilization of national defence, etc.

(4) Expenditure for public security: It refers to the spending of government on maintaining social and public security, including the expense on armed police force, public security, state security, prosecution, courts, justice, prison, labour education and rehabilitation, protection of state secrecy, anti-smuggling police, etc.

(5) Expenditure for education: It refers to the spending of government on education, including the expense on the administration of education, pre-primary education, primary education, secondary education, high school education, regular higher education, primary vocational education, secondary vocational education, technical school education, vocational high school education and higher vocational education, radio and television education, student abroad education, special education, on the job training of cadres, education authorities services, etc.

(6) Expenditure for science and technology: It refers to the spending of government on science and technology (S&T), including the expense on the administration of S&T, basic research, applied research, research and development, conditions and services of S&T, popularization of social science, science and technology, exchanges and cooperation of S&T, etc.

(7) Expenditure for culture, sport and media: It refers to the spending of government on culture, cultural heritage, sports, radio, film, television, press and publication, etc.

(8) Expenditure for social safety net and employment effort: It refers to the spending of government on social

safety net and employment, including the expense on administration of social safety net and employment, civil affairs, budgetary subsidy on the social insurance funds, subsidy on National Social Security Fund, retirees of administrative units and institutions, subsidy on enterprise reform, subsidy on employment effort, pension, placement of ex-serviceman, social welfare, the handicapped undertakings, the system of cost of living allowances for urban residents, other urban social relief, rural social relief, living relief of natural disasters, affairs of Red Cross Society, etc.

(9) Expenditure for medical and health care: It refers to the spending of government on medical and health care, including the expense on administration of medical and health care, medical services, health care, disease prevention and control, health inspection and supervision, women and children's health, rural health care, etc.

(10) Expenditure for environment protection: It refers to the spending of government on environment protection, including the expense on administration of environment protection, environment monitoring and supervision, pollution control, natural ecology protection, project of virgin forests protection, reforesting farmland, controlling the sources of dust storms, returning pastureland to grassland, returning pastureland to grassland, returning cultivated land to grassland, energy conservation, emissions reduction, comprehensive utilization of renewable energy and resources, etc.

(11) Expenditure for urban and rural community affairs: It refers to the spending of government on urban and rural community affairs, including the expense on administration of urban and rural community, planning and management of urban and rural community, public facilities of urban and rural community, housing of urban and rural community, sanitation of urban and rural community, management and supervision on the construction market, etc.

(12) Expenditure for agriculture, forestry and water conservancy: It refers to the spending of government on agriculture, forestry and water conservancy, including the expense on agriculture, forestry, water conservancy, poverty alleviation, comprehensive agricultural development, etc.

(13) Expenditure for transportation: It refers to the spending of government on transportation and postal services, including the expense on road transportation, waterway transportation, railway transportation, civil aviation transportation, and postal services.

(14) Expenditure for industry, commerce and banking: It refers to the spending of government on industry, commerce and banking, including the expense on mining, manufacturing, construction, industry and information technology supervision and administration, State-owned assets supervision and administration, commerce and circulation affairs, financial intermediation supervision and administration, tourism administration and service, etc.

Revenue of the Central Government and Revenue of the Local Governments refers to the revenue collected by the Central Government and that by the local governments as defined by the decentralized taxation system. In accordance with this system, the revenue of the Central Government includes tariff, VAT and consumption tax from imports, VAT and consumption tax rebate for exports, consumption tax, business tax and city maintenance and construct tax from the Ministry of Railways, head offices of banks, head offices of insurance company, which are handed over to the government in a centralized way, 75% of the value added tax, 60% the share part of the corporate income tax, unshared part of corporate income tax of the central enterprises, profit handed in by the central enterprises, 60% of individual income tax, vehicle purchase tax, ship tonnage tax, 97% of stamp tax on securities transactions, resource tax on the offshore petroleum resources. The revenue of the local governments includes business tax (excluding the part of the Ministry of Railways, head offices of banks, head offices of insurance company, which are handed over to the government in a centralized way), profit handed in by the local enterprises, city maintenance and construct tax (excluding the part of the Ministry of Railways, head offices of banks, head offices of insurance company, which are handed over to the government in a centralized way), house property tax, urban land use tax, land appreciation tax, tax on vehicles and boat operation, farm land occupation tax, deed tax, and tobacco leaf tax, stamp tax, 25% of the value added tax, 40% the share part of the corporate income tax, 40% of individual income tax, 3%

of stamp tax on securities transactions, resource tax other than the tax on offshore petroleum resources, local non-tax revenue, etc.

Expenditure of the Central Government and Expenditure of the Local Governments according to the different functions of the Central Government and local governments in economic and social activities, the rights of affairs administration are demarcated between those of the Central Government and those of local governments; and the classification of the expenditure between the Central Government and local governments are made on the basis of the classification of the rights of affairs administration between them. The expenditure of the Central Government includes the expenditure for general public services, expenditure for foreign affairs, expenditure for public security, and the expenditure of the Central Government for adjusting the national economic structure; coordinating the development among different regions; and exercising macroeconomic regulation. The expenditure of the local governments includes mainly the expenditure for general public services, expenditure for public security, and expenditures for social development which are planed by local governments, etc.

6 物价指数

PRICE INDICES

资料整理：李　欣　刘　青　郭菁媛
Data management:Li Xin Liu Qing Guo Jingyuan

第六部分　物价指数

一、简要说明

本章资料主要包括居民消费、零售、工业产品出厂、主要原材料购进、土地交易、房地产销售、租赁以及固定资产投资和建筑安装工程等价格指数，由国家统计局西安调查队提供。

二、主要指标

商品零售价格总指数（上年=100）	104.4	比上年提高 1.7个百分点
居民消费价格总指数（上年=100）	105.6	比上年提高 2.1个百分点

6 PRICE INDICES

Ⅰ.Brief Introduction

This chapter consists primarily of data on price indices of residents consumption, retail, industrial products dispatching sales, primary raw material purchasing, land deal, real estate selling, leasing, fixed asset investment and construction installation projects, provided by Fixed Asset Investment Division of the NBS Survey Office in Xi'an.

Ⅱ.Major Indicators

		Increase over Preceding Year
Retail Price Index(the price Preceding year=100)	104.4	1.7 percentage points
Consumer Price Index(the price Preceding year=100)	105.6	2.1 percentage points

6-1 主要年份各种价格指数

Price Indices in Representative Years

(以上年价格为100) (the price of preceding year=100)

年 份 Year	居民消费价格指数 Consumer Price Index	商品零售价格指数 Retail Price Index	工业生产者出厂价格指数 Producer Price Indices（PPI） for Manufactured Goods	工业生产者购进价格指数 Purchasing Price Indices for Industrial Producers	固定资产投资价格指数 Price Index for Investment in Fixed Assets
1980	108.7	109.3			
1981	102.4	102.7			
1982	100.9	101.0			
1983	102.6	102.0			
1984	104.7	104.8			
1985	109.7	109.3			
1986	108.5	107.4			
1987	110.6	111.4			
1988	122.8	123.2			
1989	118.3	117.8			
1990	102.5	100.9			
1991	109.4	108.3			
1992	112.2	112.4			
1993	117.2	112.8	102.5	104.3	
1994	128.5	126.2	132.2	115.0	
1995	117.0	114.6	110.8	113.1	
1996	110.9	107.9	100.7	103.8	
1997	106.0	101.5	98.6	102.5	
1998	97.9	95.5	94.4	97.5	
1999	96.8	97.4	97.5	96.9	100.8
2000	100.2	98.7	99.4	102.4	102.1
2001	99.9	98.9	99.3	101.0	101.3
2002	98.6	98.5	98.2	98.4	101.2
2003	100.5	100.0	101.5	105.3	102.4
2004	102.3	101.9	102.7	110.4	103.3
2005	100.3	99.7	103.9	109.6	102.4
2006	101.6	101.5	103.2	106.1	102.0
2007	104.7	103.7	101.9	106.2	103.5
2008	106.0	105.4	103.7	108.5	110.5
2009	99.7	99.5	99.9	100.7	97.9
2010	103.5	102.7	102.3	106.3	103.8
2011	105.6	104.4	102.5	108.8	105.4

6-2 居民消费价格指数（2011年）

Residents Consumer Price Indices（2011）

(以上年价格为100)　　(the price of preceding year=100)

类　　别	Item	2011
居民消费价格总指数	**Consumer Price Index**	**105.6**
非食品价格指数	Non-foodstuff Price Index	103.0
服务项目价格指数	Price Index of Service	105.0
工业品价格指数	Ex-factory Price Indices of Industrial Products	101.7
扣除食品烟酒和能源价格指数	Price Index with Food,Tobacco,Liquor and Energy Excluded	102.6
扣除鲜菜鲜果总指数	Price Index with Fresh Vegetables and Fruits Excluded	105.4
消费品价格指数	Price Index of Consumer Goods	105.8
一、食品	**Food**	**111.3**
1.粮食	Grain	111.0
2.淀粉及制品	Starches and Processed Products	109.6
3.干豆类及豆制品	Beans and Bean Products	100.9
4.油脂	Oil or Fat	113.7
5.肉禽及其制品	Meat,Poultry and Processed Products	126.5
6.蛋	Eggs	112.7
7 水产品	Aquatic Products	111.4
8.菜	Vegetables	105.6
9.调味品	Flavouring	108.7
10.糖	Carbohydrate	114.4
11.茶及饮料	Tea and Beverages	106.4
12.干鲜瓜果	Dried and Fresh Melons and Fruits	114.6
13.糕点饼干面包	Cake,Biscuit and Bread	109.3
14.液体乳及乳制品	Milk and Its Product	113.6
15.在外用膳食品	Dining Out	106.3
16.其他食品	Other Food	107.9
二、烟酒	**Tobacco and Liquor**	**103.0**
1.烟草	Tobacco	101.0
2.酒	Liquor	107.3
三、衣着	**Clothing**	**104.0**
1.服装	Garments	105.7
2.衣着材料	Clothing Material	101.2
3.鞋袜帽	Footgear and Hats	98.8
4.衣着加工服务费	Clothing Manufacturing Services	115.6

6-2 续表 continued

(以上年价格为100) (the price of preceding year=100)

类　　别	Item	2011
四、家庭设备用品及维修服务	**Household facilities,Articles and Services**	**101.8**
1.耐用消费品	Durable Consumer Goods	101.9
2.室内装饰品	Interior Decorations	99.7
3.床上用品	Bed Articles	95.7
4.家庭日用杂品	Daily Use Household Articles	101.4
5.家庭服务及加工维修服务	Household Service and Maintenance Renovation	109.5
五、医疗保健和个人用品	**Health Care and Personal Articles**	**105.3**
1.医疗保健	Health Care	104.3
（1）医疗器具及用品	Medical Instrument Articles	120.7
（2）中药材及中成药	Traditional Chinese Medicine	115.2
（3）西药	Western Medicine	99.2
（4）保健器具及用品	Health Care Appliances and Articles	103.0
（5）医疗保健服务	Health Care Services	100.0
2.个人用品及服务	Personal Articles and Services	107.5
六、交通和通信	**Transportation and Communication**	**100.3**
1.交通	Transportation	105.3
（1）交通工具	Transportation Facility	97.9
（2）车用燃料及零配件	Fuels and Parts	110.8
（3）车辆使用及维修费	Fees for Vehicles Use and Maintenance	105.7
（4）市区公共交通费	Incity Traffic Fare	104.7
（5）城市间交通费	Intercity Traffic Fare	107.5
2.通信	Communication	95.8
（1）通信工具	Telecommunication Facility	75.8
（2）通信服务	Telecommunication Service	100.0
七、娱乐教育文化用品及服务	**Recreation,Education and Culture Articles**	**101.0**
1.文娱用耐用消费品及服务	Durable Consumer Goods for Cultural and Recreational Use and Services	86.8
2.教育	Education	101.1
3.文化娱乐	Cultural and Recreational Articles	103.7
4.旅游	Touring	112.5
八、居住	**Residence**	**105.1**
1.建房及装修材料	Building and Building Decoration Materials	101.6
2.住房租金	Rental Housing	106.6
3.自有住房	Private Housing	111.1
4.水、电、燃料	Water, Electricity and Fuels	103.3

6-3 商品零售价格指数（2011年）

Retail Price Indices（2011）

(以上年价格为100)　　(the price of preceding year=100)

类别	Item	2011
商品零售价格总指数	**Retail Price Indices**	**104.4**
一、食品	**Food**	**111.7**
1.粮食	Grain	110.6
2.淀粉及制品	Starches and Processed Products	109.6
3.干豆类及豆制品	Beans and Bean Products	101.0
4.油 脂	Oil or Fat	113.8
5.肉禽及其制品	Meat,Poultry and Processed Products	126.4
6.蛋	Eggs	112.7
7.水产品	Aquatic Products	112.0
8.菜	Vegetables	105.5
9.调味品	Flavouring	107.4
10.糖	Carbohydrate	117.8
11.干鲜瓜果	Dried and Fresh Melons and Fruits	114.6
12.糕点饼干面包	Cake,Biscuit and Bread	109.0
13.液体乳及乳制品	Milk and Its Product	113.6
14.在外用膳食品	Dining Out	107.1
15.其它食品	Other Food and Manufacturing Services	107.9
二、饮料、烟酒	**Beverages,Tobacco and Liquor**	**105.5**
1.茶及饮料	Tea and Beverages	109.3
2.烟草	Tobacco	100.7
3.酒	Liquor	107.3
三、服装、鞋帽	**Garments,Shoes and Hats**	**103.7**
1.服装	Garments	105.3
2.鞋袜帽	Footgear and Hats	98.9
3.其他	Others	123.7
四、纺织品	**Textiles**	**97.7**
1.衣着材料	Cotton Cloth	101.6
2.床上用品	Blend Cloth	96.0
五、家用电器及音像器材	**Household Appliances,Music and Video Equipment**	**93.0**
1.家庭设备	Household facility	98.1
2.文娱用耐用消费品	Durable Consumer Goods on Cultural and Recreational Use	86.0
3.专业音像器材	Music and Video Equipment	95.3
六、文化办公用品	**Cultural and Office Appliances**	**93.7**

6-3 续表 continued

(以上年价格为100) (the price of preceding year=100)

类　　别	Item	2011
七、日用品	**Articles for Daily Use**	**102.1**
1.日用百货	General Merchandise for Daily Use	102.9
2.日用杂品	Miscellaneous for Daily Use	101.6
3.洗涤用品	Daily Use Articles For Washing	101.7
4.其它日用品	Other Daily Articles	101.8
八、体育娱乐用品	**Sports and Recreation Articles**	**102.5**
1.体育用品	Sports Goods	101.2
2.娱乐用品	Receration Goods	103.3
九、交通、通信用品	**Transportation and Communication Goods**	**91.3**
1.交通运输机械	Transportation Machinery	93.7
2.通信器材	Communication Machinery	80.0
十、家具	**Furniture**	**108.3**
十一、化妆品	**Cosmetics**	**101.6**
十二、金银珠宝	**Gold,Silver and Jewelry**	**112.4**
十三、中西药品及医疗保健用品	**Traditional Chinese and Western Medicines And Health Care Articles**	**105.0**
1.医疗器具及用品	Medical Apparatus and Article	120.7
2.中药材及中成药	Traditional Chinese Medicinal Materials and Medicines	116.4
3.西药	Western Medicine	99.1
4.保健器具及用品	Health Care Apparatus and Article	102.8
十四、书报杂志及电子出版物	**Books,Newspapers,Magazines and Electronic Publications**	**99.2**
1.教材及参考书	Teaching Materials and Reference Books	99.5
2.书报杂志	Books, Newspapers and Magazines	100.0
3.电子音像制品	Electronic Audio-video Products	96.7
十五、燃料	**Fuel**	**112.3**
1.煤炭及制品	Coal and Its Products	111.3
2.石油及制品	Oil and Its Products	112.4
十六、建筑材料及五金电料	**Building Materials and Hardware**	**104.9**
1.建筑装潢材料	Building Decoration Materials	104.6
2.五金电料	Hardware	106.1

6-4 主要年份工业生产者出厂价格指数

（上年价格=100）

类 别	Classify	1997	1998	1999	2000	2001
全部工业品	**Total Industry Products**	**98.6**	**94.4**	**97.5**	**99.4**	**99.3**
按轻重工业分	Grouped by Light Industry and Heavy Industry					
轻工业	Light Industry	98.2	91.1	95.9	97.8	99.6
以农产品为原料	Using Farm Products as Raw Materials	99.2	89.5	95.2	99.2	99.0
以非农产品为原料	Using Non-farm Products as Raw Materials	96.8	93.4	97.0	95.5	100.6
重工业	Heavy Industry	99.0	97.3	98.9	100.8	99.2
采掘	Mining & Quarrying		104.1	101.5	97.5	94.8
原料	Raw Materials	101.0	100.7	102.3	107.7	101.1
加工	Processing	97.9	95.6	98.0	98.4	98.5
按用途分	Grouped by Use					
生产资料	Means of Production	99.6	96.6	98.3	100.5	99.1
采掘	Mining & Quarrying		104.1	101.5	97.5	94.8
原料	Raw Materials	100.9	100.6	100.2	106.4	101.1
加工	Processing	98.9	94.7	97.6	98.7	98.5
生活资料	Consumer Goods	97.0	91.4	96.5	97.3	99.9
（1）食品	Food	108.2	97.8	95.8	94.4	99.6
（2）衣着	Clothing	93.0	83.9	95.2	101.6	99.4
（3）一般日用品	Articles for Daily Use	91.6	95.1	97.6	96.9	101.9
（4）耐用消费品	Durable Consumer Goods	99.7	95.4	98.0	95.9	97.0
按工业部门分	Grouped by Industrial Sector					
1.冶金工业	Metallurgical Industry	99.2	97.5	91.2	98.2	97.2
2.电力工业	Power Industry	111.3	111.2	109.3	109.6	102.4
3.煤炭及炼焦工业	Coal and Coking Industry	98.9	98.5	96.3	100.5	110.3
4.石油工业	Petroleum Industry			107.1	134.2	96.6
5.化学工业	Chemical Industry	91.8	92.9	96.6	96.7	100.5
6.机械工业	Machine Manufacturing Industry	98.8	94.6	98.1	98.0	98.3
7.建筑材料工业	Building Materials Industry	98.2	99.3	96.7	98.5	100.6
8.森林工业	Timber Industry	107.6	104.5	97.9	98.9	98.1
9.食品工业	Food Industry	106.8	95.3	95.5	94.3	99.8
10.纺织工业	Textiles Industry	94.3	82.6	93.7	103.4	97.5
11.缝纫工业	Tailoring Industry	100.1	97.3	99.1	103.5	100.0
12.皮革工业	Leather Industry	91.2	96.8	98.0	99.2	101.0
13.造纸工业	Paper Industry			95.3	96.7	102.3
14.文教艺术用品工业	Cultural,Educational & Handicrafts Articles			96.7	96.4	101.1
15.其他工业	Other Industry	109.5	109.2	98.9	104.8	107.1

注：经国务院批准，2011年起国家统计局进行统计方法制度改革，新的工业生产者价格调查方案中把“工业品价格统计”改称为“工业生产者价格统计”，相应地将“工业品出厂价格指数”和“原材料、燃料、动力购进价格指数”改为“工业生产者出厂价格指数”和“工业生产者购进价格指数”。

Producer Price Indices（PPI） for Manufactured Goods in Representative Years

(the price of preceding year=100)

2002	2003	2004	2005	2006	2007	2008	2009	2010	2011
98.2	**101.5**	**102.7**	**103.9**	**103.2**	**101.9**	**103.7**	**99.9**	**102.3**	**102.5**
98.4	101.3	103.4	99.9	100.2	101.8	103.7	100.6	102.5	107.0
98.4	104.5	108.7	97.3	100.1	103.3	106.0	98.9	104.0	109.3
98.6	99.9	100.8	101.2	100.2	100.8	102.1	101.8	101.4	100.9
98.2	101.6	101.9	107.9	105.5	101.9	103.8	99.3	102.2	101.6
101.3	103.4	140.5	107.9	100.6	111.6	122.3	90.0	150.2	102.6
101.3	111.2	109.0	114.2	111.8	104.9	110.8	99.5	108.9	111.2
97.7	100.1	100.6	106.7	104.2	101.2	101.9	99.4	100.8	100.1
98.0	101.8	102.7	105.3	104.2	101.3	103.4	99.3	102.2	101.9
101.3	103.4	140.5	107.9	100.6	111.6	122.3	90.0	150.2	102.6
101.0	108.1	106.6	111.3	111.6	104.8	110.2	99.7	109.0	111.3
97.4	100.9	102.0	104.3	103.0	100.6	102.0	99.3	101.0	100.3
99.1	100.5	102.5	100.4	100.4	103.5	104.7	101.4	102.5	104.5
101.2	101.0	103.6	100.3	100.4	105.3	106.6	100.3	103.3	109.5
100.8	99.4	102.7	102.0	103.3	104.6	105.1	102.7	101.2	111.9
97.9	101.2	101.2	101.3	100.8	100.1	102.7	102.6	101.2	101.5
98.1	97.2	98.3	99.1	99.4	100.7	100.7	103.9	101.9	99.5
98.7	103.8	107.1	103.9	106.5	103.2	104.8	92.0	105.8	116.3
100.0	103.2	104.1	110.6	107.9	105.5	110.0	109.0	101.2	104.7
106.7	136.8	131.4	97.1	95.4	106.8	104.8	101.7	110.6	109.3
100.7	118.6	110.5	121.7	117.6	104.8	115.6	96.7	114.2	108.4
99.2	100.2	100.8	103.2	100.8	101.1	104.1	102.6	100.8	104.2
97.6	99.8	100.6	104.9	103.4	101.0	101.7	99.9	100.9	99.5
99.6	99.7	100.0	98.6	98.9	98.9	101.8	101.9	99.9	100.6
98.9	100.1	100.2	101.6	101.6	101.1	101.1	101.1	101.7	105.2
101.1	102.8	107.5	98.3	99.0	106.1	109.3	98.3	104.3	110.1
94.9	117.3	119.1	89.9	102.4	98.4	99.7	97.5	108.9	107.2
101.1	100.2	103.6	100.8	103.5	104.6	105.1	102.6	101.3	113.4
101.8	98.7	99.6	101.2	100.0	99.0	99.6	99.7	99.6	98.0
95.0	96.9	100.2	101.2	100.0	100.1	104.5	98.4	100.4	103.4
103.4	97.5	96.5	98.1	100.1	99.1	99.2	102.2	99.9	100.7
99.4	103.3	105.0	103.4	105.7	111.4	104.3	99.7	100.5	104.3

Note: Approved by the State Council, from 2011, National Bureau of Statistics started statistical methods reform.In the new industrial producer price survey program , the"Price of Industrial Statistics" has been renamed to "Industrial Producer Prices Statistics".Accordingly,the "Producer price index"and "Raw materials, Fuel, Power, Price Indices" have been renamed to "Producer Price Indices for Manufactured Goods and "Purchasing Price Indices for Industrial Producers".

6-5 主要年份工业生产者购进价格指数

Purchasing Price Indices for Industrial Producers in Representative Years

(上年价格=100) (the price of preceding year=100)

类别	Item	2000	2001	2002	2003	2004	2005
全部原材料	**Total of Raw Materials**	**102.4**	**101.0**	**98.4**	**105.3**	**110.4**	**109.6**
(一)燃料、动力类	Fuel and Power	105.0	101.8	100.9	105.7	109.4	123.5
(二)黑色金属材料类	Ferrous Metals	102.7	102.1	98.5	107.4	117.4	107.6
#钢材	Steel	103.4	102.4	97.9	106.0	114.8	107.5
(三)有色金属材料和电线类	Non-ferrous Metals and Electric Wires	105.2	95.5	96.8	105.8	114.1	107.8
(四)化工原料类	Raw Chemical Materials	104.6	102.5	97.9	102.4	106.3	106.1
(五)木材及纸浆类	Timber and Paper Pulp	101.2	102.8	99.4	101.2	100.3	108.2
(六)建筑材料及非金属矿类	Building Materials and Non-metal ores	100.3	99.7	98.6	99.6	110.4	99.3
(七)其它工业原材料及半成品类	Other Industrial Raw Materials and Semi-Products	98.8	100.8	98.9	102.5	111.2	106.1
(八)农副产品类	Agricultural Products	100.4	102.8	98.2	113.7	112.7	100.9
(九)纺织原料类	Textile Materials	98.0	96.8	90.6	103.4	103.9	97.6

6-5 续表 continued

(上年价格=100) (the price of preceding year=100)

类别	Item	2006	2007	2008	2009	2010	2011
全部原材料	**Total of Raw Materials**	**106.1**	**106.2**	**108.5**	**100.7**	**106.3**	**108.8**
(一)燃料、动力类	Fuel and Power	112.6	107.0	109.8	105.1	108.6	113.5
(二)黑色金属材料类	Ferrous Metals	99.2	104.8	111.3	99.2	103.1	102.9
#钢材	Steel	98.5	104.9	111.7	98.7	103.5	102.9
(三)有色金属材料和电线类	Non-ferrous Metals and Electric Wires	116.5	110.7	99.1	93.9	113.6	118.9
(四)化工原料类	Raw Chemical Materials	101.6	105.6	111.4	95.0	103.9	108.1
(五)木材及纸浆类	Timber and Paper Pulp	111.7	105.9	106.5	102.6	101.1	105.4
(六)建筑材料及非金属矿类	Building Materials and Non-metal ores	100.7	104.0	104.8	106.8	102.1	102.9
(七)其它工业原材料及半成品类	Other Industrial Raw Materials and Semi-Products	104.3	108.8	110.6	101.4	108.1	109.4
(八)农副产品类	Agricultural Products	107.2	107.2	108.9	99.6	106.5	107.4
(九)纺织原料类	Textile Materials	101.5	100.5	99.8	97.6	104.6	107.0

6-6 土地交易价格指数（2011年）

Transactions Price Indices of Land（2011）

(上年价格=100) (the price of preceding year=100)

项　目	Item	2011
土地交易价格指数	**Transactions Price Indices of Land**	**103.1**
一、居住用地	**Land for Residential Building Use**	**102.6**
（一）经济适用房用地	Economically Affordable Housing	100.0
（二）商品住宅用地	Commercialized Housing	102.6
1.普通住宅用地	General Residential Buildings	102.5
2.高档住宅用地	Luxury Residential Buildings	101.8
二、工业用地	**Land for Industry and Storage Use**	**105.1**
三、商业营业用地	**Land for Business,Tourism and Entertainment**	**103.8**
四、其他用地	**Land for Other Uses**	**101.6**

6-7 住宅销售价格指数（2011年）

Selling Price Indices of Residential Buildings（2011）

(上年价格=100) (the price of preceding year=100)

项　目	Item	2011
新建住宅	**Newly Residential Buildings**	**104.0**
一、保障性住房	guaranteed house	
二、新建商品住宅	New commodity residential house	104.3
（一）90平方米及以下	90 square meters and less	105.8
（二）90-144平方米	90-144 square metre	103.9
（三）144平方米以上	144 square meters and more	102.8
二手住宅	**Second-hand Residential Buildings**	**102.9**
一、90平方米及以下	90 square meters and the following	102.2
二、90-144平方米	90-144 square metre	103.4
三、144平方米以上	144 square meters	103.3

6-8 房屋租赁和物业服务价格指数（2011年）

Lease and Property Service Price Index（2011）

(上年价格=100) (the price of preceding year=100)

项　　目	Item	2011
住宅租赁	**Renting Price Indices of Residential Buildings**	**111.7**
一、经济适用房	Economical Affordable Housing	100.0
二、廉租房	Tenement House	100.0
三、商品住宅	Commercialized Residential Buildings	112.0
（一）普通住宅	General Residential Buildings	113.4
（二）高档住宅	Luxury Residential Buildings	110.3
物业服务	**Property Services**	**100.0**
一、经济适用房	Economical Affordable Housing	100.0
二、商品住宅	Commercialized Residential Buildings	100.0
（一）普通住宅	General Residential Buildings	100.0
（二）高档住宅	Luxury Residential Buildings	100.0

6-9 主要年份固定资产投资价格指数

Price Indices for Investment in Fixed Assets in Representative Years

(上年价格=100) (the price of preceding year=100)

项　　目	Item	2000	2004	2005	2006	2007	2008	2009	2010	2011
固定资产投资价格指数	**Price Indices for Investment in Fixed Assets**	**102.1**	**103.3**	**102.4**	**102.0**	**103.5**	**110.5**	**97.9**	**103.8**	**105.4**
建筑安装、装饰工程	Construction,Installation and Decoration	103.9	104.6	102.3	102.6	104.9	114.9	97.1	105.5	107.2
设备、工器具购置	Purchase of Equipment and Instruments	97.9	100.5	104.5	100.8	100.7	101.0	98.6	100.0	100.6
其他费用	Others	100.0	100.6	100.5	100.5	100.6	101.9	100.9	100.8	102.8

主要统计指标解释

居民消费价格指数 是反映一定时期内城乡居民所购买的生活消费品和服务项目价格变动趋势和程度的相对数，是对城市居民消费价格指数和农村居民消费价格指数进行综合汇总计算的结果。通过该指数可以观察和分析消费品的零售价格和服务项目价格变动对城乡居民实际生活费支出的影响程度。

商品零售价格指数 是反映一定时期内城乡商品零售价格变动趋势和程度的相对数。商品零售价格的变动与国家的财政收入、市场供需的平衡、消费与积累的比例关系有关。因此，该指数可以从一个侧面对上述经济活动进行观察和分析。

工业生产者出厂价格指数 是反映一定时期内全部工业产品出厂价格总水平的变动趋势和程度的相对数，包括工业企业售给本企业以外所有单位的各种产品和直接售给居民用于生活消费的产品。该指数可以观察出厂价格变动对工业总产值及增加值的影响。

工业生产者购进价格指数 是反映工业企业作为生产投入，而从物资交易市场和能源、原材料生产企业购买原材料、燃料和动力产品时，所支付的价格水平变动趋势和程度的统计指标，是扣除工业企业物质消耗成本中的价格变动影响的重要依据。

固定资产投资价格指数 是反映一定时期内固定资产投资品及取费项目的价格变动趋势和程度的相对数。固定资产投资额是由建筑安装工程投资完成额、设备工器具购置投资完成额和其他费用投资完成额三部分组成的。编制固定资产投资价格指数应首先分别编制上述三部分投资的价格指数，然后采用加权算术平均法求出固定资产投资价格总指数。

该指数可以准确地反映固定资产投资中涉及的各类投资品和取费项目价格变动趋势和变动幅度，消除按现价计算的固定资产投资指标中的价格变动因素，真实地反映固定资产投资的规模、速度、结构和效益，为国家科学地制定、检查固定资产投资计划并提高宏观调控水平，为完善国民经济核算体系提供科学的、可靠的依据。

Explanatory Notes on Main Statistical Indicators

Consumer Price Indices reflect the trend and degree of changes in prices of consumer goods and services purchased by urban and rural households during a given period. They are obtained by combining Consumer Price Indices of Urban Household and Consumer Price Indices of Rural Household. The Indices enable the observation and analysis of the degree of impact of the changes in the prices of retailed goods and services on the actual living expenses of urban and rural residents.

Retail Price Indices reflect the trend and degree of change in retail prices of commodities during a given period. The change in retail prices of commodities is related to government revenue, the equilibrium of market supply and demand, and the ratio of consumption to accumulation. Therefore, the retail price indices are useful from an oblique perspective for observing and analyzing the changes of the above economic activities.

Producer Price Indices (PPI) for Manufactured Goods reflect the trend and degree of changes in general ex-factory prices of all manufactured goods during a given period, including sales of manufactured goods by an industrial enterprise to all units outside the enterprise, as well as sales of consumer goods to residents. It can be used to analyze the impact of ex-factory prices on gross output value and value-added of the industrial sector.

Purchasing Price Indices for Industrial Producers reflect changes in the level and degree of prices paid by industrial enterprises when they purchase production input such as raw materials, fuels and power from the market or from other energy or raw materials producing enterprises. These indices provide an important basis for measuring the material consumption of industrial enterprises after removing the influence of price changes.

Price Indices for Investment in Fixed Assets reflect the trend and degree of changes in prices of investment goods and projects in fixed assets during a given period. The investment in fixed assets consists of three components, namely the investment in construction and installation, the investment in purchases of equipment and instrument, and the investment in other items. Price indices for investment in fixed assets are calculated as the weighted arithmetic mean of the price indices for the three components of investment in fixed assets.

Removing the factor of price change in the aggregates of investment at current prices, this indicator shows the changes in the prices of commodities and fees involved in the investment of fixed assets, and can be used to observe the actual size, growth, structure, and efficiency of investment in fixed assets and provides reliable and scientific data for government planning, management, decision-making, and further improving the current national accounting system.

7 人民生活

PEOPLE'S LIVELIHOOD

资料整理：冯军魁　贾薪蓉　赵兰莉

Data management:Feng Junkui Jia Xinrong Zhao Lanli

第七部分　人民生活

一、简要说明

本章资料主要内容包括城乡居民家庭基本情况、主要商品购买数量、耐用消费品拥有数量等，由西安市统计局人口就业处提供。

二、主要指标

城镇居民人均可支配收入（元）	25981	比上年增长 16.8%
城镇居民人均消费性支出（元）	19306	比上年增长 16.7%
农村居民人均纯收入（元）	9788	比上年增长 26.3%
农村居民人均生活消费支出（元）	6705	比上年增长 19.0%

7 PEOPLE'S LIVELIHOOD

Ⅰ.Brief Introduction

Data in this chapter reflects situation of the people's daily life of Xi'an city. It consists of mainly basic condition of urban and rural households, volume of primary commodity purchasing, possession of endurable goods, etc. The data come from Population & Employment Division of the Xi'an Bureau of Statistics.

Ⅱ.Major Indicators

		Increase over Preceding Year
Per Capita Annual Disposable Income of Urban Households (yuan)	25981	16.8%
Per Capita Annual Consumption Expenditure of Urban Households (yuan)	19306	16.7%
Per Capita Living Expenditure Built(yuan)	9788	26.3%
Per Capita Net Income of Rural Residents(yuan)	6705	19.0%

7-1 主要年份城乡居民家庭人均收入及恩格尔系数

Per Capita Annual Income and Engel's Coefficient of Urban and Rural Households in Representative Years

年 份 Year	城镇居民家庭人均可支配收入 Per Capita Annual Disposable Income of Urban Households		农村居民家庭人均纯收入 Per Capita Annual Net Income of Rural Households		城镇居民家庭恩格尔系数（%） Engel's Coefficient of Urban Households	农村居民家庭恩格尔系数（%） Engel's Coefficient of Rural Households
	绝对数（元） Value(yuan)	指数（1980年=100） Indax (preceding year=100)	绝对数（元） Value(yuan)	指数（1978年=100） Index (preceding year=100)		
1978			140	100.0		
1979						
1980	414	100.0	190	135.7	53.3	53.3
1981	446	107.7	207	147.9	52.9	53.7
1982	479	115.6	254	181.4	55.1	56.7
1983	509	122.9	245	175.0	55.1	58.4
1984	540	130.3	299	213.6	54.9	51.7
1985	719	173.5	351	250.7	49.5	48.5
1986	911	219.8	390	278.6	49.9	47.9
1987	1034	249.7	434	310.0	50.6	50.3
1988	1142	275.6	482	344.3	44.9	47.5
1989	1344	324.3	530	378.6	51.7	48.2
1990	1518	366.5	610	435.7	53.1	49.5
1991	1619	390.9	707	505.0	51.6	46.7
1992	1992	481.0	783	559.3	52.5	50.9
1993	2661	642.5	870	621.4	46.4	46.0
1994	3517	849.1	1078	770.0	45.2	50.1
1995	4153	1002.5	1353	966.4	44.7	50.3
1996	5023	1212.6	1586	1132.9	42.6	49.9
1997	5344	1290.1	1846	1318.6	40.7	49.2
1998	5670	1368.7	2052	1465.7	39.8	42.4
1999	5999	1448.3	2203	1573.6	36.3	39.1
2000	6364	1536.5	2344	1674.3	36.5	36.6
2001	6705	1618.8	2490	1778.6	34.8	33.9
2002	7184	1734.3	2641	1886.4	34.4	31.1
2003	7748	1870.7	2838	2027.1	34.8	37.6
2004	8544	2062.8	3143	2245.0	36.1	35.7
2005	9628	2324.5	3460	2471.4	37.0	36.3
2006	10905	2632.9	3808	2720.0	34.4	36.8
2007	12662	3057.0	4399	3142.1	36.6	38.2
2008	15207	3671.4	5212	3722.9	36.4	37.0
2009	18963	4578.2	6275	4482.3	32.4	35.8
2010	22244	5370.4	7750	5535.7	31.3	32.5
2011	25981	6272.6	9788	6991.4	31.3	31.9

7-2 主要年份城乡居民人民币储蓄存款

Savings Deposit of Urban and Rural Households in Representative Years

单位：亿元　　(100 million yuan)

年 份 Year	年末余额 Balance at Year-end	指数（上年=100） Index(preceding year=100)
1978	3.72	
1979	4.85	130.4
1980	5.48	113.0
1981	6.36	116.1
1982	7.76	122.0
1983	10.02	129.1
1984	14.70	146.7
1985	16.70	113.6
1986	23.10	138.3
1987	32.13	139.1
1988	32.51	101.2
1989	45.78	140.8
1990	62.23	135.9
1991	78.64	126.4
1992	96.09	122.2
1993	124.61	129.7
1994	174.19	139.8
1995	230.63	132.4
1996	394.02	170.8
1997	358.78	91.1
1998	499.68	139.3
1999	586.40	117.4
2000	675.83	115.3
2001	800.86	118.5
2002	988.04	123.4
2003	1210.56	122.5
2004	1432.86	118.4
2005	1716.76	119.8
2006	1950.53	113.6
2007	2002.38	102.7
2008	2513.70	125.5
2009	3084.20	122.7
2010	3641.09	118.1
2011	4155.65	114.1

7-3 分区县城乡居民人均收入

Per Capita Income of Urban and Rural Households by Region

区县	District	城镇居民人均可支配收入 Per Capita Disposable Income of Urban Households			农村居民人均纯收入 Per Capita net Income of Rural Households		
		绝对数（元）Value(yuan)		指数（上年=100） Index(preceding year=100)	绝对数（元）Value(yuan)		指数（上年=100） Index(preceding year=100)
		2010	2011		2010	2011	
全市	**Total**	**22244**	**25981**	**116.8**	**7750**	**9788**	**126.3**
新城区	Xincheng	22554	26498	117.5			
碑林区	Beilin	22998	27025	117.5			
莲湖区	Lianhu	22940	26962	117.5			
雁塔区	Yanta	21162	24817	117.3	8849	11291	127.6
灞桥区	Baqiao	22184	26041	117.4	9712	12383	127.5
未央区	Weiyang	23517	27601	117.4	9863	12585	127.6
阎良区	Yanliang	22927	26839	117.1	8969	11426	127.4
临潼区	Lintong	18213	21271	116.8	7156	9109	127.3
长安区	Chang'an	19557	22918	117.2	7389	9421	127.5
蓝田县	Lantian	14874	17309	116.4	5316	6704	126.1
周至县	Zhouzhi	14877	17353	116.6	5238	6615	126.3
户县	Huxian	16761	19532	116.5	6549	8265	126.2
高陵县	Gaoling	17377	20313	116.9	7106	9053	127.4

7-4 主要年份城镇居民家庭及收支基本情况

Basic Conditions of Urban Households in Representative Years

指　　标	Item	2001	2002	2003	2004
一、平均每户家庭人口(人)	**Average Household Size(person)**	**3.03**	**3.01**	**3.04**	**2.99**
二、平均每户就业人口(人)	**Average Number of Employed Persons Per Housedhold (person)**	**1.38**	**1.47**	**1.46**	**1.46**
三、平均每户就业面(%)	**Proportion Percentage of Employment Per Housedhold (%)**	**45.6**	**48.8**	**48.0**	**48.8**
四、平均每一就业者负担人数(人)	**Number of Dependents per Emplyee(person)**	**2.19**	**2.05**	**2.08**	**2.05**
五、年人均家庭总收入(元)	**Per Capita Annual Income(yuan)**	**6743.12**	**7670.67**	**8315.13**	**9150.65**
#可支配收入	Disposable Income	6704.86	7183.54	7748.38	8544.03
（一）工资性收入	Income from Wages and Salaries	4288.09	5075.62	5443.21	6050.38
（二）经营性收入	Net Business Income	135.27	159.03	111.83	251.37
（三）财产性收入	Income from Properties	49.35	60.90	194.17	186.95
（四）转移性收入	Income from Transfer	2270.41	2375.12	2565.92	2661.95
六、年人均家庭总支出(元)	**Annual Actual Expenditure Per Capita (yuan)**	**6678.56**	**7819.74**	**8610.43**	**9312.05**
1.消费性支出	Consumption Expenditure	5815.66	6419.21	6805.30	7427.82
(1)食品	Food	2023.91	2205.38	2371.02	2685.10
(2)衣着	Clothing	485.93	540.52	574.56	611.03
(3)家庭设备用品及服务	Facilities,Articles and Services	628.91	467.36	403.24	493.33
(4)医疗保健	Health Care and Medical Services	406.13	535.52	602.31	641.77
(5)交通和通信	Transport and Communication Services	453.12	567.96	630.48	688.22
(6)教育和文化娱乐服务	Education,Receration and Cultural Services	908.07	1126.68	1230.60	1252.55
(7)居住	Residence	531.45	783.56	779.32	813.14
(8)杂项商品和服务	Miscellaneous Goods and Services	378.14	192.23	213.77	242.68
2.购房与建房支出	Purchase and Construction Expenditure of Houses	289.31	415.08	532.19	590.33
3.转移性支出	Transfer Expenditure	573.59	567.81	786.70	768.01
4.财产性支出	Property Expenditure				
5.社会保障支出	Social Services Expenditure		417.64	486.24	525.89
七、人均期末手存现金(元)	**Cash Reserves at Hand at the end of Year Per Capita (yuan)**	**550.39**	**587.82**	**810.60**	**882.65**

7-4 续表1 continued 1

指　　标	Item	2005	2006	2007	2008
一、平均每户家庭人口(人)	**Average Household Size(person)**	**2.93**	**2.90**	**2.91**	**2.82**
二、平均每户就业人口(人)	**Average Number of Employed Persons Per Housedhold (person)**	**1.39**	**1.40**	**1.39**	**1.35**
三、平均每户就业面(%)	**Proportion Percentage of Employment Per Housedhold (%)**	**47.4**	**48.3**	**47.8**	**47.9**
四、平均每一就业者负担人数(人)	**Number of Dependents per Emplyee(person)**	**2.11**	**2.07**	**2.09**	**2.09**
五、年人均家庭总收入(元)	**Per Capita Annual Income(yuan)**	**10387.44**	**11708.43**	**13421.45**	**16365.67**
#可支配收入	Disposable Income	9627.89	10905.39	12662.03	15206.89
（一）工资性收入	Income from Wages and Salaries	6926.28	7622.92	8897.30	10944.90
（二）经营性收入	Net Business Income	163.66	345.70	375.68	410.70
（三）财产性收入	Income from Properties	193.20	317.87	208.80	241.24
（四）转移性收入	Income from Transfer	3104.30	3421.94	3939.67	4768.83
六、年人均家庭总支出(元)	**Annual Actual Expenditure Per Capita (yuan)**	**10030.64**	**12033.94**	**12257.69**	**14380.69**
1.消费性支出	Consumption Expenditure	7899.81	8986.87	10097.95	12015.81
(1)食品	Food	2926.32	3093.12	3696.57	4374.24
(2)衣着	Clothing	712.98	783.93	950.50	1232.12
(3)家庭设备用品及服务	Facilities,Articles and Services	373.36	582.85	597.11	761.02
(4)医疗保健	Health Care and Medical Services	746.67	695.09	847.80	1161.86
(5)交通和通信	Transport and Communication Services	763.56	922.99	1145.90	1246.34
(6)教育和文化娱乐服务	Education,Receration and Cultural Services	1357.50	1666.93	1466.55	1724.63
(7)居住	Residence	719.00	946.87	1027.90	1058.11
(8)杂项商品和服务	Miscellaneous Goods and Services	300.42	295.09	365.62	457.49
2.购房与建房支出	Purchase and Construction Expenditure of Houses	722.35	1273.52	524.62	262.31
3.转移性支出	Transfer Expenditure	745.24	1043.44	933.52	1042.50
4.财产性支出	Property Expenditure		1.89	9.33	23.30
5.社会保障支出	Social Services Expenditure	663.24	728.22	692.27	1036.77
七、人均期末手存现金(元)	**Cash Reserves at Hand at the end of Year Per Capita (yuan)**	**1121.29**	**1525.31**	**1563.07**	**1296.10**

注：2007年因统计制度变化，部分数据有调整。

Note:As statistical system was changed in 2007, some data was adjusted.

7-4 续表2 continued 2

指　　标	Item	2009	2010	2011
一、平均每户家庭人口(人)	**Average Household Size(person)**	**2.84**	**2.81**	**2.83**
二、平均每户就业人口(人)	**Average Number of Employed Persons Per Housedhold (person)**	**1.51**	**1.51**	**1.55**
三、平均每户就业面(%)	**Proportion Percentage of Employment Per Housedhold (%)**	**53.2**	**53.7**	**54.8**
四、平均每一就业者负担人数(人)	**Number of Dependents per Emplyee(person)**	**1.88**	**1.86**	**1.83**
五、年人均家庭总收入(元)	**Per Capita Annual Income(yuan)**	**20299.12**	**23879.86**	**27710.24**
#可支配收入	Disposable Income	18963.31	22243.63	25981.45
(一)工资性收入	Income from Wages and Salaries	13562.24	15733.57	18240.83
(二)经营性收入	Net Business Income	715.99	979.22	1442.33
(三)财产性收入	Income from Properties	357.26	506.47	639.65
(四)转移性收入	Income from Transfer	5663.63	6660.60	7387.43
六、年人均家庭总支出(元)	**Annual Actual Expenditure Per Capita (yuan)**	**17619.36**	**20597.76**	**23991.29**
1.消费性支出	Consumption Expenditure	14250.78	16543.21	19305.83
(1)食品	Food	4621.40	5176.55	6041.18
(2)衣着	Clothing	1564.44	1837.40	2368.64
(3)家庭设备用品及服务	Facilities,Articles and Services	1037.98	1250.86	1565.74
(4)医疗保健	Health Care and Medical Services	1375.57	1572.40	1737.36
(5)交通和通信	Transport and Communication Services	1614.68	1995.20	2472.58
(6)教育和文化娱乐服务	Education,Receration and Cultural Services	2043.52	2424.51	2753.85
(7)居住	Residence	1262.83	1542.76	1594.54
(8)杂项商品和服务	Miscellaneous Goods and Services	730.36	743.53	771.94
2.购房与建房支出	Purchase and Construction Expenditure of Houses	606.42	639.83	1125.88
3.转移性支出	Transfer Expenditure	1517.15	1907.40	1961.60
4.财产性支出	Property Expenditure	23.09	53.55	119.38
5.社会保障支出	Social Services Expenditure	1221.92	1453.77	1478.60
七、人均期末手存现金(元)	**Cash Reserves at Hand at the end of Year Per Capita (yuan)**	**2553.73**	**4727.95**	**6295.60**

7-5 城镇居民家庭基本情况（2011年）

Basic Conditions of Urban Households（2011）

指　　标	Item	合计 Total
一、人均可支配收入(新算法)(元)	**Per Capita Disposable Income (New Algorithm)(yuan)**	**25981.45**
二、家庭人口数(人/户)	**Number of Family Members (Person/Household)**	**2.83**
（一）有收入者人数	Family Members Earning Income	2.18
1.就业人口数	Family Members Employed	1.55
（1）国有经济单位职工人数	Employed by State-Owned Enterprises	0.89
（2）城镇集体经济单位职工人数	Employed by Urban Collective Enterprises	0.05
（3）其他各种经济类型单位职工	Employed by Other Units	0.10
（4）城镇个体经营者人员数	Personnel of Urban Individual Business	0.09
（5）城镇个体被雇人员数	Employed by Self-Employers	0.23
（6）离退休再就业人员数	Re-Employed Resigned and Retired Personnel	0.08
（7）其他就业人员数	Others	0.11
2.离退休人数	Resigned and Retired	0.61
3.其他有收入者人数	Others	0.03
（二）无收入者人数	Family Members Without Income	0.64
三、非家庭人口在家用餐人次数	**None-Family Members Eating At Home**	**4.13**
(人次/户)	**(Person-Times/Household)**	
四、家庭人口在外用餐人次数	**Family Members Eating Outside**	**10.73**
(人次/户)	**(Person-Times/Household)**	

7-6 城镇居民家庭年人均收入情况（2011年）

Statistics on Per Capital Annual Income of Urban Residents （2011）

单位：元 (yuan)

项 目	Item	总平均 Total
一、家庭总收入	**Total Family Income**	**27710.24**
#可支配收入	Disposable Income	25981.45
（一）工薪收入	Income from Wages and Salaries	18240.83
#工资及补贴收入	Wages and Subsidies	17740.53
（二）经营性收入	Net Income from Business	1442.33
（三）财产性收入	Income from Properties	639.65
#利息收入	Interest Income	70.14
出租房屋收入	House Rents	391.34
（四）转移性收入	Transfer Income	7387.43
#养老金或离退休金	Pensions	6220.24
提取住房公积金	Withdrawal of Housing Funds	16.80
记账补贴	Book-Keeping Allowances	173.62
二、出售财物收入	**Income from Sales Of Property**	**86.31**
1.出售住房收入	Sales of Housing	78.65
2.出售其他物品收入	Sales of Other Properties	7.66
三、借贷收入	**Income For Savings and Credit**	**7765.84**

7-7 城镇居民家庭年人均支出情况（2011年）

Statistics on Per Capital Annual Living Expenditure of Urban Households（2011）

单位:元 (yuan)

项 目	Item	总平均 Total
一、家庭总支出	**Total Expenditures**	**23991.29**
（一）消费支出	Consumption Expenditures	19305.83
#服务性消费支出	Consumption on Service	5469.88
1.食品	Food	6041.18
2.衣着	Clothing	2368.64
3.家庭设备用品及服务	Household Facilities,Articles and Service	1565.74
4.医疗保健	Health Care and Medical Service	1737.36
5.交通和通信	Transport and Communications	2472.58
6.教育文化娱乐服务	Education,Receration and Cultural Services	2753.85
7.居住	Residence	1594.54
8.杂项商品和服务	Miscellaneous Goods and Services	771.94
（二）购房与建房支出	Expenditures on House Purchasing/Construction	1125.88
（三）转移性支出	Transfer Expenditures	1961.60
（四）财产性支出	Property Expenditures	119.38
（五）社会保障支出	Expenditures on Social Security	1478.60
二、借贷支出	**Expenditures on Loans and Debts**	**9500.66**

7-8 城镇居民家庭年人均消费性支出情况（2011年）

Statistics on Per Capita Annual Consumption Expenditure of Urban Households（2011）

单位:元 (yuan)

项 目	Item	总平均 Total
消费支出	**Consumption Expenditures**	**19305.83**
#服务性消费支出	Consumption on services	5469.88
食品	**Food**	**6041.18**
（一）粮油类	Grains and oil	834.83
1.粮食	Grain	530.28
2.淀粉及薯类	Starches and Tubers	59.69
3.干豆类及豆制品	Bean and Bean Products	90.73
4.油脂类	Oil or Fats	154.13
（二）肉禽蛋水产品类	Meat,Poultry,Egg and Aquatic Products	1076.78
1.肉类	Meat	635.78
2.禽类	Poultry	152.99
3.蛋类	Egg	114.12
4.水产品类	Aquatic Products	173.89
（三）蔬菜类	Vegetables	552.29
1.鲜菜	Fresh Vegetables	493.66
2.干菜	Dried Vegetables	37.24
3.菜制品	Vegetable Products	21.39
（四）调味品	Flavouring	102.04
（五）糖烟酒饮料类	Sugar,Tobacco,Liquor and Beverage	823.51
1.糖类	Sugar	60.25
2.烟草类	Tobacco	354.41
3.酒类	Liquor	231.84
4.饮料	Beverage	177.01
（六）干鲜瓜果类	Dried and Fresh Melons &Fruits	592.85
（七）糕点、奶及奶制品	Cakes, Milk and Processed Products	460.86
1.糕点	Cakes	163.61
2.奶及奶制品	Milk and Its Products	297.25
（八）其他食品	Other Food	111.53
（九）饮食服务	Catering Services	1486.49
1.食品加工服务费	Charge for Food Processing Services	0.55
2.在外饮食	Foods Consumed outside	1485.94

7-8 续表1 continued 1

单位:元 (yuan)

项　目	Item	总平均 Total
非食品类	**Non-food**	
一、衣着	**Clothing**	**2368.64**
（一）服装	Garments	1665.06
（二）衣着材料	Cloth Materials	17.53
（三）鞋类	Shoes	576.12
（四）其他衣着用品	Others	98.88
（五）衣着加工服务费	Tailoring and Laundering	11.05
二、家庭设备用品及服务	**Household Facilities,Articles and Services**	**1565.74**
（一）耐用消费品	Durable Consumer Goods	606.34
1.家具	Furniture	186.74
2.家庭设备	Household Facilities	419.60
（二）室内装饰品	Interior Decorations	64.32
（三）床上用品	Bed Articles	146.20
（四）家庭日用杂品	Daily Use Household Articles	641.81
（五）家具材料	Furniture Materials	39.81
（六）家庭服务	Household Services	67.26
三、医疗保健	**Medicine and Medical Services**	**1737.36**
（一）医疗器具	Medical Appliances and Articles	13.54
（二）保健器具	Health Care Articles	34.86
（三）药品费	Medicines	693.80
（四）滋补保健品	Tonic	177.29
（五）医疗费	Medical Care Services	787.01
（六）其他	Others	30.86
四、交通和通讯	**Transportation ,Post and Telecommumication Services**	**2472.58**
（一）交通	Trasportation	1612.53
1.家庭交通工具	Family Vehicles	852.89
2.车辆用燃料及零配件	Fuel and Accessories	247.11
3.交通工具服务支出	Expenditure on Maintenance of Vehicles	161.35
4.交通费	Transport Servi	351.18

7-8 续表2 continued 2

单位:元 (yuan)

项　目	Item	总平均 Total
（二）通信	Telecommumication	860.05
1.通信工具	Telecommunication Tools	222.55
2.通信服务	Telecommunication Services	637.50
五、教育文化娱乐服务	**Recreation,Culture and Education Services**	**2753.85**
（一）文化娱乐用品	Recreating Goods	614.90
（二）文化娱乐服务	Recreation and Culture Services	1080.52
（三）教育	Education	1058.43
六、居住	**Residence**	**1594.54**
（一）住房	Housing	584.88
1.租赁房房租	House Renting	111.90
2.住房装潢支出	Home Decorate Expenditure	299.23
3.维修用建筑材料	Building Material for Repair	113.11
4.其他	Others	60.64
（二）水电燃料及其他	Water,Electricity,Fuel and Others	848.97
1.水	Water	76.96
2.电	Electricity	317.96
3.燃料	Fuel	191.79
4.取暖费	Heating Cost	248.44
5.其他	Others	13.82
（三）居住服务费	Cost on Housing Service	160.69
1.物业管理费	Housing Management	115.37
2.维修服务费	Expenditures on House Maintenance	18.91
3.其他	Others	26.41
七、杂项商品和服务	**Miscellaneous Commodities and Services**	**771.94**
（一）杂项商品	Miscellaneous Commodities	549.12
1.金银珠宝饰品	Jewel	216.74
2.手表	Watches	36.11
3.理发美容用具	Hair-care	7.89
4.化妆品	Cosmetics	215.16
5.其他杂品	Others	73.22
（二）服务	Services	222.82
1.旅馆住宿费	Rent for Hotels	20.76
2.理发洗澡费	Hair-cutting and Bathing	61.07
3.美容费	Cosmetic	65.61
4.其他服务	Others	75.38

7-9 主要年份城镇居民家庭年人均购买主要商品数量

商品名称	Name of Commodities	2000	2001	2002	2003
食用植物油（市斤）	Vegetable Oil(500g)	10.0	9.1	9.9	9.4
猪　肉（市斤）	Pork (500g)	13.7	12.0	12.9	13.6
牛　肉（市斤）	Beef(500g)	1.7	1.6	1.4	1.5
羊　肉（市斤）	Mutton (500g)	0.7	0.5	0.8	1.0
鸡　（市斤）	Chicken (500g)	4.4	3.6	3.7	4.0
鲜　蛋（市斤）	Eggs (500g)	12.3	10.8	11.4	11.9
鱼（市斤）	Fish(500g)	3.7	3.8	4.5	5.2
鲜　菜（市斤）	Fresh Vegetables (500g)	107.0	104.5	112.3	109.7
白　酒（市斤）	Liquor(500g)	0.9	1.0	1.0	1.0
果　酒（市斤）	Fruit Wine (500g)	0.2	0.3	0.3	0.2
啤　酒（市斤）	Beer (500g)	3.0	3.6	4.7	4.0
糕　点（市斤）	Cake(500g)	4.6	4.2	4.8	5.3
鲜乳品（市斤）	Fresh Dairy Products (500g)	12.0	12.8	18.9	21.8
奶　粉（市斤）	Milk Powder (500g)	0.6	0.6	0.6	0.7
服　装（件）	Clothes(unit)	5.1	5.6	6.6	6.5
鞋（双）	Shoes(pair)	2.4	2.5	2.6	2.7
水（吨）	Water(ton)	25.7	24.5	28.6	28.8
电（度）	Electricity (degree)	307.5	309.7	390.8	385.3
煤　炭（公斤）	Coal (kg)	62.0	61.7	51.8	45.1
罐装液化石油气（公斤）	Liquified Petroleum Gas (kg)	17.9	14.5	13.3	12.2
管道天燃气（立方米）	Piping Gas (cu.m)	26.1	26.4	35.1	39.0

Per Capita Annual Purchases of Principal Goods in Urban Household in Representative Years

2004	2005	2006	2007	2008	2009	2010	2011
9.4	12.3	10.1	10.2	11.5	10.2	9.5	9.7
12.5	15.0	13.6	12.8	19.0	12.6	13.1	12.9
2.0	2.6	2.4	1.9	2.1	2.7	3.2	3.3
1.1	1.1	0.8	0.8	0.7	1.0	1.1	1
3.5	5.0	3.8	4.1	6.3	4.2	4.4	4.6
10.4	14.1	11.8	11.1	13.2	10.7	11.0	11.1
4.3	5.6	4.6	5.3	6.1	5.0	5.1	5.5
113.4	132.5	110.9	113.9	126.5	111.7	111.7	113.1
1.4	1.3	1.3	1.5	0.9	1.1	1.2	1.1
0.2	0.2	0.3	0.2	0.2	0.3	0.4	0.4
4.0	6.5	6.3	4.6	3.8	5.2	5.3	4.8
5.4	6.6	5.9	6.5	11.3	8.1	8.2	7.9
20.4	28.0	25.0	25.3	16.9	19.6	20.2	19.7
0.7	0.6	0.5	0.7	0.9	0.6	0.6	0.5
6.8	6.9	7.1	9.0	6.9	8.7	9.2	9.3
2.8	2.8	2.8	2.8	3.2	4.2	3.7	3.9
26.5	26.1	22.9	22.8	22.2	27.1	28.4	27.2
435.6	449.5	444.9	460.6	439.3	523.1	589.9	591.8
51.4	33.9	46.0	66.5	70.4	34.3	30.5	21.9
12.7	9.8	7.5	6.9	8.1	7.5	5.6	4.8
38.4	58.2	46.4	38.8	33.2	45.2	54.2	70.4

7-10 城镇居民家庭居住情况（2011年）

Conditions of Dwellings of Urban Households （2011）

住房情况	Accommodation data	2011
一、家庭人口数（人/户）	**Number of Persons Per Household(person/household)**	**2.83**
二、现住房总建筑面积（平方米/人）	**Building Area of Living Houses(sq.m/person)**	**28.9**
三、房屋产权(合计)（%）	**Proportion of Property Right of Houses(%)**	
租赁公房	Public Houses Rent	7.30
租赁私房	Private Houses Rent	4.45
原有私房	Originally Self-owned Houses	3.36
房改私房	Present Self-owned Houses	55.03
商品房	Commercial Houses	17.28
其 他	Others	12.58
四、住宅建筑式样(合计)（%）	**Proportion of Patterns of Residential Building(%)**	
单栋住宅	Flats With Complete Facilities (%)	1.01
四居室	4 Rooms	2.10
三居室	3 Rooms	27.01
二居室	2 Rooms	61.41
一居室	1 Rooms	3.69
普通楼房	Ordinary Storeyed Building	3.44
平房及其他	Single-storey Houses and Others	1.34
五、装修状况(合计)（%）	**Proportion of Decoration Condition(%)**	
有装修	Decorated	69.10
未装修	Undecorated	30.90
如果装修过,最近一次装修花费（元/户）	Expenditure of Latest Decoration(yuan/household)	20579.29
六、现有住房按市场价估计值（元/户）	**Estimated Market Price of Present Houses(yuan/household)**	**210531.63**
七、租赁房房租（元/户）	**Expenditure of Rent Houses(yuan/household)**	**409.88**
八、自有房房租折算（元/户）	**Rent of Self-owned Houses(yuan/household)**	**6580.46**
九、购房总金额（元/户）	**Total Expenditure on Purchase of Houses(yuan/household)**	**71260.57**
购房实际支出金额	Expenditure on Purchase Practice of Houses(yuan/household)	68887.27
十、饮水情况(合计)（%）	**Proportion of Water Drinking(%)**	
自来水	Tap Water	91.53
矿泉水	Mineral Water	4.61
纯净水	Pure Water	3.86
井、河水	Well Water and River Water	
其 他	Others	

7-10 续表 continued

住房情况	Accommodation data	2011
十一、用水情况(合计)（%）	**Proportion of Water Use Condition(%)**	
独用自来水	Moloply Use of Tap Water	98.24
公用自来水	Public Tap Water	1.76
井、河水	Well Water and River Water	
其 他	Others	
十二、卫生设备(合计)（%）	**Proportion of Sanitary Facilities(%)**	
无卫生设备	Without Sanitary Facilities	0.25
有厕所浴室	With Bathroom and Lavatory	82.63
有厕所无浴室	With Lavatory but without Bathroom	14.09
公 用	Common-used Sanitary Facilities	3.03
十三、取暖设备(合计)（%）	**Proportion of Heating Facilities(%)**	
无取暖设备	Without Heating Facilities (%)	7.47
空调设备	Air-conditioner	12.50
暖 气	Central Heating	64.35
其 他	Others	15.68
十四、炊用燃料使用情况(合计)（%）	**Proportion of Cooking Fuels(%)**	
管道天煤气	Pipeline Gas	62.25
罐装液化石油气	Liquefied Gas	28.52
煤 炭	Coal	6.04
其他燃料	Others	3.19
十五、除了现住房，还有几处其他住房（套/户）	**Other Living Houses besides Present Living House(unit/household)**	**0.14**
①出租房（套/户）	Houses for Rent(unit/household)	0.1
②偶尔居住房（套/户）	Houses Seldom Living in (unit/household)	0.02
③其它用途房（套/户）	Houses for other Purposes(unit/household)	0.01

7-11 主要年份城镇居民家庭平均每百户年末拥有主要耐用消费品数量

商品名称	Commodity Names	2000	2001	2002	2003
摩托车（辆）	Motorcycle (unit)	5.0	6.0	8.7	10.2
家用汽车（辆）	Car (unit)	0.0	0.0	0.3	0.3
洗衣机（台）	Washing Machine (unit)	96.7	97.7	97.3	95.7
电冰箱（台）	Refrigerator (unit)	91.0	91.3	95.7	91.8
彩色电视机（台）	Color TV Set (unit)	124.0	123.7	128.3	127.0
家用电脑（台）	Computer (unit)	11.7	15.7	19.0	23.9
组合音响（套）	Hi-Fi System (set)	16.7	19.3	23.0	22.9
摄像机（台）	Pick-up Camera (unit)	1.0	0.3	1.0	1.7
照相机（架）	Camera (set)	46.3	47.3	48.0	48.3
钢琴（架）	Piano (set)	1.3	0.3	1.7	2.0
其它中高档乐器（件）	Other High-Grade Musical Instruments (unit)	2.3	3.7	6.7	5.9
微波炉（台）	Oven (unit)	18.0	27.7	39.3	42.2
空调器（台）	Air Conditioner (unit)	51.3	54.3	75.0	82.4
淋浴热水器（台）	Shower(unit)	52.3	52.3	63.7	70.0
健身器材（件）	Health Care Equipment (unit)	3.3	3.0	1.7	2.6
消毒碗柜（台）	Disinfecting Cupboard(unit)	0.0	0.0	1.7	4.7
洗碗机（台）	Dishwasher (unit)	0.0	0.0	0.0	0.0
固定电话（部）	Telephone (unit)	81.3	86.0	88.0	87.1
移动电话（部）	Hand Telephone (unit)	7.6	19.3	48.3	74.4

Number of Durable Consumer Goods Owned Every 100 Urban Households in Representative Years

2004	2005	2006	2007	2008	2009	2010	2011
9.1	8.6	8.9	5.4	7.9	7.6	8.0	8.3
0.3	0.6	0.9	2.0	4.0	9.0	13.3	16.7
98.3	101.1	101.1	98.9	95.3	98.8	100.3	100.8
91.2	90.9	94.4	95.7	89.2	95.0	97.1	97.7
134.0	134.0	136.0	134.5	119.9	126.7	128.7	129.9
31.7	20.3	37.1	45.6	54.0	68.8	76.1	82.0
20.0	34.0	20.6	24.8	19.0	25.2	27.7	28.0
1.1	3.1	4.3	4.8	7.7	9.7	11.1	11.8
44.3	49.7	47.7	50.1	39.9	52.1	57.7	62.0
2.0	1.4	1.7	1.1	2.4	2.4	2.7	2.5
7.1	11.4	12.9	6.0	4.7	5.3	5.3	5.8
47.1	52.0	52.9	56.4	52.7	62.1	66.4	68.4
92.6	99.7	102.9	116.0	104.0	119.7	129.5	135.1
74.9	110.3	71.4	74.1	70.9	79.9	82.3	84.1
2.9	6.9	3.4	4.0	4.3	4.8	5.0	5.5
7.1	29.4	6.0	7.4	5.5	7.8	8.5	8.9
0.0	0.0	0.0	0.6	0.6	0.3	0.8	0.8
85.7	88.0	79.1	75.2	67.4	72.8	71.5	69.9
102.0	119.7	144.3	162.3	162.1	185.3	196.4	207.1

7-12 主要年份农民家庭基本情况

项　　目	Item	1998	1999
一、调查户数（户）	**Households Surveyed(household)**	**460**	**460**
二、调查人口（人）	**Residents Sueveyed(person)**		
1.常住人口	Average Number of Permanent Residents	2028	2024
2.整半劳动力	Average Number Able-bodied and Semi-able-bodied Laborers Per Households	1279	1296
3.平均每个劳动力负担人口	Persons Supported by Each Laborers	1.59	1.56
三、平均每人全年收入(元)	**Per Capita Annual Income(yuan)**		
1.总收入	Total Revenue	2597.24	2711.55
2.纯收入	Net Income	2052.07	2202.73
3.现金收入	Cash Income	2087.96	2288.00
4.可支配收入	Disposable Income		
四、按人均纯收入分组（%）	**Grouped by Per Capita Annual Net Income(%)**		
户数占总户数比重	Percentage of Households		
1000元以下	Below 1000 yuan		
1000-2000元	1000-2000 yuan		
2000-3000元	2000-3000 yuan		
3000-4000元	3000-4000 yuan		
4000-5000元	4000-5000 yuan		
5000元以上	Over 5000 yuan		
五、农民家庭房屋情况	**Rural Household Housing Condition**		
1.年末人均住房价值(元)	Average Value of Living House Per Capita of Year-end(yuan)	4813.50	4850.32
2.年末人均住房面积(m^2)	Average Floor Space of Living House Per Capita at Year-end(sq.m)	27.32	26.80
3.年内人均新建房屋面积(m^2)	Percapita Space of Building Newly Built Within the year (sq.m)	1.33	2.03
4.年内人均新建房屋价值(元)	Percapita Value of Building Newly Built Within the Year(yuan)	308.01	304.40
六、人均生活消费支出总计（元）	**Per Capita Living Expenditure Built(yuan)**	**1564.81**	**1492.43**
食品消费支出	Food	663.75	584.18
衣着	Clothing	120.76	112.83
居住	Residence	327.56	247.45
家庭设备用品及服务	Household Facilities,Articles and Services	87.43	97.79
医疗保健	Medical and Health Care Services	72.72	94.60
交通通讯	Transport and Communications	51.99	62.45
文化娱乐用品及服务	Culture,Educational and Recreational Articles and Services	196.96	230.09
其它商品及服务	Other Commodities and Services	43.64	63.04

Basic Indicators of Rural Households In Representative Years

2000	2001	2002	2003	2004	2005	2006	2007	2008	2009	2010	2011
500	**770**	**770**	**750**	**710**	**720**	**700**	**700**	**900**	**940**	**940**	**940**
2147	3214	3212	3102	2920	3040	2935	2924	3628	3828	3704	3732
1371	2008	2017	1993	1873	1904	1841	1863	2422	2557	2469	2570
1.57	1.60	1.59	1.56	1.56	1.60	1.59	1.57	1.50	1.50	1.50	1.50
2929.23	3185.54	3370.82	3571.71	3889.12	4495.44	4968.93	5605.12	6746.04	7961.26	9737.00	11910.00
2343.76	2490.27	2641.44	2837.83	3142.78	3459.60	3808.38	4398.64	5212.14	6275.22	7750.00	9788.00
2513.14	2747.00	2965.92	3042.02	3299.16	3940.24	4466.49	4969.58	6249.34	7297.58	9265.00	11278.00
2225.13	2357.30	2560.58	2729.88	3021.25	3353.43	3562.80	4167.18	4983.23	6008.41	7369.00	
		11.69	10.00	5.49	5.14	3.57	2.57	1.89	1.70	1.06	
		28.57	26.67	22.40	18.33	14.57	7.57	7.33	3.83	2.45	
		27.92	26.00	28.45	25.00	22.43	15.14	13.78	7.98	5.74	
		15.45	16.13	19.30	20.70	19.43	21.00	13.00	12.55	6.91	
		5.97	10.00	9.01	11.94	13.57	17.72	14.00	12.87	11.28	
		10.40	11.20	15.35	18.89	26.43	36.00	50.00	61.07	72.55	
5398.21	6286.53	6883.06	7354.40	7780.97	9052.30	10878.22	13145.27	20476.11	24500.32	32059.00	37103.00
28.31	29.72	32.54	33.90	34.66	36.73	40.05	42.92	54.97	56.73	67.00	63.00
1.58	1.81	2.20	0.98	1.13	1.13	1.82	2.03	1.80	2.62	4.00	2.00
408.07	475.33	484.18	239.47	309.07	365.97	746.64	787.03	784.68	1349.27	2380.00	1591.00
1605.36	**1676.42**	**1782.14**	**1802.75**	**2276.65**	**2602.68**	**2708.87**	**3380.80**	**3938.09**	**4771.06**	**5633**	**6705**
587.97	567.62	553.78	677.03	812.47	945.76	996.75	1289.61	1455.22	1708.35	1833	2138
106.80	105.53	115.02	113.15	133.97	159.09	174.81	205.85	256.92	305.46	369	483
343.71	409.90	444.92	314.04	478.37	462.21	488.47	768.16	763.44	928.87	1375	1604
87.89	74.29	83.64	98.59	104.93	133.11	152.83	191.26	276.61	332.52	368	476
111.25	115.92	136.18	128.47	173.89	213.04	216.67	257.14	316.95	405.62	481	580
67.51	88.83	115.14	143.45	191.89	213.12	236.97	256.27	308.85	469.06	476	604
232.61	241.31	275.38	296.80	340.88	420.45	387.51	352.98	489.68	531.23	631	699
67.62	73.02	58.08	31.22	40.25	55.90	54.86	59.53	70.42	89.95	100	121

7-13 主要年份农村居民家庭人均总收入和纯收入

单位：元

指　标	Item	2005	2006
一、全年总收入	Annul Total Revenue	**4495.44**	**4968.92**
1.工资性收入	Wages Income	1292.69	1498.79
2.家庭经营收入	Household Business Income	2612.18	2799.09
3.财产性收入	Property Income	330.42	388.00
4.转移性收入	Transfer Income	260.15	283.04
二、全年纯收入	Annul Net Income	**3459.60**	**3808.38**
1.工资性收入	Wages Income	1292.69	1498.79
2.家庭经营纯收入	Household Business Net Income	1629.54	1661.10
（1）第一产业收入	'Income from Primary Industry	982.81	992.79
（2）第二产业收入	Income from Secondary Industry	143.16	166.33
（3）第三产业收入	Income from Tertiary Industry	503.57	502.00
3.财产性收入	Property Income	330.42	388.00
4.转移性收入	Transfer Income	206.95	260.46

Per Capita Annual Total Revenue and Net Income of Rural Households In Representative Years

(yuan)

2007	2008	2009	2010	2011
5605.13	**6746.04**	**7961.25**	**9736.93**	**11910**
1751.84	2161.42	2587.24	3307.61	4282
3063.28	3595.63	4109.86	4734.60	5347
449.52	553.35	738.95	1025.49	1417
340.49	435.64	525.20	669.23	864
4398.64	**5212.14**	**6275.22**	**7750.35**	**9788**
1751.84	2161.42	2587.24	3307.61	4282
1887.68	2092.35	2469.83	2826.61	3413
1168.79	1232.01	1431.38	1532.79	1740
177.99	241.48	257.74	290.73	375
540.90	618.86	780.71	1003.09	1298
449.52	553.35	738.95	1025.49	1418
309.60	405.02	479.20	590.64	675

7-14 农村居民家庭平均每人总收入和纯收入（2011年）

单位：元

项　　目	Item	西安市 Xi'an	灞桥区 Baqiao	未央区 Weiyang
一、全年总收入	**Annual Total Revenue**	**11910**	**12332**	**12868**
（一）工资性收入	Income from Wages and Salaries	4282	4964	5684
（二）家庭经营收入	Income from Household Operations	5347	3962	1462
（三）财产性收入	Income from Properties	1417	2280	4783
（四）转移性收入	Income from Transfers	864	1126	939
二、全年纯收入	**Annual Net Income**	**9788**	**11291**	**12383**
（一）工资性收入	Wages Income	4282	4964	5684
（二）家庭经营纯收入	Household Business Net Income	3413	3067	1188
1.第一产业收入	Income from Primary Industry	1740	733	36
2.第二产业收入	Income from Secondary Industry	375	616	239
3.第三产业收入	Income from Tertiary Industry	1298	1718	913
（三）财产性收入	Property Income	1418	2280	4783
（四）转移性收入	Transfer Income	675	980	728
三、可支配收入	**Disposable Income**			

Per Capita Annual Total Revenue and Net Income of Rural Households（2011）

（yuan)

雁塔区 Yanta	阎良区 Yanliang	临潼区 Lintong	长安区 Chang'an	蓝田县 Lantian	周至县 Zhouzhi	户　县 Huxian	高陵县 Gaoling
13266	**17686**	**11736**	**11180**	**7659**	**8949**	**11426**	**11541**
4848	3242	4115	4910	3484	2492	4331	3770
2439	12340	6250	4663	3378	5898	6454	6144
5544	796	218	421	154	206	31	966
435	1308	1153	1186	643	353	610	661
12585	**11426**	**9110**	**9421**	**6704**	**6615**	**8265**	**9053**
4848	3242	4115	4910	3484	2492	4331	3770
1858	6465	3823	3281	2549	3648	3457	3724
	3452	2854	696	1739	2435	2373	1973
670	670	636	138	-175	515	506	36
1188	2343	333	2447	985	698	578	1715
5544	796	218	422	154	207	32	966
335	923	954	808	517	268	445	593

7-15 农村居民家庭基本情况（2011年）

项　目	Item	西安市 Xi'an	灞桥区 Baqiao	未央区 Weiyang
一、调查户数（户）	**Number of Households Surveyed (household)**	**940**	**100**	**80**
二、常住人口（人）	**Permanent Residents(person)**	**3732**	**398**	**353**
6岁及以下	6 Year-old and Below	200	22	25
7-15岁人口	7-15 Year-old	316	29	29
16-60岁人口	16-60 Year-old	2726	299	249
61岁以上人口	61 Year-old and Above	490	48	50
三、整半劳动力（人）	**Able-bodied and Semi-able-bodied Labourer(person)**	**2570**	**289**	**233**
四、常住人口外出从业人数（人）	**Permanent Residents Employed in Other Places Outside(person)**	**480**	**66**	
五、劳动力文化程度（人）	**Labourer Literacy(person)**	**2096**	**263**	**175**
1.不识字或识字很少	Illiterates or Semi-illiterates	14	3	
2.小学文化程度	Primary Schools	156	5	2
3. 初中文化程度	Junior Secondary Schools	1142	167	91
4. 高中程度	Senior Secondary Schools	573	61	47
5.中专程度	Specialized Secondary Schools	89	9	20
6. 大专及以上	Universities and Colleges and Above	122	18	15
六、人均耕地经营面积（亩）	**Area of Cultivated Land Managed per Capita(mu)**	**0.83**	**0.44**	**0.06**

Basic Conditions of Rural Households（2011）

雁塔区 Yanta	阎良区 Yanliang	临潼区 Lintong	长安区 Chang'an	蓝田县 Lantian	周至县 Zhouzhi	户 县 Huxian	高陵县 Gaoling
80	**80**	**100**	**120**	**90**	**90**	**100**	**100**
300	**281**	**388**	**490**	**338**	**385**	**418**	**381**
18	8	16	23	23	23	20	22
30	11	38	37	37	33	46	26
224	220	282	353	233	285	294	287
28	42	52	77	45	44	58	46
199	**189**	**265**	**324**	**239**	**253**	**305**	**274**
13	**12**	**89**	**54**	**46**	**32**	**94**	**74**
147	**51**	**247**	**248**	230	203	305	227
	1	3	1	2		2	2
3	1	21	30	21	21	40	12
52	21	136	149	166	100	133	127
62	22	75	49	29	57	108	63
8	3	5	11	7	8	6	12
22	3	7	8	5	17	16	11
0.02	0.82	1.3	0.81	1.03	1.29	1.12	1.22

7-16 农村居民家庭平均每人全年总支出（2011年）

单位：元

项　　目	Item	西安市 Xi'an	灞桥区 Baqiao	未央区 Weiyang
全年总支出	**Annual Total Expenditure**	**9367**	**8713**	**11488**
一、家庭经营费用支出	**Expenditure for Household Business**	**1753**	**624**	**197**
#农业支出	Farming	872	154	13
牧业支出	Animal Husbandry	526	319	11
二、购置生产用固定资产支出	**Purchasing Productive Fixed Assets**	**208**	**13**	**425**
三、建造生产性固定资产雇工支出	**Expenditure on labor hiring on building of productive fixed assets**	**2**		
四、税费支出	**Expenditure for Tax and Fee**	**12**	**4**	
五、生活消费支出	**Expenditure for Living Consumption**	**6705**	**7484**	**10248**
六、财产性支出	**Expenditure for Property**	**4**		
七、转移性支出	**Expenditure for Transfer**	**683**	**588**	**618**

7-17 农村居民家庭平均每人生活消费支出（2011年）

单位：元

项　　目	Item	西安市 Xi'an	灞桥区 Baqiao	未央区 Weiyang
生活消费支出总计	**Living Expenditure**	**6705**	**7484**	**10248**
一、食品消费支出	**Food**	**2138**	**2195**	**2504**
二、衣着	**Clothing**	**483**	**545**	**721**
三、居住	**Residence**	**1604**	**1667**	**4026**
四、家庭设备用品及服务	**Household Facilities,Articles and Service**	**476**	**446**	**457**
五、医疗保健	**Medical and Health Care Services**	**580**	**604**	**841**
六、交通通讯	**Transport,Post and Telecommunication Services**	**604**	**1061**	**617**
七、文化娱乐用品及服务	**Cultural,Educational and Recreational Articles and Services**	**699**	**813**	**919**
八、其它商品及服务	**Other Commodities and Services**	**121**	**153**	**163**
附：人均生活消费现金支出	Per Capita Cash Expenditure for Living Consumption	6556	7475	10244

Per Capita Annual Total Expenditure of Rural Households（2011）

（yuan)

雁塔区 Yanta	阎良区 Yanliang	临潼区 Lintong	长安区 Chang'an	蓝田县 Lantian	周至县 Zhouzhi	户 县 Huxian	高陵县 Gaoling
9914	13359	10976	8600	6059	7803	9848	8050
447	5710	2219	1206	685	2169	2732	2174
	5470	777	334	294	1268	720	789
	43	1085	68	133	739	1799	743
28	13	558	354	215	280	31	66
	2						20
18	2		37	3	26	21	1
8882	7037	7401	6388	4713	4520	5997	5095
		6	17	4			8
539	595	792	598	439	808	1067	686

Per Capita Living Expenditure of Rural Households（2011）

（yuan)

雁塔区 Yanta	阎良区 Yanliang	临潼区 Lintong	长安区 Chang'an	蓝田县 Lantian	周至县 Zhouzhi	户 县 Huxian	高陵县 Gaoling
8882	7037	7401	6388	4713	4522	5997	5095
3703	2519	1892	1753	1970	1535	1806	2091
733	584	514	376	298	460	375	341
1383	876	1933	1689	939	685	1793	871
552	902	664	432	387	270	466	309
652	406	764	720	460	388	468	446
512	695	907	590	323	445	439	415
1198	991	590	714	276	596	589	459
149	64	137	114	60	143	61	163
8882	6867	7255	6382	4094	4371	5688	4965

7-18 农村居民家庭人均生产情况（2011年）

单位：公斤

项　目	Item	西安市 Xi'an	灞桥区 Baqiao	未央区 Weiyang
粮食产量	Output of Grain	579		15
#1.小麦	Wheat	321		9
2.玉米	Corn	249		6
3.大豆	Soybean	1		
棉花产量	Output of Cotton			
油料产量	Output of Oil-bearing Crops			
蔬菜产量	Output of Vegetables	193		
水果产量	Output of Fruits	140		

7-19 农村居民家庭人均出售产品情况（2011年）

单位：公斤

项　目	Item	西安市 Xi'an	灞桥区 Baqiao	未央区 Weiyang
粮食	Grain	363	43	8
棉花	Cotton			
油料	Oil-bearing Corps			
蔬菜	Vegetables	193	4	
水果	Fruits	56	24	
肉猪及猪肉	Fattened Hogs & Pork	21		
菜牛及牛肉	Beef Cattle & Beef	1		
菜羊及羊肉	Mutton Sheep & Mutton			
蛋类	Poultry Eggs	4		
奶类	Milks	56	42	7

Output of Major Farm Crops Per Capita by Rural Households（2011）

（kg）

雁塔区 Yanta	阎良区 Yanliang	临潼区 Lintong	长安区 Chang'an	蓝田县 Lantian	周至县 Zhouzhi	户 县 Huxian	高陵县 Gaoling
	844	523	559	503	346	1213	926
	397	251	287	248	147	589	468
	447	205	272	242	199	623	443
				7			
				1			
	1515	143		14	83	75	449
	37	45			1238	45	3

Per Capita Product Sold by Rural Households（2011）

（kg）

雁塔区 Yanta	阎良区 Yanliang	临潼区 Lintong	长安区 Chang'an	蓝田县 Lantian	周至县 Zhouzhi	户 县 Huxian	高陵县 Gaoling
	671	674	369	427	222	444	763
	1451	175	56	25	63	66	410
	38	44	39	23	326	39	3
	32	1	7	3	34	98	27
		1		9			
						9	32
	289	213		5			65

7-20 农村居民家庭人均粮食收支情况（2011年）

单位：公斤

项　目	Item	西安市 Xi'an	灞桥区 Baqiao	未央区 Weiyang
一、粮食收入合计	**Total Grain Income**	**664**	**130**	**97**
1.家庭经营生产	Self-produced	579		15
2.购入	Purchased	84	130	82
3.借入	Borrowed			
4.收回借出粮	Grains Taken Back	1		
5.其它粮食收入	Other Grain Income			
二、粮食支出合计	**Total Grain Expenditure**	**536**	**183**	**92**
1.主食用粮	Staple Food	138	93	83
2.其它生活用粮	Other Living Uses			
3.出售	Sold Out	363	44	8
4.种籽	Seeds	9	1	
5.饲料	Fodder	26	45	1
6.借出	Lent Out			
7.归还借粮	Grains Returned			
8.其它粮食支出	Other Grain Expenditure			
三、年末粮食结存调查数	**Year-end Grain Deposite Balance**	**340**	**49**	

7-21 农村居民家庭平均每人购买商品（2011年）

单位：元

商品名称	Commodity Names	西安市 Xi'an	灞桥区 Baqiao	未央区 Weiyang
一、食品类	**Food**	**1599**	**1849**	**2049**
二、衣着类	**Clothing**	**482**	**544**	**718**
三、居住类	**Residence**	**1043**	**979**	**2623**
四、家用设备和日用品	**Household Facilities and Articles**	**453**	**415**	**450**
五、交通、通讯类	**Transport,post and Telecommunication**	**349**	**601**	**359**
六、文教类	**Cultural and Edueation**	**213**	**112**	**246**
七、医疗保健类	**Health Care and Medical Services**	**187**	**144**	**320**
八、其他杂项商品	**Other Commodities and Services**	**82**	**131**	**119**

Per Capita Annual Income and Expenditure of Grains of Rural Households（2011）

（kg)

雁塔区 Yanta	阎良区 Yanliang	临潼区 Lintong	长安区 Chang'an	蓝田县 Lantian	周至县 Zhouzhi	户 县 Huxian	高陵县 Gaoling
78	**922**	**627**	**616**	**555**	**433**	**1277**	**1045**
	844	523	559	503	346	1213	926
78	78	92	57	52	87	63	119
		12					
						1	
87	**833**	**852**	**429**	**824**	**391**	**679**	**1004**
87	137	121	50	380	150	194	118
	671	674	369	427	222	444	763
	23	8	7	10	16	15	13
	2	48	3	7	3	25	110
		1				1	
	208	**840**	**726**	**346**	**254**	**361**	**376**

Per Capita Purchase of Commodities in Rural Househlods（2011）

（yuan)

雁塔区 Yanta	阎良区 Yanliang	临潼区 Lintong	长安区 Chang'an	蓝田县 Lantian	周至县 Zhouzhi	户 县 Huxian	高陵县 Gaoling
2811	**2194**	**1353**	**1366**	**1124**	**1035**	**1078**	**1638**
730	**582**	**511**	**376**	**296**	**460**	**374**	**341**
382	**500**	**1622**	**976**	**748**	**549**	**1395**	**434**
519	**885**	**645**	**415**	**333**	**236**	**454**	**299**
128	**530**	**708**	**308**	**139**	**284**	**176**	**247**
204	**588**	**292**	**137**	**79**	**145**	**268**	**167**
240	**124**	**266**	**127**	**126**	**208**	**199**	**129**
91	**34**	**70**	**68**	**39**	**109**	**38**	**112**

7-22 农村居民家庭人均主要食品消费量（2011年）

单位：公斤

食品名称	Food Names	西安市 Xi'an	灞桥区 Baqiao	未央区 Weiyang
一、粮食	**Grain**	**138**	**93**	**83**
#小麦	Wheet	103	50	66
二、油脂类	**Oil or Fat**	**9**	**12**	**7**
三、蔬菜及菜制品	**Vegetable and Its Products**	**74**	**86**	**100**
四、瓜果类	**Melons and Fruits**	**9**	**9**	**11**
五、水果类	**Fruits**	**16**	**15**	**22**
六、肉禽及制品	**Meat,Poultry and Their Products**	**12**	**13**	**14**
七、蛋类及蛋制品	**Eggs and Its Products**	**7**	**9**	**7**
八、奶和奶制品	**Milk and Dairy Products**	**11**	**9**	**16**
九、酒	**Liquor**	**5**	**5**	**4**

Per Capita Average Food Consumption of Rural Households（2011）

（kg）

雁塔区 Yanta	阎良区 Yanliang	临潼区 Lintong	长安区 Chang'an	蓝田县 Lantian	周至县 Zhouzhi	户　县 Huxian	高陵县 Gaoling
87	**137**	**121**	**50**	**380**	**150**	**194**	**118**
24	80	102	32	317	103	161	106
9	**10**	**9**	**8**	**9**	**7**	**8**	**11**
94	**101**	**61**	**77**	**70**	**31**	**48**	**86**
9	**15**	**12**	**2**	**5**	**8**	**7**	**16**
25	**21**	**16**	**16**	**8**	**12**	**14**	**15**
18	**28**	**6**	**10**	**7**	**8**	**12**	**9**
9	**11**	**6**	**5**	**5**	**6**	**6**	**5**
13	**15**	**13**	**11**	**7**	**10**	**8**	**9**
4	**6**	**6**	**5**	**4**	**2**	**3**	**8**

7-23 农村居民家庭每百户耐用消费品年末拥有量（2011年）

品　名	Item	西安市 Xi'an	灞桥区 Baqiao	未央区 Weiyang
大型家具(件)	Large Furnitures (unit)			
洗衣机(台)	Washing Machine(unit)	100	105	103
电风扇(台)	Electric Fan(unit)			
电冰箱(台)	Refrigerator(unit)	66	82	100
空调机(台)	Air Conditioner(unit)	54	62	105
热水器(台)	Water Heater(unit)	51	62	88
自行车(辆)	Bicycle (unit)	131	122	116
摩托车(辆)	Motorcycle(unit)	35	28	1
生活用汽车(辆)	Automobile(unit)	9	8	21
电话机(部)	Telephone (unit)	57	28	43
移动电话(部)	Mobile Phone(unit)	207	241	253
彩色电视机(台)	Color TV Set(unit)	133	151	149
黑白电视机(台)	Black-white TV Set(unit)	3		13
影碟机(台)	Video Disc Player (unit)	48	91	1
照相机(架)	Camera(set)	17	21	30
家用计算机(台)	Computer(unit)	29	22	73

7-24 农村居民家庭人均住房情况（2011年）

指　标	Item	西安市 Xi'an	灞桥区 Baqiao	未央区 Weiyang
一、年末住房面积 (平方米)	**Floor Space of Houses at the End of Year (sq.m)**	**67**	**88**	**103**
二、住房类型 (平方米)	**Pattern of Houses(sq.m)**	**67**	**88**	**103**
1. 楼房面积	Floor Space of Storied Building	52	72	103
2. 砖瓦平房面积	Floor Space of Single-storey Building	15	16	
3. 其他	Others			
三、年末住房价值(元)	**Value of Houses at the End of Year (yuan)**	**37103**	**33446**	**90108**
四、年内新建（购）房屋面积(平方米)	**Floor Space Of Newly-Built Purchased Houses (sq.m)**	**2**		**11**
年内新建（购）房屋价值(元)	Value of Houses of Newly-Built Purchased (yuan)	1591		11323

Year-end Possession of Durable Consumer Goods Per 100 Rural Households（2011）

雁塔区 Yanta	阎良区 Yanliang	临潼区 Lintong	长安区 Chang'an	蓝田县 Lantian	周至县 Zhouzhi	户　县 Huxian	高陵县 Gaoling
104	100	105	97	80	100	97	112
100	78	58	46	34	50	41	91
129	65	37	23	7	34	18	89
98	30	49	12	18	51	29	92
98	180	152	125	59	114	200	133
9	59	56	20	22	71	23	55
21	4	4	2	3	10	2	22
90	70	47	72	58	38	77	47
250	211	203	118	171	248	184	228
149	131	137	103	94	143	145	138
		4	13	3			
99	21	68	58	24	42	19	46
90	10	4	5	4	10	7	9
88	24	16	7	13	17	16	41

Per Capita Housing Conditions of Rural Households（2011）

雁塔区 Yanta	阎良区 Yanliang	临潼区 Lintong	长安区 Chang'an	蓝田县 Lantian	周至县 Zhouzhi	户　县 Huxian	高陵县 Gaoling
141	**57**	**43**	**41**	**41**	**45**	**50**	**66**
141	57	43	41	41	45	50	66
140	21	10	28	18	31	45	28
1	36	33	13	23	14	5	37
							1
95945	**41955**	**14635**	**13132**	**29486**	**34312**	**18800**	**25238**
		1	**2**	**1**		**1**	**1**
		903	1018	1569		626	781

主要统计指标解释

一、城镇住户

城镇家庭人口 指居住在一起，经济上合在一起共同生活的家庭成员。凡计算为家庭人口的成员其全部收支都包括在本家庭中。

城镇就业面 指就业人口占家庭人口的百分比。

城镇就业者负担人数 指家庭人口与就业人口之比。

城镇家庭总收入 指家庭成员得到的工薪收入、经营净收入、财产性收入、转移性收入之和，不包括出售财物收入和借贷收入。

城镇家庭可支配收入 指家庭成员得到可用于最终消费支出和其它非义务性支出以及储蓄的总和，即居民家庭可以用来自由支配的收入。它是家庭总收入扣除交纳的个人所得税、个人交纳的社会保障支出以及记账补贴后的收入。计算公式为：

可支配收入=家庭总收入-交纳个人所得税-个人交纳的社会保障支出-记账补贴

城镇家庭总支出 指除借贷支出以外的全部家庭支出。包括消费性支出、购房建房支出、转移性支出、财产性支出、社会保障支出。

城镇家庭消费性支出 指家庭用于日常生活的支出，包括食品、衣着、居住、家庭设备用品及服务、医疗保健、交通和通信、娱乐教育文化服务、其他商品和服务等八大类支出。

恩格尔系数 指食物支出金额在消费性总支出金额中所占的比例。计算公式为：

$$恩格尔系数=\frac{食品支出金额}{消费性总支出金额}\times 100\%$$

二、农村住户

农村住户 指农村常住户。农村常住户指长期（一年以上）居住在乡镇（不包括城关镇）行政管理区域内的住户，以及长期居住在城关镇所辖行政村范围内的农村住户。户口不在本地而在本地居住一年及以上的住户也包括在本地农村常住户范围内；有本地户口，但举家外出谋生一年以上的住户，无论是否保留承包耕地都不包括在本地农村住户范围内。

常住人口 指全年经常在家或在家居住6个月以上，而且经济和生活与本户连成一体的人口。外出从业人员在外居住时间虽然在6个月以上，但收入主要带回家中，经济与本户连为一体，仍视为家庭常住人口；在家居住，生活和本户连成一体的国家职工、退休人员也为家庭常住人口。但是现役军人、中专及以上(走读生除外)的在校学生、以及常年在外（不包括探亲、看病等）且已有稳定的职业与居住场所的外出从业人员，不算家庭常住人口。家庭常住人口主要作为计算农村住户平均每人收入、消费和积累水平及分析家庭人口状况的依据。

整、半劳动力 整劳动力指男子18周岁到50周岁，女子18周岁到45周岁；半劳动力指男子16周岁到17周岁，51周岁到60周岁；女子16周岁到17周岁，46周岁到55周岁，同时具有劳动能力的人。虽然在劳动年龄之内，但已丧失劳动能力的人，不应算为劳动力；超过劳动年龄，但能经常参加劳动，计入半劳动力数内。常住人口中的职工，若这些职工为劳动力，就包括在本户的整半劳动力中。

总收入 指调查期内农村住户和住户成员从各种来源渠道得到的收入总和。按收入的性质划分为工资性收入、家庭经营收入、财产性收入和转移性收入。

工资性收入 指农村住户成员受雇于单位或个人，靠出卖劳动而获得的收入。

家庭经营收入 指农村住户以家庭为生产经营单位进行生产筹划和管理而获得的收入。农村住户家庭经营活动按行业划分为农业、林业、牧业、渔业、工业、建筑业、交通运输业邮电业、批发和零售贸易餐饮业、社会服务业、文教卫生业和其他家庭经营。

财产性收入 指金融资产或有形非生产性资产的所有者向其他机构单位提供资金或将有形非生产性资产供其支配，作为回报而从中获得的收入。

转移性收入 指农村住户和住户成员无须付出任何对应物而获得的货物、服务、资金或资产所有权等，不包括无偿提供的用于固定资本形成的资金。一般情况下，是指农村住户在二次分配中的所有收入。

现金收入 指农村住户和住户成员在调查期内得到以现金形态表现的收入。按来源分成工资性收入、家庭经营现金收入、财产性收入、转移性收入。

纯收入 指农村住户当年从各个来源得到的总收入相应地扣除所发生的费用后的收入总和。计算方法：

纯收入=总收入-税费支出-家庭经营费用支出-生产性固定资产折旧-赠送农村内部亲友支出

纯收入主要用于再生产投入和当年生活消费支出，也可用于储蓄和各种非义务性支出。“农民人均纯收入”是按人口平均的纯收入水平，反映的是一个地区农村居民的平均收入水平。

总支出 指农村住户用于生产、生活和再分配的全部支出。包括家庭经营费用支出、购置生产性固定资产支出、税费支出、生活消费支出、财产性支出和转移性支出。

Explanatory Notes on Main Statistical Indicators

I. Urban Households

Population of Urban Households refer to members of households living and sharing economically together in the urban areas. All the income and expenditure of all the members of such households are included in the income and expenditure of the household.

Proportion of Urban Employment refers to the proportion of employed population to the population of urban households.

Number of Dependents per Urban Employee refers to the ratio between number of persons in an urban household and the number of employed persons.

Total Income of Urban Households refers to the sum of wage and salary; net business income; income from properties; and income from transfers of members of the households. Income from selling of properties and income from borrowing are not included..

Disposable Income of Urban Households refers to the actual income at the disposal of members of the households which can be used for final consumption, other non-compulsory expenditure and savings. This equals to total income minus income tax, personal contribution to social security and subsidy for keeping diaries in being a sample household. The following formula is used:

Disposable income = total household income - income tax - personal contribution to social security - subsidy for keeping diaries for a sampled household

Total Expenditure of Urban Households refers to all expenditure of households except expenditure on lending. It includes expenditure on consumption; on purchasing or building houses; on transfers; on properties; and on social security.

Consumption Expenditure of Urban Households refers to total expenditure of households for consumption in daily life, including expenditure on the eight categories of food; clothing; housing; household appliances and services; health care and medical services; transport and communications; recreation, education and cultural services; and miscellaneous goods and services.

Expenditure of Urban Households on Consumption of Services refers to expenditure of households on various kinds of non-commercial services provided by society.

Engel's Coefficient refers to the percentage of expenditure on food in the total consumption expenditure, using the following formula:

$$\text{Engel's Coefficient}=\frac{\text{expenditure on food}}{\text{total consumption expenditure}}\times 100\%$$

II. Rural Household

Rural Households refer to usual resident households in rural areas. Usual resident households in rural areas are households residing on a long term basis(for more than one year) in the areas under the administration of township governments (not including county towns), and in the areas under the administration of villages in county towns. Households residing in the current addresses for over one year with their household registration in other places are still considered as resident households of the locality. For households with their household registration in one place but all members of the households having moved away to make a living in another place for over one year, they will not be included in the rural households of the area where they are registered, irrespective of whether they still keep their contracted land.

Usual Resident Population refers to persons staying at home regularly or for over 6 months during a year and integrated with the household economically and in terms of living.. Members of the household staying away from the household for over 6 months but keeping a close economic relation with the household by sending the majority of income to the household are regarded as usual resident of the household. Government staff and workers or retirees living as close members of the household are also considered as usual resident. However, servicemen, students of secondary technical schools or schools of higher education and persons with stable jobs and residence outside the household (excluding those visiting relatives or seeking medical service) are not included as resident population of the household. Resident population is used in calculating income, consumption, accumulation on per capita basis of rural households and in analyzing composition of rural households.

Full/Semi Labour Force Full labour force refers to persons capable of work, aged 18-50 for males and 18-45 for females. Semi labour force refers to persons capable of work, aged 16-17 and 51-60 for males and 16-17 and 46-55 for females. Persons at their working ages but not capable of work are not to be included as labour force.

Persons not at working ages but participating regularly in work are included in semi labour force. For staff and workers who are usual residents, are included as full or semi labour force of the household if they are in the labour force.

Total Income refers to the sum of income earned from various sources by the rural households and their members during the reference period, and is classified as income from wages and salaries, income from household operations, income from properties and income from transfers.

Income from Wages and Salaries refers to income from labour earned by the members of rural households employed by other units or individuals.

Income from Household Operations refers to income by the rural households as units of production and operation. Operations by rural households are classified according to their economic activities namely agriculture, forestry, animal husbandry, fishery, manufacturing, construction, transportation, post and telecommunications, wholesale, retail and catering, social service, culture, education, health, and other household operations.

Income from Properties refers to the income received as returns by owners of financial assets or tangible non-productive assets by providing capitals or tangible non-productive assets to other institutional units.

Income from Transfers refers to the receipt by rural households and their members of goods, services, capital or rights of assets without giving or repaying accordingly, excluding capital provided to them for the formation of fixed assets. In general, it refers to all income received by rural households through redistribution.

Cash Income refers to income received by rural households and their members in the form of cash during the reference period. It is classified, by source of income, into income from wages and salaries, cash income from household operations, income from properties and income from transfers.

Net Income refers to the total income of rural households from all sources minus all corresponding expenses. The formula for calculation is as follows:

Net income = total income - taxes and fees paid - household operation expenses - taxes and fees depreciation of fixed assets for production - gifts to non-rural relatives

Net income is mainly used as input for reinvestment in production and as consumption expenditure of the year, and also used for savings and non-compulsory expenses of various forms. "Per capita net income of farmers" is the level of net income averaged by population, reflecting the average income level of rural households in a given area.

Total Expenditure refers to total expenses of rural households on production, consumption and redistribution, including expenditure on household operations; purchase of productive fixed assets; taxes and fees; expenses on household consumption; expenses on properties; and expenses on transfers.

8 城市公用事业

URBAN PUBLIC UTILITIES

资料整理：陈超毅
Data management:Chen Chaoyi

第八部分　城市公用事业

一、简要说明

本章资料主要包括城市供水、售电、供燃气、供热、公共交通、市政设施、市政设施水平、城市规模及用地状况、园林绿地、环境卫生等情况，由西安市统计局社会科技处根据西安市城建委和西安市供电局等部门提供的数据整理。

二、主要指标

人均公园绿地面积（平方米）	9.89	比上年同口径增长	8.68%
人均城市道路面积（平方米）	15.87	比上年同口径增长	3.05%
用水普及率（%）	99.95	比上年同口径增加	1.18个百分点
燃气普及率（%）	97.46	比上年同口径增加	0.44个百分点
每万人拥有公共交通车辆（标台）	21.8	比上年下降	1.97%

8　URBAN PUBLIC UTILITIES

Ⅰ.Brief IntroductionData in this chapter reflects basic condition of urban public utilities of Xi'an City. Data on public utilities primarily consist of urban water supply, electricity sales, gas sales, urban heating, public transportation, municipal facilities, level of municipal construction, scale of the city, condition of land utilization, parks, greenbelt and environmental sanitation. Data in this chapter is compiled by Social Science & Technology Division of Xi'an Bureau of Statistics according to the data provided by Committee of Urban Construction and Bureau of Electricity Supply of Xi'an, and other department concerned.

Ⅱ.Major Indicators

		Increase over Preceding Year
Per Capita Public Green Areas (sq.m)	9.89	8.68%
Per Captia Area of Roads (sq.m)	15.87	3.05%
Water-Consuming Popularization (%)	99.95	1.18 percentage points
Gas-Consuming Popularization (%)	97.46	0.44 percentage points
Number of Public Transport Vehicles Per 10 000 Population (unit)	21.8	-1.97%

8-1　城市供水

Urban Water Supply

指　　标	Item	2000	2007	2008	2009	2010	2011
年末水厂个数（个）	Number of Water Factory at Year-end (unit)	8	9	9	9	9	15
供水综合生产能力（万立方米/日）	Total Volume of Water Supply (10 000 cu.m/day)	139.9	180.7	180.5	190.0	197.4	197.4
#地下水	Groundwater	73.9	53.7	52.4	55.3	55.8	54.8
年末供水管道总长度（公里）	Length of Water Supply Pipelines at Year-end (km)	2237	2424	2385	1985	2416	2721
全年供水总量（万立方米）	Total Annual Volume of Water Supply (10 000 cu.m)	30273	32959	36471	38307	41089	38934
#生产运营用水	For Productive Use	6486	5570	6292	6414	6267	5484
居民家庭用水	For Residential Use	10949	13931	17510	18513	20944	19945
用水人口（万人）	Population with Access to Tap Water (10 000 persons)	257.0	331.3	374.1	357.6	410.9	394.1

注：1.2009年部门统计制度变化，年末供水管道总长度和用水人口数调整；
　　2.2010年数据口径变化，为全市口径，与往年不可比。

Note:1.Departmental statistical system was changed in 2009,length of water supply pipelines at year-end and population with access to tap water were adjusted.
　　2.Statistic caliber of 2010 has changed to city data, not comparable with that of former years.

8-2　城市供燃气

Gas Supply in Urban Area

指　　标	Item	2000	2007	2008	2009	2010	2011
一、天然气	**Natural Gas**						
管道长度（公里）	Total Length of Gas Pipelines (km)	480	3121	3540	3932	4488	4500
供气总量（万立方米）	Total Gas Supply(10 000 cu.m)	11513	72253	84874	95885	109052	120330
# 家庭用量	Residential Households	2808	9854	13767	15473	20989	22868
用气人口（万人）	Population with Access to Gas (10 000 persons)	79.5	233.6	246.7	285.0	333.1	355.6
二、液化石油气	**Liquefied Petroleum Gas**						
供气总量（吨）	Total Gas Supply (ton)	43304	73081	74164		11469	5920
# 家庭用量	Residential Households	43303	46051	46342		7376	4352
用气人口（万人）	Population with Access to Gas (10 000 persons)	101.6	93.0	81.9		31.2	28.6

注：1.2009年部门统计制度变化，无液化石油气相关统计指标；
　　2.2010年数据为全市口径，2009年以前数据为市区口径。

Note:1.Departmental statistical system was changed in 2009,statistical indicators about liquefied petroeum gas were canceled.
　　2.Statistic caliber of 2010 has changed to data of city,while it was downtown data before 2009.

8-3 城市供热

Heating in Urban Area

指　　标	Item	2000	2007	2008	2009	2010	2011
供热能力	Heating Capacity						
蒸气（吨/小时）	Steam (ton/hour)	766	1680	1063	2118	2235	2075
热水（兆瓦）	Hot Water (1 billion kw)	405	1627	11085	11467	3531	4570
供热总量	Volume Supplied						
蒸气（万吉焦）	Steam (10 000 gigajoules)	126	1510	1192	1541	1674	1421
热水（万吉焦）	Hot Water (10 000 gigajoules)	202	1075	896	1220	2570	2901
管道长度（公里）	Length of Pipelines (km)						
蒸气	Steam	221	296	97	209	180	167
热水	Hot Water	133	263	179	289	361	500
供热面积（万平方米）	Heated Area (10 000sq.m)	854	2811	3179	5178	6094	6524
#住宅	Residential Buildings	536	2098	2616	4325	5009	5226

注：2010年数据为全市口径，2009年以前数据为市区口径。

Note:Statistic Aperture of 2010 has changed to data of city,while it was downtown data before 2009.

8-4 城市公共交通

Urban Public Traffic

指　　标	Item	2000	2007	2008	2009	2010	2011
运营车辆(辆)	Operating Vehicles (unit)	2573	5836	6123	7039	7107	7462
1.汽车	Bus	2488	5772	6059	7004	7107	7462
2.电车	Trolley	85	64	64	35		
标准运营车辆（标台）	Standard Vehicles (unit)	2509	5969	6416	7833	8139	8598
公交客运总量（万人次）	Total of Bus Passenger(10 000 person-time)	44570	114859	139924	161782	162400	175234
公交客运收入（万元）	Bus Passenger Transport Income (10 000 yuan)					129397	141505
出租汽车数（辆）	Number of Taxis (unit)	10277	11879	11879	12786	12786	13839

8-5 市政设施

Municipal Facilities

指　　标	Item	2000	2007	2008	2009	2010	2011
一、道路长度（公里）	**Length of Roads (km)**	**975**	**1842**	**2115**	**2296**	**2662**	**2755**
二、道路面积（万平方米）	**Area of Roads (10 000 sq.m)**	**1263**	**4190**	**4722**	**5057**	**5965**	**6259**
三、人行道面积（万平方米）	**Area of Sidewalks (10 000 sq.m)**	**636**	**1337**	**1470**	**1517**	**1834**	**1867**
四、桥梁数（座）	**Number of Bridges (unit)**	**79**	**259**	**305**	**314**	**347**	**402**
#立交桥	Overpasses	22	48	71	71	71	91
五、路灯盏数（盏）	**Number of Street Lights (unit)**	**27516**	**260000**	**266442**	**271444**	**291754**	**311991**
六、排水管道长度（公里）	**Length of Drainage Pipelines (km)**	**835**	**1964**	**2562**	**2848**	**3765**	**4043**
七、污水年排放量（万立方米）	**Annual Discharge Volume of Sewage (10 000 cu.m)**	**23543**	**24719**	**21886**	**31394**	**34706**	**36673**
八、污水处理厂日处理能力（万立方米/日）	**Daily Disposal Capacity of Sewage (10 000 cu.m/day)**	**29**	**44**	**78**	**80**	**107**	**112**
九、污水处理厂年处理量（万立方米）	**Yearly Disposal Capacity of Sewage Disposal Plant (10 000 cu.m)**	**5441**	**12338**	**13003**	**20386**	**25088**	**31512**
十、防洪堤长度（公里）	**Length of Flood Control Dikes (km)**	**2**	**39**	**119**	**119**	**168**	**168**

注：2010年数据为全市口径，2009年以前数据为市区口径。

Note:Statistic Aperture of 2010 has changed to data of city,while it was downtown data before 2009.

8-6 城市设施水平

Urban Municipal Facilities

指　　标	Item	2000	2007	2008	2009	2010	2011
一、人均日生活用水量（升）	**Per Capita Daily Consumption of Tap Water For Residential Use (liter)**	**241.50**	**187.00**	**179.70**	**198.40**	**186.20**	**185.20**
二、用水普及率（%）	**Water-Consuming Popularization (%)**	**99.00**	**100.00**	**111.20**	**100.00**	**98.77**	**99.95**
三、每万人拥有公共交通车辆（标台）	**Number of Public Transport Vehicles Per 10 000 Population (unit)**	**10.20**	**18.00**	**19.10**	**22.90**	**23.80**	**21.80**
四、燃气普及率（%）	**Gas-Consuming Popularization (%)**	**81.50**	**98.60**	**97.70**	**98.20**	**97.02**	**97.46**
五、人均城市道路面积（平方米）	**Per Captia Area of Roads (sq.m)**	**5.10**	**12.70**	**14.00**	**14.80**	**15.40**	**15.87**
六、建成区排水管道密度（公里/平方公里）	**Density of Drainage Pipelines in Developed Areas (km/sq.km)**	**4.50**	**6.30**	**8.00**	**10.10**	**9.50**	**9.74**
七、污水处理率（%）	**Rate of Sewerage Disposal (%)**	**23.10**	**61.60**	**65.10**	**81.00**	**84.00**	**85.93**
八、园林绿化	**Afforestation and Parks and Gardens**						
#人均公园绿地面积（平方米）	Per Capita Public Green Areas (sq.m)	5.10	7.60	7.80	7.90	9.10	9.89
建成区绿地率（%）	Rate of Green Areas in Developed Areas (%)	19.70	31.10	31.90	40.40	29.20	30.94
九、垃圾无害化处理率（%）	**Rate of No Harm Disposal of Garbage (%)**	**90.90**	**81.20**	**90.40**	**90.30**	**93.90**	**93.69**

注：1.由于用水人口包括不在城市辖区内但已经使用城市供水的人口，故有些年份用水普及率有大于100%；

2.2010年数据为全市口径，2009年以前数据为市区口径。

Note:1.As population with access to tap water contained the people who were out of urban area but had used tap water, water-consuming popularization was over 100% in some year.

2.Statistic Aperture of 2010 has changed to data of city,while it was downtown data before 2009.

8-7 城市规模及用地情况

City Scale and Land Use

指　　标	Item	2000	2007	2008	2009	2010	2011
建成区面积（平方公里）	Area of the Constructed Regions (sq.km)	187	268	273	283	395	415
城市建设用地（平方公里）	Land use for Construction (sq.km)	175	277	370	277	336	349
#工业用地	Industrial	35	61	64	61	61	80
仓储用地	Storage	8	12	4	12	12	14
对外交通用地	External Transportation	10	8	8	8	8	10
生活居住用地	Residential Area	73	66	122	122	122	90

注：2010年数据为全市口径，2009年以前数据为市区口径。

Note:Statistic Aperture of 2010 has changed to data of city,while it was downtown data before 2009.

8-8 城市园林绿化

Urban Parks,Gardens and Green Areas in Cities

指　　标	Item	2000	2007	2008	2009	2010	2011
一、公园个数（个）	**Number of Parks (unit)**	**47**	**50**	**54**	**55**	**68**	**66**
二、公园面积（公顷）	**Area of Parks (hectare)**	**880**	**1129**	**1233**	**1241**	**1335**	**1478**
三、园林绿地总面积（公顷）	**Total Area of Parks,Gardens and Green Areas (hectare)**	**4116**	**8670**	**9199**	**9553**	**12140**	**13680**
#公园绿地面积	Public Green Areas	1263	2520	2625	2700	3526	3898
四、年末绿化覆盖面积（公顷）	**Coverage Space of Green Areas at year-end (hectare)**	**6542**	**11087**	**11616**	**12059**	**15646**	**17325**
五、建成区绿化覆盖率（%）	**Coverage of Green Areas in Developed Areas (%)**	**33.3**	**39.7**	**40.3**	**40.4**	**37.5**	**39.0**

注：1.2006年统计口径发生变化，原“公共绿地面积”改为“公园绿地面积”；

2.2010年数据为全市口径，2009年以前数据为市区口径。

Note:1.As regulations of 2006 were changed, 'public green area' was replaced by 'park green area'.

2.Statistic Aperture of 2010 has changed to data of city,while it was downtown data before 2009.

8-9 城市环境卫生

Urban Environment Sanitation

指　　标	Item	2000	2007	2008	2009	2010	2011
清扫面积(万平方米)	Area Under Cleaning Program (10 000 sq.m)	1739	3646	4218	5285	6290	6411
清运生活垃圾（万吨）	Volume of Residential Garbage Disposal (10 000 tons)	98	147	152	179	237	265
清运粪便（万吨）	Volume of Excrement and Urine Disposal (10 000 tons)	5	4	4	3	3	4
公共厕所（座）	Number of Public Lavatories (unit)	430	962	1131	1131	1257	1493
市容环卫专用车辆（台）	Special Vehicles of Environmental Sanitation (unit)	330	768	716	939	1042	1200

注：2010年数据为全市口径，2009年以前数据为市区口径。

Note:Statistic Aperture of 2010 has changed to data of city,while it was downtown data before 2009.

2.Statistic Aperture of 2010 has changed to data of city,while it was downtown data before 2009.

8-10 市区及县供水（2011年）

Urban Water Supply（2011）

指　　标	Item	西安 Xi'an	市区 City	蓝田县 Lantian	周至县 ZhouZhi	户县 Huxian	高陵县 GaoLing
年末水厂个数（个）	Number of Water Factory at Year-end (unit)	15	11	1	1	1	1
供水综合生产能力（万立方米/日）	Total Volume of Water Supply (10 000 cu.m/day)	197.4	186.7	2.6	0.8	3.1	4.1
#地下水	Groundwater	54.8	51.7				3.1
年末供水管道总长度（公里）	Length of Water Supply Pipelines at Year-end (km)	2721.4	2294.6	110.4	38.0	70.6	207.8
全年供水总量（万立方米）	Total Annual Volume of Water Supply (10 000 cu.m)	38933.8	36715.4	508.6	266.6	664.1	779.1
#生产运营用水	For Productive Use	5483.7	5028.8	50.4	1.6	100.0	302.9
居民家庭用水	For Residential Use	19944.7	18771.1	251.7	220.0	374.6	327.3
用水人口（万人）	Population with Access to Tap Water (10 000 persons)	394.1	343.4	13.4	8.4	15.1	13.9

注：2009年部门统计制度变化，年末供水管道总长度和用水人口数调整。

Note:Departmental statistical system was changed in 2009,length of water supply pipelines at year-end and population with access to tap water were adjusted.

8-11 市区及县供燃气（2011年）

Gas Supply in Urban Area（2011）

指　　标	Item	西安 Xi'an	市区 City	蓝田县 Lantian	周至县 ZhouZhi	户县 Huxian	高陵县 GaoLing
一、天然气	**Natural Gas**						
管道长度（公里）	Total Length of Gas Pipelines (km)	4500.0	4341.0	13.0	25.0	42.0	79.0
供气总量（万立方米）	Total Gas Supply(10 000 cu.m)	120329.5	116649.0	360.1	2.4	564.0	2754.0
#家庭用量	Residential Households	22867.7	21047.2	85.0	2.3	233.2	1500.0
用气人口（万人）	Population with Access to Gas (10 000 persons)	355.6	342.0	0.9	0.8	5.7	6.3
二、液化石油气	**Liquefied Petroleum Gas**						
供气总量（吨）	Total Gas Supply (ton)	5920.0	2110.0	1064.0	721.0	1656.0	369.0
#家庭用量	Residential Households	4352.0	850.0	775.0	720.0	1656.0	351.0
用气人口（万人）	Population with Access to Gas (10 000 persons)	28.6	1.0	6.4	5.5	8.9	6.8

8-12 市区及县供热（2011年）

Heating in Urban Area（2011）

指　　标	Item	西安 Xi'an	市区 City	蓝田县 Lantian	周至县 ZhouZhi	户县 Huxian	高陵县 GaoLing
供热能力	Heating Capacity						
蒸气（吨/小时）	Steam (ton/hour)	2075	2075				
热水（兆瓦）	Hot Water (1 billion kw)	4570	4290				280
供热总量	Volume Supplied						
蒸气（万吉焦）	Steam (10 000 gigajoules)	1421	1421				
热水（万吉焦）	Hot Water (10 000 gigajoules)	2901	1981				920
管道长度（公里）	Length of Pipelines (km)						
蒸气	Steam	167	167				
热水	Hot Water	500	482				18
供热面积（万平方米）	Heated Area (10 000sq.m)	6524	6424				100
#住宅	Residential Buildings	5226	5126				100

8-13 市区及县市政设施（2011年）

Municipal Facilities in Urban Area（2011）

指　　标	Item	西安 Xi'an	市区 City	蓝田县 Lantian	周至县 ZhouZhi	户县 Huxian	高陵县 GaoLing
一、道路长度（公里）	**Length of Roads （km)**	**2755.0**	**2473.0**	**67.0**	**34.0**	**100.0**	**81.0**
二、道路面积（万平方米）	**Area of Roads (10 000 sq.m)**	**6259.3**	**5502.0**	**111.9**	**70.8**	**315.7**	**259.0**
三、人行道面积（万平方米）	**Area of Sidewalks (10 000 sq.m)**	**1867.0**	**1627.0**	**50.0**	**23.0**	**80.0**	**87.0**
四、桥梁数（座）	**Number of Bridges (unit)**	**402**	**368**	**10**	**2**	**1**	**21**
#立交桥	Crossroads	91	90			1	
五、路灯盏数（盏）	**Number of Street Lights (unit)**	**311991**	**294968**	**1576**	**3525**	**4252**	**7670**
六、排水管道长度（公里）	**Length of Drainage Pipelines (km)**	**4043**	**3587**	**66**	**39**	**169**	**182**
七、污水年排放量（万立方米）	**Annual Discharge Volume of Sewage (10 000 cu.m)**	**36673**	**34757**	**311**	**356**	**1070**	**179**
八、污水处理厂日处理能力（万立方米/日）	**Daily Disposal Capacity of Sewage (10 000 cu.m/day)**	**111.6**	**105.0**	**1.5**	**1.1**	**3.0**	**1.0**
九、污水处理厂年处理量（万立方米）	**Yearly Disposal Capacity of Sewage Disposal Plant (10 000 cu.m)**	**31512**	**30082**	**224**	**258**	**839**	**109**
十、防洪堤长度（公里）	**Length of Flood Control Dikes (km)**	**168**	**119**	**20**	**22**		**7**

8-14 市区及县城市设施水平（2011年）

Urban Municipal Facilities in Urban Area（2011）

指　　标	Item	西安 Xi'an	市区 City	蓝田县 Lantian	周至县 ZhouZhi	户县 Huxian	高陵县 GaoLing
一、人均日生活用水量（升）	**Per Capita Daily Consumption of Tap Water For Residential Use (liter)**	**185.2**	**200.0**	**88.9**	**87.0**	**93.1**	**73.2**
二、用水普及率（%）	**Water-Consuming Popularization (%)**	**100.0**	**100.0**	**98.5**	**100.0**	**100.0**	**100.0**
三、每万人拥有公共交通车辆（标台）	**Number of Public Transport Vehicles Per 10 000 Population (unit)**	**21.8**					
四、燃气普及率（%）	**Gas-Consuming Popularization (%)**	**97.5**	**99.9**	**53.8**	**75.5**	**96.5**	**94.8**
五、人均拥有道路面积（平方米）	**Per Captia Area of Roads (sq.m)**	**15.9**	**16.0**	**8.2**	**8.5**	**20.9**	**18.7**
六、排水管道密度（公里/平方公里）	**Density of Drainage Pipelines (km/sq.km)**	**9.7**	**10.5**	**5.5**	**4.3**	**8.3**	**5.9**
七、污水处理率（%）	**Rate of Sewerage Disposal (%)**	**85.9**	**86.6**	**72.0**	**72.5**	**78.4**	**60.9**
八、园林绿化	**Afforestation and Parks and Gardens**						
#人均公园绿地面积（平方米）	Per Capita Public Green Areas (sq.m)	9.9	10.4	4.0	10.5	5.6	6.5
建成区绿地率（%）	Rate of Green Areas in Developed Areas(%)	30.9	33.0	17.6	17.4	29.3	18.7
九、垃圾无害化处理率（%）	**Rate of No Harm Disposal of Garbage (%)**	**93.7**	**97.6**			**100.0**	**99.8**

主要统计指标解释

供水综合生产能力 指按供水设施取水、净化、送水、出厂输水干管等环节设计能力计算的综合生产能力。包括在原设计能力的基础上，经挖、革、改增加的生产能力。计算时，以四个环节中最薄弱的环节为主确定能力。

年末供水管道长度 指从送水泵至用户水表之间所有管道的长度。不包括新安装尚未使用、水厂内以及用户建筑物内的管道。

全年供水总量 指报告期供水企业(单位)供出的全部水量。包括有效供水量和漏损水量。

生活用水量 包括公共服务用水和居民家庭用水。公共服务用水指为城市社会公共生活服务的用水。包括行政事业单位、部队营区和公共设施服务、社会服务业、批发零售业、住宿餐饮业以及其他公共服务业等单位的用水。居民家庭用水指城市范围内所有居民家庭的日常生活用水。包括城市居民、农民家庭、公共供水站用水。

用水普及率 指城市用水人口数与城市人口总数的比率。计算公式：

$$用水普及率=\frac{城市用水人口数}{城市人口总数}\times 100\%$$

供气管道长度 指报告期末从气源厂压缩机的出口或门站出口至各类用户引入管之间的全部已经通气投入使用的管道长度。不包括煤气生产厂、输配站、液化气储存站、灌瓶站、储配站、气化站、混气站、供应站等厂（站）内的管道。

全年供气总量 指全年燃气企业（单位）向用户供应的燃气数量。包括销售量和损失量。

燃气普及率 指报告期末使用燃气的城市人口数与城市人口总数的比率。计算公式为：

$$燃气普及率=\frac{城市使用燃气人口数}{城市人口总数}\times 100\%$$

城市供热能力 指供热企业（单位）向城市热用户输送热能的设计能力。

城市供热总量 指在报告期供热企业（单位）向城市热用户输送全部蒸汽和热水的总热量。

城市供热管道长度 指从各类热源到热用户建筑物接入口之间的全部蒸汽和热水的管道长度。不包括各类热源厂内部的管道长度。

年末道路长度 指年末道路长度和与道路相通的桥梁、隧道的长度，按车行道中心线计算。在统计时只统计路面宽度在3.5米（含3.5米）以上的各种铺装道路，包括开放型工业区和住宅区道路在内。

城市桥梁 指为跨越天然或人工障碍物而修建的构筑物。包括跨河桥、立交桥、人行天桥以及人行地下通道等。按使用年限分为永久性桥和半永久性桥。

城市排水管道长度 指所有排水总管、干管、支管、检查井及连接井进出口等长度之和。

城市污水日处理能力 指污水处理厂（或污水处理装置）每昼夜处理污水量的设计能力。

城市园林绿地面积 指报告期末用作园林和绿化的各种绿地面积。包括公园绿地、生产绿地、防护绿地、附属绿地和其他绿地的面积。

公园绿地 城市中向公众开放的以游憩为主要功能，有一定的游憩设施和服务设施，同时兼有健全生态、美化景观、防灾减灾等综合作用的绿化用地。包括综合公园、社区公园、专类公园、带状公园和街旁绿地。其中综合公园、专类公园和带状公园面积之和为公园面积。

清扫保洁面积 指报告期末对城市道路和公共场所（主要包括城市行车道、人行道、车行隧道、人行过街地下通道、道路附属绿地、地铁站、高架路、人行过街天桥、立交桥、广场、停车场及其他设施等）进行清扫保洁的面积。一天清扫多次的，按清扫保洁面积最大的一次计算。

市容环卫专用车辆 指用于环境卫生作业、监察的专用车辆和设备，包括用于道路清扫、冲洗、洒水、除雪、垃圾粪便清运、市容监察以及与其配套使用的车辆和设备。

每万人拥有公共交通车辆 指报告期末城区内每万人平均拥有的公共交通车辆标台数。计算公式：

$$每万人拥有公共交通车辆=\frac{公共交通运营车标台数}{城市人口总数}$$

Explanatory Notes on Main Statistical Indicators

Production Capacity of Water Supply refers to the designed overall production capacity of water facilities, covering the four segments of water collection, purification, conveyance, and outflow through trunk pipelines. Increased capacity through transformation and innovation projects is included as well. The capacity is determined mainly on the weakest of the above-mentioned four segments.

Length of Water Supply Pipelines at Year-end refers to the total length of all the pipelines between the water pumps and the user water meters, excluding pipelines newly installed but not used yet, pipeline in the water factory,and pipeline in the user's buildings.

Annual Volume of Water Supply refers to the total volume of water supplied by water-works (units) during the reference period, including both the effective water supply and loss during the water supply.

Consumption of Water for Residential Use refers to water consumption of households for daily life and water consumption of public service facilities. The latter refers to water consumption for urban public services, including the consumption of government agencies and public institutions, military barracks, public facilities, wholesale and retail trades, accommodation and catering industry and other units providing public services. Household water consumption refers to consumption of water for daily life of all households within the boundary of cities, including households of urban residents and farmers, and public water supply stations.

Coverage Rate of Urban Population with Access to Tap Water refers to the ratio of the urban population with access to tap water to the total urban population. The formula is:

$$\text{Coverage of urban population with access to tap water} = \frac{\text{Urban population with access to tap water}}{\text{Urban population}} \times 100\%$$

Length of Gas Pipelines refers to the total length of pipelines in use between the outlet of the compressor of gas-work or outlet of gas stations and the leading pipe of users, excluding pipelines within gasworks, delivery stations, LPG storage stations, refilling stations, gas-mixing stations and supply stations.

Volume of Gas Supply refers to the total volume of gas provided to users by gas-producing enterprises (units) in a year, including the volume sold and the volume lost.

Coverage Rate of Urban Population with Access to Gas refers to the ratio of the urban population with access to gas to the total urban population at the end of the reference period. The formula is:

$$\text{Coverage rate of urban population with access to gas} = \frac{\text{Urban population with access to gas}}{\text{Urban population}} \times 100\%$$

Heating Capacity in Urban Areas refers to the designed capacity of heating enterprises (units) in supplying heating energy to urban users during the reference period.

Quantity of Heat Supplied in Urban Areas refers to the total quantity of heat from steam and hot water supplied to urban users by heating enterprises (units) during the reference period.

Length of Urban Heating Pipelines refers to the total length of steam or hot water pipelines for sources of heat to the leading pipelines of the buildings of the users, excluding internal pipelines in heat generating enterprises.

Length of Paved Roads at Year-end refers to the length of roads with paved surface including bridges and tunnels connected with roads by the end of the year. Length of the roads is measured by the central lines for vehicles for paved roads with a width of 3.5 meters and over, including roads in open-ended factory compounds and residential quarters.

Urban Bridges refer to bridges built to cross over natural or man-made barriers, including bridges over rivers, overpasses for traffic and for pedestrians, underpasses for pedestrians, etc. Both permanent and semi-permanent bridges are included.

Length of Urban Sewage Pipes refers to the total length of general drainage, trunks, branch and inspection wells, connection wells, inlets and outlets, etc.

Daily Disposal Capacity of Urban Sewage refers to the designed 24-hour capacity of sewage disposal by the sewage treatment works or facilities.

Area of Parks and Green Land refers to the total area occupied for green projects at the end of the reference period, including park green land, production green land, protection green land, green land attached to institutions, and other green areas.

Park Green Area refers to green areas open to the public for amusement and rest with the facilities of amusement, rest and services. Its function includes perfecting ecology, beautifying landscape, and preventing and reducing disaster. Park green areas include comprehensive park, community park, topic park, belt-shaped park and green area nearby street. Total areas of comprehensive park, topic park and belt-shaped is the area of park.

Area Cleaned refers to the area which are regularly cleaned, as at the end of the reference period, at urban roads and public places (mainly including urban roadways, pedestrian walkways, vehicular tunnels, pedestrian underpasses, underground railway stations, lifted roads, pedestrians walk bridges, overpasses, plazas, carparks and other facilities). If there are several times of cleaning in a day at a location, the area of that time of cleaning with the largest area cleaned will be taken.

Vehicles Dedicated to Urban Cleanliness and Environmental Sanitation refer to vehicles and facilities dedicated for use in the operation, management and monitoring of environmental hygiene work. They include vehicles for road cleaning, washing, showering, ice removal, disposal of garbage and human wastes, cleanliness monitoring and related activities.

Public Transportation Vehicles per 10000 Population refers to the number of public transportation vehicles, at the end of the reference period, per 10000 population in the city district. The formula for calculation is:

$$\begin{matrix}\text{PublicTransportation Vehicles}\\ \text{per 10000 Population}\end{matrix} = \frac{\begin{matrix}\text{Number of Public}\\ \text{Transportation Vehicles}\end{matrix}}{\text{City District Population}}$$

9 环境保护

ENVIRONMENT PROTECTION

资料整理：齐昆峰　刘　婷
Data management:Qi Kunfeng Liu Ting

第九部分　环境保护

一、简要说明

本章资料反映环境保护、工业污染排放及处理利用情况、危险废物集中处置情况、生活及其他污染情况和工业污染治理项目建设情况，由西安市统计局社会科技处根据西安市环保局提供的数据资料整理。

二、主要指标

工业用水重复利用率（%）	47.0
工业固体废物综合利用率（%）	97.3
污水处理厂处理能力（万吨/日）	111.0
污水处理量（万吨）	28746.2

注：因2011年环保年报统计口径变化，故与往年不可比。

9 ENVIRONMENT PROTECTION

Ⅰ.Brief Introduction

This chapter contain information that reflect environment protection, discharge and treatment of industrial pollutant, centralized treatment of dangerous wastes, domestic pollution and other pollution, construction of projects of industrial pollution treatment. Data in this chapter is compiled by Social & Science and Technology Division of the Xi'an Bureau of Statistics according to the reported data from Environment Protection Administration department of the municipal government.

Ⅱ.Major Indicators

Percentage of Industrial Water Recycled (%)	47.0
Percentage of Industrial Solid Waste Utilized (%)	97.3
Daily Disposal Capacity of Sewage(10 000 tons/day)	111.0
Volume of Sewgae Disposal(10 000 tons)	28746.2

Note: Because of the 2011 annual report of environmental protection statistical caliber changed,it was not compared with previous years.

9-1 城市环境保护（2011年）

Urban Environmental Protection（2011）

指　　标	Item	2011
一、大气环境	Air	
1.全年环境空气质量达标天数(天)	Days of Air Quality up to the Standards(day)	305
2.全年空气质量达标率(%)	Percentage of Air Quality up to the Standards(%)	84
二、声环境	Voice	
1.功能区噪声平均值(Db(A))	Average Noise Value of Functional Districts(Db(A))	
0类区	Class 0	52
1类区	Class 1	57
2类区	Class 2	59
3类区	Class 3	68
4类区	Class 4	72
2.道路交通噪声平均值(Db(A))	Average Noise Value of Road Traffic(Db(A))	69
3.区域噪声平均值(Db(A))	Average Noise Value of Region(Db(A))	55

9-2 主要年份工业"三废"排放及处理利用情况

Discharge and Treatrment of Waste Gas, Water & Solid Wastes in Repersentative Years

指　　标	Item	2000	2006	2007
一、工业废水排放量（万吨）	**Volume of Waste Water Discharge (10 000 tons)**	**9145**	**16389**	**19069**
工业废水排放达标量	Industrial Waste Wster Meeting Discharge Standards	6130	15267	18352
工业废水排放达标率(%)	Percentage of Industrial Waste Wster Meeting Discharge Standards(%)	67.03	93.15	96.24
二、工业废气排放量（万标立方米）	**Total Volume of Industrial Waste Gas Emission (10 000 cu.m)**	**2759719**	**6425076**	**11494114**
#燃料燃烧过程中排放量	Volume of Waste Gas in the Process of Fuel Burning	1942884	3885611	3731610
生产工艺过程中排放量	Volume of Waste Gas from the Process of Production	816835	2539465	7762504
废气治理设施数（套）	Number of Facilities for Treatment of Waste Gas(set)		466	846
三、工业固体废物产生量（万吨）	**Volume of Industrial Solid Wastes Produced (10 000 tons)**	**107**	**161**	**193**
工业固体废物处置量	Volume of Industrial Solid Wastes Treated	20	5	6
工业固体废物综合利用量	Volume of Industrial Solid Waste Utilized in a Comprehensive Way	63	143	171
工业固体废物综合利用率（%）	Percentage of Volume of Industrial Solid Waste Utilized in a Comprehensive Way(%)	58.88	89.07	88.48

9-2 续表 continued

指　　标	Item	2008	2009	2010	2011
一、工业废水排放量（万吨）	**Volume of Waste Water Discharge (10 000 tons)**	**18304**	**13168**	**13840**	**13148**
工业废水排放达标量	Industrial Waste Wster Meeting Discharge Standards	17862	12106	13269	
工业废水排放达标率(%)	Percentage of Industrial Waste Wster Meeting Discharge Standards(%)	98	94	96	
二、工业废气排放量（万标立方米）	**Total Volume of Industrial Waste Gas Emission (10 000 cu.m)**	**15191799**	**7372387**	**7915628**	**10184619**
#燃料燃烧过程中排放量	Volume of Waste Gas in the Process of Fuel Burning	8980681	4275975	4368727	
生产工艺过程中排放量	Volume of Waste Gas from the Process of Production	6211118	3096412	3546901	
废气治理设施数（套）	Number of Facilities for Treatment of Waste Gas(set)	920	852	816	745
三、工业固体废物产生量（万吨）	**Volume of Industrial Solid Wastes Produced (10 000 tons)**	**220**	**246**	**267**	**279**
工业固体废物处置量	Volume of Industrial Solid Wastes Treated	5	5	4	6
工业固体废物综合利用量	Volume of Industrial Solid Waste Utilized in a Comprehensive Way	215	241	262	271
工业固体废物综合利用率（%）	Percentage of Volume of Industrial Solid Waste Utilized in a Comprehensive Way(%)	97.78	97.83	98.05	97.3

9–3 工业污染排放及处理利用情况（2011年）

Discharge and Treatment of Industrial Pollution（2011）

指　　标	Item	2011
一、被调查企业基本情况	**Basic condition of Enterprises investigated**	
1.企业数（个）	Number of Enterprises (unit)	513
2.工业总产值（万元）	Gross Industry Output Value (10 000 yuan)	18279242.0
3.工业炉窑数（座）	Number of Industrial Grates (item)	1049
二、工业废水	**Industrial Waste Water**	
1.工业用水总量（万吨）	Total Volume of Industrial Water (10 000 tons)	36466.68
#新鲜水量	Volume of Fresh Water	19333.8
重复用水量	Volume of Water Recycled	17123.88
2.工业用水重复利用率（%）	Percentage of Industrial Water Recycled (%)	47
3.废水治理设施数（套）	Number of Facilities for Treatment of Waste Water (set)	314
4.废水治理设施处理能力（万吨/日）	Disposal Capacity of Facilities for Treatment of Waste Water (10 000 tons/day)	68.66
5.废水治理设施运行费用（万元）	Operating Expense of Facilities for Treatment of Waste Water (10 000 yuan)	15690.2
6.工业废水排放量（万吨）	Volume of Industrial Waste Water Discharged (10 000 tons)	13147.96
三、工业废气	**Industrial Waste Gas**	
1.煤炭消费总量（万吨）	Total Coal Consumption (10 000 tons)	826.91
2.燃料油消费量（万吨）	Fuel Oil Consumption (10 000 tons)	1.66
3.天然气消费量（万立方米）	Natural Gas Consumption (10 000 cu.m.)	14323
4.工业废气排放总量（万标立方米）	Total Volume of Industrial Waste Gas Emission (10 000 cu.m.)	10184619
5.废气治理设施数（套）	Number of Facilities for Treatment of Waste Gas (set)	745
6.废气治理设施处理能力（万标立方米/时）	Disposal Capacity of Facilities for Treatment of Waste Gas (10 000 cu.m./h)	3716.86
7.废气治理设施设备运行费用（万元）	Operating Expense of Facilities for Treatment of Waste gas(10 000 yuan)	27565.4
8.二氧化硫去除量（吨）	Volume of Sulphur Dioxide Removed (ton)	68705.74
9.二氧化硫排放量（吨）	Volume of Sulphur Dioxide Emission (ton)	97884.02
10.烟尘去除量（吨）	Volume of Soot Removed (ton)	1521363.59
11.烟尘排放量（吨）	Volume of Soot Emission (ton)	18888.18
四、工业固体废物	**Industrial Solid Waste**	
1.工业固体废物产生量（万吨）	Volume of Industrial Solid Waste Produced (10 000tons)	278.87
2.工业固体废物综合利用量（万吨）	Volume of Industrial Solid Waste Utilized (10 000tons)	271.35
3.工业固体废物综合利用率（%）	Percentage of Industrial Solid Waste Utilized (%)	97.30
4.工业固体废物贮存量（万吨）	Volume of Industrial Solid Waste Accumulated (10 000tons)	1.50
5.工业固体废物处置量（万吨）	Volume of Industrial Solid Waste Treated (10 000tons)	6.01
6.工业固体废物排放量（万吨）	Volume of Industrial Solid Waste Discharged (10 000tons)	0.02

9-4 城市污水处理情况（2011年）

Urban Sewage Disposal（2011）

指　　标	Item	2011
一、污水处理厂数（座）	**Number of Sewage Treatment Works(unit)**	**23**
污水处理厂处理能力（万吨/日）	Daily Disposal Capacity of Sewage(10 000 tons/day)	111
二、污水处理	**Sewgae Disposal**	
污水处理量（万吨）	Volume of Sewgae Disposal(10 000 tons)	**28746.2**
#处理生活污水量	Volume of Domestic Sewgae Disposal	25757.5
处理工业废水量	Volume of Industrial Sewage Disposal	2988.7
城市污水集中处理率（%）	Urban sewage centralized treatment rate （%）	93.4
三、污水再生利用量（万吨）	**Volume of Sewage Recycled(10 000 tons)**	**761**
四、化学需氧量去除量（吨）	**Volume of COD Removed (ton)**	**84754**
五、氨氮去除量（吨）	**Volume of Ammonia and Nitrogen Removed(ton)**	**9087**
六、总磷去除量（吨）	**Volume of Total Phosphorus Removed(ton)**	**1334**
七、污泥产生量（吨）	**Volume of Sludge Produced(ton)**	**249962**
八、污泥处置量（吨）	**Volume of Sludge Disposal(ton)**	**249962**
九、污泥利用量（吨）	**Volume of Sludge Utilized(ton)**	**35321**
十、本年运行费用（万元）	**Operating Expense(10 000 yuan)**	**18541.9**

注：污水处理厂数及污水处理能力为市建委部门统计数据。

Note:The number of sewage disposal plant and the disposal capacity of sewage were statistics from Municipal Construction Commission.

9-5 危险废物集中处置情况（2011年）

Condition of Collected Dangerous Wastes Treated（2011）

指　　标	Item	2011
一、危险废物集中处置厂数（座）	**Number of Colleted Dangerous Wastes Treated Plants(item)**	**3**
二、危险废物实际处置能力（吨/日）	**Actual Disposal Capacity of Dangerous Wastes (ton/day)**	**20.0**
三、危险废物处置量（吨）	**Volume of Dangerous Wastes Treated (ton)**	**10027.6**
四、危险废物综合利用量（吨）	**Volume of Dangerous Wastes Utilized in a Comprehensive Way (ton)**	**425.0**
五、焚烧残渣流向（吨）	**Flow Direction of Residuum after Burning (ton)**	
（1）焚烧残渣量	Volume of Residuum after Burning	300.8
（2）焚烧残渣利用量	Volume of Residuum after Burning Utilized	
（3）焚烧残渣填埋量	Volume of Residuum after Burning Landfilled	300.8
六、当年运行费用（万元）	**Operating Expenses in Current year(10 000 yuan)**	**2306.0**

9-6 生活及其他污染情况（2011年）

Domestic Pollution and Other conditions（2011）

指　　标	Item	2011
一、基本情况	**Basic Condition**	
1.煤炭消费总量（万吨）	Total Coal Consumption (10 000 tons)	959.19
#工业煤炭消费量	Industrial Coal Consumption	826.98
生活及其他煤炭消费量	Domestic and Other Coal Consumption	132.21
2.生活及其他煤炭含硫量（%）	Percentage of Sulphur Content in Domestic and Other Coal (%)	0.75
3.生活及其他煤炭灰份（%）	Percentage of Ash Content in Domestic and Other Coal (%)	14.60
二、污染排放情况	**Discharge of Pollutant**	
1.城镇生活污水排放量（万吨）	Volume of Urban Domestic Sewage Discharged(10 000 tons)	27458.4
2.城镇生活污水中COD去除量（吨）	Volume of COD in Urban Domestic Sewage Removed (ton)	65681.1
3.城镇生活污水中氨氮产生量（吨）	Volume of Ammonia and Nitrogen in Urban Domestic Sewage Produced (ton)	17216.0
4.城镇生活污水中氨氮排放量（吨）	Volume of Ammonia and Nitrogen in Urban Domestic Sewage Discharged (ton)	11041.2
5.污水处理厂去除生活污水中氨氮量（吨）	Sewage Disposal Plant Removing the Amount of Ammonia Nitrogen in Wastewater.(ton)	6174.8
6.生活及其他二氧化硫排放量（吨）	Volume of Domestic and Other Sulphur Dioxide Emission (ton)	16922.9
7.生活及其他烟尘排放量（吨）	Volume of Domestic and Other Soot Emission (ton)	11898.9

9–7 工业污染治理项目建设情况（2011年）

Condition of Anti-Industrial-Pollution Projects（2011）

指　　标	Item	2011
一、工业企业数（个）	**Number of Industrial Enterprises (unit)**	**27**
二、本年施工项目总数（个）	**Total Number of Projects Under Construction (unit)**	**33**
#废水治理项目	Treatment of Waste Water	16
废气治理项目	Treatment of Waste Gas	15
固体废物治理项目	Treatment of Solid Wastes	
三、施工项目本年完成投资额（万元）	**Investment Completed in Anti-pollution Projects**	**14702.7**
	Under Construction (10 000 yuan)	
#废水治理项目	Treatment of Waste Water	10303.8
废气治理项目	Treatment of Waste Gas	4314.6
固体废物治理项目	Treatment of Solid Wastes	
四、施工项目本年投资来源合计（万元）	**Investment Sources of Projects Under Construction (10 000 yuan)**	**14702.7**
#排污费补助	Pollution Charges Subsidies	79.5
政府其他补助	Other Government Subsidies	1208.0
企业自筹	Self-raising Funds	13415.2
#银行贷款	Loans	700.0
五、本年竣工项目数（个）	**Number of Projects Completed(unit)**	26
#废水治理项目	Treatment of Waste Water	14
废气治理项目	Treatment of Waste Gas	11
噪声治理项目	Treatment of Noise Pollution	
六、本年竣工项目新增设计处理能力	**Newly Increased Disposal Capacity of Projects Completed**	
#治理废水（吨/日）	Treatment of Waste Water (ton/day)	18100
治理废气（万标立方米/时）	Treatment of Waste Gas (10 000 cu.m./h)	200.46
治理固体废物（吨/日）	Treatment of Solid Wastes (ton/day)	

9–8 各区县环境保护基本情况（2011年）

区 县	Region	环境污染治理本年完成投资额（万元）Completed Investment on Environmental Pollution Treatment（10 000 yuan)	工业二氧化硫排放量（吨）Volume of Industrial Sulphur Dioxide Discharged（ton）
全 市	**Total**	**14702.7**	**97884**
#新城区	Xincheng	87	157
碑林区	Beilin	826.6	2290
莲湖区	Lianhu	24.3	2679
灞桥区	Baqiao	1728.6	18723
未央区	Weiyang	364.6	2219
雁塔区	Yanta	940	830
阎良区	Yanliang	-	2867
临潼区	Lintong	2380	3917
长安区	Chang'an	444	2887
蓝田县	Lantian	-	681
周至县	Zhouzhi	-	248
户 县	Huxian	6600	10842
高陵县	Gaoling	67.3	956

Condition of Environment Protection by Regions（2011）

工业化学需氧量排放量（吨）Volume of COD Removed (ton)	垃圾处理站数（座）Number of Rubbish Disposal Works (unit)	污水处理厂数（个）Number of Sewage Treatment Works (unit)
32729	**3**	**23**
317		
23		
561		1
1250	1	2
273		2
470		1
590	1	1
6134		2
95		7
41		2
105		1
6157		2
85	1	1

主 要 统 计 指 标 解 释

工业用水 指工矿企业在生产过程中用于制造、加工、冷却、空调、净化、洗涤等方面的用水，按新水取用量计，不包括企业内部的重复利用水量。

工业废水排放量 指经过企业厂区所有排放口排到企业外部的工业废水量。包括生产废水、外排的直接冷却水、超标排放的矿井地下水和与工业废水混排的厂区生活污水，不包括外排的间接冷却水（清污不分流的间接冷却水应计算在内）。

直接排入海的 指经企业位于海边的排放口，直接排入海的废水量。直接排放指废水经过工厂的排污口直接排入海，而未经过城市下水道或其他中间体，也不受其他水体的影响。

工业废水排放达标量 指报告期内废水中各项污染物指标都达到国家或地方排放标准的外排工业废水量，包括未经处理外排达标的，经废水处理设施处理后达标排放的，以及经污水处理厂处理后达标排放的。

生活污水排放量 指城镇居民每年排放的生活污水。用人均系数法测算。测算公式为：

$$\frac{\text{生活污水}}{\text{排放量}}=\frac{\text{城镇生活污水}}{\text{排放系数}}\times\frac{\text{市镇非}}{\text{农业人口}}\times 365$$

生活污水中化学需氧量（COD）排放量 指城镇居民每年排放的生活污水中的COD的量。用人均系数法测算。测算公式为：

$$\frac{\text{城镇生活污水}}{\text{中}COD\text{排放量}}=\frac{\text{城镇生活污水中}}{COD\text{产生系数}}\times\frac{\text{市镇非}}{\text{农业人口}}\times 365$$

化学需氧量（COD） 指用化学氧化剂氧化水中有机污染物时所需的氧量。COD值越高，表示水中有机污染物污染越重。

工业废气排放量 指报告期内企业厂区内燃料燃烧和生产工艺过程中产生的各种排入大气的含有污染物的气体的总量，以标准状态（273K，101325Pa）计算。测算公式为：

$$\frac{\text{工业废气}}{\text{排放量}}=\frac{\text{燃料燃烧过程}}{\text{中废气排放量}}+\frac{\text{生产工艺过程}}{\text{中废气排放量}}$$

生活及其他SO_2排放量 以生活及其他煤炭消费量和其含硫量为基础，根据以下公式计算：

$$\frac{\text{生活及其他}}{SO_2\text{排放量}}=\frac{\text{生活及其他}}{\text{煤炭消费量}}\times\text{含硫量}\times 0.8\times 2$$

工业SO_2排放量 指报告期内企业在燃料燃烧和生产工艺过程中排入大气的SO_2总量，计算公式为：

$$\frac{\text{工业}SO_2}{\text{排放量}}=\frac{\text{燃料燃烧过程}}{\text{中}SO_2\text{排放量}}+\frac{\text{生产工艺过程}}{\text{中}SO_2\text{排放量}}$$

工业烟尘排放量 指企业厂区内燃料燃烧过程中产生的烟气中夹带的颗粒物排放量。

生活及其他烟尘排放量 指除工业生产活动以外的所有社会、经济活动及公共设施的经营活动中燃烧所排放的烟尘纯重量。以生活及其他煤炭消费量为基础进行测算。

工业粉尘排放量 指企业在生产工艺过程中排放的能在空气中悬浮一定时间的固体颗粒物排放量。如钢铁企业的耐火材料粉尘、焦化企业的筛焦系统粉尘、烧结机的粉尘、石灰窑的粉尘、建材企业的水泥粉尘等。不包括电厂排入大气的烟尘。

工业固体废物产生量 指报告期内企业在生产过程中产生的固体状、半固体状和高浓度液体状废弃物的总量，包括危险废物、冶炼废渣、粉煤灰、炉渣、煤矸石、尾矿、放射性废物和其他废物等；不包括矿山开采的剥离废石和掘进废石（煤矸石和呈酸性或碱性的废石除外）。酸性或碱性废石指采掘的废石其流经水、雨淋水的pH值小于4或pH值大于10.5者。

危险废物 指列入国家危险废物名录或根据国家规定的危险废物鉴别标准和鉴别方法认定的，具有爆炸性、易燃性、易氧化性、毒性、腐蚀性、易传染疾病等危险特性之一的废物。

工业固体废物综合利用量 指报告期内企业通过回收、加工、循环、交换等方式，从固体废物中提取或者使其转化为可以利用的资源、能源和其他原材料的固体废物量（包括当年利用往年的工业固体废物贮存量），如用作农业肥料、生产建筑材料、筑路等。综合利用量由原产生固体废物的单位统计。

工业固体废物综合利用率 指工业固体废物综合利用量占工业固体废物产生量（包括综合利用往年贮存量）的百分率。计算公式为：

$$\frac{\text{工业固体废物}}{\text{综合利用率}}=\frac{\text{工业固体废物综合利用量}}{\text{工业固体废物产生量}+\text{综合利用往年贮存量}}\times 100\%$$

工业固体废物贮存量 指报告期内企业以综合利用或处置为目的，将固体废物暂时贮存或堆存在专设的贮存设施或专设的集中堆存场所内的数量。专设的固体废物贮存场所或贮存设施必须有防扩散、防流失、防渗漏、防止污染大气、水体的措施。

工业固体废物处置量 指报告期内企业将固体废物

焚烧或者最终置于符合环境保护规定要求的场所，并不再回取的工业固体废物量（包括当年处置往年的工业固体废物贮存量）。处置方式有填埋（其中危险废物应安全填埋）、焚烧、专业贮存场（库）封场处理、深层灌注、回填矿井及海洋处置（经海洋管理部门同意投海处置）等。

工业固体废物排放量 指报告期内企业将所产生的固体废物排到固体废物污染防治设施、场所以外的数量，不包括矿山开采的剥离废石和掘进废石(煤矸石和呈酸性或碱性的废石除外)。

“三废”综合利用产品产值 指报告期内利用“三废”作为主要原料生产的产品价值（现行价）；已经销售或准备销售的应计算产品价值，留作生产自用的不应计算产品价值。

生活垃圾清运量 指报告期内收集和运送到各生活垃圾处理厂（场）和生活垃圾最终消纳点的生活垃圾数量。生活垃圾指城市日常生活或为城市日常生活提供服务的活动中产生的固体废物以及法律行政规定的视为城市生活垃圾的固体废物。包括：居民生活垃圾、商业垃圾、集市贸易市场垃圾、街道清扫垃圾、公共场所垃圾和机关、学校、厂矿等单位的生活垃圾。

生活垃圾无害化处理率 指报告期生活垃圾无害化处理量与生活垃圾产生量的比率。在统计上，由于生活垃圾产生量不易取得，可用清运量代替。计算公式为：

$$\text{生活垃圾无害化处理率}=\frac{\text{生活垃圾无害化处理量}}{\text{生活垃圾产生量}}\times 100\%$$

Explanatory Notes on Main Statistical Indicators

Water Use by Industry refers to new withdrawals of water, excluding reuse of water within enterprises.

Waste Water Discharged by Industry refers to the volume of waste water discharged by industrial enterprises through all their outlets, including waste water from production process, directly cooled water, groundwater from mining wells which does not meet discharge standards and sewage from households mixed with waste water produced by industrial activities, but excluding indirectly cooled water discharged (It should be included if the discharge is not separated from waste water).

Waste Water Directly Discharged into Sea refers to the volume of waste water directly discharged into sea through outlets of enterprises situated by sea without going through municipal sewerage networks or any other intermediates or being affected by any other water bodies.

Industrial Waste Water Meeting Discharge Standards refers to volume of industrial waste water discharge which, with or without treatment, reaches national or local standards with regard to all pollutants.

Urban Non-industrial Waste Water Discharge refers to annual discharge of non-industrial waste water by urban households. It is estimated by per capita coefficient using the formula:

$$\text{Urban non-industrial waste water discharge} = \text{urban non-industrial waste water discharge coefficient} \times \text{urban non-alagricultur population} \times 365$$

Volume of Chemical Oxygen Demand (COD) Generated by Urban Non-industrial Waster Water refers to chemical oxygen demand generated through the annual discharge of non-industrial waste water by urban households. It is estimated as:

$$\text{Volume of chemical oxygen demand (cod) generated by urban non-industrial waster water} = \text{Coefficient of COD generated through urban non-industrial waste water} \times \text{urban non-agricultural population} \times 365$$

Chemical Oxygen Demand (COD) refers to the amount of oxygen required when chemical oxidants are used to oxidize organic pollutants in water. A higher value of COD corresponds to more serious pollution by organic pollutants.

Industrial Waste Air Emission refers to the discharge into atmosphere of waste air containing pollutants generated from fuel burning and production processes in enterprises within a given period of time. It is calculated at standard status (273K, 101325Pa) as:

$$\text{Industrial waste air emission} = \text{tnoissimehrough fuel burning} + \text{tnoissimehrough production process}$$

So_2 Emission through Non-industrial and Other Activities is calculated on the basis of consumption of coal by households and other activities and the sulphur content of coal with the following formula:

$$\text{SO}_2\text{ emission through non-industrial and other activities} = \text{of coalby households andother activities} \times \text{sulphur content} \times 0.8 \times 2$$

So_2 Emission through Industrial Activities refers to volume of sulphur dioxide emission from fuel burning and production process by enterprises during a given period of time. It is calculated as:

$$\text{SO}_2\text{ emission through industrial activities} = \text{SO}_2\text{ emission from fuel burning} + \text{SO}_2\text{ emission from production process}$$

Industrial Soot Emission refers to the volume of soot in smoke emitted in the process of fuel burning in the premises of enterprises.

Soot Emission by Consumption and Others refers to the net volume of soot emitted by fuel burning from all social and economic activities and operations of public facilities other than industrial activities. It is calculated on the basis of coal consumption by households and others.

Industrial Dust Emission refers to volume of dust emitted by production process of enterprises and suspended in the air for a given period of time, including dust from refractory material of iron and steel works, dust from coke-screening systems and sintering machines of coke plants, dust from lime kilns and dust from cement production in building material enterprises, but excluding soot and dust emitted from power plants.

Industrial Solid Wastes Produced refers to total volume of solid, semi-solid and high concentration liquid residues produced by industrial enterprises from production process in a given period of time, including hazardous wastes, slag, coal ash, gangue, tailings, radioactive residues and other wastes, but excluding stones stripped or dug out in mining - gangue and acid or alkaline stones not included (a stone is acid or alkaline according to the pH value of the water being below 4 or above 10.5 when the stone is in, or soaked by water).

Hazardous Wastes refers to those included in the national hazardous wastes catalogue or specified as any one of the following properties in the national hazardous wastes identification standards: explosive, ignitable, oxidizable, toxic, corrosive or liable to cause infectious diseases or lead to other dangers.

Industrial Solid Wastes Utilized refers to volume of solid wastes from which useful materials can be extracted or which can be converted into usable resources, energy or other materials by means of reclamation, processing, recycling and exchange (including utilizing in the year the stocks of industrial solid wastes of the previous year). Examples of such utilizations include fertilizers, building materials and road materials. The information shall be collected by the producing units of the wastes.

Rate of Utilization of Industrial Solid Wastes refers to the percentage of industrial solid wastes utilized over industrial solid wastes produced (including stocks of the previous years). It is calculated as:

$$\text{Rate of utilization of industrial solid wastes} = \frac{\text{volume of industrial solid wastes utilized}}{\text{industrial solid wastesproduced+ stock of previous years}} \times 100\%$$

Stock of Industrial Solid Wastes refers to the volume of solid wastes placed in special facilities or special sites for purposes of utilization or disposal. The sites or facilities should take measures against dispersion, loss, seepage, and air and water contamination.

Industrial Solid Wastes Disposed refers to the quantity of industrial solid wastes which are burnt or placed ultimately in the sites meeting the requirements for environmental protection and not salvaged or recycled (including disposition in the year of those wastes of previous years). The disposition includes landfill (Safe landfills should be conducted for hazardous wastes), incineration, containment spaces, deep underground disposal, backfill in mining pits and disposal at sea.

Industrial Solid Wastes Discharged refers to the volume of industrial solid wastes discharged by producing enterprises to disposal facilities or to other sites. The wastes exclude stones stripped or dug from mining (gangue and acid or alkaline waste stones not included).

Output Value of Products Made from Waste Gas, Waste Water and Solid Wastes refers to the current value of products with waste gas, waste water and solid wastes as main materials of production. Products sold and ready to sell shall be included while those produced for own use shall not be included.

Consumption Wastes Transported refers to volume of consumption wastes collected and transported to disposal factories or sites. Consumption wastes are solid wastes produced from urban households or from service activities for urban households, and solid wastes regarded by laws and regulations as urban consumption wastes, including those from households, commercial activities, markets, cleaning of streets, public sites, offices, schools, factories, mining units and other sources.

Ratio of Consumption Wastes Treated refers to consumption wastes treated over that produced. In practical statistics, as it is difficult to estimate, the volume of consumption wastes produced is replaced with that transported. It is calculated as:

$$\text{Ratio of consumption wastes treated} = \frac{\text{consumption wastes treated}}{\text{consumption wastes produced}} \times 100\%$$

10 农　业

AGRICULTURE

资料整理：张喜兰　马秋娟　薛　丰
Data management:Zhang Xilan　Ma Qiujuan　Xue Feng

第十部分　农业

一、简要说明

本章资料主要包括农村基本情况、农业生产条件与生产情况、耕地、农林牧渔及服务业产值、主要农产品产量以及各区县农业生产和农村经济效益主要指标，由西安市统计局农村处提供，其中10-21、10-23、10-30、10-32、10-35、10-36表内2006年和2007年部分数据为第二次农业普查衔接数。

二、主要指标

年末耕地面积（万亩）	377.10	比上年下降	1.6%
农林牧渔及服务业总产值（亿元）	272.66	比上年增长	6.6%
农作物播种面积（万亩）	704.17	比上年下降	0.3%
粮食产量（万吨）	182.04	比上年下降	1.0 %

注：2011年粮食产量增速仍用未调整数计算。

10 AGRICULTURE

Ⅰ.Brief Introduction

Data in this chapter reflects basic condition of agriculture production of Xi'an city. It is primarily consist of basic condition of rural area, condition of agriculture production, plow land, production value of farming, forestry, animal husbandry and fishery, gross yield of primary produce and primary Indicators of agriculture production and rural area economic performance. The data are provided and compiled by Rural Area Division of the Xi'an Bureau of Statistics.The data in this chapter in 2006 and 2007 is conformity with the second national agriculture census, except table of 10-1、10-2、10-3、10-4、10-5、10-6、10-13、10-14、10-20、10-21、10-22.

Ⅱ.Major Indicators

		Increase over Preceding Year
Cultivated Area Year-end(10 000 mu)	377.10	-1.6%
Gross Output Value of Farming, Forestry, Animal Husbandry,Fishery and Service(100 mil. yuan)	272.66	6.6%
Sown Area of Crops(10 000 mu)	704.17	-0.3%
Grain Output(10 000 tons)	182.04	-1.0%

Note：The rate of food production in 2011 was still calculated by unadjusted data.

10-1 农村基层组织、乡村户数、人口及劳动力情况

Grass-root Organizations, Households, Population and Labor Resources in Rural Area

指　　标	Item	2000	2005	2006	2007	2008	2009	2010	2011
一、农村基层组织情况	**Village Units**								
1.乡镇个数（个）	Number of Township and Towns(unit)	168	102	97	84	82	73	73	70
#镇个数	Number of Towns	52	50	45	37	35	31	31	61
2.村民委员会个数（个）	Number of Villagers' Committees(unit)	3165	3162	3161	3161	3145	3104	3063	3049
3.村民小组个数（个）	Number of Village Groups(unit)	16294	16281	16275	16260	16272	16068	15981	15703
二、乡村户数（万户）	**Number of Households (10 000 households)**	**98.77**	**101.50**	**102.35**	**100.85**	**101.02**	**101.00**	**101.43**	**102.59**
三、农村人口和从业人员情况	**Rural Population and Employment**								
1.乡村人口数（万人）	Rural Population(10 000 persons)	401.64	408.90	409.77	403.02	404.18	404.17	405.17	404.54
2.乡村劳动力资源总数（万人）	Total Number of Rural Labor Source (10 000 persons)	240.76	255.93	257.66	254.06	256.17	255.00	256.36	260.97
#劳动年龄内人口	Population at Labor Age	232.43	229.74	234.12	230.28	231.96	231.04	232.06	
3.乡村从业人员数（万人）	Rural Laborers(10 000 persons)	212.65	223.30	225.99	222.09	223.85	223.13	225.04	230.56
#劳动年龄内人口	Population at Labor Age		205.97	208.36	201.29	202.51	201.79	202.89	
#女性	Female	99.07	103.22	103.87	101.83	103.11	102.76	103.25	109.61
(1)农业	Laborers of Farming	146.07	137.69	135.64	131.96	126.46	121.78	116.58	116.15
(2)工业	Laborers of Industry	15.43	18.41	19.92	20.60	22.29	22.67	23.94	26.36
(3)建筑业	Laborers of Construction	16.45	21.73	22.37	23.28	25.27	26.24	29.20	29.78
(4)交通仓储邮电业	Laborers of Transportation,Postal and Telecommunications Services	7.64	8.74	9.26	9.22	10.45	10.92	11.91	12.57
(5)批零贸易、餐饮业	Laborers of Trade and Catering	8.14	12.70	14.14	14.18	16.61	18.09	18.91	20.52
(6)金融、保险业	Laborers of Banking and Insurance	0.45							
(7)其他	Laborers of Others	18.47	24.03	24.66	22.85	22.77	23.43	24.50	25.18
四、国有农林牧渔业从业人员数（万人）	**Number of staff and Workers in State-owned farms(10 000 persons)**	**0.29**	**0.11**	**0.11**	**0.08**	**0.07**	**0.07**	**0.06**	
五、自来水受益村数（个）	**Number of Villages Benefited from the Tap Water System (unit)**	**1527**	**1756**	**1794**	**1881**	**1934**	**2058**	**2184**	**2400**
六、通汽车村数（个）	**Number of Villages Accessible by motor Vehicles (unit)**	**2785**	**2952**	**2923**	**2973**	**2996**	**2989**	**2989**	**2978**
七、通电话村数（个）	**Number of Villages Accessible by Telephone (unit)**	**2885**	**3101**	**3113**	**3129**	**3086**	**3071**	**3052**	**3033**

注：农村基层组织数据来自民政报表，镇数不包括四县的中心镇和工矿镇。

Note:Figures of rural gross-roots organizations are from report of civil administration department. Number of townships exclude central townships and plant townships of the four counties.

10-2 各区县农村基层组织、乡村户数及人口（2011年）

Grass-root Organizations, Households and Population in Rural Area by Region（2011）

区 县	Region	乡镇个数（个）Number of Townships and Towns (unit)	镇个数 Number of Towns	村民委员会个数（个）Number of Villagers' Committees (unit)	村民小组个数（个）Number of Village Groups (unit)	乡村户数（万户）Number of Households (10000household)	乡村人数（万人）Number Rural Population (10000 person)
合 计	**Total**	**70**	**61**	**3049**	**15703**	**102.59**	**404.54**
新城区	Xincheng						
碑林区	Beilin						
莲湖区	Lianhu			5			
灞桥区	Baqiao			222	831	7.41	28.47
未央区	Weiyang			190	534	5.34	19.33
雁塔区	Yanta			98	336	4.10	11.91
阎良区	Yanliang	2	2	80	592	4.31	16.53
临潼区	Lintong	3		285	2081	14.18	57.04
长安区	Chang'an	2		668	3234	21.43	83.97
蓝田县	Lantian	21	21	519	2348	14.39	57.93
周至县	Zhouzhi	21	21	376	2535	13.92	59.60
户 县	Huxian	14	14	518	2472	11.92	47.79
高陵县	Gaoling	7	3	88	740	5.59	21.97

10-3 各区县从业人员数（2011年）

Number of Labours in Families by Region（2011）

单位：万人 (10 000 persons)

区 县	Region	乡村从业人员数合计 Rural Laborers Total	女性 Female	农林牧渔业 Farming,Forestry Animal Husbandry and Fishery	工业 Industry	建筑业 Laborers of Construction
合 计	**Total**	**230.56**	**109.61**	**116.15**	**26.36**	**29.78**
新城区	Xincheng					
碑林区	Beilin					
莲湖区	Lianhu					
灞桥区	Baqiao	15.88	6.93	6.42	1.99	1.77
未央区	Weiyang	11.20	5.11	2.55	2.74	0.97
雁塔区	Yanta	5.84	2.82	0.58	0.95	0.37
阎良区	Yanliang	9.33	4.02	5.40	0.60	1.52
临潼区	Lintong	31.56	15.42	17.32	2.86	4.67
长安区	Chang'an	46.85	19.80	19.90	5.77	8.32
蓝田县	Lantian	34.49	21.64	22.15	1.63	2.61
周至县	Zhouzhi	34.65	14.57	19.27	4.07	4.27
户 县	Huxian	28.32	13.24	16.98	4.31	2.99
高陵县	Gaoling	12.44	6.06	5.58	1.44	2.29

10–3 续表 continued

单位：万人 (10 000 persons)

区 县	Region	交通运输、仓储及邮政业 Transportation,Postal and Telecommunication Services	批零贸易餐饮业 Trade and Catering	金融、保险业 Banking and Insurance	其 他 Others
合 计	**Total**	**12.57**	**20.52**		**25.18**
新城区	Xincheng				
碑林区	Beilin				
莲湖区	Lianhu				
灞桥区	Baqiao	1.26	1.31		3.13
未央区	Weiyang	0.90	1.67		2.37
雁塔区	Yanta	0.54	1.51		1.89
阎良区	Yanliang	0.44	0.49		0.88
临潼区	Lintong	1.55	2.80		2.36
长安区	Chang'an	3.02	4.54		5.30
蓝田县	Lantian	1.30	3.06		3.74
周至县	Zhouzhi	1.68	2.66		2.70
户 县	Huxian	1.00	1.34		1.70
高陵县	Gaoling	0.88	1.14		1.11

10–4 主要年份耕地面积

Area of Cultivated Land in Representative Years

单位：万亩 (10 000 mu)

年 份 Year	年末实有耕地面积 Cultivated Area Year-end	#水 田 Paddy Field	水浇地 Irrigable Land
1970	554.09	18.20	297.05
1975	538.35	20.34	349.13
1978	530.96	16.70	370.46
1980	526.29	17.45	372.96
1985	508.88	17.63	328.10
1990	495.32	17.97	311.91
1991	492.09	17.03	309.17
1992	485.30	16.44	298.19
1993	479.04	14.36	304.49
1994	471.44	13.98	299.58
1995	463.97	17.04	278.01
1996	451.50	14.21	283.76
1997	456.62	11.90	290.49
1998	455.15	11.18	282.23
1999	450.74	11.31	281.96
2000	443.37	10.26	284.04
2001	431.69	9.00	274.73
2002	424.46	7.98	275.96
2003	413.84	6.65	263.75
2004	404.87	6.59	254.04
2005	400.17	5.55	254.04
2006	395.79	5.33	263.75
2007	391.77	4.80	255.95
2008	390.77	4.64	255.36
2009	387.89	4.39	260.71
2010	383.32	4.03	257.43
2011	377.10	3.80	253.46

10–5 各区县耕地面积（2011年）

单位：亩

区　县	Region	年末实有耕地面积 Cultivated Area Year-end	水田 Paddy Field	旱地 Dry Land	水浇地 Irrigable Land	当年增加的耕地面积 Area of Newly Increased Cultivated Land	新开荒地面积 Area of Newly Reclamation of Wasteland
合　计	**Total**	**3770990**	**38031**	**3732959**	**2534583**	**86405**	**3738**
新城区	Xincheng						
碑林区	Beilin						
莲湖区	Lianhu						
灞桥区	Baqiao	160505	430	160075	98964		
未央区	Weiyang	47700	300	47400	47400		
雁塔区	Yanta	15838		15838	4413		
阎良区	Yanliang	236928		236928	230164	1011	13
临潼区	Lintong	715985	150	715835	547385		
长安区	Chang'an	686349	23244	663105	340183	2189	465
蓝田县	Lantian	608000	9000	599000	175000	31822	500
周至县	Zhouzhi	497930	3203	494727	361410	49515	2760
户　县	Huxian	572941	1704	571237	500850	988	
高陵县	Gaoling	228814		228814	228814	880	

Area of Cultivated Land by Region（2011）

(mu)

当年减少的耕地面积 Decrease in Cultivated Area in the Year	国家基建占地 Capital Construction	乡村基建占地 Village Collective Construction	农民个人建房占地 Peasant Housing Construction	退耕改果、茶、桑面积 Area for Change into Fruit, Tea and Mulberry	退耕造林面积 Area for Change into Woods
141935	**42522**	**8636**	**4351**	**74130**	**3853**
10106	7401			2705	
4397	4397				
4361	3511			330	
1728	1283	30	76	339	
25449	9923	5000	1526	1954	
9814	6636	528	201	1947	53
36061	3900	3000	2215	23146	3800
43993	1869	66	311	41319	
2750	400	12	16	2322	
3276	3202		6	68	

10–6 主要年份农业机械拥有量（年末数）

Possession of Agricultural Machinery in Representative Years（Number of year-end）

指　标	Item	2004	2005	2006	2007
农业机械总动力(千瓦)	**Total Power of Agricultural Machinery(kw)**	**2140737**	**2239001**	**2277584**	**2348856**
大中型拖拉机(台)	Large and Medium Tractors(unit)	7500	8415	8963	10431
(千瓦)	(kw)	246978	290638	312325	387962
小型拖拉机(台)	Mini-tractors(unit)	27225	26326	23437	21555
(千瓦)	(kw)	307382	303831	263565	237550
大中型拖拉机配套农具（台）	Number of Large and Medium Tractor Towing Farm Machinery(unit)	18446	19334	18724	23487
小型拖拉机配套农具（台）	Mini-Tractor Towing Farm Machinery (unit)	47260	47883	30439	28780
农用排灌柴油机(台)	Agricultural Diesel Engines(unit)	2522	2219	3547	2709
(千瓦)	(kw)	21865	22993	29112	24445
农用排灌电动机(台)	Agricultural Motors(unit)	78542	79666	76614	84416
(千瓦)	(kw)	343230	369843	360684	387042
农用水泵（台）	Agricultural Water Pump(unit)	74701	77567	73039	80722
节水灌溉类机械（套）	Equipment in Water-saving Irrigation(set)	1141	1290	2656	1991
联合收割机（台）	Combine Harvesters(unit)	4053	4802	5026	5294
(千瓦)	(kw)	150982	173183	183313	211490
自走式机动割晒机（台）	Self-propelled Motorized Swather(unit)	3147	4226	1342	4918
(千瓦)	(kw)	150982	173183	52740	211388
机动脱粒机（台）	Motorized Huller (unit)	13060	13870	5806	11585
农用运输车（辆）	Agricultucal Transporter(unit)	42247	47348	50395	49576
(千瓦)	(kw)	545052	623859	711276	729219
#三轮运输车	Three-wheel Transporter	34736	36436	41907	40373
(千瓦)	(kw)	391455	406199	507667	507388

10-6 续表 continued

指　标	Item	2008	2009	2010	2011
农业机械总动力(千瓦)	**Total Power of Agricultural Machinery(kw)**	**2712616**	**2616053**	**2677334**	**2890247**
大中型拖拉机(台)	Large and Medium Tractors(unit)	11092	11479	14675	12585
(千瓦)	(kw)	421581	474115	568653	536087
小型拖拉机(台)	Mini-tractors(unit)	19036	18406	14194	13008
(千瓦)	(kw)	213806	204965	167724	145805
大中型拖拉机配套农具（台）	Number of Large and Medium Tractor Towing Farm Machinery(unit)	25125	26575	29215	36209
小型拖拉机配套农具（台）	Mini-Tractor Towing Farm Machinery (unit)	26984	29039	24393	29624
农用排灌柴油机(台)	Agricultural Diesel Engines(unit)	2670	2691	3309	2639
(千瓦)	(kw)	23546	23008	31859	22103
农用排灌电动机(台)	Agricultural Motors(unit)	85349	83243	79462	87461
(千瓦)	(kw)	421435	400534	333107	416555
农用水泵（台）	Agricultural Water Pump(unit)	80462	80174	77367	75426
节水灌溉类机械（套）	Equipment in Water-saving Irrigation(set)	1728	1799	1710	1733
联合收割机（台）	Combine Harvesters(unit)	5390	6155	6718	7854
(千瓦)	(kw)	220185	252976	271577	362692
自走式机动割晒机（台）	Self-propelled Motorized Swather(unit)	2174	1220	208	187
(千瓦)	(kw)	90899	52129	9877	11085
机动脱粒机（台）	Motorized Huller (unit)	23781	11960	13231	13407
农用运输车（辆）	Agricultucal Transporter(unit)	54860	50671	51665	51838
(千瓦)	(kw)	860328	730843	811064	790650
#三轮运输车	Three-wheel Transporter	44953	41899	42749	42770
(千瓦)	(kw)	572902	546660	562204	561416

10-7 各区县农业机械拥有量（2011年）

指　标	Item	西安市 Xi'an	灞桥区 Baqiao	未央区 Weiyang
农业机械总动力(千瓦)	**Total Power of Agricultural Machinery(kw)**	**2890247**	**173226**	**44694**
大中型拖拉机(台)	Large and Medium Tractors(unit)	12585	427	152
(千瓦)	(kw)	536087	20817	5930
小型拖拉机(台)	Mini-tractors(unit)	13008	63	11
(千瓦)	(kw)	145805	921	145
大中型拖拉机配套农具（台）	Number of Large and Medium Tractor Towing Farm Machinery(unit)	36209	946	510
小型拖拉机配套农具（台）	Mini-Tractor Towing Farm Machinery (unit)	29624	552	12
农用排灌柴油机(台)	Agricultural Diesel Engines(unit)	2639		
(千瓦)	(kw)	22103		
农用排灌电动机(台)	Agricultural Motors(unit)	87461	3818	958
(千瓦)	(kw)	416555	26901	3832
农用水泵（台）	Agricultural Water Pump(unit)	75426	3818	958
节水灌溉类机械（套）	Equipment in Water-saving Irrigation(set)	1733	30	95
联合收割机（台）	Combine Harvesters(unit)	7854	223	43
(千瓦)	(kw)	362692	13034	1620
自走式机动割晒机（台）	Self-propelled Motorized Swather(unit)	187	187	
(千瓦)	(kw)	11085	11085	
机动脱粒机（台）	Motorized Huller (unit)	13407	47	
农用运输车（辆）	Agricultucal Transporter(unit)	51838	3681	508
(千瓦)	(kw)	790650	60396	9681
#三轮运输车	Three-wheel Transporter	42770	2545	398
(千瓦)	(kw)	561416	30021	4731

Possession of Agricultural Machinery by Region（2011）

雁塔区 Yanta	阎良区 Yanliang	临潼区 Lintong	长安区 Chang'an	蓝田县 Lantian	周至县 Zhouzhi	户　县 Huxian	高陵县 Gaoling
98899	**159853**	**530420**	**513544**	**291670**	**396587**	**448481**	**232873**
56	920	2205	2719	997	1330	2378	1401
2205	40191	88411	108131	37104	66300	111820	55178
19	650	1204	2477	2361	4623	1393	207
261	7800	13593	30735	26436	46937	16700	2277
114	2672	6285	6051	1980	2099	9993	5559
71	1530	3640	5896	3645	7346	5946	986
		253	1476	565	289	56	
		2907	9227	6879	2522	568	
580	6010	17304	23338	3223	15718	12824	3688
4028	28033	97830	98658	18759	58467	59905	20142
		16458	17651	2485	17515	12853	3688
	55	106	1032	63	244	108	
32	580	1556	1524	264	422	2398	812
1080	30959	72155	60716	11744	19846	112576	38962
	1250	4481	775	1989	2164	2171	530
725	2244	14007	7789	4498	8337	4050	5999
30139	32310	191551	124842	64813	115099	65767	96052
536	2110	13483	4597	3754	7458	3599	4290
9112	30173	178993	69959	47690	89504	51392	49841

10-8 主要年份农业机械、化肥、水利、水电情况

Agricultural Machinery,Chemical Fertilizers,Water Conservancy, Hydropower in Representative Years

指　　标	Item	2000	2005	2006	2007
一、农业机械化水平(万亩)	**Statistics on Agricultural Machinery (10 000 mu)**				
当年实际机耕地面积	Area Ploughed by Tractors	366.81	360.68	354.05	361.62
当年作业机械播种面积	Seeded Area by Tractors	482.74	485.62	519.00	521.36
当年作业机械收获面积	Harvest Area by Tractors	272.83	271.77	280.88	296.06
二、农用化肥施用量(吨)	**Use of Agricultural Fertilizers and Insecticides(ton)**				
1.按实物量计算合计	Practicality Consumption	697243	749802	759882	762401
氮 肥	Nitrogenous Fertilizer	392366	411161	413514	408847
磷 肥	Phosphate Fertilizer	155480	161444	164781	160932
钾 肥	Potash Fertilizer	31841	34114	31414	34284
复合肥	Compound Fertilizer	78620	115458	121124	124784
2.按折纯量计算合计	Standard Consumption	196343	211790	216093	220251
氮 肥	Nitrogenous Fertilizer	102982	107645	110137	109484
磷 肥	Phosphate Fertilizer	18658	19368	19772	19311
钾 肥	Potash Fertilizer	15921	17055	15709	17141
复合肥	Compound Fertilizer	39313	57009	59731	62398
三、农用塑料薄膜使用量（公斤）	**Plastic Sheet for Agricultural Use(kg)**	**1622198**	**1855383**	**1931527**	**2096169**
四、农用柴油使用量（吨）	**Diesel Oil for Agricultural Use (ton)**	**52706**	**50832**	**49686**	**50137**
五、农药使用量（公斤）	**Pesticide (kg)**	**1559333**	**1427879**	**1471672**	**1444867**
六、年末农村办沼气池（个）	**Number of Mash Gas Pond Managed by Village Government in Year-end(unit)**	**10199**	**12445**	**16211**	**26448**
七、农村水利化情况（万亩）	**Irrigation and Water Conservancy (10 000 mu)**				
有效灌溉面积	Effective Irrigation Area	335.97	280.10	276.58	276.28
旱涝保收面积	Stable-Harvesting Arable Land	294.06	255.37	253.66	247.99
机电排灌面积	Electrical Irrigation Area	249.11	223.74	214.03	210.51
八、农村电气化情况	**Rural electrization**				
乡村及村以下办水电站（个）	Hydropower Station in Rural Areas(unit)	67	79	79	76
装机容量（千瓦）	Installed Power Generation Capacity(kw)	7236	13775	14252	24827
发 电 量（万千瓦小时）	Generating Capacity (10 000 kwh)	1138	2239	2253	10085
已配套机电井（眼）	Electricity Powered Well(unit)	50289	46505	46112	45783

10-8 续表 continued

指　　标	Item	2008	2009	2010	2011
一、农业机械化水平(万亩)	**Statistics on Agricultural Machinery (10 000 mu)**				
当年实际机耕地面积	Area Ploughed by Tractors	404.42	413.70	367.32	427.03
当年作业机械播种面积	Seeded Area by Tractors	539.81	544.86	548.28	507.55
当年作业机械收获面积	Harvest Area by Tractors	313.11	342.82	403.50	413.93
二、农用化肥施用量(吨)	**Use of Agricultural Fertilizers and Insecticides(ton)**				
1.按实物量计算合计	Practicality Consumption	767980	776319	781072	785885
氮 肥	Nitrogenous Fertilizer	413397	414481	397975	398395
磷 肥	Phosphate Fertilizer	157145	153825	152943	151005
钾 肥	Potash Fertilizer	34149	33069	37715	38195
复合肥	Compound Fertilizer	132481	142137	158062	163797
2.按折纯量计算合计	Standard Consumption	225949	230299	235532	239497
氮 肥	Nitrogenous Fertilizer	112000	112275	108868	110412
磷 肥	Phosphate Fertilizer	18855	18457	18315	18026
钾 肥	Potash Fertilizer	17077	16534	17997	18095
复合肥	Compound Fertilizer	66247	71042	78811	81764
三、农用塑料薄膜使用量（公斤）	**Plastic Sheet for Agricultural Use(kg)**	**2122310**	**2141969**	**2450496**	**2533372**
四、农用柴油使用量（吨）	**Diesel Oil for Agricultural Use (ton)**	**51097**	**51346**	**61917**	**61637**
五、农药使用量（公斤）	**Pesticide (kg)**	**1465819**	**1325459**	**1243105**	**1242773**
六、年末农村办沼气池（个）	**Number of Mash Gas Pond Managed by Village Government in Year-end(unit)**	**36540**	**46737**	**50710**	**62208**
七、农村水利化情况（万亩）	**Irrigation and Water Conservancy (10 000 mu)**				
有效灌溉面积	Effective Irrigation Area	274.48	273.17	281.28	262.32
旱涝保收面积	Stable-Harvesting Arable Land	249.31	247.60	234.15	214.62
机电排灌面积	Electrical Irrigation Area	211.01	213.42	224.60	200.36
八、农村电气化情况	**Rural electrization**				
乡村及村以下办水电站（个）	Hydropower Station in Rural Areas(unit)	76	75	44	44
装机容量（千瓦）	Installed Power Generation Capacity(kw)	24827	25047	22325	22325
发 电 量（万千瓦小时）	Generating Capacity (10 000 kwh)	10477	10678	7268	7268
已配套机电井（眼）	Electricity Powered Well(unit)	47032	46790	44310	40345

10-9 各区县农业机械、化肥、水利、水电情况（2011年）

指　　标	Item	西安市 Xi'an	灞桥区 Baqiao	未央区 Weiyang
一、农业机械化水平(万亩)	**Statistics on Agricultural Machinery (10 000 mu)**			
当年实际机耕地面积	Area Ploughed by Tractors	427	20	6
当年作业机械播种面积	Seeded Area by Tractors	508	22	4
当年作业机械收获面积	Harvest Area by Tractors	414	17	2
二、农用化肥施用量(吨)	**Use of Agricultural Fertilizers and Insecticides(Ton)**			
1.按实物量计算合计	Practicality Consumption	785885	23434	3989
氮 肥	Nitrogenous Fertilizer	398395	13040	2260
磷 肥	Phosphate Fertilizer	151005	2138	326
钾 肥	Potash Fertilizer	38195	2043	70
复合肥	Compound Fertilizer	163797	6144	1024
2.按折纯量计算合计	Standard Consumption	239497	8810	1480
氮 肥	Nitrogenous Fertilizer	110412	4427	740
磷 肥	Phosphate Fertilizer	18026	257	39
钾 肥	Potash Fertilizer	18095	1021	35
复合肥	Compound Fertilizer	81764	3072	512
三、农用塑料薄膜使用量（公斤）	**Plastic Sheet for Agricultural Use(kg)**	2533372	154934	14638
四、农用柴油使用量（吨）	**Diesel Oil for Agricultural Use (ton)**	61637	1996	821
五、农药使用量（公斤）	**Pesticide (kg)**	1242773	38683	9472
六、年末农村办沼气池（个）	**Number of Mash Gas Pond Managed by Village Government in Year-end(unit)**	62208	1640	3
七、农村水利化情况（万亩）	**Irrigation and Water Conservancy (10 000 mu)**			
有效灌溉面积	Effective Irrigation Area	262	11	3
旱涝保收面积	Stable-Harvesting Arable Land	215	10	3
机电排灌面积	Electrical Irrigation Area	200	10	5
八、农村电气化情况	**Rural electrization**			
乡村及村以下办水电站（个）	Hydropower Station in Rural Areas(unit)	44		
装机容量（千瓦）	Installed Power Generation Capacity(kw)	22325		
发 电 量（万千瓦小时）	Generating Capacity (10 000 kwh)	7268		
已配套机电井（眼）	Electricity Powered Well(unit)	40345	2029	1290

Agricultural Machinery,Chemical Fertilizers,Water Conservancy, Hydropower by Region（2011）

雁塔区 Yanta	阎良区 Yanliang	临潼区 Lintong	长安区 Chang'an	蓝田县 Lantian	周至县 Zhouzhi	户　县 Huxian	高陵县 Gaoling
	22	52	117	55	66	48	41
	29	94	108	66	81	91	14
	22	76	92	38	46	84	39
1199	53755	149034	134697	95052	143222	103139	78364
419	25554	78703	68049	52100	63334	62284	32652
75	10854	43586	24075	19320	15990	13942	20699
100	4216	2579	6634	6210	8457	3017	4869
216	13043	22253	27698	16020	41042	21271	15086
411	18409	39377	33270	36610	45100	32009	24021
54	8434	20778	9186	22640	15557	16982	11614
7	1303	5230	2889	2300	1918	1680	2403
49	2108	1288	3317	3100	3967	1508	1702
108	6521	11126	13848	8010	20403	10621	7543
	912607	211012	143855	175890	95775	612722	211939
15	2521	6359	13317	10220	3318	9901	13169
22	172608	336451	127916	78200	162601	62928	253892
	4951	4822	4249	1700	25340	12631	6872
	22	54	29	23	50	49	20
	22	46	22	16	27	47	20
2	23	41	33	11	16	47	13
			7	5	26	6	
			5065	13600	1100	2560	
			1180	5440	410	238	
377	3784	7183	5260	1800	5910	9996	2716

10-10 主要年份农林牧渔及服务业总产值及指数

Gross Output Value of Farming,Forestry,Animal Husbandry,Fishery,Service and Related Indices in Representative Years

单位：万元 （10 000yuan）

年 份 Year	农林牧渔及服务业总产值（现价）Gross Output Value (At current prices)	农业 Farming	林业 Forestry	牧业 Animal Husbandry	渔业 Fishery	农林牧渔服务业 Service of Farming, Forestry, Animal Husbandry and Fishery	指数（上年=100）（可比价） Indices(preceding year=100) (At constant prices)
1970	40617	35965	713	3896	43		111.2
1975	55322	47378	1509	6403	32		93.9
1978	65423	56519	1444	7427	33		104.7
1980	65322	54004	1177	10106	35		85.0
1985	134933	105888	2559	26186	300		106.4
1990	262073	191088	3134	65840	2011		102.5
1991	295620	208324	3362	81070	2864		108.6
1992	321155	219160	4225	94045	3725		108.6
1993	387068	261959	5031	115810	4268		112.8
1994	565056	359609	7819	192140	5488		102.4
1995	754597	513348	7185	228598	5466		106.8
1996	786003	552726	7573	219214	6490		102.1
1997	836201	585973	9226	233623	7379		110.3
1998	853279	625465	8146	212045	7623		107.5
1999	739905	530029	8883	194552	6441		100.7
2000	743712	514845	8482	212612	7773		104.3
2001	767511	527160	8427	223861	8063		102.8
2002	797444	539978	11378	238761	7327		103.0
2003	837857	551398	10550	269610	6299		101.5
2004	967946	580798	12773	314517	6728	53130	108.4
2005	1065437	657262	13086	329856	7340	57893	107.7
2006	1141484	686748	15188	346626	7017	85905	107.2
2007	1341450	798163	15845	410213	9051	108178	105.3
2008	1682725	956549	19031	564095	11084	131966	107.8
2009	1787032	1061756	22663	546191	11830	144592	106.5
2010	2270994	1438934	26787	629376	12830	163067	107.4
2011	2726608	1729295	34453	754593	14856	193411	106.6

10-11 主要年份农林牧渔及服务业总产值指数

Related Indices of Gross Output Value of Farming,Forestry,Animal Husbandry,Fishery,Service and Related Indices in Representative Years

年 份 Year	农林牧渔及服务业总产值指数（上年=100）（可比价） Indices(preceding year=100) (At constant prices)	农业 Farming	林业 Forestry	牧业 Animal Husbandry	渔业 Fishery	农林牧渔服务业 Service of Farming, Forestry, Animal Husbandry and Fishery
2005	107.7	108.0	98.7	107.3	112.6	107.9
2006	107.2	106.0	102.5	109.3	104.5	109.4
2007	105.3	106.4	101.3	102.4	106.3	108.7
2008	107.8	107.9	112.2	106.0	100.5	113.7
2009	106.5	105.4	121.3	106.8	107.4	110.2
2010	107.4	108.7	115.2	104.3	92.7	108.9
2011	106.6	108.2	105.7	102.9	102.1	107.7

10-12 主要年份农林牧渔及服务业总产值构成

Gross Output Value and Its Composition of Farming, Forestry, Animal Husbandry,Fishery and Service at Current Price in Representative Years

年 份 Year	农林牧渔及服务业总产值（%） Service of Farming, Forestry, Animal Husbandry and Fishery(%)	农业 Farming	林业 Forestry	牧业 Animal Husbandry	渔业 Fishery	农林牧渔服务业 Service of Farming, Forestry, Animal Husbandry and Fishery
2005	100.0	61.7	1.2	31.0	0.7	5.4
2006	100.0	60.9	1.3	31.5	0.6	5.7
2007	100.0	59.5	1.2	30.6	0.7	8.1
2008	100.0	56.9	1.1	33.5	0.7	7.8
2009	100.0	59.4	1.3	30.6	0.7	8.1
2010	100.0	63.4	1.2	27.7	0.6	7.2
2011	100.0	63.4	1.3	27.7	0.5	7.1

10-13 各区县农林牧渔及服务业总产值（2011年）

Gross Output Value of Farming, Forestry, Animal Husbandry, Fishery and Service by Region（2011）

单位：万元 （10 000yuan)

区县	Region	农林牧渔及服务业总产值 Gross Output Value	农业 Farming	林业 Forestry	牧业 Animal Husbandry	渔业 Fishery	农林牧渔服务业 Service of Farming, Forestry, Animal Husbandry and Fishery
全　市	**Total**	**2726608**	**1729295**	**34453**	**754593**	**14856**	**193411**
新城区	Xincheng						
碑林区	Beilin						
莲湖区	Lianhu						
灞桥区	Baqiao	219746	157939	913	42654	2240	16000
未央区	Weiyang	37534	20015	15	14093	1186	2225
雁塔区	Yanta	36907	22636	36	9235		5000
阎良区	Yanliang	259395	188735	476	50365	259	19560
临潼区	Lintong	447588	217196	7530	188659	2203	32000
长安区	Chang'an	438545	300632	1196	103354	3873	29490
蓝田县	Lantian	337450	214070	18542	78891	2602	23345
周至县	Zhouzhi	329966	241610	4044	65482	655	18175
户　县	Huxian	340026	222351	902	88597	850	27326
高陵县	Gaoling	279451	144111	799	113263	988	20290

10-14 各区县农林牧渔及服务业总产值指数及构成（2011年）

Gross Output Value and Its Composition of Farming, Forestry, Animal Husbandry,Fishery and Service at Current Price by Region（2011）

单位：%　　　　(%)

区　县	Region	农林牧渔及服务业总产值 Gross Output Value	农业 Farming	林业 Forestry	牧业 Animal Husbandry	渔业 Fishery	农林牧渔服务业 Service of Farming, Forestry, Animal Husbandry and Fishery
全市指数	**Total**	**106.6**	**108.2**	**105.7**	**102.9**	**102.1**	**107.7**
新城区	Xincheng						
碑林区	Beilin						
莲湖区	Lianhu						
灞桥区	Baqiao	108.1	109.0	108.8	102.6	110.3	114.4
未央区	Weiyang	88.6	90.7	75.2	96.2	57.2	62.8
雁塔区	Yanta	95.7	96.7	39.6	88.1	100.0	111.1
阎良区	Yanliang	107.8	109.3	87.2	102.1	91.0	109.3
临潼区	Lintong	104.0	105.8	104.3	101.1	111.5	106.1
长安区	Chang'an	107.1	108.4	59.1	105.2	119.7	103.6
蓝田县	Lantian	107.7	109.7	115.9	101.1	114.8	107.3
周至县	Zhouzhi	108.1	109.7	106.0	102.4	95.7	110.1
户　县	Huxian	108.5	108.5	100.7	107.6	93.4	112.3
高陵县	Gaoling	108.2	109.7	100.4	105.5	101.8	112.5
全市构成	**Total**	**100.0**	**63.4**	**1.3**	**27.7**	**0.5**	**7.1**
新城区	Xincheng						
碑林区	Beilin						
莲湖区	Lianhu						
灞桥区	Baqiao	100.0	71.9	0.4	19.4	1.0	7.3
未央区	Weiyang	100.0	53.3		37.5	3.2	5.9
雁塔区	Yanta	100.0	61.3	0.1	25.0		13.5
阎良区	Yanliang	100.0	72.8	0.2	19.4	0.1	7.5
临潼区	Lintong	100.0	48.5	1.7	42.2	0.5	7.1
长安区	Chang'an	100.0	68.6	0.3	23.6	0.9	6.7
蓝田县	Lantian	100.0	63.4	5.5	23.4	0.8	6.9
周至县	Zhouzhi	100.0	73.2	1.2	19.8	0.2	5.5
户　县	Huxian	100.0	65.4	0.3	26.1	0.2	8.0
高陵县	Gaoling	100.0	51.6	0.3	40.5	0.4	7.3

10-15 主要年份农林牧渔及服务业增加值

Value-Added of Farming, Forestry, Animal Husbandry, Fishery and Service in Representative Years

单位:万元 (10 000 yuan)

年份 Year	农林牧渔及服务业增加值 Farming,Forestry, Animal Husbandry, Fishery and Service	农业 Farming	林业 Forestry	牧业 Animal Husbandry	渔业 Fishery	农林牧渔服务业 Service of Farming, Forestry, Animal Husbandry and Fishery
1995	413981	329662	4413	76746	3160	
2000	446481	336777	4323	101353	4028	
2001	458720	342427	4258	108096	3939	
2002	477691	351358	6419	116591	3323	
2003	458378	312849	5473	137236	2820	
2004	582009	393349	6811	164572	2919	14358
2005	660148	444320	6888	169701	3373	35866
2006	704427	465823	8556	177431	3227	49390
2007	825053	538794	8420	210930	4467	62442
2008	1034471	639071	10592	301305	5598	77905
2009	1103793	698043	11958	303594	5913	84285
2010	1400575	935489	14362	349204	6503	95017
2011	1731398	1161249	18807	428169	7679	115494

10-16 主要年份农林牧渔及服务业增加值指数

Indices of Value-Added of Farming, Forestry, Animal Husbandry, Fishery and Service in Representative Years

年 份 Year	农林牧渔及服务业增加值指数（上年=100）（可比价） Farming,Forestry,Animal Husbandry,Fishery and Service	农 业 Farming	林 业 Forestry	牧 业 Animal Husbandry	渔 业 Fishery	农林牧渔服务业 Service of Farming, Forestry, Animal Husbandry and Fishery
2008	107.6	107.6	112.0	105.8	100.0	114.0
2009	106.3	103.6	114.6	111.2	106.3	108.8
2010	106.9	107.9	108.7	104.3	94.0	108.9
2011	106.7	108.1	106.1	102.8	102.7	108.1

10-17 各区县农林牧渔及服务业增加值（2011年）

Value-Added of Farming, Forestry, Animal Husbandry, Fishery and Service by Region（2011）

单位:万元 (10 000yuan)

区 县	Region	农林牧渔及服务业增加值 Farming,Forestry, Animal Husbandry, Fishery and Service	农 业 Farming	林 业 Forestry	牧 业 Animal Husbandry	渔 业 Fishery	农林牧渔服务业 Service of Farming, Forestry, Animal Husbandry and Fishery
全 市	**Total**	**1731398**	**1161249**	**18807**	**428169**	**7679**	**115494**
新城区	Xincheng						
碑林区	Beilin						
莲湖区	Lianhu						
灞桥区	Baqiao	144069	108030	548	25635	896	8960
未央区	Weiyang	23132	12810	3	8399	474	1446
雁塔区	Yanta	26127	16049	25	6058		3995
阎良区	Yanliang	176092	129850	243	33745	127	12127
临潼区	Lintong	282650	145521	4179	111309	1321	20320
长安区	Chang'an	289716	226677	670	42375	2595	17399
蓝田县	Lantian	204908	132654	10384	47019	1171	13680
周至县	Zhouzhi	202995	156563	1820	34705	347	9560
户 县	Huxian	212392	142305	496	54930	451	14210
高陵县	Gaoling	169317	90790	439	63994	297	13797

10-18 各区县农林牧渔及服务业增加值指数（2011年）

Indices of Value-Added of Farming, Forestry, Animal Husbandry, Fishery and Service by Region （2011）

（上年=100）（可比价） (preceding year = 100)（At constant prices）

区　县	Region	农林牧渔及服务业增加值指数（上年=100）（可比价） Farming,Forestry,Animal Husbandry,Fishery and Service	农　业 Farming	林　业 Forestry	牧　业 Animal Husbandry	渔　业 Fishery	农林牧渔服务业 Service of Farming, Forestry, Animal Husbandry and Fishery
全　市	**Total**	**106.7**	**108.1**	**106.1**	**102.8**	**102.7**	**108.1**
新城区	Xincheng						
碑林区	Beilin						
莲湖区	Lianhu						
灞桥区	Baqiao	108.2	109.0	108.8	102.4	109.9	115.1
未央区	Weiyang	90.0	92.5	75.2	96.2	56.1	62.8
雁塔区	Yanta	95.9	96.6	39.6	87.6	100.0	111.0
阎良区	Yanliang	108.0	109.4	88.0	102.4	90.2	109.3
临潼区	Lintong	104.2	105.8	105.3	101.4	110.7	106.9
长安区	Chang'an	107.2	108.2	60.7	105.2	114.5	103.5
蓝田县	Lantian	107.8	109.6	115.2	101.4	113.8	109.8
周至县	Zhouzhi	108.3	109.8	106.0	102.3	95.3	111.0
户　县	Huxian	108.2	108.2	100.7	107.7	92.7	111.1
高陵县	Gaoling	108.1	109.6	100.4	104.9	101.5	113.2

10–19 主要年份农作物播种面积

Sown Areas of Farm Crops In Representative Years

单位：万亩 （10 000 mu）

年 份 Year	总播种面积 Total Sown Area	粮 食 Grain Crops	小 麦 Wheat	玉 米 Corn	棉 花 Cotton	油 料 Oil-bearing Crops	蔬 菜 Vegetables
1980	835.43	706.35	324.17	273.14	81.23	10.01	24.02
1985	795.41	704.36	378.20	271.14	21.02	8.01	45.03
1990	816.41	731.42	387.20	282.14	15.02	12.00	51.03
1991	820.41	731.37	389.19	283.14	19.01	13.01	47.03
1992	820.65	715.50	384.60	273.60	26.70	16.20	54.60
1993	821.63	713.49	380.40	273.69	17.66	14.84	63.90
1994	821.10	719.00	375.90	272.40	19.70	13.80	59.90
1995	784.74	690.63	370.41	259.55	11.07	18.57	57.59
1996	797.40	709.00	366.30	286.80	7.70	18.80	55.50
1997	755.78	670.83	367.71	248.79	4.50	15.53	59.36
1998	789.99	705.03	370.17	285.45	3.56	14.69	60.95
1999	793.08	709.95	371.94	294.00	2.85	12.74	60.68
2000	784.94	697.55	369.89	283.70	2.48	13.46	64.35
2001	763.16	678.05	359.19	278.57	2.91	11.87	61.77
2002	751.10	655.59	350.64	271.95	2.63	11.40	67.71
2003	737.06	632.55	336.05	261.89	3.38	11.04	69.44
2004	753.83	630.63	311.52	286.50	4.94	9.74	77.55
2005	757.91	642.75	325.10	287.87	5.40	9.51	83.33
2006	769.49	648.00	313.23	307.89	6.09	8.58	87.03
2007	762.38	637.05	306.98	304.13	6.93	7.41	91.07
2008	756.06	630.31	319.39	286.69	6.35	8.59	93.02
2009	757.11	628.69	318.36	285.20	6.45	8.59	94.83
2010	751.74	621.71	317.18	279.93	6.26	8.98	95.71
2011	704.17	573.13	306.39	243.06	5.97	8.83	96.97

注：2011年农作物播种面积为陕西省统计局依据（国统字办[2011]68号）文件调整数。

Note:The crop acreage of 2011 was adjustment in accordance with the document[2011] No.68 issued by Bureau of Shaanxi Province.

10-20 各区县主要农作物播种面积（2011年）

Sown Areas of Major Farm Crops by Region（2011）

单位：万亩 (10 000 mu)

区 县 Region	总播种面积 Total Sown Area	粮 食 Grain Crops	小 麦 Wheat	玉 米 Corn	棉 花 Cotton	油 料 Oil-bearing Crops	蔬 菜 Vegetables	瓜果类 Fruits Class
合 计 Total	**704.17**	**573.13**	**306.39**	**243.06**	**5.97**	**8.83**	**96.97**	**16.22**
新城区 Xincheng								
碑林区 Beilin								
莲湖区 Lianhu								
灞桥区 Baqiao	29.40	20.89	12.73	7.36	0.14	0.48	7.04	0.75
未央区 Weiyang	8.51	6.25	3.52	2.71		0.01	2.01	0.15
雁塔区 Yanta	1.34	0.13	0.08	0.04			1.20	0.02
阎良区 Yanliang	47.58	20.52	11.33	9.16	4.46	0.10	16.20	6.29
临潼区 Lintong	131.76	110.97	61.60	45.88	1.10	2.37	14.16	1.84
长安区 Chang'an	138.70	110.66	59.95	49.14	0.03	1.55	23.99	2.24
蓝田县 Lantian	110.90	96.10	49.48	32.10	0.24	2.59	8.11	2.90
周至县 Zhouzhi	89.12	78.88	40.87	36.09		1.25	8.51	0.20
户 县 Huxian	97.83	86.65	45.06	40.65		0.48	8.98	1.65
高陵县 Gaoling	49.03	42.08	21.76	19.93			6.77	0.18

注：本表区县农作物播种面积为依据（陕统办发[2011]79号）文件调整数。

Note:The county crop acreage in this table was adjustment based on document [2011] No.79 issued by Bureau of Shaanxi Province.

10-21 主要年份农作物产品产量

Yield of Major Farm Crops in Representative Years

单位：万吨 (10 000 ton)

年　份 Year	粮食作物 Grain Crops	夏　粮 Summer Grain	小麦 Wheat	秋　粮 Autumn Grain	稻谷 Rice	玉米 Corn	棉　花 Cotton	油　料 Oil-bearing Crops	油菜籽 Rapeseeds	蔬　菜 Vegetables
1978	132.8	64.2	58.2	68.7	5.1	55.8	2.85	0.09	0.07	45.66
1979	145.7	81.8	74.2	63.9	4.5	53.4	2.63	0.33	0.29	49.11
1980	114.4	56.6	52.2	57.8	4.7	47.7	1.97	0.54	0.50	40.13
1981	116.1	78.7	74.3	37.4	3.4	31.5	1.36	0.76	0.75	34.06
1982	148.9	85.6	82.2	63.3	4.9	55.5	2.88	0.51	0.49	53.71
1983	148.1	81.8	79.6	66.3	4.8	58.5	0.85	0.36	0.34	46.99
1984	157.6	82.4	81.0	75.2	5.0	66.5	1.49	0.46	0.29	75.47
1985	150.1	76.1	74.8	74.0	5.1	65.1	0.49	0.75	0.39	86.44
1986	162.4	91.7	90.1	70.7	4.8	61.8	0.44	1.25	0.82	85.84
1987	171.2	87.0	85.2	84.2	5.0	74.3	0.47	1.57	1.22	95.16
1988	158.0	86.8	84.6	71.1	3.8	61.4	0.42	0.89	0.51	113.50
1989	173.6	93.5	91.2	80.2	4.7	70.4	0.55	1.33	0.94	129.32
1990	172.4	91.7	89.7	80.8	5.5	70.4	0.70	1.35	0.94	119.32
1991	178.8	91.1	89.2	87.7	5.0	77.5	0.97	1.20	0.74	117.41
1992	183.4	101.7	99.6	81.7	4.7	72.3	0.74	1.49	0.87	128.12
1993	190.0	101.1	99.0	88.9	4.9	78.6	0.75	1.40	1.00	145.80
1994	157.4	86.9	84.9	70.5	4.5	61.4	0.65	1.08	0.78	135.26
1995	175.3	99.8	97.4	75.5	3.4	67.8	0.29	2.17	1.90	133.60
1996	187.5	80.1	78.4	107.4	3.4	95.6	0.24	1.83	1.55	138.01
1997	190.5	114.3	112.3	76.3	3.5	69.4	0.17	1.86	1.65	142.11
1998	212.7	104.4	104.0	108.3	3.2	99.1	0.14	1.67	1.36	148.87
1999	204.4	95.5	94.4	108.9	2.9	99.7	0.15	1.30	1.00	153.24
2000	201.9	92.6	91.6	109.3	3.1	100.5	0.14	1.34	0.95	162.14
2001	197.1	98.1	97.2	98.9	2.7	91.3	0.17	1.23	0.90	152.80
2002	192.4	94.5	93.5	97.9	2.1	91.6	0.18	1.22	0.84	169.74
2003	176.3	98.2	96.7	78.2	1.6	72.3	0.22	1.13	0.70	169.67
2004	195.8	97.8	96.0	98.0	1.7	91.6	0.40	1.14	0.84	180.96
2005	205.5	100.0	99.1	105.5	1.6	99.3	0.45	1.16	0.89	195.70
2006	193.5	86.0	85.4	107.4	1.4	101.2	0.48	1.08	0.87	189.30
2007	189.1	77.3	76.7	111.8	1.5	105.6	0.59	0.96	0.77	204.30
2008	214.4	105.9	105.6	108.5	0.9	103.0	0.62	1.15	0.95	221.53
2009	218.2	103.0	102.1	115.2	0.9	109.5	0.63	1.12	0.93	242.41
2010	221.7	106.6	105.8	115.1	0.8	108.9	0.60	1.20	1.00	253.10
2011	182.0	90.5	89.7	91.5	0.7	85.3	0.56	1.17	0.95	261.66

注：2011年农作物产品产量为陕西省统计局依据（国统字办[2011]70号）文件调整数。

Note:The agricultural production of 2011 was adjustment in accordance with the document [2011] No.70 issued by Bureau of Shaanxi Province.

10-22 各区县主要农作物产品产量（2011年）

Yield of Major Farm Crops by Region（2011）

单位：万吨 (10 000 tons)

区 县	Region	粮食总产量 Total Yield of Grain Crops	夏粮 Summer Grain	小麦 Wheat	秋粮 Autumn Grain	稻谷 Rice	玉米 Corn
合 计	**Total**	**182.04**	**90.54**	**89.68**	**91.49**	**0.67**	**85.30**
新城区	Xincheng						
碑林区	Beilin						
莲湖区	Lianhu						
灞桥区	Baqiao	5.71	3.02	3.02	2.68		2.49
未央区	Weiyang	2.05	1.01	1.01	1.04		1.03
雁塔区	Yanta	0.03	0.02	0.02	0.01		0.01
阎良区	Yanliang	8.11	4.24	4.24	3.87		3.86
临潼区	Lintong	32.03	17.30	17.26	14.73		13.55
长安区	Chang'an	34.62	17.13	17.13	17.49	0.43	16.89
蓝田县	Lantian	26.58	11.76	11.46	14.82	0.21	11.22
周至县	Zhouzhi	22.60	11.23	10.92	11.38	0.04	11.08
户 县	Huxian	30.27	15.14	14.93	15.13		15.06
高陵县	Gaoling	20.03	9.69	9.69	10.34		10.12

注：本表区县农作物产品产量为依据（陕统办发[2011]79号）文件调整数。

Note:The county crop acreage in this table was adjustment based on document [2011] No.79 issued by Bureau of Shaanxi Province.

10-22 续表 continued

单位：万吨 (10 000 tons)

区 县	Region	棉花 Cotton	油料 Oil-bearing Crops	油菜籽 Rapeseeds	蔬菜 Vegetables	瓜果类 Fruits Class
合 计	**Total**	**0.56**	**1.17**	**0.95**	**261.66**	**46.10**
新城区	Xincheng					
碑林区	Beilin					
莲湖区	Lianhu					
灞桥区	Baqiao	0.01	0.06	0.05	26.47	1.00
未央区	Weiyang				5.13	0.52
雁塔区	Yanta				0.37	0.05
阎良区	Yanliang	0.42	0.01	0.01	57.44	20.63
临潼区	Lintong	0.11	0.23	0.14	36.77	5.62
长安区	Chang'an		0.28	0.26	52.78	4.93
蓝田县	Lantian	0.03	0.30	0.24	16.88	7.20
周至县	Zhouzhi		0.20	0.18	17.43	0.51
户 县	Huxian		0.09	0.07	27.50	4.83
高陵县	Gaoling				20.89	0.81

10–23 主要年份农作物单位面积产量

Yield of Farm Crops Per Hectare in Representative Years

单位：公斤/亩 (kg/mu)

年 份 Year	粮食作物 Grain Crops	夏 粮 Summer Grain	小麦 Wheat	秋 粮 Autumn Grain	玉米 Corn	棉 花 Cotton	油 料 Oil-bearing Crops	油菜籽 Rapeseeds	蔬 菜 Vegetables
1990	236	232	232	241	249	46	103	101	2349
1991	245	229	229	264	274	51	94	89	2332
1992	256	259	259	253	264	28	92	101	2344
1993	266	260	260	274	287	42	94	107	2282
1994	219	226	226	211	225	33	79	84	2260
1995	254	263	263	243	261	27	117	128	2320
1996	265	214	214	321	333	32	86	100	2489
1997	284	305	306	257	279	38	76	129	2395
1998	302	278	279	328	347	40	114	121	2443
1999	288	253	254	327	339	52	102	106	2526
2000	289	247	248	338	354	55	102	112	2520
2001	291	270	271	314	328	60	104	113	2474
2002	293	266	267	326	337	70	107	115	2507
2003	279	287	288	269	276	67	102	110	2444
2004	310	308	308	313	320	81	117	129	2333
2005	320	304	305	336	345	84	121	132	2349
2006	299	273	273	323	329	80	125	135	2175
2007	297	250	250	341	347	85	129	132	2245
2008	340	330	331	350	359	97	134	137	2382
2009	347	320	321	375	384	97	131	131	2556
2010	357	333	334	381	389	94	130	131	2644
2011	318	293	293	347	351	95	133	134	2698

注：2011年农作物单产为陕西省统计局依据（国统字办[2011]72号）文件调整数。

Note:The crop per unit area yield of 2011 was adjustment in accordance with the document [2011] No.72 issued by Bureau of Shaanxi Province.

10–24 各区县主要农作物单位面积产量（2011年）

The Output of Main Crops per Hectare by Region（2011）

单位：公斤/亩 (kg/mu)

区 县	Region	粮食作物 Grain Crops	夏 粮 Summer Grain	小 麦 Wheat	秋 粮 Autumn Grain	玉 米 Corn
合 计	**Total**	**318**	**293**	**293**	**347**	**351**
新城区	Xincheng					
碑林区	Beilin					
莲湖区	Lianhu					
灞桥区	Baqiao	273	237	237	329	339
未央区	Weiyang	328	288	288	380	379
雁塔区	Yanta	269	232	232	341	341
阎良区	Yanliang	395	374	374	422	422
临潼区	Lintong	289	280	280	299	295
长安区	Chang'an	313	286	286	345	344
蓝田县	Lantian	277	233	232	325	349
周至县	Zhouzhi	287	269	267	306	307
户 县	Huxian	349	331	331	370	371
高陵县	Gaoling	476	445	445	509	507

注：本表区县农作物产品单产为依据（陕统办发[2011]79号）文件调整数。

Note:The county crop acreage in this table was adjustment based on document [2011] No.79 issued by Bureau of Shaanxi Province.

10-24 续表 continued

单位：公斤/亩 (kg/mu)

区 县	Region	棉 花 Cotton	油 料 Oil-bearing Crops	油菜籽 Rapeseeds	蔬 菜 Vegetables	瓜果类 Fruits Class
合 计	**Total**	**95**	**133**	**134**	**2698**	**2840**
新城区	Xincheng					
碑林区	Beilin					
莲湖区	Lianhu					
灞桥区	Baqiao	60	131	132	3391	1322
未央区	Weiyang		275	250	2134	3557
雁塔区	Yanta				1145	3253
阎良区	Yanliang	95	119	116	3795	3278
临潼区	Lintong	96	96	96	2340	3050
长安区	Chang'an	82	179	181	2174	2200
蓝田县	Lantian	106	117	110	1775	2480
周至县	Zhouzhi		161	156	1839	2558
户 县	Huxian	87	180	184	2864	2921
高陵县	Gaoling				2964	4500

10-25 设施农业生产情况（2011年）

Agricultural Production Facilities（2011）

指 标	Item	种植面积（亩） planting area （mu)	产量（吨） outpot(ton)
一、蔬菜	Vegetables	227231	1100743
#芹菜	Celery	68067	339995
油菜	Rape	1795	3433
菠菜	Spinach	13401	30952
黄瓜	Cucumber	20072	94240
西红柿	Tomato	26631	97850
辣椒	Chilli	12439	34960
二、瓜果类	Fruits class	104049	371227
#草莓	Strawberry	4179	5443
三、花卉苗木	Flower seedling wood	14638	
四、食用菌	Edible Fungi	3310	15365
五、其他	Others	24424	
补充资料：蔬菜大棚个数（个）	Updates：Vegetable shed number（unit）		87555
蔬菜大棚面积	Vegetables awning area	146856	

10-26 主要年份林业生产情况

Statistics on Forestry in Representative Years

指　　标	Item	2000	2005	2006	2007	2008	2009	2010	2011
一、营林情况	**Afforestation**								
当年造林面积合计（万亩）	Build Forestry Areas(10 000 mu)	27.47	16.56	12.95	6.17	8.76	15.60	16.10	10.42
更新造林面积（万亩）	Reforestation Areas(10 000 mu)	1.08	0.62	0.63	0.65	0.45	0.48		
封山育林面积（万亩）	Hill-closeure for Afforestation Areas (10 000 mu)	18.78	18.65	20.71	23.97	30.19	37.40	55.10	41.30
零星四旁植树（万株）	Planting(10 000 plants)	731	1064	1096	1176	952	931	509	537
育苗面积（万亩）	Raise Seedlings Areas(10 000 mu)	2.05	5.99	5.34	6.03	4.72	3.41	11.95	9.93
#本年新育	New Seedling of Current Year	1.69	2.54	3.00	3.15	2.19	1.86	1.75	1.93
二、主要林产品产量（吨）	**Main Forestry Product(ton)**								
生漆	Lacquer	11	2	4	5	6	5	10	4
核桃	Walnuts	997	3351	3120	3349	4589	4306	7875	13235
板栗	Chinese Chestnut	744	2076	1944	2153	2728	3122	7736	8229
花椒	Pepper	140	525	507	575	842	689	1420	889
三、村及村以下采伐木材（万立方米）	**Timber Harvested at or below Village Level（10 000 cu.m)**	**1.62**	**1.87**	**1.41**	**0.96**	**1.23**	**0.97**	**3.3**	**1.39**

注：1.2009年迹地更新面积改为更新造林面积；

2.2010年起，根据统计制度要求，林业统计数据取自林业部门。

Note:1.Slash updating areas in 2009 were reforestation areas.

2.Since 2010, according to the requirement of statistical system, statistics on forestry were from forestry departments.

10-27 各区县林业生产情况（2011年）

Statistics On Forestry by Region（2011）

区　县	Region	当年造林面积（亩） Build Forestry Areas in The Year (mu)	零星植树（万株） Planting (10 000 plants)	育苗面积（亩） Raise Seedlings Areas (mu)	核桃产量（吨） Output of Walnuts (ton)	板栗产量（吨） Output of Chinese Chestnut (ton)	村及村以下木材采伐量（万立方米） Timber Harvesting at\under Vallage level (10 000 cu.m)
全　市	**Total**	**104160**	**536.70**	**99285**	**13235**	**8229**	**1.39**
新城区	Xincheng						
碑林区	Beilin						
莲湖区	Lianhu						
灞桥区	Baqiao	4005			250		
未央区	Weiyang	225	56.10	2280			
雁塔区	Yanta		3.00	3480			
阎良区	Yanliang	5115	35.00	450			0.58
临潼区	Lintong	10965	72.00	1125	1280	340	
长安区	Chang'an	14865	110.00	9465	425	210	
蓝田县	Lantian	39690	81.30	7095	4950	4663	0.06
周至县	Zhouzhi	16005	75.00	68145	6300	3000	0.32
户　县	Huxian	12285	74.30	5250	30	16	0.43
高陵县	Gaoling	1005	30.00	1995			

10-28 主要年份果业生产情况

Statistics on Fruits in Representative Years

指　　标	Item	2000	2005	2006	2007	2008	2009	2010	2011
果园面积(万亩)	**Areas of Orchards (10 000 mu)**	**47.86**	**55.55**	**57.68**	**60.86**	**64.31**	**71.08**	**74.95**	**74.27**
苹果园	Apple Orchards	12.15	5.96	5.95	5.94	5.82	5.66	3.55	1.53
梨　园	Pears Orchards	5.79	3.01	2.76	2.90	2.82	2.66	2.27	1.66
葡萄园	Grapes Orchards	1.89	3.02	3.20	3.18	3.55	4.59	4.83	4.91
桃　园	Peach Orchards	3.47	8.66	9.01	8.87	8.75	8.48	7.68	6.87
猕猴桃园	Chinese Goosebeery Orchards	16.83	4.33	18.39	21.04	23.61	29.01	34.92	36.97
杏　园	Apricot Orchards	0.62	2.50	2.54	2.65	2.78	2.97	3.62	3.6
柿子园	Presimmons Orchards	1.96	2.69	2.73	2.97	3.28	3.26	3.16	2.83
石榴园	Pomegranate Orchards					3.94	3.61	3.43	3.38
水果产量(吨)	**Output of Fruits (ton)**	**343551**	**512869**	**553433**	**605075**	**716902**	**789587**	**847821**	**911361**
苹　果	Apple	89416	53387	51809	52180	53194	53023	39130	34313
梨	Pears	65459	57059	51517	52869	55945	57929	55122	48026
葡　萄	Grapes	16647	30951	35504	43621	50185	56731	64885	69003
桃	Peach	27010	89755	103142	124393	139058	146651	142051	137683
猕猴桃	Chinese Goosebeery	96640	137853	153678	146301	210393	233296	296023	357066
杏	Apricot					39690	55535	48544	34340
柿　子	Persimmon					28540	34780	35287	31625
石　榴	Pomegranate					43701	42122	40211	34340

10-29 各区县果业生产情况（2011年）

Area and Output of Fruits by Region（2011）

区　　县	Region	果园（万亩） Area of Orchards(10 000 mu)	水果产量（吨） Output of Fruits(ton)
全　市	**Total**	**74.27**	**911361**
新城区	Xincheng		
碑林区	Beilin		
莲湖区	Lianhu		
灞桥区	Baqiao	6.93	89650
未央区	Weiyang	0.63	10924
雁塔区	Yanta	0.39	5800
阎良区	Yanliang	2.54	62708
临潼区	Lintong	4.50	44216
长安区	Chang'an	5.59	73682
蓝田县	Lantian	8.66	118403
周至县	Zhouzhi	37.29	364174
户　县	Huxian	4.89	90470
高陵县	Gaoling	2.85	51334

10-30 主要年份畜牧业生产情况

Statistics on Livestock Husbandry in Representative Years

指　　标	Item	2000	2005	2006	2007	2008	2009	2010	2011
一、大牲畜年末总头数(头)	**Large Animals In Stock at Year-end (head)**	**260742**	**322521**	**175435**	**181353**	**204723**	**208358**	**216043**	**212351**
#能繁殖母畜	Female Animals of Reprductive Ability	137087	176682	105042	110451	132772	136276	144104	143074
#役 畜	Draught Animals	98130	90717	44416	39968	36069	42670	42243	32877
1.牛	Cattle	256073	320773	173834	180200	203596	207237	215072	211334
#能繁殖母畜	Female Animals of Reprductive Ability	136626	176445	104391	109970	132657	136143	144012	142977
当年生仔畜	Newborn Livestock in the Year	69015	72163	39836	43313	41457	39403	40052	36093
肉 牛	Farm Cattle					60490	63804	65447	62127
奶 牛	Dairy Cattle	48164	96498	78056	96400	108164	112071	118747	117149
2.马(匹)	Horses	736	559	527	477	499	515	456	496
3.驴	Donkeys	476	175	97	108	83	87	67	71
4.骡	Mutes	3457	1014	977	568	545	519	448	450
二、猪年末头数(头)	**Hogs in Stock Year-end (head)**	**1284592**	**1472869**	**764579**	**774534**	**864083**	**918734**	**943183**	**943987**
#能繁殖母猪	Female Hogs of Reprductive Ability	93775	123543	65313	71600	85419	96522	106610	101332
三、羊年末只数(只)	**Sheeps and Goats in Stock at Year-end(head)**	**421103**	**532471**	**221809**	**234900**	**263164**	**279463**	**294539**	**295995**
1.山 羊	Goats	397121	520354	213981	226810	258287	274359	288738	288346
#奶山羊	Milch Goats	266525	358733	156429	177547	201007	229301	246442	245118
2.绵 羊	Sheeps	23982	12117	7828	8090	4877	5104	5801	7649
四、家禽年末存栏数(万只)	**Poultry in Stock at Year-end (10 000 heads)**	**1623.81**	**1372.56**	**831.25**	**849.12**	**919.91**	**980.83**	**1034.20**	**1153.76**
五、年末养蜂箱数(箱)	**Honey (box)**	**20408**	**24287**	**18871**	**18371**	**22124**	**22779**	**22984**	**17567**

10-31 各区县畜牧业生产情况（2011年）

Statistics On Livestock, Animal Husbandry by Region（2011）

区 县	Region	大牲畜年末头数（头）Large Animals In Stock at Year-end (head)	#能繁殖母畜 Female Animals of Reprductive Ability	役畜 Draught Animals	牛（头）Cattle (head)	奶牛 Dairy Cattle	马（匹）Horses (head)	驴（头）Donkeys (head)
全 市	**Total**	**212351**	**143074**	**32877**	**211334**	**117149**	**496**	**71**
新城区	Xincheng							
碑林区	Beilin							
莲湖区	Lianhu							
灞桥区	Baqiao	12596	7357	599	12580	12186	16	
未央区	Weiyang	6440	4732		6440	6217		
雁塔区	Yanta	293	210		293	293		
阎良区	Yanliang	17053	12660		17053	14975		
临潼区	Lintong	69777	56087	6838	69777	62323		
长安区	Chang'an	7928	3257	1197	7252	3909	315	
蓝田县	Lantian	45692	27878	12550	45587	2410	40	30
周至县	Zhouzhi	32909	17612	11483	32873	2880	25	
户 县	Huxian	11708	6897	28	11708	6385		
高陵县	Gaoling	7955	6384	182	7771	5571	100	41

10-31 续表 continued

区 县	Region	骡（头）Mutes (head)	猪（头）Hogs (head)	能繁殖母猪 Female Hogs of Reprductive Ability	羊（只）Sheep and Goats (head)	山羊 Goats	奶山羊 Milch Goats	家禽（万只）Poultry (10 000 head)	蜂（箱）Honey (box)
全 市	**Total**	**450**	**943987**	**101332**	**295995**	**288346**	**245118**	**1153.76**	**17567**
新城区	Xincheng								
碑林区	Beilin								
莲湖区	Lianhu								
灞桥区	Baqiao		47849	4085	11570	11505	9946	41.07	330
未央区	Weiyang		39302	4084	1148	1148	704	7.99	
雁塔区	Yanta							1.80	
阎良区	Yanliang		36809	4226	50140	50110	50110	54.94	572
临潼区	Lintong		241746	20965	116403	116403	116403	264.42	1550
长安区	Chang'an	361	100049	9676	14967	12107	4925	293.04	3763
蓝田县	Lantian	35	77956	9771	69361	69292	44942	163.70	
周至县	Zhouzhi	11	199912	25915	12938	11166	2264	89.80	7132
户 县	Huxian		150480	16407	6529	6529	6390	133.00	4220
高陵县	Gaoling	43	49884	6203	12939	10086	9434	104.00	

10-32 主要年份畜产品和水产品产量

Output of Livestock Products and Aquatic Products in Representative Years

单位：吨 (ton)

年 份 Year	肉类总产量 Output of Meat	猪 肉 Pork	牛 肉 Beef	羊 肉 Mutton	禽 肉 Poultry
1990	63273	50646	4667	1931	5885
1991	72268	55086	5623	2162	9062
1992	88994	68134	6468	2460	11290
1993	93420	71274	7249	2220	12174
1994	106691	79433	8298	2350	15681
1995	127815	86513	11251	3731	23948
1996	91468	63750	5402	2578	19324
1997	106597	75381	6672	3468	20596
1998	134152	98974	8788	4710	21424
1999	130124	93859	9827	4147	21963
2000	147571	106137	12066	4766	23760
2001	157277	113353	11900	5153	20540
2002	161092	118634	11516	5394	20515
2003	165860	122759	13241	5180	19682
2004	171545	126404	13641	5874	18493
2005	182046	136503	14031	6106	18803
2006	108634	81199	8267	2841	13417
2007	102191	73254	8589	3111	14075
2008	115352	84654	9840	3335	16060
2009	126182	94490	10142	3677	17190
2010	136501	102296	10854	3875	18338
2011	144631	104816	11860	3645	19390

注：2010年起，根据统计制度要求，水产品产量及养殖面积统计数据取自水务部门。

Note:Since 2010, according to the requirement of statistical system, statistics of aquatic product output and cultivating area were from water supply departments.

10-32 续表 continued

单位：吨 (ton)

年 份 Year	奶类总产量 Output of Milk	牛 奶 Cow Milk	禽蛋 Poultry Eggs	蜂蜜（公斤） Honey(kg)	水产品 Output of Aquatic Products	养殖面积（万亩） Water Raise Areas (10 000 mu)
1990	82017	50528	55938	1035392	4259	2.55
1991	91006	57700	90558	1022797	4949	2.63
1992	100080	63586	104970	739275	6015	2.80
1993	111070	73897	125244	662049	7132	2.97
1994	145412	99025	146503	547808	7900	3.10
1995	132909	85753	141227	535891	8517	3.21
1996	133372	86103	138044	613290	8910	3.51
1997	150964	98078	156066	713918	10054	3.46
1998	174099	119719	142519	537304	10480	3.40
1999	209144	145191	135981	541613	11061	3.38
2000	245913	176155	138305	460598	11384	3.35
2001	255437	179977	132303	479839	12480	3.17
2002	288009	202826	134336	497530	12017	3.31
2003	336296	245407	128833	537805	9967	2.48
2004	384319	289564	117597	449765	9721	2.46
2005	422229	327961	118115	421052	9370	2.38
2006	471438	374813	97816	414271	11937	1.60
2007	528037	428462	98140	401761	12402	1.38
2008	589697	475681	108515	503031	12487	1.40
2009	618186	498394	116685	528731	13044	1.52
2010	633663	509178	123793	436759	11850	2.24
2011	647978	509777	125639	217632	11800	2.20

10-33 各区县主要畜产品和水产品产量（2011年）

Output of Major Livestock Products and Aquatic Products by Region（2011）

单位：吨 (ton)

区 县	Region	肉类总产量 Output of Meat	猪肉 Pork	牛肉 Beef	羊肉 Mutton	禽肉 Poultry
全 市	**Total**	**144631**	**104816**	**11860**	**3645**	**19390**
新城区	Xincheng					
碑林区	Beilin					
莲湖区	Lianhu					
灞桥区	Baqiao	7155	5454	757	138	790
未央区	Weiyang	3656	3426	155	14	61
雁塔区	Yanta	2408	2370			38
阎良区	Yanliang	5478	3684	505	493	737
临潼区	Lintong	37467	26430	3027	1484	3802
长安区	Chang'an	19423	11877	518	254	6236
蓝田县	Lantian	17590	9411	3848	884	2205
周至县	Zhouzhi	26565	22856	2119	189	1401
户 县	Huxian	18010	14723	662	69	2337
高陵县	Gaoling	6879	4585	269	120	1783

10–33 续表 continued

单位：吨 (ton)

区 县	Region	奶类总产量 Output of Milk	牛奶 Cow Milk	禽蛋 Poultry Eggs	蜂 蜜（公斤） Honey(kg)	水产品 Output of Aquatic Products	养殖面积（亩） Water Raise Areas(mu)
全 市	**Total**	**647978**	**509777**	**125639**	**217632**	**11800**	**21958**
新城区	Xincheng						
碑林区	Beilin						
莲湖区	Lianhu						
灞桥区	Baqiao	62124	55153	5134	8300	1502	2850
未央区	Weiyang	25313	25110	492		2000	1005
雁塔区	Yanta	1290	1290	240		100	255
阎良区	Yanliang	84957	60904	6590	15640	202	180
临潼区	Lintong	338123	272564	27770	40250	1836	5023
长安区	Chang'an	22130	18856	37399	67714	3400	5580
蓝田县	Lantian	37722	10294	9959		900	3555
周至县	Zhouzhi	12986	11924	9900	67628	828	2310
户 县	Huxian	34131	31018	16576	18100	802	1020
高陵县	Gaoling	29202	22664	11579		230	180

10–34 农业科技、教育及农村经济组织情况（2011年）

Agricultural Science and Technology Education and Economic Organization（2011）

指 标	Item	2011
农业研究开发机构（个）	Agricultural research and development institutions（unit）	295
农业科技人员（人）	Agricultural scientific and technical personnel(persons)	3372
农业科研成果（个）	Agricultural scientific research achievements（unit）	32
农民技能培训人数（万人)	The number of peasants skills training(10000 persons)	18.5
良种推广面积（万亩）	Thoroughbred promotion area（10000 mu）	544.4
农业信息站（个）	information station of Agricultural（unit）	3104
农村经济合作组织（个）	rural economic cooperative organization（unit）	463
参与农村经济合作组织的农户（万户）	Participate in the rural economic cooperation organization of farmers(10000 households)	16

10-35 主要年份农产品人均占有量

Per Capita Output of Major Farm Products in Representative Years

单位：公斤/人 (kg/person)

年份 Year	粮食 Grain	棉花 Cotton	油料 Oil-bearing Crops	猪牛羊肉 Pork Beef and Mutton	禽蛋 Poultry Eggs	奶类 Milk	水果 Fruits	蔬菜 Vegetables
1978	266.7	5.7	0.2	5.4	0.9	3.3	6.8	91.7
1979	288.6	5.2	0.6	6.7	1.0	4.0	5.1	97.3
1980	223.5	3.8	1.1	5.9	1.2	4.1	6.9	78.4
1981	222.9	2.6	1.5	6.6	1.7	4.7	5.8	65.4
1982	281.5	5.5	1.0	4.9	2.7	5.6	5.9	101.6
1983	276.6	1.6	0.7	4.9	3.2	6.5	5.0	87.8
1984	289.4	2.7	0.8	4.8	6.2	8.7	4.8	138.6
1985	271.4	0.9	1.4	6.8	5.7	10.2	7.6	156.3
1986	288.0	0.8	2.2	7.8	6.4	12.1	9.6	152.2
1987	298.0	0.8	2.7	7.3	6.8	13.8	10.6	165.6
1988	269.7	0.7	1.5	8.0	8.9	15.6	11.1	193.7
1989	290.7	0.9	2.2	8.4	7.6	13.1	10.2	216.5
1990	298.7	1.2	2.1	9.4	9.2	14.2	11.5	196.0
1991	290.6	1.6	2.0	10.2	14.7	14.8	11.7	190.8
1992	294.3	1.2	2.4	12.4	16.8	16.2	17.3	205.6
1993	301.2	1.2	2.2	12.8	19.9	17.6	25.9	231.1
1994	246.1	1.0	1.7	14.1	22.9	22.7	28.0	211.5
1995	270.4	0.5	3.4	15.7	21.8	20.5	37.5	206.1
1996	286.3	0.4	3.2	11.0	21.1	20.4	43.9	210.8
1997	287.8	0.3	2.8	12.9	23.6	22.8	43.3	214.7
1998	318.3	0.2	2.5	16.8	21.3	26.1	50.0	222.8
1999	303.0	0.2	1.9	16.0	20.2	31.0	52.7	227.2
2000	293.5	0.2	1.9	17.9	20.1	35.7	49.9	235.7
2001	283.7	0.2	1.8	18.8	19.0	36.8	48.8	219.9
2002	273.8	0.3	1.7	19.3	19.1	41.0	53.5	241.6
2003	246.0	0.3	1.6	19.7	18.0	46.9	53.6	236.8
2004	270.1	0.6	1.6	20.1	16.2	53.0	63.9	249.6
2005	277.1	0.6	1.6	21.1	15.9	56.9	69.1	263.8
2006	256.9	0.6	1.4	12.3	13.0	62.6	73.5	251.4
2007	247.4	0.8	1.3	11.1	12.8	69.1	79.2	267.3
2008	256.0	0.7	1.4	11.7	13.0	70.4	85.6	264.5
2009	258.7	0.7	1.3	12.8	13.8	73.3	93.6	287.4
2010	261.8	0.7	1.4	13.8	14.6	74.8	100.1	298.9
2011	213.8	0.7	1.4	14.1	14.8	76.1	107.1	318.9

10-36 主要年份农村经济效益主要指标

Main Indicators of Rural Economic Benefit in Representative Years

年 份 Year	每一农业劳动力创造的 Average Labor Force Production 农林牧渔及服务业总产值（元） Gross Output Value of Farming,Forestry，Animal Husbandry, Fishery and Service (yuan)	粮食（公斤） Grain Crops(kg)	棉花（公斤） Cotton (kg)	油料（公斤） Oil-bearing Crops(kg)	每亩耕地种植业产值（元） Output of Each Unit of Area Planting(yuan)	每百元物耗生产的总产值（元） Output per 100-Yuan of Material Consumed(yuan)
1978	504.7	1024.6	22.0	0.7	104.3	
1979	549.0	1096.5	19.8	2.3	116.0	
1980	483.1	846.1	14.5	4.0	99.2	
1981	502.8	840.5	9.9	5.5	105.4	
1982	631.5	1058.9	20.5	3.6	139.3	
1983	606.5	1053.2	6.1	2.6	124.1	
1984	850.7	1154.2	10.9	3.4	163.6	
1985	1020.1	1134.6	3.7	5.6	183.1	
1986	1132.2	1236.4	3.4	9.5	204.6	
1987	1280.3	1277.2	3.5	11.7	231.5	
1988	1558.4	1148.0	3.0	6.5	273.2	
1989	1605.3	1231.9	3.9	9.5	295.0	
1990	1766.3	1279.1	5.2	10.0	343.4	233.3
1991	1958.8	1326.6	7.2	8.9	380.4	238.4
1992	2093.7	1360.7	5.5	11.1	451.6	241.8
1993	2528.9	1409.7	5.6	10.4	546.8	240.1
1994	3705.0	1167.8	4.8	8.0	762.8	227.6
1995	4953.0	1300.6	2.2	16.1	1106.5	225.9
1996	5154.8	1391.2	1.8	13.6	1224.2	234.5
1997	5493.0	1413.4	1.3	13.8	1283.3	239.2
1998	5615.9	1578.1	1.0	12.4	1374.3	247.0
1999	4826.5	1516.6	1.1	9.7	1175.9	251.7
2000	5091.5	1498.0	1.0	9.9	1161.1	250.2
2001	5328.5	1462.4	1.3	9.1	1221.1	248.6
2002	5617.4	1427.5	1.3	9.1	1272.0	265.9
2003	5761.2	1308.1	1.6	8.4	1332.4	254.3
2004	6885.4	1452.7	3.0	8.5	1434.6	261.7
2005	7737.9	1524.7	3.3	8.6	1642.3	262.9
2006	8415.5	1435.7	3.6	8.0	1756.9	263.1
2007	10165.6	1403.0	4.4	7.1	2037.3	259.8
2008	13306.4	1695.4	4.9	9.1	2447.9	259.6
2009	14674.3	1791.7	5.1	9.2	2737.9	261.6
2010	19480.7	1901.3	5.1	10.0	3753.4	260.9
2011	23474.6	1567.2	4.9	10.1	4585.8	274.0

主要统计指标解释

农林牧渔业总产值 指以货币表现的农、林、牧、渔业全部产品和对农林牧渔业生产活动进行的各种支持性服务活动的价值总量，它反映一定时期内农林牧渔业生产总规模和总成果。1957年以前的农林牧渔业总产值中包括了厩肥和农民自给性手工业(如农民自制衣服、鞋、袜，自己从事粮食初步加工等)。1958年及以后，林业中增加了村及村以下竹木采伐产值；牧业中取消了厩肥产值；副业中取消了农民自给性手工业产值，增加了村及村以下办的工业产值；渔业中增加了海洋捕捞水产品产值。1980年及以后，在副业中增加了农民家庭兼营工业商品部分的产值。从1984年起村及村以下工业产值划归工业。从1993年起取消副业，将野生动物的捕猎划入牧业，野生植物采集和农民家庭兼营商品性工业划归农业。从2003年起，执行新的国民经济行业分类标准，农林牧渔业总产值中包括了农林牧渔服务业产值。林业中增加了森林采运业产值。农业中取消了家庭兼营商品性工业产值，将野生林产品的采集划归林业。第一次农业普查以后，由于畜牧业产品年报数据与普查数据之间存在一定的差距，根据农业普查结果对畜牧业年报数据进行了修正，对畜牧业产值进行了相应修正。

农林牧渔业总产值的计算方法通常是按农、林、牧、渔业产品及其副产品的产量分别乘以各自单位产品价格求得；少数生产周期较长，当年没有产品或产品产量不易统计的，则采用间接方法匡算其产值；然后将四业产品产值及农林牧渔服务业产值相加即为农林牧渔业总产值。

粮食产量 指全社会的产量。包括国有经济经营的、集体统一经营的和农民家庭经营的粮食产量，还包括工矿企业办的农场和其他生产单位的产量。粮食除包括稻谷、小麦、玉米、高粱、谷子及其他杂粮外，还包括薯类和豆类。其产量计算方法，豆类按去豆荚后的干豆计算；薯类(包括甘薯和马铃薯，不包括芋头和木薯)1963年以前按每4公斤鲜薯折1公斤粮食计算，从1964年开始改为按5公斤鲜薯折1公斤粮食计算。城市郊区作为蔬菜的薯类(如马铃薯等)按鲜品计算，并且不作粮食统计。其他粮食一律按脱粒后的原粮计算。1989年以前全国粮食产量数据主要靠全面报表取得，1989年开始使用抽样调查数据。

棉花产量 指全社会的产量。包括春播棉和夏播棉。产量按皮棉计算。不包括木棉。

油料产量 指全部油料作物的生产量。包括花生、油菜籽、芝麻、向日葵籽、胡麻籽（亚麻籽）和其他油料。不包括大豆、木本油料和野生油料。花生以带壳干花生计算。

水产品产量 指人工养殖的水产品和天然生长的水产品的捕捞量。包括海水的鱼类、虾蟹类、贝类和藻类以及内陆水域的鱼类、虾蟹类和贝类，不包括淡水生植物。水产品产量是通过各级水产和统计部门逐级上报取得数据。1995年及以前，贝类中牡蛎按鲜肉计算；蚶、蛤、蛏按 5 斤鲜品折 1 斤计算。1996年以后则统一按鲜品计算。

猪、牛、羊肉产量 指当年出栏并已屠宰、除去头蹄下水后带骨肉（即胴体重）的重量。包括全社会范围内的产量。1996年前为各级逐级上报数据。1996年第一次农业普查以后，由于畜牧业产品年报数据与普查数据之间存在一定的差距，根据普查结果对畜牧业年报数据进行了修正。1999年以后，国家统计局在部分地区开展了猪、牛、羊、禽等主要畜禽品种的抽样调查，并用抽样数据作为国家定案数据使用。未开展抽样调查的地区和品种，仍使用各级统计部门逐级上报数据。2007年，根据第二次农业普查结果，对20002006年畜牧业年报数据进行了修正。2008年，建立了主要畜禽监测调查制度，猪、牛、羊、禽等主要畜牧业数据均以抽样调查数为法定数据。

期初（末）畜禽存栏头（只）数 指报告期初(末)农村各种合作经济组织和国营农场、农民个人、机关、团体、学校、工矿企业、部队等单位以及城镇居民饲养的大牲畜、猪、羊、家禽等畜禽的存栏数。数据上报方式及数据调整情况同猪、牛、羊肉产量。

常用耕地 是指耕地总资源中专门种植农作物并经常进行耕种、能够正常收获的土地。包括当年实际耕种的熟地;弃耕、休闲不满三年，随时可以复耕的地;开荒利用三年以上的地。不包括临时种植农作物的坡度在25度以上的陡坡地;在河套、湖畔、库区临时开发的成片或零星土地;也不包括已列为国家和省（区、市）退耕计划但临时耕种的土地。

农作物播种面积 指实际播种或移植有农作物的面积。凡是实际种植有农作物的面积，不论种植在耕地上还是种植在非耕地上，均包括在农作物播种面积中。在播种季节基本结束后，因遭灾而重新改种和补种的农作物面积，也包括在内。它是反映我国耕地面积利用情况的一个重要指标。目前，农作物播种面积主要包括粮食、棉花、油料、糖料、麻类、烟叶、蔬菜和瓜类、药材和其他农作物九大类。

有效灌溉面积 指具有一定的水源，地块比较平整，灌溉工程或设备已经配套，在一般年景下，当年能够进行正常灌溉的耕地面积。在一般情况下，有效灌溉面积应等于灌溉工程或设备已经配备，能够进行正常灌溉的水田和水浇地面积之和。它是反映我国耕地抗旱能力的一个重要指标。

农用化肥施用量 指本年内实际用于农业生产的化肥数量，包括氮肥、磷肥、钾肥和复合肥。化肥施用量要求按折纯量计算数量。折纯量是指把氮肥、磷肥、钾肥分别按含氮、含五氧化二磷、含氧化钾的百分之百成份进行折算后的数量。复合肥按其所含主要成分折算。公式为：

折纯量=实物量×某种化肥有效成份含量的百分比

农业机械总动力 指主要用于农、林、牧、渔业的各种动力机械的动力总和。包括耕作机械、排灌机械、收获机械、农用运输机械、植物保护机械、牧业机械、林业机械、渔业机械和其他农业机械〔内燃机按引擎马力折成瓦（特）计算、电动机按功率折成瓦（特）计算〕。不包括专门用于乡、镇、村、组办工业、基本建设、非农业运输、科学试验和教学等非农业生产方面用的动力机械与作业机械。这个指标的统计数据主要来源于农机部门。

Explanatory Notes on Main Statistical Indicators

Gross Output Value of Agriculture, Forestry, Animal Husbandry and Fishery refers to the total value of products of agriculture, forestry, animal husbandry and fishery, and total value of services in support of agriculture, forestry, animal husbandry and fishery activities. It reflects the total scale and results of agricultural production during a given period. Prior to 1957, China's gross agricultural output value included barnyard manure and handicraft products for self-consumption (clothes, shoes, stockings, and initial grain processing undertaken by peasants). Since 1958, cutting and felling of bamboo and trees by villages and other cooperative organizations under villages have been included in forestry; value of barnyard manure has been excluded from animal husbandry; self consumed handicrafts have not been included from sideline occupations, while the output value of industries run by villages and cooperative organizations under village has been included in sideline occupations; and the output value of fish catches by motor fishing boats has been added to fishery. Since 1980, the value of handicraft products made for sale by individuals in households has been added to sideline occupations. Since 1984, industries run by villages and under villages have been included in the sector of industry. Since 1993, the subdivision of sideline occupations has been cancelled, and the hunting of wild animals has been classified into animal husbandry, and the gathering of wild plants and commodity industry run by rural household have been included in farming. A new industrial classification of economic activities was introduced in 2003. Under the new classification, value of services to agriculture, forestry, animal husbandry and fishery is included in the gross output value of agriculture, value of wood felling and transport is included in forestry, value of industrial output by rural households is not included in agriculture, and the collection of wild forest products is taken from agriculture and included in forestry. The First Agriculture Census of China revealed some discrepancy between the production of animal products from the annual reports and that from the census. According to the result of the First Agriculture census, efforts were made to adjust the output value of animal husbandry to make the figures from the annual reports consistent with the census data.

Gross output value of agriculture is obtained by multiplying the output of each product or by-product by its price, resulting in the output value of each single item. For a small number of products, annual output of which is not available or difficult to get due to the long production (growing) process involved, the output value is estimated through an indirect approach. The sum of output values of all products of agriculture, forestry, animal husbandry and fishery and services in support to those industries is then equal to the gross output value of agriculture.

Grain Output refers to the total output in the whole country including grains produced by State farms, collective units, rural households, as well as by farms affiliated to industrial and mining enterprises and other production units. Grain includes rice, wheat, corn, sorghum, millet and other miscellaneous grains as well as tubers and beans. Output of beans refers to dry beans without pods. The output of tubers (sweet potatoes and potatoes, not including taros and cassava) are converted into that of grain at the ratio 4:1, i.e. 4 kilograms of fresh tubers were equivalent to 1 kilogram of grain up to 1963. Since 1964 the ratio for conversion has been 5:1. Tubers supplied as vegetables (such as potatoes) in cities and suburbs are calculated as fresh vegetables and their output is not included in the output of grain. Output of all other grains refers to husked grain. Data on grain production before 1989 were obtained through the Comprehensive Statistical Reporting System. Since 1989, data from sample surveys are used.

Cotton Output refers to cotton production in the whole country including cotton planted in spring and in autumn. Output is measured as the weight of ginned cotton. Ceiba is not included.

Output of Oil-bearing Crops refers to the total production of oil-bearing crops of various kinds, including peanuts (dry, in shell), rapeseeds, sesame, sunflower seeds, flax seeds, and other oil-bearing crops. Soybeans, oil-bearing woody plants, and wild oil-bearing crops are not included.

Output of Aquatic Products refers to catches of both artificially cultured and naturally grown aquatic products, including fish, shrimps, crabs and shellfish in sea and inland water as well as seaweed. Freshwater plants are not included. Data on output of aquatic products are reported by aquatic product and statistical agencies level by level. Before 1995, among the shellfish, oyster was counted as fresh meat; 5 kilograms of ark shell, clams and frogs are equivalent to 1 kilogram of fresh aquatic products; they have all been counted as fresh aquatic products since 1996.

Output of Pork, Beef, and Mutton refers to the meat of slaughtered hogs, cattle, sheep and goats with head, feet, and offal taken away. Data refers to the production of the whole country. The First Agricultural Census of China in 1996 revealed some discrepancy between the production of animal products from the annual reports and that from the census. Efforts were made to adjust the output value of animal husbandry to make the figures from the annual reports consistent with the census data. Since 1999, the NBS conducted sample surveys for the major animal husbandry products, such as hogs, cattle, sheep and goats and fowls, and the data from sample surveys are used as national finalized data. Those products, which are not covered by the sample survey, are still reported by statistical agencies level by level. In 2007, the data on animal husbandry from 2000 to 2006 were revised according to the results of the Second Agriculture Census of China. In 2008, A Monitoring and Survey Program was set up on main livestock, the data on the main livestock such as hog, cattle, sheep and poultry became the official data based on the sampling survey.

Number of Livestock or Poultry in Stock at Beginning (or End) of Period refers to the total number of large animals, pigs, sheep, fowls, etc. raised by rural cooperative organizations, State farms, rural individuals, government agencies, schools, industrial and mining enterprises, army, and urban residents at the beginning (or end) of the reference period. Data reporting system and data adjustment are the same as that in the output of pork, beef and mutton.

Regularly Cultivated Land refers to farmland among the total land resources which is exclusively used for farming and is under regular cultivation with harvest in normal years. Included are currently cultivated land, land that has been abandoned or put in idle for less than 3 years and could be re-used for cultivation at any time, and new-claimed land that has been put into cultivation for more than 3 years. Excluded under this category are steep slope land over 25 degrees under temporary cultivation, land (large or small plots) that is claimed along river bends, lake sides or banks of reservoirs, as well as land that has been designated under the "Green for Grain" programmes of the state and provincial governments but is still temporarily under cultivation.

Sown Area of Crops refers to area of land sown or transplanted with crops regardless of being in cultivated area or non-cultivated area. Area of land re-sown due to natural disasters is also included. This is an important indicator that can reflect the utilization condition of the cultivated land in China. At present, the sown area of crops mainly include the following 9 categories of crops: grain, cotton, oil-bearing crops, sugar crops, flax crops, tobacco, vegetables and melons, medicinal materials and other farm crops.

Irrigated Area refers to area of land that are effectively irrigated, i.e. relatively level land, where there are water sources or complete sets of irrigation facilities to lift and move adequate water for irrigation purpose under normal conditions. Under normal situations, irrigated area is the sum of watered fields and irrigated fields where irrigation systems or equipment have been installed for regular irrigation purpose. This important indicator reflects drought resistance capacity of the cultivated land in China.

Consumption of Chemical Fertilizers in Agriculture refers to the quantity of chemical fertilizers applied in agriculture in the year, including nitrogenous fertilizer, phosphate fertilizer, potash fertilizer, and compound fertilizer. The consumption of chemical fertilizers is calculated in terms of volume of effective components by means of converting the gross weight of the respective fertilizers into weight containing effective component (e.g. nitrogen content in nitrogenous fertilizer, phosphorous pentoxide contents in phosphate fertilizer, and potassium oxide contents in potash fertilizer). Compound fertilizer is converted in regard to its major components. The formula is:

Volume of effective component= physical quantity × effective component of certain chemical fertilizer (%)

Total Power of Agricultural Machinery refers to total mechanical power of machinery used in agriculture, forestry, animal husbandry and fishery, including machinery for ploughing, irrigation and drainage, harvesting, transport, plant protection, animal husbandry, forestry and fishery and other agricultural machineries. (For the power of internal combustion engines, it is converted from its horsepower into watts while for electric motors the output power is converted into watts.) Machinery employed for non-agricultural purposes, such as the machines used in township-run and village-run industry, construction, non-agricultural transport, scientific experiments and teaching, are not included. Data are mainly from agricultural machinery agencies.

11 工 业

INDUSTRY

资料整理：王风玲　席锋旭　赵　博　陈小兵　李　玫　王　玥
Data management:Wang Fengling Xi Fengxu Zhao Bo Chen Xiaobing Li Mei Wang Yue

第十一部分　工业

一、简要说明

本章资料包括全部工业总产值，规模以上工业企业单位数、总产值、主要经济指标等，由西安市统计局工业处提供。

二、主要指标

规模以上工业企业单位数（个）	891	
#大中型工业企业	218	
全部工业增加值（亿元）	1189.61	比上年增长 16.2 %
#规模以上工业增加值	1012.58	比上年增长 17.2%

11　INDUSTRY

Ⅰ.Brief Introduction

Data in this chapter reflects Gross Industrial Output Value, number of industrial enterprises above designated size and gross product, primary economic. Data in this chapter are provided and compiled by Industry Division of the Xi'an Bureau of Statistics.

Ⅱ.Major Indicators

		Increase over Preceding Year
Number of Industrial Enterprises Above Designated Size(item)	891	
Large-size and Medium-size Industrial Enterprises	218	
Value Added of Industry(100 mil. yuan)	1189.61	16.2%
Value Added of Industry Above Designated Size	1012.58	17.2%

11-1 主要年份全部工业总产值

Gross Output Value of Industry In Representative Years

单位：万元 （10 000 yuan）

年 份 Year	全部工业总产值 Gross Industrial Output Value	工业总产值指数 (上年=100) Index of Gross Industry Output Value (Preceding Year=100)	国有经济 State-owned Enterprises	集体经济 Collective-owned Enterprises	其他经济类型 Enterprises of Other Ownership
1952	23512	139.6	9917	464	13131
1962	120833	86.8	102103	17599	1131
1965	200416	132.1	183164	17252	
1970	333386	143.5	305303	28083	
1975	385509	106.1	332982	52527	
1978	483262	116.9	405376	77886	
1979	517483	106.6	438850	78633	
1980	531755	101.8	440139	91577	39
1981	524587	98.6	433740	90675	172
1982	549200	107.1	450308	98516	456
1983	603507	112.2	493773	108923	811
1984	674963	112.8	520593	153056	1314
1985	853196	120.4	632702	218893	1601
1986	976326	112.1	706380	267282	2664
1987	1142220	114.2	809186	328701	4341
1988	1429811	116.0	1012268	416217	1326
1989	1653472	106.1	1160877	486754	5814
1990	1771310	107.4	1196777	548605	25928
1991	2002727	110.0	1325242	604495	72990
1992	2300472	112.5	1488541	561369	250562
1993	3045988	121.7	1748145	1071122	226721
1994	3891584	120.6	1960533	1581321	349730
1995	4058952	108.7	2071755	1663536	323661
1996	5338510	133.4	2132140	2836176	370194
1997	5794532	121.8	1915536	2005610	1873386
1998	6738224	117.3	2593405	2077273	2067546
1999	7151528	117.1	2128243	2174220	2849065
2000	6394812	115.3	2749778	2094680	1550354
2001	7361510	116.4	3098431	2380910	1882169
2002	8379363	115.8	3472067	2312923	2594373
2003	9750800	115.1	4149015	1501372	4100413
2004	11853224	118.4	5414952	875412	5562860
2005	13085580	106.3	5916553	674900	6494127
2006	15573516	119.0	7527607	514810	7531099
2007	19798593	122.1	10179303	365329	9253961
2008	23881446	120.6	12479652	441987	10959807
2009	28270652	118.3	14440321	388777	13441554
2010	35628753	126.0	18353877	435206	16839669
2011	40933178	114.9	20654524	377199	19901455

11-1 续表 continued

单位：万元 （10 000 yuan）

年 份 Year	轻工业 Ligth Industry	重工业 Heavy Industry	大型工业 Large-size Industry Enterprises	中型工业 Medium-size Industry Enterprlses	小型工业 Small-size Industry Enterprises
1952	20800	2712			
1962	68221	52618			
1965	98631	101785			
1970	124467	208919			
1975	167285	218224	145262	130592	109655
1978	220480	262782	168397	121813	193052
1979	243043	274440	189877	133759	193847
1980	283475	248280	193092	130053	208610
1981	309199	215388	178130	140810	205639
1982	303249	246031	213015	128597	207668
1983	315785	287722	245053	127164	231290
1984	321678	353285	241842	143165	289956
1985	401748	451448	333820	147488	371888
1986	458270	518056	401037	150644	424609
1987	516776	625452	472958	171698	497572
1988	699593	730210	615946	210089	603776
1989	712743	940729	696368	258414	698690
1990	787857	983453	716421	279098	775791
1991	897676	1105051	888052	303151	844524
1992	967104	1333368			
1993	1121957	1924031	1258137	384255	1403596
1994	1578875	2312709	1479613	390233	2021738
1995	1636219	2432733	1575030	371156	2112766
1996	2347887	2990623	1693985	358913	3285612
1997	2700085	3094447	1675521	274888	3844123
1998	3232681	3505543	1821556	308424	4608244
1999	3488547	3662981	1744637	337795	5069096
2000	3121419	3273393	2320973	328494	3745345
2001	3518054	3843456	2656010	368497	4337003
2002	3935764	4443599	3038828	398834	4941701
2003	4028859	5721941	2662073	2027256	5061471
2004	4211592	7641632	3595150	3237701	5020372
2005	4078417	9007163	4640325	3228553	5216702
2006	4510970	11062546	5970535	3414468	6188513
2007	7331719	12466874	8351303	4171131	7276158
2008	6010865	17870581	10472686	5005676	8403084
2009	6636464	21634188	12309192	6186395	9775065
2010	7841869	27786884	15002737	8537140	12088876
2011	8992547	31940631	16844272	6207660	17881246

11-2 各区县、开发区规模以上工业总产值（2011年）

Gross Output Value of Industrial Enterprises above Designated Size by Region and Development Zone（2011）

单位：亿元 （100 million yuan）

区县名称	Name of District and County	单位数（个） Name of Enterprises (unit)	工业总产值 Gross Industrial Output Value	国有经济 State-owned Enterprises	集体经济 Collective-owned Enterprises	其他经济类型 Enterprises of Other Ownership
新城区	Xingcheng	20	323.64	86.39		237.25
碑林区	Beilin	21	138.72	113.73		24.99
莲湖区	Lianhu	47	457.96	183.77	0.28	273.91
灞桥区	Baqiao	130	280.52	20.84	12.33	247.35
未央区	Weiyang	147	510.39	103.34	6.70	400.35
雁塔区	Yanta	179	367.97	103.45	2.74	261.78
阎良区	Yanliang	67	176.67	5.77		170.90
临潼区	Lintong	32	277.75	67.75		210.00
长安区	Chang'an	91	350.68	21.39	3.29	326.00
蓝田县	Lantian	18	35.87	5.94	0.40	29.53
周至县	Zhouzhi	25	15.29		0.95	14.34
户　县	Huxian	51	100.42	18.00	0.80	81.62
高陵县	Gaoling	63	516.33	27.45	0.01	488.87
在总计中：	Among of Total:					
高新区	GaoXin	169	589.99	67.98		522.01
经开区	JingKai	108	755.33	31.26		724.07
航空基地	Aviation Industry Base	11	5.69	2.42		3.27
航天基地	Aerospace Base	11	53.12	18.12		35.00

11-2 续表 continued

单位：亿元 (100 million yuan)

区县名称	Name of District and County	轻工业 Ligth Industry	重工业 Heavy Industry	大型工业 Large-size Industry Enterprises	中型工业 Medium-size Industry Enterprises	小型工业 Small-size Industry Enterprises
新城区	Xingcheng	66.93	256.71	293.87	20.20	9.57
碑林区	Beilin	16.20	122.52	3.63	121.54	13.55
莲湖区	Lianhu	59.95	398.01	409.06	35.41	13.49
灞桥区	Baqiao	46.59	233.93	22.23	23.91	234.38
未央区	Weiyang	133.29	377.10	242.68	153.86	113.85
雁塔区	Yanta	63.32	304.65	158.00	113.84	96.13
阎良区	Yanliang	35.68	140.99	112.36	5.98	58.33
临潼区	Lintong	106.57	171.18	133.21	37.42	107.12
长安区	Chang'an	39.10	311.58	266.73	23.58	60.37
蓝田县	Lantian	7.28	28.59	4.89	12.42	18.56
周至县	Zhouzhi	8.55	6.74	1.62	2.48	11.19
户　县	Huxian	47.34	53.08	43.42	27.69	29.31
高陵县	Gaoling	15.06	501.27	396.58	47.81	71.94
在总计中：	Among of Total:					
高新 区	GaoXin	75.73	514.26	15.87	23.83	550.29
经开区	JingKai	110.23	645.10	520.40	234.93	
航空基地	Aviation Industry Base	0.56	5.13		2.42	3.27
航天基地	Aerospace Base	0.51	52.61	44.65		8.47

11-3 规模以上工业企业主要产品产量

Output of Major Industrial Products Of Enterprises Above Designated Size

产品名称	Name of Products	2011	比上年增长（%） Increase over Preceding Year (%)
铁矿石成品矿（吨）	Iron Ore(ton)	24712	22.6
发电量（万千瓦小时）	Electricity Generation Volume(10 000 kw.h)	950100	-0.1
#火电	Thermal Power	938160	0.1
水力发电	Hydroelectric Power	11940	-18.1
自来水生产量（万立方米）	Tap Water Production (10 000 cu.m)	32027	9.4
大米（吨）	Rice (ton)	56942	-14.0
小麦粉（万吨）	Wheat Flour (10 000 tons)	108	4.2
精制食用植物油（吨）	Edible Vegetable Oil (ton)	305100	8.2
鲜、冷藏肉(吨)	Fresh/Frozen Meat(ton)	21138	29.8
配混合饲料（吨）	Mixed Feed(ton)	657341	25.9
方便面 （吨）	Instant Noodle	101515	14.6
乳制品（吨）	Dairy Products (ton)	1146836	12.3
液体乳	Milk	1072498	12.5
罐头（吨）	Canned Food (ton)	2673	5.7
饮料酒（千升）	Beverage Wine (kiloliter)	473888	4.8
白酒（折65度，商品量）	Liquor (as 65 degree, amount of goods)	570	13.5
啤酒	Beer	473318	4.8
软饮料（吨）	Soft Beverage (ton)	2000530	-6.6
其中： 碳酸饮料 （汽水）	Carbonated Beverage	440062	30.1
果汁和蔬菜汁饮料	Juice and Fruit Beverage	224121	9.3
包装饮用水类	Canned Drinking Water	2760	-90.7
纱（吨）	Yarn (ton)	39258	3.2
1. 棉纱	Cotton Yarn	17650	-27.7
2.棉混纺纱	Blend Fabric	8354	66.2
3. 化学纤维纱	Pure Chemical-Fibre Yarn	13254	53.9
布（万米）	Cloth (10 000 m)	16344	2.7
1.棉布	Cotton Cloth	7230	-28.3
2. 棉混纺布	Blend Fabric	3358	47.0
3.化学纤维布	Pure Chemical-Fibre Cloth	5756	62.6
无纺布（无纺织物）（吨）	Non-textile fabrics(Non-extile stuff) (ton)	309	-69.1
服装（万件）	Garment (10 000 units)	776	5.7
梭织服装	Shuttle-Woven Garment	773	5.6
皮革鞋靴（万双）	Leather Shoes (10 000 pairs)	142	9.5

11-3 续表1 continued 1

产品名称	Name of Products	2011	比上年增长（%）Increase over Preceding Year (%)
人造板（立方米）	Artificial Board (cu.m)	381386	3.4
纤维板	Fibre Board	381386	3.4
家具（件）	Furniture (unit)	928952	78.9
木质家具	Wooden Furniture	808187	100.2
软体家具	Soft Furniture (inc.: Sofa ,Mattress etc.)	120765	4.6
机制纸及纸板（外购原纸加工除外）（吨）	Machine Made Paper(not including processing of procured base paper)(ton)	497882	0.7
卫生用纸原纸	Body Paper of Sanitary Paper	7546	-11.8
纸制品（吨）	Paper-Made Products (ton)	101382	-7.6
其中：瓦楞纸箱	Corrugated Paper	101382	-7.6
单色印刷（万令）	Monochrom Printed products(10000 reams)	109	44.7
多色印刷品（万对开色令）	Colored Printed products(10000 reams)	461	7.7
原油加工量（吨）	Crude Oil Processing (ton)	1531686	-12.1
汽油（吨）	Petrol(ton)	198949	-2.1
柴油（吨）	Diesel(ton)	419387	-8.1
燃料油（吨）	Fuel Oil(ton)	118784	-9.5
石油沥青（吨）	Petroleum Pitch (ton)	100621	-85.8
液化石油气（吨）	Liquefied Petroleum Gas (ton)	45108	-6.4
石油焦（吨）	Petroleum Coke (ton)		
盐酸（含量31%以上）（吨）	Salt Acid (Content over 31%) (ton)	391546	0.0
氢氧化钠（烧碱）（折100%）（吨）	Caustic Soda (100%)(ton)	19246	-44.7
碳化钙（电石）（折 300升/千克)（吨）	Calcium Carbide Lonverted into(ton)	34008	-37.7
化学农药原料药(折有效成分100%)（吨）	Chemical Pesticide(100% effective content)(ton)	37765	-23.5
涂料（吨）	Construction Paint(ton)	1930	80.4
初级形态的塑料（塑料树脂及共聚物）（吨）	Plastic,Resin and Copolymer (ton)	13593	-3.1
合成洗涤剂（吨）	Synthetic Detergents (ton)	86936	4.2
合成洗衣粉	Washing Power	22071	-3.5
化学原料药（吨）	Chemical Medicine (ton)	412	-16.6
中成药（吨）	Traditional Chinese Medicine (ton)	2559	-0.9
化学纤维（吨）	Chemical Fiber	23140	0.3
#人造纤维（纤维素纤维）	Man-made Fiber	23140	0.3
塑料制品（吨）	Plastic Product (ton)	12666	10.2
#塑料薄膜	Plastic Sheet	5579	9.7
#农用薄膜	Agricultural Sheet	5579	9.7

11-3 续表2 continued 2

产品名称	Name of Products	2011	比上年增长（%）Increase over Preceding Year (%)
水泥（吨）	Cement (ton)	4099898	-19.8
硅酸盐水泥熟料（吨）	Portland Cement Clinker (ton)	3748902	7.8
窑外分解窑水泥熟料	Outside Decomposition of Kiln Cement Clinker	35545	-52.4
水泥混凝土电杆（根）	Cement Pole(unit)	34958	-10.3
商品混凝土（万立方米）	Ready-mixed Concrete（10 000 cu.m）	1781	87.5
沥青和改性沥青防水卷材（万平方米）	Asphalt and Modified Bitumen Membrane(10 000 sq.m)	987	29.8
平板玻璃（重量箱）	Plate Glass (wt.cases)		0.0
钢化玻璃(平方米)	Toughened Glass(sq.m)	567991	0.0
日用玻璃制品（吨）	Glassware(ton)	7177	9.3
生铁（吨）	Csat iron(ton)		0.0
粗钢（吨）	Thick Steel (ton)	21413	-9.8
钢材（吨）	Rolled-steel Final Products (ton)	184753	-43.9
中小型型钢	Rolled-steel Medium and Small	9625	2.4
盘条(线材)	Wire Rod	162060	-46.2
冷轧薄板	Non-hot-roll Thin Steel	1725	-43.3
无缝钢管	Seamless Steel Pipe	9111	-0.3
焊接钢管	Welded Steel Pipes	2232	-63.5
铁合金（吨）	Ferroalloy	15304	3.4
铝材（吨）	Aluminum Material (ton)	48658	15.8
黄金（千克）	Gold (kilogramme)	275	-16.7
单晶硅（千克）	Monocrystalline Silicon	904603	13.0
工业锅炉（蒸发量吨）	Industrial Boiler steam(ton)	1089	37.7
发动机（千瓦）	Engine (kw)	956257	-25.6
汽车发动机	Motor Engine	956257	-25.6
金属切削机床（台）	Metal-cutting Machines (unit)	3963	62.8
泵（液体泵）（台）	Pump (Liquid pump)(unit)	2977	37.1
风机（台）	Fan(unit)	1174	-29.1
气体压缩机（台）	Gas Compressor(unit)	7123625	32.3
阀门（吨）	Valves (ton)	1134	38.5
铸铁件（吨）	Iron Castings (ton)	74340	14.3
铸钢件（吨）	Steel Castings (ton)	8798	0.1
锻件（吨）	Forgings (ton)	7562	-1.2
粉末冶金零件（吨）	Powder Melallurgy Products(ton)	354	46.3
矿山专用设备（吨）	Mining Equipment (ton)	7813	36.8
炼油、化工专用设备（吨）	Oil Refining and Chemical Industry Machine(ton)	5040	71.4

11-3 续表3 continued 3

产品名称	Name of Products	2011	比上年增长（%）Increase over Preceding Year (%)
金属冶炼设备（吨）	Metal Smelting Equipments(ton)	22986	11.0
金属轧制设备（吨）	Metal-rolling Machine(ton)	6745	110.4
混凝土机械（台）	Concrete Machinery(unit)	371	42.1
印刷专用设备（吨）	Printing Equipment(ton)	6070	104.4
环境保护专用设备（台、套）	Special Equipment for Environment Protection	95	-33.6
大气污染防治设备	Equipment for Preventing Atmospheric Pollution	95	-33.6
铁路货车（辆）	Freight(unit)	3600	15.4
汽车（辆）	Motor Vehicle (unit)	556664	-14.6
其中：基本型乘用车（轿车）	Basic Passenger Vehicles (Cars)	386777	-25.3
①排量≤1升	1.0L and Below Gas Displacement	82962	-44.4
②1升<排量≤1.6升	1.0L-1.6L Gas Displacement(1.6L included)	282158	-10.1
③1.6升<排量≤2.0升	1.6L-2.0L Gas Displacement(2.0L included)	20920	-58.2
④2.0升<排量≤2.5升	2.0L-2.5L Gas Displacement(2.5L included)	340	-93.2
多功能乘用车（MPV）	Multi-purpose Vehicles (MPV)	2399	-24.1
运动型多用途乘用车	Sport Utility Vehicles	60249	0.0
客车	Passenger Vehicles	10553	45.0
大型客车（车长>10）	Buses	1029	-67.2
轻型客车（车长<7）	Large(40seats and above)	9524	129.9
载货汽车	Trucks	96686	-21.7
改装汽车（辆）	Refit Trucks (unit)	18435	36.4
交流电动机（千瓦）	Alternating Current Motor (kw)	5646935	24.4
变压器（千伏安）	Transformer (kwa)	114275087	0.0
高压开关板（面）	High-voltage Switch Panel(unit)	10840	236.9
低压开关板（面）	Low-voltage Switch Panel(unit)	19446	-16.4
电力电缆（千米）	Electric Power Cables(km)	7489	84.0
通信及电子网络用电缆（对千米）	Communication Cables(pair km)	15812	571.1
光缆（光纤通迅电缆）（芯千米）	Cable (Optical Communication Cable) (Core.km)	1569274	140.2
绝缘制品（吨）	Insulating Products(ton)	5846	8.4
家用电冰箱（台）	Household refrigerator(unit)	72218	-32.9
电子计算机整机（台）	Air-conditioner Compressor(unit)	16766	-64.4
彩色显像管（只）	Color kinescope (unit)	1907200	-72.9
半导体分立器件（万只）	Semiconductor Discrete Device(10 000units)	23	-10.5
电子元件（万只）	Electronic Components(10 000units)	32723	-76.2
工业自动化调节仪表与控制系统（台、套）	Automatization meter and system (unit)	48422	-2.8
分析仪器及装置（台套）	Analysis Instruments and Apparatus(sets)	48269	-3.6

11-4 主要年份规模以上工业企业主要经济指标

Main Economic Indicators of all Industrial Enterprises above Designated Size in Representative Years

单位：亿元 （100 million yuan）

年 份 Year	企业单位数（个）Number of Enterprises (unit)	工业总产值(现价) Gross Industrial Output Value	工业增加值(现价) Value-added of Industry	从业人员年平均人数（万人）Annual Average Employed Persons (10 000 persons)
1998	793	350.38	99.20	51.71
1999	770	366.59	106.56	45.64
2000	816	417.97	130.18	43.25
2001	785	482.61	149.06	40.12
2002	771	544.78	170.39	38.48
2003	735	638.66	202.74	36.55
2004	1066	830.06	254.17	38.08
2005	902	981.02	314.01	37.92
2006	904	1187.74	370.11	37.94
2007	937	1577.05	499.96	38.55
2008	1032	2007.85	605.25	40.17
2009	1131	2468.27	700.13	43.42
2010	1126	3130.15	862.28	47.11
2011	892	3552.21	1012.58	50.42

11-4 续表 continued

单位：亿元 （100 million yuan）

年 份 Year	资产合计 Total Assets	负债合计 Total Liabilities	所有者权益 Owners' Equities	主营业务收入 Revenue from Principal Business	利润总额 Total Profits	利税总额 Total Pre-tax Profits
1998	810.56	548.68	261.88	346.84	-1.26	14.82
1999	853.90	577.94	275.96	346.26	8.26	27.30
2000	958.05	622.46	323.72	420.42	16.11	36.29
2001	1054.36	657.88	384.65	451.62	17.97	40.84
2002	1065.76	643.78	412.27	541.64	25.43	51.31
2003	1195.69	733.04	460.97	645.53	33.82	64.99
2004	1333.91	869.30	464.60	812.46	38.57	74.23
2005	1503.85	977.42	508.82	980.97	28.72	67.25
2006	1651.67	1062.11	578.33	1183.51	61.46	110.23
2007	1940.52	1254.01	686.51	1561.25	106.22	168.54
2008	2426.13	1518.86	907.27	1928.05	84.89	168.63
2009	2913.56	1779.38	1130.76	2384.52	177.20	280.68
2010	3592.13	2069.29	1515.65	3011.19	245.37	373.56
2011	3975.38	2295.49	1678.19	3381.27	172.94	312.78

11-5 规模以上工业企业分行业工业增加值（2011年）

Value Added of Industrial Enterprises Above Designated Size by Sector（2011）

单位：万元 (10 000 yuan)

分　　组	Item	2011
总　　计	**Total**	**1012.58**
煤炭开采和洗选业	Mining and Washing of Coal	
石油和天然气开采业	Extraction of Petroleum and Natural Gas	
黑色金属矿采选业	Mining and Processing of Ferrous Metal Ores	0.08
有色金属矿采选业	Mining and Processing of Non-ferrous Metal Ores	
非金属矿采选业	Mining and Processing of Nonmetal Ores	
开采辅助活动	Mining Auxiliary Activities	7.49
其他采矿业	Mining of Other Ores	
农副食品加工业	Processing of Food from Agricultural Porducts	39.16
食品制造业	Manufacture of Foods	33.22
酒、饮料和精制茶制造业	Manufacture of Alcohol,Beverages and Tea	27.29
烟草加工业	Manufacture of Tobacco	0.37
纺织业	Manufacture of Textile	5.92
纺织服装、鞋、帽制造业	Manufacture of Textile Wearing Apparel,Footwear and Caps	2.87
皮革、毛皮、羽毛(绒)及其制品业	Manufacture of Leather, Fur, Feather (eiderdown) and Related Products	0.47
木材加工及竹、藤、棕、草制品业	Processing of Timber,Manufacture of Wood,Plam and Straw Products	2.83
家具制造业	Manufacture of Furniture	1.72
造纸及纸制品业	Manufacture of Paper and Paper Products	8.15
印刷业、记录媒介的复制	Printing,Reproduction of Recording Media	20.63
文教、工美、体育和娱乐用品制造业	Manufacture of Articles For Cultural,Educational and Sports Activities	1.64
石油加工、炼焦及核燃料加工业	Processing of Petroleum, Cokeing,Processing of Nuclear and Nuclear Fuel	43.74
化学原料及化学制品制造业	Manufacture of Raw Chemical Materials and Chemical Products	36.30
医药制造业	Manufacture of Medicines	41.72
化学纤维制造业	Manufacture of Chemical Fibers	2.06
橡胶和塑料制品业	Manufacture of Rubber and Plastics	13.46
非金属矿物制品业	Manufacture of Non-metallic Mineral Products	46.55
黑色金属冶炼及压延加工业	Smelting and Pressing of Ferrous Metals	14.27
有色金属冶炼及压延加工业	Smelting and Pressing of Non-ferrous Metals	23.81
金属制品业	Manufacture of Metal Products	43.17
通用设备制造业	Manufacture of General Purpose Machinery	41.23
专用设备制造业	Manufacture of Special Equipment	62.24
汽车制造业	Manufacture of Motor Vehicle	157.60
铁路、船舶、航空航天和其他运输设备制造业	Railways,Shipbuilding,Aerospace and Other Transportation Equipment Manufacturing Industry	84.99
电气机械及器材制造业	Manufacture of Electric Equipment and Machinery	88.21
计算机、通讯和其他电子设备制造业	Manufacture of Communication Equipment, Computers and other Electronic Equipment	37.50
仪器仪表制造业	Manufacture of Measuring Instruments and Machinery	35.53
其他制造业	Manufacture of Other Manufacturing	0.47
废弃资源综合利用业	Recycling and Disposal of Waste	
金属制品、机械和设备修理业	Metal Products,Machinery and Equipment Repair Industry	1.08
电力、热力的生产和供应业	Production and Supply of Electric Power and Heat Power	72.93
燃气生产和供应业	Gas Mining and Supplying Industry	9.95
水的生产和供应业	Production and Supply of Water	3.91

11-6 各区县、开发区规模以上工业企业主要经济指标（2011年）

Main Economic Indicators of All Industrial Enterprises Above Designated Size by Region and Development Zone（2011）

区县名称	Name of District and County	企业单位数（个）Number of Enterprises（unit）	工业增加值（现价）(亿元) Value Added of Industry (At Current Prices) (100 mil.yuan)	从业人员年平均人数（万人）Annual Average Employers (10 000 persons)
新城区	Xingcheng	20	83.85	6.39
碑林区	Beilin	21	39.75	0.81
莲湖区	Lianhu	47	128.72	6.37
灞桥区	Baqiao	130	82.98	3.64
未央区	Weiyang	147	151.49	6.54
雁塔区	Yanta	179	112.47	7.65
阎良区	Yanliang	67	40.96	2.86
临潼区	Lintong	32	84.67	1.60
长安区	Chang'an	91	105.37	5.59
蓝田县	Lantian	18	10.78	0.48
周至县	Zhouzhi	25	4.52	1.04
户　县	Huxian	51	34.53	1.57
高陵县	Gaoling	63	132.49	5.86
在总计中：	Among of Total:			
高新 区	GaoXin	169	147.53	10.02
经开区	JingKai	108	185.45	7.27
航空基地	Aviation Industry Base	11	1.76	0.15
航天基地	Aerospace Base	11	13.99	0.82

11-6 续表1 continued 1

单位：亿元 （100 million yuan）

区县名称	Name of District and County	资产合计 Total Assets	负债合计 Total Liabilites	所有者权益合计 Total Owners' Equities
新城区	Xingcheng	412.33	268.87	143.45
碑林区	Beilin	165.85	102.15	63.70
莲湖区	Lianhu	688.22	313.69	374.53
灞桥区	Baqiao	141.36	70.27	70.92
未央区	Weiyang	516.13	319.71	196.26
雁塔区	Yanta	629.59	336.12	293.35
阎良区	Yanliang	343.76	220.54	122.36
临潼区	Lintong	222.45	131.65	90.72
长安区	Chang'an	266.49	150.76	115.60
蓝田县	Lantian	42.81	19.19	23.53
周至县	Zhouzhi	12.44	6.50	5.88
户县	Huxian	103.79	66.73	37.06
高陵县	Gaoling	430.16	289.31	140.83
在总计中：	Among of Total:			
高新 区	GaoXin	721.27	357.20	364.05
经开区	JingKai	646.53	432.08	214.29
航空基地	Aviation Industry Base	11.53	4.85	6.68
航天基地	Aerospace Base	68.44	37.24	31.20

11-6 续表2 continued 2

单位：亿元 （100 million yuan）

区县名称	Name of District and County	主营业务收入 Revenue from Principal Business	利润总额 Total Profits	利税总额 Total Pre-tax Profits
新城区	Xingcheng	314.47	6.51	21.93
碑林区	Beilin	137.00	8.24	11.75
莲湖区	Lianhu	444.10	13.43	30.90
灞桥区	Baqiao	276.16	34.54	48.33
未央区	Weiyang	517.26	20.80	50.58
雁塔区	Yanta	347.42	26.48	45.79
阎良区	Yanliang	184.26	8.16	9.76
临潼区	Lintong	259.98	9.71	15.17
长安区	Chang'an	332.34	17.78	33.53
蓝田县	Lantian	28.44	2.75	3.59
周至县	Zhouzhi	13.98	0.65	0.98
户县	Huxian	89.00	4.71	7.96
高陵县	Gaoling	436.86	19.18	32.51
在总计中：	Among of Total:			
高新 区	GaoXin	558.66	38.22	70.24
经开区	JingKai	643.84	31.76	54.87
航空基地	Aviation Industry Base	5.04	0.42	0.67
航天基地	Aerospace Base	51.93	8.35	9.15

11-7 主要年份规模以上工业企业经济效益指标（2011年）

Indicators of Economic Benefit of Industrial Enterprises Above Designated Size in Representative Years（2011）

年 份 Year	总资产贡献率 （%） Ratio of Total Assets to Industrial Output Value (%)	资产负债率 （%） Assets-Liability Ratio (%)	流动资产周转次数 （次/年） Rate of Annual Turnover Working Capitals (times/year)	成本费用利润率 （%） Ratio of Profits to cost (%)	全员劳动生产率 （元/人.年） Overall Labor Productivity (yuan/person yea	产品销售率 （%） Proportion of Industrial Products Sold (%)
1998		67.7	0.9	-266.1	19185	95.3
1999		67.7	0.9	2.5	22878	95.9
2000		65.0	1.0	4.2	29496	97.1
2001	5.8	62.4	0.9	4.1	38267	96.7
2002	6.2	60.4	1.1	5.1	46940	96.7
2003	7.0	61.3	1.1	5.7	58801	96.3
2004	6.9	65.2	1.2	5.0	66752	97.9
2005	8.4	65.0	1.3	3.1	82815	97.5
2006	7.8	64.3	1.4	5.5	97561	98.2
2007	10.2	64.6	1.6	7.3	129706	96.8
2008	8.6	62.6	1.5	4.6	150641	96.1
2009	11.3	61.1	1.7	8.1	161289	97.6
2010	12.2	57.6	1.7	8.8	188483	97.1
2011	8.6	57.7	1.5	5.2	194105	97.4

11-8 规模以上工业企业主要经济指标（2011年）

单位：万元

分组	Item	企业单位数（个）Number of Enterprises (unit)	亏损企业 Loss Making Enterprises	工业总产值（当年价）Gross Industrial Output Value (At Current Prices)
总　计	**Total**	**891**	**139**	**35522078.1**
#市　区	Urban Area	734	102	28842958.2
#亏损企业	Deficit Enterprises	139	139	4908002.0
按隶属关系分	Grouped by Jurisdiction of Management			
中央企业	Central Enterprises	75	12	10502652.0
省属企业	Provincial Enterprises	77	16	8046743.6
市属企业	Municipal Enterprises	739	111	16972682.5
按登记注册类型分组	Grouped by Registion Status			
内资企业	Domestic Investment Enterprises	785	120	28591864.8
国有经济	State-owned Enterprises	73	14	7578215.4
集体经济	Collective-owned Enterprises	28	2	274956.0
股份合作企业	Share-holding Corperative	10	2	140931.7
联营企业	Joint Ownership Enterprises	2		16757.2
有限责任公司	Limited Liability Corporations	385	65	16019408.6
国有独资公司	State Sole Funded Enterprises	24	4	2701875.3
其他有限责任公司	Other Limited Liability Corporation	361	61	13317533.3
股份有限公司	Share-holding Corperation Ltd.	61	10	1745354.4
私营企业	Private Enterprises	215	27	2717601.6
其他内资企业	Other Domestic Funded Enterprises	10		98639.9
港、澳、台商投资企业	Enterprises with Funds from Hong Kong,Macao and Taiwan	21	5	264063.8
外商投资企业	Enterprises with Foreign Investment	86	14	6666149.5
按轻重工业分	Grouped by Light Industry and Heavy Industry			
轻工业	Light Industry	253	41	6458647.6
重工业	Heavy Industry	638	98	29063430.5
按企业规模分	Grouped by Size of Enterprises			
大型工业	Large-size	67	7	20882833.9
中型工业	Medium-size	150	30	6261443.6
小型工业	Small-size	674	102	8377800.6

Main Economic Indicators of All Industrial Enterprises Above Designated Size（2011）

（10 000 yuan）

工业销售产值（当年价）Value of Industry Products Sales (At Current Prices)	出口交货值 Export Delivery Value	从业人员年平均人数（人）Annual Average Employers (person)	资产总计 Total Assets	流动资产合计 Total Working Capitals	固定资产合计 Total Fixed Assets	固定资产原价 Origing Value of Fixed Assets	累计折旧 Accumulative Total Depreciation
34586629.5	**1915086.4**	**504178**	**39753754.1**	**23095077.5**	**12934757.5**	**16611627.0**	**6297998.8**
28209290.8	1597002.2	414593	33861771.3	19874212.6	11036728.2	14286436.4	5506081.6
4738423.1	227043.6	73001	7768757.2	4289764.8	2768793.5	3143042.6	1138124.7
10263688.2	623780.4	179567	17388753.6	9695394.4	6817042.4	8475399.1	3196767.6
7909274.0	551168.5	89726	7237885.6	4581403.4	1756289.6	2113860.8	834974.6
16413667.3	740137.5	234885	15127114.9	8818279.7	4361425.5	6022367.1	2266256.6
27778243.5	1273712.6	430459	34980317.9	20564670.0	11219074.5	14223613.5	5429027.3
7369391.1	172412.9	106038	11536776.7	6237847.3	4631691.5	5892213.1	2055852.6
264002.7		6436	117730.7	72144.8	31658.5	48220.0	18031.4
143410.5		2207	122145.9	89453.9	18480.9	32680.4	15863.2
16656.5		188	6071.1	5064.1	742.6	1487.5	1017.5
15702613.4	987203.6	244691	18368353.7	11504111.9	5147439.6	6536804.9	2724322.9
2623564.3	232240.1	81003	4797109.3	2723657.7	1678556.0	2158208.9	901409.2
13079049.1	754963.5	163688	13571244.4	8780454.2	3468883.6	4378596.0	1822913.7
1646610.3	99944.2	31048	3116799.8	1588986.8	850007.8	957031.6	364149.8
2542500.0	14023.9	38217	1640757.2	1026611.4	514146.5	726355.2	241481.9
93059.0	128.0	1634	71682.8	40449.8	24907.1	28820.8	8308.0
276016.8	12895.0	5820	351102.8	149060.8	94754.2	162041.5	70513.2
6532369.2	628478.8	67899	4422333.4	2381346.7	1620928.8	2225972.0	798458.3
6435553.4	350305.0	93130	4381333.2	2395892.8	1388252.2	2406793.9	1127891.0
28151076.1	1564781.4	411048	35372420.9	20699184.7	11546505.3	14204833.1	5170107.8
20404388.8	1402571.3	314214	26315078.4	15571896.5	8577503.3	10566809.1	4143595.9
6125325.7	351475.8	102794	7902557.4	4003332.3	2809273.9	3714141.8	1259394.4
8056915.0	161039.3	87170	5536118.3	3519848.7	1547980.3	2330676.1	895008.5

11-8 续表1

单位：万元

分组	Item	负债合计 Total Liabilites	流动负债合计 Total Working Liabilities	非流动负债 Non-Working Liabilities
总　计	**Total**	**22954855.0**	**18845549.5**	**3780057.3**
#市　区	Urban Area	19137561.1	15607361.7	3285616.6
#亏损企业	Deficit Enterprises	4693902.8	3335482.4	1280476.9
按隶属关系分	Grouped by Jurisdiction of Management			
中央企业	Central Enterprises	10128659.1	8004168.6	2038603.4
省属企业	Provincial Enterprises	4597183.9	4045272.3	486075.6
市属企业	Municipal Enterprises	8229012.0	6796108.6	1255378.3
按登记注册类型分组	Grouped by Registion Status			
内资企业	Domestic Investment Enterprises	20360466.6	16501156.9	3551924.3
国有经济	State-owned Enterprises	7161371.1	5533747.5	1590867.5
集体经济	Collective-owned Enterprises	71154.0	64805.4	2620.1
股份合作企业	Share-holding Corperative	87148.2	84358.7	2789.4
联营企业	Joint Ownership Enterprises	4766.2	4766.2	
有限责任公司	Limited Liability Corporations	10777865.6	9145723.3	1395093.2
国有独资公司	State Sole Funded Enterprises	2264341.9	1736177.2	456570.0
其他有限责任公司	Other Limited Liability Corporation	8513523.7	7409546.1	938523.2
股份有限公司	Share-holding Corperation Ltd.	1369033.9	884156.0	475417.8
私营企业	Private Enterprises	850962.4	755436.5	76106.9
其他内资企业	Other Domestic Funded Enterprises	38165.2	28163.3	9029.4
港、澳、台商投资企业	Enterprises with Funds from Hong Kong,Macao and Taiwan	195295.5	177976.2	5662.6
外商投资企业	Enterprises with Foreign Investment	2399092.9	2166416.4	222470.4
按轻重工业分	Grouped by Light Industry and Heavy Industry			
轻工业	Light Industry	2241404.4	2040905.7	150741.7
重工业	Heavy Industry	20713450.6	16804643.8	3629315.6
按企业规模分	Grouped by Size of Enterprises			
大型工业	Large-size	15398478.2	12960963.3	2329542.0
中型工业	Medium-size	4438076.2	3134633.3	1221623.4
小型工业	Small-size	3118300.6	2749952.9	228891.9

continued 1

（10 000 yuan）

所有者权益合计 Total Owners' Equities	实收资本 Total Capital Hold	营业收入 Total Revenue	主营业务收入 Revenue from Principal Business	营业成本 Total Cost	主营业务成本 Cost of Principal Business	营业税金及附加 Taxs and Other Changes	主营业务税金及附加 Taxes and Other Charges on Principal Business
16781929.1	**6490675.3**	**34602209.1**	**33812693.2**	**29641752.6**	**28750370.4**	**341495.5**	**322491.6**
14708964.3	5288176.3	28770616.0	28129941.6	24578892.4	23828426.6	325295.6	307645.1
3072830.0	1180492.3	4572605.0	4405469.3	4190886.2	4080040.9	114215.4	113554.3
7260092.8	2342100.8	10717929.9	10522426.0	9617975.7	9234508.9	139819.4	134762.5
2638718.0	1093124.2	7518015.1	7314894.5	6547414.6	6371093.7	25185.8	24192.4
6883118.3	3055450.3	16366264.1	15975372.7	13476362.3	13144767.8	176490.3	163536.7
14604203.1	5434986.4	27668187.1	27107106.0	23934741.3	23226677.9	230999.4	212199.2
4375403.9	1282599.9	7134785.9	6955984.5	6265559.7	6114970.5	135258.5	133149.9
46391.3	15295.7	266283.0	266283.0	224604.2	224604.2	1460.7	1460.7
34448.7	14683.4	134209.2	128909.9	116060.0	116055.7	437.9	437.9
1304.9	1290.8	13625.1	13625.1	12784.2	12784.2	35.5	35.5
7579965.9	3215730.4	15930662.5	15606851.2	13956587.0	13444871.1	66683.0	51129.7
2532354.3	782157.6	2963103.7	2902889.7	2505445.0	2465301.0	11964.4	10336.1
5047611.6	2433572.8	12967558.8	12703961.5	11451142.0	10979570.1	54718.6	40793.6
1747709.3	505396.6	1650727.2	1623757.2	1257992.6	1238003.4	11099.6	10876.4
785490.8	366209.6	2442903.5	2416748.7	2019858.6	1994093.8	14819.1	14360.9
33488.3	33780.0	94990.7	94946.4	81295.0	81295.0	1205.1	748.2
155717.9	135105.3	262450.1	257665.8	179360.7	175539.6	3788.0	3780.8
2022008.1	920583.6	6671571.9	6447921.4	5527650.6	5348152.9	106708.1	106511.6
2136153.0	1036948.7	6368616.7	6272940.2	5124024.1	5049654.8	43639.9	33307.2
14645776.1	5453726.6	28233592.4	27539753.0	24517728.5	23700715.6	297855.6	289184.4
10916598.5	3417954.8	20404160.5	19871052.8	17727319.5	17063953.1	261118.9	255044.8
3458346.6	1630889.4	6122324.8	5942612.3	5183411.0	5024774.8	36736.8	26672.0
2406984.0	1441831.1	8075723.8	7999028.1	6731022.1	6661642.5	43639.8	40774.8

11-8 续表2

单位：万元

分　组	Item	销售费用 Expenses for Sales	管理费用 Expenses for Management
总　计	**Total**	**1314383.1**	**1928176.3**
#市　区	Urban Area	1124162.9	1652261.1
#亏损企业	Deficit Enterprises	215505.0	318548.4
按隶属关系分	Grouped by Jurisdiction of Management		
中央企业	Central Enterprises	236301.6	794789.2
省属企业	Provincial Enterprises	417095.9	308694.6
市属企业	Municipal Enterprises	660985.6	824692.5
按登记注册类型分组	Grouped by Registion Status		
内资企业	Domestic Investment Enterprises	864454.1	1695801.0
国有经济	State-owned Enterprises	190031.3	529040.5
集体经济	Collective-owned Enterprises	6945.7	11188.8
股份合作企业	Share-holding Corperative	4322.1	4852.6
联营企业	Joint Ownership Enterprises	180.8	204.7
有限责任公司	Limited Liability Corporations	476348.0	896208.9
国有独资公司	State Sole Funded Enterprises	89221.4	238160.6
其他有限责任公司	Other Limited Liability Corporation	387126.6	658048.3
股份有限公司	Share-holding Corperation Ltd.	105238.7	132189.0
私营企业	Private Enterprises	78853.2	116545.1
其他内资企业	Other Domestic Funded Enterprises	2534.3	5571.4
港、澳、台商投资企业	Enterprises with Funds from Hong Kong,Macao and Taiwan	37905.8	18675.5
外商投资企业	Enterprises with Foreign Investment	412023.2	213699.8
按轻重工业分	Grouped by Light Industry and Heavy Industry		
轻工业	Light Industry	565581.9	314651.4
重工业	Heavy Industry	748801.2	1613524.9
按企业规模分	Grouped by Size of Enterprises		
大型工业	Large-size	865083.9	1167827.0
中型工业	Medium-size	213895.7	386276.8
小型工业	Small-size	235403.5	374072.5

continued 2

（10 000 yuan）

财务费用 Financial cost	营业利润 Operating Profit	利润总额 Total Profits	亏损企业亏损总额 Total Loss of Deficit Enterprises	利税总额 Total Pre-tax Profits	应付职工薪酬 Salary Payable	本年应交增值税 Value Added Tax Payable
309072.2	**1778103.5**	**1729427.8**	**296684.3**	**3127753.9**	**2679607.2**	**1056830.6**
241258.7	1520106.7	1456364.1	277255.6	2677386.0	2370819.6	895726.3
71482.9	-269449.4	-296684.3	296684.3	-66688.5	413338.4	115780.4
149900.4	147160.3	213677.8	196814.9	620977.1	1206478.1	267479.9
54827.8	286608.0	213048.8	18207.3	470320.8	410247.5	232086.2
104344.0	1344335.2	1302701.2	81662.1	2036456.0	1062881.6	557264.5
283527.5	1280309.3	1240764.9	272160.8	2253450.5	2279914.0	781686.2
99831.2	75914.8	103049.6	188971.5	470852.6	722809.5	232544.5
1323.4	22392.3	21702.3	603.7	32076.2	20283.0	8913.2
2908.5	-868.7	3097.7	76.1	9112.8	6679.6	5577.2
24.2	395.7	395.7		544.6	408.5	113.4
131022.4	828600.6	760418.4	57955.9	1218929.1	1238014.1	391827.7
19030.0	92636.3	121850.8	15781.4	206019.1	389850.2	72203.9
111992.4	735964.3	638567.6	42174.5	1012910.0	848163.9	319623.8
17144.6	142653.2	160359.4	22111.5	238874.3	149633.1	67415.3
30550.5	207142.0	188643.0	2442.1	275409.4	136583.1	71947.3
722.7	4079.4	3098.8		7651.5	5503.1	3347.6
1691.8	13546.3	14442.7	5711.2	30305.7	33168.1	12075.0
23852.9	484247.9	474220.2	18812.3	843997.7	366525.1	263069.4
45350.5	438367.8	403674.3	26256.6	729018.6	438504.7	281704.4
263721.7	1339735.7	1325753.5	270427.7	2398735.3	2241102.5	775126.2
171587.3	630332.2	686474.1	190866.1	1523329.5	1873544.4	575736.5
79014.2	402147.4	419436.2	67980.2	679552.1	434978.7	223379.1
58470.7	745623.9	623517.5	37838.0	924872.3	371084.1	257715.0

11-8 续表3

单位：万元

分　组	Item	企业单位数(个) Number of Enterprises (unit)	亏损企业 Loss Making Enterprises	工业总产值（当年价） Gross Industrial Output Value (At Current Prices)
按经济组织类型分	Grouped by Economic Type of Orgnization			
独资企业	Appropratorship	155	21	9340151.5
合作、合伙企业	Partnership	24	4	261262.7
股份有限公司	Corporaton	77	12	2170673.3
有限责任公司	Limited Liability Company	635	102	23749990.6
按控股情况分	Grouped by Cast strand			
国有控股	State owned shares	196	40	20400206.2
集体控股	Collective shares	59	8	1110379.2
私人控股	Private holdings	523	69	9298807.8
港澳台控股	Hong Kong and Macao Holdings	13	4	174684.1
外商投资	Foreign Investment	54	10	3363963.0
其他	Others	46	8	1174037.8
按工业行业大类分	Grouped by Sector			
煤炭开采和洗选业	Mining and Washing of Coal			
石油和天然气开采业	Extraction of Petroleum and Natural Gas			
黑色金属矿采选业	Mining and Processing of Ferrous Metal Ores	1	1	2223.0
有色金属矿采选业	Mining and Processing of Non-ferrous Metal Ores			
非金属矿采选业	Mining and Processing of Nonmetal Ores			
开采辅助活动	Mining Auxiliary Activities	2		36315.5
其他采矿业	Mining of other Ores			
农副食品加工业	Processing of Food from Agricultural Porducts	51	6	1570922.2
食品制造业	Manufacture of Foods	26	5	985753.1
酒、饮料和精制茶制造业	Manufacture of Alcohol,Beverages and Tea	13	3	712005.0
烟草加工业	Manufacture of Tobacco	1		4624.0
纺织业	Manufacture of Textile	12	4	203430.7
纺织服装、鞋、帽制造业	Manufacture of Textile Wearing Apparel,Footwear and Caps	6		92560.9
皮革、毛皮、羽毛(绒)及其制品业	Manufacture of Leather, Fur, Feather (eiderdown) and Related Products	1		19701.9
木材加工及竹、藤、棕、草制品业	Processing of Timber,Manufacture of Wood,Plam and Straw Products	5		99359.0

continued 3

（10 000 yuan）

工业销售产值（当年价）Value of Industry Products Sales (At Current Prices)	出口交货值 Export Delivery Value	从业人员年平均人数（人）Annual Average Employers (person)	资产总计 Total Assets	流动资产合计 Total Working Capitals	固定资产合计 Total Fixed Assets	固定资产原价 Origing Value of Fixed Assets	累计折旧 Accumulative Total Depreciation
9099423.3	356318.9	129809	12638616.4	6797501.8	5071532.0	6580851.9	2325800.3
257448.3	492.0	4263	204509.1	137212.4	46495.3	64274.5	25611.2
2073967.1	286231.0	35713	3725288.0	1950974.7	1059299.3	1238543.2	437948.0
23155790.8	1272044.5	334393	23185340.6	14209388.6	6757430.9	8727957.4	3508639.3
19949364.2	1125840.5	317753	29370875.4	17104195.9	9733866.9	12087661.9	4691189.3
1102042.8	77333.8	16644	812002.4	505608.7	190335.8	293045.5	119883.6
8958295.0	140821.5	122368	6203497.0	3570644.4	1918860.4	2513269.8	829138.5
188878.7	2678.2	4125	234308.7	78218.0	71185.9	120306.2	49137.4
3244238.3	433420.9	29137	2371059.3	1330278.8	836767.9	1328978.2	514826.4
1143810.5	134991.5	14151	762011.3	506131.7	183740.6	268365.4	93823.6
2122.5		120	2062.6	1399.9	468.9	1078.9	615.1
36944.4		741	54029.5	35594.7	11434.6	18600.6	7166.0
1517582.0	5027.6	9915	657865.7	433766.3	176713.1	315513.8	147784.0
942507.0	218.5	11296	399928.3	206463.7	127083.7	213740.4	89210.0
875368.2	184938.0	8452	840953.6	390797.1	325259.1	504078.2	179953.2
4830.8		230	11650.1	8625.6	2406.5	4795.1	2388.6
186213.4	25830.8	14754	192606.0	91636.3	63392.4	114925.0	53927.6
92111.9		2127	84335.7	66939.6	16412.2	19117.0	7632.9
22174.8		724	37946.1	12599.9	3621.7	5350.7	1729.0
92701.9		900	113906.1	49152.0	56343.2	86057.7	30909.9

11-8 续表4

单位：万元

分 组	Item	负债合计 Total Liabilites	流动负债合计 Total Working Liabilities	非流动负债 Non-Working Liabilities
按经济组织类型分	Grouped by Economic Type of Orgnization			
独资企业	Appropratorship	7635543.5	5914071.1	1677096.4
合作、合伙企业	Partnership	131851.9	117977.7	11818.8
股份有限公司	Corporaton	1727479.3	1207448.9	510570.3
有限责任公司	Limited Liability Company	13459980.3	11606051.8	1580571.8
按控股情况分	Grouped by Cast strand			
国有控股	State owned shares	17532741.4	14054531.0	3294625.3
集体控股	Collective shares	480122.3	442683.1	28619.0
私人控股	Private holdings	3215192.3	2783672.9	318933.7
港澳台控股	Hong Kong and Macao Holdings	144155.5	127794.6	5115.5
外商投资	Foreign Investment	1201080.7	1099500.3	95555.4
其他	Others	381562.8	337367.6	37208.4
按工业行业大类分	Grouped by Sector			
煤炭开采和洗选业	Mining and Washing of Coal			
石油和天然气开采业	Extraction of Petroleum and Natural Gas			
黑色金属矿采选业	Mining and Processing of Ferrous Metal Ores	2996.7	608.4	
有色金属矿采选业	Mining and Processing of Non-ferrous Metal Ores			
非金属矿采选业	Mining and Processing of Nonmetal Ores			
开采辅助活动	Mining Auxiliary Activities	15540.8	15540.8	
其他采矿业	Mining of other Ores			
农副食品加工业	Processing of Food from Agricultural Porducts	436410.0	420724.8	7269.0
食品制造业	Manufacture of Foods	199984.2	188683.4	11300.7
酒、饮料和精制茶制造业	Manufacture of Alcohol,Beverages and Tea	498747.7	483399.2	14844.0
烟草加工业	Manufacture of Tobacco	6403.4	6403.4	
纺织业	Manufacture of Textile	84600.2	77859.9	6157.8
纺织服装、鞋、帽制造业	Manufacture of Textile Wearing Apparel,Footwear and Caps	63235.7	52994.2	10180.3
皮革、毛皮、羽毛(绒)及其制品业	Manufacture of Leather, Fur, Feather (eiderdown) and Related Products	18895.8	11378.9	7516.9
木材加工及竹、藤、棕、草制品业	Processing of Timber,Manufacture of Wood,Plam and Straw Products	36041.1	16255.2	19000.0

continued 4

(10 000 yuan)

所有者权益合计 Total Owners' Equities	实收资本 Total Capital Hold	营业收入 Total Revenue	主营业务收入 Revenue from Principal Business	营业成本 Total Cost	主营业务成本 Cost of Principal Business	营业税金及附加 Taxs and Other Changes	主营业务税金及附加 Taxes and Other Charges on Principal Business
5001672.8	1572979.6	8912233.3	8720503.4	7729429.4	7569531.4	145204.1	143025.3
72078.9	51063.1	247093.4	241749.8	214092.0	214087.7	1686.5	1229.6
1997627.7	578433.7	2064803.7	2014759.3	1613419.3	1573347.0	14212.2	13706.8
9710549.7	4288198.9	23378078.7	22835680.7	20084811.9	19393404.3	180392.7	164529.9
11836113.1	4298055.5	19970683.7	19456417.5	17642541.7	16982665.0	188883.5	172155.5
331680.0	146398.7	1132802.6	1112211.7	894781.9	887748.9	4858.9	4858.4
2975019.4	1228790.3	8853373.4	8672569.2	7468874.4	7301736.0	124433.4	122838.4
90093.4	92113.8	182673.0	179265.7	127496.5	125046.2	3368.1	3360.9
1168779.8	510269.0	3351880.8	3313209.2	2588794.8	2572600.3	15984.3	15904.9
380243.4	215048.0	1110795.6	1079019.9	919263.3	880574.0	3967.3	3373.5
-934.1	600.0	2137.4	2137.4	1994.6	1994.6	21.0	21.0
38488.7	4982.7	36065.8	35450.9	23730.6	23571.1	902.4	869.2
220383.3	112222.5	1493793.2	1486192.7	1388876.5	1385719.9	2137.6	1866.4
198024.6	98292.6	941777.9	933629.7	820593.2	813130.3	3613.7	3525.4
342205.8	129018.2	869113.2	847790.6	677664.2	671636.3	15569.9	6390.4
5246.7	1514.7	7194.8	6975.1	4705.1	4549.5	71.2	71.2
108005.7	30660.9	191112.0	189403.6	177516.3	169627.0	1187.9	949.9
21100.0	11600.0	109867.3	109806.8	84038.2	84023.2	2945.8	2945.8
19050.3	6000.0	43630.1	22401.2	40619.4	19556.2	58.3	58.3
77765.0	38222.0	90413.1	89052.0	84939.2	84939.2	476.2	476.2

11-8 续表5

单位：万元

分 组	Item	销售费用 Expenses for Sales	管理费用 Expenses for Management
按经济组织类型分	Grouped by Economic Type of Orgnization		
独资企业	Appropratorship	322860.0	604688.0
合作、合伙企业	Partnership	7091.1	10927.4
股份有限公司	Corporaton	116113.2	152515.5
有限责任公司	Limited Liability Company	868318.8	1160045.4
按控股情况分	Grouped by Cast strand		
国有控股	State owned shares	579822.6	1289559.8
集体控股	Collective shares	45239.3	73583.0
私人控股	Private holdings	266548.7	360004.2
港澳台控股	Hong Kong and Macao Holdings	33068.2	13684.1
外商投资	Foreign Investment	351803.6	129187.3
其他	Others	37900.7	62157.9
按工业行业大类分	Grouped by Sector		
煤炭开采和洗选业	Mining and Washing of Coal		
石油和天然气开采业	Extraction of Petroleum and Natural Gas		
黑色金属矿采选业	Mining and Processing of Ferrous Metal Ores	7.0	529.4
有色金属矿采选业	Mining and Processing of Non-ferrous Metal Ores		
非金属矿采选业	Mining and Processing of Nonmetal Ores		
开采辅助活动	Mining Auxiliary Activities	575.6	3358.4
其他采矿业	Mining of other Ores		
农副食品加工业	Processing of Food from Agricultural Porducts	36807.4	35354.4
食品制造业	Manufacture of Foods	90659.7	38655.0
酒、饮料和精制茶制造业	Manufacture of Alcohol,Beverages and Tea	80780.6	34001.0
烟草加工业	Manufacture of Tobacco	88.7	1671.6
纺织业	Manufacture of Textile	3315.6	14373.4
纺织服装、鞋、帽制造业	Manufacture of Textile Wearing Apparel,Footwear and Caps	4015.1	5798.6
皮革、毛皮、羽毛(绒)及其制品业	Manufacture of Leather, Fur, Feather (eiderdown) and Related Products	709.5	863.0
木材加工及竹、藤、棕、草制品业	Processing of Timber,Manufacture of Wood,Plam and Straw Products	2996.1	2825.5

continued 5

（10 000 yuan）

财务费用 Financial cost	营业利润 Operating Profit	利润总额 Total Profits	亏损企业亏损总额 Total Loss of Deficit Enterprises	利税总额 Total Pre-tax Profits	应付职工薪酬 Salary Payable	本年应交增值税 Value Added Tax Payable
103370.5	209360.4	238955.4	196248.1	678843.3	843497.4	294683.8
3656.0	3560.9	6546.7	121.6	17372.4	13015.0	9139.2
27874.8	179086.3	199429.0	24242.8	309411.3	173022.6	95770.1
174170.9	1386095.9	1284496.7	76071.8	2122126.9	1650072.2	657237.5
194870.2	604807.8	589745.4	246922.7	1294758.5	1865064.9	516129.6
10609.5	106116.3	106567.7	2333.2	151102.0	62889.6	39675.4
81063.4	636406.2	596428.0	25007.5	985061.6	459776.1	264200.2
780.7	4130.6	4455.4	5561.8	17002.1	25217.5	9178.6
14620.8	325198.2	329246.7	13713.0	530613.8	206772.6	185382.8
7127.6	101444.4	102984.6	3146.1	149215.9	59886.5	42264.0
172.3	-415.0	-550.5	550.5	-369.2	376.8	160.3
-6.1	7504.9	7421.5		13285.7	5007.5	4961.8
12523.4	79051.2	37385.5	8020.4	55682.5	31842.8	16159.4
-659.9	49134.5	39548.7	5590.1	64417.2	38651.3	21254.8
5093.6	80651.0	79915.4	5250.7	149773.6	63258.6	54288.3
-2.7	666.4	668.4		1336.1	2008.5	596.5
806.7	872.0	3727.8	2577.9	13011.7	39701.1	8096.0
738.5	9596.5	10280.3		16123.1	6725.3	2897.0
215.4	1326.2	1410.8		1469.1	3437.3	
1940.7	2368.7	2380.0		11679.9	3084.5	8823.7

11-8　续表6

单位：万元

分　组	Item	企业单位数（个）Number of Enterprises (unit)	亏损企业 Loss Making Enterprises	工业总产值（当年价）Gross Industrial Output Value (At Current Prices)
家具制造业	Manufacture of Furniture	7		49352.1
造纸及纸制品业	Manufacture of Paper and Paper Products	22	4	251152.4
印刷业、记录媒介的复制	Printing,Reproduction of Recording Media	19	4	469432.2
文教、工美、体育和娱乐用品制造业	Manufacture of Articles For Cultural,Educational and Sports Activities	5	2	69064.3
石油加工、炼焦及核燃料加工业	Processing of Petroleum, Cokeing,Processing of Nuclear and Nuclear Fuel	5	2	1640196.1
化学原料及化学制品制造业	Manufacture of Raw Chemical Materials and Chemical Products	42	6	1451566.4
医药制造业	Manufacture of Medicines	45	6	1128780.6
化学纤维制造业	Manufacture of Chemical Fibers	2	1	85301.8
橡胶塑料制品业	Manufacture of Rubber and Plastics	28	5	456455.6
非金属矿物制品业	Manufacture of Non-metallic Mineral Products	88	20	1423374.6
黑色金属冶炼及压延加工业	Smelting and Pressing of Ferrous Metals	27	4	510440.7
有色金属冶炼及压延加工业	Smelting and Pressing of Non-ferrous Metals	25	5	788970.9
金属制品业	Manufacture of Metal Products	60	6	803288.7
通用设备制造业	Manufacture of General Purpose Machinery	55	8	1510895.1
专用设备制造业	Manufacture of Special Equipment	74	9	1781484.8
汽车制造业	Manufacture of Motor Vehicle	28	4	7942441.7
铁路、船舶、航空航天和其他运输设备制造业	Railways,Shipbuilding,Aerospace and Other Transportation Equipment Manufacturing Industry	42	5	3276761.1
电气机械及器材制造业	Manufacture of Electric Equipment and Machinery	84	8	2968324.7
计算机、通讯和其他电子设备制造业	Manufacture of Communication Equipment, Computers and other Electronic Equipment	50	9	1457068.7
仪器仪表制造业	Manufacture of Measuring Instruments and Machinery	39	3	1035301.2
其他制造业	Manufacture of Other Manufacturing	2		20713.2
废弃资源综合利用业	Recycling and Disposal of Waste			
金属制品、机械和设备修理业	Metal Products,Machinery and Equipment Repair Industry	4	1	38274.0
电力、热力的生产和供应业	Production and Supply of Electric Power and Heat Power	13	8	2336929.8
燃气生产和供应业	Gas Mining and Supplying Industry	4		228815.2
水的生产和供应业	Production and Supply of Water	3		70796.9

continued 6

（10 000 yuan）

工业销售产值（当年价）Value of Industry Products Sales (At Current Prices)	出口交货值 Export Delivery Value	从业人员年平均人数（人）Annual Average Employers (person)	资产总计 Total Assets	流动资产合计 Total Working Capitals	固定资产合计 Total Fixed Assets	固定资产原价 Origing Value of Fixed Assets	累计折旧 Accumulative Total Depreciation
48234.7		1738	24418.2	15959.7	7503.7	11968.9	6564.7
249664.8		7445	110968.0	55710.5	51697.7	79277.7	29781.6
470206.8	1060.5	8625	530973.4	273244.2	177051.4	319851.9	173743.5
68713.2	2377.7	711	33582.6	14072.7	17364.5	14851.6	6118.6
1653406.8		1875	358272.8	188574.9	146176.5	234575.9	138438.0
1422297.0	109656.4	34265	1819929.3	901223.9	705787.0	997911.6	411298.4
1083583.7	13498.6	14974	858145.7	523847.3	175734.8	321471.6	162905.1
84652.9		435	69411.7	27189.0	32645.5	68658.8	36013.3
424630.7	2318.0	13393	487268.9	258120.8	156391.5	170508.5	57044.4
1391228.4		13860	803970.6	410808.7	338523.9	473879.6	164017.1
492335.5	1339.8	4638	206214.4	113106.2	88964.2	125531.8	37884.2
738017.6	54035.1	6825	704768.3	406351.6	203737.6	260984.8	78084.1
798538.0	20398.0	15413	841748.8	522830.6	250137.5	346044.7	136875.0
1449017.6	27443.6	18439	2428765.9	1970838.0	298248.2	424541.6	159388.0
1613535.9	107225.5	27274	2373358.4	1649628.6	488019.4	691898.7	226089.0
7821637.5	380949.6	83836	5971384.1	3395618.9	1744251.0	1831339.1	615385.5
3192205.0	410187.1	68946	6802724.0	4473440.9	1883403.2	2158713.2	953225.7
2845595.3	293334.0	35409	4320771.1	3056373.8	1184055.2	1144700.2	416443.6
1308943.3	183955.4	26127	2933351.1	1484259.6	858840.1	924777.8	309434.8
952772.8	91292.2	24054	1769339.5	1136490.7	480704.0	693752.3	298275.6
20452.9		446	19201.6	9605.4	4702.4	7543.4	3980.8
34486.6		544	35327.5	24098.0	6930.0	8085.7	2052.4
2350360.4		40131	3317673.0	660261.7	2544109.2	3571701.0	1157052.2
228758.3		2447	394371.6	175727.6	216033.8	239345.3	59409.7
70796.9		3069	142529.9	50719.1	90609.8	206453.9	137177.2

11-8 续表7

单位：万元

分 组	Item	负债合计 Total Liabilites	流动负债合计 Total Working Liabilities	非流动负债 Non-Working Liabilities
家具制造业	Manufacture of Furniture	9650.3	9204.1	403.8
造纸及纸制品业	Manufacture of Paper and Paper Products	56227.1	48309.7	5903.3
印刷业、记录媒介的复制	Printing,Reproduction of Recording Media	201538.8	158997.6	31800.0
文教、工美、体育和娱乐用品制造业	Manufacture of Articles For Cultural,Educational and Sports Activities	25239.2	18378.7	
石油加工、炼焦及核燃料加工业	Processing of Petroleum, Cokeing,Processing of Nuclear and Nuclear Fuel	361304.0	326973.6	11037.8
化学原料及化学制品制造业	Manufacture of Raw Chemical Materials and Chemical Products	870474.9	671820.2	164429.4
医药制造业	Manufacture of Medicines	354458.0	328720.1	16647.4
化学纤维制造业	Manufacture of Chemical Fibers	8349.1	8349.1	
橡胶塑料制品业	Manufacture of Rubber and Plastics	337768.1	271818.0	54626.5
非金属矿物制品业	Manufacture of Non-metallic Mineral Products	401241.0	363110.3	12301.9
黑色金属冶炼及压延加工业	Smelting and Pressing of Ferrous Metals	119017.0	106970.4	10934.5
有色金属冶炼及压延加工业	Smelting and Pressing of Non-ferrous Metals	428724.5	343585.1	45102.7
金属制品业	Manufacture of Metal Products	511578.8	395690.1	87683.6
通用设备制造业	Manufacture of General Purpose Machinery	1441911.3	1388381.2	51907.6
专用设备制造业	Manufacture of Special Equipment	1191660.3	1048448.2	122465.0
汽车制造业	Manufacture of Motor Vehicle	3543994.9	3195817.3	343596.8
铁路、船舶、航空航天和其他运输设备制造业	Railways,Shipbuilding,Aerospace and Other Transportation Equipment Manufacturing Industry	4116529.7	3509575.5	548490.7
电气机械及器材制造业	Manufacture of Electric Equipment and Machinery	2114572.2	1737815.9	373286.6
计算机、通讯和其他电子设备制造业	Manufacture of Communication Equipment, Computers and other Electronic Equipment	1738102.9	1071417.9	650936.2
仪器仪表制造业	Manufacture of Measuring Instruments and Machinery	879847.8	733489.4	144853.0
其他制造业	Manufacture of Other Manufacturing	9772.3	9772.3	
废弃资源综合利用业	Recycling and Disposal of Waste			
金属制品、机械和设备修理业	Metal Products,Machinery and Equipment Repair Industry	22573.6	18517.8	4055.8
电力、热力的生产和供应业	Production and Supply of Electric Power and Heat Power	2574164.8	1580287.7	976278.3
燃气生产和供应业	Gas Mining and Supplying Industry	211793.3	185713.9	26079.4
水的生产和供应业	Production and Supply of Water	61505.5	40537.2	20968.3

continued 7

(10 000 yuan)

所有者权益合计 Total Owners' Equities	实收资本 Total Capital Hold	营业收入 Total Revenue	主营业务收入 Revenue from Principal Business	营业成本 Total Cost	主营业务成本 Cost of Principal Business	营业税金及附加 Taxs and Other Changes	主营业务税金及附加 Taxes and Other Charges on Principal Business
14767.8	8761.9	47735.4	47440.1	36648.8	36458.5	175.1	175.1
54595.0	29398.1	250900.1	249982.9	220181.5	220107.0	995.4	995.4
329372.2	160849.8	459583.2	450492.2	331206.1	326336.9	4270.2	3770.4
8343.4	4661.0	67872.0	67872.0	58339.7	58339.7	396.3	396.3
-3788.9	75751.5	1626179.2	1624460.1	1576036.7	1575964.5	91803.7	91803.6
948516.3	365357.7	1482221.0	1416409.2	1177664.2	1128611.6	6420.6	5623.5
503544.1	214589.8	1022631.5	1019817.7	554198.8	551429.2	8780.5	8771.1
61062.6	50800.0	84663.6	84556.3	71100.9	71097.9	324.1	324.1
149486.7	115000.3	421796.4	416273.7	345339.6	332395.4	7064.5	7064.5
400293.9	168897.4	1339792.1	1332267.4	1088943.6	1082722.2	10791.7	10749.0
86830.1	43358.9	563087.0	558153.2	494898.0	487926.0	2755.4	2461.0
275970.0	119939.7	687465.8	672666.9	577568.6	563533.3	2740.9	2740.9
329229.2	129013.2	750886.9	746945.0	614547.6	608267.5	3312.6	3261.0
986631.3	176092.5	1349064.6	1334512.1	1029266.1	1018288.1	7235.7	7031.2
1174516.3	607108.7	1681345.0	1666904.5	1344574.3	1330610.7	11100.5	11000.1
2427388.8	930813.2	7362291.0	7097182.1	6569516.1	6313525.3	97456.3	97069.1
2686187.3	816621.4	3730810.2	3672258.9	3409392.9	3127438.4	15417.3	11800.3
2206051.7	463735.1	2586892.7	2486554.5	2161222.7	2082662.9	18168.1	18144.8
1194982.2	465803.2	1436582.9	1402605.2	1202616.4	1171817.3	6872.4	5568.6
889319.0	431528.9	1058235.2	1042290.8	829821.1	820104.4	6139.9	5147.1
9429.2	3620.0	19732.6	18888.4	16516.0	15871.4	156.1	156.1
12753.9	7370.4	36239.3	36159.3	29169.8	29115.1	163.8	163.7
743508.3	498763.1	2408352.3	2347204.3	2320200.0	2286299.8	9332.1	8486.4
182578.3	125180.0	265949.4	226796.1	212165.7	189837.1	1896.1	1896.1
81024.4	44545.9	76794.9	71160.3	65940.1	62862.9	742.2	718.4

11-8 续表8

单位：万元

分　　组	Item	销售费用 Expenses for Sales	管理费用 Expenses for Management
家具制造业	Manufacture of Furniture	3405.5	3100.1
造纸及纸制品业	Manufacture of Paper and Paper Products	4491.3	6469.5
印刷业、记录媒介的复制	Printing,Reproduction of Recording Media	12160.4	46198.1
文教、工美、体育和娱乐用品制造业	Manufacture of Articles For Cultural,Educational and Sports Activities	862.1	2580.5
石油加工、炼焦及核燃料加工业	Processing of Petroleum, Cokeing,Processing of Nuclear and Nuclear Fuel	8191.9	18959.5
化学原料及化学制品制造业	Manufacture of Raw Chemical Materials and Chemical Products	51756.0	137694.6
医药制造业	Manufacture of Medicines	293969.1	72051.6
化学纤维制造业	Manufacture of Chemical Fibers	210.5	2677.9
橡胶塑料制品业	Manufacture of Rubber and Plastics	21496.5	36297.9
非金属矿物制品业	Manufacture of Non-metallic Mineral Products	31987.6	32859.4
黑色金属冶炼及压延加工业	Smelting and Pressing of Ferrous Metals	7983.4	12359.2
有色金属冶炼及压延加工业	Smelting and Pressing of Non-ferrous Metals	8270.2	29175.6
金属制品业	Manufacture of Metal Products	16571.6	47681.4
通用设备制造业	Manufacture of General Purpose Machinery	56062.8	143116.7
专用设备制造业	Manufacture of Special Equipment	70209.9	133215.9
汽车制造业	Manufacture of Motor Vehicle	208139.3	210572.0
铁路、船舶、航空航天和其他运输设备制造业	Railways,Shipbuilding,Aerospace and Other Transportation Equipment Manufacturing Industry	76269.0	288992.2
电气机械及器材制造业	Manufacture of Electric Equipment and Machinery	148073.0	209679.6
计算机、通讯和其他电子设备制造业	Manufacture of Communication Equipment, Computers and other Electronic Equipment	31576.5	117244.5
仪器仪表制造业	Manufacture of Measuring Instruments and Machinery	27044.0	115621.1
其他制造业	Manufacture of Other Manufacturing	528.2	1553.8
废弃资源综合利用业	Recycling and Disposal of Waste		
金属制品、机械和设备修理业	Metal Products,Machinery and Equipment Repair Industry	1745.8	3154.5
电力、热力的生产和供应业	Production and Supply of Electric Power and Heat Power	1007.2	96119.4
燃气生产和供应业	Gas Mining and Supplying Industry	9286.4	15393.9
水的生产和供应业	Production and Supply of Water	3129.6	7977.1

continued 8

(10 000 yuan)

财务费用 Financial cost	营业利润 Operating Profit	利润总额 Total Profits	亏损企业亏损总额 Total Loss of Deficit Enterprises	利税总额 Total Pre-tax Profits	应付职工薪酬 Salary Payable	本年应交增值税 Value Added Tax Payable
240.1	3251.4	3245.6		5061.2	4086.5	1640.5
1592.5	16134.9	13229.1	55.4	19515.3	24228.1	5290.8
3673.7	65385.5	65342.7	2274.9	95898.4	62312.2	26285.5
351.9	4275.4	4157.6	258.5	5586.1	4232.2	1032.2
7087.3	13585.4	-87310.4	90681.0	13129.3	12705.8	8636.0
13596.8	115713.4	130116.9	21722.5	185923.7	146999.3	49386.2
13751.6	83890.5	98784.1	913.1	217532.4	105817.3	109967.8
-137.3	10975.4	10976.2	84.9	13733.9	3926.1	2433.6
8281.1	19548.4	19736.4	318.0	38530.2	43883.5	11729.3
7456.3	166709.9	165018.7	3514.4	247884.3	49156.6	72073.9
3617.2	41345.8	39351.6	1461.0	57474.6	22264.0	15367.6
15700.2	50809.3	51037.4	2877.7	78424.0	33228.3	24645.7
9644.8	63935.2	60515.1	1216.1	81678.1	82226.9	17850.4
-3886.2	126016.2	131282.7	2431.7	191146.0	137750.1	52627.6
9722.1	134619.4	130459.5	9253.3	206872.9	146405.9	65312.9
34745.7	269059.5	273848.5	7521.2	523620.0	369068.7	152315.2
48537.1	137912.8	185607.2	2874.2	255206.3	466428.8	54181.8
22972.1	27764.3	17089.9	69878.5	139462.5	244949.8	104204.5
14675.4	76476.2	92530.6	26882.7	126994.2	128946.0	27591.2
5711.5	72557.1	79225.3	2146.1	140429.5	202369.2	55064.3
220.1	753.8	996.4		1929.8	1116.2	777.3
779.4	1382.7	1552.0	242.5	3023.4	2641.4	1307.6
71972.5	17065.7	29371.7	28087.0	107749.4	149241.5	69045.6
-2332.9	29415.0	28594.1		37081.9	24549.1	6591.7
277.3	-1236.1	2481.0		7456.8	16980.0	4233.6

11-9 规模以上国有及国有控股工业企业主要经济指标（2011年）

单位：万元

分　　组	Item	企业单位数（个）Number of Enterprises (unit)	亏损企业 Loss Making Enterprises	工业总产值（当年价）Gross Industrial Output Value (At Current Prices)
总　　计	**Total**	**196**	**40**	**20400206.2**
#亏损企业	Deficit Enterprises	40	40	3537825.4
按隶属关系分	Grouped by Jurisdiction of Management			
中央企业	Central Enterprises	70	12	10447280.6
省属企业	Provincial Enterprises	42	7	6701663.7
市属企业	Municipal Enterprises	84	21	3251261.9
按轻重工业分	Grouped by Light Industry and Heavy Industry			
轻工业	Light Industry	36	8	1030609.0
重工业	Heavy Industry	160	32	19369597.2
按企业规模分	Grouped by Size of Enterprises			
大型工业	Large-size	44	6	15173159.3
中型工业	Medium-size	67	19	3284195.0
小型工业	Small-size	85	15	1942851.9
按工业行业大类分	Grouped by Sector			
煤炭开采和洗选业	Mining and Washing of Coal			
石油和天然气开采业	Extraction of Petroleum and Natural Gas			
黑色金属矿采选业	Mining and Processing of Ferrous Metal Ores			
有色金属矿采选业	Mining and Processing of Non-ferrous Metal Ores			
非金属矿采选业	Mining and Processing of Nonmetal Ores			
开采辅助活动	Mining Auxiliary Activities	1		7438.5
其他采矿业	Mining of Other Ores			
农副食品加工业	Processing of Food from Agricultural Porducts	3	1	25615.1
食品制造业	Manufacture of Foods	4	1	246574.7
酒、饮料和精制茶制造业	Manufacture of Alcohol,Beverages and Tea	2	1	95022.8
烟草加工业	Manufacture of Tobacco	1		4624.0
纺织业	Manufacture of Textile	6	3	133921.7
纺织服装、鞋、帽制造业	Manufacture of Textile Wearing Apparel, Footwear and Caps	1		5880.0
皮革、毛皮、羽毛(绒)及其制品业	Manufacture of Leather, Fur, Feather (eiderdown) and Related Products	1		19701.9
木材加工及竹、藤、棕、草制品业	Processing of Timber,Manufacture of Wood,Plam and Straw Products			

Economic Indicators of all State-owned and State-holding Share Industrial Enterprises above Designated Size（2011）

（10 000 yuan）

工业销售产值（当年价）Value of Industry Products Sales (At Current Prices)	出口交货值 Export Delivery Value	从业人员年平均人数（人）Annual Average Employers (person)	资产总计 Total Assets	流动资产合计 Total Working Capitals	固定资产合计 Total Fixed Assets	固定资产原价 Origing Value of Fixed Assets	累计折旧 Accumulative Total Depreciation
19949364.2	**1125840.5**	**317753**	**29370875.4**	**17104195.9**	**9733866.9**	**12087661.9**	**4691189.3**
3474886.2	192746.0	53609	6673725.6	3612407.3	2489398.6	2709696.3	952660.9
10207803.9	618858.6	178025	17320385.8	9653046.0	6801311.7	8449101.6	3185661.5
6542960.7	354336.1	76201	6130827.6	3832918.6	1466918.8	1690467.2	678462.2
3198599.6	152645.8	63527	5919662.0	3618231.3	1465636.4	1948093.1	827065.6
1155679.4	27103.0	28032	1034556.5	515302.7	380357.9	772320.0	445428.8
18793684.8	1098737.5	289721	28336318.9	16588893.2	9353509.0	11315341.9	4245760.5
14801289.8	973406.2	245868	22596205.2	13671547.5	7242638.3	8755574.8	3517025.7
3270773.5	116429.8	59297	5326532.7	2443463.9	2143130.3	2798987.8	950016.7
1877300.9	36004.5	12588	1448137.5	989184.5	348098.3	533099.3	224146.9
8067.4		103	6656.8	5255.2	1170.8	1688.3	517.5
24167.8	5027.6	751	49748.1	19520.2	25065.8	31656.8	6739.8
242715.6		2349	53455.2	22168.5	27389.6	56504.9	29144.9
230280.4		832	147727.8	97714.9	22688.5	54603.2	32879.7
4830.8		230	11650.1	8625.6	2406.5	4795.1	2388.6
124386.5	21014.9	13365	134085.6	69064.7	27559.4	70152.2	44987.8
5880.0		112	2861.8	2723.5	42.4	60.7	18.3
22174.8		724	37946.1	12599.9	3621.7	5350.7	1729.0

11-9 续表1

单位：万元

分　组	Item	负债合计 Total Liabilites	流动负债合计 Total Working Liabilities	非流动负债 Non-Working Liabilities
总　计	**Total**	**17532741.4**	**14054531.0**	**3294625.3**
#亏损企业	Deficit Enterprises	3884533.4	2601957.2	1244489.6
按隶属关系分	Grouped by Jurisdiction of Management			
中央企业	Central Enterprises	10087509.1	7966137.3	2035484.7
省属企业	Provincial Enterprises	3852237.9	3342836.8	460340.3
市属企业	Municipal Enterprises	3592994.4	2745556.9	798800.3
按轻重工业分	Grouped by Light Industry and Heavy Industry			
轻工业	Light Industry	415615.7	354023.0	54616.8
重工业	Heavy Industry	17117125.7	13700508.0	3240008.5
按企业规模分	Grouped by Size of Enterprises			
大型工业	Large-size	13276111.8	11055580.5	2149320.8
中型工业	Medium-size	3223703.4	2079873.3	1081664.4
小型工业	Small-size	1032926.2	919077.2	63640.1
按工业行业大类分	Grouped by Sector			
煤炭开采和洗选业	Mining and Washing of Coal			
石油和天然气开采业	Extraction of Petroleum and Natural Gas			
黑色金属矿采选业	Mining and Processing of Ferrous Metal Ores			
有色金属矿采选业	Mining and Processing of Non-ferrous Metal Ores			
非金属矿采选业	Mining and Processing of Nonmetal Ores			
开采辅助活动	Mining Auxiliary Activities	3579.4	3579.4	
其他采矿业	Mining of Other Ores			
农副食品加工业	Processing of Food from Agricultural Porducts	26567.5	20171.9	
食品制造业	Manufacture of Foods	31615.9	29013.8	2602.0
酒、饮料和精制茶制造业	Manufacture of Alcohol,Beverages and Tea	69362.3	69232.3	130.0
烟草加工业	Manufacture of Tobacco	6403.4	6403.4	
纺织业	Manufacture of Textile	58142.7	51510.6	6052.1
纺织服装、鞋、帽制造业	Manufacture of Textile Wearing Apparel, Footwear and Caps	1149.2	1088.2	61.0
皮革、毛皮、羽毛(绒)及其制品业	Manufacture of Leather, Fur, Feather (eiderdown) and Related Products	18895.8	11378.9	7516.9
木材加工及竹、藤、棕、草制品业	Processing of Timber,Manufacture of Wood,Plam and Straw Products			

continued 1

(10 000 yuan)

所有者权益合计 Total Owners' Equities	实收资本 Total Capital Hold	营业收入 Total Revenue	主营业务收入 Revenue from Principal Business	营业成本 Total Cost	主营业务成本 Cost of Principal Business	营业税金及附加 Taxs and Other Changes	主营业务税金及附加 Taxes and Other Charges on Principal Business
11836113.1	**4298055.5**	**19970683.7**	**19456417.5**	**17642541.7**	**16982665.0**	**188883.5**	**172155.5**
2788327.2	834647.7	3312976.3	3156336.3	3009401.7	2905649.1	110861.8	110205.7
7232875.2	2328591.8	10654422.7	10459358.7	9562098.1	9179025.3	139513.1	134456.2
2276606.2	923913.4	6070450.3	5882725.0	5469111.0	5302125.2	14733.3	14206.3
2326631.7	1045550.3	3245810.7	3114333.8	2611332.6	2501514.5	34637.1	23493.0
618911.1	345469.5	1188915.1	1150337.0	951187.5	910136.9	15793.8	6248.8
11217202.0	3952586.0	18781768.6	18306080.5	16691354.2	16072528.1	173089.7	165906.7
9320091.9	2866869.7	14744490.5	14398653.8	13031109.4	12527027.9	158651.7	153171.3
2102799.4	1097329.8	3312877.0	3193453.7	2874561.2	2763892.9	22733.4	13013.7
413221.8	333856.0	1913316.2	1864310.0	1736871.1	1691744.2	7498.4	5970.5
3077.4	1800.0	8067.4	8067.4	5880.3	5880.3	28.8	28.8
23150.9	12152.7	24332.0	23494.0	19331.2	19095.4	150.6	150.6
21839.3	22835.1	243394.1	241964.4	200658.2	199822.5	678.7	591.3
78365.5	31481.5	231005.2	230292.2	181429.8	180946.8	9231.2	58.0
5246.7	1514.7	7194.8	6975.1	4705.1	4549.5	71.2	71.2
75942.8	15812.9	127656.2	125949.6	122275.6	114386.3	938.3	700.3
1712.6	1000.0	5933.6	5879.8	5425.3	5410.3	14.7	14.7
19050.3	6000.0	43630.1	22401.2	40619.4	19556.2	58.3	58.3

11–9 续表2

单位：万元

分　　组	Item	销售费用 Expenses for Sales	管理费用 Expenses for Management
总　　计	**Total**	**579822.6**	**1289559.8**
#亏损企业	Deficit Enterprises	137481.0	244644.8
按隶属关系分	Grouped by Jurisdiction of Management		
中央企业	Central Enterprises	235036.1	792047.9
省属企业	Provincial Enterprises	201591.4	229594.0
市属企业	Municipal Enterprises	143195.1	267917.9
按轻重工业分	Grouped by Light Industry and Heavy Industry		
轻工业	Light Industry	60944.9	83083.3
重工业	Heavy Industry	518877.7	1206476.5
按企业规模分	Grouped by Size of Enterprises		
大型工业	Large-size	469112.0	988689.0
中型工业	Medium-size	79388.5	236632.3
小型工业	Small-size	31322.1	64238.5
按工业行业大类分	Grouped by Sector		
煤炭开采和洗选业	Mining and Washing of Coal		
石油和天然气开采业	Extraction of Petroleum and Natural Gas		
黑色金属矿采选业	Mining and Processing of Ferrous Metal Ores		
有色金属矿采选业	Mining and Processing of Non-ferrous Metal Ores		
非金属矿采选业	Mining and Processing of Nonmetal Ores		
开采辅助活动	Mining Auxiliary Activities	523.6	609.7
其他采矿业	Mining of Other Ores		
农副食品加工业	Processing of Food from Agricultural Porducts	983.5	1592.6
食品制造业	Manufacture of Foods	27422.8	15405.7
酒、饮料和精制茶制造业	Manufacture of Alcohol,Beverages and Tea	13631.7	6071.6
烟草加工业	Manufacture of Tobacco	88.7	1671.6
纺织业	Manufacture of Textile	1771.8	11156.1
纺织服装、鞋、帽制造业	Manufacture of Textile Wearing Apparel, Footwear and Caps	50.0	209.9
皮革、毛皮、羽毛(绒)及其制品业	Manufacture of Leather, Fur, Feather (eiderdown) and Related Products	709.5	863.0
木材加工及竹、藤、棕、草制品业	Processing of Timber,Manufacture of Wood,Plam and Straw Products		

continued 2

（10 000 yuan）

财务费用 Financial cost	营业利润 Operating Profit	利润总额 Total Profits	亏损企业亏损总额 Total Loss of Deficit Enterprises	利税总额 Total Pre-tax Profits	应付职工薪酬 Salary Payable	本年应交增值税 Value Added Tax Payable
194870.2	**604807.8**	**589745.4**	**246922.7**	**1294758.5**	**1865064.9**	**516129.6**
55968.6	-243830.3	-246922.7	246922.7	-38516.2	340547.2	97544.7
149968.7	141983.5	208653.8	196814.9	612533.9	1202643.1	264367.0
36195.7	220222.2	139889.2	8505.7	265697.5	308008.4	111075.0
8705.8	242602.1	241202.4	41602.1	416527.1	354413.4	140687.6
1472.8	98792.8	97740.4	4648.2	163120.8	135630.5	49586.6
193397.4	506015.0	492005.0	242274.5	1131637.7	1729434.4	466543.0
132571.6	275092.8	334053.2	188298.3	852518.7	1530980.0	359813.8
52656.4	174006.0	192589.4	48781.4	320314.5	266447.0	104991.7
9642.2	155709.0	63102.8	9843.0	121925.3	67637.9	51324.1
1.1	1023.9	907.1		1285.9	303.0	350.0
843.2	1331.3	2321.3	199.6	3381.2	2448.8	909.3
-22.3	9492.1	-196.7	1637.4	4763.4	7502.5	4281.4
-1581.9	23041.4	23132.2	9.5	42284.0	12924.0	9920.6
-2.7	666.4	668.4		1336.1	2008.5	596.5
444.8	-1972.3	958.2	2536.2	7663.2	35570.0	5766.7
17.4	176.7	192.5		341.2	652.5	134.0
215.4	1326.2	1410.8		1469.1	3437.3	

11-9 续表3

单位：万元

分组	Item	企业单位数(个) Number of Enterprises (unit)	亏损企业 Loss Making Enterprises	工业总产值（当年价） Gross Industrial Output Value (At Current Prices)
家具制造业	Manufacture of Furniture			
造纸及纸制品业	Manufacture of Paper and Paper Products			
印刷业、记录媒介的复制	Printing,Reproduction of Recording Media	4		241179.6
文教、工美、体育和娱乐用品制造业	Manufacture of Articles For Cultural,Educational and Sports Activities			
石油加工、炼焦及核燃料加工业	Processing of Petroleum, Cokeing,Processing of Nuclear and Nuclear Fuel	2	1	1597042.0
化学原料及化学制品制造业	Manufacture of Raw Chemical Materials and Chemical Products	14	3	829762.7
医药制造业	Manufacture of Medicines	4		55339.3
化学纤维制造业	Manufacture of Chemical Fibers	2	1	85301.8
橡胶和塑料制品业	Manufacture of Rubber and Plastics	4	1	180553.7
非金属矿物制品业	Manufacture of Non-metallic Mineral Products	12	4	84731.4
黑色金属冶炼及压延加工业	Smelting and Pressing of Ferrous Metals	2	1	110874.1
有色金属冶炼及压延加工业	Smelting and Pressing of Non-ferrous Metals	8	1	333472.3
金属制品业	Manufacture of Metal Products	10	1	352072.8
通用设备制造业	Manufacture of General Purpose Machinery	8	2	1019265.2
专用设备制造业	Manufacture of Special Equipment	22	3	1016851.2
汽车制造业	Manufacture of Motor Vehicle	7	1	4926197.7
铁路、船舶、航空航天和其他运输设备制造业	Railways,Shipbuilding,Aerospace and Other Transportation Equipment Manufacturing Industry	24	2	3107891.9
电气机械及器材制造业	Manufacture of Electric Equipment and Machinery	12	3	1829861.0
计算机、通讯和其他电子设备制造业	Manufacture of Communication Equipment, Computers and other Electronic Equipment	18	2	786233.8
仪器仪表制造业	Manufacture of Measuring Instruments and Machinery	9		722189.6
其他制造业	Manufacture of Other Manufacturing			
废弃资源综合利用业	Recycling and Disposal of Waste			
金属制品、机械和设备修理业	Metal Products,Machinery and Equipment Repair Industry			
电力、热力的生产和供应业	Production and Supply of Electric Power and Heat Power	11	8	2324103.5
燃气生产和供应业	Gas Mining and Supplying Industry	1		187707.0
水的生产和供应业	Production and Supply of Water	3		70796.9

continued 3

(10 000 yuan)

工业销售产值（当年价）Value of Industry Products Sales (At Current Prices)	出口交货值 Export Delivery Value	从业人员年平均人数（人）Annual Average Employers (person)	资产总计 Total Assets	流动资产合计 Total Working Capitals	固定资产合计 Total Fixed Assets	固定资产原价 Origing Value of Fixed Assets	累计折旧 Accumulative Total Depreciation
249164.7	1060.5	3267	293532.3	154543.0	113420.3	198970.1	114145.0
1610508.0		1706	325769.1	163453.6	140380.3	226544.6	136132.7
815898.9	72540.6	28051	1366925.7	626458.9	604731.3	823437.5	336093.6
53177.0		1480	44562.1	26761.5	13337.2	22986.0	9648.8
84652.9		435	69411.7	27189.0	32645.5	68658.8	36013.3
180361.3	1954.0	10392	338040.1	171147.1	101512.7	100538.3	36940.9
82079.6		2293	106552.5	74302.1	24979.9	32629.9	11391.8
110874.1		973	39710.7	29634.8	9512.9	10825.5	2172.5
311032.1	19664.0	2684	333660.8	198526.8	113633.9	131965.8	33524.4
351808.6	18892.4	8765	595311.2	374282.1	184056.3	252454.5	104855.8
968763.0	11024.7	11553	2039038.8	1680583.2	223727.2	305103.2	106286.6
900627.4	51549.1	14787	1567432.3	1133470.4	297383.0	426460.7	143052.8
4855123.6	305108.9	44719	4356384.6	2634160.3	1094498.1	1134231.4	441723.1
3013916.1	395173.8	65128	6593611.2	4313775.8	1856413.1	2110582.7	929193.3
1764300.3	122617.9	21921	3449218.0	2474373.2	970653.7	873231.7	333525.2
688846.2	58825.1	17021	2271184.9	1091500.7	624568.2	597050.8	200805.2
649689.1	41387.0	19065	1385867.7	837306.4	426920.7	617495.7	274252.1
2337534.1		39964	3296128.7	653371.7	2540030.2	3562862.8	1152293.0
187707.0		2014	311871.6	150963.7	160907.9	160366.1	33556.4
70796.9		3069	142529.9	50719.1	90609.8	206453.9	137177.2

11-9 续表4

单位：万元

分组	Item	负债合计 Total Liabilites	流动负债合计 Total Working Liabilities	非流动负债 Non-Working Liabilities
家具制造业	Manufacture of Furniture			
造纸及纸制品业	Manufacture of Paper and Paper Products			
印刷业、记录媒介的复制	Printing,Reproduction of Recording Media	69931.5	53650.5	16280.9
文教、工美、体育和娱乐用品制造业	Manufacture of Articles For Cultural,Educational and Sports Activities			
石油加工、炼焦及核燃料加工业	Processing of Petroleum, Cokeing,Processing of Nuclear and Nuclear Fuel	340544.4	306214.0	11037.8
化学原料及化学制品制造业	Manufacture of Raw Chemical Materials and Chemical Products	610305.0	433383.2	143361.7
医药制造业	Manufacture of Medicines	19234.9	18846.9	388.0
化学纤维制造业	Manufacture of Chemical Fibers	8349.1	8349.1	
橡胶和塑料制品业	Manufacture of Rubber and Plastics	249767.4	200815.6	48951.8
非金属矿物制品业	Manufacture of Non-metallic Mineral Products	78208.6	69896.6	1005.9
黑色金属冶炼及压延加工业	Smelting and Pressing of Ferrous Metals	29362.3	29362.3	
有色金属冶炼及压延加工业	Smelting and Pressing of Non-ferrous Metals	231460.4	198967.7	32492.7
金属制品业	Manufacture of Metal Products	390981.1	291741.3	76421.6
通用设备制造业	Manufacture of General Purpose Machinery	1234133.3	1193012.7	41120.6
专用设备制造业	Manufacture of Special Equipment	832973.0	756292.7	63802.6
汽车制造业	Manufacture of Motor Vehicle	2568293.8	2305120.1	263129.0
铁路、船舶、航空航天和其他运输设备制造业	Railways,Shipbuilding,Aerospace and Other Transportation Equipment Manufacturing Industry	4015660.2	3409705.1	547491.6
电气机械及器材制造业	Manufacture of Electric Equipment and Machinery	1667118.2	1352583.8	314042.9
计算机、通讯和其他电子设备制造业	Manufacture of Communication Equipment, Computers and other Electronic Equipment	1427107.2	858528.0	565628.8
仪器仪表制造业	Manufacture of Measuring Instruments and Machinery	725030.1	592137.8	132825.8
其他制造业	Manufacture of Other Manufacturing			
废弃资源综合利用业	Recycling and Disposal of Waste			
金属制品、机械和设备修理业	Metal Products,Machinery and Equipment Repair Industry			
电力、热力的生产和供应业	Production and Supply of Electric Power and Heat Power	2570354.9	1579384.5	976232.4
燃气生产和供应业	Gas Mining and Supplying Industry	186704.3	163623.4	23080.9
水的生产和供应业	Production and Supply of Water	61505.5	40537.2	20968.3

continued 4

(10 000 yuan)

所有者权益合计 Total Owners' Equities	实收资本 Total Capital Hold	营业收入 Total Revenue	主营业务收入 Revenue from Principal Business	营业成本 Total Cost	主营业务成本 Cost of Principal Business	营业税金及附加 Taxs and Other Changes	主营业务税金及附加 Taxes and Other Charges on Principal Business
223600.8	102584.4	250577.3	246984.1	167263.4	164300.1	3136.6	3136.6
-14775.3	65910.9	1589357.2	1587703.3	1544042.9	1544035.9	91720.7	91720.6
756180.8	294393.9	864111.4	807043.9	705732.0	658521.2	4091.9	3303.9
25327.2	15402.3	47572.7	47434.3	33162.9	30875.1	245.1	245.1
61062.6	50800.0	84663.6	84556.3	71100.9	71097.9	324.1	324.1
88272.7	71970.4	184213.8	180239.4	157041.5	146955.9	6111.2	6111.2
27479.0	21469.4	80930.0	79923.8	71764.3	70517.2	562.6	531.3
10348.4	10500.0	127319.2	123899.7	125287.9	119786.2	188.4	66.3
102200.3	59025.7	248977.6	234684.3	189770.3	176016.0	724.5	724.5
204329.9	84716.5	311005.1	307516.7	260311.6	254367.8	658.2	606.6
804905.3	70250.3	865619.1	853074.2	634369.5	624082.2	5180.6	4982.8
734045.8	414907.4	950504.8	942536.8	752317.0	746861.4	6795.9	6750.2
1788090.8	726447.2	4314713.6	4190989.8	3877248.7	3760885.2	10134.7	10065.9
2577944.7	772796.1	3550928.2	3494433.4	3277585.8	2996731.3	13787.4	10170.4
1782099.7	215851.3	1543938.8	1470879.9	1304663.3	1254189.5	14642.5	14619.9
843811.8	258525.6	806575.5	798251.0	702375.7	692173.9	3696.1	3136.5
660837.5	340989.0	759632.8	748349.2	632655.9	625403.7	3902.7	3047.4
725773.9	484372.3	2395526.0	2334378.0	2309836.3	2275936.1	9292.8	8447.1
125167.3	100000.0	226508.7	187355.4	179746.8	157418.2	1773.5	1773.5
81024.4	44545.9	76794.9	71160.3	65940.1	62862.9	742.2	718.4

11-9 续表5

单位：万元

分　组	Item	销售费用 Expenses for Sales	管理费用 Expenses for Management
家具制造业	Manufacture of Furniture		
造纸及纸制品业	Manufacture of Paper and Paper Products		
印刷业、记录媒介的复制	Printing,Reproduction of Recording Media	5505.0	27363.1
文教、工美、体育和娱乐用品制造业	Manufacture of Articles For Cultural,Educational and Sports Activities		
石油加工、炼焦及核燃料加工业	Processing of Petroleum, Cokeing,Processing of Nuclear and Nuclear Fuel	6591.6	17420.8
化学原料及化学制品制造业	Manufacture of Raw Chemical Materials and Chemical Products	20558.9	96335.8
医药制造业	Manufacture of Medicines	5724.5	3676.4
化学纤维制造业	Manufacture of Chemical Fibers	210.5	2677.9
橡胶和塑料制品业	Manufacture of Rubber and Plastics	14670.4	9018.1
非金属矿物制品业	Manufacture of Non-metallic Mineral Products	1329.9	3875.2
黑色金属冶炼及压延加工业	Smelting and Pressing of Ferrous Metals	529.3	1879.9
有色金属冶炼及压延加工业	Smelting and Pressing of Non-ferrous Metals	2941.0	15729.5
金属制品业	Manufacture of Metal Products	5755.4	29809.3
通用设备制造业	Manufacture of General Purpose Machinery	27220.2	119617.6
专用设备制造业	Manufacture of Special Equipment	38591.5	81732.4
汽车制造业	Manufacture of Motor Vehicle	173917.5	140321.9
铁路、船舶、航空航天和其他运输设备制造业	Railways,Shipbuilding,Aerospace and Other Transportation Equipment Manufacturing Industry	71171.6	274678.0
电气机械及器材制造业	Manufacture of Electric Equipment and Machinery	114288.0	149236.2
计算机、通讯和其他电子设备制造业	Manufacture of Communication Equipment, Computers and other Electronic Equipment	23012.9	76633.3
仪器仪表制造业	Manufacture of Measuring Instruments and Machinery	10199.4	84730.9
其他制造业	Manufacture of Other Manufacturing		
废弃资源综合利用业	Recycling and Disposal of Waste		
金属制品、机械和设备修理业	Metal Products,Machinery and Equipment Repair Industry		
电力、热力的生产和供应业	Production and Supply of Electric Power and Heat Power	895.8	95792.9
燃气生产和供应业	Gas Mining and Supplying Industry	8398.0	13473.3
水的生产和供应业	Production and Supply of Water	3129.6	7977.1

continued 5

（10 000 yuan）

财务费用 Financial cost	营业利润 Operating Profit	利润总额 Total Profits	亏损企业亏损总额 Total Loss of Deficit Enterprises	利税总额 Total Pre-tax Profits	应付职工薪酬 Salary Payable	本年应交增值税 Value Added Tax Payable
133.0	47802.3	47775.8		65941.2	38036.1	15028.8
6621.1	11752.5	-88321.1	90660.4	10932.9	11994.5	7533.3
6508.0	36971.5	51509.9	21373.1	86776.5	124169.2	31174.7
734.6	6547.9	6406.4		9132.3	5136.7	2480.8
-137.3	10975.4	10976.2	84.9	13733.9	3926.1	2433.6
3917.3	4942.0	5404.7	152.1	16129.6	32034.9	4613.7
158.6	719.6	495.1	687.7	3620.2	5205.6	2562.5
511.5	951.4	1088.9	1026.7	7781.4	3556.9	6504.1
7685.5	28890.6	29482.0	707.9	41835.4	17019.7	11628.9
8055.5	21853.0	20760.3	457.3	25037.8	50684.2	3619.3
-6579.7	98498.9	104288.5	1944.5	147588.4	109474.3	38119.3
5677.9	75043.4	71942.2	7897.0	117914.9	96029.8	39176.8
19859.1	99837.3	103031.3	3756.1	203646.4	215580.0	90480.4
48247.3	112481.0	159706.5	1618.4	215868.0	454112.6	42374.1
10227.7	-48574.0	-58638.7	65776.3	15061.7	185610.6	59057.9
9334.5	1169.8	12712.3	18310.6	32747.3	88328.1	16338.9
4467.4	21611.2	28049.4		74758.0	172156.8	42805.9
71877.5	14108.6	26415.7	28087.0	104177.9	148371.6	68469.4
-2621.6	25375.8	24785.2		32093.8	21810.6	5535.1
277.3	-1236.1	2481.0		7456.8	16980.0	4233.6

11-10 规模以上股份制工业企业主要经济指标（2011年）

单位：万元

分　　组	Item	企业单位数（个） Number of Enterprises (unit)	工业总产值（当年价） Gross Industrial Output Value (At Current Prices)
总　　计	**Total**	**713**	**25920663.9**
#亏损企业	Deficit Enterprises	114	166.0
按隶属关系分	Grouped by Jurisdiction of Management		
中央企业	Central Enterprises	39	4387099.9
省属企业	Provincial Enterprises	60	7704225.0
市属企业	Municipal Enterprises	614	13829339.0
按轻重工业分	Grouped by Light Industry and Heavy Industry		
轻工业	Light Industry	208	5328461.3
重工业	Heavy Industry	505	20592202.6
按企业规模分	Grouped by Size of Enterprises		
大型工业	Large-size	42	14484804.5
中型工业	Medium-size	113	4220138.2
小型工业	Small-size	558	7215721.2
按工业行业大类分	Grouped by Sector		
煤炭开采和洗选业	Mining and Washing of Coal		
石油和天然气开采业	Extraction of Petroleum and Natural Gas		
黑色金属矿采选业	Mining and Processing of Ferrous Metal Ores	1	2223.0
有色金属矿采选业	Mining and Processing of Non-ferrous Metal Ores		
非金属矿采选业	Mining and Processing of Nonmetal Ores		
开采辅助活动	Mining Auxiliary Activities	2	36315.5
其他采矿业	Mining of Other Ores		
农副食品加工业	Processing of Food from Agricultural Porducts	44	1428855.9
食品制造业	Manufacture of Foods	21	468474.4
酒、饮料和精制茶制造业	Manufacture of Alcohol,Beverages and Tea	10	598690.8
烟草加工业	Manufacture of Tobacco		
纺织业	Manufacture of Textile	9	166313.4
纺织服装、鞋、帽制造业	Manufacture of Textile Wearing Apparel, Footwear and Caps	5	86680.9
皮革、毛皮、羽毛(绒)及其制品业	Manufacture of Leather, Fur, Feather (eiderdown) and Related Products		
木材加工及竹、藤、棕、草制品业	Processing of Timber,Manufacture of Wood,Plam and Straw Products	5	99359.0

Main Indicators of Share-holding Corporation Industrial Enterprises Above Designated Size（2011）

（10 000 yuan）

工业销售产值（当年价） Value of Industry Products Sales (At Current Prices)	出口交货值 Export Delivery Value	从业人员年平均人数（人） Annual Average Employers (person)	资产总计 Total Assets	流动资产合计 Total Working Capitals	固定资产合计 Total Fixed Assets	固定资产原价 Origing Value of Fixed Assets	累计折旧 Accumulative Total Depreciation
25229757.9	**1558275.5**	**37**	**26910628.6**	**16160363.3**	**7816730.2**	**9966500.6**	**3946587.3**
157.3	9.9	4	329.8	154.7	111.5	138.4	53.0
4295204.9	473963.9	102669	9019901.2	5662829.0	2778460.3	3302125.5	1383677.9
7588288.1	548160.1	81107	6563500.0	4167378.8	1629957.8	1961118.1	782534.8
13346264.9	536151.5	186330	11327227.4	6330155.5	3408312.1	4703257.0	1780374.6
5304197.1	338614.3	74668	3609187.4	1953724.5	1164962.9	2033878.0	958375.1
19925560.8	1219661.2	295438	23301441.2	14206638.8	6651767.3	7932622.6	2988212.2
14177517.0	1127244.7	217085	16712246.7	10003176.6	5120073.7	6164322.6	2476320.5
4117056.2	317333.4	80887	5417208.8	3105125.4	1378980.3	1751131.8	668794.0
6935184.7	113697.4	72134	4781173.1	3052061.3	1317676.2	2051046.2	801472.8
2122.5		120	2062.6	1399.9	468.9	1078.9	615.1
36944.4		741	54029.5	35594.7	11434.6	18600.6	7166.0
1370749.3	5027.6	8394	562732.1	364351.1	161329.2	290200.5	137495.4
455423.4	218.5	6930	200255.4	70894.9	74833.3	115691.0	43169.2
742703.6	184938.0	6037	747429.5	355444.5	276491.8	427898.3	152033.8
154803.6	25830.8	13514	159171.2	78446.8	51498.2	98656.5	47226.5
86231.9		2015	81473.9	64216.1	16369.8	19056.3	7614.6
92701.9		900	113906.1	49152.0	56343.2	86057.7	30909.9

11-10 续表1

单位：万元

分组	Item	负债合计 Total Liabilites	流动负债合计 Total Working Liabilities	非流动负债 Non-Working Liabilities
总　计	**Total**	**15187459.6**	**12813500.7**	**2091142.1**
#亏损企业	Deficit Enterprises	204.1	133.9	64.1
按隶属关系分	Grouped by Jurisdiction of Management			
中央企业	Central Enterprises	5095555.4	4267799.9	744087.4
省属企业	Provincial Enterprises	4100974.2	3668093.5	387314.8
市属企业	Municipal Enterprises	5990930.0	4877607.3	959739.9
按轻重工业分	Grouped by Light Industry and Heavy Industry			
轻工业	Light Industry	1842580.7	1687847.2	108331.8
重工业	Heavy Industry	13344878.9	11125653.5	1982810.3
按企业规模分	Grouped by Size of Enterprises			
大型工业	Large-size	9713502.8	8437662.8	1168567.0
中型工业	Medium-size	2811862.0	2030449.0	720972.5
小型工业	Small-size	2662094.8	2345388.9	201602.6
按工业行业大类分	Grouped by Sector			
煤炭开采和洗选业	Mining and Washing of Coal			
石油和天然气开采业	Extraction of Petroleum and Natural Gas			
黑色金属矿采选业	Mining and Processing of Ferrous Metal Ores	2996.7	608.4	
有色金属矿采选业	Mining and Processing of Non-ferrous Metal Ores			
非金属矿采选业	Mining and Processing of Nonmetal Ores			
开采辅助活动	Mining Auxiliary Activities	15540.8	15540.8	
其他采矿业	Mining of Other Ores			
农副食品加工业	Processing of Food from Agricultural Porducts	368215.4	353200.8	7053.4
食品制造业	Manufacture of Foods	103387.7	92502.9	10884.7
酒、饮料和精制茶制造业	Manufacture of Alcohol,Beverages and Tea	443054.9	431598.3	11456.6
烟草加工业	Manufacture of Tobacco			
纺织业	Manufacture of Textile	59576.2	57849.6	1144.2
纺织服装、鞋、帽制造业	Manufacture of Textile Wearing Apparel, Footwear and Caps	62086.5	51906.0	10119.3
皮革、毛皮、羽毛(绒)及其制品业	Manufacture of Leather, Fur, Feather (eiderdown) and Related Products			
木材加工及竹、藤、棕、草制品业	Processing of Timber,Manufacture of Wood,Plam and Straw Products	36041.1	16255.2	19000.0

continued 1

(10 000 yuan)

所有者权益合计 Total Owners' Equities	实收资本 Total Capital Hold	营业收入 Total Revenue	主营业务收入 Revenue from Principal Business	营业成本 Total Cost	主营业务成本 Cost of Principal Business	营业税金及附加 Taxs and Other Changes	主营业务税金及附加 Taxes and Other Charges on Principal Business
11708177.4	**4866632.6**	**25442882.4**	**24850440.0**	**21698231.2**	**20966751.3**	**194604.9**	**178236.7**
125.5	75.1	161.6	153.2	150.3	144.2	0.7	0.6
3924345.2	1324393.0	4934513.6	4857660.9	4387920.3	4095199.3	18730.7	15265.5
2460542.3	1027221.9	7158104.1	6995385.9	6247865.2	6110697.4	22904.8	22689.4
5323289.9	2515017.7	13350264.7	12997393.2	11062445.7	10760854.6	152969.4	140281.8
1763379.9	873237.0	5200194.0	5143966.2	4149574.0	4106742.3	35162.8	24837.3
9944797.5	3993395.6	20242688.4	19706473.8	17548657.2	16860009.0	159442.1	153399.4
6998743.4	2417654.6	14427719.2	14004770.4	12557866.9	11983637.8	129865.5	125449.3
2599212.6	1167342.0	4079029.0	3971301.8	3366231.2	3266159.5	27766.1	17983.8
2110221.4	1281636.0	6936134.2	6874367.8	5774133.1	5716954.0	36973.3	34803.6
-934.1	600.0	2137.4	2137.4	1994.6	1994.6	21.0	21.0
38488.7	4982.7	36065.8	35450.9	23730.6	23571.1	902.4	869.2
193444.3	101424.0	1358651.7	1355380.4	1270104.7	1266952.4	1889.7	1618.5
95497.1	64616.2	441500.7	440066.3	364695.0	363854.6	1720.7	1633.3
304374.5	95683.6	734377.0	715269.0	585202.5	580935.0	12539.8	3366.6
99594.9	17242.9	157034.2	155734.3	145818.9	137929.6	1047.8	809.8
19387.4	10600.0	103933.7	103927.0	78612.9	78612.9	2931.1	2931.1
77765.0	38222.0	90413.1	89052.0	84939.2	84939.2	476.2	476.2

11-10 续表2

单位：万元

分　　组	Item	销售费用 Expenses for Sales	管理费用 Expenses for Management
总　　计	**Total**	**984432.0**	**1312560.9**
#亏损企业	Deficit Enterprises	5.4	13.5
按隶属关系分	Grouped by Jurisdiction of Management		
中央企业	Central Enterprises	94994.4	432078.1
省属企业	Provincial Enterprises	407348.7	266013.3
市属企业	Municipal Enterprises	482088.9	614469.5
按轻重工业分	Grouped by Light Industry and Heavy Industry		
轻工业	Light Industry	448626.1	265256.9
重工业	Heavy Industry	535805.9	1047304.0
按企业规模分	Grouped by Size of Enterprises		
大型工业	Large-size	593202.9	746327.0
中型工业	Medium-size	184904.0	248530.4
小型工业	Small-size	206325.1	317703.5
按工业行业大类分	Grouped by Sector		
煤炭开采和洗选业	Mining and Washing of Coal		
石油和天然气开采业	Extraction of Petroleum and Natural Gas		
黑色金属矿采选业	Mining and Processing of Ferrous Metal Ores	7.0	529.4
有色金属矿采选业	Mining and Processing of Non-ferrous Metal Ores		
非金属矿采选业	Mining and Processing of Nonmetal Ores		
开采辅助活动	Mining Auxiliary Activities	575.6	3358.4
其他采矿业	Mining of Other Ores		
农副食品加工业	Processing of Food from Agricultural Porducts	32976.9	31984.5
食品制造业	Manufacture of Foods	36170.2	28134.7
酒、饮料和精制茶制造业	Manufacture of Alcohol,Beverages and Tea	56025.7	25944.6
烟草加工业	Manufacture of Tobacco		
纺织业	Manufacture of Textile	2765.0	11512.8
纺织服装、鞋、帽制造业	Manufacture of Textile Wearing Apparel, Footwear and Caps	3965.1	5588.7
皮革、毛皮、羽毛(绒)及其制品业	Manufacture of Leather, Fur, Feather (eiderdown) and Related Products		
木材加工及竹、藤、棕、草制品业	Processing of Timber,Manufacture of Wood,Plam and Straw Products	2996.1	2825.5

continued 2

(10 000 yuan)

财务费用 Financial cost	营业利润 Operating Profit	利润总额 Total Profits	亏损企业亏损总额 Total Loss of Deficit Enterprises	利税总额 Total Pre-tax Profits	应付职工薪酬 Salary Payable	本年应交增值税 Value Added Tax Payable
202045.7	**1565182.2**	**1483925.7**	**100314.6**	**2431538.2**	**1823094.8**	**753007.6**
2.9	**-8.2**	**-10.0**	**10.0**	**-5.3**	**17.7**	**4.1**
54632.0	187179.2	242298.7	16421.1	348505.1	654128.8	87475.7
48307.9	277737.4	195654.7	16879.7	445535.1	376489.4	226975.6
99105.8	1100265.6	1045972.3	67013.8	1637498.0	792476.6	438556.3
42257.8	381098.9	341188.6	21800.6	618602.9	351971.9	242251.5
159787.9	1184083.3	1142737.1	78514.0	1812935.3	1471122.9	510756.1
112817.5	591300.2	634221.8	12600.4	1130365.7	1205406.4	366278.4
38999.5	305730.4	304086.9	53925.4	505516.8	311136.0	173663.8
50228.7	668151.6	545617.0	33788.8	795655.7	306552.4	213065.4
172.3	-415.0	-550.5	550.5	-369.2	376.8	160.3
-6.1	7504.9	7421.5		13285.7	5007.5	4961.8
9631.7	78281.8	32688.0	8020.4	45194.9	26752.3	10617.2
1555.9	22708.4	12286.0	3022.3	23759.6	16623.0	9752.9
5535.8	73888.8	73064.7	5241.2	132754.9	44175.8	47150.4
469.3	2097.2	5025.4	913.6	13048.6	34952.0	6975.4
721.1	9419.8	10087.8		15781.9	6072.8	2763.0
1940.7	2368.7	2380.0		11679.9	3084.5	8823.7

11-10 续表3

单位：万元

分　　组	Item	企业单位数(个) Number of Enterprises (unit)	工业总产值（当年价）Gross Industrial Output Value (At Current Prices)
家具制造业	Manufacture of Furniture	6	44852.1
造纸及纸制品业	Manufacture of Paper and Paper Products	15	184999.6
印刷业、记录媒介的复制	Printing,Reproduction of Recording Media	15	417597.8
文教、工美、体育和娱乐用品制造业	Manufacture of Articles For Cultural,Educational and Sports Activities	3	57762.5
石油加工、炼焦及核燃料加工业	Processing of Petroleum, Cokeing,Processing of Nuclear and Nuclear Fuel	3	838799.9
化学原料及化学制品制造业	Manufacture of Raw Chemical Materials and Chemical Products	36	1358005.1
医药制造业	Manufacture of Medicines	41	1030479.8
化学纤维制造业	Manufacture of Chemical Fibers	2	85301.8
橡胶和塑料制品业	Manufacture of Rubber and Plastics	21	253308.7
非金属矿物制品业	Manufacture of Non-metallic Mineral Products	74	1250815.6
黑色金属冶炼及压延加工业	Smelting and Pressing of Ferrous Metals	18	331682.6
有色金属冶炼及压延加工业	Smelting and Pressing of Non-ferrous Metals	19	535962.3
金属制品业	Manufacture of Metal Products	44	514941.0
通用设备制造业	Manufacture of General Purpose Machinery	47	807470.0
专用设备制造业	Manufacture of Special Equipment	62	1281076.2
汽车制造业	Manufacture of Motor Vehicle	24	7875906.0
铁路、船舶、航空航天和其他运输设备制造业	Railways,Shipbuilding,Aerospace and Other Transportation Equipment Manufacturing Industry	30	2827588.9
电气机械及器材制造业	Manufacture of Electric Equipment and Machinery	65	1085442.4
计算机、通讯和其他电子设备制造业	Manufacture of Communication Equipment, Computers and other Electronic Equipment	44	1168094.8
仪器仪表制造业	Manufacture of Measuring Instruments and Machinery	30	667324.3
其他制造业	Manufacture of Other Manufacturing	2	20713.2
废弃资源综合利用业	Recycling and Disposal of Waste		
金属制品、机械和设备修理业	Metal Products,Machinery and Equipment Repair Industry	3	36428.8
电力、热力的生产和供应业	Production and Supply of Electric Power and Heat Power	6	63214.5
燃气生产和供应业	Gas Mining and Supplying Industry	4	228815.2
水的生产和供应业	Production and Supply of Water	2	67167.9

continued 3

（10 000 yuan）

工业销售产值（当年价）Value of Industry Products Sales (At Current Prices)	出口交货值 Export Delivery Value	从业人员年平均人数（人）Annual Average Employers (person)	资产总计 Total Assets	流动资产合计 Total Working Capitals	固定资产合计 Total Fixed Assets	固定资产原价 Origing Value of Fixed Assets	累计折旧 Accumulative Total Depreciation
43734.7		1478	21769.8	14584.4	7064.2	11270.3	6305.6
183400.0		5419	65262.1	30131.4	32461.4	58063.2	25800.0
418978.2	1060.5	6900	440878.5	223047.0	159730.7	276115.4	145891.2
57603.2	2377.7	631	26537.8	9841.8	14568.6	11808.3	5871.2
838799.9		428	151512.0	104612.5	23917.9	103011.7	79097.6
1331455.8	109101.1	32006	1698150.5	819795.0	674902.3	957288.2	398786.1
973883.9	1386.1	12023	747380.6	462481.7	140863.7	259511.8	131572.2
84652.9		435	69411.7	27189.0	32645.5	68658.8	36013.3
225575.8	1954.0	3098	183108.4	120699.2	55481.3	73943.6	23661.2
1224921.2		11234	661925.8	355519.3	263075.1	377948.4	138710.8
319197.2		3038	144313.2	68347.1	74958.5	96480.7	21809.7
514009.7	19882.4	5367	475662.2	265838.0	129303.6	166401.1	46235.3
518987.3	3056.3	9362	461657.7	280338.5	135332.2	188211.7	80470.4
753591.4	18849.4	12528	825301.7	611117.2	186907.2	235312.6	81497.7
1181716.3	57782.0	19592	1745996.6	1290334.1	278960.1	406584.0	139616.9
7755822.7	380949.6	83020	5945378.4	3383602.4	1734860.0	1813255.6	606693.0
2747557.7	392049.3	56606	5917551.4	3979085.2	1584890.5	1808175.7	806261.0
1026446.0	170716.1	12727	845127.3	580636.1	200115.0	268726.3	92045.8
1029602.7	95312.9	19809	2346415.3	1216658.4	664371.5	657395.4	218159.8
645810.8	87783.2	16681	1252556.0	797297.5	357297.8	457394.3	185321.6
20452.9		446	19201.6	9605.4	4702.4	7543.4	3980.8
32641.4		351	33495.7	22828.4	6390.0	7155.4	1662.1
63309.4		12943	389433.1	245634.5	107870.2	158598.3	50728.1
228758.3		2447	394371.6	175727.6	216033.8	239345.3	59409.7
67167.9		2886	127169.3	45911.6	81257.7	201061.3	134755.7

11-10 续表4

单位：万元

分　组	Item	负债合计 Total Liabilites	流动负债合计 Total Working Liabilities	非流动负债 Non-Working Liabilities
家具制造业	Manufacture of Furniture	8780.4	8335.8	402.2
造纸及纸制品业	Manufacture of Paper and Paper Products	30569.8	23337.6	5798.2
印刷业、记录媒介的复制	Printing,Reproduction of Recording Media	148787.3	132734.6	5311.6
文教、工美、体育和娱乐用品制造业	Manufacture of Articles For Cultural,Educational and Sports Activities	21151.3	14290.8	
石油加工、炼焦及核燃料加工业	Processing of Petroleum, Cokeing,Processing of Nuclear and Nuclear Fuel	108652.3	74359.7	11000.0
化学原料及化学制品制造业	Manufacture of Raw Chemical Materials and Chemical Products	807768.5	632347.3	159643.7
医药制造业	Manufacture of Medicines	330625.7	304896.1	16639.1
化学纤维制造业	Manufacture of Chemical Fibers	8349.1	8349.1	
橡胶和塑料制品业	Manufacture of Rubber and Plastics	107096.0	92892.5	5404.7
非金属矿物制品业	Manufacture of Non-metallic Mineral Products	350992.5	316037.2	10248.7
黑色金属冶炼及压延加工业	Smelting and Pressing of Ferrous Metals	77423.5	69162.1	8037.6
有色金属冶炼及压延加工业	Smelting and Pressing of Non-ferrous Metals	264370.0	213477.6	10855.8
金属制品业	Manufacture of Metal Products	260491.9	212336.8	22141.5
通用设备制造业	Manufacture of General Purpose Machinery	459616.0	419401.0	38592.5
专用设备制造业	Manufacture of Special Equipment	882268.3	777580.3	84818.6
汽车制造业	Manufacture of Motor Vehicle	3529063.6	3182619.3	342177.3
铁路、船舶、航空航天和其他运输设备制造业	Railways,Shipbuilding,Aerospace and Other Transportation Equipment Manufacturing Industry	3645962.0	3126096.5	463504.5
电气机械及器材制造业	Manufacture of Electric Equipment and Machinery	445522.2	384737.4	57961.0
计算机、通讯和其他电子设备制造业	Manufacture of Communication Equipment, Computers and other Electronic Equipment	1320556.0	802761.6	502045.6
仪器仪表制造业	Manufacture of Measuring Instruments and Machinery	683642.9	544054.4	139122.1
其他制造业	Manufacture of Other Manufacturing	9772.3	9772.3	
废弃资源综合利用业	Recycling and Disposal of Waste			
金属制品、机械和设备修理业	Metal Products,Machinery and Equipment Repair Industry	21876.8	17876.8	4000.0
电力、热力的生产和供应业	Production and Supply of Electric Power and Heat Power	307808.5	208216.2	96731.5
燃气生产和供应业	Gas Mining and Supplying Industry	211793.3	185713.9	26079.4
水的生产和供应业	Production and Supply of Water	53620.1	32651.8	20968.3

continued 4

(10 000 yuan)

所有者权益合计 Total Owners' Equities	实收资本 Total Capital Hold	营业收入 Total Revenue	主营业务收入 Revenue from Principal Business	营业成本 Total Cost	主营业务成本 Cost of Principal Business	营业税金及附加 Taxs and Other Changes	主营业务税金及附加 Taxes and Other Charges on Principal Business
12989.3	7261.9	43908.7	43613.4	33199.6	33009.3	156.3	156.3
34546.4	23602.8	180737.9	180628.8	157568.3	157567.8	834.0	834.0
292028.8	143386.1	405989.0	398728.0	295411.0	291006.7	2965.5	2465.7
5386.5	4131.0	56822.7	56822.7	49458.2	49458.2	195.0	195.0
42859.6	24988.1	811037.8	811037.8	788831.4	788831.4	448.9	448.9
889443.9	347581.3	1354292.6	1324800.4	1076192.8	1059134.3	5943.9	5149.6
416611.3	178442.8	912051.1	910056.0	487915.0	485616.8	7779.8	7770.4
61062.6	50800.0	84663.6	84556.3	71100.9	71097.9	324.1	324.1
75998.4	54431.0	219742.8	217659.7	172919.5	169994.9	786.5	786.5
308497.9	148025.4	1188634.7	1181485.6	980199.8	974068.4	9565.6	9523.7
66889.6	27353.2	376670.4	371736.6	318274.1	313178.3	2336.4	2164.1
211218.4	80677.1	478340.2	463681.3	417455.0	403419.7	1969.1	1969.1
200265.2	79938.6	508410.9	505786.3	413146.8	411827.3	2436.0	2436.0
365647.9	154013.3	733428.3	726380.2	605742.6	600759.2	2744.2	2735.5
856546.6	434096.1	1205893.1	1196066.9	961672.4	950784.9	6937.1	6855.3
2416314.5	926852.3	7294774.7	7029902.5	6513683.4	6257807.1	97085.1	96706.0
2271583.5	708131.0	3270738.2	3220901.4	3037610.4	2764427.8	13713.5	10998.7
399535.3	239578.4	990504.9	957640.8	822850.9	786902.8	3498.9	3475.6
1025593.3	387249.6	1156247.8	1125248.1	959394.8	934161.2	5327.5	4988.3
568740.4	227019.7	745345.9	734777.4	559325.7	552356.5	3027.5	2279.5
9429.2	3620.0	19732.6	18888.4	16516.0	15871.4	156.1	156.1
11618.9	6915.9	32316.7	32238.7	26892.3	26837.7	134.4	134.4
81624.6	106985.6	109745.2	66821.4	102490.0	79961.0	2097.3	1368.5
182578.3	125180.0	265949.4	226796.1	212165.7	189837.1	1896.1	1896.1
73549.2	43000.0	72789.6	67167.9	63116.2	60044.2	717.4	693.6

11-10 续表5

单位：万元

分 组	Item	销售费用 Expenses for Sales	管理费用 Expenses for Management
家具制造业	Manufacture of Furniture	3403.9	2844.4
造纸及纸制品业	Manufacture of Paper and Paper Products	2916.7	4745.4
印刷业、记录媒介的复制	Printing,Reproduction of Recording Media	8197.7	39877.8
文教、工美、体育和娱乐用品制造业	Manufacture of Articles For Cultural,Educational and Sports Activities	786.1	1598.0
石油加工、炼焦及核燃料加工业	Processing of Petroleum, Cokeing,Processing of Nuclear and Nuclear Fuel	5797.7	3449.7
化学原料及化学制品制造业	Manufacture of Raw Chemical Materials and Chemical Products	48135.3	123954.4
医药制造业	Manufacture of Medicines	268224.6	62517.8
化学纤维制造业	Manufacture of Chemical Fibers	210.5	2677.9
橡胶和塑料制品业	Manufacture of Rubber and Plastics	8413.6	28410.9
非金属矿物制品业	Manufacture of Non-metallic Mineral Products	29051.4	27208.1
黑色金属冶炼及压延加工业	Smelting and Pressing of Ferrous Metals	5333.8	9127.8
有色金属冶炼及压延加工业	Smelting and Pressing of Non-ferrous Metals	5159.7	17986.2
金属制品业	Manufacture of Metal Products	12944.9	31562.9
通用设备制造业	Manufacture of General Purpose Machinery	33830.9	42588.0
专用设备制造业	Manufacture of Special Equipment	53463.0	96226.4
汽车制造业	Manufacture of Motor Vehicle	206772.9	208171.8
铁路、船舶、航空航天和其他运输设备制造业	Railways,Shipbuilding,Aerospace and Other Transportation Equipment Manufacturing Industry	67135.3	234120.1
电气机械及器材制造业	Manufacture of Electric Equipment and Machinery	29291.2	55598.8
计算机、通讯和其他电子设备制造业	Manufacture of Communication Equipment, Computers and other Electronic Equipment	25432.0	89118.7
仪器仪表制造业	Manufacture of Measuring Instruments and Machinery	20561.6	89407.5
其他制造业	Manufacture of Other Manufacturing	528.2	1553.8
废弃资源综合利用业	Recycling and Disposal of Waste		
金属制品、机械和设备修理业	Metal Products,Machinery and Equipment Repair Industry	822.6	2225.6
电力、热力的生产和供应业	Production and Supply of Electric Power and Heat Power	341.7	4888.9
燃气生产和供应业	Gas Mining and Supplying Industry	9286.4	15393.9
水的生产和供应业	Production and Supply of Water	2908.7	7427.5

continued 5

(10 000 yuan)

财务费用 Financial cost	营业利润 Operating Profit	利润总额 Total Profits	亏损企业亏损总额 Total Loss of Deficit Enterprises	利税总额 Total Pre-tax Profits	应付职工薪酬 Salary Payable	本年应交增值税 Value Added Tax Payable
230.8	3157.7	3151.9		4796.7	3551.0	1488.5
1453.4	12040.5	8999.8	55.4	13574.5	18620.7	3740.7
3015.4	60685.0	60635.4	2252.8	88645.7	54152.3	25044.8
267.7	3451.6	3333.8	258.5	4426.3	4004.3	897.5
980.3	103339.5	3337.4	20.6	6059.1	1757.8	2272.8
12328.5	104440.2	115869.1	21564.1	167459.4	138141.5	45646.4
12454.6	77183.8	91794.5	913.1	202069.2	93607.8	102494.9
-137.3	10975.4	10976.2	84.9	13733.9	3926.1	2433.6
4201.1	9331.8	9633.0	275.1	16285.0	12626.9	5865.5
5782.4	142430.8	137006.2	3179.1	210807.9	43250.4	64236.1
2756.4	37071.1	35323.4	1388.0	45951.0	15440.0	8291.2
11479.2	22767.2	23554.9	2347.0	40476.1	22755.2	14952.1
4304.2	46577.5	41465.5	1216.1	55988.0	49881.3	12086.5
5816.2	37978.1	39922.0	2431.7	62625.8	57212.4	19959.6
4999.7	104933.1	100025.2	1356.3	156608.7	96054.7	49646.4
34407.3	261783.8	266941.3	7521.2	513841.1	365188.9	149814.7
44601.5	99835.5	138592.6	2874.2	200142.1	383903.6	47836.0
11330.1	71794.3	72268.1	1258.0	118669.3	55793.5	42902.3
10229.8	72129.1	81615.6	26882.7	113907.4	97098.9	26964.3
7079.9	61583.4	65260.1	1470.1	83100.9	114943.9	14813.3
220.1	753.8	996.4		1929.8	1116.2	777.3
776.2	1622.3	1794.5		2992.5	1830.9	1063.6
5493.2	-4320.8	-1672.6	5217.7	8377.8	10232.8	7953.1
-2332.9	29415.0	28594.1		37081.9	24549.1	6591.7
287.2	-1632.1	2104.4		6851.8	16409.9	4030.0

11-11 规模以上外商及港澳台商工业企业主要经济指标（2011年）

单位：万元

分　组	Item	企业单位数（个）Number of Enterprises (unit)	亏损企业 Loss Making Enterprises	工业总产值（当年价）Gross Industrial Output Value (At Current Prices)
总　计	**Total**	**107**	**19**	**6930213.3**
#亏损企业	Deficit Enterprises	19	19	526812.4
按隶属关系分	Grouped by Jurisdiction of Management			
中央企业	Central Enterprises	3		123750.4
省属企业	Provincial Enterprises	11	2	993733.3
市属企业	Municipal Enterprises	93	17	5812729.6
按登记注册类型分组	Grouped by Type of Registration			
港、澳、台商投资企业	Enterprises with Funds from Hong Kong, Macao &Taiwan	21	5	264063.8
与港、澳、台商合作经营	Cooperative Enterprises			
与港、澳、台商合资经营	Joint-venture Enterprises	14	3	137609.3
港、澳、台商独资	Enterprises with Sole Investment	6	1	124732.2
港、澳、台商投资股份有限公司	Share-holding Corporations Ltd. With their Investment	1	1	1722.3
外商投资企业	Foreign Funded Enterprises	86	14	6666149.5
中外合资经营	Joint-venture Enterprises	61	9	5366370.6
中外合作经营	Cooperation Enterprises	1	1	2202.2
外资企业	Foreign Funded Enterprises	22	4	1103987.9
外商投资股份有限公司	Share-holding Corporations Ltd. With Foreign Funds	2		193588.8
按轻重工业分	Grouped by Light Industry and Heavy Industry			
轻工业	Light Industry	40	9	2688333.0
重工业	Heavy Industry	67	10	4241880.3
按企业规模分	Grouped by Size of Enterprises			
大型工业	Large-size	15	1	4931409.3
中型工业	Medium-size	17	4	931584.8
小型工业	Small-size	75	14	1067219.2
按工业行业大类分	Grouped by Sector			
煤炭开采和洗选业	Mining and Washing of Coal			
石油和天然气开采业	Extraction of Petroleum and Natural Gas			
黑色金属矿采选业	Mining and Processing of Ferrous Metal Ores			
有色金属矿采选业	Mining and Processing of Non-ferrous Metal Ores			
非金属矿采选业	Mining and Processing of Nonmetal Ores			
开采辅助活动	Mining Auxiliary Activities			
其他采矿业	Mining of Other Ores			
农副食品加工业	Processing of Food from Agricultural Porducts	4		182494.2
食品制造业	Manufacture of Foods	5	2	738895.8
酒、饮料和精制茶制造业	Manufacture of Alcohol,Beverages and Tea	8	2	606998.7
烟草加工业	Manufacture of Tobacco			
纺织业	Manufacture of Textile	1	1	2143.1

Economic Indicators of Foreign Fund Industrial Enterprises Above Designated Size（2011）

（10 000 yuan）

工业销售产值（当年价）Value of Industry Products Sales (At Current Prices)	出口交货值 Export Delivery Value	从业人员年平均人数（人）Annual Average Employers (person)	资产总计 Total Assets	流动资产合计 Total Working Capitals	固定资产合计 Total Fixed Assets	固定资产原价 Origing Value of Fixed Assets	累计折旧 Accumulative Total Depreciation
6808386.0	**641373.8**	**73719**	**4773436.2**	**2530407.5**	**1715683.0**	**2388013.5**	**868971.5**
482410.6	17397.7	6428	402706.2	199764.8	106556.5	182738.0	78622.4
123627.9	4911.5	1377	97789.6	53367.2	35217.7	80603.5	45385.8
1016428.8	186143.8	7727	805142.0	538425.8	202064.7	331619.9	133577.7
5668329.3	450318.5	64615	3870504.6	1938614.5	1478400.6	1975790.1	690008.0
276016.8	12895.0	5820	351102.8	149060.8	94754.2	162041.5	70513.2
130009.0	10216.8	2741	224558.1	98149.2	35787.0	70652.2	38089.1
143532.9	2678.2	2679	98373.2	37973.9	49254.7	78551.8	29299.1
2474.9		400	28171.5	12937.7	9712.5	12837.5	3125.0
6532369.2	628478.8	67899	4422333.4	2381346.7	1620928.8	2225972.0	798458.3
5237638.4	261949.0	53771	3226599.7	1747601.7	1148119.2	1503192.2	528630.3
1590.6	364.0	72	3681.9	1496.3	2185.6	856.7	172.5
1072851.8	181227.8	12030	819833.6	420041.0	327271.4	522919.7	214004.7
220288.4	184938.0	2026	372218.2	212207.7	143352.6	199003.4	55650.8
2671116.7	316805.5	23917	1623915.9	872724.0	520543.0	902063.9	395631.1
4137269.3	324568.3	49802	3149520.3	1657683.5	1195140.0	1485949.6	473340.4
4858754.8	395303.7	54758	3090666.9	1483561.0	1267484.1	1659838.3	564034.8
903433.3	172815.3	8620	665953.9	406187.5	192940.1	263665.9	87849.4
1046197.9	73254.8	10341	1016815.4	640659.0	255258.8	464509.3	217087.3
179671.2		1021	60578.5	38774.0	9679.4	20956.4	13070.0
707416.7		5320	272171.7	148937.8	63583.2	140434.8	76851.6
634769.3	184938.0	7296	683182.7	287932.6	299955.6	446222.1	146266.5
1932.0		212	5143.2	4111.7	1031.5	6892.0	5927.7

11-11 续表1

单位：万元

分组	Item	负债合计 Total Liabilites	流动负债合计 Total Working Liabilities	非流动负债 Non-Working Liabilities
总　计	**Total**	**2594388.4**	**2344392.6**	**228133.0**
#亏损企业	Deficit Enterprises	288378.4	268695.1	4350.6
按隶属关系分	Grouped by Jurisdiction of Management			
中央企业	Central Enterprises	42275.3	39750.9	2524.4
省属企业	Provincial Enterprises	510340.3	488619.6	10979.8
市属企业	Municipal Enterprises	2041772.8	1816022.1	214628.8
按登记注册类型分组	Grouped by Type of Registration			
港、澳、台商投资企业	Enterprises with Funds from Hong Kong, Macao &Taiwan	195295.5	177976.2	5662.6
与港、澳、台商合作经营	Cooperative Enterprises			
与港、澳、台商合资经营	Joint-venture Enterprises	117350.7	105166.9	1031.6
港、澳、台商独资	Enterprises with Sole Investment	58480.7	54550.4	3425.8
港、澳、台商投资股份有限公司	Share-holding Corporations Ltd. With their Investment	19464.1	18258.9	1205.2
外商投资企业	Foreign Funded Enterprises	2399092.9	2166416.4	222470.4
中外合资经营	Joint-venture Enterprises	1821664.6	1679281.7	133681.6
中外合作经营	Cooperation Enterprises	1082.8		
外资企业	Foreign Funded Enterprises	321350.8	243047.1	77881.7
外商投资股份有限公司	Share-holding Corporations Ltd. With Foreign Funds	254994.7	244087.6	10907.1
按轻重工业分	Grouped by Light Industry and Heavy Industry			
轻工业	Light Industry	853772.9	812602.9	24921.5
重工业	Heavy Industry	1740615.5	1531789.7	203211.5
按企业规模分	Grouped by Size of Enterprises			
大型工业	Large-size	1742130.3	1567031.7	174594.2
中型工业	Medium-size	355927.2	323297.1	21055.9
小型工业	Small-size	496330.9	454063.8	32482.9
按工业行业大类分	Grouped by Sector			
煤炭开采和洗选业	Mining and Washing of Coal			
石油和天然气开采业	Extraction of Petroleum and Natural Gas			
黑色金属矿采选业	Mining and Processing of Ferrous Metal Ores			
有色金属矿采选业	Mining and Processing of Non-ferrous Metal Ores			
非金属矿采选业	Mining and Processing of Nonmetal Ores			
开采辅助活动	Mining Auxiliary Activities			
其他采矿业	Mining of Other Ores			
农副食品加工业	Processing of Food from Agricultural Porducts	23111.2	22700.0	
食品制造业	Manufacture of Foods	132173.1	131749.1	424.0
酒、饮料和精制茶制造业	Manufacture of Alcohol,Beverages and Tea	424953.5	410166.1	14282.9
烟草加工业	Manufacture of Tobacco			
纺织业	Manufacture of Textile	1426.9	1426.9	

continued 1

(10 000 yuan)

所有者权益合计 Total Owners' Equities	实收资本 Total Capital Hold	营业收入 Total Revenue	主营业务收入 Revenue from Principal Business	营业成本 Total Cost	主营业务成本 Cost of Principal Business	营业税金及附加 Taxs and Other Changes	主营业务税金及附加 Taxes and Other Charges on Principal Business
2177726.0	**1055688.9**	**6934022.0**	**6705587.2**	**5707011.3**	**5523692.5**	**110496.1**	**110292.4**
113850.1	164429.7	469019.4	463157.8	447336.4	442958.1	1125.2	1120.2
55514.3	34194.0	127834.5	127398.8	110210.6	109816.9	533.0	533.0
294801.7	108916.3	1021973.3	1014975.5	707889.4	704522.5	6663.1	6653.6
1827410.0	912578.6	5784214.2	5563212.9	4888911.3	4709353.1	103300.0	103105.8
155717.9	135105.3	262450.1	257665.8	179360.7	175539.6	3788.0	3780.8
107118.1	94304.4	113338.8	111363.4	75303.2	73715.0	698.7	698.7
39892.4	34330.4	146636.4	144338.3	102195.0	100367.7	3052.3	3045.1
8707.4	6470.5	2474.9	1964.1	1862.5	1456.9	37.0	37.0
2022008.1	920583.6	6671571.9	6447921.4	5527650.6	5348152.9	106708.1	106511.6
1404460.4	669983.8	5341770.7	5128747.2	4388121.6	4216160.0	101593.0	101459.5
2599.1	1108.9	1590.6	1590.6	1411.5	1411.5	1.2	1.2
497725.1	227912.9	1115512.0	1105187.4	938574.5	931093.0	4216.5	4153.5
117223.5	21578.0	212698.6	212396.2	199543.0	199488.4	897.4	897.4
769612.6	372350.2	2667979.1	2621210.6	2056325.6	2026778.2	15586.2	15491.5
1408113.4	683338.7	4266042.9	4084376.6	3650685.7	3496914.3	94909.9	94800.9
1348536.5	540641.6	4976715.1	4776929.8	4133002.5	3974707.2	98729.8	98642.4
309997.1	167702.3	905446.1	887728.2	748019.4	731204.0	5730.5	5699.2
519192.4	347345.0	1051860.8	1040929.2	825989.4	817781.3	6035.8	5950.8
37437.7	29173.8	211297.1	210277.0	194559.0	194168.5	229.5	229.5
139938.9	71651.3	715570.1	707636.5	635464.2	628191.5	2457.8	2369.5
258229.1	95856.5	627543.2	606933.6	489767.5	484222.6	5857.4	5851.1
3716.3	3768.7	2188.7	2188.7	1722.9	1466.4	14.4	14.4

11-11 续表2

单位：万元

分　组	Item	销售费用 Expenses for Sales	管理费用 Expenses for Management
总　计	**Total**	**449929.0**	**232375.3**
#亏损企业	Deficit Enterprises	57385.6	32682.8
按隶属关系分	Grouped by Jurisdiction of Management		
中央企业	Central Enterprises	544.4	3880.1
省属企业	Provincial Enterprises	206168.8	51240.1
市属企业	Municipal Enterprises	243215.8	177255.1
按登记注册类型分组	Grouped by Type of Registration		
港、澳、台商投资企业	Enterprises with Funds from Hong Kong，Macao &Taiwan	37905.8	18675.5
与港、澳、台商合作经营	Cooperative Enterprises		
与港、澳、台商合资经营	Joint-venture Enterprises	10606.7	8970.6
港、澳、台商独资	Enterprises with Sole Investment	26691.5	7410.9
港、澳、台商投资股份有限公司	Share-holding Corporations Ltd. With their Investment	607.6	2294.0
外商投资企业	Foreign Funded Enterprises	412023.2	213699.8
中外合资经营	Joint-venture Enterprises	310557.6	154344.0
中外合作经营	Cooperation Enterprises	36.9	183.8
外资企业	Foreign Funded Enterprises	95229.8	49809.9
外商投资股份有限公司	Share-holding Corporations Ltd. With Foreign Funds	6198.9	9362.1
按轻重工业分	Grouped by Light Industry and Heavy Industry		
轻工业	Light Industry	376302.3	102942.4
重工业	Heavy Industry	73626.7	129432.9
按企业规模分	Grouped by Size of Enterprises		
大型工业	Large-size	377111.6	134950.2
中型工业	Medium-size	32287.5	36287.9
小型工业	Small-size	40529.9	61137.2
按工业行业大类分	Grouped by Sector		
煤炭开采和洗选业	Mining and Washing of Coal		
石油和天然气开采业	Extraction of Petroleum and Natural Gas		
黑色金属矿采选业	Mining and Processing of Ferrous Metal Ores		
有色金属矿采选业	Mining and Processing of Non-ferrous Metal Ores		
非金属矿采选业	Mining and Processing of Nonmetal Ores		
开采辅助活动	Mining Auxiliary Activities		
其他采矿业	Mining of Other Ores		
农副食品加工业	Processing of Food from Agricultural Porducts	3954.1	3046.7
食品制造业	Manufacture of Foods	79166.4	22812.0
酒、饮料和精制茶制造业	Manufacture of Alcohol,Beverages and Tea	65965.3	25891.1
烟草加工业	Manufacture of Tobacco		
纺织业	Manufacture of Textile	259.9	352.9

continued 2

(10 000 yuan)

财务费用 Financial cost	营业利润 Operating Profit	利润总额 Total Profits	亏损企业亏损总额 Total Loss of Deficit Enterprises	利税总额 Total Pre-tax Profits	应付职工薪酬 Salary Payable	本年应交增值税 Value Added Tax Payable
25544.7	**497794.2**	**488662.9**	**24523.5**	**874303.4**	**399693.2**	**275144.4**
5217.7	**-24605.6**	**-24523.5**	**24523.5**	**-17089.0**	**32740.8**	**6309.3**
-151.9	14812.2	14384.2		19628.6	4867.9	4711.4
13997.9	61953.8	66297.2	5776.9	184138.3	83895.5	111178.0
11698.7	421028.2	407981.5	18746.6	670536.5	310929.8	159255.0
1691.8	13546.3	14442.7	5711.2	30305.7	33168.1	12075.0
1831.7	8558.1	9465.1	3042.5	14773.8	10936.9	4610.0
-410.4	7585.0	6970.3	676.0	17412.8	20827.1	7390.2
270.5	-2596.8	-1992.7	1992.7	-1880.9	1404.1	74.8
23852.9	484247.9	474220.2	18812.3	843997.7	366525.1	263069.4
17197.6	395743.3	379763.5	12772.5	684103.9	287007.9	202747.4
0.2	-42.9	-42.9	42.9	-25.9	112.0	15.8
-519.7	76990.4	81325.4	5996.9	122466.8	68382.9	36924.9
7174.8	11557.1	13174.2		37452.9	11022.3	23381.3
12202.7	179679.7	169914.4	11124.8	354309.6	168120.6	168809.0
13342.0	318114.5	318748.5	13398.7	519993.8	231572.6	106335.4
17565.8	307825.0	300372.6	2567.8	592220.5	307277.1	193118.1
4043.0	79779.6	79477.3	10495.1	124948.1	39222.3	39740.3
3935.9	110189.6	108813.0	11460.6	157134.8	53193.8	42286.0
-7.7	2009.9	2057.7		5212.9	3506.2	2925.7
-2241.3	36417.4	27379.3	3405.7	44682.4	25461.7	14845.3
6439.7	57450.3	56607.0	5241.2	106574.9	49589.7	44110.5
-0.1	-161.3	-149.4	149.4	-15.2	553.9	119.8

11-11　续表3

单位：万元

分　　组	Item	企业单位数(个) Number of Enterprises (unit)	亏损企业 Loss Making Enterprises	工业总产值（当年价） Gross Industrial Output Value (At Current Prices)
纺织服装、鞋、帽制造业	Manufacture of Textile Wearing Apparel, Footwear and Caps			
皮革、毛皮、羽毛(绒)及其制品业	Manufacture of Leather, Fur, Feather (eiderdown) and Related Products			
木材加工及竹、藤、棕、草制品业	Processing of Timber,Manufacture of Wood,Plam and Straw Products			
家具制造业	Manufacture of Furniture			
造纸及纸制品业	Manufacture of Paper and Paper Products	2		25422.4
印刷业、记录媒介的复制	Printing,Reproduction of Recording Media	2	1	29882.6
文教、工美、体育和娱乐用品制造业	Manufacture of Articles For Cultural,Educational and Sports Activities			
石油加工、炼焦及核燃料加工业	Processing of Petroleum, Cokeing,Processing of Nuclear and Nuclear Fuel	1		4354.2
化学原料及化学制品制造业	Manufacture of Raw Chemical Materials and Chemical Products	4	2	20112.7
医药制造业	Manufacture of Medicines	9	1	655013.7
化学纤维制造业	Manufacture of Chemical Fibers	1		82830.9
橡胶和塑料制品业	Manufacture of Rubber and Plastics	5	1	33675.4
非金属矿物制品业	Manufacture of Non-metallic Mineral Products	6		306485.1
黑色金属冶炼及压延加工业	Smelting and Pressing of Ferrous Metals	2		52493.3
有色金属冶炼及压延加工业	Smelting and Pressing of Non-ferrous Metals	3		101078.5
金属制品业	Manufacture of Metal Products	3		12698.0
通用设备制造业	Manufacture of General Purpose Machinery	5		124879.7
专用设备制造业	Manufacture of Special Equipment	7		305238.0
汽车制造业	Manufacture of Motor Vehicle	4	1	2609163.2
铁路、船舶、航空航天和其他运输设备制造业	Railways,Shipbuilding,Aerospace and Other Transportation Equipment Manufacturing Industry	4	1	76001.2
电气机械及器材制造业	Manufacture of Electric Equipment and Machinery	13	3	430257.4
计算机、通讯和其他电子设备制造业	Manufacture of Communication Equipment, Computers and other Electronic Equipment	7	2	209474.3
仪器仪表制造业	Manufacture of Measuring Instruments and Machinery	7	1	100238.9
其他制造业	Manufacture of Other Manufacturing	1		5900.2
废弃资源综合利用业	Recycling and Disposal of Waste			
金属制品、机械和设备修理业	Metal Products,Machinery and Equipment Repair Industry	2	1	26774.8
电力、热力的生产和供应业	Production and Supply of Electric Power and Heat Power			
燃气生产和供应业	Gas Mining and Supplying Industry	1		187707.0
水的生产和供应业	Production and Supply of Water			

continued 3

(10 000 yuan)

工业销售产值（当年价） Value of Industry Products Sales (At Current Prices)	出口交货值 Export Delivery Value	从业人员年平均人数（人） Annual Average Employers (person)	资产总计 Total Assets	流动资产合计 Total Working Capitals	固定资产合计 Total Fixed Assets	固定资产原价 Origing Value of Fixed Assets	累计折旧 Accumulative Total Depreciation
27127.1		391	18503.0	10637.6	6990.7	7861.3	3026.2
30830.0	1060.5	837	72204.7	32540.1	13997.9	25156.0	12521.7
4098.9		40	8526.2	5297.3	2689.1	4257.2	1634.5
21366.0		312	23042.7	14523.9	7038.6	10077.1	3603.1
652250.4	13498.6	6516	366610.2	257277.9	74671.7	157704.7	89860.5
82182.0		265	44249.7	22376.8	21173.5	57086.4	35912.9
29296.4	364.0	562	41495.5	25526.4	15133.3	20791.1	7917.3
293647.8		995	186239.5	47410.7	122632.5	167593.3	49204.9
53006.2	1339.8	343	18150.3	6165.0	11985.3	25867.2	13881.9
102130.3	23030.9	454	48762.6	38509.4	7490.0	19479.6	11999.6
12016.5	1761.3	496	15716.3	9724.9	4817.1	12851.3	8162.1
124291.7	16098.8	1589	107403.5	83438.5	19709.9	47516.4	28096.1
290510.0	52954.6	3113	250738.3	177692.7	37482.5	76110.7	38628.3
2542952.5	74962.6	32849	1364019.2	589215.3	584033.6	609823.2	148869.6
74252.8	15013.3	554	86632.0	73072.9	9772.8	28156.9	18384.2
424848.7	118792.1	3138	230706.7	162619.7	48105.0	77594.2	29779.9
204932.0	101380.1	3569	418985.9	231249.9	174431.5	235882.1	79972.2
98331.6	36179.2	1338	113993.1	91895.7	15116.6	24730.8	10495.5
5666.4		226	5686.3	2810.6	2491.4	3280.2	788.8
23152.5		269	18822.8	17702.4	762.4	1322.4	560.0
187707.0		2014	311871.6	150963.7	160907.9	160366.1	33556.4

11-11 续表4

单位：万元

分组	Item	负债合计 Total Liabilites	流动负债合计 Total Working Liabilities	非流动负债 Non-Working Liabilities
纺织服装、鞋、帽制造业	Manufacture of Textile Wearing Apparel, Footwear and Caps			
皮革、毛皮、羽毛(绒)及其制品业	Manufacture of Leather, Fur, Feather (eiderdown) and Related Products			
木材加工及竹、藤、棕、草制品业	Processing of Timber,Manufacture of Wood,Plam and Straw Products			
家具制造业	Manufacture of Furniture			
造纸及纸制品业	Manufacture of Paper and Paper Products	7182.9	7182.9	
印刷业、记录媒介的复制	Printing,Reproduction of Recording Media	50182.3	39441.4	
文教、工美、体育和娱乐用品制造业	Manufacture of Articles For Cultural,Educational and Sports Activities			
石油加工、炼焦及核燃料加工业	Processing of Petroleum, Cokeing,Processing of Nuclear and Nuclear Fuel	928.0	928.0	
化学原料及化学制品制造业	Manufacture of Raw Chemical Materials and Chemical Products	11307.3	9444.5	1233.8
医药制造业	Manufacture of Medicines	152447.1	149082.6	484.5
化学纤维制造业	Manufacture of Chemical Fibers	8239.9	8239.9	
橡胶和塑料制品业	Manufacture of Rubber and Plastics	21549.7	17127.5	3339.3
非金属矿物制品业	Manufacture of Non-metallic Mineral Products	37436.5	28207.9	3832.8
黑色金属冶炼及压延加工业	Smelting and Pressing of Ferrous Metals	11462.6	3307.1	8155.5
有色金属冶炼及压延加工业	Smelting and Pressing of Non-ferrous Metals	19188.7	10171.7	9016.9
金属制品业	Manufacture of Metal Products	6254.9	6254.9	
通用设备制造业	Manufacture of General Purpose Machinery	34697.8	34526.9	170.9
专用设备制造业	Manufacture of Special Equipment	123265.0	101520.1	21744.8
汽车制造业	Manufacture of Motor Vehicle	865812.3	795708.5	70103.8
铁路、船舶、航空航天和其他运输设备制造业	Railways,Shipbuilding,Aerospace and Other Transportation Equipment Manufacturing Industry	56885.3	56883.6	1.7
电气机械及器材制造业	Manufacture of Electric Equipment and Machinery	121808.7	113352.7	8237.7
计算机、通讯和其他电子设备制造业	Manufacture of Communication Equipment, Computers and other Electronic Equipment	233479.9	173759.5	59720.4
仪器仪表制造业	Manufacture of Measuring Instruments and Machinery	47807.2	43559.9	4247.3
其他制造业	Manufacture of Other Manufacturing	2883.1	2883.1	
废弃资源综合利用业	Recycling and Disposal of Waste			
金属制品、机械和设备修理业	Metal Products,Machinery and Equipment Repair Industry	13200.2	13144.4	55.8
电力、热力的生产和供应业	Production and Supply of Electric Power and Heat Power			
燃气生产和供应业	Gas Mining and Supplying Industry	186704.3	163623.4	23080.9
水的生产和供应业	Production and Supply of Water			

continued 4

(10 000 yuan)

所有者权益合计 Total Owners' Equities	实收资本 Total Capital Hold	营业收入 Total Revenue	主营业务收入 Revenue from Principal Business	营业成本 Total Cost	主营业务成本 Cost of Principal Business	营业税金及附加 Taxs and Other Changes	主营业务税金及附加 Taxes and Other Charges on Principal Business
11320.1	2738.2	27303.7	26469.9	22242.9	22168.9	80.0	80.0
22022.4	24437.9	27542.8	26547.7	20834.9	20141.2	162.4	162.4
6840.6	6840.6	4561.0	4495.8	3099.0	3033.8	33.6	33.6
11317.6	10823.5	21457.6	21457.4	18108.2	18108.2	239.2	239.2
214139.9	94305.2	634384.0	631732.3	318049.8	317573.4	5803.3	5803.3
36009.8	24800.0	82192.7	82182.0	68543.0	68543.0	324.1	324.1
19945.6	16158.9	27382.5	26115.8	22716.9	21556.2	154.5	154.5
148769.7	27709.2	282292.4	282292.4	212733.6	212733.6	2730.5	2730.5
6687.7	5569.7	52980.6	52980.6	45781.3	45781.3	112.3	112.3
29573.9	22181.3	99501.9	99257.2	86103.5	85257.0	465.9	465.9
9461.4	6947.0	12941.8	12920.9	9454.8	9454.7	75.6	75.6
72705.6	34997.1	139502.0	139057.4	121362.3	121362.3	176.1	176.1
127473.3	58855.7	303603.9	302333.0	258964.1	258188.1	562.2	521.2
498206.9	164235.7	2609557.1	2474681.0	2335740.8	2208705.3	85740.9	85740.9
29746.6	17196.5	73993.2	72925.0	53425.7	52369.7	900.3	900.3
108897.9	92523.3	417832.6	404938.1	359156.4	344462.7	584.1	584.0
185506.0	115466.5	205036.6	203420.3	163157.9	162752.3	1643.5	1638.6
66185.9	24197.8	98593.8	97313.1	61511.9	61324.4	244.1	181.1
2803.2	1800.0	4946.1	4848.2	4067.4	4067.4	37.1	37.1
5622.6	3454.5	25307.9	25227.9	20696.5	20641.8	93.8	93.7
125167.3	100000.0	226508.7	187355.4	179746.8	157418.2	1773.5	1773.5

11-11 续表5

单位：万元

分组	Item	销售费用 Expenses for Sales	管理费用 Expenses for Management
纺织服装、鞋、帽制造业	Manufacture of Textile Wearing Apparel, Footwear and Caps		
皮革、毛皮、羽毛(绒)及其制品业	Manufacture of Leather, Fur, Feather (eiderdown) and Related Products		
木材加工及竹、藤、棕、草制品业	Processing of Timber,Manufacture of Wood,Plam and Straw Products		
家具制造业	Manufacture of Furniture		
造纸及纸制品业	Manufacture of Paper and Paper Products	596.9	788.3
印刷业、记录媒介的复制	Printing,Reproduction of Recording Media	1564.9	2195.6
文教、工美、体育和娱乐用品制造业	Manufacture of Articles For Cultural,Educational and Sports Activities		
石油加工、炼焦及核燃料加工业	Processing of Petroleum, Cokeing,Processing of Nuclear and Nuclear Fuel	769.6	561.4
化学原料及化学制品制造业	Manufacture of Raw Chemical Materials and Chemical Products	1776.9	1649.4
医药制造业	Manufacture of Medicines	221922.2	36717.6
化学纤维制造业	Manufacture of Chemical Fibers	180.5	2109.4
橡胶和塑料制品业	Manufacture of Rubber and Plastics	930.5	1771.5
非金属矿物制品业	Manufacture of Non-metallic Mineral Products	1896.2	3241.1
黑色金属冶炼及压延加工业	Smelting and Pressing of Ferrous Metals	778.3	976.5
有色金属冶炼及压延加工业	Smelting and Pressing of Non-ferrous Metals	1644.2	3634.5
金属制品业	Manufacture of Metal Products	403.4	1544.1
通用设备制造业	Manufacture of General Purpose Machinery	5122.2	5403.8
专用设备制造业	Manufacture of Special Equipment	7643.1	18662.6
汽车制造业	Manufacture of Motor Vehicle	21977.2	38570.3
铁路、船舶、航空航天和其他运输设备制造业	Railways,Shipbuilding,Aerospace and Other Transportation Equipment Manufacturing Industry	1444.8	5794.5
电气机械及器材制造业	Manufacture of Electric Equipment and Machinery	11467.2	17950.4
计算机、通讯和其他电子设备制造业	Manufacture of Communication Equipment, Computers and other Electronic Equipment	3017.6	12223.2
仪器仪表制造业	Manufacture of Measuring Instruments and Machinery	7515.5	10563.6
其他制造业	Manufacture of Other Manufacturing	185.7	288.7
废弃资源综合利用业	Recycling and Disposal of Waste		
金属制品、机械和设备修理业	Metal Products,Machinery and Equipment Repair Industry	1348.4	2152.8
电力、热力的生产和供应业	Production and Supply of Electric Power and Heat Power		
燃气生产和供应业	Gas Mining and Supplying Industry	8398.0	13473.3
水的生产和供应业	Production and Supply of Water		

continued 5

(10 000 yuan)

财务费用 Financial cost	营业利润 Operating Profit	利润总额 Total Profits	亏损企业亏损总额 Total Loss of Deficit Enterprises	利税总额 Total Pre-tax Profits	应付职工薪酬 Salary Payable	本年应交增值税 Value Added Tax Payable
39.9	3551.9	3529.4		4882.2	1189.1	1272.8
1519.8	1419.4	1782.6	2055.2	3105.1	3262.5	1160.1
-42.1	832.7	12.6		778.9	333.7	732.7
75.2	266.3	446.4	190.5	1448.8	697.7	763.2
6077.7	45242.8	47607.1	198.3	139335.8	75418.4	85925.4
-26.7	11062.4	11061.1		13818.8	3010.9	2433.6
454.6	1354.7	1371.1	42.9	2568.7	1935.5	1043.1
396.4	58058.4	60650.9		79021.2	3748.6	15639.8
71.0	5958.8	5429.2		7628.5	2925.8	2087.0
492.3	7802.1	7451.6		11408.1	2877.4	3490.6
-17.6	1446.0	1474.7		2203.5	2592.7	653.2
585.2	7390.2	7422.7		9342.0	7225.5	1743.2
-152.5	19980.6	19681.0		29468.0	17373.5	9224.8
11514.1	128789.9	129134.0	3721.7	259606.3	126204.4	44731.4
-92.5	11773.2	11873.3	1057.4	19349.1	3958.7	6575.5
1017.6	28281.9	25240.5	3285.7	46656.6	16377.0	20832.0
1383.3	23285.4	23674.2	4257.0	30240.8	18394.8	4923.1
523.5	18982.8	18862.8	676.0	22503.1	9288.1	3396.2
44.2	318.5	318.5		582.6	614.1	227.0
112.3	904.1	959.4	242.5	1806.5	1342.7	753.3
-2621.6	25375.8	24785.2		32093.8	21810.6	5535.1

11-12 规模以上大中型工业企业主要经济指标（2011年）

单位：万元

分组	Item	企业单位数（个） Number of Enterprises (unit)	亏损企业 Loss Making Enterprises	工业总产值（当年价） Gross Industrial Output Value (At Current Prices)
总计	**Total**	**217**	**37**	**27144277.5**
#市区	Urban Area	186	31	21367820.9
#亏损企业	Deficit Enterprises	37	37	4208551.3
按隶属关系分	Grouped by Jurisdiction of Management			
中央企业	Central Enterprises	51	10	10146155.0
省属企业	Provincial Enterprises	31	6	6775419.7
市属企业	Municipal Enterprises	135	21	10222702.8
按登记注册类型分组	Grouped by Registion Status			
内资企业	Domestic Investment Enterprises	186	32	21281283.4
国有经济	State-owned Enterprises	45	11	7196318.6
集体经济	Collective-owned Enterprises	4		45975.8
股份合作企业	Share-holding Corperative	1		92663.9
联营企业	Joint Ownership Enterprises			
有限责任公司	Limited Liability Corporations	83	16	11777148.3
国有独资公司	State Sole Funded Enterprises	18	3	2666904.4
其他有限责任公司	Other Limited Liability Corporation	65	13	9110243.9
股份有限公司	Share-holding Corperation Ltd.	32	4	1403456.3
私营企业	Private Enterprises	18	1	722444.1
其他内资企业	Other Domestic Funded Enterprises	2		43276.4
港、澳、台商投资企业	Enterprises with Funds from Hong Kong,Macao and Taiwan	5	1	145987.0
外商投资企业	Enterprises with Foreign Investment	27	4	5717007.1
按轻重工业分	Grouped by Light Industry and Heavy Industry			
轻工业	Light Industry	66	10	4464492.0
重工业	Heavy Industry	151	27	22679785.5
按企业规模分	Grouped by Size of Enterprises			
大型工业	Large-size	67	7	20882833.9
中型工业	Medium-size	150	30	6261443.6

Economic Indicators of Large and Medium-sized Industrial Enterprises Above Designated Size（2011）

（10 000 yuan）

工业销售产值（当年价）Value of Industry Products Sales (At Current Prices)	出口交货值 Export Delivery Value	从业人员年平均人数（人）Annual Average Employers (person)	资产总计 Total Assets	流动资产合计 Total Working Capitals	固定资产合计 Total Fixed Assets	固定资产原价 Origing Value of Fixed Assets	累计折旧 Accumulative Total Depreciation
26529714.5	**1754047.1**	**417008**	**34217635.8**	**19575228.8**	**11386777.2**	**14280950.9**	**5402990.3**
20960284.4	1440754.0	359147	29244632.1	16845581.3	9892763.1	12507682.2	4756076.7
4095917.1	198578.1	59017	6662115.2	3643190.0	2434112.7	2706065.8	996859.3
9919069.3	613741.2	175847	17101877.3	9500304.9	6757242.1	8366189.8	3142824.5
6653496.6	539690.6	83599	6628553.4	4150474.4	1624965.6	1866324.4	708064.9
9957148.6	600615.3	157562	10487205.1	5924449.5	3004569.5	4048436.7	1552100.9
20767526.4	1185928.1	353630	30461015.0	17685480.3	9926353.0	12357446.7	4751106.1
6998926.2	172412.9	101454	11177555.9	6015890.6	4510488.8	5773079.5	2025042.6
45364.4		3237	21181.3	7569.7	13268.5	15132.3	1964.1
98748.8		973	80958.6	63170.1	7719.6	15883.0	8163.4
11646683.2	913537.7	207319	15800829.0	9809640.1	4499565.9	5532781.1	2334890.3
2594470.0	232240.1	80286	4757770.0	2692691.9	1672854.0	2150183.9	898247.4
9052213.2	681297.6	127033	11043059.0	7116948.2	2826711.9	3382597.2	1436642.9
1303761.1	93971.7	27000	2764242.0	1391221.1	727573.1	783778.8	303985.3
636023.1	6005.8	12728	586022.9	381942.6	156254.4	220978.0	71292.6
38019.6		919	30225.3	16046.1	11482.7	15814.0	5767.8
166287.8	1060.5	3436	165635.6	69027.9	63091.6	104250.1	42522.1
5595900.3	567058.5	59942	3590985.2	1820720.6	1397332.6	1819254.1	609362.1
4535774.2	333383.3	67818	3251771.0	1815573.2	983487.4	1742632.8	832896.4
21993940.3	1420663.8	349190	30965864.8	17759655.6	10403289.8	12538318.1	4570093.9
20404388.8	1402571.3	314214	26315078.4	15571896.5	8577503.3	10566809.1	4143595.9
6125325.7	351475.8	102794	7902557.4	4003332.3	2809273.9	3714141.8	1259394.4

11-12　续表1

单位：万元

分　组	Item	负债合计 Total Liabilites	流动负债合计 Total Working Liabilities	非流动负债 Non-Working Liabilities
总　计	**Total**	**19836554.4**	**16095596.6**	**3551165.4**
#市　区	Urban Area	16456203.9	13210813.0	3056065.4
#亏损企业	Deficit Enterprises	3834092.7	2571401.1	1228602.1
按隶属关系分	Grouped by Jurisdiction of Management			
中央企业	Central Enterprises	9963309.7	7847701.9	2030440.3
省属企业	Provincial Enterprises	4159050.2	3655841.0	468063.9
市属企业	Municipal Enterprises	5714194.5	4592053.7	1052661.2
按登记注册类型分组	Grouped by Registion Status			
内资企业	Domestic Investment Enterprises	17738496.9	14205267.8	3355515.3
国有经济	State-owned Enterprises	6896597.8	5296059.2	1579966.2
集体经济	Collective-owned Enterprises	15859.0	15278.9	
股份合作企业	Share-holding Corperative	64620.8	64570.8	50.0
联营企业	Joint Ownership Enterprises			
有限责任公司	Limited Liability Corporations	9185816.8	7764968.0	1271213.3
国有独资公司	State Sole Funded Enterprises	2231032.3	1702917.6	456520.0
其他有限责任公司	Other Limited Liability Corporation	6954784.5	6062050.4	814693.3
股份有限公司	Share-holding Corperation Ltd.	1226223.8	757820.0	462419.1
私营企业	Private Enterprises	326614.9	291276.8	34397.0
其他内资企业	Other Domestic Funded Enterprises	22763.8	15294.1	7469.7
港、澳、台商投资企业	Enterprises with Funds from Hong Kong,Macao and Taiwan	104753.2	89720.8	3375.8
外商投资企业	Enterprises with Foreign Investment	1993304.3	1800608.0	192274.3
按轻重工业分	Grouped by Light Industry and Heavy Industry			
轻工业	Light Industry	1716503.3	1583891.7	112868.9
重工业	Heavy Industry	18120051.1	14511704.9	3438296.5
按企业规模分	Grouped by Size of Enterprises			
大型工业	Large-size	15398478.2	12960963.3	2329542.0
中型工业	Medium-size	4438076.2	3134633.3	1221623.4

continued 1

(10 000 yuan)

所有者权益合计 Total Owners' Equities	实收资本 Total Capital Hold	营业收入 Total Revenue	主营业务收入 Revenue from Principal Business	营业成本 Total Cost	主营业务成本 Cost of Principal Business	营业税金及附加 Taxs and Other Changes	主营业务税金及附加 Taxes and Other Charges on Principal Business
14374945.1	**5048844.2**	**26526485.3**	**25813665.1**	**22910730.5**	**22088727.9**	**297855.7**	**281716.8**
12782292.5	4058951.9	21558240.8	20997674.2	18520804.9	17840360.2	285366.5	269493.3
2828022.1	875112.8	3894470.6	3769133.6	3570136.1	3484887.5	110713.1	110610.5
7138566.2	2258963.8	10345787.0	10153665.9	9287173.7	8911723.5	138236.7	133326.3
2469503.1	947806.0	6239379.0	6046290.1	5356958.6	5191433.7	22044.0	21569.5
4766875.8	1842074.4	9941319.3	9613709.1	8266598.2	7985570.7	137575.0	126821.0
12716411.5	4340500.3	20644324.1	20149007.1	18029708.6	17382816.7	193395.4	177375.2
4280956.6	1218786.1	6764123.9	6596844.6	5933763.7	5794859.4	133312.1	131378.0
5322.3	4414.6	46537.1	46537.1	42987.7	42987.7	193.4	193.4
16337.8	6544.5	88740.8	84411.6	80046.8	80042.5	9.8	9.8
6608963.5	2589247.6	11792159.5	11515840.3	10439234.9	9969719.1	48019.3	34246.7
2526737.7	772008.5	2930645.0	2870821.5	2479153.4	2439324.8	11621.3	9993.0
4082225.8	1817239.1	8861514.5	8645018.8	7960081.5	7530394.3	36398.0	24253.7
1537962.0	406902.7	1304156.4	1280404.2	986006.8	969075.5	8830.3	8613.4
259407.8	102604.8	609236.3	585601.0	512865.4	491329.2	2871.3	2774.7
7461.5	12000.0	39370.1	39368.3	34803.3	34803.3	159.2	159.2
60852.8	56734.0	165017.9	161610.7	116234.7	113568.4	3206.2	3199.9
1597680.8	651609.9	5717143.3	5503047.3	4764787.2	4592342.8	101254.1	101141.7
1535181.7	663265.9	4497544.1	4409063.1	3552776.8	3486617.3	35960.8	25877.4
12839763.4	4385578.3	22028941.2	21404602.0	19357953.7	18602110.6	261894.9	255839.4
10916598.5	3417954.8	20404160.5	19871052.8	17727319.5	17063953.1	261118.9	255044.8
3458346.6	1630889.4	6122324.8	5942612.3	5183411.0	5024774.8	36736.8	26672.0

11-12 续表2

单位：万元

分　组	Item	销售费用 Expenses for Sales	管理费用 Expenses for Management
总　计	**Total**	**1078979.6**	**1554103.8**
#市　区	Urban Area	916598.5	1372049.6
#亏损企业	Deficit Enterprises	193543.2	257990.4
按隶属关系分	Grouped by Jurisdiction of Management		
中央企业	Central Enterprises	230043.4	779408.6
省属企业	Provincial Enterprises	400077.0	272466.6
市属企业	Municipal Enterprises	448859.2	502228.6
按登记注册类型分组	Grouped by Registion Status		
内资企业	Domestic Investment Enterprises	669580.5	1382865.7
国有经济	State-owned Enterprises	183947.8	507291.8
集体经济	Collective-owned Enterprises	910.4	1611.3
股份合作企业	Share-holding Corperative	3198.4	2098.0
联营企业	Joint Ownership Enterprises		
有限责任公司	Limited Liability Corporations	356657.8	731656.5
国有独资公司	State Sole Funded Enterprises	88592.1	234301.7
其他有限责任公司	Other Limited Liability Corporation	268065.7	497354.8
股份有限公司	Share-holding Corperation Ltd.	95017.7	115684.0
私营企业	Private Enterprises	29185.9	21904.2
其他内资企业	Other Domestic Funded Enterprises	662.5	2619.9
港、澳、台商投资企业	Enterprises with Funds from Hong Kong,Macao and Taiwan	26370.3	9386.1
外商投资企业	Enterprises with Foreign Investment	383028.8	161852.0
按轻重工业分	Grouped by Light Industry and Heavy Industry		
轻工业	Light Industry	489118.5	203671.8
重工业	Heavy Industry	589861.1	1350432.0
按企业规模分	Grouped by Size of Enterprises		
大型工业	Large-size	865083.9	1167827.0
中型工业	Medium-size	213895.7	386276.8

continued 2

（10 000 yuan）

财务费用 Financial cost	营业利润 Operating Profit	利润总额 Total Profits	亏损企业亏损总额 Total Loss of Deficit Enterprises	利税总额 Total Pre-tax Profits	应付职工薪酬 Salary Payable	本年应交增值税 Value Added Tax Payable
250601.5	**1032479.6**	**1105910.3**	**258846.3**	**2202881.6**	**2308523.1**	**799115.6**
195695.1	825152.5	893291.1	251779.1	1850241.0	2062882.6	671583.4
60222.8	-228519.1	-258846.3	258846.3	-55418.0	364911.7	92715.2
149326.0	124476.5	190524.9	196517.5	581714.5	1184872.8	252952.9
50960.0	167785.8	192537.1	8541.9	428924.1	383512.0	214343.0
50315.5	740217.3	722848.3	53786.9	1192243.0	740138.3	331819.7
228992.7	644875.0	726060.4	245783.4	1485713.0	1962023.7	566257.2
97212.9	66156.7	88820.4	186724.5	436567.1	700406.4	214434.6
169.1	656.4	668.0		1740.5	6702.2	879.1
2558.0	-3495.1	433.7		4693.8	3685.4	4250.3
103639.7	429721.9	473388.4	39765.8	799761.1	1075430.5	278353.4
18698.0	93699.7	122751.2	14036.0	205464.3	385781.1	71091.8
84941.7	336022.2	350637.2	25729.8	594296.8	689649.4	207261.6
14544.2	107090.7	125771.7	18923.1	182662.4	132158.9	48060.4
10472.5	43985.0	36363.3	370.0	57913.1	40269.5	18678.5
396.3	759.4	614.9		2375.0	3370.8	1600.9
1088.8	8722.1	9132.3	2055.2	21001.5	23484.9	8663.0
20520.0	378882.5	370717.6	11007.7	696167.1	323014.5	224195.4
31043.3	307177.2	289594.8	19175.8	566412.6	351164.8	240857.0
219558.2	725302.4	816315.5	239670.5	1636469.0	1957358.3	558258.6
171587.3	630332.2	686474.1	190866.1	1523329.5	1873544.4	575736.5
79014.2	402147.4	419436.2	67980.2	679552.1	434978.7	223379.1

11-12 续表3

单位：万元

分组	Item	企业单位数（个）Number of Enterprises (unit)	亏损企业 Loss Making Enterprises	工业总产值（当年价）Gross Industrial Output Value (At Current Prices)
按经济组织类型分	Grouped by Economic Type of Orgnization			
独资企业	Appropratorship	60	13	8303394.5
合作、合伙企业	Partnership	3		135940.3
股份有限公司	Corporaton	35	4	1697802.0
有限责任公司	Limited Liability Company	119	20	17007140.7
按控股情况分	Grouped by Cast strand			
国有控股	State owned shares	111	25	18457354.3
集体控股	Collective shares	12	1	599660.2
私人控股	Private holdings	58	5	4300709.1
港澳台控股	Hong Kong and Macao Holdings	3	1	112488.5
外商投资	Foreign Investment	22	4	2800571.6
其他	Others	11	1	873493.8
按工业行业大类分	Grouped by Sector			
煤炭开采和洗选业	Mining and Washing of Coal			
石油和天然气开采业	Extraction of Petroleum and Natural Gas			
黑色金属矿采选业	Mining and Processing of Ferrous Metal Ores			
有色金属矿采选业	Mining and Processing of Non-ferrous Metal Ores			
非金属矿采选业	Mining and Processing of Nonmetal Ores			
开采辅助活动	Mining Auxiliary Activities	1		28877.0
其他采矿业	Mining of other Ores			
农副食品加工业	Processing of Food from Agricultural Porducts	8	1	828137.8
食品制造业	Manufacture of Foods	9	3	837909.5
酒、饮料和精制茶制造业	Manufacture of Alcohol,Beverages and Tea	6	1	682791.6
烟草加工业	Manufacture of Tobacco			
纺织业	Manufacture of Textile	5	2	149961.3
纺织服装、鞋、帽制造业	Manufacture of Textile Wearing Apparel,Footwear and Caps	1		30223.4
皮革、毛皮、羽毛(绒)及其制品业	Manufacture of Leather, Fur, Feather (eiderdown) and Related Products	1		19701.9
木材加工及竹、藤、棕、草制品业	Processing of Timber,Manufacture of Wood,Plam and Straw Products	1		77633.3

continued 3

(10 000 yuan)

工业销售产值（当年价）Value of Industry Products Sales (At Current Prices)	出口交货值 Export Delivery Value	从业人员年平均人数（人）Annual Average Employers (person)	资产总计 Total Assets	流动资产合计 Total Working Capitals	固定资产合计 Total Fixed Assets	固定资产原价 Origing Value of Fixed Assets	累计折旧 Accumulative Total Depreciation
8098372.9	309469.0	117144	11976996.4	6387710.6	4868520.9	6333799.5	2243944.6
136768.4		1892	111183.9	79216.2	19202.3	31697.0	13931.2
1607642.2	280258.5	29783	3227723.2	1648156.5	907565.3	1026587.3	366801.7
16686931.0	1164319.6	268189	18901732.3	11460145.5	5591488.7	6888867.1	2778312.8
18072063.3	1089836.0	305165	27922737.9	16115011.4	9385768.6	11554562.6	4467042.4
591657.0	77333.8	10478	507063.3	314504.9	118552.0	172927.9	68106.3
4168334.8	89185.2	64029	3308752.8	1795400.6	1011652.2	1201066.8	362725.0
131264.5		2671	122612.2	47238.2	49833.7	82413.0	32594.4
2699023.4	375391.5	25070	1877642.8	994902.7	708028.3	1104423.3	416366.4
867371.5	122300.6	9595	478826.8	308171.0	112942.4	165557.3	56155.8
28877.0		638	47372.7	30339.5	10263.8	16912.3	6648.5
797737.6	5027.6	5057	463191.2	326485.0	109195.8	174813.6	72371.6
805848.4		8623	295062.3	178631.7	102328.2	181098.0	80147.6
845055.8	184938.0	7328	807068.1	375393.0	312424.4	478224.9	166258.7
137280.1	18552.7	13458	139179.4	67948.0	33771.0	73113.6	41669.4
31411.5		1324	67052.7	57885.3	8279.4	6129.5	2766.1
22174.8		724	37946.1	12599.9	3621.7	5350.7	1729.0
73677.6		495	78694.9	26695.5	44168.2	61035.0	18062.2

11-12 续表4

单位：万元

分组	Item	负债合计 Total Liabilites	流动负债合计 Total Working Liabilities	非流动负债 Non-Working Liabilities
按经济组织类型分	Grouped by Economic Type of Orgnization			
独资企业	Appropratorship	7223805.0	5547619.9	1654106.2
合作、合伙企业	Partnership	87384.6	79864.9	7519.7
股份有限公司	Corporaton	1516491.3	1017180.4	493326.2
有限责任公司	Limited Liability Company	11008873.5	9450931.4	1396213.3
按控股情况分	Grouped by Cast strand			
国有控股	State owned shares	16499815.2	13135453.8	3230985.2
集体控股	Collective shares	315026.3	290695.3	23750.8
私人控股	Private holdings	1741733.9	1521919.2	182615.3
港澳台控股	Hong Kong and Macao Holdings	80291.8	65670.6	3375.8
外商投资	Foreign Investment	960714.0	875411.4	84880.7
其他	Others	238973.2	206446.3	25557.6
按工业行业大类分	Grouped by Sector			
煤炭开采和洗选业	Mining and Washing of Coal			
石油和天然气开采业	Extraction of Petroleum and Natural Gas			
黑色金属矿采选业	Mining and Processing of Ferrous Metal Ores			
有色金属矿采选业	Mining and Processing of Non-ferrous Metal Ores			
非金属矿采选业	Mining and Processing of Nonmetal Ores			
开采辅助活动	Mining Auxiliary Activities	11961.4	11961.4	
其他采矿业	Mining of other Ores			
农副食品加工业	Processing of Food from Agricultural Porducts	356325.8	348582.9	1347.3
食品制造业	Manufacture of Foods	140569.0	134762.6	5806.3
酒、饮料和精制茶制造业	Manufacture of Alcohol,Beverages and Tea	483359.0	468453.2	14401.3
烟草加工业	Manufacture of Tobacco			
纺织业	Manufacture of Textile	64828.5	58196.4	6052.1
纺织服装、鞋、帽制造业	Manufacture of Textile Wearing Apparel,Footwear and Caps	55416.7	48416.7	7000.0
皮革、毛皮、羽毛(绒)及其制品业	Manufacture of Leather, Fur, Feather (eiderdown) and Related Products	18895.8	11378.9	7516.9
木材加工及竹、藤、棕、草制品业	Processing of Timber,Manufacture of Wood,Plam and Straw Products	30201.4	11201.4	19000.0

continued 4

(10 000 yuan)

所有者权益合计 Total Owners' Equities	实收资本 Total Capital Hold	营业收入 Total Revenue	主营业务收入 Revenue from Principal Business	营业成本 Total Cost	主营业务成本 Cost of Principal Business	营业税金及附加 Taxs and Other Changes	主营业务税金及附加 Taxes and Other Charges on Principal Business
4753189.8	1445303.1	7891626.2	7713813.0	6871782.3	6724084.8	140055.1	138114.7
23799.3	18544.5	128110.9	123779.9	114850.1	114845.8	169.0	169.0
1711175.7	444780.7	1601169.8	1554940.5	1255984.3	1219430.7	9842.8	9625.9
7886780.3	3140215.9	16905578.4	16421131.7	14668113.8	14030366.6	147788.8	133807.2
11422891.3	3964199.5	18057367.5	17592107.5	15905670.6	15290920.8	181385.1	166185.0
192036.9	65311.3	611049.7	592037.0	468506.8	461643.0	1701.8	1701.3
1560970.3	482012.4	4107502.3	3942972.4	3580423.0	3431193.6	97295.3	96964.0
42320.4	47581.3	133063.8	130651.9	92950.7	91184.4	2997.8	2991.5
916928.7	366748.1	2777332.1	2742171.2	2142337.1	2127995.8	11822.2	11815.3
239797.5	122991.6	840169.9	813725.1	720842.3	685790.3	2653.5	2059.7
35411.3	3182.7	27998.4	27383.5	17850.3	17690.8	873.6	840.4
106835.7	55769.3	790862.3	784633.1	742889.9	742487.6	919.2	855.8
154493.0	64584.7	813077.0	805004.1	715400.1	708012.5	3149.3	3061.9
323709.2	116886.8	841808.3	820826.4	658117.2	652317.2	14961.8	5782.3
74350.8	19854.2	141619.9	139959.9	136101.4	128493.6	987.2	749.2
11636.0	7500.0	49112.3	49105.6	34865.7	34865.7	2654.0	2654.0
19050.3	6000.0	43630.1	22401.2	40619.4	19556.2	58.3	58.3
48493.5	12500.0	71015.9	70097.6	70091.2	70091.2	248.6	248.6

11-12 续表5

单位：万元

分 组	Item	销售费用 Expenses for Sales	管理费用 Expenses for Management
按经济组织类型分	Grouped by Economic Type of Orgnization		
独资企业	Appropratorship	297011.8	554528.5
合作、合伙企业	Partnership	3860.9	4717.9
股份有限公司	Corporaton	101345.3	127509.1
有限责任公司	Limited Liability Company	676761.6	867348.3
按控股情况分	Grouped by Cast strand		
国有控股	State owned shares	548500.5	1225321.3
集体控股	Collective shares	29015.9	51597.4
私人控股	Private holdings	130744.1	124610.9
港澳台控股	Hong Kong and Macao Holdings	24624.8	7421.1
外商投资	Foreign Investment	333957.3	101411.9
其他	Others	12137.0	43741.2
按工业行业大类分	Grouped by Sector		
煤炭开采和洗选业	Mining and Washing of Coal		
石油和天然气开采业	Extraction of Petroleum and Natural Gas		
黑色金属矿采选业	Mining and Processing of Ferrous Metal Ores		
有色金属矿采选业	Mining and Processing of Non-ferrous Metal Ores		
非金属矿采选业	Mining and Processing of Nonmetal Ores		
开采辅助活动	Mining Auxiliary Activities	52.0	2748.7
其他采矿业	Mining of other Ores		
农副食品加工业	Processing of Food from Agricultural Porducts	23087.0	12333.1
食品制造业	Manufacture of Foods	85917.1	27073.0
酒、饮料和精制茶制造业	Manufacture of Alcohol,Beverages and Tea	78051.6	28564.0
烟草加工业	Manufacture of Tobacco		
纺织业	Manufacture of Textile	1227.6	11353.3
纺织服装、鞋、帽制造业	Manufacture of Textile Wearing Apparel,Footwear and Caps	2691.8	4373.5
皮革、毛皮、羽毛(绒)及其制品业	Manufacture of Leather, Fur, Feather (eiderdown) and Related Products	709.5	863.0
木材加工及竹、藤、棕、草制品业	Processing of Timber,Manufacture of Wood,Plam and Straw Products	1897.5	1828.6

continued 5

(10 000 yuan)

财务费用 Financial cost	营业利润 Operating Profit	利润总额 Total Profits	亏损企业亏损总额 Total Loss of Deficit Enterprises	利税总额 Total Pre-tax Profits	应付职工薪酬 Salary Payable	本年应交增值税 Value Added Tax Payable
95830.2	138184.7	166553.0	192320.5	559930.3	784924.5	253322.2
2954.3	-2735.7	1048.6		7068.8	7056.2	5851.2
23651.3	127888.9	148727.1	18923.1	230793.9	146794.0	72224.0
128165.7	769141.7	789581.6	47602.7	1405088.6	1369748.4	467718.2
185228.0	449098.8	526642.6	237079.7	1172833.2	1797427.0	464805.5
7216.9	60082.9	62248.8	185.4	83557.7	35539.1	19607.1
39658.3	194505.8	181806.4	8390.5	393304.9	229291.6	114203.2
494.3	4543.4	4805.0	2055.2	14593.8	19227.1	6791.0
13127.5	251214.0	256985.9	11007.7	427341.6	183690.3	158533.5
4876.5	73034.7	73421.6	127.8	111250.4	43348.0	35175.3
-7.2	6481.0	6514.4		11999.8	4704.5	4611.8
9600.5	27346.0	2113.0	7064.4	14710.3	17567.8	11678.1
-1680.3	42978.1	33774.8	4224.0	55588.4	31431.6	18664.3
4857.4	81888.5	81059.6	3147.4	148796.9	59052.1	52775.5
442.6	-1534.1	1055.2	2386.8	8557.7	35094.2	6515.3
249.5	1271.8	2363.0		5583.1	3780.0	566.1
215.4	1326.2	1410.8		1469.1	3437.3	
1927.4	676.1	687.4		9031.9	1104.0	8095.9

11-12 续表6

单位：万元

分组	Item	企业单位数（个） Number of Enterprises (unit)	亏损企业 Loss Making Enterprises	工业总产值（当年价） Gross Industrial Output Value (At Current Prices)
家具制造业	Manufacture of Furniture	1		15927.3
造纸及纸制品业	Manufacture of Paper and Paper Products	6		117562.9
印刷业、记录媒介的复制	Printing,Reproduction of Recording Media	11	2	397645.4
文教、工美、体育和娱乐用品制造业	Manufacture of Articles For Cultural,Educational and Sports Activities			
石油加工、炼焦及核燃料加工业	Processing of Petroleum, Cokeing,Processing of Nuclear and Nuclear Fuel	1	1	797042.0
化学原料及化学制品制造业	Manufacture of Raw Chemical Materials and Chemical Products	14	2	1196451.0
医药制造业	Manufacture of Medicines	11		851384.6
化学纤维制造业	Manufacture of Chemical Fibers			
橡胶塑料制品业	Manufacture of Rubber and Plastics	3		187894.0
非金属矿物制品业	Manufacture of Non-metallic Mineral Products	6	2	210617.1
黑色金属冶炼及压延加工业	Smelting and Pressing of Ferrous Metals	1	1	7426.5
有色金属冶炼及压延加工业	Smelting and Pressing of Non-ferrous Metals	6	1	401705.7
金属制品业	Manufacture of Metal Products	8	2	329139.6
通用设备制造业	Manufacture of General Purpose Machinery	7	1	1091018.6
专用设备制造业	Manufacture of Special Equipment	25	3	1370438.7
汽车制造业	Manufacture of Motor Vehicle	14	1	7719970.9
铁路、船舶、航空航天和其他运输设备制造业	Railways,Shipbuilding,Aerospace and Other Transportation Equipment Manufacturing Industry	19	1	2932198.9
电气机械及器材制造业	Manufacture of Electric Equipment and Machinery	15	4	2367214.4
计算机、通讯和其他电子设备制造业	Manufacture of Communication Equipment, Computers and other Electronic Equipment	21	5	1194876.1
仪器仪表制造业	Manufacture of Measuring Instruments and Machinery	7		756007.8
其他制造业	Manufacture of Other Manufacturing			
废弃资源综合利用业	Recycling and Disposal of Waste			
金属制品、机械和设备修理业	Metal Products,Machinery and Equipment Repair Industry			
电力、热力的生产和供应业	Production and Supply of Electric Power and Heat Power	8	4	2292805.8
燃气生产和供应业	Gas Mining and Supplying Industry	1		187707.0
水的生产和供应业	Production and Supply of Water	1		64007.4

continued 6

(10 000 yuan)

工业销售产值（当年价）Value of Industry Products Sales (At Current Prices)	出口交货值 Export Delivery Value	从业人员年平均人数（人）Annual Average Employers (person)	资产总计 Total Assets	流动资产合计 Total Working Capitals	固定资产合计 Total Fixed Assets	固定资产原价 Origing Value of Fixed Assets	累计折旧 Accumulative Total Depreciation
15596.9		800	1585.6	985.6	600.0	670.0	70.0
118385.6		5230	51090.5	18932.3	30125.6	49928.1	19848.5
401993.4	1060.5	7415	494508.2	254458.7	164915.1	298491.9	164519.8
810508.0		1407	198234.6	78665.1	119569.5	127307.0	57705.9
1168511.3	106252.4	31767	1638828.1	779835.2	665044.6	925888.9	378680.2
838714.2	6815.2	10192	607652.7	372306.4	106875.8	201962.4	107052.0
188859.4	1954.0	10476	332067.4	166291.4	99538.2	96901.3	35278.4
207612.6		2674	166242.9	64741.9	92527.7	110884.9	31402.3
7426.5		678	8410.9	6111.3	1736.6	2237.8	501.2
364438.5	22444.7	4392	497378.4	264936.6	144937.6	180412.3	47770.8
340436.9	18636.7	9466	616452.8	380623.2	185753.8	248774.0	99473.9
1033039.9	27123.5	12714	2114092.4	1738242.2	238466.5	339842.8	131914.6
1220242.5	80195.4	20905	2003162.5	1392707.9	402213.8	582080.3	193494.8
7596479.0	380797.6	81356	5848948.0	3320592.5	1707448.4	1771958.4	591807.4
2869637.4	387807.8	66129	6442544.3	4166838.5	1846750.4	2100328.7	927917.4
2286508.7	282969.3	28210	3836438.1	2708123.0	1076830.1	991855.1	365137.8
1072085.3	165325.6	21740	2576450.2	1208461.1	808868.0	851598.0	282868.6
688734.6	64146.1	19600	1389923.8	848553.7	432381.2	627311.0	279486.0
2306726.6		39427	3039167.9	536912.1	2410184.9	3431684.2	1133158.1
187707.0		2014	311871.6	150963.7	160907.9	160366.1	33556.4
64007.4		2769	107017.5	39968.5	67049.0	183790.1	131693.1

11-12 续表7

单位：万元

分组	Item	负债合计 Total Liabilites	流动负债合计 Total Working Liabilities	非流动负债 Non-Working Liabilities
家具制造业	Manufacture of Furniture	11.4	11.4	
造纸及纸制品业	Manufacture of Paper and Paper Products	30962.4	24906.7	4534.5
印刷业、记录媒介的复制	Printing,Reproduction of Recording Media	179462.0	141337.7	27383.2
文教、工美、体育和娱乐用品制造业	Manufacture of Articles For Cultural,Educational and Sports Activities			
石油加工、炼焦及核燃料加工业	Processing of Petroleum, Cokeing,Processing of Nuclear and Nuclear Fuel	251723.7	251685.9	37.8
化学原料及化学制品制造业	Manufacture of Raw Chemical Materials and Chemical Products	776181.5	584718.0	158389.5
医药制造业	Manufacture of Medicines	230975.4	218837.0	12138.3
化学纤维制造业	Manufacture of Chemical Fibers			
橡胶塑料制品业	Manufacture of Rubber and Plastics	249479.4	200527.6	48951.8
非金属矿物制品业	Manufacture of Non-metallic Mineral Products	58224.8	56499.6	1303.3
黑色金属冶炼及压延加工业	Smelting and Pressing of Ferrous Metals	9089.2	9089.2	
有色金属冶炼及压延加工业	Smelting and Pressing of Non-ferrous Metals	298918.5	232663.4	29997.0
金属制品业	Manufacture of Metal Products	378885.7	279192.1	76875.4
通用设备制造业	Manufacture of General Purpose Machinery	1255826.4	1214706.3	41120.1
专用设备制造业	Manufacture of Special Equipment	967359.0	846366.8	102022.8
汽车制造业	Manufacture of Motor Vehicle	3465587.0	3131027.6	334514.7
铁路、船舶、航空航天和其他运输设备制造业	Railways,Shipbuilding,Aerospace and Other Transportation Equipment Manufacturing Industry	3858612.5	3255673.9	544475.3
电气机械及器材制造业	Manufacture of Electric Equipment and Machinery	1881371.1	1531165.0	350206.0
计算机、通讯和其他电子设备制造业	Manufacture of Communication Equipment, Computers and other Electronic Equipment	1550127.2	916946.1	633180.9
仪器仪表制造业	Manufacture of Measuring Instruments and Machinery	697403.6	565934.0	131469.6
其他制造业	Manufacture of Other Manufacturing			
废弃资源综合利用业	Recycling and Disposal of Waste			
金属制品、机械和设备修理业	Metal Products,Machinery and Equipment Repair Industry			
电力、热力的生产和供应业	Production and Supply of Electric Power and Heat Power	2303381.6	1350489.6	952892.1
燃气生产和供应业	Gas Mining and Supplying Industry	186704.3	163623.4	23080.9
水的生产和供应业	Production and Supply of Water	44710.1	27241.8	17468.3

continued 7

(10 000 yuan)

所有者权益合计 Total Owners' Equities	实收资本 Total Capital Hold	营业收入 Total Revenue	主营业务收入 Revenue from Principal Business	营业成本 Total Cost	主营业务成本 Cost of Principal Business	营业税金及附加 Taxs and Other Changes	主营业务税金及附加 Taxes and Other Charges on Principal Business
1574.2	910.1	15596.9	15596.9	12165.6	12165.6	17.9	17.9
20128.1	18500.3	122023.7	122023.7	111705.9	111705.9	242.5	242.5
314990.2	151624.3	390294.8	382165.4	275794.0	270924.8	3941.5	3472.9
-53489.1	43922.8	810580.4	808926.5	784106.3	784099.3	91321.2	91321.1
862646.5	317175.2	1225798.5	1160283.3	974101.3	925303.6	4684.9	3897.0
376677.3	122613.6	771782.2	768998.5	381146.6	380633.9	7412.1	7412.1
82588.0	68630.4	192607.8	189046.8	167196.3	157110.7	6052.1	6052.1
108017.7	26750.0	188631.9	184696.6	149398.9	145520.3	920.4	920.4
-678.3	1000.0	10846.0	7426.5	10698.4	7072.9	66.3	66.3
198459.8	67792.9	351508.1	338990.1	287606.4	278353.7	1422.9	1422.9
237567.1	81306.3	299063.6	295170.1	250945.8	244665.8	617.1	617.1
858265.7	96307.0	932059.2	920908.9	688216.0	679055.4	5190.2	4991.9
1029755.5	528463.8	1293271.2	1282793.3	1029197.9	1022407.9	8747.8	8683.3
2383360.9	897625.0	7128699.5	6866881.0	6379299.8	6125794.0	96643.5	96256.3
2583930.7	767406.1	3392484.2	3337176.7	3133212.4	2859986.1	12588.8	9673.1
1955066.9	286971.6	2045101.0	1950260.5	1725574.6	1653762.9	15661.5	15638.8
1026322.9	331773.9	1164567.2	1132802.4	1010091.5	980025.8	4304.3	3754.9
692520.2	345020.9	789011.2	779130.0	645243.3	639099.7	4042.8	3210.9
735786.3	469772.3	2327763.3	2299613.7	2239479.5	2222945.6	7673.2	7385.9
125167.3	100000.0	226508.7	187355.4	179746.8	157418.2	1773.5	1773.5
62307.4	39000.0	69161.7	64007.4	59868.0	57161.0	679.2	655.4

11-12 续表8

单位：万元

分　组	Item	销售费用 Expenses for Sales	管理费用 Expenses for Management
家具制造业	Manufacture of Furniture	782.4	1637.0
造纸及纸制品业	Manufacture of Paper and Paper Products	1915.4	1894.3
印刷业、记录媒介的复制	Printing,Reproduction of Recording Media	10153.9	41450.2
文教、工美、体育和娱乐用品制造业	Manufacture of Articles For Cultural,Educational and Sports Activities		
石油加工、炼焦及核燃料加工业	Processing of Petroleum, Cokeing,Processing of Nuclear and Nuclear Fuel	1624.6	14948.4
化学原料及化学制品制造业	Manufacture of Raw Chemical Materials and Chemical Products	43355.4	125508.6
医药制造业	Manufacture of Medicines	258952.3	50017.1
化学纤维制造业	Manufacture of Chemical Fibers		
橡胶塑料制品业	Manufacture of Rubber and Plastics	14444.7	7952.7
非金属矿物制品业	Manufacture of Non-metallic Mineral Products	11439.5	6100.1
黑色金属冶炼及压延加工业	Smelting and Pressing of Ferrous Metals		1079.5
有色金属冶炼及压延加工业	Smelting and Pressing of Non-ferrous Metals	3093.9	15931.5
金属制品业	Manufacture of Metal Products	7913.0	29290.0
通用设备制造业	Manufacture of General Purpose Machinery	33041.7	120262.4
专用设备制造业	Manufacture of Special Equipment	57595.6	113002.8
汽车制造业	Manufacture of Motor Vehicle	201687.0	192853.2
铁路、船舶、航空航天和其他运输设备制造业	Railways,Shipbuilding,Aerospace and Other Transportation Equipment Manufacturing Industry	64806.9	271599.8
电气机械及器材制造业	Manufacture of Electric Equipment and Machinery	127540.5	179448.4
计算机、通讯和其他电子设备制造业	Manufacture of Communication Equipment, Computers and other Electronic Equipment	21520.9	88413.6
仪器仪表制造业	Manufacture of Measuring Instruments and Machinery	13487.8	90378.6
其他制造业	Manufacture of Other Manufacturing		
废弃资源综合利用业	Recycling and Disposal of Waste		
金属制品、机械和设备修理业	Metal Products,Machinery and Equipment Repair Industry		
电力、热力的生产和供应业	Production and Supply of Electric Power and Heat Power	760.4	92641.3
燃气生产和供应业	Gas Mining and Supplying Industry	8398.0	13473.3
水的生产和供应业	Production and Supply of Water	2831.6	7083.8

continued 8

(10 000 yuan)

财务费用 Financial cost	营业利润 Operating Profit	利润总额 Total Profits	亏损企业亏损总额 Total Loss of Deficit Enterprises	利税总额 Total Pre-tax Profits	应付职工薪酬 Salary Payable	本年应交增值税 Value Added Tax Payable
19.8	974.2	974.2		1447.3	1173.6	455.2
1303.6	6317.6	3551.0		5496.7	17303.3	1703.2
2764.5	60652.5	60825.7	2172.6	88337.8	56247.1	23570.6
6149.1	-90586.8	-90660.4	90660.4	6291.3	10614.3	5630.5
10851.8	85220.6	99671.6	19411.1	140796.9	136498.5	36440.4
10631.0	65708.2	80845.1		188908.5	91782.3	100651.3
3988.3	4395.9	4883.4		14880.5	32759.2	3945.0
952.9	26336.5	29872.4	335.3	45951.6	7248.0	15158.8
31.7	-1032.3	-1026.7	1026.7	-279.8	2657.9	680.6
12448.6	34054.6	33624.2	707.9	48923.0	19649.6	13875.9
7303.6	18196.6	17558.6	585.1	22340.8	53404.0	4165.1
-6478.1	102209.3	107848.4	199.1	152663.6	113297.7	39625.0
5493.1	102983.4	100123.1	7897.0	161330.7	122847.6	52459.8
32561.7	248928.1	253977.8	3756.1	495797.3	354510.7	145176.0
46489.6	108915.9	156403.8	1616.4	203710.3	452501.2	34717.7
17537.6	-18407.6	-29724.0	69564.4	71655.9	212483.4	85718.4
11351.9	40644.9	53852.6	21130.3	79343.3	109995.6	21186.4
4296.4	29935.6	36148.1		83733.4	175299.4	43542.5
70007.1	22447.9	31541.4	22961.3	97345.3	144322.1	58130.7
-2621.6	25375.8	24785.2		32093.8	21810.6	5535.1
-86.4	-1224.9	1856.6		6376.2	15945.5	3840.4

11–13 规模以上工业高技术产业企业主要经济指标（2011年）

单位：万元

分 组	Item	企业单位数（个） Number of Enterprises (unit)	亏损企业 Loss Making Enterprises	工业总产值（当年价） Gross Industrial Output Value (At Current Prices)
总 计	**Total**	**151**	**20**	**6348022.5**
一、信息化学品制造	**Information Chemical Products**	**2**		**275537.0**
二、医药制造业	**Medicines Manufacturing**	**45**	**6**	**1128780.6**
#化学药品原药制造业	Chemical Medicine Manufacturing			
中成药制造业	Traditional Chinese Midicine	20	3	210567.0
生物、生化制品的制造业	Biology,Biochemistry Products			
三、航空航天器制造业	**Aviation and Aircrafts Manufacturing**	**12**	**1**	**2442834.2**
1.飞机制造及修理业	Manufacture and Repairing of Aircrafts			
2.航天器制造业	Aircrafts Manufacturing	4		233305.0
四、电子及通讯设备制造业	**Electronic and Communication Equipment**	**48**	**9**	**1446014.9**
1.通信设备制造业	Communication Equipment Manufacturing	12	2	333517.6
#通信传输设备制造业	Communication Transmitting Equipment			
通信交换设备制造业	Communication Exchanging Equipment			
通信终端设备制造业	Communication Terminal Equipment	2	1	4855.9
移动通信及终端设备制造业	Mobile Communication and Terminal Equipment			
2.雷达及配套设备制造业	Rader Equipments	2		220015.6
3.广播电视设备制造业	Broadcast and Television Equipments	2		23878.7
4.电子器件制造业	Electronic Appliances Manufacturing	16	3	573874.2
电子真空器件制造业	Electronic Vacuum Appliances	3	1	83136.6
半导体分立器件制造	Semiconductor Discreting Appliances	8		390503.4
集成电路制造	Integrate Circuit	3	2	83491.6
光电子器件及其他电子器件制造	Photoelectron Appliances and Other Electronic Appliances	2		16742.6
5.电子元件制造	Electronic Components Manufacturing	15	4	270760.6
6.家用视听设备制造	Household Audiovisual			
7.其他电子设备制造	Other Electronic Equipment	1		23968.2
五、电子计算机及办公设备制造业	**Computers and Office Equipment Manufacturing**	**2**		**11053.8**
1.电子计算机整机制造	Entired Computer Manufacturing			
2.计算机网络设备制造	Computer Network Equipment			
3.电子计算机外部设备制造	Computer Peripheral Equipment			
4.办公设备维修	Repairing of Office Equipment			
六、医疗设备及仪器仪表	**Medical Equipments and Meters**	**41**	**4**	**1041375.8**
1.医疗仪器设备及器械制造	Medical Equipments and Instruments	2	1	6074.6
2.仪器仪表制造业	Instruments and Meters	39	3	1035301.2
七、其他	**Others**	**1**		**2426.2**

Economic Indicators of High Technology Industry

Industrial Enterprises Above Designated Size（2011）

（10 000 yuan）

工业销售产值（当年价）Value of Industry Products Sales (At Current Prices)	从业人员年平均人数（人）Annual Average Employers (person)	资产合计 Total Assets	流动资产小计 Total Working Capitals	固定资产小计 Total Fixed Assets	固定资产原价合计 Origing Value of Fixed Assets	累计折旧 Accumulative Total Depreciation
6037223.3	**121974**	**11665685.4**	**7085406.5**	**3937529.2**	**1645566.7**	**1517531.4**
267004.2	**1861**	**222591.0**	**115300.5**	**102006.3**	**38476.0**	**19787.6**
1083583.7	**14974**	**858145.7**	**523847.3**	**321471.6**	**162905.1**	**118781.1**
189090.9	3551	214654.8	133050.3	60228.6	22969.1	28453.2
2416096.4	**54662**	**5861600.6**	**3813988.6**	**1886894.5**	**834245.0**	**585327.3**
224633.7	6444	582740.4	280054.6	277781.3	108895.1	63027.3
1298352.3	**25916**	**2919463.0**	**1475571.3**	**917855.9**	**307119.7**	**401677.4**
321998.1	3429	304392.0	248981.6	64166.4	21930.8	136065.3
5608.5	457	30823.4	15095.5	13426.6	3220.1	6403.2
148353.4	3775	452958.3	347892.7	114186.9	35671.1	46820.4
22957.6	255	24389.5	19029.5	3386.8	1589.3	8900.7
529079.7	10262	1646250.7	575615.1	618815.1	201839.6	124444.3
80761.2	4069	950217.7	222577.0	246897.5	102249.0	25146.4
357478.0	3345	382958.8	273429.8	96882.4	30738.2	80447.4
75111.4	1749	293909.9	70202.1	263870.2	65226.3	15677.4
15729.1	1099	19164.3	9406.2	11165.0	3626.1	3173.1
251995.3	8102	479109.5	272943.9	116533.9	45820.7	78919.5
23968.2	93	12363.0	11108.5	766.8	268.2	6527.2
10591.0	**211**	**13888.1**	**8688.3**	**6921.9**	**2315.1**	**1576.2**
959195.6	**24290**	**1787370.6**	**1146480.9**	**700446.3**	**299669.9**	**389574.6**
6422.8	236	18031.1	9990.2	6694.0	1394.3	3630.8
952772.8	24054	1769339.5	1136490.7	693752.3	298275.6	385943.8
2400.1	**60.0**	**2626.4**	**1529.6**	**1932.7**	**835.9**	**807.2**

11-13 续表1

单位：万元

分组	Item	负债合计 Total Liabilites	流动负债小计 Total Working Liabilities	非流动负债合计 Non-Working Liabilities
总　计	**Total**	**6633612.0**	**5195983.8**	**1335457.2**
一、信息化学品制造	**Information Chemical Products**	**140999.2**	**107768.0**	**14811.3**
二、医药制造业	**Medicines Manufacturing**	**354458.0**	**328720.1**	**16647.4**
#化学药品原药制造业	Chemical Medicine Manufacturing			
中成药制造业	Traditional Chinese Midicine	127036.6	104657.8	13288.3
生物、生化制品的制造业	Biology,Biochemistry Products			
三、航空航天器制造业	**Aviation and Aircrafts Manufacturing**	**3506806.8**	**2944495.5**	**505804.9**
1.飞机制造及修理业	Manufacture and Repairing of Aircrafts			
2.航天器制造业	Aircrafts Manufacturing	280334.8	198867.9	81466.8
四、电子及通讯设备制造业	**Electronic and Communication Equipment**	**1735254.8**	**1068569.8**	**650936.2**
1.通信设备制造业	Communication Equipment Manufacturing	172690.9	164587.5	5806.3
#通信传输设备制造业	Communication Transmitting Equipment			
通信交换设备制造业	Communication Exchanging Equipment			
通信终端设备制造业	Communication Terminal Equipment	21561.5	20355.7	1205.8
移动通信及终端设备制造业	Mobile Communication and Terminal Equipment			
2.雷达及配套设备制造业	Rader Equipments	322090.3	278980.6	43109.7
3.广播电视设备制造业	Broadcast and Television Equipments	18215.7	17825.5	390.2
4.电子器件制造业	Electronic Appliances Manufacturing	844252.3	330684.9	500768.9
电子真空器件制造业	Electronic Vacuum Appliances	467371.8	71164.2	396207.5
半导体分立器件制造	Semiconductor Discreting Appliances	241862.7	195712.3	46150.3
集成电路制造	Integrate Circuit	127280.4	57145.0	57337.1
光电子器件及其他电子器件制造	Photoelectron Appliances and Other Electronic Appliances	7737.4	6663.4	1074.0
5.电子元件制造	Electronic Components Manufacturing	375740.4	274226.2	100861.1
6.家用视听设备制造	Household Audiovisual			
7.其他电子设备制造	Other Electronic Equipment	2265.2	2265.1	
五、电子计算机及办公设备制造业	**Computers and Office Equipment Manufacturing**	**2848.1**	**2848.1**	
1.电子计算机整机制造	Entired Computer Manufacturing			
2.计算机网络设备制造	Computer Network Equipment			
3.电子计算机外部设备制造	Computer Peripheral Equipment			
4.办公设备维修	Repairing of Office Equipment			
六、医疗设备及仪器仪表	**Medical Equipments and Meters**	**891624.5**	**742596.1**	**146623.0**
1.医疗仪器设备及器械制造	Medical Equipments and Instruments	11776.7	9106.7	1770.0
2.仪器仪表制造业	Instruments and Meters	879847.8	733489.4	144853.0
七、其他	**Others**	**1620.6**	**986.2**	**634.4**

continued 1

(10 000 yuan)

所有者权益合计 Total Owners' Equities	实收资本 Total Capital Hold	主营业务收入 Revenue from Principal Business	主营业务成本 Cost of Principal Business	主营业务税金及附加 Taxes and Other Charges on Principal Business
5031484.7	**1726042.1**	**6599649.7**	**5225659.0**	**32207.4**
81591.8	**26268.0**	**263396.7**	**211096.5**	**301.3**
503544.1	**214589.8**	**1019817.7**	**551429.2**	**8780.5**
87558.0	55744.3	186173.3	118099.7	1103.9
2354787.4	**582852.2**	**2862904.3**	**2465366.9**	**10027.0**
302399.3	20226.9	243242.3	193507.4	1036.4
1183942.2	**457303.2**	**1392661.9**	**1164450.6**	**6833.6**
131435.2	123088.6	354083.3	286595.4	1874.3
9261.8	6770.5	5097.7	3827.3	362.0
130868.0	27678.0	233676.8	192673.4	230.3
6173.8	2500.0	22957.6	19851.6	492.2
801998.3	244447.0	505084.6	443096.5	2067.8
482845.9	79684.2	80636.9	67019.8	344.1
141096.1	65454.1	334759.3	292158.0	1615.3
166629.4	89308.7	74086.2	72491.5	9.6
11426.9	10000.0	15602.2	11427.2	98.8
103369.1	58789.6	252891.4	205213.5	2029.7
10097.8	800.0	23968.2	17020.2	139.3
11040.0	**8500.0**	**9943.3**	**7366.7**	**38.8**
895573.4	**435628.9**	**1048728.0**	**824190.6**	**6220.5**
6254.4	4100.0	6437.2	4086.2	80.6
889319.0	431528.9	1042290.8	820104.4	6139.9
1005.8	**900.0**	**2197.8**	**1758.5**	**5.7**

11-13 续表2

单位：万元

分组	Item	销售费用 Expenses for Sales	管理费用 Expenses for Management
总 计	**Total**	**410541.9**	**547157.4**
一、信息化学品制造	**Information Chemical Products**	**1256.2**	**21110.7**
二、医药制造业	**Medicines Manufacturing**	**293969.1**	**72051.6**
#化学药品原药制造业	Chemical Medicine Manufacturing		
中成药制造业	Traditional Chinese Midicine	41987.9	14047.5
生物、生化制品的制造业	Biology,Biochemistry Products		
三、航空航天器制造业	**Aviation and Aircrafts Manufacturing**	**55967.0**	**219861.0**
1.飞机制造及修理业	Manufacture and Repairing of Aircrafts		
2.航天器制造业	Aircrafts Manufacturing	3657.5	27759.1
四、电子及通讯设备制造业	**Electronic and Communication Equipment**	**30939.4**	**116139.5**
1.通信设备制造业	Communication Equipment Manufacturing	8580.3	25728.2
#通信传输设备制造业	Communication Transmitting Equipment		
通信交换设备制造业	Communication Exchanging Equipment		
通信终端设备制造业	Communication Terminal Equipment	932.6	2524.5
移动通信及终端设备制造业	Mobile Communication and Terminal Equipment		
2.雷达及配套设备制造业	Rader Equipments	3924.0	19538.7
3.广播电视设备制造业	Broadcast and Television Equipments	806.6	1138.4
4.电子器件制造业	Electronic Appliances Manufacturing	8935.5	39367.8
电子真空器件制造业	Electronic Vacuum Appliances	5334.7	15036.9
半导体分立器件制造	Semiconductor Discreting Appliances	2955.9	15252.2
集成电路制造	Integrate Circuit	92.3	6621.4
光电子器件及其他电子器件制造	Photoelectron Appliances and Other Electronic Appliances	552.6	2457.3
5.电子元件制造	Electronic Components Manufacturing	8598.1	29020.4
6.家用视听设备制造	Household Audiovisual		
7.其他电子设备制造	Other Electronic Equipment	94.9	1346.0
五、电子计算机及办公设备制造业	**Computers and Office Equipment Manufacturing**	**637.1**	**1105.0**
1.电子计算机整机制造	Entired Computer Manufacturing		
2.计算机网络设备制造	Computer Network Equipment		
3.电子计算机外部设备制造	Computer Peripheral Equipment		
4.办公设备维修	Repairing of Office Equipment		
六、医疗设备及仪器仪表	**Medical Equipments and Meters**	**27710.4**	**116787.0**
1.医疗仪器设备及器械制造	Medical Equipments and Instruments	666.4	1165.9
2.仪器仪表制造业	Instruments and Meters	27044.0	115621.1
七、其他	**Others**	**62.7**	**102.6**

continued 2

(10 000 yuan)

财务费用 Financial Cost	营业利润 Operating Profit	利润总额 Total Profits	亏损企业亏损总额 Total Loss of Deficit Enterprises	利税总额 Total Pre-tax Profits	本年应交增值税 Value Added Tax Payable
78219.7	**368742.6**	**452118.2**	**30535.0**	**696409.9**	**212084.3**
2753.9	**45593.6**	**46819.4**		**50337.3**	**3216.6**
13751.6	**83890.5**	**98784.1**	**913.1**	**217532.4**	**109967.8**
2437.6	6573.9	6463.3	707.9	16601.4	9034.2
40672.1	**90451.7**	**135004.6**	**2.0**	**160864.7**	**15833.1**
2944.7	26513.1	34009.3		36998.2	1952.5
14478.0	**75116.5**	**90835.9**	**26882.7**	**124932.8**	**27263.3**
1807.4	29913.4	35183.4	4257.0	45483.3	8425.6
270.6	-2417.1	-1813.2	1992.7	-1092.7	358.5
870.9	16105.2	20148.4		20983.4	604.7
388.5	862.6	1000.7		1796.4	303.5
6331.1	13891.6	18587.0	21749.4	33916.6	13261.8
1263.6	-7276.7	-5915.5	14787.3	-3370.4	2201.0
3200.0	23249.9	25271.9		37502.5	10615.3
1586.8	-2918.6	-1903.4	6962.1	-1885.0	8.8
280.7	837.0	1134.0		1669.5	436.7
4993.4	9668.9	11237.3	876.3	16541.4	3274.4
86.7	4674.8	4679.1		6211.7	1393.3
197.4	**1359.7**	**1694.7**		**2061.4**	**327.9**
6356.3	**72272.7**	**78921.6**	**2737.2**	**140611.3**	**55469.2**
644.8	-284.4	-303.7	591.1	181.8	404.9
5711.5	72557.1	79225.3	2146.1	140429.5	55064.3
10.4	**57.9**	**57.9**		**70.0**	**6.4**

11-14 规模以上工业企业主要经济效益指标（2011年）

分组	Item	总资产贡献率（%） Ratio of Total Assets to Industrial Output Value (%)	资产负债率（%） Assets-Liability Ratio (%)
总 计	**Total**	**8.6**	**57.7**
按工业行业大类分	Grouped by Sector		
煤炭开采和洗选业	Mining and Washing of Coal		
石油和天然气开采业	Extraction of Petroleum and Natural Gas		
黑色金属矿采选业	Mining and Processing of Ferrous Metal Ores	-9.6	145.3
有色金属矿采选业	Mining and Processing of Non-ferrous Metal Ores		
非金属矿采选业	Mining and Processing of Nonmetal Ores		
开采辅助活动	Mining Auxiliary Activities	24.6	28.8
其他采矿业	Mining of other Ores		
农副食品加工业	Processing of Food from Agricultural Porducts	10.4	66.3
食品制造业	Manufacture of Foods	15.8	50.0
酒、饮料和精制茶制造业	Manufacture of Alcohol,Beverages and Tea	18.4	59.3
烟草加工业	Manufacture of Tobacco	11.5	55.0
纺织业	Manufacture of Textile	7.0	43.9
纺织服装、鞋、帽制造业	Manufacture of Textile Wearing Apparel,Footwear and Caps	19.9	75.0
皮革、毛皮、羽毛(绒)及其制品业	Manufacture of Leather, Fur, Feather (eiderdown) and Related Products	4.4	49.8
木材加工及竹、藤、棕、草制品业	Processing of Timber,Manufacture of Wood,Plam and Straw Products	11.7	31.6
家具制造业	Manufacture of Furniture	21.6	39.5
造纸及纸制品业	Manufacture of Paper and Paper Products	18.8	50.7
印刷业、记录媒介的复制	Printing,Reproduction of Recording Media	18.7	38.0
文教、工美、体育和娱乐用品制造业	Manufacture of Articles For Cultural,Educational and Sports Activities	17.6	75.2

Main Indicators of Economic Benefit of Industrial Enterprises Above Designated Size（2011）

流动资产周转率（次）Rate of Annual Turnover Working Capitals (times)	成本费用利润率（%）Ratio of Profits to Cost (%)	工业产品销售率（%）Proportion of Industrial Products Sold (%)	产值利税率（%）Ratio of Output Value to Profits and Tax (%)	每百元固定资产实现利税（元）Profit and Tax per 100 yuan of Fixed Assets (yuan)	每百元销售收入实现利税（元）Profit and Tax per 100 yuan of Sales Revenue (yuan)
1.5	**5.2**	**97.4**	**8.8**	**18.8**	**9.3**
1.5	-20.4	95.5	-16.6	-34.2	-17.3
1.0	26.8	101.7	36.6	71.4	37.5
3.4	2.5	96.6	3.5	17.7	3.8
4.6	4.2	95.6	6.5	30.1	6.9
2.2	10.0	122.9	21.0	29.7	17.7
0.8	10.3	104.5	28.9	27.9	19.2
2.1	1.9	91.5	6.4	11.3	6.9
1.6	10.9	99.5	17.4	84.3	14.7
3.5	3.3	112.6	7.5	27.5	6.6
1.8	2.6	93.3	11.8	13.6	13.1
3.0	7.5	97.7	10.3	42.3	10.7
4.5	5.7	99.4	7.8	24.6	7.8
1.7	16.6	100.2	20.4	30.0	21.3
4.8	6.7	99.5	8.1	37.6	8.2

11-14 续表

分　　组	Item	总资产贡献率（%） Ratio of Total Assets to Industrial Output Value (%)	资产负债率（%） Assets-Liability Ratio (%)
石油加工、炼焦及核燃料加工业	Processing of Petroleum, Cokeing,Processing of Nuclear and Nuclear Fuel	5.5	100.9
化学原料及化学制品制造业	Manufacture of Raw Chemical Materials and Chemical Products	10.9	47.8
医药制造业	Manufacture of Medicines	26.1	41.3
化学纤维制造业	Manufacture of Chemical Fibers	19.6	12.0
橡胶和塑料制品业	Manufacture of Rubber and Plastics	9.5	69.3
非金属矿物制品业	Manufacture of Non-metallic Mineral Products	31.5	49.9
黑色金属冶炼及压延加工业	Smelting and Pressing of Ferrous Metals	29.2	57.7
有色金属冶炼及压延加工业	Smelting and Pressing of Non-ferrous Metals	12.9	60.8
金属制品业	Manufacture of Metal Products	10.8	60.8
通用设备制造业	Manufacture of General Purpose Machinery	7.6	59.4
专用设备制造业	Manufacture of Special Equipment	9.1	50.2
汽车制造业	Manufacture of Motor Vehicle	9.3	59.4
铁路、船舶、航空航天和其他运输设备制造业	Railways,Shipbuilding,Aerospace and Other Transportation Equipment Manufacturing Industry	4.4	60.5
电气机械及器材制造业	Manufacture of Electric Equipment and Machinery	3.7	48.9
计算机、通讯和其他电子设备制造业	Manufacture of Communication Equipment, Computers and other Electronic Equipment	4.8	59.3
仪器仪表制造业	Manufacture of Measuring Instruments and Machinery	8.2	49.7
其他制造业	Manufacture of Other Manufacturing	11.2	50.9
废弃资源综合利用业	Recycling and Disposal of Waste		
金属制品、机械和设备修理业	Metal Products,Machinery and Equipment Repair Industry	10.8	63.9
电力、热力的生产和供应业	Production and Supply of Electric Power and Heat Power	5.4	77.6
燃气生产和供应业	Gas Mining and Supplying Industry	8.9	53.7
水的生产和供应业	Production and Supply of Water	5.4	43.2

continued

流动资产周转率（次）Rate of Annual Turnover Working Capitals (times)	成本费用利润率（%）Ratio of Profits to Cost (%)	工业产品销售率（%）Proportion of Industrial Products Sold (%)	产值利税率（%）Ratio of Output Value to Profits and Tax (%)	每百元固定资产实现利税（元）Profit and Tax per 100 yuan of Fixed Assets (yuan)	每百元销售收入实现利税（元）Profit and Tax per 100 yuan of Sales Revenue (yuan)
8.6	-5.4	100.8	0.8	5.6	0.8
1.6	9.4	98.0	12.9	18.8	13.2
2.0	10.6	96.0	19.3	67.7	21.3
3.1	14.9	99.2	16.1	20.0	16.2
1.6	4.8	93.0	8.4	22.6	9.3
3.3	14.2	97.7	17.4	52.3	18.6
5.0	7.6	96.5	11.3	45.8	10.3
1.7	8.1	93.5	9.9	30.1	11.7
1.4	8.8	99.4	9.5	22.0	10.2
0.7	10.7	95.9	12.7	45.0	14.3
1.0	8.4	90.6	11.6	29.9	12.4
2.2	3.9	98.5	6.6	28.6	7.4
0.8	4.9	97.4	7.9	12.0	7.1
0.9	0.7	95.9	4.7	12.2	5.6
1.0	6.8	89.8	8.7	13.7	9.1
0.9	8.1	92.0	13.6	20.2	13.5
2.1	5.3	98.7	9.3	25.6	10.2
1.5	4.5	90.1	7.9	37.4	8.4
3.7	1.2	100.6	4.6	3.0	4.6
1.5	12.2	100.0	16.2	15.5	16.4
1.5	3.2	100.0	10.5	3.6	10.5

主要统计指标解释

工业 指从事自然资源的开采，对采掘品和农产品进行加工和再加工的物质生产部门。具体包括：（1）对自然资源的开采，如采矿、晒盐等（但不包括禽兽捕猎和水产捕捞）；（2）对农副产品的加工、再加工，如粮油加工、食品加工、缫丝、纺织、制革等；（3）对采掘品的加工、再加工，如炼铁、炼钢、化工生产、石油加工、机器制造、木材加工等，以及电力、自来水、煤气的生产和供应等；（4）对工业品的修理、翻新，如机器设备的修理、交通运输工具（如汽车）的修理等。

工业统计调查单位为独立核算法人工业企业。

独立核算法人工业企业指从事工业生产经营活动的单位。独立核算法人工业企业应同时具备以下条件：①依法成立，有自己的名称、组织机构和场所，能够承担民事责任；②独立拥有和使用资产，承担负债，有权与其他单位签订合同；③独立核算盈亏，并能够编制资产负债表。

国有及国有控股企业 指国有企业加上国有控股企业。国有企业（即原全民所有制工业或国营工业）指企业全部资产归国家所有，并按《中华人民共和国企业法人登记管理条例》规定登记注册的非公司制的经济组织。包括国有企业、国有独资公司和国有联营企业。1957年以前的公私合营和私营工业，后均改造为国营工业，1992年改为国有工业，这部分工业的资料不单独分列时，均包括在国有企业内。国有控股企业是对混合所有制经济的企业进行的“国有控股”分类。它是指这些企业的全部资产中国有资产（股份）相对其他所有者中的任何一个所有者占资（股）最多的企业。该分组反映了国有经济控股情况。

本篇涉及的其他企业登记注册类型的解释详见综合篇。

轻工业 指主要提供生活消费品和制作手工工具的工业。按其所使用的原料不同，可分为两大类：（1）以农产品为原料的轻工业，是指直接或间接以农产品为基本原料的轻工业。主要包括食品制造、饮料制造、烟草加工、纺织、缝纫、皮革和毛皮制作、造纸以及印刷等工业；（2）以非农产品为原料的轻工业，是指以工业品为原料的轻工业。主要包括文教体育用品、化学药品制造、合成纤维制造、日用化学制品、日用玻璃制品、日用金属制品、手工工具制造、医疗器械制造、文化和办公用机械制造等工业。

重工业 指为国民经济各部门提供物质技术基础的主要生产资料的工业。按其生产性质和产品用途，可以分为下列三类：（1）采掘（伐）工业，是指对自然资源的开采，包括石油开采、煤炭开采、金属矿开采、非金属矿开采等工业；（2）原材料工业，指向国民经济各部门提供基本材料、动力和燃料的工业。包括金属冶炼及加工、炼焦及焦炭、化学、化工原料、水泥、人造板以及电力、石油和煤炭加工等工业；（3）加工工业，是指对工业原材料进行再加工制造的工业。包括装备国民经济各部门的机械设备制造工业、金属结构、水泥制品等工业，以及为农业提供的生产资料如化肥、农药等工业。

根据上述划分原则，修理业中以重工业产品为修理作业对象的划为重工业，反之划为轻工业。

工业总产值

（1）定义：

工业总产值是工业企业在一定时期内生产的以货币形式表现的工业最终产品和提供工业性劳务活动的总价值量。它反映一定时间内工业生产的总规模和总水平。

（2）计算原则：

工业生产的原则，即凡是企业在报告期生产的经检验合格的产品，不管是否在报告期销售，均包括在内。

最终产品的原则，即凡是计入工业总产值的产品，必须是本企业生产的经检验合格的，不需要再进行任何加工的最终产品。如果企业有中间产品（半成品）对外销售，则对外销售的中间产品应视为企业的最终产品。

工厂法原则，即工业总产值是以工业企业作为基本计算（核算）单位，即按企业的最终产品计算工业总产值。按这种方法计算的工业总产值，不允许同一产品价值在企业内部重复计算，不能把企业内部各个车间（分厂）生产的成果相加，但允许企业间的重复计算。

（3）内容及计算方法：

1995年全国工业普查对工业总产值（原规定）的内容及计算原则和方法做了某些修订，修订后的工业总产值（新规定）包括三项内容：即本期生产成品价值、对外加工费收入、在制品半成品期末期初差额价值三部分。

本期生产成品价值指企业本期生产，并在报告期内不再进行加工，经检验、包装入库的全部工业成品（半成品）价值合计，包括企业生产的自制设备及提供给本企业在建工程、其他非工业部门和福利部门等单位使用的成品价值。本期生产成品价值为按自备原材料生产的产品的数量乘以本期不含增值税（销项税额）的产品实际销售平均单价计算；会计核算中按成本价格转帐的自制设备和自产自用的成品，按成本价格计算生产成品价值。生产成品价值中不包括用定货者来料加工的成品（半成品）价值。

对外加工费收入指企业在报告期内完成的对外承接的工业品加工（包括用定货者来料加工产品）的加工费收入和对外工业修理作业所取得的加工费收入。对外加工费收入按不含增值税（销项税额）的价格计算，可根据会计“产品销售收入”科目的有关资料取得。

对于本企业对内非工业部门提供的加工修理、设备安装的劳务收入，如果企业会计核算基础较好，能取得这部分资料，而且这部分价值所占比重较大，应包括在对外加工费收入中。

自制半成品在制品期末期初差额价值指企业报告期在制品期末减期初的差额价值，本指标一般可以从会计核算资料中取得。如果会计产品成本核算中不计算半成品、在制品的成本，则总产值中也不包括这部分价值，反之则包括。

（4）工业总产值统计范围变化和计算方法修订情况：

1984年以前工业总产值不包括村办工业，村办工业总产值划归农业。1984年以后工业总产值包括村办工业。

1995年工业普查对工业总产值计算方法做了修订，即从1995年始按新修订（新规定）方法计算工业总产值。新规定与原规定的区别如下：

全价与加工费的计算原则不同：新规定为凡自备原材料，不论其生产繁简程度如何，一律按全价计算工业总产值；凡来料加工，允许按加工费计算工业总产值。原规定则视生产加工的繁简程度不同，规定哪些行业按全价，哪些行业按加工费计算工业总产值。

自制半成品、在产品期末期初差额价值的计算原则不同：新规定要求，凡会计产品成本核算时计算了成本的差额价值，总产值中就应包括，否则可不包括；原规定则按生产周期六个月的界限区分，凡生产周期六个月以上的企业，总产值计算中应包括这部分差额价值，否则可不包括。

计算价格不同：新规定按不含增值税（销项税额）的价格计算；原规定则按含增值税（销项税额）的价格计算。

工业增加值 指工业企业在报告期内以货币表现的工业生产活动的最终成果。

工业增加值有两种计算方法：一是生产法，即工业总产出减去工业中间投入加上应交增值税；二是收入法，即从收入的角度出发，根据生产要素在生产过程中应得到的收入份额计算，具体构成项目有固定资产折旧、劳动者报酬、生产税净额、营业盈余，这种方法也称要素分配法。本年鉴中的工业增加值是以收入法计算的。

生产法工业增加值的计算方法为：

工业增加值=工业总产出-工业中间投入+应交增值税

（1）工业总产出：指工业企业在一定时期内工业生产活动的总成果。工业总产出包括：成品生产价值，对外加工费收入，自制半成品、在产品期末期初差额价值。1995年后用新规定计算的工业总产值代替。

（2）工业中间投入：指工业企业在工业生产活动中消耗的外购物质产品和对外支付的服务费用。服务费用包括支付给物质生产部门（工业、农业、批发零售贸易业、建筑业、运输邮电业）的服务费用和支付给非物质生产部门（如保险、金融、文化教育、科学研究、医疗卫生、行政管理等）的服务费用。工业中间投入的确定须遵循以下原则：必须从外部购入的，并已计入工业总产出的产品和服务价值；必须是本期投入生产，并一次性消耗掉（包括本期摊销的低值易耗品等）的产品和服务价值。

工业中间投入包括直接材料费用、制造费用中的工业中间投入、管理费用中的工业中间投入、销售费用中的工业中间投入和利息支出五部分。

资产总计 指企业拥有或控制的能以货币计量的经济资源，包括各种财产、债权和其他权利。资产按流动性分为流动资产、长期投资、固定资产、无形资产、递延资产和其他资产。该指标根据企业会计“资产负债表”中“资产总计”项目的期末数增列。

流动资产 指企业可以在一年内或者超过一年的一个生产周期内变现或者耗用的资产，包括现金及各种存款、短期投资，应收及预付款项、存货等。

固定资产原价 指企业在建造、购置、安装、改建、扩建、技术改造某项固定资产时所支出的全部货币总额。它一般包括买价、包装费、运杂费和安装费等。

固定资产净值 指固定资产原价减去历年已提折旧额后的净额。计算公式为：

固定资产净值=固定资产原价-累计折旧

负债合计 指企业所承担的能以货币计量，将以资产或劳务偿付的债务，偿还形式包括货币、资产或提供劳务。负债一般按偿还期长短分为流动负债和长期负债。根据会计“资产负债表”中“负债合计”的年末数填列。

所有者权益合计 指企业投资人对企业净资产的所有权。企业净资产为企业全部资产与企业全部负债的差额，包括实收资本、资本公积、盈余公积、未分配利润等。根据会计“资产负债表”中“所有者权益”项的期末数填列。

主营业务收入 指会计“利润表”中对应指标的本年累计数。未执行2001年《企业会计制度》的企业，用“产品销售收入”的本期累计数代替。

主营业务成本 指会计“利润表”中对应指标的本年累计数。未执行2001年《企业会计制度》的企业，用“产品销售成本”的本期累计数代替。

主营业务税金及附加 指会计“利润表”中对应指标的本年累计数。未执行2001年《企业会计制度》的企业，用“产品销售税金及附加”的本期累计数代替。

利润总额 指企业在生产经营过程中各种收入扣除各种耗费后的盈余，反映企业在报告期内实现的盈亏总额，包括营业利润、补贴收入、投资净收益和营业外收支净额。根据会计“利润表”中的对应指标的本期累计数填列。

本年应交增值税 指企业按税法规定，从事货物销售或提供加工、修理修配劳务等增加货物价值的活动本期应交纳的税金。指企业在报告期应交增值税额。计算公式为：

本年应交增值税=销项税额-（进项税额-进项税额转出）-出口抵减内销产品应纳税额-减免税款+出口退税

本年进项税额 指工业企业在报告期内购入货物或接受应税劳务而支付的、准予从销项税额中抵扣的增值税额。

本年销项税额 指工业企业在报告期内销售货物或提供应税劳务应收取的增值税额。

从业人员平均人数 是指报告期内每天拥有的从业人员人数。其计算公式为：

月平均人数=报告月内每天实有人数之和/报告月日历日数

季平均人数=季内各月平均人数之和/3

年平均人数=年内各月平均人数之和/12

总资产贡献率 反映企业全部资产的获利能力，是企业经营业绩和管理水平的集中体现，是评价和考核企业盈利能力的核心指标。计算公式为：

总资产贡献率（%）=（利润总额+税金总额+利息支出）/平均资金总额×100%

公式中：税金总额为产品销售税金及附加与应交增值税之和；平均资产总额为期初期末资产之和的算术平均值。

资产负债率 该指标既反映企业经营风险的大小，也反映企业利用债权人提供的资金从事经营活动的能力。计算公式为：

资产负债率（%）=负债总额/资产总额×100%

资产与负债均为报告期期末数。

流动资产周转次数 指一定时期内流动资产完成的周转次数，反映投入工业企业流动资金的周转速度。计算公式为：

流动资产周转次数=产品销售收入/全部流动资产平均余额

公式中：全部流动资产平均余额为期初和期末的流动资产之和的算术平均值。

成本费用利润率 反映企业投入的生产成本及费用的经济效益，同时也反映企业降低成本所取得的经济效益。计算公式为：

成本费用利润率（%）=利润总额/成本费用总额×100%

公式中：成本费用总额为产品销售成本、销售费用、管理费用、财务费用之和。

产品销售率 该指标反映工业产品已实现销售的程度，是分析工业产销衔接情况，研究工业产品满足社会需求的指标。计算公式为：

产品销售率（%）=工业销售产值/工业总产值（现价）×100%

Explanatory Notes on Main Statistical Indicators

Industry refers to the material production sector which is engaged in the extraction of natural resources and processing and reprocessing of minerals and agricultural products, including (1) extraction of natural resources, such as mining, salt production (but not including hunting and fishing); (2) processing and reprocessing of farm and sideline produces, such as rice husking, flour milling, wine making, oil pressing, silk reeling, spinning and weaving, and leather making; (3) manufacture of industrial products, such as steel making, iron smelting, chemicals manufacturing, petroleum processing, machine building, timber processing; water and gas production and electricity generation and supply; (4)repairing of industrial products such as the repairing of machinery and means of transport (including cars).

In industrial statistics surveys, the units of enquiry are corporate industrial enterprises with independent accounting systems.

Corporate industrial enterprises with independent accounting systems refer to enterprises engaging in industrial production activities, which meet the following requirements: (1) They are established legally, having their own names, organizations, location and able to take civil liability; (2) They possess and use their assets independently, assume liabilities and are entitled to sign contracts with other units; (3) They are financially independent and compile their own balance sheets.

State-owned and State-holding Enterprises refer to state-owned enterprises plus State-holding enterprises. State-owned enterprises (originally known as State-run enterprises with ownership by the whole society) are non-corporate economic entities registered in accordance with the Regulation of the People's Republic of China on the Management of Registration of Legal Enterprises, where all assets are owned by the State. Included in this category are State-owned enterprises, State-funded corporations and State-owned joint-operation enterprises. Joint State-private industries and private industries, which existed before 1957, were transformed into state-run industries since 1957, and into State-owned industries after 1992. Statistics on those enterprises are included in the State-owned industries instead of being grouped them separately. State-holding enterprises are a sub-classification of enterprises with mixed ownership, referring to enterprises where the percentage of State assets (or shares by the State) is larger than any other single share holder of the same enterprise. This sub-classification illustrates the control of the State over a particular industry.

For explanation of enterprises of other types of registration covered in this chapter, please refer to General Survey.

Light Industry refers to the industry that produces consumer goods and hand tools. It consists of two categories, depending on the materials used:

(1) Industries using farm products as raw materials. These are the branches of light industry which directly or indirectly use farm products as basic raw materials, including the manufacture of food and beverages, tobacco processing, textile, clothing, fur and leather manufacturing, paper making, printing, etc.

(2) Industries using non-farm products as raw materials. These are the branches of light industry which use manufactured goods as raw materials, including the manufacture of cultural, educational articles and sports goods, chemicals, synthetic fibre, chemical products for daily use, glass products for daily use, metal products for daily use, hand tools, medical apparatus and instruments, and the manufacture of cultural and office machinery.

Heavy Industry refers to the industry which produces capital goods, and provides various sectors of the national economy with necessary material and technical basis for production. It consists of the following three branches according to the purpose of production or the use of products:

(1) Mining, quarrying and logging industry, which refers to the industry that extracts natural resources, including extraction of petroleum, coal, metal and non-metal ores.

(2) Raw materials industry refers to the industry that provides various sectors of the national economy with raw materials, fuels and power. It includes smelting and processing of metals, coking and coke chemistry, chemical materials and building materials such as cement, plywood, and power, petroleum refining and coal dressing.

(3) Manufacturing industry which refers to the industry that processes raw materials. It includes machine-building industries which equip sectors of the national economy; industries producing metal structure and cement products; and industries producing means of

agricultural production, such as chemical fertilizers and pesticides.

In accordance with the above principles of classification, the repairing trades, which are engaged primarily in repairing products of heavy industry, are classified as heavy industry while those which are engaged in repairing products of light industry are classified as light industry.

Gross Industrial Output Value

(1) Definition: Gross industrial output value is the total volume of final industrial products produced and industrial services provided during a given period in monetary terms. It reflects the total achievements and overall scale of industrial production during a given period.

(2) Principles for calculation:

Statistics on industrial production follow the principle that all products produced by the enterprises and accepted through quality check during the reference period are to be included no matter whether they are sold or not during the reference period.

Determination of final products follows the principle that all products that are included in the calculation of gross industrial output value are the final products of the enterprise which have been accepted through quality check and require no further processing. If an enterprise has intermediate (semi-finished) products to sell, these intermediate products are considered as the final products of the enterprise.

Gross industrial output value is calculated following the principle of factory approach, i.e. industrial enterprise is used as the basic accounting unit in calculating the gross industrial output value. By this approach, value of the same product is not to be double-counted, and the output value of different workshops (branch factories) within the enterprise should not be added. However, this approach allows the possibility of double counting between enterprises.

(3) Content and method of calculation: The old definition of gross industrial output value was modified during the 1995 National Industrial Census. The revised (new) definition of gross industrial output value consists of 3 components: value of the finished products during the reference period, income from processing for external parties, and value of change in semi-finished products between the end and the beginning of the reference period.

Value of finished products during the reference period: refers to the value of all finished (semi-finished) industrial products that are produced during the reference period without the need for further processing, checked for acceptance, packed and put into the warehouse of the enterprise, including the value of own-produced equipment and the value of products provided to the projects under construction of the enterprise, and to other non-industrial or welfare units. Value of finished products during the reference period is calculated by the quantity of products produced using own materials multiplied by the average unit prices at which products are sold (excluding value-added tax). Own-produced equipment and products produced for own use are valued at cost prices as in the case of enterprise accounting. Value of finished products does not include the value of finished products (semi-finished products) that are produced using the materials from the clients who place the orders.

Income from external processing: refers to income from contracted external processing of industrial products (including processing of industrial products using materials from the clients), and the income from industrial repairing work provided to other parties. Income from external processing is calculated using information from the item "products sales income" in the enterprise accounting at the prices with value-added tax excluded.

For income from services such as processing, repairing and installation of equipment provided to non-industrial units within the enterprise, if the accounting work of the enterprise is good enough to separate it from other records, and the share of such services is significant, it should also be included in the income from external processing.

Value of change in semi-finished products between the end and the beginning of the reference period: refers to the value of change in semi-finished products between the end and the beginning of the reference period, which generally can be obtained from accounting records of enterprises. If the enterprise accounting excludes the cost of semi-finished products, then it should not be included in the gross industrial output value, and the reverse if otherwise.

(4) Changes in the scope and method of calculation of the gross industrial output value

Prior to 1984, the value of rural industry run by villages was classified into agriculture instead of industry. Since 1984, it has been included in the gross industrial output value. Method of calculation for the gross industrial output value was modified in the industrial census in 1995. The difference in the new method as compared with the old one is outlined below:

Principle in using full value vs. processing fee: The new method stipulates that all products produced using own materials are to be calculated with full value in reporting the gross industrial output value irrespective of the complexity of production, and for external processing, it allows calculation using processing fee. In the old method, however, the use of full value or processing fee was determined by the degree of complexity of production in different branches of industries.

Principle in determining the value of change in semi-finished products: The new method requires that value of change in semi-finished products should be included in the gross industrial output value if it is included in the accounting record of the enterprise, otherwise it should not be included. In the old method, it is determined by the type of enterprises in terms of production cycle. If the production cycle is over 6 months, the value of change in semi-finished products is included in the gross industrial output value, otherwise it is not.

Difference in prices: The new method uses prices excluding value-added tax in the calculation of gross industrial output value, while the old method used prices including value-added tax.

Value-added of Industry refers to the final results of industrial production of industrial enterprises in money terms during the reference period.

Industrial value-added can be calculated by two approaches: the production approach, i.e. gross industrial output value minus intermediate input plus value-added tax, and the income approach, i.e. income for various factors used in the course of production, including depreciation of fixed assets, remuneration of labourers, net of production tax, and operating surplus. Value-added of industry in the Yearbook is calculated by the income approach as follows:

Value-added of industry = gross industrial output - industrial intermediate input + value-added tax

(1) Gross industrial output: refers to the total achievements of industrial production activities during a given period. Gross industrial output includes value of finished products, income from external processing, and value of change in semi-finished products between the end and the beginning of the reference period. Since 1995, the gross industrial output value obtained by the new method is used in the calculation.

(2) Industrial intermediate input: refers to purchased goods and paid services consumed during the industrial production of enterprises. Fees paid for services include fees paid for the services provided by material production sectors (industry, agriculture, wholesale and retail trade, construction, transport, post and telecommunications) and by non-material production sectors (insurance, banking, culture, education, scientific research, health and medical care, public administration, etc.). The determination of industrial intermediate input follows the principle that the goods and services must be purchased from outside and included in the gross industrial output, and that the goods and services are inputted into production and consumed (include low-value consumables) during the reference period.

Industrial intermediate input includes 5 components, namely direct consumption of materials, industrial intermediate input in manufacturing cost, industrial intermediate input in management cost, industrial intermediate input in marketing cost and expenditure on interest.

Total Assets refer to all economic resources, in monetary term, these are owned or controlled by enterprises, including properties, creditor's equity and other economic rights of all forms. Classified by the degree of liquidity, total assets include working capitals, long-term investment, fixed assets, intangible assets, deferred assets and other assets. Data on this indicator can be obtained by the year-end figures of total assets in the Assets and Liability Table of accounting records of enterprises.

Working Capital refers to capital that an enterprise can cash or use during one year or one production cycle that may exceed one year, including cash and savings deposits of various forms, short-term investment, money receivable and prepaid money, inventories, etc.

Original Value of Fixed Assets refers to the total value, in monetary terms, that an enterprise spent on fixed assets, through construction, purchase, installation, transformation, expansion or technical upgrading. Generally, it covers cost of purchase, packing, transportation and installation, etc.

Net Value of Fixed Assets refers to the original value of fixed assets minus depreciation over the years, i.e.:

Net value of fixed assets = original value of fixed assets - cumulative depreciation

Total Liabilities refer to payable liabilities of enterprises that have to be repaid in terms of money, assets or labour services. In terms of payment, it can be divided into liquid liabilities and long-term liabilities. Data on this item is obtained from the ending figures on total liabilities from the Assets and Liability Table from the enterprises.

Total Equity refers to the ownership of net assets of enterprise by its investors. Net assets equal total assets minus total liabilities of the enterprise, including the paid-in capital, accumulation of capital and operating surplus and non-distributed profits. Data are obtained from the ending figures on "total equity" from the "balance sheets".

Revenue from Principal Business refers to the annual accumulation of the corresponding item in the "profit table" of the accountant. For enterprises that do not follow the 2001 Enterprise Accounting Standards, the year-end accumulation of revenue from the sales of products is used as a substitute.

Cost of Principal Business refers to the annual accumulation of the corresponding item in the "profit table" of the accountant. For enterprises that do not follow the 2001 Enterprise Accounting Standards, the year-end accumulation of cost for the sales of products is used as a substitute.

Tax and Extra Charges from Principal Business refer to the annual accumulation of the corresponding item in the "profit table" of the accountant. For enterprises that do not follow the 2001 Enterprise Accounting Standards, the year-end accumulation of tax and extra charges from the sales of products is used as a substitute.

Total Profits refers to the balance of various incomes minus various spendings in the course of operation, reflecting the total profits and losses of enterprises in reporting period. It includes: operating profits, income from subsidies, net investment income and net income from activities other than operation. Data are obtained from the annual accumulation of the corresponding item in the "profit table" of the accountant.

Value-added Tax Payable in the Current Year refers to the payable tax of enterprises which engaged in selling of goods or providing services that bring added value to the goods, such as processing, repairing, fitting and other activities should be paid according to Tax Law. It refers to the amount of the value-added tax which should be paid by the enterprises during the reference period. The formula is as follows:

Value-added Tax Payable in the Current Year = tax on sales-(tax on purchase-transferred tax on purchase)-exports deduct tax payable on domestic sales-tax relief+the export tax rebate.

Tax on Purchase in Current Year refers to goods purchased by industrial enterprises or value added tax that should be paid but being granted the right to deduct from the tax on sales.

Tax on Sales in Current Year refers to value added tax on industrial enterprises from sales of goods or taxable services that should be charged value added tax.

Average number of employed persons refers to the number of employee everyday during the reference period, calculated with the following formula:

$$\text{Monthly average number} = \frac{\text{sum of actual employees everyday in reference month}}{\text{number of calendar dates in reference month}}$$

$$\text{Quarterly average number} = \frac{\text{sum of monthly average number in reference quarter}}{3}$$

$$\text{Annual average number} = \frac{\text{sum of monthly average number in reference year}}{12}$$

Ratio of Profits, Taxes and Interests to Average Assets reflects the profit-making capability of all assets of the enterprise and is a key indicator manifesting the performance and management and evaluating the profit-making potential of the enterprise. It is calculated as follows:

$$\text{Ratio of Profits, Taxes and Interests toAverageAssets(\%)} = \frac{\text{total profits+ total taxes+ interest payment}}{\text{average assets}} \times 100\%$$

In the above formula, total taxes is the sum of tax and extra charges on the sales of products and value-added tax payable; and average assets is the arithmetic mean of the sum of beginning assets and ending assets.

Ratio of Debts to Assets reflects both the operation risk and the capability of the enterprise in making use of the capital from the creditors. It is calculated as follows:

$$\text{Ratio of Debts toAssets(\%)} = \frac{\text{total debts}}{\text{total assets}} \times 100\%$$

Both assets and debts are figures at the end of the reference period.

Turnover of Working Capital refers to the number of times of turnover of working capital in a given period of time, which reflects the speed of the turnover of working capital of industrial enterprises, and is calculated as follows:

$$\text{Turnover of Working Capital} = \frac{\text{sales revenue of products}}{\text{average balance of total working capital}}$$

In the above formula, average balance of total working capital refers to the arithmetic mean of the sum of working capital at the beginning and at the end of the reference period.

Ratio of Profits to Total Industrial Costs refers to the ratio of profits realized in a given period to the total costs in the same period, which reflects the economic efficiency of input cost and is calculated as follows:

$$\text{Ratio of Profits to Total Industrial Cost (\%)} = \frac{\text{total profits}}{\text{total costs}} \times 100\%$$

Total costs in the above formula are the sum of cost of products sold, marketing cost, management cost and financial cost.

Sales Ratio of Products is an indicator reflecting the actual sale of industrial products, analyzing the production-selling and supply-demand relations. It is calculated as:

$$\text{Sales Ratio of Products (\%)} = \frac{\text{value of industrial sales}}{\text{gross industrial output value (current prices)}} \times 100\%$$

12 能　源

ENERGY

资料整理：雷稳强　于元英
Data management:Lei Wenqiang Yu Yuanying

第十二部分　能源

一、简要说明

本章资料包括规模以上工业能源购销存情况、全市单位GDP能耗、单位GDP电耗、规模以上工业单位增加值能耗、规模以上工业企业用水情况等，由西安市统计局能源处提供。

二、主要指标

规模以上工业综合能源消费量（吨标准煤）	4905405	比上年减少	221125吨标准煤
单位GDP能耗（吨标准煤/万元）	0.610	比上年下降	3.56%
单位GDP电耗（千瓦时/万元）	587.77	比上年下降	4.43%
规模以上工业单位增加值能耗（吨标准煤/万元）	0.502	比上年下降	15.44%

12　ENERGY

Ⅰ.Brief Introduction

Data in this chapter reflects Energy Purchases Consumption and Inventory of Industrial Enterprises Above Designated size,Energy Consumption per Unit of GDP in Whole City,Electricity Consumption per Unit of GDP,Energy Consumption per Unit of Industrial Value-added above Designated Size and Statistics on Water Use of Industrial Enterprises above Designated Size. Data in this chapter are provided and compiled by Transportation Division of the Xi'an Bureau of Statistics.

Ⅱ.Major Indicators

		Increase over Preceding Year
Comprehensive Energy Consumption Above Designated Size(Tons of Standard Coal)	4905405	-221125
Energy Consumption of GDP per Unit (Tons of Standard Coal /10 000 yuan)	0.610	-3.56%
Power Consumption of GDP per Unit (kilowatt-hour/10 000 yuan)	587.77	-4.43%
Energy Consumption of value added per Unit of Industrial Enterprises Above Designated Size (Tons of Standard Coal /10 000 yuan)	0.502	-15.44%

12-1 全市及分区县单位GDP能耗

Energy Consumption Per Unit of GDP by City（District）

单位：吨标准煤/万元 (ton of SCE/10 000 yuan)

地　区	Region	单位GDP能耗 Energy Consumption Per Unit of GDP							
		GDP按2005年价格计算 GDP are calculated at 2005 constant prices						GDP按2010年价格计算 GDP are calculated at 2010 constant prices	
		2005	2006	2007	2008	2009	2010	2010	2011
西安市	**Xi'an**	**1.030**	**0.987**	**0.930**	**0.869**	**0.820**	**0.803**	**0.633**	**0.610**
新城区	Xincheng	0.828	0.794	0.749	0.705	0.664	0.656	0.524	0.506
碑林区	Beilin	0.801	0.768	0.726	0.685	0.644	0.639	0.454	0.437
莲湖区	Lianhu	0.942	0.904	0.862	0.794	0.749	0.722	0.543	0.522
灞桥区	Baqiao	1.803	1.757	1.648	1.545	1.456	1.394	0.819	0.788
未央区	Weiyang	1.026	0.985	0.932	0.870	0.817	0.806	0.678	0.654
雁塔区	Yanta	0.929	0.885	0.835	0.787	0.739	0.708	0.541	0.522
阎良区	Yanliang	0.831	0.783	0.745	0.700	0.661	0.644	0.516	0.499
临潼区	Lintong	1.035	1.004	0.946	0.869	0.829	0.789	0.597	0.576
长安区	Chang'an	1.339	1.257	1.187	1.125	1.063	1.041	0.634	0.611
蓝田县	Lantian	1.698	1.645	1.579	1.492	1.420	1.446	1.228	1.186
周至县	Zhouzhi	1.831	1.786	1.689	1.596	1.508	1.464	1.120	1.083
户　县	Huxian	2.532	2.454	2.311	2.133	2.015	1.978	1.307	1.257
高陵县	Gaoling	0.953	0.907	0.845	0.798	0.753	0.725	0.567	0.545

12-1 续表

Continued

地　区	Region	比上年增长(%) Growth Rates over Preceding Year(%)					
		2006	2007	2008	2009	2010	2011
西安市	**Xi'an**	**-4.15**	**-5.75**	**-6.65**	**-5.56**	**-2.06**	**-3.56**
新城区	Xincheng	-4.15	-5.67	-5.79	-5.80	-1.15	-3.51
碑林区	Beilin	-4.18	-5.44	-5.65	-5.95	-0.91	-3.89
莲湖区	Lianhu	-4.07	-4.60	-7.93	-5.65	-3.58	-3.84
灞桥区	Baqiao	-2.54	-6.20	-6.24	-5.80	-4.20	-3.81
未央区	Weiyang	-3.97	-5.44	-6.63	-6.05	-1.31	-3.60
雁塔区	Yanta	-4.71	-5.64	-5.80	-6.08	-4.18	-3.61
阎良区	Yanliang	-5.77	-4.80	-6.08	-5.62	-0.61	-3.38
临潼区	Lintong	-3.03	-5.73	-8.16	-4.58	-4.81	-3.52
长安区	Chang'an	-6.15	-5.53	-5.22	-5.50	-2.08	-3.60
蓝田县	Lantian	-3.13	-4.01	-5.50	-4.84	-2.06	-3.39
周至县	Zhouzhi	-2.46	-5.43	-5.51	-5.50	-2.06	-3.30
户　县	Huxian	-3.07	-5.85	-7.70	-5.50	-2.99	-3.85
高陵县	Gaoling	-4.85	-6.85	-5.50	-5.70	-3.82	-3.93

12-2 全市及分区县单位GDP电耗

Electricity Consumption Per Unit of GDP by City（District）

单位：千瓦时/万元 (kw.h/10 000 yuan)

地 区	Region	单位GDP电耗 Electricity Consumption Per Unit of GDP							
		GDP按2005年价格计算 GDP are calculated at 2005 constant prices						GDP按2010年价格计算 GDP are calculated at 2010 constant prices	
		2005	2006	2007	2008	2009	2010	2010	2011
西安市	**Xi'an**	**963.34**	**920.19**	**856.29**	**796.92**	**754.45**	**761.98**	**615.07**	**587.77**
新城区	Xincheng	740.68	714.54	624.76	590.40	544.38	529.86	450.10	417.16
碑林区	Beilin	578.78	557.34	536.48	520.04	477.09	469.01	376.07	337.21
莲湖区	Lianhu	735.51	697.56	677.92	635.02	590.14	567.40	489.95	451.03
灞桥区	Baqiao	1606.69	1534.34	1483.26	1367.56	1275.24	1309.49	968.39	895.00
未央区	Weiyang	1112.49	1055.75	1007.35	936.19	940.23	921.64	723.10	686.76
雁塔区	Yanta	1043.36	998.03	871.48	814.97	776.04	827.95	684.87	654.82
阎良区	Yanliang	632.75	620.65	574.19	535.33	517.29	497.13	398.54	398.71
临潼区	Lintong	1019.71	997.91	952.62	878.57	792.07	780.29	601.65	587.27
长安区	Chang'an	1055.34	996.57	910.94	844.84	774.85	797.92	590.44	621.09
蓝田县	Lantian	1135.17	1104.82	1087.11	1010.23	992.80	1031.64	754.15	684.77
周至县	Zhouzhi	815.19	788.52	756.79	714.80	709.39	688.20	537.35	607.54
户 县	Huxian	848.39	824.19	810.60	773.10	742.15	769.32	636.22	628.20
高陵县	Gaoling	1065.50	972.08	828.71	726.45	638.98	651.46	509.28	438.84

注：GDP为第二次经济普查调整后数据。

Note:GDP was from the second national economic census.

12-2 续表

Continued

地 区	Region	比上年增长(%) Growth Rates over Preceding Year(%)					
		2006	2007	2008	2009	2010	2011
西安市	**Xi'an**	**-4.48**	**-6.94**	**-6.93**	**-5.33**	**1.00**	**-4.43**
新城区	Xincheng	-3.53	-12.57	-5.50	-7.80	-2.67	-7.32
碑林区	Beilin	-3.70	-3.74	-3.06	-8.26	-1.69	-10.33
莲湖区	Lianhu	-5.16	-2.82	-6.33	-7.07	-3.85	-7.94
灞桥区	Baqiao	-4.50	-3.33	-7.80	-6.75	2.69	-7.58
未央区	Weiyang	-5.10	-4.59	-7.06	0.43	-1.98	-5.03
雁塔区	Yanta	-4.34	-12.68	-6.49	-4.78	6.69	-4.39
阎良区	Yanliang	-1.91	-7.49	-6.77	-3.37	-3.90	0.04
临潼区	Lintong	-2.14	-4.54	-7.77	-9.85	-1.49	-2.39
长安区	Chang'an	-5.57	-8.59	-7.26	-8.28	2.98	5.19
蓝田县	Lantian	-2.67	-1.60	-7.07	-1.73	3.91	-9.20
周至县	Zhouzhi	-3.27	-4.02	-5.55	-0.76	-2.99	13.06
户 县	Huxian	-2.85	-1.65	-4.63	-4.00	3.66	-1.26
高陵县	Gaoling	-8.77	-14.75	-12.34	-12.04	1.95	-13.83

12-3 全市及分区县规模以上单位工业增加值能耗

Energy Consumption Per Unit of Industrial Value Added Above Designated Size by City（District）

单位：吨标准煤/万元 (ton of SCE/10 000 yuan)

地 区	Region	单位工业增加值能耗 Energy Consumption Per Unit of Industrial Value Added							
		工业增加值按2005年价格计算 VAI are calculated at 2005 constant prices						工业增加值按2010年价格计算 VAI are calculated at 2010 constant prices	
		2005	2006	2007	2008	2009	2010	2010	2011
西安市	**Xi'an**	**1.220**	**1.100**	**1.092**	**0.915**	**0.800**	**0.703**	**0.593**	**0.502**
新城区	Xincheng	0.822	0.798	0.716	0.663	0.420	0.379	0.329	0.361
碑林区	Beilin	0.876	0.846	0.782	0.763	0.293	0.246	0.115	0.073
莲湖区	Lianhu	0.861	0.832	0.775	0.639	0.269	0.232	0.226	0.207
灞桥区	Baqiao	3.029	2.871	2.446	2.078	2.072	2.032	1.447	1.106
未央区	Weiyang	1.030	1.000	0.876	0.770	1.008	0.936	0.786	0.651
雁塔区	Yanta	1.358	1.308	1.123	1.000	0.578	0.414	0.359	0.341
阎良区	Yanliang	0.876	0.849	0.761	0.625	0.354	0.271	0.255	0.209
临潼区	Lintong	1.031	0.992	0.882	0.715	0.644	0.371	0.203	0.166
长安区	Chang'an	1.370	1.300	1.208	1.087	0.725	0.698	0.366	0.323
蓝田县	Lantian	2.579	2.515	2.133	2.084	3.670	3.487	2.534	2.087
周至县	Zhouzhi	1.946	1.900	1.891	1.842	0.364	0.336	0.257	0.237
户 县	Huxian	7.467	7.168	5.857	4.910	4.514	4.036	3.570	3.135
高陵县	Gaoling	0.966	0.905	0.719	0.693	0.239	0.221	0.223	0.189

注：1.本表2005-2010年（工业增加值按2005年价格）统计范围为主营业务收入500万元及以上的法人工业企业；2010-2011年（工业增加值按2010年价格）统计范围为主营业务收入2000万元及以上的法人工业企业。

2.能源消耗按当量值计算。

Note:1.Statistical range in this table between 2005 to 2010(VAI are calculated at 2005 constant prices) were for the main business income of 500 million yuan and above legal industrial enterprises,whereas that of the year of 2010 to 2011(VAI are calculated at 2010 constant prices) were for the main business income of 500 million yuan and above legal industrial enterprises.

2.Energy consumption was calculated by the equivalent value.

12-3 续表

Continued

地 区	Region	比上年增长(%) Growth Rates over Preceding Year(%)					
		2006	2007	2008	2009	2010	2011
西安市	**Xi'an**	**-3.04**	**-12.56**	**-13.43**	**-10.48**	**-12.18**	**-15.44**
新城区	Xincheng	-2.92	-10.26	-7.38	-2.68	-9.69	9.68
碑林区	Beilin	-3.42	-7.59	-2.45	-0.44	-15.89	-36.63
莲湖区	Lianhu	-3.47	-6.91	-17.61	0.89	-13.63	-8.19
灞桥区	Baqiao	-5.22	-14.79	-15.04	0.29	-1.92	-23.61
未央区	Weiyang	-2.91	-10.63	-12.15	-15.20	-7.18	-17.17
雁塔区	Yanta	-3.68	-14.14	-10.98	-13.98	-28.43	-4.88
阎良区	Yanliang	-3.05	-10.42	-17.83	-18.36	-23.44	-18.11
临潼区	Lintong	-3.82	-11.06	-18.99	3.05	-42.41	-18.32
长安区	Chang'an	-5.11	-4.06	-10.05	-18.68	-3.67	-11.88
蓝田县	Lantian	-2.48	-15.18	-2.29	-3.39	-5.00	-17.63
周至县	Zhouzhi	-2.38	-0.48	-2.62	-12.27	-7.71	-7.56
户 县	Huxian	-4.01	-18.29	-16.17	-18.48	-10.58	-12.19
高陵县	Gaoling	-6.32	-20.52	-3.56	-18.90	-7.65	-15.26

12-4 主要年份全社会用电量

Electricity Consumption of the Whole Society in Representative Years

单位：万千瓦时 (10 000 kw.h)

指　标	Item	2000	2007	2008	2009	2010	2011
总　计	**Total**	**732373**	**1482896**	**1605089**	**1724067**	**1993751**	**2167453**
#行业用电量合计	Total of Industry of Electricity	599855	1215799	1293574	1358483	1499903	1590486
1.第一产业	Primary Industry	77579	120134	127054	99083	108720	117984
2.第二产业	Secondary Industry	354245	700026	724852	766029	883259	910360
3.第三产业	Tertiary Industry	168031	395639	441668	493371	507924	562142
一、农、林、牧、渔业	**Agriculture ,Forestry,Animal Husbandry and Fishery**	**77579**	**120134**	**127054**	**99083**	**108720**	**117984**
二、工业	**Industry**	**345175**	**674990**	**696291**	**724920**	**838317**	**859796**
1.轻工业	Light Industry	152125	187323	182176	167144	177362	183766
2.重工业	Heavy Industry	193050	487667	514115	557776	660955	676030
三、信息传输、计算机服务和软件业	**Information Transmission,Computer Service and Software**		**21938**	**26680**	**29328**	**30760**	**33191**
四、建筑业	**Construction**	**9070**	**25036**	**28561**	**41108**	**44942**	**50564**
五、交通运输、仓储及邮政业	**Traffic,Transport,Storage and Post**	**22904**	**53825**	**56614**	**62031**	**58509**	**66684**
六、公共事业及管理组织	**Public Utilities and Management Organization**		**144859**	**165024**	**177409**	**154074**	**164473**
七、商业、住宿和餐饮业	**Commercial,Hotels and Catering Services**		**107343**	**111676**	**122203**	**148418**	**166558**
八、金融、房地产、商务及居民服务业	**Finance,Real Estate,Business Affairs and Households Services**		**67674**	**81674**	**102400**	**116163**	**131236**
九、城乡居民生活用电	**Electricity Consumption of Urban and Rural Residents**	**132518**	**267097**	**311515**	**365585**	**493848**	**576966**
1.乡村	Rural	31281	38395	63072	99941	142059	169898
2.城市	City	101237	228702	248443	265644	351789	407068

12-5 规模以上工业企业能源购进、消费及库存（2011年）

Energy Purchases Consumption and Inventory of Industrial Enterprises Above Designated size（2011）

能源名称	Name(unit)	年初库存 Stock (year-beginning)	购进量 实物量 Quantity	Purchases 金额（万元） Sum (10 000 yuan)
原煤(吨)	Raw Coal（ton）	545694	7577401	430425
洗精煤(吨)	Washed Coal(ton)	96	740	55
其他洗煤(吨)	Other Washed Coals(ton)		142	10
煤制品(吨)	Briquettes(ton)	1385	11014	766
焦炭(吨)	Coke(ton)	2335	40904	7162
其他焦化产品(吨)	Other Coking Products(ton)		8100	1210
焦炉煤气(万立方米)	Other Gases(10 000cu.m)			
天然气（气态）(万立方米)	Natural Gas(10 000cu.m)		12114	25806
液化天然气（液态）(吨)	Liquefied Natural Gas (Liquid)(ton)		3	3
原油(吨)	Crude Oil(ton)	48555	1549928	875709
汽油(吨)	Gasoline(ton)	341	26290	20999
煤油(吨)	Kerosene(ton)	868	14173	10262
柴油(吨)	Diesel Oil(ton)	1126	53809	42235
燃料油(吨)	Fuel Oil(ton)	153	703	410
液化石油气(吨)	LPG(ton)		961	657
其他石油制品(吨)	Other Petroleum Products(ton)	47	5246	5808
热力(百万千焦)	Heat (1 million kilo-joule)		7882823	36956
电力(万千瓦时)	Electricity(10 000kwh)		743580	434296
其他燃料(吨标准煤)	Other Fuels(ton of SCE)	60	2010	805
能源合计(吨标准煤)	Total Energy(ton of SCE)			

12-5 续表 Cointinued

能源名称	Name(unit)	消费量 Consumption 合 计 Total	工业生产消费 Industrial Production Consume	用于原材料 as Raw Material	非工业生产消费 Non-industrial Production Consume	年末库存 Stock year-end
原煤(吨)	Raw Coal（ton）	7548194	7435220	52781	112974	570310
洗精煤(吨)	Washed Coal(ton)	701	701			135
其他洗煤(吨)	Other Washed Coals(ton)	142			142	
煤制品(吨)	Briquettes(ton)	11770	10688		1082	773
焦炭(吨)	Coke(ton)	38940	38940	36		4299
其他焦化产品(吨)	Other Coking Products(ton)	6200	6200			1900
焦炉煤气(万立方米)	Other Gases(10 000cu.m)					
天然气（气态）(万立方米)	Natural Gas(10 000cu.m)	12108	11594	39	514	6
液化天然气（液态）(吨)	Liquefied Natural Gas (Liquid)(ton)	3			3	
原油(吨)	Crude Oil(ton)	1531686	1531686			66797
汽油(吨)	Gasoline(ton)	26419	21050	315	5369	431
煤油(吨)	Kerosene(ton)	14617	14609		8	424
柴油(吨)	Diesel Oil(ton)	53353	52659	1432	694	1691
燃料油(吨)	Fuel Oil(ton)	760	752		8	82
液化石油气(吨)	LPG(ton)	961	960		1	
其他石油制品(吨)	Other Petroleum Products(ton)	5246	5246	571		47
热力(百万千焦)	Heat (1 million kilo-joule)	11882546	10711142		1171404	
电力(万千瓦时)	Electricity(10 000kwh)	831207	814649		16558	
其他燃料(吨标准煤)	Other Fuels(ton of SCE)	2040	2040			30
能源合计(吨标准煤)	Total Energy(ton of SCE)	9110122	8951912		158210	

12-6 规模以上工业分行业主要能源品种消费量（2011年）

Major Energy Consumption Above Designated Size by Sector（2011）

行 业	Sector	原煤（吨）Raw Coal (ton)	天然气（万立方米）Natural Gas(10 000cu.m)	原油（吨）Crude Oil (ton)
总 计	**Total**	**7548194**	**12108**	**1531686**
按工业行业大类分列	Grouped by Sector			
煤炭开采和洗选业	Coal Mining and Dressing			
石油和天然气开采业	Petroleum and Natural Gas Extraction		98	
黑色金属矿采选业	Ferrous Metals Mining and Dressing			
有色金属矿采选业	Nonferrous Metals Mining and Dressing		168	
非金属矿采选业	Nonmetal Minerals Mining and Dressing			
其他采矿业	Other Mining Industry			
农副食品加工业	Agricultural Products and Non-stable Food Processing Industry	261590	2	
食品制造业	Food Production	58018	120	
饮料制造业	Beverage Production	109363	227	
烟草制品业	Tobacco Processing	7		
纺织业	Textile Industry	9384		
纺织服装、鞋、帽制造业	Textile Clothing, Footwear and Headgear Industry		13	
皮革、毛皮、羽毛(绒)及其制品业	Leather, Fur, Feather (eiderdown) and Their Products Industry			
木材加工及木、竹、藤、棕、草制品制造	Timber Processing,Bamboo,Cane,Palm Fiber and Straw Products	5998		
家具制造业	Furniture Manufacturing			
造纸及纸制品业	Papermaking and Paper products	308775		
印刷业和记录媒介的复制	Printing,Record Medium Reproduction	495	157	
文教体育用品制造业	Cultural,Educational and Sports Goods			
石油加工、炼焦及核燃料加工业	Petroleum Refining, Ccoke Making and Nuclear Fuel Processing Industry	25861	128	1531686
化学原料及化学制品制造业	Raw Chemical Materials and Chemical Products	77912	525	
医药制造业	Medical and Pharmaceutical Products	53488	739	
化学纤维制造业	Chemical Fiber			
橡胶制品业	Rubber Products			
塑料制品业	Plastic Products	53629	10	
非金属矿物制品业	Nonmetal Mineral Products	353926	35	
黑色金属冶炼及压延加工业	Smelting and Pressing of Ferrous Metals	51913	1105	
有色金属冶炼及压延加工业	Smelting and Pressing of Nonferrou Metals	2044	751	
金属制品业	Metal Products	9845	139	
通用设备制造	General Equipment Manufacturing Industry	23636	176	
专用设备制造业	Special Purpose Equipment	79118	605	
交通运输设备制造业	Transport Equipment	301977	4306	
电气机械及器材制造业	Electric Equipment and Machinery	25415	1854	
通信设备、计算机及其他电子设备制造业	Communication Equipment, Computer and Other Electronic Equipment Manufacturing Industry	2689	353	
仪器仪表及文化办公用机械制造业	Instruments,Meters,Cultural and Office	1958	169	
工艺品及其他制造业	Handicraft and Other Stuff Manufacturing Industry			
废弃资源和废旧材料回收加工业	Discarded Resources and Waste Materials Salvaging and Processing Industry			
电力、热力的生产和供应业	Electric Power, Heating Power Generating and Supplying Industry	5731153	1	
燃气生产和供应业	Gas Mining and Supplying Industry		170	
水的生产和供应业	Water Processing and Supplying Industry		258	

12-6 续表 Continued

行 业	Sector	汽油（吨）Gasoline (ton)	柴油（吨）Diesel Oil (ton)	热能（百万千焦）Heat (million kilo-joule)	电力（万千瓦时）Electricity (10 000kwh)
总 计	**Total**	**26419**	**53353**	**11882546**	**831207**
按工业行业大类分列	Grouped by Sector				
煤炭开采和洗选业	Coal Mining and Dressing				
石油和天然气开采业	Petroleum and Natural Gas Extraction	124	986		423
黑色金属矿采选业	Ferrous Metals Mining and Dressing				83
有色金属矿采选业	Nonferrous Metals Mining and Dressing			17213	2181
非金属矿采选业	Nonmetal Minerals Mining and Dressing				
其他采矿业	Other Mining Industry				
农副食品加工业	Agricultural Products and Non-stable Food Processing Industry	1201	1563	1951770	26777
食品制造业	Food Production	3150	621	377592	10446
饮料制造业	Beverage Production	337	405	581511	20273
烟草制品业	Tobacco Processing	9		11532	105
纺织业	Textile Industry	57	21	427282	30466
纺织服装、鞋、帽制造业	Textile Clothing, Footwear and Headgear Industry	111			1161
皮革、毛皮、羽毛(绒)及其制品业	Leather, Fur, Feather (eiderdown) and Their Products Industry	75		14608	161
木材加工及木、竹、藤、棕、草制品制造	Timber Processing,Bamboo,Cane,Palm Fiber and Straw Products	254	6		5691
家具制造业	Furniture Manufacturing	149	104		904
造纸及纸制品业	Papermaking and Paper products	928	106	751933	21424
印刷业和记录媒介的复制	Printing,Record Medium Reproduction	581	111	69229	7947
文教体育用品制造业	Cultural,Educational and Sports Goods	35			284
石油加工、炼焦及核燃料加工业	Petroleum Refining, Ccoke Making and Nuclear Fuel Processing Industry		77		33833
化学原料及化学制品制造业	Raw Chemical Materials and Chemical Products	595	620	1240742	47231
医药制造业	Medical and Pharmaceutical Products	786	140	160055	11883
化学纤维制造业	Chemical Fiber	19	9	666663	2712
橡胶制品业	Rubber Products	91	6		1283
塑料制品业	Plastic Products	256	2026	3785	15807
非金属矿物制品业	Nonmetal Mineral Products	1448	21012	84148	43133
黑色金属冶炼及压延加工业	Smelting and Pressing of Ferrous Metals	41	34	24021	17922
有色金属冶炼及压延加工业	Smelting and Pressing of Nonferrou Metals	483	444	182562	26917
金属制品业	Metal Products	731	121	26730	6111
通用设备制造	General Equipment Manufacturing Industry	1164	394	13777	18565
专用设备制造业	Special Purpose Equipment	2758	2300	1029636	35011
交通运输设备制造业	Transport Equipment	6513	14698	1368457	140980
电气机械及器材制造业	Electric Equipment and Machinery	1693	864	1019204	35620
通信设备、计算机及其他电子设备制造业	Communication Equipment, Computer and Other Electronic Equipment Manufacturing Industry	569	84	629343	25676
仪器仪表及文化办公用机械制造业	Instruments,Meters,Cultural and Office	1284	4001	151849	5416
工艺品及其他制造业	Handicraft and Other Stuff Manufacturing Industry	48	9		346
废弃资源和废旧材料回收加工业	Discarded Resources and Waste Materials Salvaging and Processing Industry				
电力、热力的生产和供应业	Electric Power, Heating Power Generating and Supplying Industry	237	2437	1078904	223920
燃气生产和供应业	Gas Mining and Supplying Industry	439	139		3323
水的生产和供应业	Water Processing and Supplying Industry	254	19		7190

12-7 规模以上工业分行业综合能源消费量（2011年）

Comprehensive Energy Consumption by Sector Above Designated Size（2011）

单位：吨标准煤 (ton of SCE)

指　　标	Item	2011	比上年增长（%） Increase over Preceding Year (%)
总　计	**Total**	**4905405**	**-0.9**
煤炭开采和洗选业	Coal Mining and Dressing		-100.0
石油和天然气开采业	Petroleum and Natural Gas Extraction	3410	-19.8
黑色金属矿采选业	Ferrous Metals Mining and Dressing	102	-1.1
有色金属矿采选业	Nonferrous Metals Mining and Dressing	5451	-10.4
非金属矿采选业	Nonmetal Minerals Mining and Dressing		-100.0
其他采矿业	Other Mining Industry		-100.0
农副食品加工业	Agricultural Products and Non-stable Food Processing Industry	213170	-4.7
食品制造业	Food Production	76331	12.9
饮料制造业	Beverage Production	126096	0.9
烟草制品业	Tobacco Processing	541	44.4
纺织业	Textile Industry	51861	-6.6
纺织服装、鞋、帽制造业	Textile Clothing, Footwear and Headgear Industry	1762	16.1
皮革、毛皮、羽毛(绒)及其制品业	Leather, Fur, Feather (eiderdown) and Their Products Industry	806	81.7
木材加工及木、竹、藤、棕、草制品制造	Timber Processing,Bamboo,Cane,Palm Fiber and Straw Products	11317	6.4
家具制造业	Furniture Manufacturing	1483	7.6
造纸及纸制品业	Papermaking and Paper products	222453	-14.4
印刷业和记录媒介的复制	Printing,Record Medium Reproduction	15536	12.1
文教体育用品制造业	Cultural,Educational and Sports Goods	342	-27.7
石油加工、炼焦及核燃料加工业	Petroleum Refining, Ccoke Making and Nuclear Fuel Processing Industry	276067	-14.2
化学原料及化学制品制造业	Raw Chemical Materials and Chemical Products	179245	-20.4
医药制造业	Medical and Pharmaceutical Products	67762	22.7
化学纤维制造业	Chemical Fiber	26107	-3.3
橡胶制品业	Rubber Products	2939	6.6
塑料制品业	Plastic Products	61157	204.0
非金属矿物制品业	Nonmetal Mineral Products	340676	-10.7
黑色金属冶炼及压延加工业	Smelting and Pressing of Ferrous Metals	80818	-2.5
有色金属冶炼及压延加工业	Smelting and Pressing of Nonferrou Metals	50946	90.4
金属制品业	Metal Products	17861	-2.8
通用设备制造	General Equipment Manufacturing Industry	50603	2.2
专用设备制造业	Special Purpose Equipment	184073	0.9
交通运输设备制造业	Transport Equipment	423789	0.6
电气机械及器材制造业	Electric Equipment and Machinery	122771	5.2
通信设备、计算机及其他电子设备制造业	Communication Equipment, Computer and Other Electronic Equipment Manufacturing Industry	39155	19.7
仪器仪表及文化办公用机械制造业	Instruments,Meters,Cultural and Office	21699	-3.4
工艺品及其他制造业	Handicraft and Other Stuff Manufacturing Industry	1481	-9.1
废弃资源和废旧材料回收加工业	Discarded Resources and Waste Materials Salvaging and Processing Industry		-100.0
电力、热力的生产和供应业	Electric Power, Heating Power Generating and Supplying Industry	2209871	1.7
燃气生产和供应业	Gas Mining and Supplying Industry	7130	1.7
水的生产和供应业	Water Processing and Supplying Industry	10594	-0.5

12-8 规模以上工业企业用水情况

Statistics on Water Use of Industrial Enterprises Above Designated Size

指 标	Item	取水量（立方米） Water Use (Cubic meter)	支付费用的取水量（立方米） Paid Water Use (Cubic meter)	取水支付金额（千元） Money Paid for Water Use (1 000yuan)	外供水量（立方米） Outward Water Supply (Cubic meter)
合 计	**Total**	**515907400**	**425693200**	**486828**	**407493200**
1.陆地地表水	Surface Water	340965400	333106500	255261	488800
#陆地湖咸水	Land lake Salt water	8333500	8333500	10834	
2.地下水	Ground-water	83948900	19743200	16715	5674800
#地下咸水	Ground-Salt water	413600	413500	110	
3.自来水	Tap Water	78993800	61326100	201363	401329500
4.其他水	Other Water	11999300	11517400	13489	
#雨水收集利用	Rain Water Collected	1600			
再生水（中水）	Reclaimed Water	8864400	8584000	10079	

12-9 规模以上工业企业分行业用水量（2011年）

Volume of Water Use of Industrial Enterprises Above Designated Size by Sector（2011）

行　业	Sector	取水量（立方米）Water Use (Cubic meter)	支付费用的取水量 Paid Water Use
总　计	**Total**	**515907400**	**425693200**
按工业行业大类分列	Grouped by Sector		
煤炭开采和洗选业	Coal Mining and Dressing		
石油和天然气开采业	Petroleum and Natural Gas Extraction	12700	12700
黑色金属矿采选业	Ferrous Metals Mining and Dressing	97600	96400
有色金属矿采选业	Nonferrous Metals Mining and Dressing	65400	65400
非金属矿采选业	Nonmetal Minerals Mining and Dressing		
其他采矿业	Other mining industry		
农副食品加工业	Agricultural products and non-stable food processing industry	2190700.00	2066200
食品制造业	Food Production	2457900.00	2388300
饮料制造业	Beverage Production	9427400.00	6966900
烟草制品业	Tobacco Processing	5700	5700
纺织业	Textile Industry	1549500	1523900
纺织服装、鞋、帽制造业	Textile clothing, footwear and headgear industry	95400	95300
皮革、毛皮、羽毛(绒)及其制品业	Leather, fur, feather (eiderdown) and their products industry	11900	11900
木材加工及木、竹、藤、棕、草制品制造	Timber Processing,Bamboo,Cane,Palm Fiber and Straw Products	18600	13800
家具制造业	Furniture Manufacturing	26500	26500
造纸及纸制品业	Papermaking and Paper products	8344300	6775300
印刷业和记录媒介的复制	Printing,Record Medium Reproduction	627700	626900
文教体育用品制造业	Cultural,Educational and Sports Goods	4400	2500
石油加工、炼焦及核燃料加工业	Petroleum refining, coke making and nuclear fuel processing industry	791800	714500
化学原料及化学制品制造业	Raw Chemical Materials and Chemical Products	10180900	8770100
医药制造业	Medical and Pharmaceutical Products	4189300	4126600
化学纤维制造业	Chemical Fiber	250000	250000
橡胶制品业	Rubber Products	36000	36000
塑料制品业	Plastic Products	1693700	1690500
非金属矿物制品业	Nonmetal Mineral Products	2335000	1203000
黑色金属冶炼及压延加工业	Smelting and Pressing of Ferrous Metals	305600	275700
有色金属冶炼及压延加工业	Smelting and Pressing of Nonferrou Metals	1567100	1562300
金属制品业	Metal Products	468100	418200
通用设备制造	General equipment manufacturing industry	1028400	954200
专用设备制造业	Special Purpose Equipment	5955800	4730400
交通运输设备制造业	Transport Equipment	15578900	15561300
电气机械及器材制造业	Electric Equipment and Machinery	4727900	4699800
通信设备、计算机及其他电子设备制造业	Communication equipment, computer and other electronic equipment manufacturing industry	2808100	2807300
仪器仪表及文化办公用机械制造业	Instruments,Meters,Cultural and Office	1595900	1595900
工艺品及其他制造业	Handicraft and other stuff manufacturing industry	28200	28200
废弃资源和废旧材料回收加工业	Discarded resources and waste materials salvaging and processing industry		
电力、热力的生产和供应业	Electric power, heating power generating and supplying industry	29486500	29146900
燃气生产和供应业	Gas mining and supplying industry	170800	65500
水的生产和供应业	Water processing and supplying industry	407773700	326379100

12-9 续表 Continued

行 业	Sector	取水支付金额（千元）Money Paid for Water Use (1 000yuan)	外供水量（立方米）Outward Water Supply (Cubic meter)
总 计	**Total**	**486829**	**407493200**
按工业行业大类分列	Grouped by Sector		
煤炭开采和洗选业	Coal Mining and Dressing		
石油和天然气开采业	Petroleum and Natural Gas Extraction	63	
黑色金属矿采选业	Ferrous Metals Mining and Dressing	19	
有色金属矿采选业	Nonferrous Metals Mining and Dressing	257	
非金属矿采选业	Nonmetal Minerals Mining and Dressing		
其他采矿业	Other mining industry		
农副食品加工业	Agricultural products and non-stable food processing industry	2303	
食品制造业	Food Production	6233	
饮料制造业	Beverage Production	23135	12100
烟草制品业	Tobacco Processing	20	
纺织业	Textile Industry	5089	
纺织服装、鞋、帽制造业	Textile clothing, footwear and headgear industry	285	
皮革、毛皮、羽毛(绒)及其制品业	Leather, fur, feather (eiderdown) and their products industry	43	
木材加工及木、竹、藤、棕、草制品制造	Timber Processing,Bamboo,Cane,Palm Fiber and Straw Products	47	
家具制造业	Furniture Manufacturing	79	
造纸及纸制品业	Papermaking and Paper products	8433	
印刷业和记录媒介的复制	Printing,Record Medium Reproduction	2326	
文教体育用品制造业	Cultural,Educational and Sports Goods	3	
石油加工、炼焦及核燃料加工业	Petroleum refining, coke making and nuclear fuel processing industry	2601	
化学原料及化学制品制造业	Raw Chemical Materials and Chemical Products	15115	1396600
医药制造业	Medical and Pharmaceutical Products	12289	
化学纤维制造业	Chemical Fiber	353	
橡胶制品业	Rubber Products	91	
塑料制品业	Plastic Products	3462	
非金属矿物制品业	Nonmetal Mineral Products	2510	
黑色金属冶炼及压延加工业	Smelting and Pressing of Ferrous Metals	778	
有色金属冶炼及压延加工业	Smelting and Pressing of Nonferrou Metals	3845	
金属制品业	Metal Products	1400	
通用设备制造	General equipment manufacturing industry	3238	
专用设备制造业	Special Purpose Equipment	16468	22300
交通运输设备制造业	Transport Equipment	49467	121900
电气机械及器材制造业	Electric Equipment and Machinery	16939	
通信设备、计算机及其他电子设备制造业	Communication equipment, computer and other electronic equipment manufacturing industry	10772	
仪器仪表及文化办公用机械制造业	Instruments,Meters,Cultural and Office	4985	48300
工艺品及其他制造业	Handicraft and other stuff manufacturing industry	95	
废弃资源和废旧材料回收加工业	Discarded resources and waste materials salvaging and processing industry		
电力、热力的生产和供应业	Electric power, heating power generating and supplying industry	45673	
燃气生产和供应业	Gas mining and supplying industry	249	
水的生产和供应业	Water processing and supplying industry	248163	405892200

主要统计指标解释

能源消费总量 指一定时期内，地区各行业和居民生活消费的各种能源的总和。该指标是观察能源消费水平、构成和增长速度的总量指标。能源消费总量包括原煤和原油及其制品、天然气、电力等，不包括低热值燃料、生物质能和太阳能等的利用。能源消费总量分为终端能源消费量、能源加工转换损失量和能源损失量三部分。

（1）终端能源消费量：指一定时期内，全国生产和生活消费的各种能源在扣除了用于加工转换二次能源消费量和损失量以后的数量。

（2）能源加工转换损失量：指一定时期内，全国投入加工转换的各种能源数量之和与产出各种能源产品之和的差额。该指标是观察能源在加工转换过程中损失量变化的指标。

（3）能源损失量：指一定时期内，能源在输送、分配、储存过程中发生的损失和由客观原因造成的各种损失量，不包括各种气体能源放空、放散量。

工业生产能源消费 指工业企业为进行工业生产活动所消费的能源。

非工业生产能源消费 指在工业企业能源消费中，除"工业生产能源消费"以外的能源消费，即非工业生产用能和工业企业附属的不从事工业生产活动的非独立核算单位用能。

运输工具消费 指在厂区内、外进行交通运输活动的交通运输工具所消费的能源。

能源加工转换投入 能源的加工、转换是指为了特定的用途，将一种能源（一般为一次能源），经过一定的工艺，加工或转换成另外一种能源（一般为二次能源）。能源加工转换的投入即能源加工、转换消费。

一次能源 是指自然界中以现成形式存在，不经任何改变或转换的天然能源资源，即从自然界直接取得并不改变其形态和品位的能源。如原煤、原油、天然气、核燃料、植物燃料、风能、水能、太阳能、地热能、海洋能、潮汐能等。

二次能源 是指为了满足生产工艺和生活的特定需要以合理利用能源，将一次能源直接或间接加工转换产生的其它种类和形式的人工能源。如原煤加工产出的洗煤；由煤炭加工转换产出的焦炭，煤气；由原油加工产出的汽油、煤油、柴油、燃料油、液化石油气、炼厂干气等；由煤炭、石油、天然气转换产出的电力。

综合能源消费量 报告期内工业企业在工业生产活动中实际消费的各种能源的总和净值。计算综合能源消费量时，需要先将使用的各种能源折算成标准燃料后再进行计算。

单位生产总值能耗 指一定时期内，一个国家或地区每生产一个单位的生产总值所消耗的能源。计算公式为：

单位生产总值能耗=能源消费总量/生产总值

单位生产总值电耗 指一定时期内，一个国家或地区每生产一个单位的生产总值所消耗的电力。计算公式为：

单位生产总值电耗=全社会用电量/生产总值

单位工业增加值能耗 指一定时期内，一个国家或地区每生产一个单位的工业增加值所消耗的能源。计算公式为：

单位工业增加值能耗=工业能源消费量/工业增加值

Explanatory Notes on Main Statistical Indicators

Total Energy Consumption refers to the total consumption of energy of various kinds by the production sectors and the households in the country in a given period of time. It is a comprehensive indicator to show the scale, composition and pace of increase of energy consumption. Total energy consumption includes that of coal, crude oil and their products, natural gas and electricity. However, it does not include the consumption of fuel of low calorific value, bio-energy and solar energy. Total energy consumption can be divided into three parts: end-use energy consumption; loss during the process of energy conversion; and energy loss.

(1)End-use Energy Consumption: It refers to the total energy consumption by the production sectors and the households in the country (region) in a given period of time. It does not include the consumption during the conversion of primary energy into secondary energy and the loss in the process of energy conversion.

(2)Loss During the Process of Energy Conversion: It refers to the total input of various kinds of energy for conversion, minus the total output of various kinds of energy in the country in a given period of time. It is an indicator to show the loss that occurs during the process of energy conversion.

(3)Energy Loss: It refers to the total of the loss of energy during the course of energy transport, distribution and storage and the loss caused by any objective reason in a given period of time. The loss of various kinds of gas due to gas discharges and stocktaking is not included.

Industry Consumption Energy refers to the volume of energy consumed by Industrial enterprises for industrial production activities.

Non-industry Consumption Energy refers to the energy consumed by industrial enterprises except for industrial production activities , means that energy consumed by non-industry production and not independent accounting units which was not engaged in industrial production activities affiliated to industrial enterprises.

Vehicle Energy refers to the energy consumed by vehicles which carried out transport activities in and out of factories.

Energy Processing Conversion Devoted energy processing conversion refers to for specialized application , a source of energy (normally primary energy), after a certain technology , processed or converted to another kind of energy (normally secondary energy). The input of energy conversion processing that is energy processing, and conversion consumption.

Primary Energy Source refers to natural energy resources as found naturally in the form of ready-made , without any change or conversion , as energy obtained directly from natural and not change its shape and grade, such as raw coal, crude oil, natural gas, nuclear fuel, plant fuel, wind energy, water energy, solar energy, geothermal energy, oceanic energy, tidal energy and so on .

Secondary Energy refers to other types and forms of artificial energy which was processed and conversed from primary energy sources directly or indirectly , in order to meet the specific needs in production process and life to use energy more effectively. Such as washing coal processed from raw coal; coke and coal gas processed and transformed from raw coal; gasoline, kerosene, diesel oil, fuel oil, liquefied petroleum gas, dry gas refinery processed from crude oil; electric power conversed from coal, oil and natural gas.

Comprehensive energy consumption refers to the total and net energy actually consumed in industrial production activities by industrial enterprises in the reference period. When calculated the volume of consumption of comprehensive energy , should converted sorts of energy which was used into standards fuel firstly.

Energy Consumption per Unit of GDP refers to the energy consumption per unit of Gross Domestic Product in a country or the Gross Regional Product in a region in the same reference period. The formula is:

$$\text{Energy Consumption per Unit of GDP} = \frac{\text{Total Energy Consumption}}{\text{Gross Domestic Product}}$$

Electricity Consumption per Unit of GDP refers to the electricity consumption per unit of Gross Domestic Product in a country or the Gross Regional Product in a region in the same reference period. The formula is:

$$\text{Electricity Consumption per Unit ofGDP} = \frac{\text{Total Electricity Consumption}}{\text{Gross Domestic Product}}$$

Energy Consumption per Unit of Industrial Value-added refers to the energy consumption per unit of industrial value-added in a country or region in the same reference period. The formula is:

$$\text{Energy Consumption per Unit of Industrial Value-added} = \frac{\text{Total Energy Consumption}}{\text{Industrial Value-added}}$$

13 建筑业

CONSTRUCTION

资料整理：陈海生
Data management:Chen Haisheng

第十三部分　建筑业

一、简要说明

本章资料主要包括建筑业基本情况，建筑业施工企业生产情况和财务状况，由西安市统计局固定资产投资处提供。

二、主要指标

企业个数（个）	336	比上年增加	12个
建筑业总产值（亿元）	1619.08	比上年下降	11.0%
#国有及国有控股企业	1278.33	比上年下降	15.9%
房屋建筑竣工面积（万平方米）	2392.39	比上年增长	71.9%
房屋建筑面积竣工率（%）	38.5	比上年提高	8.3个百分点

13 CONSTRUCTION

Ⅰ.Brief Introduction

This chapter consists of primarily the data basic situation of the construction industry, production situation and financial situation of the construction enterprises, provided by Fixed Asset Investment Division of the Xi'an Bureau of Statistics.

Ⅱ.Major Indicators

		Increase over Preceding Year
Number of Enterprises(item)	336	12
Total Output Value of Construction(100 mil. yuan)	1619.08	-11.0%
State-owned Or State Holding Majority Shares	1278.33	-15.9%
Floor Space of Buildings Completed(10 000 sq.m)	2392.39	71.9%
Rate of Floor Space of Buildings Completed(%)	38.5	8.3 percentage points

13-1 主要年份建筑业总产值

Total Output Value of Construction in Representative Year

单位:万元 （10 000 yuan）

年 份 Year	建筑业总产值 Total Output Value of Construction	国有及国有控股企业 State-owned Or State Holding Majority Shares	集体企业 Collective-owned Enterprises
2000	1059250	788704	148709
2001	1148091	918169	154749
2002	1334713	850278	153482
2003	1771126	1199911	134010
2004	2444242	2016792	165922
2005	3266535	2766785	196111
2006	4164782	3482016	236493
2007	6047524	4326279	326658
2008	9151199	6761190	4601423
2009	12965787	10672178	471533
2010	18203450	15203874	583928
2011	16190888	12783270	794189

注：1.1996年以后建筑业年报统计范围由往年的县及县以上（含县级建制镇）各种经济类型的建筑企业，改为具有建筑业资质等级四级及四级以上的各种经济类型的建筑施工企业；2002年改为具有建筑业资质等级的各种经济类型的建筑施工企业。

2.本表资料含劳务分包企业。

Note:1.Since 1996, the boundary of annual report of construstion had change from enterprises of all economic types of county and above (including towns of county level) to enterprises at fourth or higher quality grades. Since 2002, it has changed to enterprises of all economic types with qualification grades.

2.Data in this table includes labor subcontracting enterprises.

13-2 全市建筑施工企业基本情况（2011年）

Main Indicators on Construction Enterprise of Xi'an（2011）

指 标	Item	合 计 Total	国有及国有控股 State-owned Or State Holding Majority Shares
企业个数(个)（施工总承包）	Number of Enterprises (unit) (Overall Contractor For Construction)	221	69
#二级以上企业	First and Second Class Enterprise	166	63
计算劳动生产率的平均人数（人）（施工总承包）	Average Number of Employed Persons in Calculation of Labor Productivity (person) (Overall Contractor For Construction)	457587	328207
#二级以上企业	First and Second Class Enterprise	437506	326833
建筑业总产值（万元）（施工总承包）	Total Output Value of Construction(10 000 yuan) (Overall Contractor For Construction)	15291309	12189604
#二级以上企业	First and Second Class Enterprise	14870209	12158898
全员劳动生产率(元/人) 按总产值计算	Overall Labor Productivity (yuan/person) Calculated by Total Output Value	334172	371399

13–3 施工总承包和专业承包建筑业企业生产情况（2011年）

分　组	Item	签定的合同额（万元）Contract Value (1 0000 yuan)
总　计	**Total**	**36971659**
#国有及国有控股	State-Owned and State Holding Majority Shares	31782374
一、按登记注册类型分	**Grouped by Registion Status**	
内资	Domestic Investment Enterprises	36970792
国有企业	State-owned Enterprises	20998426
集体企业	Collective-owned Enterprises	1416843
股份合作企业	Share-holding Corperative Enterprises	284079
联营企业	Joint Ownership Enterprises	5843
有限责任公司	Limited Liability Corporations	13294047
股份有限公司	Share-holding Corperation Ltd.	
私营企业	Private Enterprises	971554
其他企业	Others	
港澳台商投资企业	Enterprises with Funds from Hong Kong,Macao and Taiwan	868
外商投资企业	Enterprises with Foreign Investment	
二、按国民经济行业分	**Grouped by Sector**	
房屋和土木工程建筑业	Building Engineering and Civil Engineering Construction	34799332
房屋工程建筑	Building Engineering Construction	10662596
土木工程建筑	Civil Engineering Construction	24136737
建筑安装业	Installation of Construction	1293645
建筑装饰业	Fitting and Decoration	165981
其他建筑业	Others	233116
三、按隶属关系分	**Grouped by Administrative Relationship**	
中　央	Central	24257935
地　方	Region	4625654
四、按企业资质等级分	**Grouped by Class of Enterprises**	
1.施工总承包	Overall Contractor for Construction	3555685
#特级	Special Class	1081775
一级	First Class	108877
二级	Second Class	52571
2.专业承包	Special Contractor	55806
#一级以上	First Class	22578

Main Indicators on Overall Constructing Contractors and Professional Contractors by Registration Status（2011）

建筑业总产值（万元）Total Output Value of Constrution (1 0000 yuan)	建筑工程产值 Output Value of Constrution	安装工程产值 Output Value of Installation	其他产值 Others	计算劳动生产率的平均人数（人）Average Number of Employed Persons in Calculation of Labour Productivity(person)	期末从业人数（人）Number of Employment at Year-end (person)	工程技术人员 Technical Personnel	企业总产值（万元）Total Output Value of Enterprises (1 0000 yuan)
16190888	**14480902**	**1484322**	**225664**	**492123**	**372088**	**55568**	**166220777**
12783270	11681321	905357	196592	347014	238903	38096	131229307
16190021	14480103	1484254	225664	492052	372011	55550	166212102
7543512	7020179	455120	68213	163905	124424	17421	77152765
794190	721577	59750	12863	31896	33669	3974	8157089
152000	111146		40854	1748	986	444	1594426
4216	3376	840		274	286	52	42160
6983225	6020601	863895	98729	251290	183792	27954	71791732
				14263	7702	2168	
712879	603224	104650	5005	27899	20618	3493	7473930
				777	534	44	
868	800	68		71	77	18	8675
14662153	13506351	1027819	127983	443930	340298	50338	150662737
5959302	5297560	612006	49736	217917	140734	20192	61155516
8702851	8208791	415813	78247	226013	199564	30146	89507221
1084023	634586	433477	15960	37397	22677	3682	11023143
145891	45030	19909	80952	8445	6238	698	1546682
186556	183420	3116	20	2351	2875	850	1865556
8648802	8009064	496527	143211	227148	172137	24439	89693596
2612533	2426241	173155	13137	264975	199951	31129	76527181
1602408	1360885	230343	11180	457587	346609	51424	156164264
785435	679815	81254	24366	81792	85910	9611	24826354
116645	115621	1024		296149	193388	31690	104068029
49556	39269	10287		59565	53193	8013	22845344
48253	48253			34536	25479	4144	10056513
17187	17187			20921	10544	2439	7323734

13-3 续表

分　组	Item	房屋建筑施工面积（平方米）Number of Projects under Constrution (sq.m)	本年新开工 Beginning Projects in this year
总　计	**Total**	**62186985**	**25563308**
#国有及国有控股	State-Owned and State Holding Majority Shares	41224041	14433202
一、按登记注册类型分	**Grouped by Registion Status**		
内资	Domestic Investment Enterprises	62186985	25563308
国有企业	State-owned Enterprises	33337711	11697514
集体企业	Collective-owned Enterprises	7241993	3588461
股份合作企业	Share-holding Corperative Enterprises		
联营企业	Joint Ownership Enterprises	28680	
有限责任公司	Limited Liability Corporations	16855791	8294326
股份有限公司	Share-holding Corperation Ltd		
私营企业	Private Enterprises	4722810	1983007
其他企业	Others		
港澳台商投资企业	Enterprises with Funds from Hong Kong,Macao and Taiwan		
外商投资企业	Enterprises with Foreign Investment		
二、按国民经济行业分	**Grouped by Sector**		
房屋和土木工程建筑业	Building Engineering and Civil Engineering Construction	61813489	25446727
房屋工程建筑	Building Engineering Construction	54934676	22513894
土木工程建筑	Civil Engineering Construction	6878813	2932833
建筑安装业	Installation of Construction	336680	116581
建筑装饰业	Fitting and Decoration	10849	
其他建筑业	Others		
三、按隶属关系分	**Grouped by Administrative Relationship**		
中　央	Central	13898404	4404989
地　方	Region	48288581	21158319
四、按企业资质等级分	**Grouped by Class of Enterprises**		
1.施工总承包	Overall Contractor for Construction	60421038	24141982
#特级	Special Class	4634556	1110012
一级	First Class	47714352	18940924
二级	Second Class	6426895	3184169
2.专业承包	Special Contractor	1765947	1421326
#一级以上	First Class	547772	250000

continued

房屋建筑 竣工面积 (平方米) Floor Space of Buildings Completed (sq.m)	自有机械设备 年末净值 (万元) Net Value of Mechanical Equipment owned by Constructions Enterprises at Year-end(1 0000yuan)	自有机械设备 年末总台数 (台) Number of Mechanical Equipment Owned By Construction Enterprises at Year-end(unit)	自有机械设备 年末总功率 (千瓦) Total Power of Mechanical Equipment Owned by Construction Enterprises at Year-end(kw)
23923932	**1066748**	**9829**	**450304**
15869814	950129	5471	343776
23923932	1066748	9829	450304
8027220	767929	4251	268431
3451047	25205	1549	17918
	6443	46	1461
12781	503	5	43
11441397	241045	3600	153310
991487	25624	379	9142
23226661	1021920	8831	283121
21572093	636778	5311	89707
1654568	385142	3519	193414
225929	31058	684	14528
42	4356	104	34391
471300	4662	208	9469
2655788	875011	3288	292778
	191738	6541	157526
22757764	1004284	9054	379974
1215056	98933	1632	60922
18197717	831130	5122	277615
2695201	62222	1678	30761
1166168	62465	775	70330
599500	42353	406	15888

13-4　施工总承包和专业承包建筑业企业财务状况（2011年）

单位: 万元

指　　标	Item	总　计 Total
一、年末存货	**Stocks at the end of year**	**2544592**
二、期末资产负债	**Total Assets and Liabilities of the final**	
流动资产合计	Total Circulating Funds	12739920
#应收工程款	Receivable Project Money	3825184
#存货	Stock	2639603
固定资产合计	Fixed Assets	1279083
固定资产原价	Original Value of Fixed Assets	2032175
累计折旧	Accumulative Total Depreciation	915808
#本年折旧	Depreciation Within the Year	194468
在建工程	Projects Under Construction	65445
资产总计	Total Assets	15415498
流动负债合计	Total Liquid Liabilities	11523719
#应付账款	Accounts Payable	5338489
非流动负债合计	Total Non-Liquid Liabilities	617056
负债合计	Total Liabilities	12203893
所有者权益合计	Owner Rights and Interests	3211605
#实收资本	Actual Capital Hold	2360166
三、损益及分配	**Profit or Loss and the Distribution**	
营业收入	Total Revenue	18992300
#主营业务收入	Revenue from Principal Business	18785183
营业成本	Total Cost	16987568
#主营业务成本	Cost of Principal Business	16816168
营业税金及附加	Taxs and Other Changes	596878
#主营业务税金及附加	Taxs and Other Changes on Principal Business	582295
其他业务利润	Profits from Other Operation	34282
销售费用	Sale Expenses	
管理费用	Managenment Expenses	652665
财务费用	Financial Expenses	65536
营业利润	Business Profits	721305
利润总额	Total Profits	718500
四、人工成本	**Cost of Labor**	
应付职工薪酬	Salary Payable	2279705

Financial Status of Overall Constructing Contractors and Professional Contractors（2011）

(1 0000yuan)

国有及国有控股 State-Owned and State Holding Majority Shares Enterprises	中央企业 Enterprises Central	省属企业 Province Enterprises	市属企业 Municipal Enterprises
2193991	**1789827**	**235021**	**519744**
10558700	7658141	1674691	3407088
2895338	1733464	645455	1446264
2285132	1710152	382463	546988
961882	725007	149572	404503
1672071	1347754	174862	509559
791558	670460	51509	193839
173045	141486	12972	40010
19046	4579	8514	52353
12718631	9288034	1966274	4161189
9991960	7366093	1576045	2581581
4751238	3711300	656870	970320
561527	506776	22795	87485
10572977	7888102	1598843	2716948
2145654	1399932	367432	1444241
1500880	1000323	271923	1087920
15616468	10997107	2722856	5272338
15419619	10825594	2716578	5243012
14073653	9817232	2521312	4649024
13910652	9687002	2515958	4613209
493682	348925	84886	163067
479601	335716	84547	162033
24430	22012	3236	9033
537467	413308	79556	159802
51425	34619	3237	27680
508589	436690	30277	254338
507000	436107	30003	252390
1853974	1216628	431527	631550

13-5 劳务分包建筑业企业基本情况（2011年）

Basic Statistic on Enterprises of Work Subcontractors（2011）

单位: 万元 (10 000 yuan)

指　　标	Item	2011
一、期末资产负债	**Total Assets and Liabilities of the final**	
固定资产原值	Original Value of Fixed Assets	12
本年折旧	Depreciation In The Year	
资产总计	Total Assets	1021
负债合计	Total Liabilities	207
实收资本	Paid in Capital	1000
二、损益及分配	**Profit or Loss and the Distribution**	
营业收入	Total Revenue	
#主营业务收入	Revenue from Principal Business	
营业成本	Total Cost	
#主营业务成本	Cost of Principal Business	
营业税金及附加	Taxs and Other Changes	
#主营业务税金及附加	Taxs and Other Changes on Principal Business	
其他业务利润	Profits from Other Operation	
销售费用	Sale Expenses	71
管理费用	Managenment Expenses	
财务费用	Financial Expenses	
营业利润	Business Profits	71
利润总额	Total Profits	

13-6 各区县建筑业主要经济指标（2011年）

Main Indicators of Construction Enterprises by Region（2011）

区县名称	Name of District and County	企业个数（个） Number of Enterprises (unit)	总产值（万元） Total Output Value (1 0000 yuan)	计算劳动生产率的平均人数（人） Average Number of Employed Persons in Calculation of Labor Productivity(person)	全员劳动生产率（万元/人） Overall Labor Productivity (10 000 yuan/person)	利税总额（万元） Total Pre-tax Profits (1 0000yuan)
新城区	Xincheng	28	2255459	42599	52.95	88066
碑林区	Beilin	35	3754043	117288	32.01	213307
莲湖区	Lianhu	30	1727659	44633	38.71	68613
灞桥区	Baqiao	28	303086	13340	22.72	26707
未央区	Weiyang	52	3337613	146316	22.81	224758
雁塔区	Yanta	89	3271043	55085	59.38	235303
阎良区	Yanliang	15	181730	10157	17.89	10250
临潼区	Lintong	12	97431	4531	21.50	10257
长安区	Chang'an	17	362476	12526	28.94	24542
蓝田县	Lantian	9	131124	6522	20.10	15807
周至县	Zhouzhi	7	49276	6999	7.04	4185
户　县	Huxian	6	120374	2593	46.42	9295
高陵县	Gaoling	6	599575	25335	23.67	69025

13-7 各区县建筑业房屋施工及竣工面积（2011年）

Floor Space of Buildings under Construction & Completed by Region（2011）

区 县	Region	房屋建筑施工面积（万平方米）Floor Space under Construction	本年新开工面积 Newly Started This Year	房屋建筑竣工面积（万平方米）Floor Space of Buildings Completed	竣工房屋价值（亿元）Value of Buildings Completed
新城区	Xincheng	985.21	314.64	246.9	48.08
碑林区	Beilin	1983.92	791.64	1135.18	103.29
莲湖区	Lianhu	1048.1	215.79	218.12	39.12
灞桥区	Baqiao	97.1	43.51	24.29	4.21
未央区	Weiyang	578.69	265.62	73.89	13.93
雁塔区	Yanta	490.22	223.59	200.66	27.4
阎良区	Yanliang	95.33	25.92	26.66	2.78
临潼区	Lintong	110.1	37.1	71.27	6.39
长安区	Chang'an	250.05	139.03	91.8	8.49
蓝田县	Lantian	137.79	94.73	46.7	6.36
周至县	Zhouzhi	37.94	26.47	15.52	2.16
户 县	Huxian	109.05	83.09	41.13	4.71
高陵县	Gaoling	295.2	295.2	201.62	30.24

13-8 各区县建筑业企业主要经济效益指标（2011年）

Main Economic Benefit Indicators on Construction Enterprises by Region（2011）

区 县	Region	人均利润总额（元/人）Per Profit (yuan/person)	人均利税（元/人）Per Pre-tax Profits (yuan/person)	人均竣工产值（元/人）Per Output Value of Buildings Completed (yuan/person)	人均施工面积（平方米/人）Per Floor Space of Buildings Under Construcyion (sq.m/person)	人均竣工面积（平方米/人）Per Floor Space of Buildings Completed (sq.m/person)
新城区	Xincheng	5614	15076	112875	231	58
碑林区	Beilin	5392	12858	88068	169	97
莲湖区	Lianhu	5476	11660	87645	235	49
灞桥区	Baqiao	12034	7989	31532	73	18
未央区	Weiyang	8185	7193	9521	40	5
雁塔区	Yanta	24384	19326	49741	89	36
阎良区	Yanliang	4144	6003	27418	94	26
临潼区	Lintong	8512	14393	140960	243	157
长安区	Chang'an	10121	9472	67752	200	73
蓝田县	Lantian	19289	4948	97519	211	72
周至县	Zhouzhi	3860	2120	30879	54	22
户 县	Huxian	18732	17113	181484	421	159
高陵县	Gaoling	17274	9972	119371	117	80

13-8 续表 continued

区 县	Region	产值利润率（%）Ratio of Profits to Output Value (%)	产值利税率（%）Ratio of Pre-tax Profits to Output Value (%)	资本利润率（%）Ratio of Profits to Assets (%)	资本利税率（%）Ratio of Pre-tax Profits to Assets (%)	资产负债率（%）Ratio of Debts to Assets (%)
新城区	Xincheng	1.1	2.8	1.6	4.3	82.5
碑林区	Beilin	1.7	4.0	1.8	4.3	74.4
莲湖区	Lianhu	1.4	3.0	1.7	3.7	75.5
灞桥区	Baqiao	5.3	3.5	11.1	7.4	67.4
未央区	Weiyang	3.6	3.2	4.6	4.1	77.4
雁塔区	Yanta	4.1	3.3	3.5	2.8	73.7
阎良区	Yanliang	2.3	3.4	2.4	3.5	69.3
临潼区	Lintong	4.0	6.7	13.2	22.2	30.7
长安区	Chang'an	3.5	3.3	8.4	7.8	55.3
蓝田县	Lantian	9.6	2.5	29.7	7.6	34.5
周至县	Zhouzhi	5.5	3.0	9.1	5.0	33.0
户 县	Huxian	4.0	3.7	6.8	6.2	50.0
高陵县	Gaoling	7.3	4.2	9.8	5.6	17.8

主要统计指标解释

建筑业统计单位 指从事房屋、构筑物建造和设备安装活动的法人企业。建筑业法人企业应具有建筑业资质并能够独立核算，同时其应具备以下条件：①依法成立，有自己的名称、组织机构和场所，能够承担民事责任；②独立拥有和使用资产，承担负债，有权与其他单位签订合同；③独立核算盈亏，能够编制资产负债表。

建筑业总产值 是以货币形式表现的建筑业企业在一定时期内生产的建筑业产品和提供的服务的总和。建筑业总产值包括：

（1）建筑工程产值：指列入建筑工程预算内的各种工程价值。

（2）安装工程产值：指设备安装工程价值，不包括被安装设备本身的价值。

（3）其他产值：建筑业总产值中除建筑工程、安装工程以外的产值。包括房屋构筑物修理产值、非标准设备制造产值、总包企业向分包企业收取的管理费以及不能明确划分的施工活动所完成的产值。

a.房屋构筑物修理产值：指房屋和构筑物修理所完成的产值，但不包括被修理房屋、构筑物本身价值和生产设备的修理价值。

b.非标准设备制造产值：指加工制造没有定型的非标准生产设备的加工费和原材料价值（如化工厂、炼油厂用的各种罐、槽，矿井生产统一使用的各种漏斗、三角槽、阀门等）以及附属加工厂为本企业承建工程制作的非标准设备的价值。

建筑业增加值 指建筑业企业在报告期内以货币形式表现的建筑业生产经营活动的最终成果。

从2004年第一次全国经济普查开始，建筑业现价增加值按生产法和分配法（收入法）两种方法计算，以收入法的计算结果为准，即从收入的角度出发，根据生产要素在生产过程中应得的收入份额计算。具体计算方法：经济普查年度建筑业增加值按照《经济普查年度GDP核算方案》计算，非经济普查年度建筑业增加值按照《非经济普查年度GDP核算方案》计算。

房屋建筑施工面积 指在报告期内施过工的全部房屋建筑面积，包括本期新开工的房屋面积、上期施工跨入本期继续施工的房屋面积、上期停缓建在本期恢复施工的房屋面积、本期竣工的房屋面积及本期施工后又停缓建的房屋面积。

房屋建筑竣工面积 指在报告期内房屋建筑按照设计要求全部完工，达到了使用条件，经验收鉴定合格，正式移交使用单位的房屋建筑面积。

Explanatory Notes on Main Statistical Indicators

Statistical Unit in the Construction Industry refers to a corporate enterprise engaged in the construction of buildings and structures and in the installation of equipment. A corporate construction enterprise should have qualification certificates with independent accounting system, and should meet the following 3 requirements: a) being set up in line with relevant legal basis, having its full name, organization and location, and capable of taking civil liabilities; b) independently possessing and using its assets and assuming its liabilities, and entitled to sign contracts with other institutions; and c) making independent accounts of its profits and losses, and capable of compiling its own balance sheet.

Gross Output Value of Construction refers to total of construction products and services, expressed in money terms, produced or rendered by construction and installation enterprises during a given period of time. It includes:

(1) Output value of construction projects: the value of projects covered by the project budgets;

(2) Output value of installation projects: the value of the installation of equipment, (excluding the value of the equipment to be installed);

(3) Other output values: the output value of construction industry apart from that of construction projects and installation projects. It includes: output value of repair of buildings and structures; output value of non-standard equipment manufacturing; overhead expenses received by contracted enterprises from the sub-contracted enterprises and the completed output value of construction activities for which there is no clear definition.

a. Output value of repair of buildings and structures: the value created through the repairs of buildings or structures. It does not include the value of buildings or structures being repaired and the value of the repair of production equipment;

b. Output value of manufactured non-standard equipment: the value of non-standard production equipment, including raw materials and manufacturing cost, made for the construction project (i.e., chemical plant; kettles or tanks used by refineries; various fillers, triangle tanks, valves used by mines). It also includes the output value of equipment manufactured by subsidiary workshops.

Value-added of Construction refers to the final result of the activities of production and operation of enterprises of the construction industry in monetary terms during the reference period.

Starting from the 2004 economic census, value-added of construction is calculated by both production approach and income approach, with the figures from the income approach as the final figures. Under the income approach, calculation starts from the perspective of income and is based on the share of income derived from the production process by the relevant factors of production. Specifically, value-added of construction for the Census years is calculated in accordance with the Programme of Compilation of GDP and National Accounts for the Year of Economic Census, and value-added of construction for other years is calculated in accordance with the Programme of Compilation of GDP and National Accounts for the Non Economic Census Years.

Floor Space of Buildings Under Construction refers to floor space of buildings under construction during the reference period, including the floor space of buildings for which construction has newly started; buildings for which construction has started earlier and is continuing during the reference period; and buildings for which construction has been suspended earlier but has restarted during the reference period; buildings completed during the reference period; and buildings under construction but construction has subsequently been during the reference period.

Floor Space of Buildings Completed refers to the floor space of buildings that are completed in the reference period in accordance with the requirements of the design, up to the standard for being put into use, and having been checked and accepted by departments concerned as qualified ones.

14 运输和邮电

TRANSPORT, POSTAL AND TELECOMMUNICATION SERVICE

资料整理：曾文元

Data management:Zeng Wenyuan

第十四部分　运输和邮电

一、简要说明

本章资料包括交通运输业和邮电通信业的基本情况，主要是交通运输工具、货物和旅客运输量、邮电业务、邮政局所及服务点等基本情况。资料由西安市统计局社会科技处根据有关部门提供资料整理。

二、主要指标

旅客周转量（亿人公里）	322.35	比上年增长 9.5%
货物周转量（亿吨公里）	512.20	比上年增长 21.2%
邮电业务总量（亿元）	200.50	
全社会车辆数（万辆）	144.58	比上年增长 15.3%
#民用小轿车	61.89	比上年增长 25.8%

注：2011年邮电业务总量按2010年不变价格计算，故与以往年份不可比。。

14 TRANSPORT,POSTAL AND TELECOMMUNICATION SERVICES

Ⅰ.Brief Introduction

Data in this chapter consists of primarily basic data of communication, transportation and postal service industry, transportation facility, amount of goods and passenger transportation, basic data of postal service, post offices and service establishments of Xi'an City. Data in this chapter is compiled by Social & Science and Technology Division of the Xi'an Bureau of Statistics according to the data provided by department concerned of the municipal government.

Ⅱ.Major Indicators

		Increase over Preceding Year
Passenger-Km (100 mil. person-km)	322.35	9.5%
Freight Ton-Km (100 mil. ton-km)	512.20	21.2%
Amount of Postal and Telecommunication Service(100 mil. yuan)	200.50	
Civil Motor Vehicles(10 000 units)	144.58	15.3%
Small Saloon Car	61.89	25.8%

Note: 2011 Postal and Telecommunication Services are calculated at 2010 constant prices,then can not be compared with previous years.

14-1 主要年份各种交通线路和桥梁

Transportation Routes and Number of Bridges in Representative Years

年 份 Year	铁路营业 里程（公里） Length of Railways in Operation (km)	公路里程 （公里） Length of Highways (km)	桥 梁 （座） Bridges (seat)
1978	555		
1979	555		
1980	555		
1981	569		
1982	569		
1983	569		
1984	569		
1985	697		
1986	697		
1987	1333		
1988	1339		
1989	1339	2563	
1990	1339	2586	
1991	1357	2785	
1992	1357	2786	
1993	1356	2801	
1994	1357	2830	
1995	1357	2852	
1996	1358	2877	
1997	1489	3026	
1998	1492	3047	
1999	1478	2789	
2000	1540	3010	
2001	1536	3298	
2002	1543	7862	629
2003	1522	8360	629
2004	1608	8360	629
2005	202	8500	634
2006	269	9530	634
2007	269	9672	1319
2008	269	11895	1710
2009	269	12378	1856
2010	269	12378	1856
2011	269	12599	1863

注：2005年开始，铁路统计执行新的统计口径。

Note: Since 2005, Railway statistics has followed the renewed data.

14-1 续表 continued

年 份 Year	桥梁长度 （米） Length of Bridge (m)	永久式桥梁 （座） Permanent Bridges (seat)	永久式桥梁长度 （米） Length of Permanent Bridges (m)	民航通航里程 （重复航线）（公里） Length of Total Civil Aviation Routes(km)
1978				
1979				
1980				
1981				
1982				
1983				
1984				
1985				
1986				
1987				
1988				
1989				
1990				
1991				
1992				65007
1993				83215
1994				100800
1995				119753
1996				126433
1997				173010
1998				180000
1999				141284
2000				139764
2001				154614
2002	29799	629	29799	211000
2003	29799	629	29799	381800
2004	29799	629	29799	386953
2005	46973	632	46915	485749
2006	46973	632	46915	418852
2007	91412	1275	90716	553355
2008	151996	1657	150980	515524
2009	154866	1803	153850	587904
2010	154866	1803	153850	742375
2011	149743	1811	148810	898628

14-2 各种交通线路里程和桥梁数（2011年）

Length of Transportation Routes and Number of Bridges（2011）

指　　标	Item	2011
铁路营业里程（公里）	**Length of Railways in Operation (km)**	**269**
电气化营业里程	Length of Electrified Railways in Operation	
复线里程	Double-Tracking Length	
公路里程(公里)	**Length of Highways (km)**	**12599**
等级公路	Expressways and Class Ⅰ to Ⅳ Highways	12142
高速	Expressway	382
一级	First Class	269
二级	Second Class	1006
三级	Third Class	1204
四级	Forth Class	9280
等外公路	Highways below Class Ⅳ	457
桥梁	**Bridges**	
永久式桥梁	Permanent	
座 (座)	Seat (seat)	1863
长度 (米)	Length (m)	149743
民航通航里程(公里)（重复航线）	**Length of Total Civil Aviation Routes(km)**	**898628**
国际航线	International routes	
民航航线条数（条）	**Length of Civil Aviation routes(Article)**	**169**
国际航线	International routes	10

14–3 主要年份全社会车辆数

Possession of Civil Vehicles in Representative Years

单位：辆、台 (unit)

年 份 Year	合 计 Total	汽车 Motor	载客汽车 Passenget Vehicles	载货汽车 Ordinary Trucks	摩托车 Motorcycles	拖拉机 Tractors
1999	279335	133192	63772	44348		38023
2000	310252	138318	89783	44974		37177
2001	369988	172436	110744	55453		31355
2002	454998	206653	134527	64623	176960	36083
2003	516719	242599	163872	70781	191834	34733
2004	512802	276012	195524	74557	156709	34755
2005	544586	377628	240923	82463	131440	34741
2006	608155	393778	296078	89772	131449	33236
2007	840376	522616	360081	97614	284594	32028
2008	875005	595735	430472	89093	247079	30176
2009	1012937	754803	567326	113430	224121	31347
2010	1253461	961283	739038	145740	259239	29151
2011	1445811	1174874	928669	171649	241132	25600

14-4 全社会车辆数（2011年）

Possession of Civil Vehicles（2011）

指　标	Item	2011
合　计	**Total**	**1445811**
民用汽车 (辆)	Motor(unit)	1174874
#私人汽车拥有量	Possession of Private Vehicles	976686
载客汽车	Passenget Vehicles	928669
#大　型	Large	14260
轿　车	Car	618906
普通载货汽车	Ordinary Trucks	171649
#重、中型	Heavy and Medium	67444
其他汽车	Others	74556
#三　轮	Three Wheelers	35437
拖拉机 (台)	Tractors(unit)	25600
#大中型	Large and Medium	12590
小　型	Small-sized	13010
摩托车 (辆)	Motorcycle (unit)	241132
普通摩托车	Bicycle Motor	229969
挂车 (辆)	Articulated Trailers (unit)	4131
其他类型车 (辆)	Others (unit)	74

14–5　主要年份交通运输量及周转量

Passenger Traffic and Kilometers and Freight Traffic and Ton-kilometers in Representative Years

年　份 Year	客运量 （万人次） Passenger Traffic (10 000 person-times)	旅客周转量 （万人公里） Passenger-Km (10 000 person-Km)	货运量 （万吨） Freight Traffic (10 000 tons)	货物周转量 （万吨公里） Freight Ton-Km (10 000 ton-Km)
1978	1334		3723	
1979	1420		3919	
1980	1508		3655	
1981	1839		3379	
1982	2340		4067	
1983	3054		4225	
1984	2899		4966	
1985	2404		5681	
1986	2186		5409	
1987	3781		6294	
1988	5721		6968	
1989	6092		8742	
1990	5748		6980	
1991	4193		3389	
1992	4368		8233	
1993	8036		8406	
1994	8321		8754	
1995	9069		9590	
1996	9854		10577	
1997	8922		9358	
1998	9223		9429	
1999	10311	2130383	9766	3452383
2000	10756	2507896	10191	3691963
2001	9078	2658037	7728	4229430
2002	12527	2524444	9484	4544040
2003	11413	2596402	9392	5037684
2004	10832	3112374	14845	5850029
2005	10479	1607568	12051	1249525
2006	11245	1721217	11832	1354318
2007	12466	1753464	15124	1473182
2008	26501	2529007	27560	3490707
2009	28693	2582025	30606	3766806
2010	30294	2942957	34323	4301680
2011	33375	3223544	39231	5212010

14-6 交通运输量及周转量（2011年）

Passenger Traffic and Kilometers and Freight Traffic and Ton-kilometers（2011）

指　标	Item	2011	2011年比2010年增长(%) Increase Rate in 2011 over 2010(%)
一、客运量（万人次）	**Passenger Traffic(10 000 person-times)**	**33375**	**10.2**
铁路	Railway	2861	2.9
公路	Highway	29358	10.6
航空	Civil Aviation	1156	18.3
二、旅客周转量（万人公里）	**Passenger-Km (10 000 person-Km)**	**3223544**	**9.5**
铁路	Railway	595409	7.8
公路	Highway	1603259	19.1
民用航空	Civil Aviation	1024876	-1.9
三、货运量（万吨）	**Freight Traffic(10 000 tons)**	**39231**	**14.3**
铁路	Railway	823	16.6
公路	Highway	38399	14.2
航空	Civil Aviation	9	28.6
四、货物周转量（万吨公里）	**Freight Ton-Km (10 000 ton-Km)**	**5212010**	**21.2**
铁路	Railway	2089554	16.1
公路	Highway	3110908	25.1
航空	Civil Aviation	11548	-17.0

14–7 主要年份邮政电信情况

年 份 Year	邮电业务总量（万元） Business Volume of Postal and Telecommunication Services(10 000 yuan)	电信业务总量 Business Volume of Telecommunication Services	邮政业务总量 Business Volume of Postal Services
1978	1420		
1979	1616		
1980	1640		
1981	1713		
1982	2154		
1983	2250		
1984	2484		
1985	2972		
1986	3244		
1987	3911		
1988	5327		
1989	5973		
1990	7843		
1991	5700		
1992	6610		
1993	36581		
1994	54034		
1995	76450		
1996	104566		
1997	124601		
1998	204927		
1999	306457		
2000	461628		
2001	367620		
2002	515259	470492	44767
2003	820943	770673	50270
2004	1027415	975045	52370
2005	1320447	1261033	59414
2006	1867560	1796533	71027
2007	2267633	2191250	76383
2008	2646662	2564524	82138
2009	2989246	2900836	88410
2010	3231059	3167750	63309
2011	2005025	1944329	60696

注：2002年及以后，邮政电信机构分离；2001-2010年邮电业务总量按2000年不变价格计算；2011年邮电业务总量按2010年不变价格计算，故与以往年份不可比。

Basic Statistic on Postal and Telecommunication Service in Representative Years

固定电话年末户数（户） Number of Immobile Telephone at Year-end (subscriber)	#农村电话年末户数 Number of Telephone in Rural Areas at Year-end	移动电话用户年末数（户） Number of Mobile Phone at Year-end (subscriber)	互联网年末宽带用户（户） Number of Broad Band Net User (subscriber)
12828	1062		
13487	1052		
14024	1086		
14497	1125		
15357	1129		
16922	1156		
18611	1203		
21624	1239		
26373	1235		
30200	1290		
34265	1357		
39506	1498		
45267	1668		
49516	2479		
60727	2613		
101327	2671		
197398	5067		
299485	8386		
430270	13654		
573244	21202		
736998	37863		
874586	74761		
1242637	170199		
1711500	259374	1277400	17183
2095230	358803	1964200	35230
2538393	415593	2412392	160900
2934424	480276	3500900	243448
3214806	500847	4199570	339280
3159639	467526	5510720	508775
3145819	419446	6645863	586213
3068807	383869	7377575	813987
2891009	358238	11200566	1167916
2617691	335048	14230800	1461804
2703640	320189	16141463	1841027

Note: Since 2002, the postal service and telecommunication service have been seperated.2001-2010 Postal and Telecommunication Services are calculated at 2000 constant prices.2011 Postal and Telecommunication Services are calculated at 2010 constant prices,then can not be compared with previous years.

14-8 邮政业务及服务网点

Postal service and branch post office

指 标	Item	2010	2011
一、邮政业务总量（万元）	**Business Volume of Postal Services(10 000 yuan)**	**63309**	**60696**
二、邮政业务总收入（万元）	**Gross Income of Post Services (10 000 yuan)**	**58831**	**65174**
三、函件（万件）	**Number of Letters (10 000 pcs)**	**8176**	**3061**
四、包件（万件）	**Parcels (10 000 pcs)**	**59**	**91**
五、汇票（万张）	**Money Order (10 000 pcs)**	**123**	**112**
六、报纸订销累计份数（万份）	**Accumulated Newspaper Prescribing and Sales Volume (10 000 pcs)**	**11724**	**12603**
七、杂志订销累计份数（万份）	**Accumulated Magazine Prescribing and Sales Volume (10 000 pcs)**	**550**	**564**
八、特快专递类业务（万件）	**Express Mail Service Volume (10 000 pcs)**	**582**	**1901**
九、集邮业务量（万枚）	**Stamps For Collection (10 000 pcs)**	**860**	**1060**
十、邮政营销网点（处）	**Number of Post Office Branch Establishments (unit)**	**305**	**277**
#设在农村的局所	In it: number of post offices in rural area	50	50
十一、邮政信筒信箱（个）	**Number of Mailboxes(unit)**	**1108**	**1108**

注：2010年邮政储蓄业务归入金融业。

Note: Since 2010, post saving service has been included in finance.

14-9 电信业务情况

Telecommunication service

指 标	Item	2010	2011
一、电信业务总量（万元）	**Business Volume of Telecommunication Services (10 000 yuan)**	**3167750**	**1944329**
二、电信业务总收入（万元）	**Gross Income of Telecommunication Services (10 000 yuan)**	**1038865**	**1029629**
三、固定电话年末户数（万户）	**Number of Immobile Telephone at Year-end (10 000 subscribers)**	**261.77**	**270.36**
#农村电话年末户数	Number of Telephone in Rural Areas at Year-end	33.50	32.02
四、长途电话通话总数（万次）	**Number of Long-distance Telephone Call (10 000 times)**	**101935.00**	**299828.81**
五、电话交换机容量（万门）	**Capacity (number) of Telephone Switchboard (10 000 lines)**	**449.05**	**441.49**
六、移动电话用户年末数（万户）	**Number of Mobile Phone at Year-end(10 000 subscribers)**	**1423.08**	**1614.15**
#3G电话用户数	3G Mobile Phone Subscribers	33.40	177.37
七、互联网年末宽带用户（万户）	**Number of Broad Band Net User (10 000 subscribers)**	**146.18**	**184.10**

主要统计指标解释

铁路营业里程 又称营业长度（包括正式营业和临时营业里程），指办理客货运输业务的铁路正线总长度。凡是全线或部分建成双线及以上的线路，以第一线的实际长度计算;复线、站线、段管线、岔线和特殊用途线以及不计算运费的联络线都不计算营业里程。铁路营业里程是反映铁路运输业基础设施发展水平的重要指标，也是计算客货周转量、运输密度和机车车辆运用效率等指标的基础资料。

公路里程 指在一定时期内实际达到《公路工程技术标准JTJ01-88》规定的等级公路，并经公路主管部门正式验收交付使用的公路里程数。包括大中城市的郊区公路以及通过小城镇街道部分的公路里程和桥梁、隧道渡口的长度，不包括大中城市的街道、厂矿、林区生产用道和农业生产用道的里程。两条或多条公路共同经由同一路段，只计算一次，不得重复计算里程长度。它是反映公路建设发展规模的重要指标，也是计算运输网密度等指标的基础资料。

民用航空航线里程 指民航运输定期班机飞行的航线长度的总和。航线长度按机场之间的距离计算，通常有两种计算方法：一是将每条航线长度相加称为重复计算航线里程；一是将两线或两条以上航线经过同一区段里程，只计算一次航线长度称为不重复计算航线里程。一般常用的是后者，它能确切反映民航运输网的规模，是表明民航事业为国民经济服务和方便人民生活程度的主要指标。

货（客）运量 指在一定时期内，各种运输工具实际运送的货物（旅客）数量。它是反映运输业为国民经济和人民生活服务的数量指标，也是制定和检查运输生产计划、研究运输发展规模和速度的重要指标。货运按吨计算，客运按人计算。货物不论运输距离长短、货物类别，均按实际重量统计。旅客不论行程远近或票价多少，均按一人一次客运量统计;半价票、小孩票也按一人统计。

货物（旅客）周转量 指在一定时期内，由各种运输工具运送的货物（旅客）数量与其相应运输距离的乘积之总和。它是反映运输业生产总成果的重要指标，也是编制和检查运输生产计划，计算运输效率、劳动生产率以及核算运输单位成本的主要基础资料。计算货物周转量通常按发出站与到达站之间的最短距离，也就是计费距离计算。计算公式为:

货物（旅客）周转量 = Σ货物（旅客）运输量 × 运输距离

民用汽车拥有量 指报告期末，在公安交通管理部门按照《机动车注册登记工作规范》，已注册登记领有民用车辆牌照的全部汽车数量。汽车拥有量统计的主要分类：根据汽车结构分为载客汽车、载货汽车及其他汽车；根据汽车所有者不同分为个人(私人)汽车、单位汽车；根据汽车的使用性质分为营运汽车、非营运汽车；根据汽车大小规格不同载客汽车分为大型、中型、小型和微型，载货汽车分为重型、中型、轻型和微型。

邮电业务总量 指以价值量形式表现的邮电通信企业为社会提供各类邮电通信服务的总数量。邮电业务量按专业分类包括函件、包件、汇票、报刊发行、邮政快件、特快专递、邮政储蓄、集邮、公众电报、用户电报、传真、长途电话、出租电路、无线寻呼、移动电话、分组交换数据通信、出租代维等。计算方法为各类产品乘以相应的平均单价（不变价）之和，再加上出租电路和设备、代用户维护电话交换机和线路等的服务收入。它综合反映了一定时期邮电业务发展的总成果，是研究邮电业务量构成和发展趋势的重要指标。计算公式为:

邮电业务总量 = Σ（各类邮电业务量 × 不变单价）+ 出租代维及其他业务收入

移动电话用户 是指通过移动电话交换机进入移动电话网、占用移动电话号码的电话用户。用户数量以报告期末在移动电话营业部门实际办理登记手续进入移动电话网的户数进行计算，一部移动电话统计为一户。

电话用户 指接入国家公众固定电话网，并按固定电话业务进行经营管理的电话用户。1997年以前，电话用户分为市内电话用户和农村电话用户。“市内电话用户”是指接入县城及县以上城市的电话网上的电话用户;“农村电话用户”是指接入县邮电局农话台及县以下农村电话交换点，以县城为中心（除市话用户外）联通县、乡（镇）、行政村、村民小组的用户。从1997年起，电话用户数分组调整为以用户所在区域划分为“城市电话用户”和“乡村电话用户”，与过去的按市内电话和农村电话划分方法不同。而电话用户总数、电话机总部数统计范围不变。

农村电话用户 指县城关区以下的集镇和农村接入局用交换机的电话用户数。

局用交换机容量 是指安装在本地电信运营商内用于接续本地固定电话的电话交换机容量，有倍增设备按倍增后的数量计数。包括现用和备用的人工或自动交换机的全部容量。

互联网宽带接入端口 指用于接入互联网用户的各类实际安装运行的接入端口的数量，包括xDSL用户接入端口、LAN接入端口以及其他类型接入端口等，不包括窄带拨号接入端口。

Explanatory Notes on Main Statistical Indicators

Length of Railways in Operation refers to the total length of the trunk line under passenger and freight transportation (including both full operation and temporary operation). The calculation is based on the actual length of the first line even if this line has a full or partial double track or more tracks, excluding double tracks, station sidings, tracks under the charge of stations, branch lines, special-purpose lines and the non-payable connecting lines. The length of railways in operation is an important indicator to show the development of the infrastructure for the railway transport, and also the essential data to calculate volume of passenger freight transport, traffic density and utilization efficiency of the locomotives and carriages.

Length of Highways refers to the length of highways which are built in conformity with the grades specified by the highway engineering standard formulated by the Ministry of Communications, and have been formally checked and accepted by the departments of highways and put into use. The length of highways includes that of the suburb highways at large and medium-sized cities, highways passing through streets at small cities and towns, and also the length of bridges、 tunnel and ferries. It does not include the length of streets in big and medium-sized cities and highways built for the production purpose at factories, mines, forest areas and agricultural areas. If two or more highways go the same section of the way, the length of the section is only calculated for once and no duplication is allowed. The length of highways is an important indicator to show the development of the highway construction and to provide essential information to calculate the transport network density.

Length of Civil Aviation Routes refers to the length of all routes for regular civil aviation flights. There are usually two ways to calculate the distance between airports connected by the route length: one is to put the length of all air routes together, called duplicated calculation of the length of the routes; the other is not to allow the duplication in calculation when two or more routes passing the same section of aviation routes. The latter is usually used, as it can precisely show the size of the civil aviation network and indicate the extent of civil aviation serving the national economy and the people.

Freight (Passenger) Traffic refers to the volume of freight (passenger) transported with various means. Freight transport is calculated in tons and passenger traffic is calculated in the number of persons. Despite the type of freight and travelling distance, the freight transport is calculated in the actual weight of the goods: and despite the travelling distance and ticket price, the passenger traffic is calculated by the principle that one person can be counted only once in one travel. The passenger who travel with a half price ticket or a child ticket is also calculated as one person. The freight (passenger) traffic provides a quantitative measure to show how the transport industry serves the national economy and people, and is also an important indicator for planning the transport industry and for studying the development scale and speed of the transport industry.

Freight Ton-kilometers (Passenger-kilometers) refer to the sum of the products of the volume of transported cargo (passengers) multiplying by the transport distance, usually using ton-kilometer and passenger-kilometer as units for measurement. Normally, the shortest distance between the departure station and the destination station (i.e., the payable distance) is the basis to calculate the freight ton-kilometers. This is an important indicator to show the total results of the transport industry, to prepare and examine the transport plan and to measure the efficiency, the labour productivity and the unit cost of transport.

The formula is as follows:

Freight Ton-kilometers (Passenger-kilometers) =Σ {Freight (Passenger) Traffic x Distance of Transportation}

Measuring unit: ton-kilometer (person-kilometer)

Possession of Civil Motor Vehicles refer to the total numbers of vehicles that are registered and received vehicles license tags according to the Work Standard for Motor Vehicles Registration formulated by the Transport Management Office under the department of public security at the end of the reference period. They are divided into categories. According to the structure of motor vehicles, they are divided into passenger vehicles, trucks and others; according to ownership into private vehicles and vehicles for the unit' s use; according to kind of usage into working vehicles and non-working vehicles; and according to size of vehicles into large passenger vehicles, medium-sized passenger vehicles, small passenger vehicles and mini passenger vehicles,heavy trucks, light-heavy trucks, light trucks and mini-trucks.

Business Volume of Post and Telecommunications refers to the total amount of post and telecommunications services, expressed in value terms, provided by the post and telecommunications departments for the society. Post and telecommunication services can be classified asletters, parcels, remittance, issue of newspapers and magazines, fast mail service, express mail service, savings deposits, stamps for collection, public and individual telegraph service, facsimiles, long-distance telephone service,leasing of telephone lines, urban paging service, mobile telephone service, data transfer and transmission, etc. The accounting approach is to multiply the service products of all types with their average unit price (constant price) to get sum of business value, plus income from other services such as leasing of telephone lines and equipment, maintenance of telephone switchboards and lines on behalf of customers. This indicator reflects the overall results of post and telecommunications service during a given period, and is important to study the composition of business service and the development of post and telecommunications service.

The formula is as follows:

Business Volume of Post and Telecommunications=Σ (Transaction of Post and Telecommunication Service x Constant Price) + Income from Leasing, Maintenance and other Services

Mobile Telephone Subscribers refer to the persons who own mobile telephone numbers and are connected with the mobile telephone communication network through the mobile telephone switchboards. The number of subscribers is calculated by the subscribers who have completed registration at mobile communication business centers and entered into the mobile telephone network. One mobile telephone is taken as a subscriber.

Telephone Subscribers refer to subscribers that are connected to the public line telephone network provided with telephone services. Before 1997, telephone subscribers were classified as city subscribers and village subscribers. City subscribers referred to those connected to city telephone networks in county towns and cities, while village subscribers referred to those connected to village telephone stations at and below counties. Since 1997, the classification of telephone subscribers was modified on the basis of physical location of the subscribers as Urban telephone subscribers and rural telephone subscribers , which is different from the previous classification of categorizing local telephones and rural telephones , while the definition of total subscribers and total number of telephones remain unchanged.

Rural Telephone Subscribers refer to telephone subscribers, located at towns under county town and country, that are connected to the public line telephone network.

Capacity of Office Telephone Exchanges refers to the capacity (measured in gate) of telephone exchanges installed in the offices of local telecommunication service providers for communication between fixed telephones. It includes the capacity of both manual and automatic exchanges in use and for stand-by purpose. Equipment with expansion function is to be counted by the expanded capacity.

Broadband Connection Terminals refer to the connection terminals to internet users actually installed and put into operation, including connection terminals for xDSL, connection terminals for LAN, and other connection terminals for xDSL. N-ISDN connection terminals are not included.

15 国内贸易

DOMESTIC TRADE

资料整理：马晓庆　杨　骏　左　宇　赵琳瑛　胡树建

Data management:Ma Xiaoqing　Yang Jun　Zuo Yu　Zhao Linying　Hu Shujian

第十五部分 国内贸易

一、简要说明

本章资料主要包括社会消费品零售总额，批发零售贸易业商品购、销等情况，限额以上批发零售贸易业主要商品销售情况，限额以上批发零售贸易和住宿餐饮企业财务状况、经济效益，以及交易市场情况，由西安市统计局贸易外经处提供。

二、主要指标

批发零售贸易业网点（万个）	21.12	比上年增长 5.0%
餐饮业网点（万个）	4.37	比上年增长 5.8%
社会消费品零售总额（亿元）	1965.98	比上年增长 20.1%
#批发零售贸易业零售额	1725.03	比上年增长 20.5%

15 DOMESTIC TRADE

Ⅰ.Brief Introduction

Content of this chapter consists of total retail sales of consumer goods, sails data on commodity purchasing and sails of wholesale and retail trade, sales data on primary goods exceeds quotation, financial, economic performance and market data on wholesale and retail trade and food services industry exceeds quotation. Data in this chapter is compiled and provided by Trade and Foreign Economy Division of the Xi'an Bureau of Statistics.

Ⅱ.Major Indicators

		Increase over Preceding Year
Establishments Engaged in Whole-sale and Retail Trade(10 000 unit)	21.12	5.0%
Establishments Engaged in Trade(10 000 unit)	4.37	5.8%
Establishments Engaged in Catering Trade(10 000 unit)	1965.98	20.1%
Total Retail Sales of Consumer Goods (100 mil. yuan)	1725.03	20.5%
Retail Sales of Wholesale and Retail Enterprises		

15-1 主要年份社会消费品零售总额

Total Retail Sales of Consumer Goods in Representative Years

单位:亿元　　　　(100 million yuan)

年份 Year	社会消费品零售总额 Total Retail Sales of Consumer Goods	城镇 Urban	乡村 Village	批发零售贸易业 Wholesale Trades and Retail Trades	住宿餐饮业 Accommodation and Catering Trade	其他行业 Others
1978	12.70	8.82	3.88	11.01	0.53	0.21
1979	13.94	9.88	4.06	11.88	0.60	0.21
1980	15.88	11.53	4.35	13.05	0.80	0.20
1981	17.41	12.85	4.56	14.31	0.80	0.19
1982	18.54	13.79	4.75	15.25	0.88	0.27
1983	20.82	15.14	5.68	16.95	1.03	0.32
1984	24.87	19.13	5.74	19.47	1.29	0.46
1985	32.92	26.09	6.83	25.04	1.69	0.48
1986	37.50	29.25	8.25	28.88	1.97	0.64
1987	43.86	34.62	9.24	33.32	2.50	0.49
1988	59.65	47.74	11.91	44.84	2.97	0.78
1989	68.05	54.60	13.45	54.41	2.98	0.76
1990	72.77	59.42	13.35	57.46	3.79	0.90
1991	81.04	66.93	14.11	60.35	4.43	1.26
1992	100.84	89.17	11.67	71.86	6.13	2.30
1993	115.38	104.41	10.97	75.99	7.49	2.71
1994	144.64	131.56	13.08	89.79	9.12	3.43
1995	186.60	165.98	20.62	115.46	11.97	3.73
1996	222.94	198.19	24.75	145.05	15.83	4.02
1997	264.47	238.17	26.30	169.08	22.12	4.17
1998	291.45	257.39	34.06	183.43	30.97	4.27
1999	323.37	283.32	40.05	207.96	34.78	4.85
2000	360.42	317.12	43.30	232.89	41.42	5.43
2001	406.21	358.97	47.24	265.25	48.87	5.86
2002	459.76	409.86	49.90	309.36	51.42	6.45
2003	502.65	449.62	53.03	440.28	53.30	9.07
2004	578.60	520.94	57.66	509.60	56.87	12.13
2005	670.56	604.63	65.93	592.77	63.59	14.20
2006	784.95	708.31	76.64	694.03	74.77	16.15
2007	936.21	845.59	90.62	828.63	89.32	18.26
2008	1176.58	1063.93	112.65	1033.00	122.90	20.68
2009	1381.12	1249.79	131.33	1222.98	134.54	23.60
2010	1637.04	1570.16	66.88	1431.23	179.82	25.99
2011	1965.98	1908.65	57.33	1725.03	210.15	30.80

注：1.依据2008年第二次经济普查数据，对2005-2007年数据进行调整。

2. 2009年以前按经营单位所在地分为市和县及县以下。

3. 2002年以前按行业分组中不包括制造业零售额和农业对非农业居民零售额。

Note:1.According to the Secong Economic Census statistics,datas from 2005 to 2007 were adjusted.

2.Before 2009, the sales was categorized into city and county and below by location of operation units.

3.Before 2002,the categories by sector did not include the retailing sales of manufacture and agricultural over non-agricultural residents.

15-2 社会消费品零售总额（2011年）

Total Retail Sales of Consumer Goods（2011）

单位:亿元 (100 million yuan)

分 类	Classify	金 额 Sum
社会消费品零售总额	**Total Retail Sales of Consumer Goods**	**1965.98**
（一）按销售单位所在地分:	Grouped by Region	
（1）城镇	Urban	1908.65
其中：城区	District	1586.30
（2）乡村	Village	57.33
（二）按行业分:	Grouped by Sector	0.00
（1）批发业	Wholesale Enterprises	277.44
限额以上企业	Enterprises Above Designated Size	243.90
限额以下企业和个体户	Enterprises Below Designated Size and Self-employed Laborers	33.54
#个体户	Self-employed Laborers	
（2）零售业	Retail Enterprises	1447.59
限额以上企业	Enterprises Above Designated Size	1127.27
限额以下企业和个体户	Enterprises Below Designated Size and Self-employed Laborers	320.32
#个体户	Self-employed Laborers	0.00
（3）住宿和餐饮业	Accommodation and Catering Trade	210.15
限额以上企业	Enterprises Above Designated Size	97.48
限额以下企业和个体户	Enterprises Below Designated Size and Self-employed Laborers	112.67
#个体户	Self-employed Laborers	
（4）其他行业	Others	30.80

15-3 各区县社会消费品零售总额（2011年）

Total Retail Sales of Consumer Goods by Region（2011）

单位：亿元 (100 million yuan)

区县名称	Name of District and County	社会消费品零售总额 Total Retail Sales of Consumer Goods	批发零售贸易业 Wholesale and Retail Trade of Retail Sales	住宿餐饮业 Accommodation and Catering Trade of Retail Sales
新城区	Xincheng	341.82	316.16	19.90
碑林区	Beilin	342.07	296.91	41.73
莲湖区	Lianhu	281.61	251.18	28.91
灞桥区	Baqiao	46.40	39.72	6.34
未央区	Weiyang	278.26	260.29	17.50
雁塔区	Yanta	380.19	320.26	46.54
阎良区	Yanliang	23.21	18.85	4.11
临潼区	Lintong	48.54	41.76	5.76
长安区	Chang'an	109.97	83.74	24.11
蓝田县	Lantian	35.45	30.43	4.55
周至县	Zhouzhi	23.72	20.98	2.23
户 县	Huxian	38.85	32.57	5.85
高陵县	Gaoling	15.89	12.18	2.62

15-4 主要年份批发零售贸易业、餐饮业网点和人员

Wholesale and Retail Trade, Catering Outlets and Staff in Representative Years

单位:个、人 (unit,person)

年份 Year	批发业 Wholesale Trade		零售业 Retail Trade		餐饮业 Catering Services	
	网点 Branch Shop	人员 Personnel	网点 Branch Shop	人员 Personnel	网点 Branch Shop	人员 Personnel
1978	586	22136	5862	51462	442	9043
1979	462	14002	5387	49252	815	10349
1980	1505	28320	6312	51927	1893	16297
1981	597	17780	8800	74095	3397	25626
1982	881	25023	9811	68734	6422	25879
1983	1642	32597	17130	77863	6387	28054
1984	1875	34906	27043	136852	8484	25977
1985	1247	43311	35860	223076	11907	41025
1986	1706	42270	37503	241052	11977	48335
1987	3351	44475	42484	260450	13673	51361
1988	1829	40324	44330	282911	9576	47131
1989	1638	80078	46613	229705	10228	46420
1990	1558	37077	43244	219413	9800	34561
1991	1918	45583	48171	236235	10369	36813
1992	1864	36012	48422	258491	9916	38935
1993	5177	54255	43289	226572	11804	38318
1994	6338	58154	60292	318287	14296	56502
1995	6564	63337	69623	364430	15485	68782
1996	8008	67840	76828	437655	15668	78313
1997	8414	71178	80379	468811	20259	82917
1998	10780	85420	95056	515723	22500	100862
1999	10865	86630	96516	516163	24977	118442
2000	10393	81519	93928	492083	27531	124988
2001	10534	78285	95414	497448	28219	128738
2002	12220	107352	96815	465320	29219	140623
2003	13274	117740	99764	490169	32899	150883
2004	19696	102779	106477	281221	27905	132855
2005	20392	106138	112541	298285	30156	142176
2006	21243	110595	117168	312426	31694	148317
2007	21835	114497	122810	330583	34249	161517
2008	26813	148403	164642	470886	38134	201978
2009	26403	154777	165921	507706	39515	205364
2010	27887	166735	173218	544487	41289	219793
2011	30441	253618	180782	585680	43728	232552

15-5 批发贸易业机构、网点、人员（2011年）

单位:个、人

分 类	Classify	合计 Total 法人单位 Constitutional Unit	活动单位 Movemental Unit	网点 Branch Shop	人员 Personnel
总计	**Total**	**11145**	**11504**	**30441**	**253618**
一、按登记注册类型分组	**Grouped by Registered Kind**				
内资企业	Civil Funded Enterprises	10977	11321	12547	187480
国有企业	State-owned Enterprises	355	409	641	17237
集体企业	Collective-owned Enterprises	265	270	536	3936
股份合作企业	Cooperative Enterprises	213	235	237	7643
联营企业	Joint Ownership Enterprises	20	24	24	442
有限责任公司	Limited Liability Corporations	3760	3867	4061	72766
股份有限公司	Share-holding Corporations Ltd.	811	839	881	31660
私营企业	Private Enterprises	5135	5245	5517	49132
其他企业	Other Enterprises	418	432	650	4664
港澳台商投资企业	Enterprises with Funds from Hong Kong，Macao &Taiwan	111	122	122	4623
外商投资企业	Foreign Funded Enterprises	57	61	61	1679
个体经济	Individuals			17711	59836
二、按国民经济行业分组	**Grouped by Sector**				
农畜产品批发	Wholesale of Farm Produce and Livestock Products	286	303	1635	11047
食品、饮料及烟草制品批发	Wholesale of Food, Beverages and Tobaccos	632	655	5159	29058
纺织、服装及日用品批发	Wholesale of Textiles, Garments and Daily Articles	937	952	3672	33120
文化、体育用品及器材批发	Wholesale of Culture , Sports Articles and Equipments	715	734	2912	22861
医药及医疗器材批发	Wholesale of Medicines and Medical Appliances	642	725	1269	16924
矿产品、建材及化工产品批发	Wholesale of Mineral Products, Building Materials and Chemical Products	2776	2828	6061	48030
机械设备、五金交电及电子产品批发	Wholesale of Machinery, Hardwares, Transport Means and Electronic Equipment	3929	4047	7557	69648
贸易经纪与代理	Trade Broker and Agency	394	407	450	9437
其他批发	Other Wholesales	834	853	1726	13493

Organizations, Establishments and Persons Engaged in Whole-sale Trade（2011）

（unit,person）

城镇 Urban				城区 County				乡村 Village			
法人单位 Constitutional Unit	活动单位 Movemental Unit	网点 Branch Shop	人员 Personnel	法人单位 Constitutional Unit	活动单位 Movemental Unit	网点 Branch Shop	人员 Personnel	法人单位 Constitutional Unit	活动单位 Movemental Unit	网点 Branch Shop	人员 Personnel
10978	**11319**	**28752**	**247713**	**10782**	**11073**	**26900**	**241161**	**167**	**185**	**1689**	**5905**
10810	11136	12360	184702	10614	10890	12034	181671	167	185	187	2778
312	356	588	15718	270	289	476	14486	43	53	53	1519
219	223	489	3289	183	187	418	2755	46	47	47	647
213	235	236	7643	210	232	232	7581			1	
20	24	24	442	20	24	24	442				
3755	3862	4056	72550	3743	3849	4042	72303	5	5	5	216
811	839	881	31660	805	833	875	31635				
5065	5169	5440	48754	4971	5052	5325	47857	70	76	77	378
415	428	646	4646	412	424	642	4612	3	4	4	18
111	122	122	4623	111	122	122	4623				
57	61	61	1679	57	61	61	1679				
		16209	56709			14683	53188			1502	3127
245	257	1434	10302	201	205	1209	9526	41	46	201	745
601	619	4983	27374	574	586	4525	25684	31	36	176	1684
931	945	3631	32866	913	924	3176	31527	6	7	41	254
715	734	2872	22771	712	728	2775	22514			40	90
642	722	1237	16857	635	700	1192	16219		3	32	67
2730	2782	5545	46793	2682	2722	5225	45773	46	46	516	1237
3928	4046	7386	69315	3912	4030	7199	68821	1	1	171	333
391	404	427	9397	390	403	426	9391	3	3	23	40
795	810	1237	12038	763	775	1173	11706	39	43	489	1455

15-6 零售贸易业机构、网点、人员（2011年）

单位：个、人

分 类	Classify	合 计 法人单位 Constitutional Unit	活动单位 Movemental Unit	网 点 Branch Shop	Total 人 员 Personnel
总计	**Total**	**8389**	**9613**	**180782**	**585680**
一、按登记注册类型分组	**Grouped by Registered Kind**				
内资企业	Civil Funded Enterprises	8256	9431	10190	158614
国有企业	State-owned Enterprises	223	288	377	17410
集体企业	Collective-owned Enterprises	296	372	473	4239
股份合作企业	Cooperative Enterprises	90	112	112	7962
联营企业	Joint Ownership Enterprises	25	40	40	356
有限责任公司	Limited Liability Corporations	2426	3042	3259	65217
股份有限公司	Share-holding Corporations Ltd.	157	200	230	6417
私营企业	Private Enterprises	4817	5131	5453	54833
其他企业	Other Enterprises	222	246	246	2180
港澳台商投资企业	Enterprises with Funds from Hong Kong，Macao & Taiwan	42	65	65	6070
外商投资企业	Foreign Funded Enterprises	91	117	123	7296
个体经济	Individuals			170404	413700
二、按国民经济行业分组	**Grouped by Sector**				
综合零售	Intergrated Retail	760	875	30473	97026
食品、饮料及烟草制品专门零售	Retail of Food,Beverages and Tobaccos	567	682	36208	100462
纺织、服装及日用品专门零售	Special Retail of Textiles,Garments and Daily Consumer Articles	1061	1240	41361	141042
文化、体育用品及器材专门零售	Retail of Culture, Sports Appliances and Equipments	724	746	8856	33869
医药及医疗器材专门零售	Retail of Medicines and Medical Appliances	787	1104	7642	26536
汽车、摩托车、燃料及零售配件专门零售	Retail of Motor Vehicles, Motorcycles, Fuel and Parts	966	1078	14391	67868
家用电器及电子产品专门零售	Special Retail of Household Electric Appliances and Electronic Products	1763	1977	14276	49545
五金、家具及室内装修材料专门零售	Special Retail of Hardware, Furniture and Decoration Materials	1203	1341	17750	42032
无店铺及其他零售	Non-shop and Other Retail	558	570	9825	27300

Organizations, Establishments and Persons Engaged in Retail Trade（2011）

（unit,person）

城镇 Urban				城区 County				乡村 Village			
法人单位 Constitutional Unit	活动单位 Movemental Unit	网点 Branch Shop	人员 Personnel	法人单位 Constitutional Unit	活动单位 Movemental Unit	网点 Branch Shop	人员 Personnel	法人单位 Constitutional Unit	活动单位 Movemental Unit	网点 Branch Shop	人员 Personnel
8186	**9382**	**147952**	**516002**	**7774**	**8887**	**127264**	**470853**	**203**	**231**	**32830**	**69678**
8053	9200	9871	155597	7641	8705	9311	149908	203	231	319	3017
213	274	349	16877	191	232	262	16371	10	14	28	533
261	337	372	3786	228	256	273	3262	35	35	101	453
90	112	112	7962	84	106	106	7770				
22	37	37	316	21	36	36	310	3	3	3	40
2412	3025	3240	65059	2375	2988	3202	64660	14	17	19	158
157	200	230	6417	155	185	215	6149				
4685	4978	5294	53171	4381	4672	4987	49408	132	153	159	1662
213	237	237	2009	206	230	230	1978	9	9	9	171
42	65	65	6070	42	65	65	6070				
91	117	123	7296	91	117	123	7296				
		137893	347039			117765	307579			32511	66661
701	812	17194	70342	568	675	12591	57849	59	63	13279	26684
545	655	29820	88657	519	623	24694	78662	22	27	6388	11805
1044	1217	37891	135382	984	1155	29969	120927	17	23	3470	5660
720	742	7939	31981	699	721	7587	31138	4	4	917	1888
770	1081	6814	25095	731	1004	6258	23545	17	23	828	1441
922	1033	10840	56918	880	966	9932	54570	44	45	3551	10950
1743	1952	12211	43242	1704	1912	11578	41481	20	25	2065	6303
1196	1333	17336	41266	1157	1286	16856	40037	7	8	414	766
545	557	7907	23119	532	545	7799	22644	13	13	1918	4181

15-7 餐饮业机构、网点、人员（2011年）

单位:个、人

分类	Classify	合计 法人单位 Constitutional Unit	活动单位 Movemental Unit	网点 Branch Shop	Total 人员 Personnel
总计	**Total**	**1724**	**1975**	**43728**	**232552**
一、按登记注册类型分组	**Grouped by Type of Registration**				
内资企业	Domestic Funded Enterprises	1686	1852	1996	76265
国有企业	State-owned Enterprises	32	42	43	3494
集体企业	Collective-owned Enterprises	16	17	17	495
股份合作企业	Share-holding Cooperative Enterprises	5	5	5	216
联营企业	Joint Ownership Enterprises	24	24	24	759
有限责任公司	Limited Liability Corporations	407	462	516	25238
股份有限公司	Share-holding Corporations Ltd.	45	64	64	6001
私营企业	Private Enterprises	1112	1183	1250	38458
其他企业	Other Enterprises	45	55	77	1604
港、澳、台商投资企业	Enterprises with Funds from Hong Kong，Macao & Taiwan	14	89	89	6164
外商投资企业	Foreign Funded Enterprises	24	34	34	1959
个体经济	Individuals			41609	148164
二、按餐饮业行业分组	**Grouped by Sector of Catering Trade**				
正餐服务	Restaurant	1406	1533	24038	158258
快餐服务	Fast Food	99	182	4094	13818
饮料及冷料服务	Beverages and Cold Drinks	97	114	1481	5031
其他餐饮服务	Others	122	146	14115	55445

Organizations Staff and Branch Shopes of Catering Trade（2011）

(unit,person)

城镇			Urban	城区			County	乡村 Village			
法人单位 Constitutional Unit	活动单位 Movemental Unit	网点 Branch Shop	人员 Personnel	法人单位 Constitutional Unit	活动单位 Movemental Unit	网点 Branch Shop	人员 Personnel	法人单位 Constitutional Unit	活动单位 Movemental Unit	网点 Branch Shop	人员 Personnel
1637	**1881**	**38470**	**213933**	**1481**	**1717**	**33874**	**195672**	**87**	**94**	**5258**	**18619**
1600	1759	1903	74631	1444	1595	1738	70983	86	93	93	1634
31	41	42	3380	28	38	38	3144	1	1	1	114
16	17	17	495	16	17	17	495				
5	5	5	216	4	4	4	206				
21	21	21	669	18	18	18	565	3	3	3	90
406	461	515	25071	398	449	503	24325	1	1	1	167
45	64	64	6001	43	60	60	5911				
1035	1099	1166	37255	898	960	1027	34815	77	84	84	1203
41	51	73	1544	39	49	71	1522	4	4	4	60
13	88	88	6078	13	88	88	6078	1	1	1	86
24	34	34	1959	24	34	34	1959				
		36445	131265			32014	116652			5164	16899
1323	1443	22340	148046	1181	1292	20952	140760	83	90	1698	10212
95	178	3409	12533	93	177	2577	11000	4	4	685	1285
97	114	1481	5031	97	114	1481	5031				
122	146	11240	48323	110	134	8864	38881			2875	7122

15-8 各区县批发、零售、餐饮业机构、网点、人员（2011年）

Organizations, Branch Shops and Staff of Wholesale,Retail and Catering Trade by Region（2011）

单位：个、人 (unit,person)

分　　类	Classify	法人单位 Constitutional Unit	活动单位 Movemental Unit	网 点 Branch Shop	人 员 Personnel
一、批发业	**Wholesale Trade**	**11145**	**11504**	**30441**	**253618**
新城区	Xincheng	1249	1265	9405	47165
碑林区	Beilin	2006	2079	3469	34696
莲湖区	Lianhu	1529	1538	5131	25578
灞桥区	Baqiao	447	467	617	5017
未央区	Weiyang	4018	4158	5354	98501
雁塔区	Yanta	1436	1458	2143	26268
阎良区	Yanliang	58	60	395	1406
临潼区	Lintong	85	102	602	3715
长安区	Chang'an	61	66	734	3019
蓝田县	Lantian	61	68	908	2454
周至县	Zhouzhi	49	69	758	1810
户　县	Huxian	111	127	693	2869
高陵县	Gaoling	35	47	232	1120
二、零售业	**Retail Trade**	**8389**	**9613**	**180782**	**585680**
新城区	Xincheng	1240	1402	23838	113078
碑林区	Beilin	2029	2356	22610	74492
莲湖区	Lianhu	883	901	17141	52783
灞桥区	Baqiao	346	441	7014	20311
未央区	Weiyang	1679	1975	21779	78826
雁塔区	Yanta	1407	1607	23011	101412
阎良区	Yanliang	77	82	5089	9038
临潼区	Lintong	95	117	7736	12877
长安区	Chang'an	179	184	21194	61713
蓝田县	Lantian	78	78	8510	14871
周至县	Zhouzhi	72	72	10229	13876
户　县	Huxian	234	313	9731	26003
高陵县	Gaoling	70	85	2900	6400

15-8 续表 continued

单位：个、人 (unit,person)

分 类	Classify	法人单位 Constitutional Unit	活动单位 Movemental Unit	网 点 Branch Shop	人 员 Personnel
三、餐饮业	**Catering Trade**	**1724**	**1975**	**43728**	**232552**
新城区	Xincheng	145	167	2525	16866
碑林区	Beilin	341	463	5415	39945
莲湖区	Lianhu	190	199	4243	24815
灞桥区	Baqiao	127	133	2341	9816
未央区	Weiyang	116	129	4742	29795
雁塔区	Yanta	464	521	9346	55018
阎良区	Yanliang	32	33	1243	5009
临潼区	Lintong	27	33	1793	5944
长安区	Chang'an	103	110	6430	25255
蓝田县	Lantian	84	84	1736	5226
周至县	Zhouzhi	10	10	1480	3083
户 县	Huxian	47	51	1807	8891
高陵县	Gaoling	38	42	627	2889

15-9 限额以上批发零售贸易企业财务状况（2011年）

单位：万元

分　　类	Classify	单位数（个）Number (unit)	资产总计 Total Assets	流动资产合　计 Circulating Funds	固定资产合　计 Total Fixed Assets
总　　计	**Total**	**497**	**10190279.4**	**7390833.9**	**1070540.0**
一、批发企业	**Wholesale Enterprises**	**200**	**5834948.5**	**4495162.0**	**429774.5**
#国有控股	State-holding Majority Shares	45	2455742.1	1814245.1	245113.5
1.按登记注册类型分组	Grouped by Category of Commodities				
内资企业	Domestic Funded Enterprises	194	4726528.8	3663874.6	421897.8
国有企业	State-owned Enterprises	31	1720590.2	1223977.2	206117.8
集体企业	Collective-owned Enterprises	3	62698.1	30671.7	4930.3
股份合作企业	Corperative Enterprises				
联营企业	Joint Ownership Enterprises	1	292.3	225.8	66.5
国有联营企业	State Joint Ownership Enterprises				
集体联营企业	Collective Joint Ownership Enterprises	1	292.3	225.8	66.5
国有与集体联营企业	Joint State-collective Enterprises				
其他联营企业	Others Joint Ownership Enterprises				
有限责任公司	Limited Liability Corporrations	98	2063980.5	1826670.4	136216.6
国有独资	State Funded Corporations	1	19548.9	18811.3	212.9
其他有限责任公司	Other Limited Liability Corporrations	97	2044431.6	1807859.1	136003.7
股份有限公司	Share-holding Corporations Ltd.	2	296151.5	190405.7	34168.5
私营企业	Private Enterprises	58	582674.1	391893.8	40298.1
私营独资企业	Private-funded Enterprises	3	18002.3	6746.6	7869.1
私营有限责任公司	Private Limited Liability Corporations	52	496712.3	330686.1	28034.6
私营股份有限公司	Private Share-holding Corporations Ltd.	3	67959.5	54461.1	4394.4
其他企业	Other Enterprises	1	142.1	30.0	100.0
港、澳、台商投资企业	Enterprises with Funds from Hong Kong，Macao &Taiwan	3	50119.6	47770.8	1275.7
与港澳台商合资经营	Joint-venture Enterprises	1	17610.9	17566.1	44.7
港澳台商独资	Enterprises with Sole Investment	2	32508.7	30204.7	1231.0
外商投资企业	Foreign Funded Enterprises	3	1058300.1	783516.6	6601.0
中外合资经营	Joint-venture Enterprises	3	1058300.1	783516.6	6601.0
外资企业	Foreign Owned Enterprises				
2.按国民经济行业分组	Grouped by Sector				
农畜产品批发业	Wholesale of Farm produce and Livestock Products	4	76368.5	41253.8	7046.2
食品、饮料及烟草制品批发	Wholesale of Beverages and Tobaccos	13	391930.2	276740.1	72259.9
烟草制品批发业	Wholesale of Tobaccos	1	263756.9	195379.7	63644.0
纺织、服装及日用品批发业	Wholesale of Textiles, Garments and Daily Consumer Articles	11	89192.9	60424.5	22984.0
文化、体育用品及器材批发	Wholesale of Culture, Sports Appliences and Equipments	6	125685.6	67245.5	5317.6

Financial Status of Enterprises Above Designated Size in Wholesale and Retail（2011）

(10 000 yuan)

固定资产原价 Original Value of Fixed Assets	累计折旧 Accumulated Depreciation	负债合计 Total Liabilities	流动负债合计 Circulating Liabilities	非流动负债 Non-Circulating Liabilities	所有者权益合计 Total Owners' Equities	实收资本 Paid in Capital	营业收入 Total Revenue	主营业务收入 Revenue from Principal Business
1553251.5	**488132.5**	**7738039.8**	**7328923.1**	**409116.7**	**2452239.6**	**1472237.2**	**26259580.3**	**26100965.7**
606184.4	**181596.8**	**4665768.0**	**4527284.2**	**138483.8**	**1169180.5**	**784296.7**	**15781025.9**	**15745338.5**
332533.3	87419.8	1787754.6	1763395.2	24359.4	667987.5	376902.6	7755146.3	7732542.0
596397.1	179686.2	3740175.4	3602542.3	137633.1	986353.4	637803.7	13720285.0	13686988.8
266033.4	59915.6	1122969.0	1108888.4	14080.6	597621.2	316344.7	4837349.5	4821802.1
7942.7	3012.4	64375.6	36641.4	27734.2	-1677.5	5358.0	19844.5	19844.0
69.4	2.9				292.3	292.3	2005.5	2005.5
69.4	2.9				292.3	292.3	2005.5	2005.5
203980.0	67842.0	1812313.0	1768182.7	44130.3	251667.5	168423.0	6311754.5	6306878.6
713.9	501.0	14533.3	14533.3		5015.6	5015.6	96218.8	96188.2
203266.1	67341.0	1797779.7	1753649.4	44130.3	246651.9	163407.4	6215535.7	6210690.4
58372.0	24203.5	268591.0	263246.7	5344.3	27560.5	27560.5	1315700.4	1309114.6
59889.6	24699.8	471916.8	425573.1	46343.7	110757.3	119693.1	1228910.6	1222624.0
3598.3	837.5	10594.3	8788.3	1806.0	7408.0	6372.3	93812.4	93812.4
50887.4	22852.8	407210.6	400600.7	6609.9	89501.7	100353.8	960445.6	954159.0
5403.9	1009.5	54111.9	16184.1	37927.8	13847.6	12967.0	174652.6	174652.6
110.0	10.0	10.0	10.0		132.1	132.1	4720.0	4720.0
2099.4	823.7	44563.6	43794.9	768.7	5556.0	1410.0	317760.6	317760.6
179.9	135.2	16769.3	16769.3		841.6	1000.0	239960.6	239960.6
1919.5	688.5	27794.3	27025.6	768.7	4714.4	410.0	77800.0	77800.0
7687.9	1086.9	881029.0	880947.0	82.0	177271.1	145083.0	1742980.3	1740589.1
7687.9	1086.9	881029.0	880947.0	82.0	177271.1	145083.0	1742980.3	1740589.1
11093.5	4047.3	74559.2	46764.0	27795.2	1809.3	8908.2	20581.5	20581.5
99842.7	27582.8	95273.6	81499.9	13773.7	296656.6	30518.8	903985.7	903344.3
85895.2	22251.2	27571.6	27571.6		236185.3	2283.1	723316.5	723316.5
54479.4	31495.4	63833.5	63833.5		25359.4	23559.4	1152023.8	1150920.0
9699.8	4382.2	66109.5	66109.5		59576.1	33000.0	155176.6	154151.9

15-9 续表1

单位：万元

分类	Classify	营业成本 Total Cost	主营业务成本 Cost of Principal Business	营业税金及附加 Taxs and Other Changes	主营业务税金及附加 Taxs and Other Changes on Principal Business
总计	**Total**	**23882246.2**	**23743502.0**	**206723.1**	**205681.7**
一、批发企业	**Wholesale Enterprises**	**14841662.6**	**14795483.1**	**81449.9**	**81221.5**
#国有控股	State-holding Majority Shares	7223981.3	7184572.6	55430.3	55212.8
1.按登记注册类型分组	Grouped by Category of Commodities				
内资企业	Domestic Funded Enterprises	12803431.6	12757983.8	79599.9	79371.5
国有企业	State-owned Enterprises	4471237.4	4443578.7	53580.7	53375.1
集体企业	Collective-owned Enterprises	18782.8	18782.8	28.3	28.3
股份合作企业	Corperative Enterprises				
联营企业	Joint Ownership Enterprises	1740.3	1740.3	62.2	62.2
国有联营企业	State Joint Ownership Enterprises				
集体联营企业	Collective Joint Ownership Enterprises	1740.3	1740.3	62.2	62.2
国有与集体联营企业	Joint State-collective Enterprises				
其他联营企业	Others Joint Ownership Enterprises				
有限责任公司	Limited Liability Corporations	5955564.3	5947570.1	23813.6	23806.5
国有独资	State Funded Corporations	94660.3	94629.7	6.9	6.9
其他有限责任公司	Other Limited Liability Corporations	5860904.0	5852940.4	23806.7	23799.6
股份有限公司	Share-holding Corporations Ltd.	1178619.0	1172692.6	1163.7	1151.8
私营企业	Private Enterprises	1175487.8	1171619.3	901.4	897.6
私营独资企业	Private-funded Enterprises	92286.7	92286.7	23.5	19.7
私营有限责任公司	Private Limited Liability Corporations	914965.8	911097.3	824.4	824.4
私营股份有限公司	Private Share-holding Corporations Ltd.	168235.3	168235.3	53.5	53.5
其他企业	Other Enterprises	2000.0	2000.0	50.0	50.0
港、澳、台商投资企业	Enterprises with Funds from Hong Kong，Macao &Taiwan	299691.7	299691.7	1210.3	1210.3
与港澳台商合资经营	Joint-venture Enterprises	231958.5	231958.5	131.0	131.0
港澳台商独资	Enterprises with Sole Investment	67733.2	67733.2	1079.3	1079.3
外商投资企业	Foreign Funded Enterprises	1738539.3	1737807.6	639.7	639.7
中外合资经营	Joint-venture Enterprises	1738539.3	1737807.6	639.7	639.7
外资企业	Foreign Owned Enterprises				
2.按国民经济行业分组	Grouped by Sector				
农畜产品批发业	Wholesale of Farm Produce and Livestock Products	18532.2	18532.2	20.2	20.2
食品、饮料及烟草制品批发	Wholesale of Beverages and Tobaccos	670304.4	670285.8	44594.7	44594.7
烟草制品批发业	Wholesale of Tobaccos	530146.8	530146.8	43982.0	43982.0
纺织、服装及日用品批发业	Wholesale of Textiles, Garments and Daily Consumer Articles	983868.8	982859.9	18566.8	18566.8
文化、体育用品及器材批发	Wholesale of Culture, Sports Applionces and Equipments	140957.4	139954.0	190.1	190.1

continued 1

(10 000 yuan)

销售费用 Sale Expenses	管理费用 Management Expenses	财务费用 Financial Expenses	营业利润 Business Profits	利润总额 Total Profits	应付职工薪酬 Salary Payable	本年应交增值税 Value Added Tax Payable
865557.1	**464263.3**	**67445.5**	**915798.8**	**913250.7**	**354210.6**	**490958.2**
328996.5	**174360.8**	**14281.3**	**364561.9**	**362496.4**	**132764.6**	**161993.5**
164225.3	93105.3	17190.8	228296.2	227926.6	69155.9	65128.9
318024.0	169370.2	32892.7	361685.6	359583.2	126301.1	146327.1
108632.9	81589.6	12387.4	131008.9	131188.0	46332.4	48897.0
394.8	1107.1	101.2	190.0	367.7	431.5	54.5
19.5	23.2	6.3	154.0	154.0	12.0	6.9
19.5	23.2	6.3	154.0	154.0	12.0	6.9
142130.4	63095.3	9525.7	132259.2	132768.8	50369.1	75085.0
583.0	196.7	375.6	528.5	407.3	165.0	31.3
141547.4	62898.6	9150.1	131730.7	132361.5	50204.1	75053.7
38378.0	5018.5	1937.4	90583.8	89290.3	18325.3	12299.5
28463.4	18534.5	8934.6	4826.8	3151.5	10760.8	9606.6
598.8	491.7	198.4	217.1	216.4	53.5	324.6
24096.6	15448.5	8357.9	-1061.7	-2651.9	9576.6	8932.2
3768.0	2594.3	378.3	5671.4	5587.0	1130.7	349.8
5.0	2.0	0.1	2662.9	2662.9	70.0	377.6
9367.7	2084.2	-23.4	5444.5	5439.6	5517.4	15039.1
6123.4	472.5	-24.6	1299.8	1294.4	1910.6	1303.2
3244.3	1611.7	1.2	4144.7	4145.2	3606.8	13735.9
1604.8	2906.4	-18588.0	-2568.2	-2526.4	946.1	627.3
1604.8	2906.4	-18588.0	-2568.2	-2526.4	946.1	627.3
1865.8	1231.1	100.2	-403.9	398.2	659.7	261.9
30593.2	39292.4	1489.7	119168.0	120007.2	28396.7	33737.6
14600.4	24880.7	-623.7	111189.6	111350.3	17020.9	31866.2
29011.6	21999.3	424.7	100936.2	100948.8	20764.5	40097.7
8549.9	5177.4	-87.3	1105.1	1045.7	2900.1	1636.7

15-9 续表2

单位：万元

分类	Classify	单位数（个）Number (unit)	资产总计 Total Assets	流动资产合计 Circulating Funds	固定资产合计 Total Fixed Assets
医药及医疗器材批发	Wholesale of Medicines and Medical Appliances	26	320152.6	297452.4	7156.2
矿产品、建材及化工产品批发	Wholesale of Mineral Products, Building Materials and Chemical Products	92	4025166.9	2991997.4	293192.1
煤炭及制品批发	Wholesale of Coal and Related Products	10	478895.1	413947.5	45644.8
石油及制品批发业	Wholesale of Petrolem and Related Products	24	1336511.3	765348.3	182190.6
金属及金属矿批发业	Wholesale of Metals and Metals Minerals	44	1744694.7	1433881.8	17374.3
建材批发业	Wholesale of Building Materials	7	413662.0	329861.4	46290.7
化肥批发业	Wholesale of Chemicel Fertilizer	5	27419.7	25034.2	1631.8
其他化工产品批发	Wholesale of Other Chemical Products	1	643.7	600.7	43.0
机械设备、五金交电及电子产品批发业	Wholesale of Machinery, Hardware, and Electronic Equipment	46	791612.1	745716.5	21665.1
汽车、摩托车及零配件批发业	Wholesale of Motor Vehicles, Motocycles and Parts	10	287431.3	266686.7	10855.8
家用电器批发业	Wholesale of Household Electrical Appliances	5	195194.3	193496.7	1551.0
计算机、软件及辅助设备批发业	Wholesale of Computers,Software and Assisant Appliances	5	91267.3	81100.5	2307.9
贸易经纪与代理	Trade Borker and Agency	2	14839.7	14331.8	153.4
其他批发业	Other wholesale not Classified Elsewhere				
二、零售企业	**Retail Trade**	**297**	**4355330.9**	**2895671.9**	**640765.5**
#国有控股	State-holding Majority Shares	18	221167.9	185757.7	23021.6
1.按登记注册类型分组	Grouped by Category of Commodities				
内资企业	Domestic Funded Enterprises	270	3358706.8	2241067.8	531681.5
国有企业	State-owned Enterprises	15	161701.6	141457.8	8935.1
集体企业	Collective-owned Enterprises	18	8758.5	4702.7	1876.1
股份合作企业	Share-holding Cooperative Enterprises				
联营企业	Joint Ownership Enterprises	1	254.9	96.3	86.3
国有联营企业	State Joint Ownership Enterprises				
集体联营企业	Collective Joint Ownership Enterprises	1	254.9	96.3	86.3
国有与集体联营企业	Joint State-collective Enterprises				
其他联营企业	Others Joint Ownership Enterprises				
有限责任公司	Limited Liability Corporations	126	1601263.5	1011817.9	310096.8
国有独资公司	State Funded Corporations	2	43251.6	28982.9	13197.8
其他有限责任公司	Other Limited Liability Corporations	124	1558011.9	982835.0	296899.0
股份有限公司	Share-holding Corporations Ltd.	8	861839.8	576885.6	124801.6
私营企业	Private Enterprises	99	713746.8	502956.7	84174.7
私营独资企业	Private-funded Enterprises	10	7259.9	5140.1	982.0
私营合伙企业	Private Partnership Enterprises	3	1110.7	892.3	206.0
私营有限责任公司	Private Limited Liability Corporations	79	669697.3	469401.0	76490.0
私营股份有限公司	Private Share-holding Corporations Ltd.	7	35678.9	27523.3	6496.7
其他企业	Other Enterprises	3	11141.7	3150.8	1710.9

continued 2

(10 000 yuan)

固定资产原价 Original Value of Fixed Assets	累计折旧 Accumulated Depreciation	负债合计 Total Liabilities	流动负债合计 Circulating Liabilities	非流动负债 Non-Circulating Liabilities	所有者权益合计 Total Owners' Equities	实收资本 Paid in Capital	营业收入 Total Revenue	主营业务收入 Revenue from Principal Business
12629.8	5473.6	290868.3	287967.2	2901.1	29284.3	26244.3	610549.9	608773.3
384859.3	96854.1	3314554.5	3224081.2	90473.3	710612.4	622179.8	11208308.3	11186973.9
60781.4	15136.6	406962.1	401999.9	4962.2	71933.0	29435.6	977403.6	977344.7
241684.2	64601.9	1024249.3	979009.2	45240.1	312262.0	333144.0	6164715.1	6150691.8
25089.3	7793.6	1489929.4	1482092.0	7837.4	254765.3	227469.3	3018166.3	3012910.1
54885.5	8594.8	352321.6	319888.0	32433.6	61340.4	22983.6	938143.4	938121.7
2090.0	458.2	17600.4	17600.4		9819.3	8597.3	77028.6	75054.3
298.3	255.3	60.5	60.5		583.2	500.0	2024.9	2024.9
33382.4	11717.3	746720.8	743500.7	3220.1	44891.3	38830.3	1694256.1	1684449.6
15690.9	4835.1	276741.6	276161.6	580.0	10689.7	10932.0	637973.3	637427.9
2188.1	637.1	194041.6	194041.6		1152.7	2200.0	285088.7	284448.6
2782.4	474.5	88393.3	85818.6	2574.7	2874.0	5042.3	341473.5	340773.5
197.5	44.1	13848.6	13528.2	320.4	991.1	1055.9	36144.0	36144.0
947067.1	**306535.7**	**3072271.8**	**2801638.9**	**270632.9**	**1283059.1**	**687940.5**	**10478554.4**	**10355627.2**
36177.4	13155.8	165308.5	127684.4	37624.1	55859.4	10678.6	432986.9	428435.5
792020.1	260507.6	2434598.7	2171946.1	262652.6	924108.1	508307.6	8418045.1	8317866.8
14925.1	5990.0	121515.8	84861.7	36654.1	40185.8	7113.2	294259.3	290416.9
2764.8	888.7	8178.6	7661.8	516.8	579.9	2210.2	71129.3	63479.9
166.4	80.1	128.6	128.6		126.3	50.0	4202.4	4202.4
166.4	80.1	128.6	128.6		126.3	50.0	4202.4	4202.4
446581.7	136647.9	1061333.8	941309.3	120024.5	539929.7	345723.9	4956733.6	4918653.7
20059.9	6862.1	32637.3	31667.3	970.0	10614.3	3065.4	44381.7	43869.4
426521.8	129785.8	1028696.5	909642.0	119054.5	529315.4	342658.5	4912351.9	4874784.3
194734.0	69932.4	666833.5	596014.9	70818.6	195006.3	57124.9	1034109.6	1002661.6
129329.0	45160.3	570208.1	540069.5	30138.6	143538.7	91885.4	1787578.6	1768420.0
1230.1	248.1	2462.5	2170.9	291.6	4797.4	3085.6	36415.5	36415.5
281.3	75.3	984.8	924.5	60.3	125.9	220.0	4076.4	4076.4
117813.5	41329.5	536100.4	512160.4	23940.0	133596.9	85629.8	1625239.9	1607978.1
10004.1	3507.4	30660.4	24813.7	5846.7	5018.5	2950.0	121846.8	119950.0
3519.1	1808.2	6400.3	1900.3	4500.0	4741.4	4200.0	270032.3	270032.3

15-9 续表3

单位：万元

分类	Classify	营业成本 Total Cost	主营业务成本 Cost of Principal Business	营业税金及附加 Taxs and Other Changes	主营业务税金及附加 Taxs and Other Changes on Principal Business
医药及医疗器材批发	Wholesale of Medicines and Medical Appliances	589266.5	582867.9	628.0	622.2
矿产品、建材及化工产品批发	Wholesale of Mineral Products, Building Materials and Chemical Products	10784030.2	10770124.6	16074.3	16062.2
煤炭及制品批发	Wholesale of Coal and Related Products	906129.3	906129.3	1401.7	1401.5
石油及制品批发业	Wholesale of Petrolem and Related Products	5896322.0	5886971.1	3693.5	3681.6
金属及金属矿批发业	Wholesale of Metals and Metals Minerals	2961366.6	2956878.2	9023.2	9023.2
建材批发业	Wholesale of Building Materials	914351.4	914287.1	1883.4	1883.4
化肥批发业	Wholesale of Chemicel Fertilizer	75698.5	75696.5	62.2	62.2
其他化工产品批发	Wholesale of Other Chemical Products	1877.3	1877.3	4.1	4.1
机械设备、五金交电及电子产品批发业	Wholesale of Machinery, Hardware, and Electronic Equipment	1621289.6	1601080.4	1321.4	1110.9
汽车、摩托车及零配件批发业	Wholesale of Motor Vehicles, Motocycles and Parts	618681.8	605215.9	308.0	307.8
家用电器批发业	Wholesale of Household Electrical Appliances	272132.5	271543.2	160.1	159.0
计算机、软件及辅助设备批发业	Wholesale of Computers,Software and Peripherals	329249.9	329209.9	205.1	201.3
贸易经纪与代理	Trade Borker and Agency	33413.5	29778.3	54.4	54.4
其他批发业	Other wholesale not Classified Elsewhere				
二、零售企业	**Retail Trade**	**9040583.6**	**8948018.9**	**125273.2**	**124460.2**
#国有控股	State-owned ding Majority Shares	370339.6	360277.2	1538.8	1529.0
1.按登记注册类型分组	Grouped by Category of Commodities				
内资企业	Domestic Funded Enterprises	7229723.0	7178128.3	113416.0	112705.0
国有企业	State-owned Enterprises	250383.5	240321.1	1205.9	1205.9
集体企业	Collective-owned Enterprises	64459.9	58215.5	613.8	613.8
股份合作企业	Share-Holding Cooperative Enterprises				
联营企业	Joint Ownership Enterprises	1691.0	1691.0	4.5	4.5
国有联营企业	State Joint Ownership Enterprises				
集体联营企业	Collective Joint Ownership Enterprises	1691.0	1691.0	4.5	4.5
国有与集体联营企业	Joint State-collective Enterprises				
其他联营企业	Others Joint Ownership Enterprises				
有限责任公司	Limited Liability Corporations	4296325.9	4272274.0	67774.3	67288.8
国有独资	State Funded Corporations	33602.7	33602.7	163.3	163.3
其他有限责任公司	Other Limited Liability Corporrations	4262723.2	4238671.3	67611.0	67125.5
股份有限公司	Share-holding Corporations Ltd.	862004.0	860177.7	8853.1	8787.5
私营企业	Private Enterprises	1518922.5	1509512.8	21592.1	21432.2
私营独资企业	Private-funded Enterprises	28800.4	28781.5	486.6	477.2
私营合伙企业	Private Partnership Enterprises	3481.7	3481.7	52.8	52.8
私营有限责任公司	Private Limited Liability Corporations	1386299.1	1376908.3	17441.7	17318.2
私营股份有限公司	Private Share-holding Corporations Ltd.	100341.3	100341.3	3611.0	3584.0
其他企业	Other Enterprises	235936.2	235936.2	13372.3	13372.3

continued 3

(10 000 yuan)

销售费用 Sale Expenses	管理费用 Managenment Expenses	财务费用 Financial Expenses	营业利润 Business Profits	利润总额 Total Profits	应付职工薪酬 Salary Payable	本年应交增值税 Value Added Tax Payable
14256.4	7462.5	2329.3	3017.9	3317.2	6708.3	6054.4
189539.8	75333.4	10726.4	127046.7	122920.5	56622.0	61480.8
53188.8	7338.5	2088.8	11856.9	11979.5	8357.3	5304.4
103860.5	44302.9	21316.0	103419.8	99413.2	39070.4	26450.7
26813.7	16474.0	-14547.2	1578.6	1665.0	6772.5	7634.5
1010.3	6071.9	1540.4	14242.5	13901.8	1785.3	16598.1
2144.5	925.3	332.9	-4098.7	-4097.0	499.2	4699.8
60.0	65.5		18.0	18.0	36.1	38.0
51829.8	23453.1	-577.8	11018.3	11193.0	16546.7	18303.6
21848.4	10082.6	997.7	722.3	823.2	3558.2	3227.5
8839.2	3225.0	-2041.3	2811.6	2776.5	3095.5	1397.0
8443.6	924.9	-65.8	2723.5	2706.2	2933.8	11115.2
3350.0	411.6	-123.9	2673.6	2665.8	166.6	420.8
536560.6	**289902.5**	**53164.2**	**551236.9**	**550754.3**	**221446.0**	**328964.7**
25738.7	33024.3	1496.0	10324.4	10168.2	19694.2	9170.3
397632.8	239158.8	47634.5	447743.2	445395.7	178870.2	267391.2
17318.0	26032.1	1332.8	7434.3	7275.9	14461.7	6339.6
1684.9	2090.5	88.1	843.3	842.6	1512.1	679.6
2461.4	54.1		-8.6	-8.6	35.0	15.7
2461.4	54.1		-8.6	-8.6	35.0	15.7
231577.6	111118.9	17248.7	273753.5	274568.2	91702.0	183282.3
5875.0	4572.3	-148.2	354.1	361.1	2759.4	501.4
225702.6	106546.6	17396.9	273399.4	274207.1	88942.6	182780.9
49641.8	45165.5	14209.7	54945.0	58173.5	29222.5	23646.8
87837.7	51400.0	14544.5	100671.7	94440.5	40428.6	45249.1
999.6	797.8	122.3	9759.4	9771.6	643.0	620.6
347.4	127.7	0.5	70.9	70.4	359.3	113.4
84709.4	37902.7	14242.4	89283.0	82960.1	31740.2	41143.2
1781.3	12571.8	179.3	1558.4	1638.4	7686.1	3371.9
7111.4	3297.7	210.7	10104.0	10103.6	1508.3	8178.1

15-9 续表4

单位：万元

分　　类	Classify	单位数（个）Number (unit)	资产总计 Total Assets	流动资产合　计 Circulating Funds	固定资产合　计 Total Fixed Assets
港、澳、台商投资企业	Enterprises with Funds from Hong Kong，Macao &Taiwan	10	491462.3	292919.0	40503.4
与港澳台商合资经营企业	Joint-venture Enterprises	2	77414.0	59955.1	11930.7
港澳抬商独资	Wholly Funded from Hong Kong, Macao and Taiwan	8	414048.3	232963.9	28572.7
港、澳、台商投资股份有限公司	Share-holding Corporations Ltd.				
外商投资企业	Foreign Funded Enterprises	17	505161.8	361685.1	68580.6
中外合资经营企业	Joint-venture Enterprises	2	77414.0	59955.1	11930.7
外资企业	Enterprises with Sole Fund	8	414048.3	232963.9	28572.7
外商投资股份有限公司	Share-holding Corporations Ltd.				
2.按国民经济行业分组	Grouped by Sector				
综合零售	Integrated Retail	69	1633782.6	981110.9	240425.4
百货零售	Retail of General Merchandise	34	1064070.6	629166.3	184330.8
超级市场零售	Retail of Supermarkets	27	566690.0	350744.5	54544.5
其他综合零售	Other Integrated Retail	8	3022.0	1200.1	1550.1
食品、饮料及烟草制品专门零售	Food, Beverages and Tobaccos Special Retail Trade	9	325654.4	215584.6	77742.5
纺织、服装及日用品专门零售	Textiles, Garments and Daily Consumer Articles Special Retail Trade	25	249376.6	88754.1	73932.9
#服装零售	Retail of Garments	16	209752.2	60709.9	67302.9
文化、体育用品及器材专门零售	Culture,Sports Appliances and Equipments Special Retail Trade	15	125427.9	104574.8	14975.9
#图书零售	Retail of Book	4	58580.7	43237.5	13856.8
医药及医疗器材专门零售	Medinces and Medical Appliances Special Retail Trade	11	75114.2	68530.3	3855.7
#药品零售	Retail of Medinces	11	75114.2	68530.3	3855.7
汽车、摩托车、燃料及零配件专门零售	Motor Vehicles, Motorcycle,Fuel and Parts Special Retail Trade	127	1360352.3	1029545.7	134585.3
#汽车零售业	Retail of Motorcar Vehicles	101	1226853.1	983319.3	112420.4
家用电器及电子产品专门零售	Household Appliances and Electronic products Special retail trade	23	374156.6	281992.5	53853.0
#家用电器零售	Retail of Household Electric Appliances	13	296206.3	232376.4	40074.8
计算机、软件及辅助设备零售	Retail of Computer, Software and Peripherals	8	66586.5	38534.7	13616.6
通讯设备零售	Retail of Communication Equipment	2	11363.8	11081.4	161.6
五金、家具及室内装修材料专门零售	Ironware, Furniture and Room fitting stuff Special Retail Trade	14	192909.0	108923.6	39492.9
无店铺及其他零售	Retail of No Stores and Others	4	18557.3	16655.4	1901.9

continued 4

(10 000 yuan)

固定资产原价 Original Value of Fixed Assets	累计折旧 Accumulated Depreciation	负债合计 Total Liabilities	流动负债合计 Circulating Liabilities	非流动负债 Non-Circulating Liabilities	所有者权益合计 Total Owners' Equities	实收资本 Paid in Capital	营业收入 Total Revenue	主营业务收入 Revenue from Principal Business
68770.4	28267.0	310260.3	302323.8	7936.5	181202.0	65278.7	956170.4	947904.1
18392.6	6461.9	27680.1	26273.6	1406.5	49733.9	5150.0	222187.9	219402.3
50377.8	21805.1	282580.2	276050.2	6530.0	131468.1	60128.7	733982.5	728501.8
86276.6	17761.1	327412.8	327369.0	43.8	177749.0	114354.2	1104338.9	1089856.3
18392.6	6461.9	27680.1	26273.6	1406.5	49733.9	5150.0	222187.9	219402.3
50377.8	21805.1	282580.2	276050.2	6530.0	131468.1	60128.7	733982.5	728501.8
378516.0	138155.7	1178584.5	1061263.8	117320.7	455198.1	223328.5	2419080.1	2364739.8
277902.6	93636.9	728979.4	612824.2	116155.2	335091.2	183690.9	1293437.2	1257961.0
98652.0	44107.5	447471.0	446538.4	932.6	119219.0	38912.1	1103306.3	1084442.2
1961.4	411.3	2134.1	1901.2	232.9	887.9	725.5	22336.6	22336.6
101893.2	24150.7	272933.6	222464.1	50469.5	52720.8	15221.7	161642.9	156764.1
115611.6	41678.7	145551.3	93339.4	52211.9	103825.3	88433.3	1142843.2	1129142.5
105956.3	38653.4	118694.5	72293.9	46400.6	91057.7	83061.2	986954.5	977817.3
23412.0	8436.1	81731.8	80591.8	1140.0	43696.1	23814.2	205604.2	196970.5
21566.9	7710.1	46510.6	45540.6	970.0	12070.1	5109.1	50381.6	49304.3
5566.4	1710.7	69321.7	66871.2	2450.5	5792.5	16599.8	120208.5	119434.8
5566.4	1710.7	69321.7	66871.2	2450.5	5792.5	16599.8	120208.5	119434.8
181118.0	46701.7	1008697.9	990340.2	18357.7	351654.4	219120.8	4394512.5	4378483.0
155063.1	42805.7	930441.0	912743.3	17697.7	296412.1	148676.6	4083228.7	4067217.1
75153.8	21300.8	180720.5	179779.2	941.3	193436.1	56880.3	1184724.4	1162259.6
52024.4	11949.6	147517.2	146973.5	543.7	148689.1	17906.0	1067052.3	1044680.5
22436.2	8819.6	26916.7	26519.1	397.6	39669.8	37895.3	81109.4	81109.4
693.2	531.6	6286.6	6286.6		5077.2	1079.0	36562.7	36469.7
62617.6	23124.7	122579.1	95033.8	27545.3	70329.9	36047.0	796061.5	795643.7
3178.5	1276.6	12151.4	11955.4	196.0	6405.9	8494.9	53877.1	52189.2

15-9 续表5

单位：万元

分　　类	Classify	营业成本 Total Cost	主营业务成本 Cost of Principal Business	营业税金及附加 Taxs and Other Changes	主营业务税金及附加 Taxs and Other Changes on Principal Business
港、澳、台商投资企业	Enterprises with Funds from Hong Kong，Macao &Taiwan	830608.6	817490.4	6327.4	6327.4
与港澳台商合资经营企业	Joint-venture Enterprises	191513.4	183674.3	866.7	866.7
港澳台商独资	Wholly Funded from Hong Kong, Macao and Taiwan	639095.2	633816.1	5460.7	5460.7
港澳台商投资股份有限公司	Share-holding Corporations Ltd.				
外商投资企业	Foreign Funded Enterprises	980252.0	952400.2	5529.8	5427.8
中外合资经营企业	Joint-venture Enterprises	191513.4	183674.3	866.7	866.7
外资企业	Enterprises with Sole Fund	639095.2	633816.1	5460.7	5460.7
外商投资股份有限公司	Share-holding Corporations Ltd.				
2.按国民经济行业分组	Grouped by Sector				
综合零售	Integrated Retail	2040093.9	1982016.6	23478.2	23012.6
百货零售	Retail of General Merchandise	1063376.0	1024641.4	14713.1	14666.2
超级市场零售	Retail of Supermarkets	956887.0	937544.3	8462.2	8043.5
其他综合零售	Other Integrated Retail	19830.9	19830.9	302.9	302.9
食品、饮料及烟草制品专门零售	Food, Beverages and Tobaccos Special Retail Trade	130802.0	125797.9	2500.3	2500.3
纺织、服装及日用品专门零售	Textiles, Garments and Daily Consumer Articles Special Retail Trade	888420.5	882446.4	28665.8	28542.6
#服装零售	Retail of Garments	767315.2	761341.1	24960.1	24836.9
文化、体育用品及器材专门零售	Culture,Sports Appliances and Equipments Special Retail Trade	164339.1	158247.6	1297.5	1297.5
#图书零售	Retail of Book	37650.8	37650.8	153.0	153.0
医药及医疗器材专门零售	Medinces and Medical Appliances Special Retail Trade	100372.7	100347.0	334.5	334.5
#药品零售	Retail of Medinces	100372.7	100347.0	334.5	334.5
汽车、摩托车、燃料及零配件专门零售	Motor Vehicles, Motorcycle,Fuel and Parts Special Retail Trade	4059560.1	4052803.2	25676.3	25526.7
#汽车零售业	Retail of Motorcar Vehicles	3770138.3	3763718.5	25379.5	25256.9
家用电器及电子产品专门零售	Household Appliances and Electronic products Special retail trade	996840.9	995703.6	21513.9	21445.8
#家用电器零售	Retail of Household Electric Appliances	893430.4	892386.9	20593.7	20526.0
计算机、软件及辅助设备零售	Retail of Computer, Software and Peripherals	72703.0	72702.1	714.4	714.0
通讯设备零售	Retail of Communication Equipment	30707.5	30614.6	205.8	205.8
五金、家具及室内装修材料专门零售	Ironware, Furniture and Room fitting stuff Special Retail Trade	609824.4	609658.1	21486.3	21486.3
无店铺及其他零售	Retail of No Stores and Others	50330.0	40998.5	320.4	313.9

continued 5

(10 000 yuan)

销售费用 Sale Expenses	管理费用 Managenment Expenses	财务费用 Financial Expenses	营业利润 Business Profits	利润总额 Total Profits	应付职工薪酬 Salary Payable	本年应交增值税 Value Added Tax Payable
67452.9	19920.6	1176.0	63664.6	65820.9	24918.6	44307.4
9207.6	7251.7	-534.6	25199.6	24669.2	1959.1	2260.0
58245.3	12668.9	1710.6	38465.0	41151.7	22959.5	42047.4
71474.9	30823.1	4353.7	39829.1	39537.7	17657.2	17266.1
9207.6	7251.7	-534.6	25199.6	24669.2	1959.1	2260.0
58245.3	12668.9	1710.6	38465.0	41151.7	22959.5	42047.4
217445.9	106388.9	12995.0	130501.8	132948.9	93516.6	54615.8
81887.3	87539.9	12928.1	72950.1	71643.6	51007.4	43394.2
134891.7	18182.4	14.6	56734.7	60488.3	41778.9	10556.1
666.9	666.6	52.3	817.0	817.0	730.3	665.5
13396.8	7825.8	7436.4	465.7	482.1	8907.8	7087.4
62038.8	39102.1	4125.3	118747.7	115861.0	23706.0	31489.7
50091.6	25759.7	3379.2	114555.4	111572.6	13754.5	26616.7
14678.1	12594.9	-262.8	16036.8	16193.0	6728.2	3134.5
5224.2	7148.7	-136.8	374.2	383.3	3207.1	194.1
11706.2	7996.4	-982.2	1200.7	3183.9	6492.1	2149.2
11706.2	7996.4	-982.2	1200.7	3183.9	6492.1	2149.2
117328.7	69295.7	22349.8	100790.7	101901.5	53369.8	142684.8
97155.9	60260.3	20289.7	109897.2	111213.6	45592.9	139768.4
70545.1	29736.5	1647.4	65600.5	65856.1	17846.0	10504.7
61295.5	26978.9	970.8	63847.3	64094.0	14429.5	8265.6
4176.5	2179.5	658.7	696.8	719.8	1458.4	1279.5
5073.1	578.1	17.9	1056.4	1042.3	1958.1	959.6
23279.4	12542.1	5837.2	115945.1	112451.2	7876.6	75353.4
6141.6	4420.1	18.1	1947.9	1876.6	3002.9	1945.2

15-10 限额以上住宿和餐饮业企业主要财务状况（2011年）

单位：万元

分　类	Classify	单位数（个）Number (unit)	资产总计 Total Assets	流动资产合计 Circulating Funds	固定资产合计 Total Fixed Assets
总　计	**Total**	**475**	**1721397.6**	**525685.3**	**805742.2**
一、住宿业	**Hotel Services**	**189**	**1147962.5**	**301957.5**	**662008.9**
#国有控股	State-holding Majority Shares	58	358055.1	63589.9	235292.5
1.按登记注册类型分组	Grouped by Type of Registration				
内资企业	Domestic Funded Enterprises	174	911230.5	232027.7	523484.3
国有企业	State-owned Enterprises	45	284579.9	47330.2	185869.4
集体企业	Collective-owned Enterprises	4	4058.4	220.2	2798.8
股份合作企业	Cooperative Enterprises	1	597.8	417.3	80.3
联营企业	Joint Ownership Enterprises				
国有联营企业	State Joint Ownership Enterprises				
集体联营企业	Collective Joint Ownership Enterprises				
国有与集体联营企业	Joint State-collective Enterprises				
其他联营企业	Others Joint Ownership Enterprises				
有限责任公司	Limited Liability Corporations	67	350554.3	100963.5	183977.8
国有独资企业	State Sole Funded Corporations	1	1910.2	760.0	1150.2
其他有限责任公司	Other Limited Liability Corporations	66	348644.1	100203.5	182827.6
股份有限公司	Share-holding Corporations Ltd.	4	14398.9	1990.5	12004.7
私营企业	Private Enterprises	47	226682.6	68598.5	121601.7
私营独资企业	Private-funded Enterprises	5	5054.0	3888.1	1032.0
私营合伙企业	Private Partnership Enterprises				
私营有限责任公司	Private Limited Liability Corporations	41	218719.9	64302.6	118142.9
私营股份有限公司	Private Share-holding Corporations Ltd.	1	2908.7	407.8	2426.8
其他企业	Other Enterprises	6	30358.6	12507.5	17151.6
港、澳、台商投资企业	Enterprises with Funds from Hong Kong, Macao &Taiwan	7	101646.8	31913.5	50403.0
合资经营企业（港或澳、台资）	Joint-venture Enterprises	4	70483.1	27007.0	25656.9
合作经营企业（港或澳、台资）	Cooperative Enterprises	2	27032.2	4607.9	22424.3
港澳台商独资	Enterprise with Sole Fund	1	4131.5	298.6	2321.8
港澳台商独资股份有限公司	Share-holding Corporations Ltd. With their Investment				
外商投资企业	Foreign Funded Enterprises	8	135085.2	38016.3	88121.6
中外合资经营企业	Joint-venture Enterprises	3	40117.7	6074.7	29262.0
中外合作经营企业	Cooperation Enterprises	2	8501.6	6293.7	2207.9
外资企业	Foreign Funded Enterprises	3	86465.9	25647.9	56651.7
外商投资股份有限公司	Share-holding Corporations Ltd. With Foreign Funds				
2.按住宿行业小类分组	Grouped by Major Group of Hotel Services				
旅游饭店	Tourist Hotel	153	1042758.8	265874.9	614871.8
一般旅馆	Normal Hotel	33	51952.8	16994.0	22799.6
其他住宿服务	Others	3	53250.9	19088.6	24337.5

Finacial Status of Catering Enterprises Above Designated Size（2011）

(10 000 yuan)

固定资产原价 Original Value of Fixed Assets	累计折旧 Accumulated Depreciation	负债合计 Total Liabilities	流动负债合计 Circulating Liabilities	非流动负债 Non-Circulating Liabilities	所有者权益合计 Total Owners' Equities	实收资本 Paid in Capital	营业收入 Total Revenue	
								主营业务收入 Revenue from Principal Business
1286287.0	**523151.4**	**1250891.0**	**804408.6**	**446482.4**	**470506.6**	**822388.0**	**1241432.1**	**1229696.0**
1030978.2	**403601.3**	**936979.1**	**522564.3**	**414414.8**	**210983.4**	**494170.5**	**534760.8**	**529644.1**
373907.4	149561.2	248972.2	153554.5	95417.7	109082.9	171770.3	169445.2	168033.7
773677.1	265021.4	694777.4	450236.4	244541.0	216453.1	370353.5	430034.1	426868.6
304897.7	129841.6	209694.7	127316.7	82378.0	74885.2	138502.8	125350.5	124293.4
4770.2	2374.9	768.0	768.0		3290.4	790.8	2252.3	2252.3
142.7	62.4	522.6	522.6		75.2	50.0	1921.5	1921.5
250508.1	67509.1	295521.2	202332.7	93188.5	55033.1	111813.0	183712.4	181872.9
1150.2	147.2	3001.9	3001.9		-1091.7	1000.0	3716.2	3716.2
249357.9	67361.9	292519.3	199330.8	93188.5	56124.8	110813.0	179996.2	178156.7
16224.0	4219.3	12243.7	12040.1	203.6	2155.2	2577.5	6010.9	6008.6
172767.2	53798.5	163433.2	103933.8	59499.4	63249.4	100865.1	95146.7	94880.8
2070.7	1038.7	5594.0	5384.2	209.8	-540.0	8820.7	4746.4	4746.4
168246.5	52736.6	154696.6	95407.0	59289.6	64023.3	91933.4	89047.0	88781.1
2450.0	23.2	3142.6	3142.6		-233.9	111.0	1353.3	1353.3
24367.2	7215.6	12594.0	3322.5	9271.5	17764.6	15754.3	15639.8	15639.1
101924.6	52920.6	58695.7	32369.6	26326.1	42951.1	48341.9	34747.0	34365.5
47918.7	22272.4	26117.3	23318.1	2799.2	44365.8	33798.5	22672.2	22672.2
52378.3	29954.0	30582.0	7055.1	23526.9	-3549.8	11902.4	11117.1	10735.6
1627.6	694.2	1996.4	1996.4		2135.1	2641.0	957.7	957.7
155376.5	85659.3	183506.0	39958.3	143547.7	-48420.8	75475.1	69979.7	68410.0
45709.8	33625.9	69995.0	9817.2	60177.8	-29877.3	15352.7	22835.3	22707.3
28826.4	27844.8	67816.9	19022.0	48794.9	-59315.3	6701.1	8253.9	8253.9
80840.3	24188.6	45694.1	11119.1	34575.0	40771.8	53421.3	38890.5	37448.8
967250.4	386445.4	878640.8	468940.7	409700.1	164118.0	450358.2	477915.5	473742.7
34179.1	11934.2	42953.8	38239.1	4714.7	8999.0	15612.3	45056.2	44112.3
29548.7	5221.7	15384.5	15384.5		37866.4	28200.0	11789.1	11789.1

15-10 续表1

单位：万元

分类	Classify	营业成本 Total Cost	主营业务成本 Cost of Principal Business
总 计	**Total**	**503733.3**	**489416.1**
一、住宿业	**Hotel Services**	**163544.5**	**152554.4**
#国有控股	State-holding Majority Shares	59466.9	51103.2
1.按登记注册类型分组	Grouped by Type of Registration		
内资企业	Domestic Funded Enterprises	135700.5	125435.6
国有企业	State-owned Enterprises	48045.0	39778.5
集体企业	Collective-owned Enterprises	1602.2	1602.2
股份合作企业	Cooperative Enterprises	854.8	854.8
联营企业	Joint Ownership Enterprises		
国有联营企业	State Joint Ownership Enterprises		
集体联营企业	Collective Joint Ownership Enterprises		
国有与集体联营企业	Joint State-collective Enterprises		
其他联营企业	Others Joint Ownership Enterprises		
有限责任公司	Limited Liability Corporations	52677.8	50720.2
国有独资企业	State Sole Funded Corporations	1065.2	1065.2
其他有限责任公司	Other Limited Liability Corporations	51612.6	49655.0
股份有限公司	Share-holding Corporations Ltd.	1153.5	1153.5
私营企业	Private Enterprises	28012.3	27994.7
私营独资企业	Private-funded Enterprises	1910.4	1910.4
私营合伙企业	Private Partnership Enterprises		
私营有限责任公司	Private Limited Liability Corporations	25300.5	25282.9
私营股份有限公司	Private Share-holding Corporations Ltd.	801.4	801.4
其他企业	Other Enterprises	3354.9	3331.7
港、澳、台商投资企业	Enterprises with Funds from Hong Kong, Macao &Taiwan	8970.7	8781.8
合资经营企业（港或澳、台资）	Joint-venture Enterprises	4971.8	4971.8
合作经营企业（港或澳、台资）	Cooperative Enterprises	3704.1	3515.2
港澳台商独资	Enterprise with Sole Fund	294.8	294.8
港澳台商独资股份有限公司	Share-holding Corporations Ltd. With their Investment		
外商投资企业	Foreign Funded Enterprises	18873.3	18337.0
中外合资经营企业	Joint-venture Enterprises	6840.3	6832.0
中外合作经营企业	Cooperation Enterprises	1550.1	1550.1
外资企业	Foreign Funded Enterprises	10482.9	9954.9
外商投资股份有限公司	Share-holding Corporations Ltd. With Foreign Funds		
2.按住宿行业小类分组	Grouped by Major Group of Hotel Services		
旅游饭店	Tourist Hotel	147040.6	136241.1
一般旅馆	Normal Hotel	13395.9	13205.3
其他住宿服务	Others	3108.0	3108.0

continued 1

(10 000 yuan)

营业税金及附加 Taxs and Other Changes	主营业务税金及附加 Taxs and Other Changes on Principal Business	销售费用 Sale Expenses	管理费用 Management Expenses	财务费用 Financial Expenses	营业利润 Business Profits	利润总额 Total Profits	应付职工薪酬 Salary Payable	本年应交增值税 Value Added Tax Payable
67786.5	**66721.6**	**375976.5**	**215110.5**	**19407.1**	**74277.6**	**66236.1**	**203079.1**	**743.7**
29219.9	**28936.0**	**159598.4**	**148340.6**	**12880.0**	**29724.5**	**22325.7**	**97462.4**	**158.2**
8919.0	8799.8	54518.9	45729.0	5109.0	3634.9	2479.7	39001.9	112.5
23488.1	23256.8	136598.4	114990.0	12841.5	15135.5	7821.8	83760.0	117.9
6829.6	6710.4	39799.3	35272.5	4108.3	-835.3	-856.9	28470.3	57.0
100.0	100.0	123.0	322.1	10.8	106.1	-3.3	450.5	1.5
106.3	106.3	728.4	388.2	4.3	-160.5	-158.5	646.9	
10002.8	9900.8	59170.0	46563.4	5529.9	10570.2	5458.1	34115.9	55.9
208.0	208.0	1720.2	880.6	10.6	-168.4	-188.5	1070.9	
9794.8	9692.8	57449.8	45682.8	5519.3	10738.6	5646.6	33045.0	55.9
331.3	331.3	2716.4	441.7	13.2	1349.4	1228.4	1193.1	
5234.5	5233.9	27770.3	27821.2	1969.1	4333.0	2253.5	16026.6	1.5
406.3	406.3	1628.7	617.6	87.0	96.4	96.4	1380.8	0.3
4749.8	4749.2	25840.5	26992.6	1882.1	4275.2	2195.7	14458.8	1.2
78.4	78.4	301.1	211.0		-38.6	-38.6	187.0	
883.6	874.1	6291.0	4180.9	1205.9	-227.4	-99.5	2856.7	2.0
1746.7	1699.0	9981.2	13329.1	242.7	322.8	259.0	5067.8	17.4
1256.0	1256.0	7227.2	8471.7	208.0	373.3	387.9	2855.7	3.2
438.1	390.4	2733.0	4382.5	-59.9	-70.3	-147.6	2134.5	14.2
52.6	52.6	21.0	474.9	94.6	19.8	18.7	77.6	
3985.1	3980.2	13018.8	20021.5	-204.2	14266.2	14244.9	8634.6	22.9
1268.6	1263.7	5125.4	7328.3	-480.0	2765.7	2813.2	2552.6	7.3
578.7	578.7	1919.2	1280.2	376.3	2544.5	2544.5	1614.7	
2137.8	2137.8	5974.2	11413.0	-100.5	8956.0	8887.2	4467.3	15.6
26220.2	25952.2	141915.9	133092.7	11806.3	26606.3	20404.5	85798.7	99.6
2332.6	2316.7	14140.4	11313.6	897.5	2753.8	1527.0	9424.1	58.6
667.1	667.1	3542.1	3934.3	176.2	364.4	394.2	2239.6	

15-10 续表2

单位：万元

分 类	Classify	单位数（个） Number (unit)	资产总计 Total Assets	流动资产合计 Circulating Funds	固定资产合计 Total Fixed Assets
二、餐饮业	**Catering Trade**	**286**	**573435.1**	**223727.8**	**143733.3**
#国有及国有控股	State-owned and State-holding Majority Shares	7	20555.1	6404.5	9083.0
1.按登记注册类型分组	Grouped by Type of Registration				
内资企业	Domestic Funded Enterprises	269	443764.9	176205.1	106532.9
国有企业	State-owned Enterprises	4	8334.6	2231.6	4982.5
集体企业	Collective-owned Enterprises	2	324.9	150.5	154.5
股份合作企业	Share-Holding Cooperative Enterprises	1	400.0	207.8	103.5
有限责任公司	Limited Liability Corporations	106	177626.5	87053.9	36479.1
其他有限责任公司	Others Limited Liability Corporations	106	177626.5	87053.9	36479.1
股份有限公司	Corporations Ltd.	6	68390.4	13769.7	21792.3
私营企业	Private Enterprises	146	184326.2	71130.3	42484.2
私营独资企业	Private-funded Enterprises	17	4708.4	1264.9	2038.9
私营合伙企业	Private Partnership Enterprises	7	4442.0	2889.6	316.2
私营有限责任公司	Private Limited Liability Corporations	118	173667.2	66190.9	40067.9
私营股份有限公司	Private Share-holding Corporations Ltd.	4	1508.6	784.9	61.2
其他企业	Other Enterprises	4	4362.3	1661.3	536.8
港、澳、台商投资企业	Enterprises with Funds from Hong Kong，Macao &Taiwan	7	72151.9	26892.3	18852.4
合资经营企业（港或澳、台资）	Joint-venture Enterprises	3	17597.1	8897.2	7960.0
合作经营企业（港或澳、台资）	Cooperative Enterprises	1	9159.2	1408.8	3648.1
独资经营企业	Enterprise with Sole Fund	3	45395.6	16586.3	7244.3
外商投资企业	Foreign Funded Enterprises	10	57518.3	20630.4	18348.0
中外合资经营企业	Joint-venture Enterprises	3	1676.5	878.2	69.8
中外合作经营企业	Cooperation Enterprises	1	134.3	76.9	8.7
外资企业	Foreign Funded Enterprises	5	52017.9	16773.0	17482.2
外商投资股份有限公司	Share-holding Corporations Ltd.	1	3689.6	2902.3	787.3
2.按餐饮行业小类分组	Grouped by Sector of Catering Trade				
正餐服务业	Dinner	277	500148.9	190308.7	131550.6
快餐服务业	Fast Food	8	71909.1	32169.8	12066.2
饮料及冷料服务	Beverages and Cold Drinks				
其他餐饮服务业	Other Catering Services	1	1377.1	1249.3	116.5

continued 2

(10 000 yuan)

固定资产原价 Original Value of Fixed Assets	累计折旧 Accumulated Depreciation	负债合计 Total Liabilities	流动负债合计 Circulating Liabilities	非流动负债 Non-Circulating Liabilities	所有者权益合计 Total Owners' Equities	实收资本 Paid in Capital	营业收入 Total Revenue	主营业务收入 Revenue from Principal Business
255308.8	**119550.1**	**313911.9**	**281844.3**	**32067.6**	**259523.2**	**328217.5**	**706671.3**	**700051.9**
14316.1	5440.3	13556.7	11158.2	2398.5	6998.4	6253.7	17209.5	17209.5
185090.4	86393.4	260407.6	234656.4	25751.2	183357.3	276237.9	537167.7	536154.7
5924.0	1088.7	7445.9	5047.4	2398.5	888.7	453.6	7031.5	7031.5
174.5	20.0	311.9	311.9		13.0	155.0	908.7	908.7
103.5	10.8	314.0	314.0		86.0	50.0	656.3	656.3
70261.5	39385.7	104707.5	98065.8	6641.7	72919.0	203069.7	227017.9	226914.9
70261.5	39385.7	104707.5	98065.8	6641.7	72919.0	203069.7	227017.9	226914.9
36388.5	13974.1	24285.3	23211.5	1073.8	44105.1	20330.6	58204.6	58155.3
69530.3	29742.7	121433.7	105796.5	15637.2	62892.5	51726.0	231811.1	230950.4
2551.1	1135.8	2651.6	2651.6		2056.8	1875.5	15422.5	15422.5
1008.2	703.9	1599.2	1599.2		2842.8	1484.2	7340.0	7320.0
65560.2	27534.7	116296.9	100659.7	15637.2	57370.3	47666.3	205145.4	204824.4
410.8	368.3	886.0	886.0		622.6	700.0	3903.2	3383.5
2708.1	2171.4	1909.3	1909.3		2453.0	453.0	11537.6	11537.6
40212.9	21499.2	30954.2	27327.8	3626.4	41197.7	29209.3	78198.8	78198.8
17749.2	9796.7	10150.4	9950.4	200.0	7446.7	6591.2	19636.4	19636.4
5598.1	1972.9	5362.9	5362.9		3796.3	1738.1	15688.2	15688.2
16865.6	9729.6	15440.9	12014.5	3426.4	29954.7	20880.0	42874.2	42874.2
30005.5	11657.5	22550.1	19860.1	2690.0	34968.2	22770.3	91304.8	85698.4
265.7	195.9	865.9	865.9		810.6	1810.0	2865.8	2865.8
69.7	61.0	110.4	110.4		23.9	100.0	473.7	473.4
26384.7	8902.5	19670.4	16980.4	2690.0	32347.5	18860.3	84486.3	78880.2
3285.4	2498.1	1903.4	1903.4		1786.2	2000.0	3479.0	3479.0
229217.7	105618.8	284319.5	258368.3	25951.2	215829.4	304714.1	623357.0	622330.7
25924.2	13880.9	28939.9	22823.5	6116.4	42969.2	22503.4	82709.7	77116.6
166.9	50.4	652.5	652.5		724.6	1000.0	604.6	604.6

15-10 续表3

单位：万元

分类	Classify	营业成本 Total Cost	主营业务成本 Cost of Principal Business
二、**餐饮业**	**Catering Trade**	340188.8	336861.7
#国有及国有控股	State-owned and State-holding Majority Shares	8899.2	8504.2
1.按登记注册类型分组	Grouped by Type of Registration		
内资企业	Domestic Funded Enterprises	267575.2	265372.5
国有企业	State-owned Enterprises	4271.1	4271.1
集体企业	Collective-owned Enterprises	579.0	579.0
股份合作企业	Share-Holding Cooperative Enterprises	328.0	328.0
有限责任公司	Limited Liability Corporations	104413.9	103263.9
其他有限责任公司	Others Limited Liability Corporations	104413.9	103263.9
股份有限公司	Corporations Ltd.	24703.2	24688.2
私营企业	Private Enterprises	127173.3	126135.6
私营独资企业	Private-funded Enterprises	11205.7	10480.0
私营合伙企业	Private Partnership Enterprises	3906.3	3906.3
私营有限责任公司	Private Limited Liability Corporations	110367.8	110055.8
私营股份有限公司	Private Share-holding Corporations Ltd.	1693.5	1693.5
其他企业	Other Enterprises	6106.7	6106.7
港、澳、台商投资企业	Enterprises with Funds from Hong Kong，Macao &Taiwan	29225.1	29225.1
合资经营企业（港或澳、台资）	Joint-venture Enterprises	8203.2	8203.2
合作经营企业（港或澳、台资）	Cooperative Enterprises	5591.7	5591.7
独资经营企业	Enterprise with Sole Fund	15430.2	15430.2
外商投资企业	Foreign Funded Enterprises	43388.5	42264.1
中外合资经营企业	Joint-venture Enterprises	1590.3	1590.3
中外合作经营企业	Cooperation Enterprises	218.4	218.4
外资企业	Foreign Funded Enterprises	40269.6	39145.2
外商投资股份有限公司	Share-holding Corporations Ltd.	1310.2	1310.2
2.按餐饮行业小类分组	Grouped by Sector of Catering Trade		
正餐服务业	Dinner	302824.8	301017.1
快餐服务业	Fast Food	36464.5	35340.1
饮料及冷料服务	Beverages and Cold Drinks		
其他餐饮服务业	Other Catering Services	899.5	504.5

continued 3

(10 000 yuan)

营业税金及附加 Taxs and Other Changes	主营业务税金及附加 Taxs and Other Changes on Principal Business	销售费用 Sale Expenses	管理费用 Managenment Expenses	财务费用 Financial Expenses	营业利润 Business Profits	利润总额 Total Profits	应付职工薪酬 Salary Payable	本年应交增值税 Value Added Tax Payable
38566.6	37785.6	216378.1	66769.9	6527.1	44553.1	43910.4	105616.7	585.5
932.5	932.5	5577.6	1212.1	7.5	974.3	973.2	3501.5	
29265.5	28766.8	162061.9	52770.9	5821.8	25613.4	24143.0	86262.4	541.8
364.2	364.2	1347.7	785.1	17.9	245.3	174.2	1552.5	
44.0	44.0	55.9	240.0		-10.2	-12.6	175.9	
30.0	30.0	4.4	207.2	1.8	84.9	85.3	124.8	
12444.5	12300.7	74123.8	22042.5	1887.9	13432.1	12787.4	37476.5	45.1
12444.5	12300.7	74123.8	22042.5	1887.9	13432.1	12787.4	37476.5	45.1
2998.1	2998.1	23998.8	3310.5	553.6	5955.0	6197.1	10933.4	354.6
12673.7	12318.8	60265.9	25964.3	3266.5	3767.8	2772.4	34741.9	142.1
872.3	800.3	2567.4	936.5	60.6	577.7	577.8	2458.0	5.1
376.3	376.3	1644.5	686.2	360.1	346.6	351.7	1289.6	
11214.5	10931.6	54959.9	24029.9	2830.6	2785.1	1784.5	30408.8	137.0
210.6	210.6	1094.1	311.7	15.2	58.4	58.4	585.5	
711.0	711.0	2265.4	221.3	94.1	2138.5	2139.2	1257.4	
4234.1	4234.1	33532.5	5733.6	982.1	4869.4	5688.6	10730.9	42.9
974.9	974.9	6558.3	2393.4	433.5	1073.1	1618.9	3432.7	41.7
862.8	862.8	7642.4	577.9	156.8	856.6	589.1	1470.0	
2396.4	2396.4	19331.8	2762.3	391.8	2939.7	3480.6	5828.2	1.2
5067.0	4784.7	20783.7	8265.4	-276.8	14070.3	14078.8	8623.4	0.8
140.3	140.3	1100.8	186.8	11.6	-158.9	-159.6	341.0	
26.5	26.5	78.1	167.5		-17.1	-17.1	97.5	
4718.9	4436.6	18259.0	7376.9	-329.2	14179.6	14188.6	7685.4	0.8
181.3	181.3	1345.8	534.2	40.8	66.7	66.9	499.5	
34048.8	33550.1	185754.1	62173.5	6218.9	37861.9	36642.8	95009.2	584.3
4484.0	4201.7	30398.2	4461.9	307.9	6986.6	7493.0	10438.0	1.2
33.8	33.8	225.8	134.5	0.3	-295.4	-225.4	169.5	

15-11 限额以上批发和零售业商品购进、销售和库存总额（2011年）

单位：个、万元

分　　类	Classify	单位数 Number of Enterprises	商品购进额 Total Purchases	进口 Exports
总　　计	**Total**	**596**	**27583259.4**	**582091.0**
一、批发企业	**Wholesale Enterprises**	**209**	**16901331.5**	**331451.6**
#国有控股	State-holding Enterprises	45	8077862.8	268378.9
1.按登记注册类型分组	Grouped by Registration Status			
内资企业	Domestic Funded Enterprises	196	14872993.3	331451.6
国有企业	State-owned Enterprises	31	4953050.8	76165.8
集体企业	Collective-owned Enterprises	3	20136.5	
股份合作企业	Cooperative Enterprises			
联营企业	Joint Ownership Enterprises	1	2739.4	
国有联营企业	State Joint Ownership Enterprises			
集体联营企业	Collective Joint Ownership Enterprises	1	2739.4	
国有与集体联营企业	Joint State-collective Ownership Enterprises			
其他联营企业	Other Joint Ownership Enterprises			
有限责任公司	Limited Liability Corporations	98	7103062.5	225578.3
国有独资公司	State-funded Corporations	1	113951.4	113951.4
其他有限责任公司	Other Limited Liability Corporations	97	6989111.1	111626.9
股份有限公司	Stock Limited Corporation	4	1476245.8	
私营企业	Private Enterprises	58	1312453.3	29707.5
私营独资企业	Private-funded Enterprises	3	94169.4	
私营有限责任公司	Private Limited Liability Corporations	52	942767.6	29707.5
私营股份有限公司	Private Share Holding Corporations	3	275516.3	
其他企业	Others	1	5305.0	
港、澳、台商投资企业	Enterprises Funded by Hong Kong, Macao and Taiwan	4	378858.5	
与港澳台商合资经营	Joint-venture with Funds from Hong Kong, Macao and Taiwan	1	271391.4	
港澳台商独资	Enterprises with Sole Investment from Hong Kong Macau and Taiwan	3	107467.1	
外商投资企业	Foreign Funded Enterprises	3	1622550.5	
中外合资企业	Sino-foreign Joint Ventures	3	1622550.5	
外资企业	Foreign Owned Enterprises			
个体工商户	Individually-owned Business	6	26929.2	
2.按国民经济行业分组	Grouped by Economic Sector			
农林牧产品批发业	Wholesale of Agricultural,Forestry and Animal Husbandry Products	4	25687.3	
#种子批发	Wholesale of Seed	1	2977.8	
食品、饮料及烟草制品批发	Wholesale of Food, Beverages and Tobacco Products	14	787438.0	
#烟草制品批发业	Wholesale of Tobacco and Tobacco Products	1	610632.0	

Total Sales of Enterprises Above Designated Size in Wholesale and Retail Trades Grouped by Category of Commodities（2011）

(unit,10 000 yuan)

商品销售额 Sales Value	批发额 Wholesale Trade	出口 Exports	零售额 Retail Trade	期末商品库存额 Value of Stock at Final goods
31233567.1	**17364948.6**	**682832.6**	**13868618.5**	**1636744.1**
18954529.0	**16734448.3**	**676481.7**	**2220080.7**	**737996.7**
8736588.5	7577610.2	578277.8	1158978.3	331995.9
16519500.1	14379312.9	676481.7	2140187.2	686702.7
5354598.3	4875035.7	350142.9	479562.6	247354.6
23273.1	23273.1			2286.8
3192.4	3168.5		23.9	265.8
3192.4	3168.5		23.9	265.8
8080979.7	7120714.7	285427.7	960265.0	298569.0
112540.1	112540.1	112540.1		5953.0
7968439.6	7008174.6	172887.6	960265.0	292616.0
1546595.9	958900.2		587695.7	48971.4
1505560.7	1392920.7	40911.1	112640.0	89247.1
109844.2	97747.6		12096.6	103.1
1114872.3	1064037.2	38492.5	50835.1	88732.1
280844.2	231135.9	2418.6	49708.3	411.9
5300.0	5300.0			8.0
390168.3	310644.8		79523.5	21477.0
280753.9	203903.4		76850.5	0.1
109414.4	106741.4		2673.0	21476.9
2014200.6	2014200.6			26517.7
2014200.6	2014200.6			26517.7
30660.0	30290.0		370.0	3299.3
22762.9	22730.4		32.5	12543.1
3116.6	3116.6			1299.5
1070200.2	1018305.8		51894.4	47525.0
846280.3	846280.3			26544.0

15-11 续表1

单位：个、万元

分类	Classify	单位数 Number of Enterprises	商品购进额 Total Purchases	进口 Exports
纺织、服装及家庭用品批发业	Wholesale of Textiles, Garments and Daily Articles	12	1231630.1	
文化、体育用品及器材批发	Wholesale of Culture, Sports Articles and Equipments	6	164720.8	
#体育用品及器材批发	Wholesale of Sports Articles and Equipments			
医药及医疗器材批发	Wholesale of Medicines and Medical Appliances	26	1250601.7	
#西药批发	Wholesale of Western Medicine	18	1107892.0	
中药批发	Wholesale of Chinese Medicine	8	142709.7	
矿产品、建材及化工产品批发	Wholesale of Mineral Products, Building Materials and Chemical Products	92	11586942.9	289962.6
#煤炭及制品批发	Wholesale of Coal and Related Products	10	885509.5	
石油及制品批发	Wholesale of Petroleum and Related Products	24	6735113.3	
金属及金属矿批发	Wholesale of Metals and Metal Minerals	44	2901944.6	288306.8
建材批发业	Wholesale of Building Materials	7	951235.2	
化肥批发	Wholesale of Chemical Fetilizers	5	79747.3	
其他化工产品批发	Wholesale of Other Chemical Products	1	2604.9	
机械设备、五金交电及电子产品批发业	Wholesale of Machinery, Hardwares, Transport Means and Electronic Products	47	1795185.5	40718.3
#农业机械批发	Wholesale of Agricultural Machinery	2	12442.0	
汽车批发	Wholesale of Automobile			
汽车、摩托车及零配件批发业	Wholesale of Motor Vehicles, Motorcycles and Parts	10	661682.9	
家用电器批发	Wholesale of Electronic Household Equipments	5	338915.9	
计算机、软件及辅助设备批发业	Wholesale of Computers,Softwares and Peripherals	5	372489.3	
贸易经纪与代理	Trade Manage and Agent	7	53504.6	770.7
其他批发业	Other Wholesales	1	5620.6	
3.经营形式分组	Grouped by Means of Operation			
独立门店	Independent Shop	154	10132741.2	309272.6
连锁总店	Headquarter of Chain Store	1	610632.0	
连锁门店	Chain Store			
其他	Other	54	6157958.3	22179.0
二、零售企业	**Retail Trade**	**387**	**10681927.9**	**250639.4**
#国有控股	State-holding Enterprises	18	509423.9	1559.0
1.按登记注册类型分组	Grouped by Registration Status			
内资企业	Domestic Funded Enterprises	274	8527968.3	173089.9
国有企业	State-owned Enterprises	18	368392.3	1559.0
集体企业	Collective-owned Enterprises	18	38263.5	
股份合作企业	Cooperative Enterprises	1	3459.3	

continued 1

(unit,10 000 yuan)

商品销售额 Sales Value	批发额 Wholesale Trade	出口 Exports	零售额 Retail Trade	期末商品库存额 Value of Stock at Final goods
1297277.1	803878.7		493398.4	41133.8
175772.1	174429.9	2374.7	1342.2	34869.1
1655934.0	1562523.2		93410.8	69923.5
1497294.0	1414249.4		83044.6	58337.1
158640.0	148273.8		10366.2	11586.4
12728146.4	11399697.8	386022.7	1328448.6	386122.4
1166516.8	954315.1	2418.6	212201.7	98649.3
7011532.2	5979019.7		1032512.5	216399.1
3459272.4	3458461.6	352486.6	810.8	55252.0
971670.8	888771.1	2334.6	82899.7	6545.3
85982.5	85958.6		23.9	8885.3
2227.4	2227.4			377.5
1937052.3	1685868.5	256660.3	251183.8	139250.5
14258.1	14258.1			1608.2
713482.1	564658.9	189918.8	148823.2	35244.3
332661.2	332661.2			46014.9
408267.0	316646.9		91620.1	108.8
64884.0	64514.0	31424.0	370.0	3508.7
2500.0	2500.0			3120.6
11369324.0	9312825.3	665896.3	2056498.7	519870.3
846280.3	846280.3			26544.0
6738924.7	6575342.7	10585.4	163582.0	191582.4
12279038.1	**630500.3**	**6350.9**	**11648537.8**	**898747.4**
490904.8			490904.8	91629.9
9598597.1	586337.4	6350.9	9012259.7	741346.4
341180.9			341180.9	70171.5
75474.4			75474.4	3240.2
3459.2			3459.2	0.1

15-11 续表2

单位：个、万元

分　　类	Classify	单位数 Number of Enterprises	商品购进额 Total Purchases	进口 Exports
联营企业	Joint Ownership Enterprises	1	3325.5	
国有联营企业	State Joint Ownership Enterprises			
集体联营企业	Collective Joint Ownership Enterprises	1	3325.5	
国有与集体联营企业	Joint State-collective Ownership Enterprises			
其他联营企业	Other Joint Ownership Enterprises			
有限责任公司	Limited Liability Corporations	126	5052382.8	62133.0
国有独资公司	State-funded Corporations	2	53571.7	
其他有限责任公司	Other Limited Liability Corporations	124	4998811.1	62133.0
股份有限公司	Stock Limited Corporation	8	990617.3	26908.4
私营企业	Private Enterprises	99	1787288.9	82489.5
私营独资企业	Private-funded Enterprises	10	13012.2	
私营合伙企业	Private Partnership Enterprises	3	4826.0	
私营有限责任公司	Private Limited Liability Corporations	79	1650041.3	82489.5
私营股份有限公司	Private Share Holding Corporations	7	119409.4	
其他企业	Others	3	284238.7	
港、澳、台商投资企业	Enterprises Funded by Hong Kong, Macao and Taiwan	10	841726.6	77549.5
与港澳台商合资经营	Joint-venture with Funds from Hong Kong, Macao and Taiwan	2	204015.0	
港澳台商独资	Enterprises with Sole Investment from Hong Kong Macau and Taiwan	8	637711.6	77549.5
港澳台商投资股份有限公司	Share Holding Enterprises Funded by Overseas Chinese from Hong Kong, Macao & Taiwan			
外商投资企业	Foreign Funded Enterprises	19	1087337.3	
中外合资营企业	Sino-foreign Joint Ventures	2	204015.0	
外资企业	Foreign Owned Enterprises	8	637711.6	77549.5
外商投资股份有限公司	Limited Company Funded by Foreign Investment	1		
个体工商户	Individually-owned Business	84	224895.7	
2.按国民经济行业分组	Grouped by Registered Kind			
综合零售	General Retail Sales Trade	92	2443878.0	8.5
#百货零售	Retail of Daily Goods	40	1243482.9	8.5
超级市场零售	Retail of Supermarkets	40	1126459.1	
其他综合零售	Other General Retail Sales Trade	12	73936.0	
食品、饮料及烟草制品专门零售	Retail of Food，Beverage and Tobaccos	23	81516.7	
纺织、服装及日用品专门零售	Retail of Textiles，Garments and Daily Articles	46	1251543.1	
#服装零售	Retail of Garments	30	1069324.8	
文化、体育用品及器材专门零售	Retail of Culture , Sports Articles and Equipments	23	175975.9	
#图书零售	Retail of Books and Mangzines	4	71626.3	

continued 2

(unit,10 000 yuan)

商品销售额 Sales Value	批发额 Wholesale Trade	出口 Exports	零售额 Retail Trade	期末商品库存额 Value of Stock at Final goods
4748.7			4748.7	247.0
4748.7			4748.7	247.0
5698807.7	386341.7		5312466.0	429229.7
52108.4			52108.4	16771.4
5646699.3	386341.7		5260357.6	412458.3
1154529.4	125855.5		1028673.9	76342.3
2021972.2	40772.5	6350.9	1981199.7	160555.3
41262.8			41262.8	4741.5
4760.3			4760.3	579.3
1838769.0	40652.7	6350.9	1798116.3	146352.1
137180.1	119.8		137060.3	8882.4
298424.6	33367.7		265056.9	1560.3
1047155.7	12900.3		1034255.4	89778.4
258118.7			258118.7	18089.2
789037.0	12900.3		776136.7	71689.2
1302512.9			1302512.9	47100.7
258118.7			258118.7	18089.2
789037.0	12900.3		776136.7	71689.2
10070.7			10070.7	0.1
330772.4	31262.6		299509.8	20521.9
2881776.7	11091.1		2870685.6	218355.8
1522378.0	28.8		1522349.2	75994.7
1280515.6	11062.3		1269453.3	137992.7
78883.1			78883.1	4368.4
200772.4	7794.4		192978.0	48729.4
1323227.4	98712.9		1224514.5	80554.7
1118717.1	98045.8		1020671.3	57174.4
247021.2	42531.2		204490.0	67317.7
59206.3			59206.3	27325.8

15-11 续表3

单位：个、万元

分　类	Classify	单位数 Number of Enterprises	商品购进额 Total Purchases	进口 Exports
医药及医疗器材专门零售	Retail of Medicines and Medical Appliances	11	128825.5	
#药品零售	Retail of Medicines	11	128825.5	
汽车、摩托车、燃料及零配件专门零售	Retail of Motor Vehicles, Motorcycles, Feuls and Parts	133	4568277.1	219430.9
#汽车零售	Retailof Motor Vehicles	101	4228010.8	219430.9
家用电器及电子产品专门零售	Retail of Household Electronic Equipments and Products	30	1180325.3	
#日用家电设备零售	Retail of Household Electronic Equipments	18	1014175.1	
计算机、软件及辅助设备零售	Retail of Computer , Software and Auxiliary Equipments	8	79714.7	
通讯设备零售	Retail of Communications	4	86435.5	
五金、家具及室内装修材料专门零售	Retail of Hardwares , Furniture and Room Decorative Building	21	791143.3	31200.0
货摊、无店铺及其他零售	No Fixed Stores and Other Retails	8	60443.0	
3.按经营形式分	Grouped by Means of Operation			
独立门店	Independent Shop	333	7905641.6	245446.4
连锁总店	Headquarter of Chain Store	13	669133.1	
连锁门店	Chain Store	10	1261266.2	
其他	Other	31	845887.0	5193.0
4.按零售业态分	Grouped by Retail Size			
有店铺	Retail of Shop	384	10595713.8	250639.4
便利店	Convenience Store	4	10211.2	
食杂店	Grocery Store			
折扣店	Dime Store			
超市	Supermarket	33	156013.1	
大型超市	Larget Supermarket	14	945494.2	
仓储会员店	Warehouse Club			
百货店	Department Store	49	1448051.6	8.5
专业店	Special Store	172	3931388.6	39980.5
专卖店	Monopoly Store	83	1771971.8	175816.4
家居建材商店	Home-building Material Store	13	693561.9	31200.0
购物中心	Shopping Center	10	1344625.3	
厂家直销中心	Factory Outlet Center	6	294396.1	3634.0
无店铺零售	Retail of No-shop	3	86214.1	
电视购物	TV Shopping	2	38447.8	
邮购	Mail Order			
网上商店	Online Stores	1	47766.3	
自动售货亭	Vending Machine			
电话购物	Tele Shopping			

continued 3

商品销售额 Sales Value	批发额 Wholesale Trade	出口 Exports	零售额 Retail Trade	期末商品库存额 Value of Stock at Final goods
138841.5	17548.3		121293.2	21888.8
138841.5	17548.3		121293.2	21888.8
5093043.6	258668.7		4834374.9	378528.9
4700283.9	245224.0		4455059.9	367658.8
1322001.9	173216.9	6350.9	1148785.0	57442.8
1135968.3	159728.2		976240.1	38115.4
92749.7	13488.7	6350.9	79261.0	5567.7
93283.9			93283.9	13759.7
1007372.0	20880.8		986491.2	24192.8
64981.4	56.0		64925.4	1736.5
8978650.3	510694.0		8467956.3	627814.4
760978.4	17269.3		743709.1	48040.3
1409883.4	75556.3		1334327.1	145237.7
1129526.0	26980.7	6350.9	1102545.3	77655.0
12176572.1	617011.6		11559560.5	895731.3
12726.6	28.8		12697.8	2205.4
201434.0	119.8		201314.2	20283.2
1036825.8	11534.2		1025291.6	123304.9
1765416.2			1765416.2	82205.3
4313073.3	371023.6		3942049.7	359728.6
2133002.8	25626.0		2107376.8	231633.2
907119.3	20844.8		886274.5	17544.9
1478061.0	187834.4		1290226.6	39328.7
328913.1			328913.1	19497.1
102466.0	13488.7	6350.9	88977.3	3016.1
47568.9			47568.9	95.0
54897.1	13488.7	6350.9	41408.4	2921.1

15-12 限额以上住宿和餐饮业经营情况（2011年）

Statistic on Hotel Services and Catering Services above Designed Size（2011）

单位：个、万元　　　　(unit、10 000 yuan)

分　　类	Classify	单位数 Number of Enterprises	营业额 Business Revenue	客房收入 From Hotel Room	餐费收入 From Meals	商品销售收入 From Commodities
总　　计	**Total**	**598**	**1373424**	**316299**	**927696**	**66499**
一、住宿业	**Lodging Services**	**199**	**571828**	**288470**	**233917**	**11760**
#国有控股	State-holding Enterprises	58	167362	77139	69866	4171
(一)按登记注册类型分组	Grouped by Registration Status					
内资企业	Domestic Funded Enterprises	184	465166	229714	197099	9267
国有企业	State-owned Enterprises	51	136942	63318	58516	3128
集体企业	Collective-owned Enterprises	4	3098	1181	1303	245
股份合作企业	Cooperative Enterprises	1	1922	426	1235	21
联营企业	Joint Ownership Enterprises					
国有联营企业	State Joint Ownership Enterprises					
集体联营企业	Collective Joint Ownership Enterprises					
国有与集体联营企业	Joint State-collective Ownership Enterprises					
其他联营企业	Other Joint Ownership Enterprises					
有限责任公司	Limited Liability Corporations	71	206312	105310	86319	3385
国有独资企业	State-funded Corporations	1	3716	1356	1565	
其他有限责任公司	Other Limited Liability Corporations	70	202595	103954	84754	3385
股份有限公司	Stock Limited Corporation	4	6011	3166	889	28
私营企业	Private Enterprises	47	95318	48144	42796	1948
私营独资企业	Private-funded Enterprises	5	4671	1814	2581	27
私营合伙企业	Private Partnership Enterprises					
私营有限责任公司	Private Limited Liability Corporations	41	89294	45873	39319	1921
私营股份有限公司	Private Share Holding Corporations	1	1353	458	896	
其他企业	Others	6	15563	8169	6041	513

15-12 续表1 continued 1

单位：个、万元 (unit、10 000 yuan)

分 类	Classify	单位数 Number of Enterprises	营业额 Business Revenue	客房收入 From Hotel Room	餐费收入 From Meals	商品销售收入 From Commodities
港、澳、台商投资企业	Enterprises Funded by Hong Kong, Macao and Taiwan	7	35694	15639	12736	572
合资经营企业 (港或澳、台资)	Joint-venture with Funds from Hong Kong, Macao and Taiwan	4	22672	8275	7566	511
合作经营企业 (港或澳、台资)	Cooperative Enterprises with Funds from Hong Kong Macau and Taiwan	2	11117	6407	4264	20
港澳台商独资	Enterprises with Sole Investment from Hong Kong Macau and Taiwan	1	1904	958	906	41
港澳台商投资股份有限公司	Share Holding Enterprises Funded by Overseas Chinese from Hong Kong, Macao & Taiwan					
外商投资企业	Foreign Funded Enterprises	8	70969	43117	24082	1921
中外合资经营企业	Sino-foreign Joint Ventures	3	22827	16242	5742	231
中外合作经营企业	Sino-Foreign Cooperative Operation Enterprises	2	9251	3890	4146	1170
外资企业	Foreign Owned Enterprises	3	38891	22985	14195	520
外商投资股份有限公司	Limited Company Funded by Foreign Investment					
个体工商户	Individually-owned Business					
（二）按住宿行业小类分组	Grouped in Classes According to Lodging Industry					
旅游饭店	Tour Restaurant	161	513945	262254	209773	10362
一般旅馆	Common Hotel	35	46094	22429	20328	1008
其他住宿服务	Others	3	11789	3788	3816	390

15-12 续表2 continued 2

单位：个、万元 (unit,10 000 yuan)

分类	Classify	单位数 Number of Enterprises	营业额 Business Revenue	客房收入 From Hotel Room	餐费收入 From Meals	商品销售收入 From Commodities
二、餐饮业	**Catering Trade**	**399**	**801596**	**27828**	**693780**	**54738**
#国有及国有控股	State-holding Enterprises	8	18242	1555	11528	1695
1.按登记注册类型分组	Grouped by Registration Status					
内资企业	Domestic Funded Enterprises	283	566373	23936	479455	46087
国有企业	State-owned Enterprises	6	15003	1626	7978	3840
集体企业	Collective-owned Enterprises	2	909		909	
股份合作企业	Cooperative Enterprises	1	656	59	570	27
有限责任公司	Limited Liability Corporations	114	244290	18775	187833	30174
其他有限责任公司	Other Limited Liability Corporations	114	244290	18775	187833	30174
股份有限公司	Stock Limited Corporation	6	58305	1550	42291	7516
私营企业	Private Enterprises	149	235245	1683	228355	4327
私营独资企业	Private-funded Enterprises	18	15921	35	14840	1004
私营合伙企业	Private Partnership Enterprises	7	7793		7595	153
私营有限责任公司	Private Limited Liability Corporations	120	207637	1553	202666	3143
私营股份有限公司	Private Share Holding Corporations	4	3895	95	3254	27
其他企业	Others	5	11966	243	11520	203
港、澳、台商投资企业	Enterprises Funded by Hong Kong, Macao and Taiwan	7	77915	1216	73808	1917
合资经营企业(港或澳、台资)	Joint-venture with Funds from Hong Kong, Macao and Taiwan	3	19636	483	16636	1550
合作经营企业(港或澳、台资)	Cooperative Enterprises with Funds from Hong Kong Macau and Taiwan	1	15622		15622	
独资经营企业	Enterprises with Sole Investment	3	42657	734	41550	367
外商投资企业	Foreign Funded Enterprises	11	82751	186	76188	772
中外合资经营企业	Sino-foreign Joint Ventures	4	3312		3292	20
中外合作经营企业	Sino-Foreign Cooperative Operation Enterprises	1	474		474	
外资企业	Foreign Owned Enterprises	5	75486	186	69672	22
个体工商户	Individually-owned Business	98	74557	2491	64329	5962
2.按餐饮行业小类分组	Grouped by Catering Middle Sector					
正餐服务	Dinner Services	380	713547	27095	612232	54738
快餐服务	Fast Food Services	12	84459	734	78126	
饮料及冷饮服务	Beverage and Cold Beverage Services					
其他餐饮服务	Other Catering Services	7	3591		3421	

15-13 限额以上批发和零售业主要商品分类销售额（2011年）

Sale Values of Enterprises above Designated Size of Wholesale and Retail Trades by Category of Main Commodities（2011）

单位：万元 (10 000 yuan)

分　类	Classify	销售合计 Total Sales Value	批发 Wholesale Value	零售 Retail Value
总　计	**Total**	**28629990**	**14918325**	**13711665**
粮油、食品、饮料、烟酒类	Grain and Oil, Food and Beverages, Alcoholic Drinks and Tobacco	2128998	1064082	1064916
粮油、食品类	Cereals, Oils and Foodstuffs	786245	113858	672387
#粮油类	Grain and Oil	357710	40608	317102
肉禽蛋类	Meat, Poultry and Eggs	66824	5	66820
水产品类	Aquatic Products	83837		83837
蔬菜类	Vegetables	61783	26584	35199
干鲜瓜果类	Fresh and Dried Fruit Category	71966	21423	50544
饮料类	Beverages	298227	79507	218720
烟酒类	Tobacco and Liquor	1044526	870717	173809
服装、鞋帽、针纺织品类	Clothing, Shoes, Hats and Textiles	3357520	679909	2677612
服装类	Clothing	2825241	609130	2216111
鞋帽类	Shoes and Hats	336357	9487	326871
针纺织品类	Knitwear and Textiles	195922	61292	134630
化妆品类	Cosmetics	237775	31161	206614
金银珠宝类	Gold,Silver and Jewelry	420536	11987	408550
日用品类	Articles for Daily Use	537324	101155	436169
#洗涤用品类	Bathing and Washing	166185	77607	88578
儿童玩具类	Children's Toys	70193	12267	57926
五金、电料类	Hardwear and Electrical Materials	164148	61076	103072
体育、娱乐用品类	Sports and Recreation Articles	204390	30603	173787
书报杂志类	Newspapers and Magazines	178256	115685	62571
电子出版物及音像制品类	E-journal and Video Products	5102		5102
家用电器和音像器材类	Household Appliances and Video Products	1185599	441787	743812
中西药品类	Traditional Chinese and Western Medicine	829041	611928	217114
#西药类	Western Medicine	621082	432864	188218
中草药及中成药类	Chinese Herbal Medicine and Traditional Chinese Medicine	71261	58555	12707
文化办公用品类	Cultural and Official Goods	658190	361313	296877
家具类	Furniture	544173	6617	537557
通讯器材类	Communication Appliances	264099	44571	219527
煤炭及制品类	Coal and Related Products	1035486	722292	313194
木材及制品类	Wood and Wooden Products	21	21	
石油及制品类	Petroleum and Related Products	6527767	5061651	1466116
化工材料及制品类	Raw Chemical Materials	69581	69581	
#化肥类	Chemical Fertilizers	56170	56170	
金属材料类	Metal Materials	4165276	4165276	
建筑及装潢材料类	Buildings and Decoration Materials	765802	209676	556126
机电产品及设备类	Mechanical and Electrical Products	419992	419387	604
#农机类	Agricultural Machinery			
汽车类	Automobile	4852732	692017	4160715
种子饲料类	Seeds and Feedstuff	22	22	
棉麻类	Cotton,Hemp	5844	5844	
其他类	Others	72314	10684	61630

15-14 亿元以上商品交易市场成交情况（2011年）

Basic Statistics on Commodity Exchange Markets of Transaction Value over 100 Million Yuan（2011）

分 类	Classify	年末出租摊位数（个）Number of Rental Booths at Year-end (unit)	成交额（万元）Turnover (10 000 yuan)
粮油、食品、饮料、烟酒类	Grain and Oil, Food and Beverages, Alcoholic Drinks and Tobacco	4392	694039
粮油、食品类	Cereals, Oils and Foodstuffs	2484	620567
#粮油类	Grain and Oil	328	298556
肉禽蛋类	Meat, Poultry and Eggs	271	62798
水产品类	Aquatic Products	77	5149
蔬菜类	Vegetables	1277	190258
干鲜果品类	Fresh and Dried Fruit Category	531	63806
饮料类	Beverages	1812	70461
烟酒类	Tobacco and Liquor	96	3011
服装、鞋帽、针纺织品类	Clothing, Shoes, Hats and Textiles	8204	406841
服装类	Clothing	5968	178662
鞋帽类	Shoes and Hats	1113	155129
针纺织品类	Knitwear and Textiles	1123	73050
化妆品类	Cosmetics	50	1409
金银珠宝类	Gold,Silver and Jewelry		
日用品类	Articles for Daily Use	102	1721
#洗涤用品类	Bathing and Washing	99	1458
儿童玩具类	Children's Toys	3	3
五金、电料类	Hardwear and Electrical Materials	321	13817
体育、娱乐用品类	Sports and Recreation Articles	35	680
书报杂志类	Newspapers and Magazines	2	35
电子出版物及音像制品类	E-journal and Video Products	2	36
家用电器和音像器材类	Household Appliances and Video Products	184	28056
中西药品类	Traditional Chinese and Western Medicine	422	35435
#西药类	Western Medicine		
中草药及中成药类	Chinese Herbal Medicine and Traditional Chinese Medicine	422	35435
文化办公用品类	Cultural and Official Goods	1545	109648
家具类	Furniture		
通讯器材类	Communication Appliances	177	2360
煤炭及制品类	Coal and Related Products		
木材及制品类	Wood and Wooden Products		
石油及制品类	Petroleum and Related Products		
化工材料及制品类	Raw Chemical Materials		
#化肥类	Chemical Fertilizers		
金属材料类	Metal Materials		
建筑及装潢材料类	Buildings and Decoration Materials	306	14388
机电产品及设备类	Mechanical and Electrical Products		
#农机类	Agricultural Machinery		
汽车类	Automobile	1396	625183
种子饲料类	Seeds and Feedstuff		
棉麻类	Cotton,Hemp		
其他类	Others	20	1294

15-15 批发和零售业连锁经营情况（2011年）

Basic Statistics on Chain Business of Wholesale and Retail Trades（2011）

指　　标	Item	本年合计 Total	上年合计 Total Last Year	本年直营店 Ragular Chain
一、门店总数（个）	**Number of Stores(unit)**	**485**	**454**	**401**
二、年末从业人员数（人）	**Employees at Year-end(person)**	**13509**	**13521**	**11627**
三、年末零售营业面积（平方米）	**Operating Area of Retail at Year-end(sq.m)**	**611786**	**409983**	**447386**
四、连锁门店商品购进额（万元）	**Purchases Value of Chain Stores(1 0000 yuan)**	**1275149**	**978607**	**1205011**
#统一配送商品购进额	Centralized Purchases and Delivery	898863	677559	898863
#自有配送中心配送商品购进额	Self Centralized Purchases and Delivery	658626	494670	658626
非自有配送中心配送商品购进额	Non-self Centralized Purchases and Delivery	52496	29554	52496
五、连锁门店商品销售额（万元）	**Sales Value of Chain Store(1 0000 yuan)**	**1636871**	**1278806**	**1533883**
#零售额	Retail Value	790590	628185	687602

15-15 续表 continued

指　　标	Item	上年直营店 Ragular Chain Last Year	本年加盟店 Franchise	上年加盟店 Franchise Last Year
一、门店总数（个）	**Number of Stores(unit)**	**390**	**84**	**64**
二、年末从业人员数（人）	**Employees at Year-end(person)**	**12072**	**1882**	**1449**
三、年末零售营业面积（平方米）	**Operating Area of Retail at Year-end(sq.m)**	**315983**	**164400**	**94000**
四、连锁门店商品购进额（万元）	**Purchases Value of Chain Stores(1 0000 yuan)**	**940076**	**70138**	**38531**
#统一配送商品购进额	Centralized Purchases and Delivery	677559		
#自有配送中心配送商品购进额	Self Centralized Purchases and Delivery	494670		
非自有配送中心配送商品购进额	Non-self Centralized Purchases and Delivery	29554		
五、连锁门店商品销售额（万元）	**Sales Value of Chain Store(1 0000 yuan)**	**1220730**	**102988**	**58076**
#零售额	Retail Value	570109	102988	58076

15-16 住宿和餐饮业连锁经营情况（2011年）

Basic Statistics on Chain Business of Hotels and Catering Services（2011）

指　　标	Item	本年合计 Total	上年合计 Total Last Year
一、门店总数（个）	**Number of Stores(unit)**	**109**	**77**
二、年末从业人员数（人）	**Employees at Year-end(person)**	**6292**	**6778**
三、年末餐饮营业面积（平方米）	**Operating Area of Retail at Year-end(sq.m)**	**59856**	**45800**
四、客房总数（间）	**Guest Rooms(room)**		
五、床位数（张）	**Guest Beds(bed)**		
六、餐位数（位）	**Dining Seats(set)**	**18149**	**14988**
七、连锁门店商品购进额（万元）	**Operating Area of Catering Services at Year end(room)(1 0000 yuan)**	**65501**	**39391**
#统一配送商品购进额	Centralized Purchases and Delivery	60279	34488
#自有配送中心配送商品购进额	Self Centralized Purchases and Delivery	11348	10984
非自有配送中心配送商品购进额	Non-self Centralized Purchases and Delivery		
八、连锁门店商品营业额（万元）	**Sales Value of Chain Store(1 0000 yuan)**	**102252**	**75028**
#餐费收入	Catering Revenues	101831	74667
商品销售额	Sales Value	421	361

15-16 续表 continued

指　　标	Item	本年直营店 Ragular Chain	上年直营店 Ragular Chain Last Year
一、门店总数（个）	**Number of Stores(unit)**	**109**	**77**
二、年末从业人员数（人）	**Employees at Year-end(person)**	**6292**	**6778**
三、年末餐饮营业面积（平方米）	**Operating Area of Retail at Year-end(sq.m)**	**59856**	**45800**
四、客房总数（间）	**Guest Rooms(room)**		
五、床位数（张）	**Guest Beds(bed)**		
六、餐位数（位）	**Dining Seats(set)**	**18149**	14988
七、连锁门店商品购进额（万元）	**Operating Area of Catering Services at Year end(room)(1 0000 yuan)**	**65501**	**39391**
#统一配送商品购进额	Centralized Purchases and Delivery	60279	34488
#自有配送中心配送商品购进额	Self Centralized Purchases and Delivery	11348	10984
非自有配送中心配送商品购进额	Non-self Centralized Purchases and Delivery		
八、连锁门店商品营业额（万元）	**Sales Value of Chain Store(1 0000 yuan)**	**102252**	**75028**
#餐费收入	Catering Revenues	101831	74667
商品销售额	Sales Value	421	361

15-17 成品油批发企业（单位）能源购进、销售与库存（2011年）

Purchases,Sales and Stock of Refined Oil Wholesale Enterprises（2011）

指　　标	Item	年初库存量 Stock at Beginning of the Year	本年购进量 Purchases This Year	购自省（区、市））外 From Other Provinces (Regions,Cities)	本年销售量 Sales This Year	销往省(区、市)外 For Other Provinces (Regions,Cities)	售予批发和零售业 For Wholesale and Retail Trades	年末库存量 Stock at End of the Year
汽油(吨)	Gasoline(ton)	36304	2279175	113902	2241095	227322	1240990	71560
#93″	#93″	14084	1501297	98785	1486681	138491	806806	33512
柴油(吨)	Diesel Oil(ton)	54105	4077582	820891	4011014	639757	1740990	95938
#0″	#0″	44133	3671471	730629	3638346	601836	1547145	49324
煤油(吨)	Kerosene(ton)	17627	738659	299105	735470	301898		28010
燃料油(吨)	Fuel Oil(ton)		12325	12325	12325	12325		
润滑油(吨)	Lube(ton)	232	16301	13969	16332	8100	7877	224

15-18 成品油零售企业（单位）能源商品销售与库存（2011年）

Purchases,Sales and Stock of Refined Oil Retail Enterprises（2011）

指　　标	Item	年初库存量 Stock at Beginning of the Year	本年销售量 Sales This Year	年末库存量 Stock at End of the Year
汽油(吨)	Gasoline(ton)	13883	685415	12927
#93″	#93″	8372	557754	8322
柴油(吨)	Diesel Oil(ton)	15006	676385	13558
#0″	#0″	13443	629157	11458
煤油(吨)	Kerosene(ton)		13	
燃料油(吨)	Fuel Oil(ton)			
润滑油(吨)	Lube(ton)	57	1620	108

主要统计指标解释

批发业 指批发商向批发、零售单位及其他企事业、机关单位批量销售生活用品和生产资料的活动，以及从事进出口贸易和贸易经纪与代理的活动。批发商可以对所批发的货物拥有所有权，并以本单位、公司的名义进行交易活动；也可以不拥有货物的所有权，而以中介身份做代理销售商。还包括各类商品批发市场中固定摊位的批发活动。

零售业 指百货商店、超级市场、专门零售商店、品牌专卖店、售货摊等主要面向最终消费者（如居民等）的销售活动。包括以互联网、邮政、电话、售货机等方式的销售活动，还包括在同地点，后面加工生产，前面销售的店铺（如前店后厂的面包房）。不包括：谷物、种子、饲料、牲畜、矿产品、生产用原料、化工原料、农用化工产品、机械设备（用车、计算机及通信设备等除外）等生产资料的销售（批发业）；非零售单位附带的零售活动（如汽车修理单位销售汽车零件）；商业零售单位所在商厦的物业管理（物业管理）；商业零售单位所在的商品市场、商业大厦的市场管理活动（市场管理）。

住宿业 指有偿为顾客提供临时住宿的服务活动，不包括提供长期住宿场所的活动（如出租房屋、公寓等）。

餐饮业 指在一定场所，对食物进行现场烹饪、调制，并出售给顾客主要供现场消费的服务活动。

社会消费品零售总额 指批发和零售业、餐饮业、新闻出版业、邮政业和其他服务业等，售予城乡居民用于生活消费的商品和社会集团用于公共消费的商品之总量。社会消费品零售总额包括：

一、批发和零售业企业（单位）售予城乡居民用于生活消费和社会集团用于公共消费的商品。包括：

1.售予城乡居民的各种生活消费品；

2.售予入境旅游的外国人、华侨、港澳台同胞的各类商品；

3.售予行政事业单位、社会团体、军队和武警等机构的商品，以及以零售方式售予各类企业的商品。具体包括：用于非生产和社会交往的办公用品，如通讯设备、计算器具和设备、电讯网络设备、文印设备、音像视听器材和设备、纸张、本册、文具及装订文印材料、家具、日用电器、针纺织品、清洁卫生用品、文体用品、奖品、纪念品、礼品等；供内部人员乘坐的交通工具和燃料；用于办公设施修缮的各类配件、材料、工具等；用于取暖和防暑降温的设备、燃料、材料及食品等；专用于教学的用品和设备；非营利医疗机构的中、西药品、中药材和医疗设备器材；非专用的劳动保护用品；不对外营业的内部食堂用的餐具、炊具、设备、清洁卫生工具和食品、燃料等；军队、武警用于其人员生活的衣着品和个人用品；其他各类非生产性设备和用品。

二、餐饮业出售的主食、菜肴、烟酒饮料和其他商品。

三、新闻出版业、邮政业售予城乡居民、企事业单位、军队和武警等机构的书报杂志、音像制品、邮品等。

四、其他服务业出售的食品、烟酒饮料、服装鞋帽、日常生活用品、医药保健用品、艺术品、工艺美术品、玩具、殡葬用品以及其他消费品。

批发和零售业商品购进、销售、库存总额 指各种登记注册类型的批发和零售业企业（单位）以本企业（单位）为总体的，从国内、国外市场购进的商品总量，销售和出口的商品总量、库存的商品总量等情况。该指标可以反映商品流转过程中商品的购进、销售、库存之间的比例关系和存在的问题。

购进总额 指从本企业（单位）以外的单位和个人购进（包括从境外直接进口）作为转卖或加工后转卖的商品总额。它反映批发和零售业从国内、国外市场上购进商品的总量。商品购进包括：（1）从工农业生产者购进的商品；（2）从出版社、报社的出版发行部门购进的图书、杂志和报纸；（3）从各种登记注册类型的批发和零售业企业（单位）购进的商品；（4）从其他单位购进的商品，如从机关、团体、企业等单位购进的剩余物资，从住宿和餐饮业、其他服务业购进的商品，从海关、市场管理部门购进的缉私和没收的商品，从居民手中收购的废旧商品等；（5）从国（境）外直接进口的商品。不包括企业（单位）为自身经营用和未通过买卖行为而收入的商品以及销售退回、商品升溢等。

销售总额 指对本企业（单位）以外的单位和个人出售（包括对境外直接出口）的商品总额。它反映批发和零售业在国内市场上销售商品以及出口商品的总量。商品销售包括：（1）售给城乡居民和社会集团消费用的商品；（2）售给工业、农业、建筑业、运输邮电业、批发和零售业、住宿和餐饮业、其他服务业等作为生产、经营使用的商品；（3）售给批发和零售业作为转卖或加工后转卖的商品；（4）对国（境）外直接出口的商品。不包括出售本企业（单位）自用的废旧包装用品，未通过买卖行为付出的商品，经本单位介绍、由买卖双方直接结算、本单位只收取手续费的业务，购货退出的商品以及商品损耗和损失等。

库存总额 指报告期末各种登记注册类型的批发和零售业企业（单位）已取得所有权的商品。它反映批发和零售业企业（单位）的商品库存情况和对市场商品供应的保证程度。商品库存包括：（1）存放在批发和零售业经营单位（如门市部、批发站、经营处）仓库、货场、货柜和货架中的商品；（2）挑选、整理、包装中的商品；（3）已记入购进而尚未运到本单位的商品，即发货单或银行承兑凭证已到而货未到的商品；（4）寄放他处的商品，如因购货方拒绝承付而暂时存放在购货方的商品和已办完加工成品收回手续而未提回的商品；（5）委托其他单位代销（未作销售或调出）尚未售出的商品；（6）代其他单位购进尚未交付的商品。不包括所有权不属于本单位的商品、委托外单位加工生产尚未收回成品的商品、外贸企业代理其他单位从国外进口尚未付给订货单位的商品、代国家物资储备部门保管的商品等。

住宿和餐饮业营业额 指住宿和餐饮业法人企业（单位）在经营活动中因提供服务或销售商品等取得的收入。包括：客房收入、餐费收入、商品销售额和其他收入。客房收入指住宿和餐饮业法人企业（单位）在经营活动中因提供住宿服务取得的收入。餐费收入指住宿和餐饮业法人企业、（单位）因为顾客提供就餐服务取得的收入，包括经烹饪、调制加工后出售的各种食品，如主食、炒菜、凉拌菜等的收入。商品销售额指住宿和餐饮业法人企业（单位）伴随服务而出售商品所取得的收入（含增值税）。其他收入指营业收入中除客房收入、餐费收入、商品销售额以外的其他收入，包括娱乐、健身和商务服务等。

连锁企业（或称连锁店、连锁公司） 指在核心企业或总店的领导下，由分散的、经营同类商品或服务的企业或活动单位，采取共同方针，实行集中采购和分散销售的有机结合，通过规范化经营，实现规模效益的经济联合组织形式。一般连锁店应由若干个分店组成。其经营特征：（1）经营同类商品；（2）使用统一商号；（3）统一采购配送，采购与销售相分离（部分商品可根据物流合理和保质保鲜原则，由供应商直接送货到门店，其余均由总部统一配送）。

连锁门店的形式分为直营连锁和加盟连锁。

直营连锁也叫正规连锁。指连锁门店均由总部独资或控股开设，在总部的直接领导下统一经营。总部采取纵深似的管理方式，直接下令掌管所有的零售门店，零售门店也必须完全接受总部指挥。这是大型垄断商业资本通过吞并、兼并或独资、控股等途径，发展壮大自身实力和规模的一种形式。

加盟连锁包括特许连锁和自由连锁两种形式。

特许连锁指各连锁门店（被特许人）通过合同形式，取得使用总部（特许人）商标、商号、经营技术和销售总部开发的商品的特许权，各加盟连锁门店为独立法人，在总部指导下统一经营。

自由连锁也称自愿连锁。指连锁公司的门店均为独立法人，各自的资产所有权关系不变，在公司总部的指导下共同经营。各成员店使用共同的店名，与总部订阅有关购、销、宣传等方面的合同，并按合同开展经营活动。在合同规定的范围之外，各成员店可以自由活动。根据自愿原则，各成员店可自由加入连锁体系，也可自由退出。

Explanatory Notes on Main Statistical Indicators

Wholesale Trade refers to the activities of wholesaler selling at wholesale commodities for daily use and capital goods to enterprises of wholesale and retail trades and other enterprises, institutions and government offices, including the activities of wholesaler engaged in import and export and acting as a trade agent. The wholesaler may have the right of ownership over the commodities of wholesale and trade in the name of its own or a company, the wholesaler may not have the right of ownership, only acts an agent. The wholesale trade also include the activities of wholesaler at the fixed stalls of the wholesale market of different commodities.

Retail Trade refers to the activities of department store, supermarket, franchised store, brand store, retail stall and on-the-spot-making-selling store selling commodities to the final consumers (citizens) by any means including internet, post, telephone, sales machine. Retail trade excludes the activities of sales of capital goods such a grain, seed, feed, livestock, mineral products, raw material for production, industrial chemicals, chemical products for farm, machine and equipment (vehicle, computer and communication equipment), and the activities of supplementary sales of non-retailer such as the sales of spare parts of car repair business

Hotel Services refer to the activities of enterprises providing paid services of lodging to the customer, excluding the activities of providing long period of services of lodging (such as leased house and apartments).

Catering Services refer to the activities of enterprises providing on-the-spot services of selling food cooked and prepared to the customer in certain sites

Total Retail Sales of Consumer Goods refer to the sum of retail sales of commodities sold by wholesale and retail trades, catering services, publishing, post and telecommunications and other service industries to urban and rural households for household consumption and to social institutions for public consumption. Retail sales of consumer goods include:

1) Sales sold by wholesale and retail trades to urban and rural households for household consumption and to social institutions for public consumption.

a) of commodities to urban and rural households;

b) of commodities to foreigners, overseas Chinese and Chinese compatriots from Hong Kong, Macao and Taiwan visiting China;

c) of commodities to government agencies, institutions, social organizations, military and armed police units, and commodities to enterprises in the form of retail sales. More specifically, `they include: office facilities and articles for non-production purposes such as communications equipment, computing equipment and instruments, TV and network equipment, printing and copying equipment, audio-visual equipment and instruments, paper, notebooks, stationeries, furniture, electric appliances, knitwear, sanitation and cleaning articles, cultural and sport articles, articles for prizes, souvenirs, etc.; transport vehicles and fuels for employees; materials, spare parts and tools for the maintenance of office facilities; equipment, fuels, materials and food for winter heating or summer cooling purposes; articles and equipment for teaching purpose; Chinese and western medicines and medical equipment and facilities purchased by non profit-making medical institutes; non-specialized work safety articles; cooking utensils, tableware, equipment, cleaning articles, food and fuels purchased by in-house cafeterias; clothes and personal articles purchased by military or armed police units for their officials and soldiers; and other equipment and articles for non-production purposes.

2) Sales of stable food, cooked dishes, beverages, tobaccos and other articles by catering units.

3) Sales of books, newspapers, magazines, audio-visual products and post products by publishing, post and telecommunications departments to urban and rural households and to enterprises, institutions, military and armed police units.

4) Sales of food, beverages, tobaccos, clothing, hats, footwear, articles for daily use, medicines, medical and

health articles, work of art, handicrafts, toys, funeral articles and other articles by other service industries.

Purchase, Sales and Stock of Commodities by Wholesale and Retail Trades refer to the total volume of commodities purchased, total volume of sales and exports, and the stock of commodities by wholesale and retail enterprises (establishments) of different status of registration from domestic and overseas markets. This indicator reflects the relationship among purchase, sales and stock of commodities in the circulation of goods and reveals the existing problems.

Total Purchases of Commodities refer to the total value of purchases of commodities by enterprises (establishments) from other establishments or individuals (including direct import from abroad) for the purpose of re-selling, either with or without further processing of the commodities purchased. The commodities include: (1) commodities purchased from agricultural and industrial producer, wholesaler, retailer, publishing house and other service business; (2) commodities purchased from institutions and government departments; (3) confiscated goods purchased from the customs authorities or market management agencies; (4) second-hand goods and wastes purchased from residents; The commodities exclude 1 commodities purchased by enterprises (establishments) for use in their own business operation, commodities obtained without buying or selling procedures such as materials, consumable goods of low value, office appliances, etc. 2 received goods without trading, such as goods handed over from others, borrowed goods, preserved goods for others, donated goods from others, processed and retrieved goods, etc. 3. goods of direct settlement between buyer and seller with handling fees introduced by others, 4. goods returned or refused to pay by the buyer, 5. excessive goods.

Total Sales of Commodities refer to value of commodities sold by the establishments to other establishments and individuals (including goods sold for self consumption, including the value-added tax). The commodities include: (1) commodities sold to urban and rural residents and social groups for their consumption; (2) commodities sold to establishments in all industries for their production and operation, including agriculture, industry, construction, transportation, post and telecommunications, catering services, and public utility including commodities sold to wholesale and retail establishments for re-selling, with or without further processing; and (3) commodities for direct export to abroad. Excluded are (1) extended commodities without trading, such as goods handed over to other enterprises and institutions because of the change of organizations, lent goods, returned goods preserved for others, extended processing materials and samples donated to others, (2) goods of direct settlement between buyer and seller with handling fees introduced by others, 3. goods returned after purchase, (4) damaged and spoiled goods, (5) waste and used goods of self use,

Total Stock of Commodities refers to total commodities possessed by wholesaler and retailer of various types of registration status at the end of the reference period, reflecting the commodity stock level of various wholesaler and retailer and the potential for market supply. It includes: (1) commodities located in storage, garages, counters, and shelves of operating places (such as sale stores, wholesale centres, and operating offices); (2) commodities in the process of being selected, sorted, and packed; (3) commodities not arrived but recorded as purchase in the account, i.e. commodities not arrived but payment receipts for the commodities from the sellers or the banks arrived; (4) commodities deposited in other places rather than places mentioned above, for instance: commodities in the hold of purchasers temporarily due to the refusal of payment and commodities not taken back after going through the formalities; (5) commodities entrusted to other units to sell but not sold yet; (6) commodities purchased for other units but not delivered yet. Commodities not included as stock are those not owned by the enterprises (units), commodities on commission for processing but not yet delivered, imported commodities of agency of foreign trade enterprise but not yet delivered to ordering units and finally those put in stock on behalf of the state material reserves units.

Business Revenue of Hotels and Catering Services refers to revenue received from providing services or selling commodities by corporate enterprises and establishments engaged in hotels and catering services, including income from hotels, from catering services, from selling of commodities and from other services. Income from hotels refers to income of corporate enterprises and establishments engaged in hotels and catering services by providing lodging services. Income from catering services refers to income of corporate enterprises and establishments engaged in hotels and catering services by providing catering services, including selling of cooked or prepared foods such as staple food, cooked dishes or cold dishes. Income from selling of commodities refers to income of corporate, enterprises and establishments engaged in hotels and catering services by selling commodities (including value-added tax) that accompany the services they provide. Income from other activities refers to income received other than income from hotels, catering services or selling of commodities, such as income from providing recreation, fitness or business services.

Chain Head Stores (headquarter) refer to the core leading stores responsible for development, allocation, administration and utilization of resources (name of stores, brand of stores, operation model, service standard, management way, ect.) of chain stores. Chain stores refers to the stores engaged in providing homogeneous commodities or services, with the central leadership of head store and guided by common policies, conduct centralized purchase and distributed selling of commodities, in order to gain better efficiency through standardized operation. The chain stores include regular chain stores, franchise chain stores and voluntary chain stores.

Regular Chain store refers to chain stores that are invested or controlled by the headquarters. They operate under direct and unified management from the headquarters.

Franchise chain store refers to the chain stores (franchisees) which are franchised with operation resources such as trade marks, names, patent and operation know-how by the franchisors in form of contract and pay the operation fees to the franchisors

Voluntary chain store refers the stores operate jointly on the voluntary bases while maintaining their status of independent legal entities with full ownership of their assets. They sell goods of same brand from same channel of resource to the consumers.

16 对外经济贸易和旅游

FOREIGN TRADE AND ECONOMIC COOPERATION TOURISM

资料整理：马晓庆　赵琳瑛

Data management:Ma Xiaoqing　Zhao Linying

第十六部分　对外经济贸易和旅游

一、简要说明

本章资料包括对外经济贸易、利用外资以及与国外友好城市交流和旅游等方面资料，由西安市统计局贸易外经处根据西安市商务局、海关、政府对外办公室和旅游局提供资料整理。

二、主要指标

进出口总额（亿美元）	126.02	比上年增长	21.3%
#出　口	58.27	比上年增长	9.6%
实际利用外商直接投资额（亿美元）	20.05	比上年增长	28.0%
国际旅游人数（万人次）	100.23	比上年增长	19.1%
国际旅游收入（亿美元）	6.41	比上年增长	20.9%

16 FOREIGN TRADE AND ECONOMIC COOPERATION,TOURISM

Ⅰ.Brief Introduction

Data in this chapter consists of data on foreign trade, using of foreign capital and fund and tourism. Data on foreign economy and trade, intercommunion to foreign cities of friendship and tourism are compiled and provided by Foreign Economy Division of the Xi'an Bureau of Statistics according to the data from Xi'an Bureau of Commerce, Xi'an Custom Office, Foreign Affairs Office of the Xi'an Municipal Government and Xi'an Bureau of Tourism.

Ⅱ.Major Indicators

		Increase over Preceding Year
Total Imports and Exports (USD 100 mil.)	126.02	21.3%
Toal Exports	58.27	9.6%
Total Amount of Foreign Capital Actually Used(USD 100 mil.)	20.05	28.0%
Total Number of International Tourists (10 000 persons)	100.23	19.1%
Total Foreign Exchange Earnings (100 mil. Yuan)	6.41	20.9%

16-1 主要年份外资、外贸和国际旅游基本情况

Main Indicators on Foreign Investments,International Trading and International Tourism In Representative Years

指标	Item	1990	1995	2000	2004	2005
一、利用外资签订协议项目(个)	**Number of Projects of Foreign Capital Used through the Signed Agreements and Contracts (unit)**	**11**	**184**	**135**	**159**	**157**
利用外资签订协议金额(万美元)	Value of Foreign Capital Used through the Signed Agreements and Contracts(USD 10 000)	415	28956	54123	78312	121499
外商实际直接投资额(万美元)	Value of Foreign Direct Investment (USD 10 000)	1154	18653	15633	27595	57113
二、进出口总额(万美元)	**Total Imports and Exports (USD 10 000)**	**38229**	**137510**	**173696**	**309295**	**390146**
#进口总额	Total Imports	9939	27347	67634	105756	126705
出口总额	Total Exports	28290	110163	106062	203539	263441
进出口差额	Balance of Imports and Exports	18351	82816	38428	97783	136736
三、国际旅游人数总计(万人次)	**Total Number of International Tourists (10 000 person-times)**	**25.88**	**41.35**	**65.03**	**65.03**	**77.56**
#外国人	Foreigners	15.40	37.11	54.65	52.75	65.86
港澳台同胞	Chinese Compatriot From Hong Kong, Macao and Taiwan	10.07	4.16	10.38	12.28	11.70
四、国际旅游者人天数总计(万人天)	**Total Number of Days of International Tourists (10 000 person/day)**	**55.03**	**84.44**	**162.69**	**186.80**	**224.93**
#外国人	Foreigners	33.48	75.71	131.44	151.11	190.99
港澳台同胞	Chinese Compatriot From Hong Kong, Macao and Taiwan	21.55	8.56	31.15	35.69	33.94
五、国际旅游收入(亿元)	**Earning of International Tourism (100 millon yuan)**	**1.96**	**10.38**	**22.41**	**27.39**	**33.54**
#商品收入	Income from Mercantile	0.44	2.57	7.71	10.44	11.25
劳务收入	Income from Labour Service	1.52	7.81	14.70	16.95	22.29
六、旅游者在西安人均停留天数(天)	**Number of Days of Average Tourists Staying in Xi'an (day)**	**2.1**	**2.0**	**2.5**	**2.9**	**2.9**

注：1990年和1995年国际旅游者中含华侨。

Note:The international tourists included overseas Chinese in 1990 and 1995.

16-1 续表 continued

指　　标	Item	2006	2007	2008	2009	2010	2011
一、利用外资签订协议项目(个)	**Number of Projects of Foreign Capital Used through the Signed Agreements and Contracts (unit)**	**190**	**135**	**100**	**65**	**82**	**99**
利用外资签订协议金额(万美元)	Value of Foreign Capital Used through the Signed Agreements and Contracts(USD 10 000)	182525	143978	118230	60027	119689	120083
外商实际直接投资额(万美元)	Value of Foreign Direct Investment (USD 10 000)	82463	111567	114738	121872	156653	200522
二、进出口总额(万美元)	**Total Imports and Exports (USD 10 000)**	**415403**	**536162**	**704029**	**724618**	**1039273**	**1260179**
#进口总额	Total Imports	142541	189029	256916	391504	507544	677517
出口总额	Total Exports	272862	347133	447113	333114	531729	582662
进出口差额	Balance of Imports and Exports	130321	158104	190197	-58390	24185	-94855
三、国际旅游人数总计(万人次)	**Total Number of International Tourists (10 000 person-times)**	**86.73**	**100.01**	**63.20**	**67.29**	**84.18**	**100.23**
#外国人	Foreigners	73.40	85.09	53.58	59.09	73.21	88.63
港澳台同胞	Chinese Compatriot From Hong Kong, Macao and Taiwan	13.33	14.92	9.62	8.20	10.97	11.60
四、国际旅游者人天数总计(万人天)	**Total Number of Days of International Tourists (10 000 person/day)**	**253.17**	**290.02**	**162.93**	**195.14**	**241.67**	**287.09**
#外国人	Foreigners	214.10	246.76	138.72	171.36	211.48	254.78
港澳台同胞	Chinese Compatriot From Hong Kong, Macao and Taiwan	39.07	43.26	24.21	23.78	30.19	32.31
五、国际旅游收入(亿元)	**Earning of International Tourism (100 millon yuan)**	**37.83**	**42.43**	**28.72**	**31.05**	**42.40**	**51.28**
#商品收入	Income from Mercantile	15.93	15.19	9.74	8.94	11.87	11.38
劳务收入	Income from Labour Service	21.90	27.24	18.98	22.11	30.53	39.90
六、旅游者在西安人均停留天数(天)	**Number of Days of Average Tourists Staying in Xi'an (day)**	**2.9**	**2.9**	**2.6**	**2.9**	**2.9**	**2.9**

16-2 主要年份利用外资情况

Utilization of Foreign Capital In Representative Years

单位：万美元 (USD 10 000)

年 份 Year	利用外资签定协议金额 Value of Foreign Capital Used through the Signed Agreements and Contracts	外商实际直接投资额 Direct Foreign Investment
1983	3500	800
1984	8	
1985	8361	1106
1986	19919	4010
1987	3218	5552
1988	2423	6758
1989	1645	11632
1990	415	1154
1991	591	1094
1992	24165	5200
1993	57289	8996
1994	20321	15240
1995	28956	18653
1996	35978	20510
1997	27214	22057
1998	40034	22286
1999	40390	13801
2000	54123	15633
2001	60736	17687
2002	70692	20281
2003	96380	25557
2004	78312	27595
2005	121499	57113
2006	182525	82463
2007	143978	111567
2008	118230	114738
2009	60027	121872
2010	119689	156653
2011	120083	200522

16-3 外国和港澳台地区在西安直接投资（2011年）

Direct Investments from Foreign Countries and Hong Kong, Macao and Taiwan in Xi'an（2011）

分　类	Classity	新签协议情况 New-signed Agreement Circumstances		外商实际直接投资额（万美元）Value of Foreign Direct Investment (USD10 000)
		合同数(个) Number of Constracts (unit)	利用外资签订协议金额(万美元) Value of Foreign Captial Used through the Signed (USD10 000)	
合　计	**Total**	**99**	**120083**	**200522**
一、按投资方式分	**Grouped by Investment Mode**			
1.中外合资经营企业	Joint-venture Enterprises	35	33243	73091
2.中外合作经营企业	Cooperation Enterprises	1	4724	
3.外资企业	Wholly Foreign-owned Enterprises	63	82116	118544
4.外资企业再投资	Re-investment from Foreign-funded Enterprises			8887
二、按国民经济行业分组	**Grouped by Sector**			
1.农林牧渔水利业	Agriculture,Forestry,Animal,Husbandy and Fishery	1	3000	1608
2.制造业	Manufacturing	52	36201	91020
3.电力、煤气及水的生产和供应业	Production and Distribution of Electricity,Gas and Water			4921
4.建筑业	Construction	1	45	
5.交通运输、仓储及邮电通信业	Transporation,Storage,Postal and Telecommunications		8886	5443
6.批发和零售贸易、餐饮业	Wholesale, Retail Trads and Catering Services	2	2301	24961
7.房地产业	Real Estate	10	44742	53609
8.社会服务业	Social Services	32	24609	16713
9.其他行业	Others	1	300	2247
三、按投资国别、地区分组	**Grouped by Different Countries and Regions**			
香港	Hong Kong	33	66885	110678
澳门	Macao	1	3041	3040
台湾	Taiwan	8	-54	28
日本	Japan	4	2461	1739
泰国	Tailand			
马来西亚	Malaysia			
新加坡	Singapore	7	16331	1355
韩国	Korea	4	76	
德国	Germany	4	1341	1711
意大利	Italy	3	582	236
法国	France	1	879	442
英国	England	4	1446	4302
捷克	Czechoslovakia			
加拿大	Canada	1	-58	80
美国	America	7	4608	7564
澳大利亚	Australia	2	313	
维尔京群岛	Virgin Islands	6	6145	35306
其它	Others	14	16087	34041

16-4 各区县、开发区外商实际直接投资（2011年）

Direct Investment by Foreign Entrepreneurs by Region and Development Zone（2011）

单位：万美元 （USD 10 000）

区县及开发区名称	Name of Region and Economic Zone	2009	2010	2011
区县合计	**Sum of Region**	**29766**	**38855**	**49726**
新城区	Xincheng	3740	4900	6765
碑林区	Beilin	4780	5150	6273
莲湖区	Lianhu	3953	5471	7405
灞桥区	Baqiao	4300	5215	6001
未央区	Weiyang	3902	5023	6202
雁塔区	Yanta	4087	5488	6912
阎良区	Yanliang	675	1208	2070
临潼区	Lintong	970	1200	2000
长安区	Chang'an	1219	1680	2300
蓝田县	Lantian	605	950	1089
周至县	Zhouzhi	315	550	600
户　县	Huxian	560	970	1050
高陵县	Gaoling	660	1050	1060
开发区合计	**Sum of Development Zones**	**92107**	**117798**	**150797**
高新区	GaoXin	40613	51130	64935
经开区	JingKai	33661	42608	54201
曲江新区	Qujiang	12589	17187	21002
浐灞生态区	Chanba Eco-District	2400	3070	3856
航空基地	Aviation Industry Base	1016	1239	1701
航天基地	Aerospace Base	1208	1554	2030
国际港务区	International Trade&Logistic Park	620	1010	1571
沣东新城	FengDongXinCheng			1500

16-5 主要年份进出口总额

Total Imports and Exports In Representative Years

单位：万美元 (USD 10 000)

年 份 Year	进出口总额 Total Imports and Exports	出口总额 Total Exports	进口总额 Total Imports
1987	13596	7540	6056
1988	36750	24632	12118
1989	32715	21564	11151
1990	38229	28290	9939
1991	55356	41511	13845
1992	70467	53060	17407
1993	93330	62393	30937
1994	104752	76897	27855
1995	137510	110163	27347
1996	143187	91745	51442
1997	150668	107753	42915
1998	180589	100492	80097
1999	172919	94495	78424
2000	173696	106062	67634
2001	169914	87948	81966
2002	186966	112479	74487
2003	230932	140327	90605
2004	309295	203539	105756
2005	390146	263441	126705
2006	415403	272862	142541
2007	536162	347133	189029
2008	704029	447113	256916
2009	724618	333114	391504
2010	1039273	531729	507544
2011	1260179	582662	677517

16-6 外贸商品进出口总额分国别和地区（2011年）

Total Value of Imports and Exports by Country and Region（2011）

单位：万美元 (USD10 000)

国别和地区	Country and Region	进出口总额 Total Imports and Exports	出口 Exports
亚洲	**Asia**	**480719**	**240808**
#香港	Hong kong	55858	51275
台湾	Taiwan	86666	12583
日本	Japan	78181	30706
菲律宾	Phiilippines	10878	4263
马来西亚	Malaysia	8193	5452
韩国	Korea	47957	27905
非洲	**Africa**	**75983**	**73147**
#埃及	Egypt	7130	7042
突尼斯	Tunisia	457	431
埃塞俄比亚	Ethiopia	813	780
博茨瓦那	Botswana	47	47
南非	South Africa	8456	7892
欧洲	**Europe**	**307747**	**126632**
#德国	Germany	88691	18970
法国	France	22093	10608
意大利	Italy	19136	7848
荷兰	Netherland	29763	23843
英国	England	25794	13708
瑞士	Switzerland	10945	311
西班牙	Spain	5062	3428
俄罗斯联邦	Russia	19628	17293
拉丁美洲	**Latin America**	**74229**	**19428**
#哥伦比亚	Colombia	1034	1034
巴西	Brazil	18084	4222
阿根廷	Argentina	3387	3343
北美洲	**North America**	**276402**	**115494**
#加拿大	Canada	16562	4859
美国	America	259840	110635
大洋洲及太平洋岛屿	**Oceanic and Pacific Islands**	**45097**	**7154**
#澳大利亚	Australia	43745	6073
新西兰	New Zealand	848	584

16-7 主要商品分大类出口金额

Export Value of Major Merchandise by Type

单位：万美元 (USD 10 000)

商品分类	HS Section and Division	2000	2001	2002	2003
食用蔬菜、根及块茎	Edible Vegetables, Certain,Roots amd Tubers	1095	1957	1275	1379
蔬菜、水果、坚果或植物其它部分的制品	Vegetables, Fruits, Nuts, or Products Made of Other Parts of Plants	2076	2684	3470	4490
矿砂、矿渣及矿灰	Ores,Slags and Ash	4083	4649	8714	11224
无机化学品；贵金属、稀土金属、放射性元素及其同位素的有机及无机化合物	Inorganic Chemicals,Organic or Inorganic Compounds of Precious Metals,of Rare Earth Metals,of Radioactive Elements or of Isotopes	3714	4141	4141	5814
有机化学品	Organic Chemicals	2367	3279	4883	4757
羊毛、动物细毛或粗毛、马毛纱线及其机织物	Wool ,Fine or Coarse Animal Hair; Horsehair Yarn and Woven Fabric	810	829	1313	1600
棉花	Cotton	3197	2734	3826	3984
化学纤维短纤	Short Staple Chemical' Fibers	5061	3612	2512	2120
针织或钩编的服装及衣着附件	Articles of Apparel and Clothing Accessories, Knitted or Crocheted	6753	1632	2660	341
非针织或非钩编的服装及衣着附件	Articles of Apparel and Clothing Accessories, not Knitted or Crocheted	7269	3319	3629	4981
其它纺织制成品；成套物品；旧衣着及旧纺织品	Other Made Up Textile Articles;Sets;Worn Clothing and Worn Textile Articles;Rags Articles	1649	1002	1432	2203
鞋靴、护腿和类似品及其零件	Footwear,Gaiters and The Like;Parts of Such Articles Headgear and Parts Thereof	1347	279	296	585
玻璃及其制品	Glass and Glassware	3376	3838	5542	6667
钢铁	Iron and Steel	3534	1197	2167	2779
钢铁制品	Articles of Iron or Steel	5535	6401	7414	8474
铅及制品	Lead Areticles Thereof	1371	1363	444	232
锌及制品	Zinc Areticles Thereof	4031	1945	1895	2200
其它贱金属、金属陶瓷及其制品	Other Base Metals,Germets;Areticles Thereof	1066	1704	1546	3150
贱金属工具、器具、利口器、餐匙、餐叉及其零件	Tools,Implements,Cutlery,Spons and Forks, of Base Metal;Parts Thereof of Base Metal	2933	2669	2613	3232
核反应堆、锅炉、机器、机械器具及其零件	Nuclear Reactors ,Boilers, Machinery and Mechanical Appliances; and Parts Thereof	10915	11979	16140	21281
电机、电气设备及其零件；录音机及放声机、电视图像、声音的录制和重放设备及其零件、附件	Electrical Machinery and Equipment and Parts Thereof;Sound Recorders and Repreducers, Television Image and Sound Recordes and Repreducers,and Parts and Accessories of Such Articles	8339	8696	8962	15106
光学、照相、电影、计量、检验、医疗或外科用仪器及设备、精密仪器及设备；上述物品的零件、附件	Optical,Photographic,Cinematographic,Measuring, Checking,Precision Medical or Surgical Instruments and Apparatus;Parts and Accessories Thereof	2020	2818	5395	3339
家具、寝具、褥垫、弹簧床垫、软床垫及类似的填充制品；未列名灯具及照明装置；发光标志、发光名牌及类似品；活动房屋	Mattresses,Mattress Supports,Cushions and Similar Stuffed Furnishings;Lamps and Lighting Fittings, not Elsewhere Spcified or Included;Illumihated Signs,Illuminated	2587	2150	2715	3994

16-7 续表1 continued 1

单位：万美元 (USD 10 000)

商品分类	HS Section and Division	2004	2005	2006	2007
食用蔬菜、根及块茎	Edible Vegetables, Certain,Roots amd Tubers	1386	1190	1136	1232
蔬菜、水果、坚果或植物其它部分的制品	Vegetables, Fruits, Nuts, or Products Made of Other Parts of Plants	7786	10531	15374	37426
矿砂、矿渣及矿灰	Ores,Slags and Ash	30590	63247	52046	47378
无机化学品；贵金属、稀土金属、放射性元素及其同位素的有机及无机化合物	Inorganic Chemicals,Organic or Inorganic Compounds of Precious Metals,of Rare Earth Metals,of Radioactive Elements or of Isotopes	5806	10997	10916	16508
有机化学品	Organic Chemicals	4837	8569	11923	11182
羊毛、动物细毛或粗毛、马毛纱线及其机织物	Wool ,Fine or Coarse Animal Hair; Horsehair Yarn and Woven Fabric	1640	903	1400	1065
棉花	Cotton	3133	3240	3808	3255
化学纤维短纤	Short Staple Chemical Fibers	1987	1471	1556	1767
针织或钩编的服装及衣着附件	Articles of Apparel and Clothing Accessories, Knitted or Crocheted	7465	5736	5332	5345
非针织或非钩编的服装及衣着附件	Articles of Apparel and Clothing Accessories, not Knitted or Crocheted	5543	5068	4078	3875
其它纺织制成品；成套物品；旧衣着及旧纺织品	Other Made Up Textile Articles;Sets;Worn Clothing and Worn Textile Articles;Rags Articles	2667	3000	3342	3090
鞋靴、护腿和类似品及其零件	Footwear,Gaiters and The Like;Parts of Such Articles Headgear and Parts Thereof	2687	1368	216	348
玻璃及其制品	Glass and Glassware	8083	8576	8272	6246
钢铁	Iron and Steel	5244	5314	4900	11366
钢铁制品	Articles of Iron or Steel	10398	13959	16903	17329
铅及制品	Lead Areticles Thereof	43	12	158	1650
锌及制品	Zinc Areticles Thereof	522	135	4119	2470
其它贱金属、金属陶瓷及其制品	Other Base Metals,Germets;Areticles Thereof	6419	11233	17695	23414
贱金属工具、器具、利口器、餐匙、餐叉及其零件	Tools,Implements,Cutlery,Spons and Forks, of Base Metal;Parts Thereof of Base Metal	3406	3052	3607	3917
核反应堆、锅炉、机器、机械器具及其零件	Nuclear Reactors ,Boilers, Machinery and Mechanical Appliances; and Parts Thereof	24696	30832	36174	47381
电机、电气设备及其零件；录音机及放声机、电视图像、声音的录制和重放设备及其零件、附件	Electrical Machinery and Equipment and Parts Thereof;Sound Recorders and Repreducers, Television Image and Sound Recordes and Repreducers,and Parts and Accessories of Such Articles	19812	23605	22801	33393
光学、照相、电影、计量、检验、医疗或外科用仪器及设备、精密仪器及设备；上述物品的零件、附件	Optical,Photographic,Cinematographic,Measuring, Checking,Precision Medical or Surgical Instruments and Apparatus;Parts and Accessories Thereof	1847	2341	3521	4230
家具、寝具、褥垫、弹簧床垫、软床垫及类似的填充制品；未列名灯具及照明装置；发光标志、发光名牌及类似品；活动房屋	Mattresses,Mattress Supports,Cushions and Similar Stuffed Furnishings;Lamps and Lighting Fittings, not Elsewhere Spcified or Included;Illumihated Signs,Illuminated	4955	4773	5086	8301

16-7 续表2 continued 2

单位：万美元 (USD 10 000)

商品分类	HS Section and Division	2008	2009	2010	2011
食用蔬菜、根及块茎	Edible Vegetables, Certain,Roots amd Tubers	1374	803	4740	2016
蔬菜、水果、坚果或植物其它部分的制品	Vegetables, Fruits, Nuts, or products made of other parts of plants	29270	21920	41289	36763
矿砂、矿渣及矿灰	Ores,Slags and Ash	40502	6141	325	4709
无机化学品；贵金属、稀土金属、放射性元素及其同位素的有机及无机化合物	Inorganic Chemicals,Organic or Inorganic Compounds of Precious Metals,of Rare Earth Metals,of Radioactive Elements or of Isotopes	15882	9774	24875	11735
有机化学品	Organic Chemicals	13954	16294	982	20067
羊毛、动物细毛或粗毛、马毛纱线及其机织物	Wool ,Fine or Coarse Animal Hair; Horsehair Yarn and Woven Fabric	720	460	10133	796
棉花	Cotton	3213	2346	98	2628
化学纤维短纤	Short staple chemical fibers	1181	2217	479	2586
针织或钩编的服装及衣着附件	Articles of Apparel and Clothing Accessories, Knitted or Crocheted	4371	3617	3209	3366
非针织或非钩编的服装及衣着附件	Articles of Apparel and Clothing Accessories, not Knitted or Crocheted	3623	2919	3394	3262
其它纺织制成品；成套物品；旧衣着及旧纺织品	Other Made Up Textile Articles;Sets;Worn Clothing and Worn Textile Articles;Rags Articles	3187	2813	544	2838
鞋靴、护腿和类似品及其零件	Footwear,Gaiters and The Like;Parts of Such Articles Headgear and Parts Thereof	380	367	150	1003
玻璃及其制品	Glass and Glassware	6538	5574	928	8073
钢铁	Iron and Steel	11966	4254	18549	16681
钢铁制品	Articles of Iron or Steel	26568	11943	5998	25319
铅及制品	Lead Areticles Thereof	2	1	10	2
锌及制品	Zinc Areticles Thereof	46	78	28545	10
其它贱金属、金属陶瓷及其制品	Other Base Metals,Germets;Areticles Thereof	27576	11276	3556	28092
贱金属工具、器具、利口器、餐匙、餐叉及其零件	Tools,Implements,Cutlery,Spons and Forks, of Base Metal;Parts Thereof of Base Metal	4083	2777	2893	3641
核反应堆、锅炉、机器、机械器具及其零件	Nuclear Reactors ,Boilers, Machinery and Mechanical Appliances; and Parts Thereof	75911	52372	130296	99631
电机、电气设备及其零件；录音机及放声机、电视图像、声音的录制和重放设备及其零件、附件	Electrical Machinery and Equipment and Parts Thereof;Sound Recorders and Repreducers, Television Image and Sound Recordes and Repreducers,and Parts and Accessories of Such Articles	56758	53355	136	137105
光学、照相、电影、计量、检验、医疗或外科用仪器及设备、精密仪器及设备；上述物品的零件、附件	Optical,Photographic,Cinematographic,Measuring, Checking,Precision Medical or Surgical Instruments and Apparatus;Parts and Accessories Thereof	6348	5255	196	11066
家具、寝具、褥垫、弹簧床垫、软床垫及类似的填充制品；未列名灯具及照明装置；发光标志、发光名牌及类似品；活动房屋	Mattresses,Mattress Supports,Cushions and Similar Stuffed Furnishings;Lamps and Lighting Fittings, not Elsewhere Spcified or Included;Illumihated Signs,Illuminated	8296	4769	5328	3860

16–8 主要商品分大类进口金额

Import Value of Major Merchandise by Type

单位:万美元 (USD 10 000)

商品分类	HS Section and Division	2000	2003	2004	2005	2006
无机化学品；贵金属、稀土金属、放射性元素及其同位素的有机及无机化合物	Inorganic Chemicals,Organic or Inorganic Compounds of Precious Metals,of Rare Earth Metals,of Radioactive Elements or of Isotopes	1467	4082	89	317	709
有机化学品	Organic Chemicals	7257	11852	14829	15237	13521
塑料及其制品	Plastic and Articles Thereof	2559	2358	2560	4317	2889
钢铁	Iron and Steel	2467	2086	1205	752	1014
铜及制品	Copper and Articles Thereof	2367	1487	842	689	8035
铝及制品	Aluminium and Articles Thereof	2652	1194	1634	3627	3172
核反应堆、锅炉、机器、机械器具及其零件	Nuclear Reactors ,Boilers, Machinery and Mechanical Appliances; and Parts Thereof	12990	31100	37185	38050	33065
电机、电气设备及其零件；录音机及放声机、电视图像、声音的录制和重放设备及其零件、附件	Electrical Machinery and Equipment and Parts Thereof;Sound Recorders and Repreducers, Television Image and Sound Recordes and Repreducers,and Parts and Accessories of Such Articles	5911	12200	16102	23337	21279
车辆及其零件、附件，铁道及电车道车辆除外	Vehicles Other Than Railway or Tramway Rolling-Stock, and Rarts and Accessories Thereof	1530	2759	3291	1387	1228
航空器、航天器及其零件	Aircraft,Spacecraft and Parts Thereof	10443	768	814	8800	17879
光学、照相、电影、计量、检验、医疗或外科用仪器及设备、精密仪器及设备	Optical,Photographic,Cinematographic,Measuring, Checking,Precision Medical or Surgical	3673	8111	10358	10424	12152

16–8 续表 continued

单位:万美元 (USD 10 000)

商品分类	HS Section and Division	2007	2008	2009	2010	2011
无机化学品；贵金属、稀土金属、放射性元素及其同位素的有机及无机化合物	Inorganic Chemicals,Organic or Inorganic Compounds of Precious Metals,of Rare Earth Metals,of Radioactive Elements or of Isotopes	1039	6001	5040	7513	19766
有机化学品	Organic Chemicals	14536	15692	14186	13949	18100
塑料及其制品	Plastic and Articles Thereof	5149	2553	3134	4091	3250
钢铁	Iron and Steel	1270	3888	2537	10949	10643
铜及制品	Copper and Articles Thereof	22683	11097	41195	43343	78482
铝及制品	Aluminium and Articles Thereof	3223	4767	6505	3116	5913
核反应堆、锅炉、机器、机械器具及其零件	Nuclear Reactors ,Boilers, Machinery and Mechanical Appliances; and Parts Thereof	55243	68504	87493	134753	135240
电机、电气设备及其零件；录音机及放声机、电视图像、声音的录制和重放设备及其零件、附件	Electrical Machinery and Equipment and Parts Thereof;Sound Recorders and Repreducers, Television Image and Sound Recordes and Repreducers,and Parts and Accessories of Such Articles	25164	48008	113034	207937	230957
车辆及其零件、附件，铁道及电车道车辆除外	Vehicles Other Than Railway or Tramway Rolling-Stock, and Rarts and Accessories Thereof	1529	3789	1798	3109	1527
航空器、航天器及其零件	Aircraft,Spacecraft and Parts Thereof	2463	26148	13057	3620	4654
光学、照相、电影、计量、检验、医疗或外科用仪器及设备、精密仪器及设备	Optical,Photographic,Cinematographic,Measuring, Checking,Precision Medical or Surgical	17026	17737	24210	37414	39317

16-9 主要年份旅游人数及收入

Number of Tourists and Tourism Earnings In Representative Years

年 份 Year	接待旅游人数（万人次） Number of Tourists (10 000 person-times)	#国际人数旅游 Number of International Tourists	旅游总收入（万元） Total Tourism Earnings (10 000 yuan)	#国际旅游收入 Earning of International Tourists	国际旅游者在西安人均停留天数（天） Number of Days of Average International Tourists Staying in Xi'an(day)
1980	4.00	4.00	1757	1757	3.8
1981	6.71	6.71	2314	2314	3.4
1982	9.09	9.09	3172	3172	2.8
1983	12.38	12.38	3720	3720	2.5
1984	15.13	15.13	4579	4579	2.3
1985	21.15	21.15	7029	7029	2.2
1986	25.78	25.78	10886	10886	2.2
1987	30.15	30.15	16588	16588	2.1
1988	36.58	36.58	21152	21152	2.0
1989	21.20	21.20	14125	14125	1.9
1990	25.88	25.88	19628	19628	2.1
1991	31.00	31.00	29051	29051	2.3
1992	40.16	40.16	40966	40966	2.2
1993	43.50	43.50	48951	48951	1.9
1994	41.49	41.49	82000	82000	2.2
1995	791.35	41.35	440000	103818	2.0
1996	925.39	45.39	470000	149400	2.6
1997	1010.53	48.53	510000	166359	2.6
1998	1105.80	47.98	560000	160244	2.6
1999	1260.40	55.41	830000	186282	2.5
2000	1567.00	65.03	1050000	224100	2.5
2001	1752.20	67.20	1130000	240700	2.4
2002	1984.13	74.13	1310000	260000	2.2
2003	1647.67	33.66	1064200	121200	2.5
2004	2149.03	65.03	1544000	273900	2.9
2005	2423.60	77.56	1785000	335380	2.9
2006	2738.70	86.73	2043000	378270	2.9
2007	3118.01	100.01	2372000	424263	2.9
2008	3232.20	63.20	2435200	287200	2.6
2009	3929.29	67.29	2974000	310500	2.9
2010	5285.18	84.18	4051800	424000	2.9
2011	6653.23	100.23	5301500	512800	2.9

16-10 主要年份国际旅游收入

Earning of International Tourism In Representative Years

单位:万美元 （USD10 000）

项 目	Item	2000	2001	2002	2003	2004	2005	2006	2007	2008	2009	2010	2011
合 计	**Total**	**27000**	**29002**	**32000**	**14600**	**33000**	**40900**	**46700**	**54323**	**35900**	**39000**	**53000**	**64100**
一、长途交通费	**Long Distance Transportation**	**7047**	**7946**	**6816**	**3109**	**8415**	**12311**	**11442**	**14286**	**10016**	**12597**	**19292**	**26153**
1.飞机	Airplane	6011	7395	5536	2526	7524	9407	9527	10918	7467	9438	15264	19807
2.火车	Train	273	203	288	131	264	858	561	2009	1436	2262	2968	2692
3.汽车	Highway	763	348	992	452	627	2046	1354	1359	1113	897	1060	3654
二、游览	**Sightseeing**	**1296**	**1276**	**1120**	**511**	**1155**	**2045**	**2335**	**2335**	**1831**	**2262**	**3445**	**3846**
三、住宿	**Accommodation**	**3051**	**3684**	**4480**	**2044**	**4752**	**4621**	**5977**	**6573**	**4523**	**5343**	**6572**	**6859**
四、餐饮	**Food and Beverage**	**2673**	**3074**	**3264**	**1489**	**2673**	**3823**	**2195**	**3804**	**2908**	**3471**	**4929**	**2436**
五、娱乐	**Entertainment**	**1512**	**1074**	**896**	**409**	**990**	**1779**	**747**	**1847**	**2046**	**1833**	**2120**	**3526**
六、购物	**Shopping**	**6615**	**7047**	**9600**	**4380**	**9900**	**9897**	**17466**	**15645**	**9262**	**7761**	**9911**	**11794**
七、邮电通讯	**Post and Communication Services**	**1350**	**899**	**1120**	**512**	**957**	**2454**	**1261**	**1794**	**1652**	**1131**	**1272**	**1474**
八、市内交通	**Local Transportation**	**1566**	**899**	**768**	**350**	**726**	**858**	**841**	**1249**	**1041**	**975**	**2120**	**2564**
九、其他	**Others**	**1890**	**3103**	**3936**	**1796**	**3432**	**3112**	**4436**	**6790**	**2621**	**3627**	**3339**	**5449**

16–11 主要年份涉外星级宾馆接待海外旅游者情况

Mainly Concerning Oversea Tourists Reception in Star Hotels in Representative Years

单位：人次 (person-time)

项　　目	Item	2004	2005	2006	2007	2008	2009	2010	2011
海外旅游者人数合计	**International Tourists**	**650325**	**775620**	**867273**	**1000063**	**632036**	**672909**	**841819**	**1002326**
外国人	Foreigners	527480	658578	733963	850905	535837	590870	732065	886276
#日本	Japan	99614	75639	85708	93135	43017	60192	70368	61844
菲律宾	Philippines	876	2165	1910	2162	1466	1708	2213	2587
新加坡	Singapore	3990	6148	6395	7309	6335	7570	10158	12759
美国	America	89499	116913	121788	146089	104742	100445	106042	117485
加拿大	Canada	13132	16807	20075	29193	19047	21901	28409	37511
英国	England	36279	45956	50046	56560	40299	43068	41023	44386
法国	France	30837	49414	49113	58216	37415	39350	42337	42114
德国	Germany	29051	37527	41446	50882	32892	36371	40166	40777
意大利	Italy	7693	16909	16493	21444	9445	15316	15868	19737
瑞士	Switzerland	2390	3748	4080	5047	3763	4479	5528	5933
澳大利亚	Australia	19231	28645	30146	36581	24784	26349	30507	34411
新西兰	New Zealand	2451	4522	3296	4978	4027	4238	5005	5248
港澳和台湾同胞	Chinese Compatriots from Hong Kong, Macao and Taiwan	122845	117042	133310	149158	96199	82039	109754	116050
#台湾同胞	Taiwan	64209	57958	66601	74962	44552	37464	54119	58197

16–12 主要年份旅行社及A级景点

Statistics of Travel Agencies and Level-A Scenic Spots in Representative Years

项　　目	Item	2005	2006	2007	2008	2009	2010	2011
旅行社数（个）	Number of Travel Agencies (unit)	221	240	262	271	303	334	365
旅行社营业收入（万元）	Revenue of Travel Agencies (10000yuan)	178171	199843	264800	178500	213417	312229	443100
旅游A级景点数（个）	Number of Level-A Scenic Spots(unit)	18	23	23	23	24	34	43
旅游A级景点年接待客人数（千人次）	Number of Tourists Received at Level-A Scenic Spots (1 000 person times)	9300	13140	14100	14200	15040	27262	42950

主要统计指标解释

进出口总额 指实际进出我国国境的货物总金额。包括对外贸易实际进出口货物，来料加工装配进出口货物，国家间、联合国及国际组织无偿援助物资和赠送品，华侨、港澳台同胞和外籍华人捐赠品，租赁期满归承租人所有的租赁货物，进料加工进出口货物，边境地方贸易及边境地区小额贸易进出口货物（边民互市贸易除外），中外合资企业、中外合作经营企业、外商独资经营企业进出口货物和公用物品，到、离岸价格在规定限额以上的进出口货样和广告品（无商业价值、无使用价值和免费提供出口的除外），从保税仓库提取在中国境内销售的进口货物，以及其他进出口货物。该指标可以观察一个国家在对外贸易方面的总规模。我国规定出口货物按离岸价格统计，进口货物按到岸价格统计。

商品经营单位所在地进、出口额 指在所在地海关注册登记的有进出口经营权的企业实际进、出口额。

商品目的地进口额和商品货源地出口额 目的地进口额指进口货物的消费、使用或最终抵运地的实际进口额；货源地出口额指出口货物的产地或原始发货地的实际出口额。

利用外资 指我国各级政府、部门、企业和其他经济组织通过对外借款、吸收外商直接投资以及用其他方式筹措的境外现汇、设备、技术等。

外商直接投资 指外国企业和经济组织或个人（包括华侨、港澳台胞以及我国在境外注册的企业）按我国有关政策、法规，用现汇、实物、技术等在我国境内开办外商独资企业、与我国境内的企业或经济组织共同举办中外合资经营企业、合作经营企业或合作开发资源的投资（包括外商投资收益的再投资），以及经政府有关部门批准的项目投资总额内企业从境外借入的资金。

旅游人数：

（1）入境旅游人数：指报告期内来我国观光、度假、探亲访友、就医疗养、购物、参加会议或从事经济、文化、体育、宗教活动的外国人、港澳台同胞等入境游客。统计时，外国人、港澳台同胞每入境一次统计1人次。

（2）出境人数：指中国（大陆）居民因公或因私出境前往其他国家、中国香港特别行政区、澳门特别行政区和台湾省观光、度假、探亲访友、就医疗养、购物、参加会议或从事经济、文化、体育、宗教活动的人数，即出境游客。统计时，按每出境一次统计1人次。

（3）国内旅游人数：指在报告期内在中国（大陆）观光游览、度假、探亲访友、就医疗养、购物、参加会议或从事经济、文化、体育、宗教活动的中国（大陆）居民人数，其出游的目的不是通过所从事的活动谋取报酬。统计时，国内游客按每出游一次统计1人次。

国际旅游（外汇）收入 指入境游客在中国（大陆）境内旅行、游览过程中用于交通、参观游览、住宿、餐饮、购物、娱乐等全部花费。

国内旅游收入 又称旅游总花费指国内游客在国内旅行、游览过程中用于交通、参观游览、住宿、餐饮、购物、娱乐等全部花费。

国际旅行社 指经营业务范围包括入境旅游业务、出境旅游业务和国内旅游业务的旅行社。

国内旅行社 指经营范围仅限于国内旅游业务的旅行社。

星级饭店 指设备、设施、服务符合《旅游饭店星级的划分与评定》（GB/T14308-2003），通过相关旅游管理部门评定，并取得星级饭店称号的饭店（含预备星级饭店）。

Explanatory Notes on Main Statistical Indicators

Total Imports and Exports at Customs refer to the real value of commodities imported and exported across the border of China. They include the actual imports and exports through foreign trade, imported and exported goods under the processing and assembling trades and materials, supplies and gifts as aid given gratis between governments and by the United Nations and other international organizations, and contributions donated by overseas Chinese, compatriots in Hong Kong and Macao and Chinese with foreign citizenship, leasing commodities owned by tenant at the expiration of leasing period, the imported and exported commodities processed with imported materials, commodities trading in border areas (excluding mutual exchange goods), the imported and exported commodities and articles for public use of the Sino-foreign joint ventures, cooperative enterprises and ventures with sole foreign investment. Also included is import or export of samples and advertising goods for which CIF or FOB value are beyond the permitted ceiling (excluding goods of no trading or use value and free commodities for export), imported goods sold in China from bonded warehouses and other imported or exported goods. The indicator of the total imports and exports at customs can be used to observe the total size of external trade in a country. In accordance with the stipulation of the Chinese government, imports are calculated at CIF, while exports are calculated at FOB.

Import Export Value by Location of China's Foreign Trade Managing Units refers to actual value of imports and exports carried out by corporations which have been registered by the local Customs house and are vested with right to run import export business.

Import Value of Commodities by Place of Destination and Export Value of Commodities by Place of Origin in China The former indicator refers to the value of import commodities of the places of their consumption, utilization or the places of their final destination. The latter indicator refers to the value of export commodities of the places of their origin or the places of the commodities dispatched.

Utilization of Foreign Capitals refers to remittance, equipment and technology financed from abroad, by loans, foreign direct investment and other forms undertaken by the Chinese governments at all levels, by various departments, enterprises and other economic units.

Foreign Borrowings refer to funds borrowed from abroad through formal signing of borrowing agreements with foreign institutions, including loans of foreign governments, loans of international financial institutions, commercial loans of foreign banks, export credit, and funds raised by Chinese bonds (and shares before 1996) issued abroad. It is an important part of China's utilization of foreign capitals.

Foreign Direct Investment refers to the investments inside China by foreign enterprises and economic organizations or individuals (including overseas Chinese, compatriots from Hong Kong, Macao and Taiwan, and Chinese enterprises registered abroad), following the relevant policies and laws of China, for the establishment of ventures exclusively with foreign own investment, Sino-foreign joint ventures and cooperative enterprises or for co-operative exploration of resources with enterprises or economic organizations in China.

Number of Tourists

(1) Visitor arrivals refer to the number of foreigners, Chinese compatriots from Hong Kong, Macao and Taiwan Chinese (mainland) who come to China (mainland) for sight-seeing, vacation, visiting relatives, medical treatment, shopping, attending conference, or to engage in economic, cultural, sports and religious activities. In compiling statistics, each time of entering China is counted as one person-time.

(2) Number of Chinese residents going abroad refer to the number of Chinese (mainland) residents going to other countries, Hong Kong Special Administrative region, Macao Special Administrative region and Taiwan for on official or private purposes, for sight-seeing, vacation, visiting relatives, medical treatment, shopping, attending conference, or to engage in economic, cultural, sports and religious activities. In compiling statistics,

each time of leaving is counted as one person-time.

(3) Number of domestic tourists refers to the number of Chinese (mainland) residents who travel within China (mainland) for sight-seeing, vacation, visiting relatives, medical treatment, shopping, attending conference, or to engage in economic, cultural, sports and religious activities. In compiling statistics, each time of travelling is counted as one person-time.

Foreign Exchange Earnings from International Tourism refer to the total expenditure of foreigners, overseas Chinese, Chinese compatriots from Hong Kong, Macao and Taiwan during their stay in the mainland of China on transportation, sighting, accommodation, food, shopping and entertainment.

Income from Domestic Tourism refer to expenditure of domestic tourists on transportation, sighting, accommodation, food, shopping and entertainment while they travel.

International Travel Agencies refer to travel agencies engaged in tourism entering China, Chinese residents going abroad and domestic tourism.

Domestic Travel Agencies refer to travel agencies only engaged in domestic tourism.

Star-rated Hotels refer to hotels rated with stars as assessed by the relevant tourism authorities according to GB/T14308-2003 standard with reference to their infrastructure, facilities and service levels.

17 金融业

FINANCIAL INTERMEDIATION

资料整理：刘　婷
Data management:Liu Ting

第十七部分　金融业

一、简要说明

本章资料包括金融、证券和保险业情况，由西安市统计局综合处根据省银监局、省证监局、省保监局、人民银行西安分行营业管理部和市金融办提供资料整理。

二、主要指标

金融机构人民币（含外资）存款余额（亿元）	10430.27	比年初增加	1514.97亿元
金融机构人民币（含外资）贷款余额（亿元）	7564.93	比年初增加	1104.75亿元
保费收入（亿元）	162.57	比上年增长	25.7%

17　FINANCIAL INTERMEDIATION

Ⅰ.Brief Introduction

This chapter includes information of the financial, securities and insurance, compiled by Integration Division of the Xi'an Bureau of Statistics, according to data from Xi'an Branch Management Department of the People's Bank of China, Securities Supervisory Authority, Insurance Supervisory Authority,Provincial Banking Bureau and Xi'an Financial Office.

Ⅱ.Major Indicators

		Increase over Preceding Year
Deposit in Financial Institution(100 mil. yuan)	10430.27	1514.97
Loans in Financial Institutions(100 mil. yuan)	7564.93	1104.75
Premiums(100 mil. Yuan)	162.57	25.7%

17-1 西安银行系统机构、人员数

Number of Institution and Employed Person in Finance System in Xi'an

机构名称	Name of Institution	2010 机构数（个）Number of Institution (unit)	2010 年末人数（人）Number of Staff and Workers (person)	2011 机构数（个）Number of Institution (unit)	2011 年末人数（人）Number of Staff and Workers (person)
合　计	**Total**	**1741**	**29233**	**1763**	**31450**
人民银行西安分行营业管理部	Management Department of the People's Bank of China Xi'an Branch	1	401	**1**	**403**
国家开发银行陕西省分行	National Development Bank Shaanxi Branch	1	162	1	171
进出口银行陕西省分行	Export Import Bank of Shaanxi Branch	1	58	1	66
农业发展银行陕西省分行	Agricultural Development Bank of China Shaanxi Branch	10	258	10	258
工商银行陕西省分行	Industrial and Commercial Bank of China Shaanxi Branch	193	4974	193	4946
农业银行陕西省分行	Agricultural Bank of China Shaanxi Branch	165	3033	165	3038
中国银行陕西省分行	Bank of China Shaanxi Branch	120	3073	122	3266
建设银行陕西省分行	Construction Bank of China Shaanxi Branch	175	3694	177	3851
中国光大银行西安分行	China Everbright Bank Xi'an Branch	16	499	17	573
华夏银行西安分行	China Huaxia Bank Xi'an Branch	9	290	10	321
招商银行西安分行	China Merchants Bank Xi'an Branch	23	981	24	1053
浦发银行西安分行	Pufa Bank Xi'an Branch	11	480	12	567
民生银行西安分行	China Minsheng Banking Corp., Ltd Xi'an Branch	14	698	15	781
福建兴业银行西安分行	Fujian Industrial Bank Xi'an Branch	13	378	13	755
西安银行	Bank of Xi'an	114	2284	114	2283
东亚银行西安分行	Dongya Bank Xi'an Branch	5	218	6	303
汇丰银行西安分行	Huifeng Bank Xi'an Branch	3	63	3	60
交通银行西安分行	Bank of Communication Xi'an Branch	48	1066	49	1062
中信实业银行西安分行	CITIC Industrial Bank Xi'an Branch	17	639	19	659
浙商银行西安分行	China Zheshang Bank Xi'an Branch	2	164	2	161
恒丰银行西安分行	Evergrowing Bank Xi'an Branch			1	80
北京银行西安分行	Bank of Beijing, Xi'an Branch	3	218	4	286
齐商银行西安分行	Qi Commercial Bank Xi'an Branch	1	39	2	63
成都银行西安分行	Bank of Chengdu, Xi'an Branch			1	78
重庆银行西安分行	Bank of Chongqing, Xi'an Branch			1	72
长安银行西安分行	Xi'an Branch of Bank of Changan	2	71	3	108
昆仑银行西安分行	Kunlun Xi'an Branch Bank	1	63	1	147
邮政储蓄银行西安分行	The postal savings bank branch in Xi'an	272	701	274	734
英国标准渣打银行西安分行	British Standard Chartered bank Xi'an Branch			1	42
农村信用社联合社	Rural Credit Cooperatives Association	520	4702	520	5237
西安高陵阳光村镇银行	Xi'an Gaoling sunshine village bank	1	26	1	26

17-2 金融机构（含外资）本外币存贷款年末余额（2011年）

Financial institution Including Foreign-funded Balance of Bisic Currency and Foreign Currency at Year-end（2011）

单位：亿元 (100 million yuan)

指 标	Item	2011	比年初增减数 Increase or decrease compared with the beginning of the Year
存款余额合计（汇率：6.3009）	**Total Deposit （Exchange Rate：6.3009）**	**10526.32**	**1498.31**
一、单位存款	**Company Deposit**	**6054.20**	**943.34**
#活期存款	Demand Deposits	3219.78	497.35
定期存款	Time Deposits	1486.97	417.52
二、个人存款	**Personal Deposits**	**4231.82**	**551.46**
#储蓄存款	Savings Deposits	4191.14	531.48
三、财政性存款	**Fiscal Deposits**	**60.25**	**24.25**
四、临时性存款	**Temporary Deposit**	**14.50**	**-10.68**
五、委托存款	**Consignment Deposits**	**36.38**	**-29.55**
六、其他存款	**Other Deposits**	**129.17**	**19.49**
贷款余额合计（汇率：6.3009）	**Total Loans（Exchange Rate：6.3009）**	**7700.19**	**1130.57**
一、境内贷款	**Domestic Loans**	**7682.01**	**1119.39**
短期贷款	Short-term Loans	1474.11	345.75
中长期贷款	Medium-term and Long-term loans	5847.72	700.02
融资租赁	Financial Leasing	1.85	-1.42
票据融资	Bill Financing	354.84	72.12
各项垫款	Various Advance Funds	3.49	2.92
二、境外贷款	**Foreign Loans**	**18.18**	**11.18**

17–3 金融机构（不含外资）本外币存贷款年末余额（2011年）

Domestic Funded Financial institution balance of Bisic Currency and Foreign Currency at Year-end（2011）

单位：亿元 (100 million yuan)

指　　标	Item	2011	比年初增减数 Increase or decrease compared with the beginning of the Year
存款余额合计（汇率：6.3009）	**Total Deposit （Exchange Rate：6.3009）**	**10443.15**	**1488.20**
一、单位存款	**Company Deposit**	**5995.03**	**939.81**
#活期存款	Demand Deposits	3192.56	496.02
定期存款	Time Deposits	1455.03	415.33
二、个人存款	**Personal Deposits**	**4207.82**	**544.87**
#储蓄存款	Savings Deposits	4167.13	524.89
三、财政性存款	**Fiscal Deposits**	60.25	24.25
四、临时性存款	**Temporary Deposit**	**14.50**	**-10.68**
五、委托存款	**Consignment Deposits**	**36.38**	**-29.55**
六、其他存款	**Other Deposits**	**129.17**	**19.49**
贷款余额合计（汇率：6.3009）	**Total Loans（Exchange Rate：6.3009）**	**7626.63**	**1122.07**
一、境内贷款	**Domestic Loans**	**7608.49**	**1110.88**
短期贷款	Short-term Loans	1455.48	339.06
中长期贷款	Medium-term and Long-term loans	5793.01	697.78
融资租赁	Financial Leasing	1.85	-1.42
票据融资	Bill Financing	354.66	72.54
各项垫款	Various Advance Funds	3.49	2.92
二、境外贷款	**Foreign Loans**	**18.14**	**11.19**

17-4 主要年份金融机构（含外资）人民币存款年末余额

Year-end Balance of Deposit in Financial Institutions Including Foreign-funded in Representative Years

单位：亿元 (100 million yuan)

年 份 Year	合 计 Total	其 中：Among 单位存款 Company Deposit	储蓄存款 Savings Deposits
1978	12.82		3.72
1980	20.99		5.48
1985	40.68		16.70
1990	112.37	31.10	62.23
1995	359.51	114.54	230.63
1996	619.98	199.85	394.02
1997	602.50	227.61	358.78
1998	799.54	245.44	499.68
1999	1014.27	347.49	586.40
2000	1335.63	540.19	675.83
2001	1629.72	674.49	800.86
2002	2191.47	884.69	988.04
2003	2665.87	1041.43	1210.56
2004	3061.66	1159.98	1432.86
2005	3599.70	1237.37	1716.76
2006	4066.16	1374.91	1950.53
2007	4582.71	1702.12	2002.38
2008	5749.35	2213.67	2513.70
2009	7522.08	3077.99	3084.20
2010	8933.23	3556.78	3641.09
2011	10430.27	5997.60	4155.65

17-5 主要年份金融机构（含外资）人民币贷款年末余额

Year-end Balance of Loans in Financial Institutions Including Foreign-funded in Representative Years

单位：亿元 (100 million yuan)

年 份 Year	合 计 Total	其 中：Among	
		短期贷款 Short-term Loans	中长期贷款 Medium-term&Long-term Loans
1978	23.56		
1980	26.40		
1985	48.60		
1990	131.67	101.13	23.78
1995	334.50	252.30	73.32
1996	477.97	333.88	90.12
1997	443.76	342.79	87.27
1998	597.34	448.74	118.42
1999	786.20	589.52	150.64
2000	972.51	652.00	241.27
2001	1185.97	666.41	387.82
2002	1598.42	780.69	502.03
2003	1954.18	946.61	743.72
2004	2052.33	950.50	850.01
2005	2158.10	830.68	1013.32
2006	2344.77	812.33	1310.57
2007	2683.77	883.32	1593.37
2008	3275.12	1031.62	1905.08
2009	4482.63	1155.83	2908.75
2010	6482.28	1097.60	5075.98
2011	7564.93	1431.29	5776.48

17-6 金融机构（含外资）人民币存贷款年末余额（2011年）

Year-end Balance of Deposit and Loans in Financial Institutions Including Foreign-funded（2011）

单位：亿元 (100 million yuan)

指　　标	Item	2011	比年初增减数 Increase or decrease compared with the beginning of the Year
存款余额合计	**Total Deposit**	**10430.27**	**1514.97**
一、单位存款	**Company Deposit**	**5997.60**	**959.37**
#活期存款	Demand Deposits	3181.93	500.72
定期存款	Time Deposits	1482.71	426.36
二、个人存款	**Personal Deposits**	**4194.70**	**551.10**
#储蓄存款	Savings Deposits	4155.65	531.27
三、财政性存款	**Fiscal Deposits**	**60.25**	**24.25**
四、临时性存款	**Temporary Deposit**	**12.24**	**-9.97**
五、委托存款	**Trusted Deposits**	**36.32**	**-29.36**
六、其他存款	**Other Deposits**	**129.16**	**19.58**
贷款余额合计	**Total Loans**	**7564.93**	**1104.75**
一、境内贷款	**Domestic Loans**	**7564.53**	**1104.71**
（一）短期贷款	Short-term Loans	1431.29	348.40
1.个人贷款及透支	Individual Loans and Overdrafts	111.91	38.53
2.单位普通贷款及透支	Unit Loans and Overdrafts	1247.41	282.04
3.普通并购贷款	Ordinary Merging Loans	0.80	0.80
4.银团贷款	Syndicated Loans	4.20	-4.00
5.贸易融资	Trade Finance	66.97	31.03
（二）中长期贷款	Medium-term&Long-term Loans	5776.48	686.12
1.个人贷款	Individual Loans and Overdrafts	1317.15	307.49
2.单位普通贷款	Unit Loans and Overdrafts	3812.15	308.89
3.普通并购贷款	Ordinary Merging Loans	7.25	1.65
4.银团贷款	Syndicated Loans	639.94	68.90
5.贸易融资	Trade Finance		-0.81
（三）融资租赁	Financial Leasing	1.85	-1.43
（四）票据融资	Bill Financing	354.72	72.00
（五）各项垫款	Various Advance Funds	0.19	-0.38
二、境外贷款	**Foreign Loans**	**0.40**	**0.04**

17-7 金融机构（不含外资）人民币存贷款年末余额（2011年）

Year-end Balance of Deposit and Loans in Financial Institutions Not Including Foreign-funded（2011）

单位：亿元 (100 million yuan)

指　标	Item	2011	比年初增减数 Increase or decrease compared with the beginning of the Year
存款余额合计	**Total Deposit**	**10350.80**	**1505.38**
一、单位存款	**Company Deposit**	**5940.53**	**955.84**
#活期存款	Demand Deposits	3156.70	499.34
定期存款	Time Deposits	1450.86	424.21
二、个人存款	**Personal Deposits**	**4172.31**	**545.04**
#储蓄存款	Savings Deposits	4133.26	525.21
三、财政性存款	**Fiscal Deposits**	**60.25**	**24.25**
四、临时性存款	**Temporary Deposit**	**12.24**	**-9.96**
五、委托存款	**Trusted Deposits**	**36.32**	**-29.36**
六、其他存款	**Other Deposits**	**129.15**	**19.59**
贷款余额合计	**Total Loans**	**7496.25**	**1097.64**
一、境内贷款	**Domestic Loans**	**7495.88**	**1097.59**
（一）短期贷款	Short-term Loans	1414.64	342.10
1.个人贷款及透支	Individual Loans and Overdrafts	111.91	39.00
2.单位普通贷款及透支	Unit Loans and Overdrafts	1230.76	275.27
3.普通并购贷款	Ordinary Merging Loans	0.80	0.80
4.银团贷款	Syndicated Loans	4.20	-4.00
5.贸易融资	Trade Finance	66.97	31.03
（二）中长期贷款	Medium-term&Long-term Loans	5724.68	684.88
1.个人贷款	Individual Loans and Overdrafts	1307.73	303.96
2.单位普通贷款	Unit Loans and Overdrafts	3769.76	311.18
3.普通并购贷款	Ordinary Merging Loans	7.25	1.65
4.银团贷款	Syndicated Loans	639.94	68.90
5.贸易融资	Trade Finance		-0.81
（三）融资租赁	Financial Leasing	1.85	-1.43
（四）票据融资	Bill Financing	354.53	72.42
（五）各项垫款	Various Advance Funds	0.18	-0.38
二、境外贷款	**Foreign Loans**	**0.37**	**0.05**

17-8 保险业务情况

Indicators of Insurance Business

指　　标	Item	2010	2011
保险金额（亿元）	**Amount Insured(100 million yuan)**	**29955.5**	**44511.2**
保费收入（万元）	**Premiums(10 000 yuan)**	**1293677.5**	**1625666.2**
一、财产险	**Property Insurance**	**338594.6**	**449625.3**
（一）财产保险	Property Insurance	325077.2	422738.7
1.机动车辆及第三者责任	Motor Vehicle and Outside Person Liability	278322.2	364584.6
2.企业财产险	Enterprise Property Insurance	28685.2	37452.1
3.货物运输保险	Freight Transport Insurance	3750.6	4208.2
4.家庭财产保险	Family Property Insurance	208.9	365.5
5.建工及安工保险及其责任险	Construction and Installation Projects Insurance and Related Libility Insurance	13176.7	15004.0
6.其他	Others	933.5	1124.3
（二）责任保险	Liability Insurance	6983.8	8987.7
（三）信用保险	Export Credit Insurance	3528.5	8187.5
（四）保证保险	Guarantee Insurance	2453.5	8798.3
（五）农业保险	Agriculture Insurance	551.6	913.1
二、人身险	**Personnel Insurance**	**955083.0**	**1176040.9**
（一）人寿保险	Life Insurance	869729.9	1072364.2
1.非分红保险	Non Dividend Insurance	93819.4	95292.4
2.分红保险	Dividend Insurance	763660.7	966023.7
3.投资连接保险	Insurance Connection Insurance	468.7	361.5
4.万能保险	Universal Insurance	11781.1	10686.6
（二）意外伤害保险	Unforeseen Injury Insurance	28967.8	37064.2
（三）健康保险	Health Insurance	56385.3	66612.6
赔款支出和各项给付（万元）	**Indemnity and Other Expenditure(10 000 yuan)**	**263886.8**	**371420.9**
一、财产险	**Property Insurance**	**141038.0**	**199915.5**
（一）财产保险	Property Insurance	135480.0	192899.6
1.机动车辆及第三者责任	Motor Vehicle and Outside Person Liability	115094.8	163878.3
2.企业财产险	Enterprise Property Insurance	14914.9	15150.8
3.家庭财产保险	Freight Transport Insurance	109.4	130.1
4.货物运输保险	Family Property Insurance	973.8	1341.7
5.建工及安工保险及其责任险	Construction and Installation Projects Insurance and Related Libility Insurance	4317.8	11345.1
6.其他	Others	69.4	1053.7
（二）责任保险	Liability Insurance	2314.0	3114.1
（三）信用保险	Export Credit Insurance	1160.9	2324.1
（四）保证保险	Guarantee Insurance	107.8	578.5
（五）农业保险	Agriculture Insurance	1975.4	999.2
二、人身险	**Personnel Insurance**	**122848.8**	**171505.4**
（一）人寿保险	Life Insurance	96704.5	140239.9
1.非分红保险	Non Dividend Insurance	34451.8	40016.8
2.分红保险	Dividend Insurance	61107.2	98168.6
3.投资连接保险	Insurance Connection Insurance	52.4	595.1
4.万能保险	Universal Insurance	1093.2	1459.4
（二）意外伤害保险	Unforeseen Injury Insurance	7479.9	7571.9
（三）健康保险	Health Insurance	18664.4	23693.5
退保金（万元）	**Withdrawal(10 000 yuan)**	**48108.4**	**90545.9**
#人寿保险	Life Insurance	46397.0	89150.4
1.非分红保险	Ordinary Life Insurance	4287.7	4302.5
2.分红保险	Dividend Insurance	42159.2	84803.5
3.投资连接保险	Insurance Connection Insurance	-3.4	1.6
4.万能保险	Universal Insurance	-46.6	42.8

注：2010年及以后统计口径调整。

Note:2010 and later statistic caliber changing.

17-9 西安证券期货系统机构、人员数

Number of Institution and Employed Person in Securities and Futures System in Xi'an

机构名称	Name of Institution	2010		2011	
		机构数（个）Number of Institution (unit)	年末人数（人）Number of Staff and Workers (person)	机构数（个）Number of Institution (unit)	年末人数（人）Number of Staff and Workers (person)
证券经营机构	**Securities Company and the Sales Department**				
一、证券公司	**Securities Company**				
西部证券股份有限公司	Western Securities Company Ltd.	56	2183	60	2344
开源证券有限责任公司	KaiYuan Securities Company Ltd.	4	163	8	224
中邮证券有限责任公司	ZhongYou Securities Company Ltd.	4	204	6	238
二、证券营业部（含外地公司在西安营业部）	**Sales Department (include Xi'an departments of nonlocal companies.)**	**61**	**2698**	**66**	**2989**
期货经纪机构	**Futures Company**	**3**	**271**	**3**	**345**
迈科期货经纪有限公司	Maike Futures Company Ltd.	1	139	1	177
陕西长安期货经纪有限公司	Shaanxi ChangAn Futures Company Ltd.	1	46	1	77
西部期货经纪有限公司	Western Futures Brokerage Co., Ltd.	1	86	1	91

注：证券公司包括三家证券公司在西安和外地的营业部。

Note:Securities companies include departments in and out of Xi'an of the three securities companies.

17–10 证券期货市场基本情况（2011年）

Basic Facts on Securities and Futures Markets（2011）

指　标	Item	2011
一、上市证券公司情况	**Listed Securities Companies**	
拥有上市股份公司（个）	Number of Listed Share-holding Companies(unit)	28
占全国比重（%）	Percentage to National Total(%)	1.2
上市股份公司总股本（亿股）	Total Capital of Listed Share-holding Companies (100 millon shares)	194
#流通股（亿股）	Negotiable Shares(100 million shares)	144
总市值（亿元）	Total Market Capitalization(100 million yuan)	1593
累计证券市场筹措资金（亿元）	Accumulated Capital Raised by Securities Markets(100 millon yuan)	503.14
二、证券经营机构情况	**Securities Trading Organizations**	
拥有证券公司（个）	Number of Securities Companies(unit)	3
证券营业部(含外地公司在西安营业部）（个）	Number of Securities Business Departments(unit)	66
投资者开户数（万户）	Number of Investors Who have Opened an Account(10 000 accounts)	165
证券交易总额（亿元）	Total Turnover(100 million yuan)	9851
三、期货市场情况	**Futures Market**	
拥有期货经纪公司（个）	Number of Futures Business Management Companies(unit)	3
期货营业部（个）	Number of Futures Business Departments(unit)	12
期货代理交易额（亿元）	Total Transaction Value in Futures Commissioning (100 million yuan)	40101.68
每个经纪公司平均拥有注册资金（万元）	Average Registered Capital of Each Business Management Company(10 000 yuan)	7666.66

主要统计指标解释

信贷资金 指金融机构以信用方式积聚和分配的货币资金。金融机构信贷资金的来源有各项存款、金融债券、对国际金融机构负债、流通中现金、其他项目等；信贷资金的运用有各项贷款、有价证券及投资、金银占款、外汇占款、财政借款及在国际金融机构中的资产等。

存款 指企业、机关、团体或居民根据资金必须收回的原则，把货币资金存入银行或其他信贷机构保管并取得一定利息的一种信用活动形式。根据存款对象或性质的不同可划分为企业存款、财政存款、机关团体存款、城乡储蓄存款、农业存款、信托及委托类存款、其他存款等科目。它是银行信贷资金的主要来源。

贷款 指银行或其他信贷机构根据资金必须归还的原则，按一定利率，为企业、个人等提供资金的一种信用活动形式。我国银行贷款分为短期贷款、委托及信托类贷款、其他类贷款等。

保险公司 在中国境内的、经过保险监督管理部门批准设立，并依法登记注册的各类商业保险公司。

保险金额 指保险人承担赔偿或者给付保险金责任的最高限额。

保费 指投保人为取得保险人在约定范围内所承担赔偿责任而支付给保险人的费用。

赔款 指保险人根据保险合同的规定，向被保险人支付的赔偿保险责任损失的金额。

给付 包括死伤医疗给付和满期给付。死伤医疗给付是指保险人根据人寿保险及长期健康保险合同的规定，因被保险人在保险期内发生保险责任范围内的保险事故支付给被保险人(或受益人)的金额。满期给付是指被保险人生存期满，保险人按人寿保险合同规定支付给被保险人的满期保险金额。

Explanatory Notes on Main Statistical Indicators

Credit Funds refer to the monetary funds accumulated and distributed in the means of credit by the financial institutions. The sources of credit funds include various deposits, financial bonds, liabilities to international financial institutions, currency in circulation, other items. The uses of credit funds include loans, securities and investment, position for bullion and silver purchase, position for foreign exchange purchase, advances to treasury, and assets with international financial institutions..

Deposit is a form of credit by which enterprises, institutions, organizations or households can put money into banks and other credit institutions for safekeeping and interest earning under the principle of free withdrawal. According to different depositors, deposits are divided into enterprise deposits, fiscal deposits, deposits of government agencies and organizations, savings deposits of rural and urban households, agricultural savings deposits, entrusted deposits and other deposits. Deposits are major sources of the credit funds of banks.

Loan is a form of credit by which banks and other credit institutions provide funds at certain interest rate to enterprises and individuals in the light of the principle of unconditional repayment. Loans from Chinese banks include short-term loan, medium- term and long-term loans, entrusted loans, and other loans.

Insurance Companies refer to commercial insurance companies of various forms registered by law and established in China with the approval of insurance regulatory agencies.

Amount Insured refers to the maximum that the insurant will get for the claim of the case insured.

Premium is the fee paid by the insurant to the insurer to obtain the obligation of compensation from the insurance within the agreed terms.

Settled Claim is the compensation paid by the insurer to the insurant in accordance with the insurance contract.

Payment includes payment for death, injury or medical treatment and payment at maturity. Payment for death, injury or medical treatment refers to the money paid to the insurant (or the beneficiary) in accordance with the life or health insurance contract when the insurant encounters accidents within the insured period covered in the contract. Payment at maturity refers to the payment to the insurant in accordance with the life insurance contract at the end of the insured period.

18 教育和科技

EDUCATION,SCIENCE AND TECHNOLOGY

资料整理：陈超毅　齐昆峰
Data management:Chen Chaoyi Qi Kunfeng

第十八部分　教育和科技

一、简要说明

本章资料包括教育事业、科技事业基本情况，由西安市统计局社会科技处根据西安市教委等有关部门提供资料整理。

二、主要指标

普通高等学校数（所）	61	比上年增加	11所
普通高等学校（本专科）在校学生（万人）	68.52	比上年增长	4.2%
研究生在校人数（万人）	8.17	比上年增长	24.3%

18　EDUCATION,SCIENCE AND TECHNOLOGY

Ⅰ.Brief Introduction

Data in this chapter consists of primarily data of educational undertakings, science and technology Activities of Xi'an city, compiled by Social & Science and Technology Division of the Xi'an Bureau of Statistics according to data from Xi'an Municipal Government Departments concerned.

Ⅱ.Major Indicators

		Increase over Preceding Year
Number of Schools Regular Institutions of Higher Education(unit)	61	11
Student Enrollment of Regular Institutions of Higher Education(10 000 persons)	68.52	4.2%
Postgraduates(10 000 persons)	8.17	24.3%

18-1 主要年份各类普通教育基本情况

Basic Statistics on Regular Eduction in Representative Years

指 标	Item	2000	2005	2006	2007	2008	2009	2010	2011
学校数(所)	**Number of Schools (unit)**								
普通高等教育	Regular Institutions of Higher Education	25	44	47	48	48	49	50	61
普通中等专业学校	Regular Specialized Secondary Schools	47	32	31	30	29	28	28	24
普通中等教育学校	Regular Secondary Education Schools	466	460	457	453	442	439	436	423
小学	Primary Schools	2323	1980	1929	1872	1781	1666	1531	1424
学前教育	Preschool Education	367	737	863	830	905	896	1004	1122
毕业生数(万人)	**Graduates (10 000 persons)**								
普通高等教育	Regular Institutions of Higher Education	3.0	11.1	13.0	15.8	17.6	16.9	18.3	19.7
普通中等专业学校	Regular Specialized Secondary Schools	1.6	1.4	1.8	2.0	2.6	2.7	2.5	2.3
普通中等教育学校	Regular Secondary Education Schools	12.0	18.8	18.0	18.4	18.0	17.8	17.0	16.4
小学	Primary Schools	13.8	11.9	11.5	11.4	10.6	10.0	9.6	8.9
学前教育	Preschool Education								6.4
招生数(万人)	**New Enrollment (10 000 persons)**								
普通高等教育	Regular Institutions of Higher Education	7.5	16.5	17.1	19.0	21.5	21.3	21.7	23.1
普通中等专业学校	Regular Specialized Secondary Schools	1.9	2.3	2.6	2.9	2.6	2.2	2.1	2.0
普通中等教育学校	Regular Secondary Education Schools	17.9	18.5	18.6	18.0	17.2	16.6	16.2	15.4
小学	Primary Schools	11.5	8.5	9.2	8.7	8.3	7.8	8.6	8.8
学前教育	Preschool Education	8.7	6.6	6.9	6.7	7.7	7.2	8.4	10.0
在校学生(万人)	**Total Enrollment (10 000 persons)**								
普通高等教育	Regular Institutions of Higher Education	19.4	53.1	57.1	62.3	66.7	70.3	73.3	76.6
普通中等专业学校	Regular Specialized Secondary Schools	6.0	6.2	7.3	8.0	8.1	7.4	6.8	6.1
普通中等教育学校	Regular Secondary Education Schools	48.3	55.7	56.1	54.7	52.8	50.6	48.9	47.2
小学	Primary Schools	77.8	60.5	59.3	56.8	54.7	52.5	51.6	51.4
学前教育	Preschool Education	12.9	12.8	13.4	14.1	15.5	16.3	18.4	24.0
教职工（人）	**Staff and Teachers (person)**								
普通高等教育	Regular Institutions of Higher Education	38067	57285	61414	65624	69048	70818	72247	72739
普通中等专业学校	Regular Specialized Secondary Schools	6964	3924	3621	3548	3417	2965	3249	2868
普通中等教育学校	Regular Secondary Education Schools	34385	39456	39341	39171	39088	39002	39207	41135
小学	Primary Schools	35336	33907	34460	34901	34653	34389	34118	32457
学前教育	Preschool Education	6346	10528	12335	13468	14932	15928	18710	23680
专任教师(人)	**Number of Full-time Teachers (person)**								
普通高等教育	Regular Institutions of Higher Education	15679	29498	32891	36717	38926	40605	42098	42734
普通中等专业学校	Regular Specialized Secondary Schools	3172	2130	2014	2011	1904	1720	1845	1723
普通中等教育学校	Regular Secondary Education Schools	26230	31094	31203	31373	31425	31415	31506	33122
小学	Primary Schools	30215	29674	30018	30533	30382	30334	29944	28453
学前教育	Preschool Education	2995	5959	7106	7951	8704	9240	10638	12577

注：普通高等教育含高校研究生。

Note:Regular institution of higher education includes postgraduates.

18-2 各级普通教育教师情况（2011年）

Basic Facts on Regular Education Teacher by School Type（2011）

指　标	Item	学校数（所）Number of Schools (unit)	教职工数(人) Number of Staff and Teachers (person)	专任教师(人) Full-time Teachers (person)
一、高等教育	**Higher education**	**77**	**76218**	**44703**
（一）研究生（不计校数）	Postgraduates(Regardless the number of school)			
1.高等学校	Institutions of Higher Schools			
2.科研机构	Scientific Research Institution			
（二）普通高等学校	Regular Institutions of Higher Schools	61	72739	42734
1. 本科院校	Universities and Colleges of Undergraduate Course	39	61547	36589
2.高职（专科）院校	Higher Vocational Colleges	22	11192	6145
（三）成人高等学校	Adult Higher Schools	16	3479	1969
（四）民办的其他高等教育	Private Higher Learning Institutions		729	305
机构（不计校数）	（Regardless 0f the school）			
二、中等职业教育	Secondary Occupation Education	**226**	**19731**	**14257**
1.普通中等专业学校	Regular Specialized Secondary Schools	24	2868	1723
2.成人中等专业学校	Adult Secondary Specialized Schools	6	1361	733
3.职业高中学校	Vocational Hight Schools	78	4849	3173
4.技工学校	Technical Schools	118	10653	8628
三、基础教育	**Elementary Education**	**2978**	**97660**	**74410**
（一）普通中等教育	Regular Institutions Education	423	41135	33122
1.高中	Senior High Schools	172	22796	17922
2.初中	Junior Middle Schools	251	18339	15200
（二）普通初等教育	Regular Primary Education	1424	32457	28453
小学	Primary Schools	1424	32457	28453
（三）特殊教育	Special Education Schools	8	343	231
（四）工读学校	Reformatory Schools	1	45	27
（五）学前教育	Preschool Education	1122	23680	12577

18–3 各级教育学生情况（2011年）

Basic Facts on Education Student by School Type（2011）

指　标	Item	学校数（所）Number of Schools (unit)	毕业生数（人）Number of Graduates (persons)	招生数（人）New Enrollment (persons)	在校学生数（人）Total Enrollment (persons)
一、高等教育	**Higher education**	**77**	**278825**	**335904**	**1044480**
（一）研究生（不计校数）	Postgraduates(Regardless the number of school)		20965	26686	81696
1.普通高校	Ordinary Colleges and Universities		20605	26256	80332
2.科研机构	Scientific Research Institution		360	430	1364
（二）普通高等学校	Regular Institutions of Higher Education	61	176754	205175	685232
1.本科	Undergraduate Course Schools	39	91540	130604	456186
2.专科	Junior Colleges	22	85214	74571	229046
（三）成人高等学校	Adult Higher Schools	16	45741	53548	161123
（四）网络本专科生	Network Undergraduate and college students		33598	50495	114169
（五）民办的其他高等教育机构（不计校数）	Private Higher Learning Institutions（Regardless of the school）		1767		2260
二、中等职业教育	Secondary Occupation Education	**226**	**100692**	**102523**	**304778**
1.普通中等专业学校	Regular Specialized Secondary Schools	24	23398	19550	61116
2.成人中等专业学校	Adult Secondary Specialized Schools	6	610	3834	13725
3.职业高中学校	Vocational High Schools	78	23468	28756	80360
4.技工学校	Technical Schools	118	53216	50383	149577
三、基础教育	**Elementary Education**	**2978**	**317776**	**341704**	**1227606**
（一）普通中等教育	Regular Institutions Education	423	164350	154164	471968
1.高中	Senior Middle Schools	172	58046	62678	185236
2.初中	Junior Middle Schools	251	106304	91486	286732
（二）普通初等教育	Regular Primary Education	1424	89184	87699	513916
小学	Primary Schools	1424	82950	80507	474874
（三）特殊教育学校	Special Education Schools	8	280	222	1393
（四）工读学校	Reformatory Schools	1	20	20	51
（五）幼儿园	Kindergarten	1122	63942	99599	240278

18-4 主要年份普通高等学校和科研机构研究生情况

Basic Statistics on Regular Institutions Schools and Post-graduates of Scientific Research Institution in Representative Years

单位：人 (persons)

年份	毕业生数		招生数		在校学生数	
	Number of Graduates	高等学校 Higher Schools	New Enrollment	高等学校 Higher Schools	Total Enrollment	高等学校 Higher Schools
Year						
1978						
1980					651	651
1985					4799	4799
1990	2051	2051	1662	1662	5275	5275
1995	1769	1769	2712	2712	7974	7974
1998	2316	2316	3888	3888	10833	10833
1999	2903	2903	5020	5020	12986	12986
2000	3236	3236	6924	6924	16620	16620
2001	3881	3770	9274	8966	22564	21855
2002	4103	3952	11282	10882	28446	27471
2003	5971	5765	14322	13882	36936	35790
2004	8384	8127	17310	16871	45402	44169
2005	10416	10127	18583	18106	52699	51310
2006	12914	12552	19581	19105	58433	56951
2007	15506	15124	20570	20167	64137	62801
2008	17234	16788	21892	21443	67296	65834
2009	19025	18574	24879	24400	72366	70908
2010	19526	19129	25971	25477	76993	75483
2011	20965	20605	26686	26256	81696	80332

18-5 主要年份普通高等教育基本情况

Baisc Statistics on Regular Higher Education in Representative Years

单位：万人 (10 000 person)

年 份 Year	学校数(所) Number of Schools (unit)	毕业生数 Number of Graduates	招生数 New Enrollment	在校学生数 Total Enrollment	教职工数 Number of Staff and Teachers	专任教师 Full-time Teachers
1978	21			2.88		0.87
1980	25			4.17		0.97
1985	28			6.49		1.28
1990	31	2.17	2.15	8.02	4.15	1.56
1995	32	3.04	3.40	10.87	4.21	1.59
1998	29	2.84	3.69	12.66	3.91	1.50
1999	29	3.13	5.62	15.09	3.95	1.52
2000	25	3.03	7.49	19.41	3.80	1.57
2001	32	3.69	9.24	25.49	4.30	1.75
2002	35	4.23	11.88	33.00	4.67	2.06
2003	37	6.49	13.65	40.12	4.92	2.21
2004	41	7.66	13.17	40.29	5.45	2.69
2005	44	10.08	14.68	47.79	5.73	2.95
2006	47	11.75	15.15	51.40	6.14	3.29
2007	48	14.33	16.96	56.03	6.56	3.67
2008	48	15.82	19.31	60.10	6.90	3.89
2009	49	15.04	18.84	63.22	7.08	4.06
2010	50	16.33	19.16	65.74	7.22	4.21
2011	61	17.68	20.52	68.52	7.27	4.27

18–6 主要年份普通中等专业学校基本情况

Baisc Statistics on Regular Specialized Secondary Schools in Representative Years

单位：万人 （10 000 persons）

年 份 Year	学校数(所) Number of Schools (unit)	毕业生数 Number of Graduates	招生数 New Enrollment	在校学生数 Total Enrollment	教职工数（人） Number of Staff and Teachers(person)	专任教师 Full-time Teachers
1978	19			0.87		1110
1980	33			1.50		1474
1985	37			1.70		2363
1990	44	0.56	0.68	2.09	7136	2891
1995	46	0.97	1.37	3.74	5903	2533
1996	47	1.15	1.61	4.18	5940	2573
1997	47	1.20	1.65	4.63	6124	2731
1998	47	1.26	1.62	5.08	6181	2840
1999	46	1.42	2.11	5.75	6385	2865
2000	47	1.63	1.90	6.02	6964	3172
2001	47	1.70	1.58	5.63	5252	2467
2002	46	1.60	1.69	5.57	5170	2508
2003	34	1.62	1.80	5.28	4562	2302
2004	35	1.40	2.09	5.71	4676	2388
2005	32	1.44	2.26	6.16	3924	2130
2006	31	1.84	2.61	7.30	3621	2014
2007	30	2.03	2.91	7.97	3548	2011
2008	29	2.58	2.55	8.06	3278	1814
2009	28	2.70	2.15	7.44	2965	1720
2010	28	2.45	2.08	6.75	3249	1845
2011	24	2.34	1.96	6.11	2868	1723

18-7 主要年份普通中学基本情况

Baisc Statistics on Regular Secondary Schools in Representative Years

单位：万人 （10 000 persons）

年 份 Year	学校数(所) Number of Schools (unit)	毕业生数 Number of Graduates	招生数 New Enrollment	在校学生数 Total Enrollment	教职工数（人） Number of Staff and Teachers(person)	专任教师 Full-time Teachers
1978	962			44.16		20660
1980	1002	12.33	14.03	44.08	29867	22530
1985	563	10.72	13.05	38.24	30063	22050
1990	518	9.11	10.49	30.03	30739	22386
1995	485	8.13	12.40	32.32	30423	21984
1996	462	8.67	13.03	35.25	30902	22478
1997	466	9.96	13.83	37.16	31682	23129
1998	467	10.64	15.00	39.79	32371	23884
1999	469	11.21	16.58	43.49	33387	25114
2000	466	12.01	17.88	48.31	34385	26230
2001	470	13.85	18.98	52.50	35442	27190
2002	467	15.76	19.68	55.36	36706	28335
2003	467	16.76	18.78	56.44	38252	29887
2004	461	18.01	18.85	56.54	39121	30600
2005	460	18.82	18.83	55.74	39456	31094
2006	457	18.04	18.61	56.11	39341	31203
2007	453	18.37	17.96	54.68	39171	31373
2008	442	17.99	17.16	52.83	39088	31425
2009	439	17.80	16.57	50.63	39002	31415
2010	436	17.01	16.15	48.89	39207	31506
2011	423	16.44	15.42	47.20	41135	33122

18-8 各区县普通中学基本情况（2011年）

Baisc Statistics on Regular Secondary Schools by Region （2011）

单位：所、人 （unit,person）

区县	Region	学校数 Number of Schools	毕业生数 Number of Graduates	高中 Senior	招生数 New Enrollment	高中 Senior	在校学生数 Total Enrollment	高中 Senior	教职工数 Number of Staff and Teachers	专任教师 Full-time Teachers
合 计	**Total**	**423**	**164350**	**58046**	**154164**	**62678**	**471968**	**185236**	**41135**	**31675**
新城区	Xincheng	25	11747	3910	12322	4337	37211	13006	2694	1980
碑林区	Beilin	36	16976	6893	16769	7393	50391	21700	4077	3013
莲湖区	Lianhu	21	11537	4199	11595	4198	35064	12563	2932	2095
灞桥区	Baqiao	28	8010	2708	7416	2608	22891	8258	2163	1619
未央区	Weiyang	28	8571	3555	10120	4397	28763	12423	3108	1933
雁塔区	Yanta	45	15364	5328	16220	5757	48630	17456	4512	3092
阎良区	Yanliang	12	5174	2152	4373	1832	13765	5741	1248	1011
临潼区	Lintong	32	14948	4665	13054	5116	40950	14905	3466	2908
长安区	Chang'an	48	18015	6994	15051	6787	47739	20853	4341	3680
蓝田县	Lantian	46	14342	4384	13530	5052	40860	14022	3391	2628
周至县	Zhouzhi	36	17217	5213	14068	6719	44269	18668	3644	2911
户 县	Huxian	39	13711	5382	11910	5563	37939	17188	3258	2871
高陵县	Gaoling	15	4889	1675	4456	2072	13535	5903	1213	1058
沣东新城	Fengdong xincheng	12	3849	988	3280	847	9961	2550	1088	876

18-9 主要年份职业中学基本情况

Basic Statistics on Vocational Secondary Schools in Representative Years

年 份 Year	学校数(所) Number of Schools (unit)	毕业生数(人) Number of Graduates (person)	招生数(人) New Enrollment (person)	在校学生数(人) Total Enrollment (person)	教职工数(人) Number of Teachers and Staff (person)	专任教师 Full-time Teachers
1985	40	1661	8346	17621	1375	868
1990	58	5936	8095	20151	2674	1574
1995	71	8976	12490	32673	2394	1877
1996	67	9235	10563	25955	3098	1735
1997	73	8756	13390	29068	2993	1709
1998	89	7753	13949	31264	3152	1823
1999	91	8480	13062	31973	3217	1908
2000	95	9949	13903	32188	3311	1997
2001	85	10300	15591	34336	3517	2113
2002	78	8659	17231	39428	3461	2192
2003	87	10755	17310	44033	4036	2458
2004	83	12177	17865	46358	4101	2515
2005	91	15092	20603	51766	4750	2892
2006	96	14887	21158	53828	5193	3126
2007	86	14881	24434	56012	4899	3064
2008	84	15813	30201	62963	4878	3008
2009	84	14691	31042	72388	5129	3179
2010	84	18100	30042	78244	5222	3178
2011	78	22493	27641	75108	4849	3173

18-10 各区县职业中学基本情况（2011年）

Basic Statistics on Vocational Secondary Schools by Region（2011）

区 县	Region	学校数（所）Number of Schools (unit)	毕业生数（人）Number of Graduates (person)	招生数（人）New Enrollment (person)	在校学生数（人）Total Enrollment (person)	教职工数（人）Number of Teachers and Staff (person)	专任教师 Full-time Teachers
合 计	**Total**	**78**	**22493**	**27641**	**75108**	**4849**	**3173**
新城区	Xincheng	10	4310	3590	10627	764	479
碑林区	Beilin	7	2105	3123	7122	500	340
莲湖区	Lianhu	6	2246	2703	7585	471	259
灞桥区	Baqiao	10	1326	1843	5023	485	235
未央区	Weiyang	7	2065	2227	7891	452	295
雁塔区	Yanta	12	3491	2486	8666	606	345
阎良区	Yanliang	1	404	1110	1739	112	100
临潼区	Lintong	5	1502	2268	4672	295	230
长安区	Chang'an	7	2126	2683	7270	676	472
蓝田县	Lantian	1	706	1052	1797	17	13
周至县	Zhouzhi	5	788	2055	5130	169	138
户 县	Huxian	5	779	1712	4481	238	207
高陵县	Gaoling	1	528	723	2780	64	60
沣东新城	Fengdong xincheng	1	117	66	325		

注：沣东新城老师数在相关区县数中。

Note:Fengdongxincheng Teachers in the Number of Related Region.

18-11 主要年份小学基本情况

Basic Statistics on Primary Schools in Representative Years

单位：万人 （10 000 persons）

年 份 Year	学校数(所) Number of Schools (unit)	毕业生数 Number of Graduates	招生数 New Enrollment	在校学生数 Total Enrollment	教职工数（人） Number of Staff and Teachers(person)	专任教师 Full-time Teachers
1978	2667			74.03	29744	26428
1980	2337	11.91	12.57	73.36	31770	28360
1985	2337	11.21	9.57	62.16	31075	26430
1990	2343	8.67	10.85	61.87	37788	29090
1995	2360	9.93	14.09	79.36	35568	30270
1996	2362	10.48	13.63	81.81	35821	30267
1997	2368	10.98	12.48	82.67	35767	30117
1998	2361	12.18	11.88	82.03	35576	30089
1999	2354	13.65	11.61	79.81	35639	30196
2000	2323	13.83	11.51	77.81	35336	30215
2001	2277	14.20	11.07	74.51	34257	29281
2002	2137	13.89	10.13	70.78	34143	29428
2003	2084	12.97	9.28	66.78	34080	29531
2004	2016	12.37	9.12	63.75	33794	29367
2005	1980	11.92	8.47	60.47	33907	29674
2006	1929	11.53	9.16	59.33	34460	30018
2007	1872	11.38	8.67	56.83	34901	30533
2008	1781	10.58	8.33	54.66	34653	30382
2009	1666	9.96	7.84	52.52	34389	30334
2010	1531	9.61	8.64	51.56	34118	29944
2011	1424	8.92	8.77	51.39	32457	29900

18-12 各区县小学基本情况（2011年）

Basic Statistics on Primary Schools by Region （2011）

单位：所、人 (unit、person)

区 县	Region	学校数 Number of Schools	毕业生数 Number of Graduates	招生数 New Enrollment	在校学生数 Total Enrollment	教职工数 Number of Teachers and Staff	专任教师 Full-time Teachers
合 计	**Total**	**1424**	**89184**	**87699**	**513916**	**32457**	**29900**
新城区	Xincheng	34	6992	5917	38594	1907	1757
碑林区	Beilin	43	6713	6681	38958	2252	1872
莲湖区	Lianhu	50	7342	7722	44424	2359	2136
灞桥区	Baqiao	79	5327	6070	33768	2011	1677
未央区	Weiyang	49	6492	8223	43524	1700	1963
雁塔区	Yanta	69	10483	12183	68354	3190	3204
阎良区	Yanliang	34	2528	2306	13552	1157	1042
临潼区	Lintong	181	8282	6344	40634	3366	3111
长安区	Chang'an	176	8077	8239	45552	3793	3178
蓝田县	Lantian	275	8103	6094	41044	2982	2843
周至县	Zhouzhi	158	7091	6217	38047	2689	2517
户 县	Huxian	140	6179	5399	33953	2332	2246
高陵县	Gaoling	86	2432	2616	13767	1548	1359
沣东新城	Fengdong xincheng	50	3143	3688	19745	1171	995

18-13 主要年份幼儿园基本情况

Basic Statistics on Kindergartens in Representative Years

年 份 Year	园 数(所) Number of Kindergartens (unit)	班 数(个) Number of Class (unit)	在园幼儿数(万人) Student Enrollment (10000 person)	教职工数(人) Number of Staff and Teachers (person)	专任教师 Full-time Teachers
1978	363		4	3568	1315
1980	186		10	5525	2657
1985	310	3135	10	6887	2770
1990	256	3816	14	6123	2058
1995	257	4464	16	6173	2659
1996	244	4313	15	5918	2661
1997	228	4243	15	6065	2748
1998	235	4195	13	6272	2910
1999	234	4222	13	6329	2982
2000	367	4142	13	6346	2995
2001	366	4306	12	6224	3069
2002	378	4186	12	6541	3397
2003	610	4470	12	8959	4853
2004	660	4507	12	9870	5577
2005	737	4712	13	10528	5959
2006	863	5037	13	12335	7106
2007	830	5081	14	13468	7951
2008	905	5506	15	14932	8704
2009	896	5710	16	15928	9240
2010	1004	6420	18	18710	10638
2011	1122	8010	24	23680	12577

注:幼儿园中包括学前班。

Note:"Kindergartens" here including units providing pre-school education.

18-14 主要年份特殊教育学校基本情况

Basic Statistics on Special Education Schools in Representative Years

单位：所、人 (unit,person)

年 份 Year	学校数 Number of Schools	毕业生数 Number of Graduates	招生数 New Enrollment	在校学生数 Total Enrollment	教职工数 Number of Teachers and Staff	专任教师 Full-time Teachers
1978						
1980	1	48	64	315	66	43
1985	2	14	36	318	94	59
1990	5	35	111	451	142	96
1995	5	27	147	1363	204	141
1996	5	60	164	1520	210	150
1997	5	153	164	1655	210	148
1998	5	266	140	2145	232	157
1999	5	349	115	1912	235	160
2000	5	269	145	1880	230	156
2001	5	237	209	1915	238	162
2002	5	216	148	1661	232	157
2003	5	156	161	1380	237	166
2004	5	137	142	1290	236	167
2005	5	184	182	1445	240	169
2006	6	171	143	1425	254	178
2007	6	169	114	1342	259	190
2008	6	83	96	1286	259	190
2009	7	311	202	1523	335	234
2010	8	214	402	1529	340	235
2011	8	280	222	1393	343	231

注:包括盲、聋、哑、弱智儿童教育在内。

Note:Including schools providing education for blind, deaf and dumb children and children with weak intelligence .

18-15 基础教育监测评价情况

Monitoring and Evaluation of Basic Education

指　标	Item	2010	2011
入学率(%)	Enrollment Rate		
小学	Primary Schools	100.0	100.0
初中	Junior Middle Schools	99.6	99.6
重读率(%)	Restduy-Rate		
小学	Primary schools	0.2	0.2
初中	Junior Middle Schools	0.1	
巩固率(%)	The Consolidation Rate（%）		
小学(六年)	Primary Schools（six years）	105.4	105.2
初中(三年)	Junior Middle Schools（three years）	96.1	96.8
毕业率(%)	The Graduate Rate		
小学	Primary school	100.4	100.2
初中	Junior middle school	99.7	100.6
专任教师学历合格率(%)	Qualified Rate Of Full-time Teacher Education（%）		
小学	Primary Schools	99.8	99.9
初中	Junior Middle Schools	99.2	99.3
高中	Senior Middle Schools	95.8	96.5
幼儿园	Kindergartens	98.4	97.4
小学教师专科以上学历达到率(%)	Rate of Primary School Teachers with College degree or Above（%）	86.9	89.5
初中教师本科以上学历达到率(%)	Rate of Junior Middle SchoolTeachers with Bachelor degree or Above（%）	76.2	80.1
高中教师研究生以上学历达到率(%)	Rate of Senior Middle School Teachers with Postgraduate degree or Above（%）	8.6	9.9

18-16　主要年份平均每万人口在校学生数及构成

单位：人、%

年 份 Year	平均每万人 高等学校在校学生数 Per 10000 people on average Hight Education Students in the school	平均每万人 中学在校学生数 Per 10000 people on average Number of Secondary School students in the school	平均每万人 高中阶段在校学生 Per 10000 people on average Number of Senior Hight School Students in the school
1978	58	886	
1980	84	906	
1985	117	692	
1990	123	493	
1995	168	639	
1996	177	672	
1997	180	701	
1998	189	740	
1999	224	798	
2000	282	854	
2001	366	903	
2002	470	940	
2003	560	939	
2004	618	980	463
2005	715	981	492
2006	760	1018	534
2007	817	1009	543
2008	863	1015	571
2009	901	1032	619
2010	939	996	635
2011	1090	912	576

The Number of Students in the School in Major Years Per 10000 Pepole on Average

（person,%）

平均每万人 初中阶段在校学生 Per 10000 people on average Number of Junior Secondary School Students in the school	平均每万人 小学在校学生数 Per 10000 people on average Number of Primary School Students in the school	高等学校在校学生 占学生总数比重 Senior Hight School Students in the school in accounting for the proportion of the total number of students	中学在校学生 占学生总数比重 Junior Secondary School students in the school in accounting for the proportion of the total number of students	小学中在校学生 占学生总数 Primary School students in the school in accounting for the proportion of the total number of students
	1486	2.3	34.9	58.6
	1434	3.1	33.2	55.3
	1124	5.3	31.3	50.9
	1016	6.7	25.1	51.7
	1224	7.3	28.0	53.6
	1249	7.6	28.8	53.5
	1249	7.6	29.8	53.1
	1228	8.0	31.3	52.0
	1183	9.3	33.2	49.2
	1131	11.5	34.8	46.0
	1072	14.6	35.9	42.6
	1007	18.2	36.4	39.0
	932	20.1	33.8	33.5
517	879	22.2	35.2	31.6
489	815	26.4	36.2	30.1
484	788	27.7	37.1	28.7
466	744	29.3	36.3	26.7
444	708	30.8	36.1	25.2
413	672	31.8	36.5	23.7
361	660	33.0	35.0	23.2
337	604	29.8	30.1	19.9

18-17 民办教育情况（2011年）

Private Education Situation（2011）

单位：所、人 (unit,person)

指 标	Item	学校、机构数 Number of Schools	毕业生数 Number of Graduates	招生数 New Enrollment
一、民办高等教育(机构）	Private higher Education (Institutions)	25	67248	78002
高等学校	Colleges and Universities	16	65481	78002
民办其他高等教育机构	Other Private higher Education Institutions	9	1767	
二、民办中等教育	Private Secondary Education	115	38038	38280
普通高中	Ordinary High School	50	6031	6585
中等专业学校	Specialized Secondary Schools	1	2288	1952
职业高中	Vocational hight school	45	12695	11231
普通初中	Ordinary Junior middle school	19	17024	18512
三、民办小学	Private Primary School	34	6252	7988
四、民办幼儿园	Private kindergarten	915	38736	68557

18-17 续表 continued

单位：所、人 (unit,person)

指 标	Item	在校学生数 Total Enrollment	教职工数 Number of Teachers and Staff	专任教师 Full-time Teachers	聘请外校教师 Teachers hired from Outside Schools
一、民办高等教育(机构）	Private higher Education (Institutions)	254879	21517	12339	4089
高等学校	Colleges and Universities	252619	20788	12034	3647
民办其他高等教育机构	Other Private higher Education Institutions	2260	729	305	442
二、民办中等教育	Private Secondary Education	117985	2802	1621	466
普通高中	Ordinary High School	19857			
中等专业学校	Specialized Secondary Schools	7970	224	136	
职业高中	Vocational hight school	34785	2578	1485	466
普通初中	Ordinary Junior middle school	55373			
三、民办小学	Private Primary School	43767	2143	1579	46
四、民办幼儿园	Private kindergarten	162562	17324	9137	87

18-18 研究与试验发展（R&D）情况

Research and Experiment Development Facts

指标名称	Item	2010	2011
一、单位数（个）	**Number of Units(unit)**	**358**	**1546**
科研单位	Units of Scientific Research	100	77
高等院校	Institutions of Higher Education	50	47
大中型工业企业	Large-scale and Medium-scale Industrial Enterprises	208	216
#有R&D活动单位数	Number of Units with R&D Activities	**163**	**341**
科研单位	Units of Scientific Research	52	46
高等院校	Institutions of Higher Education	26	47
大中型工业企业	Large-scale and Medium-scale Industrial Enterprises	85	92
二、科技活动人员（人）	**Personnel Eagaged in Scientific and Technical Activities (person)**	**128559**	**147814**
科研单位	Units of Scientific Research	40482	35407
高等院校	Institutions of Higher Education	36380	40821
大中型工业企业	Large-scale and Medium-scale Industrial Enterprises	51697	48110
三、R&D经费内部支出（万元）	**Interier Expenditures for R&D(10 000 yuan)**	**1672712**	**2025288**
科研单位	Units of Scientific Research	1010424	1039723
高等院校	Institutions of Higher Education	213382	282926
大中型工业企业	Large-scale and Medium-scale Industrial Enterprises	448906	574223
四、R&D项目（课题）（个）	**Number of Projects of R&D(item)**	**26814**	**26433**
科研单位	Units of Scientific Research	1601	1463
高等院校	Institutions of Higher Education	23393	21708
大中型工业企业	Large-scale and Medium-scale Industrial Enterprises	1820	2086

注：因口径变化，2011年单位数含规模以上小型工业企业、非工业企业和事业单位。

Note:Because of the caliber changes, the 2011 unit number containing small industrial enterprises above designated size, non-industrial enterprises and institutions.

18–19 科研院所研究与试验发展（R&D）情况

Research and Experiment Development Facts in Scientific Research Institutions

指标名称	Item	2010	2011
一、基本情况	**Basic Facts**		
单位数（个）	Number of Unit(unit)	100	77
#有（R&D）活动的单位数	Number of Units with Scientific and Technical Activities	52	46
科技活动人员（人）	Number of Personnel Engaged in Scientific Research (person)	40482	35407
#（R&D）人员	R&D Personnel	27333	25869
其中：女性	Female	8742	8025
其中：博士毕业	Doctor	765	887
硕士毕业	Master	6177	6375
本科毕业	Undergraduate	11578	10943
二、R&D人员折合全时当量（人/年）	**Full Time Equivalent of R&D Personnel (person/year)**	**25596**	**24251**
其中：研究人员	Personnel Engaged in Research	15610	14744
其中：基础研究	Basic Research	367	2081
应用研究生	Applied Research	8970	7159
试验发展	Experiment Development	16259	15010
三、R&D经费内部支出（万元）	**Raising and Use of Funds for Scientific and(10 000 yuan) Technical Activities**	**1010424**	**1039723**
在支出中：1.基础研究	Expenditure on: Basic Research	21750	34883
2.应用研究	Applied Research	210624	209314
3.试验发展	Experiment Development	778050	795526
在支出中：1.日常支出	Expenditure on: Daily Expenditure	752936	784907
#人员劳务费	Service Fees of Personnel	149753	186747
2.资产性支出	Assets Expenditure	257488	254816
#仪器和设备	Instruments and Equipment	177899	168340
在支出中：1.政府资金	Expenditure on: Government Funds	930234	955814
2.企业资金	Enterpreises Funds	13810	19389
3.境外资金	Overseas Funds		1814
4.其他资金	Others	66380	62706
四、R&D产出	**Achievements of R&D**		
专利申请数（件）	Number of Patent Applications (item)	1240	1275
#发明专利	Number of Invention Patents	867	891
专利授权数（件）	Number of Patents Awarded (item)	655	656
#发明专利	Number of Invention Patents	292	413
有效发明专利数（件）	Number of Effective Invention Patents	775	903
发表科技论文（篇）	Scientific and Technical Thesis (piece)	5155	5031
出版科技著作（种）	Scientific and Technical Works Published (book)	78	69

18–20 大专院校研究与试验（R&D）情况

Research and Experiment Development Facts in Universities

指 标 名 称	Item	2010	2011
一、基本情况	**Basic Facts**		
单位数（个）	Number of Unit(unit)	50	47
#有（R&D）活动的单位数	Number of Units with Scientific and Technical Activities	26	47
从事科技活动人员（人）	Number of Personnel Engaged in Scientific Research (person)	36380	40821
#（R&D）人员	R&D Personnel	15431	17074
其中：女性	Female	4861	5415
其中：博士毕业	Doctor	4119	4828
硕士毕业	Master	5611	5893
本科毕业	Undergraduate	4434	4887
二、R&D人员折合全时当量（人/年）	**Full Time Equivalent of R&D Personnel (person/year)**	**7747**	**11110**
其中：研究人员	Personnel Engaged in Research	6891	7257
其中：基础研究	Basic Research	3168	3707
应用研究生	Applied Research	3236	3736
试验发展	Experiment Development	1343	969
三、R&D经费内部支出（万元）	**Raising and Use of Funds for Scientific and Technical Activities(10 000 yuan)**	**213382**	**282926**
在支出中：1.基础研究	Expenditure on: Basic Research	60974	84050
2.应用研究	Applied Research	98367	130622
3.试验发展	Experiment Development	54041	68252
在支出中：1.日常支出	Expenditure on: Daily Expenditure	179886	229332
#人员劳务费	Service Fees of Personnel	32250	35910
2.资产性支出	Assets Expenditure	33496	53592
#仪器和设备	Instruments and Equipment	29788	34660
在支出中：1.政府资金	Expenditure on: Government Funds	127480	168748
2.企业资金	Enterpreises Funds	76701	100161
3.境外资金	Overseas Funds	1029	1002
4.其他资金	Others	8172	13015
四、R&D产出	**Achievements of R&D**		
专利申请数（件）	Number of Patent Applications (item)	3741	4976
#发明专利	Number of Invention Patents	2185	3189
专利授权数（件）	Number of Patents Awarded (item)	1954	2765
#发明专利	Number of Invention Patents	865	1508
有效发明专利数（件）	Number of Effective Invention Patents	6200	8358
发表科技论文（篇）	Scientific and Technical Thesis (piece)	37116	43260
出版科技著作（种）	Scientific and Technical Works Published (book)	984	986

18-21 大中型企业研究与试验发展（R&D）情况

Research and Experiment Development Facts in Large-size and Medium-size Industrial Enterprises

指 标 名 称	Item	2010	2011
一、基本情况	**Basic Facts**		
单位数（个）	Number of Unit(unit)	208	216
#有（R&D）活动的单位数	Number of Units with Scientific and Technical Activities	85	92
从事科技活动人员（人）	Number of Personnel Engaged in Scientific Research (person)	51697	48110
#（R&D）人员	R&D Personnel	23571	23635
其中： 女性	Female	6775	7152
二、R&D人员折合全时当量（人/年）	**Full Time Equivalent of R&D Personnel (person/year)**	**17416**	**17622**
其中：研究人员	Personnel Engaged in Research	10348	8586
其中：基础研究	Basic Research	35	
应用研究生	Applied Research	226	539
试验发展	Experiment Development	17155	17083
三、R&D经费内部支出（万元）	**Raising and Use of Funds for Scientific and Technical Activities(10 000 yuan)**	**448906**	**574223**
在支出中：1.基础研究	Expenditure on: Basic Research	912	
2.应用研究	Applied Research	8824	53936
3.试验发展	Experiment Development	439170	520287
在支出中：1.日常支出	Expenditure on: Daily Expenditure	371893	480859
#人员劳务费	Service Fees of Personnel	62356	87728
2.资产性支出	Assets Expenditure	77013	93364
#仪器和设备	Instruments and Equipment	74701	5113
在支出中：1.政府资金	Expenditure on: Government Funds	79730	91593
2.企业资金	Enterpreises Funds	361121	473774
3.境外资金	Overseas Funds		363
4.其他资金	Others	8055	8493
四、R&D产出	**Achievements of R&D**		
专利申请数（件）	Number of Patent Applications (item)	1612	2057
#发明专利	Number of Invention Patents	610	878
专利授权数（件）	Number of Patents Awarded (item)		
有效发明专利数（件）	Number of Effective Invention Patents	670	1103
发表科技论文（篇）	Scientific and Technical Thesis (piece)	1372	1693

18–22 主要年份企事业单位知识产权情况

Intellectual Property Right of Enterprises and Institutions in Representative Years

指标名称	Name of Item	2005	2006	2007	2008	2009	2010	2011
一、科技活动情况	**Science and technology activities**							
1.科技活动人员（人）	People involved into activities(person)	82789	86978	87095	91994	137934	128559	147814
2.科技活动机构数（个）	Units involved into activities(unit)	358	365	380	411	569	490	625
二、知识产权拥有量情况	**Number of IPR**							
1.专利情况（件）	Patents(item)							
（1）累计申请专利	Accumulated patent applications	21912	26084	32852	42436	55208	74694	102411
当年申请专利	Patent applictions in this year	2950	4172	6768	9584	12772	19486	27717
#发明专利	Invention patents	1268	1325	1886	3049	5014	7176	11689
（2）累计授权专利	Accumulated patents awarded	11670	13442	15971	19256	23962	31999	41273
当年授权专利	Patents awarded in this year	1280	1772	2529	3285	4706	8037	9274
#发明专利	Invention patents	331	461	595	749	1121	1651	2738
2.商标情况（件）	Trade marks(item)							
（1）当年注册商标申请	Trade mark registration claimed in this year	3682	7132	5559	7613	8972	21562	15620
（2）累计注册商标	Accumulated trade mark registrations	18461	20808	22860	26386	23078	52387	39381
#当年注册商标	Trade mark registrations in this year	2330	2347	2052	3526	5278	18107	12278
三、民事知识产权维权情况（件）	**IPR controversy(item)**	**106**	**108**	**131**	**212**	**427**	**241**	**512**
1.专利纠纷	Patent controversies	27	30	44	47	37	69	104
2.商标纠纷	Trade mark controversies	19	24	32	51	42	29	49
3.著作权纠纷	Copyright controversies	53	49	36	91	319	110	315
4.技术合同纠纷	Technological contract controversies	1	1	3	3	9	6	15
5.发现权与发明权纠纷	Discover and invention controversies	1						
6.其他知识产权纠纷	Others IPR controvers	5	4	16	20	20	27	29

注：本表数据由市科技局、陕西省工商局、陕西省新闻出版局、西安市中级人民法院等提供。

Note:Figures in this table are provided by Xi'an Bureau of Science and Technology, Industrial and Commercial Bureau of Shaanxi Province, Press and Publication Bureau of Shaanxi Province, Xi'an Intermediate People's Court and other department concerned.

18–23　主要年份高新技术产业开发区情况

Basic Statistics of Hi-Tech Development Zone in Representative Years

指　　标	Item	2005	2006	2007	2008	2009	2010	2011
1.高新技术企业数	Number of High-tech Enterprises	1029	1062	1311	1324	592	672	774
2.年末从业人员(人)	Number of Persons Employed at year-end (person)	296401	346000	368757	388644	275141	287140	296723
从事技术开发人数	Number of Persons Engaged in Technology Development	28792	34600	39248	48355	64212	67708	78636
3.技术开发经费支出总额 （万元）	Expenditures on Technology Development (10 000 yuan)	254161	565166	705066	777516	756767	1031223	1322923
研究与发展支出	Expenditures on Research and Development	115026	414537	533924	581716	585449	669083	831822
4.利润总额（万元）	Total Profits (10 000 yuan)	388404	654258	1087311	1231146	1308432	1707925	2224850
5.上缴税费总额（万元）	Sum of tax (10 000yuan)	356599	464700	1394194	1576472	1486556	1964820	2586712
6.出口创汇总额 （千美元）	Foreign Exchange Earnings of Exports (USD 1 000)	527014	1460251	1927114	2188721	1177000	4951265	6447050

18–24　高新技术产业开发区发展规模（2011年）

Development Status of Hi-Tech Development Zone（2011）

指　　标	Item	合计 Total	新 建 区 Newlyconstructed Zone
累计已开发面积（平方公里）	Accumulated Areas Developed (sq.km)	35	35
高新区工商注册（个）	Registered Enterprises in Hi-tech Zones (unit)	15236	13070
#工业型技术开发技术服务型企业数	Number of industrial technology developing enterprises	8088	7698
#三资企业数	Enterprises of Joiut Venture,Cooperation and Foreign-funded	1055	1031
已认定的高新技术企业数	Hi-tech Enterprises Designated	774	672

注：此表数据来源于西安市高新技术开发区。

Note:Date on this bable is from Hi-Tech Development Zone of Xi'an.

18–25 主要年份高新技术产业开发区建设与集资情况

Capital Construction and Funds-Raising of Hi-Tech Development Zone in Representative Years

指　　标	Item	2005	2006	2007	2008	2009	2010	2011
一、基建投资（亿元）	**Investment on Capital Construction (100 million yuan)**							
本年基建投资	Investment on Capital Construction of this year	91.26	114.59	132.17	159.78	196.90	255.57	266.51
1.生产业务用房	Building for Production	31.81	50.76	59.69	60.53	69.23	94.74	105.35
2. 住宅	Residential Buildings	41.35	40.61	47.75	77.05	79.00	97.30	86.32
3.公用设施	Public Installations	6.36	10.15	11.94	6.72	4.91	7.35	5.99
4.基础设施	Fundamental Facilities	8.63	8.53	7.50	9.60	24.66	32.98	32.41
5.征地拆迁	Resettlement	3.11	4.54	5.29	5.88	17.00	13.59	36.44
二、开发面积	**Area Developed**							
新建区累计开发土地面积（平方公里）	Accumulated Area Developed in Newly Constructed Zone (sq.km)	22.00	35.00	35.00	35.00	35.00	35.00	35.00
#当年新开发土地面积	Area Developed in this year		1.27					
累计竣工建筑面积（万平方米）	Accumulated Floor Space Completed (10 000 sq.m)	1104.72	1325.98	1558.70	1782.43	2085.66	2419.87	2748.09
#当年竣工建筑面积	Floor Space Completed in this year	188.60	221.30	232.70	223.76	303.23	334.20	328.22
三、当年内资金筹集情况（亿元）	**Funds Raised in this year (100 million yuan)**							
当年内资金筹集总额	Total Funds Raised in this year	160.20	155.58	152.85	179.57	202.58	300.30	291.82
#政府拨款	Allocations from the Government	5.50	6.50	11.66	21.41	25.98	33.07	45.35
贷款	Loans	108.20	108.34	100.00	106.18	125.47	165.68	154.01
四、吸引外资（亿美元）	**Foreign Investment(100 million USD)**							
年末累计境外客商协议投资额	Contracted Foreign Investment Accumulated at Year-end	21.92	28.14	32.35	36.26	43.76	52.76	56.71
年末累计境外客商实际投资额	Actual Foreign Investment Accumulated at Year-end	9.26	12.18	16.08	20.29	24.63	29.75	36.24
#当年实际投资额	Actual Investmen in this year	1.98	2.92	3.90	4.21	4.34	5.11	6.49

注：此表数据来源于西安市高新技术开发区。

Note:Date on this bable is from Hi-Tech Development Zone of Xi'an.

主 要 统 计 指 标 解 释

普通高等学校 指按国家规定的设置标准和审批程序批准举办的，通过全国普通高等学校统一招生考试，招收高中毕业生为主要培养对象，实施高等学历教育的全日制大学、独立设置的学院和高等专科学校、高等职业学校及其他机构（独立学院和分校、大专班）。

大学、独立设置的学院主要实施本科层次以上教育。高等专科学校、高等职业学校实施专科层次教育。其他机构是承担国家普通招生计划任务不计校数的机构，包括独立学院、普通高等学校分校、大专班和批准筹建的普通高等学校等。独立学院指由普通本科高校按新机制、新模式举办的本科层次的二级学院，一些普通本科高校按公办机制和模式建立的二级学院，"分校"或其他类似的二级办学机构不属此范畴。

成人高等学校 指按照国家规定的设置标准和审批程序批准举办的，通过全国成人高等教育统一招生考试，招收具有高中毕业或同等学历的人员为主要培养对象，利用函授、业余、脱产等多种形式对其实施高等学历教育的学校。包括职工高等学校、农民高等学校、管理干部学院、教育学院、独立函授学院、广播电视大学、其他机构等。其他机构是承担国家成人招生计划任务不计校数的机构。

小学学龄儿童净入学率 指调查范围内已入小学学习的学龄儿童占校内外学龄儿童总数（包括弱智儿童，不包括盲聋哑儿童）的比重。计算公式为：

小学学龄儿童净入学率（%）=已入学的小学学龄儿童数/校内外小学学龄儿童总数×100%

研究与试验发展（R&D） 指在科学技术领域，为增加知识总量，以及运用这些知识去创造新的应用进行的系统的创造性的活动，包括基础研究、应用研究、试验发展三类活动。国际上通常采用R&D活动的规模和强度指标反映一国的科技实力和核心竞争力。

基础研究 指为了获得关于现象和可观察事实的基本原理的新知识（揭示客观事物的本质、运动规律，获得新发现、新学说）而进行的实验性或理论性研究，它不以任何专门或特定的应用或使用为目的。其成果以科学论文和科学著作为主要形式。用来反映知识的原始创新能力。

应用研究 指为获得新知识而进行的创造性研究，主要针对某一特定的目的或目标。应用研究是为了确定基础研究成果可能的用途，或是为达到预定的目标探索应采取的新方法（原理性）或新途径。其成果形式以科学论文、专著、原理性模型或发明专利为主。用来反映对基础研究成果应用途径的探索。

试验发展 指利用从基础研究、应用研究和实际经验所获得的现有知识，为产生新的产品、材料和装置，建立新的工艺、系统和服务，以及对已产生和建立的上述各项作实质性的改进而进行的系统性工作。其成果形式主要是专利、专有技术、具有新产品基本特征的产品原型或具有新装置基本特征的原始样机等。在社会科学领域，试验发展是指把通过基础研究、应用研究获得的知识转变成可以实施的计划（包括为进行检验和评估实施示范项目）的过程。人文科学领域没有对应的试验发展活动。主要反映将科研成果转化为技术和产品的能力，是科技推动经济社会发展的物化成果。

R&D人员 指参与研究与试验发展项目研究、管理和辅助工作的人员，包括项目（课题）组人员，企业科技行政管理人员和直接为项目（课题）活动提供服务的辅助人员。反映投入从事拥有自主知识产权的研究开发活动的人力规模。

R&D人员全时当量 指全时人员数加非全时人员按工作量折算为全时人员数的总和。例如：有两个全时人员和三个非全时人员（工作时间分别为20%、30%和70%），则全时当量为2+0.2+0.3+0.7=3.2人年。为国际上比较科技人力投入而制定的可比指标。

R&D经费内部支出合计 指调查单位用于内部开展R&D活动（基础研究、应用研究和试验发展）的实际支出。包括用于R&D项目（课题）活动的直接支出，以及间接用于R&D活动的管理费、服务费、与R&D有关的基本建设支出以及外协加工费等。不包括生产性活动支出、归还贷款支出以及与外单位合作或委托外单位进行R&D活动而转拨给对方的经费支出。

R&D经费内部支出中政府资金 指R&D经费内部支出中来自各级政府部门的各类资金，包括财政科学技术拨款、科学基金、教育等部门事业费以及政府部门预算外资金的实际支出。

R&D经费内部支出中企业资金 指R&D经费内部支出中来自本企业的自有资金和接受其他企业委托而获得的经费，以及科研院所、高校等事业单位从企业获得的资金的实际支出。

R&D项目（课题）数 指在当年立项并开展研究工作、以前年份立项仍继续进行研究的研发项目（课题）数，包括当年完成和年内研究工作已告失败的研发项目（课题），但不包括委托外单位进行的研发项目（课题）数。

R&D项目（课题）人员全时当量 指实际参加研发项目（课题）活动人员折合的全时当量。

R&D项目（课题）经费内部支出 指调查单位内部在报告年度进行研发项目（课题）研究和试制等的实际支出。包括劳务费、其他日常支出、固定资产购建费、外协加工费等，不包括委托或与外单位合作进行项目（课题）研究而拨付给对方使用的经费。

新产品产值 指报告期企业生产的新产品的产值。新产品是指采用新技术原理、新设计构思研制、生产的全新产品，或在结构、材质、工艺等某一方面比原有产品有明显改进，从而显著提高了产品性能或扩大了使用功能的产品。新产品产值、新产品销售收入既包括经政府有关部门认定并在有效期内的新产品，也包括企业自行研制开发，未经政府有关部门认定，从投产之日起一年之内的新产品。

新产品销售收入 指报告期企业销售新产品实现的销售收入。

专利 是专利权的简称，是对发明人的发明创造经审查合格后，由专利局依据专利法授予发明人和设计人对该项发明创造享有的专有权。包括发明、实用新型和外观设计。反映拥有自主知识产权的科技和设计成果情况。

发明（专利） 指对产品、方法或者其改进所提出的新的技术方案。是国际通行的反映拥有自主知识产权技术的核心指标。

实用新型（专利） 指对产品的形状、构造或者其结合所提出的适于实用的新的技术方案。反映具有一定技术含量的技术成果情况。

外观设计（专利） 指对产品的形状、图案、色彩或者其结合所作出的富有美感并适于工业上应用的新设计。反映拥有自主知识产权的外观设计成果情况。

工业企业R&D投入强度 指研究与试验发展经费内部支出与主营业务收入的比值。

Explanatory Notes on Main Statistical Indicators

Regular Institutions of Higher Education refer to educational establishments set up according to the government evaluation and approval procedures, recruiting graduates from senior secondary schools as the main target by National Matriculation TEST. They include full-time universities, colleges, institutions of higher professional education, institutions of higher vocational education, institutions of higher vocational education and others (non-university tertiary, branch schools and undergraduate classes).

Universities and colleges primarily provide undergraduate courses; institutions of higher professional education and institutions of higher vocational education primarily provide professional trainings; and others refer to educational establishments, which are responsible for enrolling higher education students under the State Plan but not enumerated in the total number of schools, including: branch schools of universities and colleges, and universities and colleges that have been approved and under plan for construction. Non-university tertiary refers to the regular undergraduate branch college which is running in new mechanism and mode, excluding the branch schools and other similar branches of educational institutions.

Institutions of Higher Education for Adults refer to educational establishments, set up in line with relevant rules approved by the government, enrolling staff and workers with senior secondary school or equivalent education, and providing higher education courses in many forms of correspondence, spare time, or full time for adults. Professionals thus trained receive a qualification equivalent to graduates studying regular courses at regular universities, colleges and professional colleges. Institutions of higher learning for adults include schools of higher education for staff and workers, schools of higher education for peasants, colleges for management cadres, pedagogical colleges, independent correspondence colleges, Radio and TV universities and other educational establishments. Other educational establishments have undertakings to enrol adult students but not enumerated in the schools under the State Plan.

Net Enrolment Ratio of Primary Schools refers to the proportion of school age children enrolled at schools to the total number of school age children both in and outside schools (including retarded children, but excluding blind, deaf and mute children). The formula is:

$$\text{Net Enrolment Ratio of PrimarySchools} = \frac{\text{Total Primary School-age Children at Schools}}{\text{Total Primary School-age WnerdlihChether or Not Attending School}} \times 100\%$$

Research and Development (R&D) refers to systematic and creative activities in the field of science and technology aiming at increasing the knowledge and using the knowledge for new application. R&D includes 3 categories of activities: basic research, applied research and experimentation for development. The scale and intensity of R&D are widely used internationally to reflect the strength of S&T and the core competitiveness of a country in the world.

Basic Research refers to empirical or theoretical research aiming at obtaining new knowledge on the fundamental principles regarding phenomena or observable facts to reveal the intrinsic nature and underlying laws and to acquire new discoveries or new theories. Basic research takes no specific or designated application as the aim of the research. Results of basic research are mainly released or disseminated in the form of scientific papers or monographs. This indicator reflects the innovation capacity for original knowledge.

Applied Research refers to creative research aiming at obtaining new knowledge on a specific objective or target. Purpose of the applied research is to identify the possible uses of results from basic research, or to explore new (fundamental) methods or new approaches. Results of applied research are expressed in the form of scientific papers, monographs, fundamental models or invention patents. This indicator reflects the exploration of ways to apply the results of basic research.

Experiments and Development refer to systematic activities aiming at using the knowledge from basic and applied researches or from practical experience to develop new products, materials and equipment, to establish new production process, systems and services, or to make substantial improvement on the existing products, process or services. Results of experiment and development activities are embodied in patents, exclusive technology, and monotype of new products or equipment. In social sciences, experiment and development activities refer to the process of converting the knowledge from basic or applied researches into feasible programmes (including conduct of demonstration projects for assessment and evaluation). There are no experiment and development activities in the science of humanities. This indicator reflects the capability of transferring the results of S&T into technique and products, and measures the realization of S&T in spearheading the economic and social development.

R&D Personnel refer to persons engaged in research, management and supporting activities of R & D, including persons in the project teams, persons engaged in the management of S&T activities of enterprises and supporting staff providing direct service to the research projects. This indicator reflects the size of personnel engaged in R&D activities with independent intellectual property.

Full-time Equivalent of R&D Personnel refers to the sum of the full-time persons and the full-time equivalent of part-time persons converted by workload. For instance, if there are 2 full-time persons and 3 part-time workers (20%, 30% and 70% of working hours respectively on R&D activities), the full-time equivalent are 2+0.2+0.3+0.7=3.2 person-years. This is an internationally comparable indicator of S&T manpower input.

Total Internal Expenditure of Funds on R&D refers to the real expenditure of surveyed units on their own R&D activities (basic research, application study, test and development) including direct expenditure on R&D activities, indirect expenditure of management and services on R&D activities, expenditure on capital construction and material processing by others. Excluding the expenditure on production activities, return of loan, and fees transferred to cooperated and entrusted agencies on R&D activities.

Internal Expenditure of Government Funds refersto the expenditure of funds on R&D activities from government agencies at different levels, including appropriate funds on science and technology from financial departments, scientific funds, operating expenses from education departments and the real expenditure of extra budgetary funds from government agencies.

Internal Expenditure of Funds of Enterprises refers to the expenditure of funds on R&D activities from self-raised funds of enterprises and funds from other enterprises through entrustment, and the expenditure of funds of institutions, such as institution of scientific research and universities, from enterprises.

Number of R&D Projects (subjects) refers to the number of R&D projects (subjects) set up and implemented at the reference year, and the number of R&D projects (subjects) set up in former years and under implementation, including the projects (subjects) finished and failed at the reference year, excluding the projects (subjects) implemented by others through entrustment.

Full-time Equivalent of R&D Personnel refers to the full-time equivalent of persons actually engaged in R&D projects.(subjects)

Internal Expenditure of Funds on R&D Projects (subjects) refers to the real expenditure of internal funds of the surveyed units on research and test of R&D projects (subjects) at the reference year, including service fee, other daily expenditure, cost for capital goods, cost of external process; excluding expenditure of funds transferred to other cooperated and entrusted units of the projects.

Output Value of New Products refers to the output value of new products during the reporting period. The new products refer to brand new products produced with new technology and new design, or product that represent noticeable improvement in terms of structure, material, or production process for improving significantly the character of function of the older versions. The output value and sales income of the new products include those of new products certified by relevant government agencies within the period of certification, as well as new products designed and produced by enterprises within a year without certification by government agencies.

Sales Income of New Products refers to the real sales income of new products of the enterprises at the reporting period.

Patent is an abbreviation for the patent right and refers to the exclusive right of ownership by the inventors or designers for the creation or inventions, given from the patent offices after due process of assessment and approval in accordance with the Patent Law. Patents are granted for inventions, utility models and designs. This indicator reflects the achievements of S&T and design with independent intellectual property.

Patented Inventions refer to new technical proposals to the products or methods or their modifications. This is universal core indicator reflecting the technologies with independent intellectual property.

Patented Utility Models refer to the practical and new technical proposals on the shape and structure of the product or the combination of both. This indicator reflects the condition of technological results with certain technical content.

Designs refer to the aesthetics and industrially applicable new designs for the shape, pattern and colour of the product, or their combinations. This indicator reflects the appearance design achievements with independent intellectual property.

Intensity of Input into R&D of Industrial Enterprises refers to the percentage of main operation income spent on R&D activities by industrial enterprises.

19 文化、体育、卫生、社会福利和其他

CULTURE,SPORTS,PUBLIC HEALTH,SOCIAL WELFARE INSTITUTIONS AND OTHER SOCIAL ACTIVITIES

资料整理：陈超毅
Data management:Chen Chaoyi

第十九部分　文化、体育、卫生、社会福利和其他

一、简要说明

本章资料主要包括文化、卫生、民政、体育、计划生育、共青团、妇联以及公检法等方面的内容，由西安市统计局社会科技处根据西安市文广新局、卫生局、民政局、体育局、妇联、共青团市委、计划生育委员会以及公安局、检察院、法院等部门提供资料整理。

二、主要指标

图书馆总藏量（千册件）	4907	比上年增加	442千册件
医院数（所）	268	比上年增加	7所
医院床位数（万张）	3.60	比上年增加	3600张

19 CULTURE,SPORTS,PUBLIC HEALTH,SOCIAL WELFARE INSTITUTIONS AND OTHER SOCIAL ACTIVITIES

Ⅰ.Brief IntroductionData in this chapter primarily consists of data of culture, sanitation, civil administration, physical education, family planning, Communist Youth League, the Women's Federation, public security organs, procuratorial organs and people's court, compiled by Social Science & Technology Division of Xi'an Bureau of Statistics according to data from Xi'an Bureau of Cuture, Bureau of Sanitation, Bureau of Civial Adnimistration, Bureau of PE, the Women's Federation, Municipal Committee of Communist Youth League, Committee of Family Planning, Bureau of Public Security, Procuratorate, People's Court and other department concerned.

Ⅱ.Major Indicators

		Increase over Preceding Year
Number of Collections in Libraries (1 000 volumes)	4907	442
Number of Hospitals(unit)	268	7
Number of Beds(10 000 units)	3.60	3600 units

19-1 文化事业机构和人数（2011年）

Number of Institutions and Personnel in Culture and Art（2011）

项　　目	Item	机构数（个） Number of Institutions (unit)	人员数（人） Number of Personnel (person)
一、电影事业	**Career of Film**		
制片厂	Studio	1	
发行放映管理机构	Number of Film Projection and Publication Administrating Institutions	2	8
电影放映单位	Unit of Film shows	156	1204
#电影院	Cinema	24	966
影剧院	Theaters	4	71
放映队	Film Projection Team	128	167
二、艺术事业	**Art**		
艺术表演团体	Art Performance Troupes	30	2754
艺术表演场所	Art Centers	17	921
三、艺术科研机构	**Art Scientific Research Institution**	**2**	**69**
四、图书馆事业	**Libraries**	**15**	**482**
五、群众文化事业	**Mass Culture**	**2248**	**5001**
#文化馆	Cultural Centers	13	233
文化站	Culture Stations	181	658
农村文化室	Rural Cultural Center	2054	4110
五、教育事业	**Educations**	**2**	**124**

19–2 主要年份文化事业发展情况

Basic Statistics on Culture Development in Representative Years

指　　标	Item	2005	2006	2007	2008	2009	2010	2011
电影放映场数 (千场)	Number of Film Shows (1 000 shows)	33	32	29	25	44	196	230
观众人数(千人次)	Number of Spectators (1 000 person-times)	3186	2568	1890	1295	1299	5960	6753
艺术表演团体演出场次(国内)(千场)	Number of Art Performance Troupes Performers (1 000 shows)	4	4	4	4	5	6	6
观众人数(千人次)	Number of Spectators (1 000 person-times)	6138	22765	4416	3972	5573	12316	6932
图书馆总藏量(千册件)	Number of Collections in Libraries (1000 volumes)	3671	3807	3893	4040	4324	4465	4907
书刊文献外借人次(千人次)	Books, Journals and Documents Borrowing (1 000 person-times)	384	416	432	478	435	682	780
书刊文献外借册次(千册次)	Books, Journals and Documents Borrowing (1 000 Volume-time)	656	884	813	917	727	1368	1930

19–3 主要年份群众艺术馆、文化馆（站）活动情况

Basic Statistics on Activities of Mass Art Centers and Cultural Centers in Representative Years

指　　标	Item	2005	2006	2007	2008	2009	2010	2011
机构数(个)	Number of Insititutions (unit)	192	193	197	197	197	197	196
举办展览个数(个)	Number of Exhibitions (unit)	458	667	511	520	716	705	592
组织文艺活动次数(次)	Art Performances and Story-telling Sessions (time)	1439	2251	2884	2378	3158	3729	4544
举办训练班班次(个)	Number of Training Courses (unit)	1137	1327	1625	1109	1467	3018	2224
培训人次(千人次)	Number of Trained Persons (1 000 person-times)	37	43	67	87	96	133	115
藏　书(千册)	Collections (1 000 volumes)	322	336	227	270	299	331	443
本年收入(千元)	Income of this year (1 000 yuan)	11257	12981	21111	22571	40891	42937	55367
本年支出(千元)	Expenditure of this year (1 000 yuan)	10924	12706	21007	22458	42826	45160	62368

19-4 文物保护业基本情况（2011年）

Basic Statistics on Cultural Relics Protection（2011）

指　标	Item	机构（个）Insititution (unit)	人员（人）Personnel (person)	文物藏品 实际数量（件）Factual Number of Collections(piece)	一级品 Grade One	参观人员（千人次）Number of Visitors (1000 person-times)
总　计	**Total**	**138**	**3535**	**733123**	**4526**	**12530**
文物保护管理机构	Protection and Management Agencies	43	628	14761	32	380
其他文物机构	Other Agencies	7	265	39736		
博物馆	Museums	85	2395	650786	4286	12150
文物商店	Cultural Relics Agencies					
文物科研机构	Scientific Research of Historical Relics Preservation	3	247	27840	208	

注：2010年发前为省市直属文物单位数据，2011年为全口径数据（含民营、院校等）。

Note:Before the data for the provinces and cities directly under the historical monuments in 2010, 2011 for the whole caliber data (including private institutions).

19-5 主要年份广播电台及节目制作情况

Basic Statistics of Broadcasting Stations and Program Production in Representative Years

指　标	Item	2005	2006	2007	2008	2009	2010	2011
省、地广播电台(座)	Broadcasting Stations at the Province and District Level(set)	2	2	2	2	2	2	1
县级广播电视台(座)	Number of Wire Broadcasting Stations and TV Relaying Stations(set)	6	6	6	6	6	6	6
中短波、调频发射台及转播台(座)	Medium/Short Ware and FM Broadcast Transmission Stations and Relaying Stations(set)	280	290	40	46	51	55	54
节目(套)	Number of Programs(set)	14	15	17	17	18	18	19
平均每日播出时间(时)	Broadcasting Hours per Day(hour:minute)	244	248	297	312	337	340	333
广播人口覆盖率(%)	Listener Rating(%)	99.35	99.36	99.37	99.37	99.37	99.4	99.42
制作广播节目(时)	Productions of Broadcasting(hour)	81840	84083	97013	103328	110455	110639	83368
#新闻资讯类	News Programs						13786	13821
专题服务类	Special Subject Programs						24451	16318
综艺类	Variety Programs						37720	28679
广播剧类	Literature Programs						2406	2014
广告类	Advertisements						28339	14202
其他类	Service Programs						3937	8334

注：2010年制作广播节目时间分类发生变化，故2009年及以前无数据。

Note: 2010 broadcast time classification change, so before 2009 and no data.

19-6 主要年份电视台及节目制作情况

Basic Statistics of TV Stations and Production of TV Program in Representative Years

指　　标	Item	2005	2006	2007	2008	2009	2010	2011
电视台(座)	Number of Television Stations（set）	2	2	2	2	2	2	1
发射台及转播台(座)	Number of Television Transmission Stations and Relaying Stations（set）	297	297	8	8	10	10	10
无线电视节目(套)	Program Productions of Non-cable television Stations（set）	6	5	5	5	7	6	6
有线电视节目(套)	Program Productions of cable television Stations（set）	9	10	16	17	15	16	16
平均每周播出时间(时)	Average Broadcasting Hours per Week（hour）	22934	2289	2505	2704	2661	2728	2827
电视人口覆盖率(%)	Viewer Rating（%）	97.67	97.85	98.33	98.35	98.41	98.57	98.6
卫星电视地面站(座)	Earth Stations of Satellite TV（set）	1319	1251		32638	26167	41163	
制作电视节目 (时)	Productions of TV Programs(hour)	27377	36337	25883	26897	27131	29626	43925
#新闻资讯类	News and Information Programs						8930	10656
专题服务类	Special Subject Programs						7762	19191
综艺类	Variety Programs						3942	5202
影视剧类	Literature Programs						1729	3781
广告类	Advertisement						3313	3200
其他类	Service Programs						3950	1894
有线电视用户(万户)	Users of Cable television Stations（10 000 households）	102.21	115.16	125.28	138.79	146.84	164.64	179.29

注：2010年制作电视节目时间分类发生变化，故2009年及以前无数据。

Notes:In 2010 the production of television programs time classification change, so before 2009 and no data.

19-7 体育事业基本情况（市属）（2011年）

The Basic Situations of Sports (Under Municipality)（2011）

单位：人、枚　　(person、unit)

指　　标	Item	2011
一、体育系统职工人数	**Number of Staffs and Workers in Physical Education System**	**1020**
#运动员	Athletes	665
教练员	Coaches	70
二、等级裁判员发展人数	**Number of the Development of Grade Referees**	**144**
三、等级运动员发展人数	**Number of the Development of Grade Athletes**	**208**
四、全年获得奖牌数	**Number of Full-year Medals**	**450**
#国家级金牌	National Gold	42
国家级银牌	National Silver	24
省级金牌	Provincial Gold	131
省级银牌	Provincial Silver	203

19-8 少年儿童分项业余体校情况（市属）（2011年）

Basic Statistics of Youth Part-time Physical Training School（2011）

单位：人 （person）

指　标	Items	2011
一、在读学生数	**Total Enrollment**	
总　计	**Total**	**6025**
田　径	Track and Field	1500
游　泳	Swimming	360
体　操	Gymnastics	70
举　重	Weightlifting	96
国际式摔跤	Wrestling	80
柔　道	Judo	75
射　击	Shooting	150
射　箭	Archery	160
足　球	Football	1600
蓝　球	Basketball	960
排　球	Volleyball	90
乒乓球	Table Tennis	320
拳　击	Boxing	50
武　术	Wu Shu	200
跆拳道	Kickboxing	180
跳　水	Diving	56
棒　球	Baseball	78
二、职工数	**Number of Staff and Workers**	

19-9 群众体育事业（2011年）

Mass Sports（2011）

指　标	Item	2011
全民健身广场（个）	Number of National fitness square(unit)	594
社会体育指导员（人）	Social Sports Instructor(person)	7376
晨晚健身站点（个）	Morning and Evening Fitness sites(unit)	1800
社区建有体育组织比重（%）	The community has a sports organization proportion (%)	88.2
全国、全省体育先进社区（个）	National, provincial advanced sports community (unit)	21
全国农村体育先进示范站（个）	Advanced model of the National Rural Sports Station (unit)	15

19-10 主要年份卫生机构、床位、人员数

Number of Health Care Institutions, Beds and Employed Persons in Health Care Institutions in Representative Years

年 份 Year	卫生机构数（个） Number of Health Care Institutions (unit)	医院数（个） Number of Health Care Hospital (unit)	卫生机构床位数（张） Number of Health Care Bed (unit)	医院床位数（张） Number of Hospital Bed (unit)	卫生技术人员数（人） Number of Medical Technical Personnel (person)	医师、护士数（人） Number of Physicians and Nurses (person)
2008	2239	276	34618	30582	47433	18066
2009	2162	261	36849	32371	51641	19284
2010	2385	258	39407	34274	56579	18763
2011	5554	268	41010	35976	61281	21551

19-11 卫生机构、床位及人员数（2011年）

卫生机构	Health Care Institutions	机构数（个）Number of Institutions (unit)	床位数（张）Number of Beds (unit)
总　计	**Total**	**5554**	**41010**
一、医院	**Hospitals**	**268**	**35976**
综合医院	General Hospitals	201	28937
中医医院	Hospitals Specialized in Traditional Chinese Medicine	35	2877
中西医结合医院	Hospitals Integrating Traditional Chinese Medicine with Western Therapeutics in Practice	1	20
民族医院	Nationalities Hospitals		
专科医院	Specialized Hospitals	31	4142
口腔医院	Dental Hospitals	3	76
眼科医院	Eye Hospitals	5	194
耳鼻喉科医院	ENT Hospitals		
肿瘤医院	Cancer Hospitals	1	610
心血管病医院	Cardiovascular Hospitals	1	80
胸科医院	Chest Hospitals		
血液病医院	Blood Disease Hospitals		
妇产（科）医院	Obstetrics and Gynecologist Hospitals	2	68
儿童医院	Children's Hospitals	1	826
精神病医院	Psychiatric Hospitals	5	920
传染病医院	Hospitals for Infectious Diseases	1	237
皮肤病医院	Skin Hospitals		
结核病医院	Tuberculosis Hospitals	1	600
麻风病医院	Leprosy Hospitals		
职业病医院	Occupational Diseases Hospitals		
骨科医院	Orthopedic Hospitals	3	191
康复医院	Rehabilitation Hospitals	3	28
整形外科医院	Plastic Surgery Hospitals		
美容医院	Beauty Hospitals		
其他专科医院	Other Specialized Hospitals	5	312
护理院	Nursing Centets		
二、基层医疗卫生机构	**Commuting health care service centre**	**5213**	**3250**
社区卫生服务中心(站)	Community Health Care Center(Station)	202	1906
社区卫生服务中心	Community Health Care Center	129	1831
社区卫生服务站	Community Health Care Station	73	75

Number of Health Care Institutions, Beds and Employed Persons in Health Care Institutions（2011）

人员合计 （人） Total Number of Employed Persons (person)	卫生技术人员 Medical Technical Personnel	执业(助理)医师数 Licensed（Assistant） Doctors	#执业医师 Chartered Doctors
79999	**61281**	**21551**	**18904**
55132	**43944**	**14058**	**13163**
45394	36559	11754	11062
3896	3079	1071	969
46	37	14	13
5796	4269	1219	1119
368	282	112	109
251	189	61	53
903	641	179	178
97	79	24	23
166	143	52	34
1581	1308	342	333
788	496	126	119
400	233	54	52
450	341	83	80
222	176	65	44
96	55	28	20
474	326	93	74
19926	**13975**	**6516**	**4855**
4975	4192	1470	1069
4433	3698	1248	885
542	494	222	184

19-11 续表1

卫生机构	Health Care Institutions	人员合计 卫生技术人员中 注册护士 Registered Nurses	药师（士） Junior Paramedics
总　计	**Total**	**25043**	**3127**
一、医院	**Hospitals**	**19998**	**2307**
综合医院	General Hospitals	16743	1803
中医医院	Hospitals Specialized in Traditional Chinese Medicine	1149	298
中西医结合医院	Hospitals Integrating Traditional Chinese Medicine with Western Therapeutics in Practice	17	4
民族医院	Nationalities Hospitals		
专科医院	Specialized Hospitals	2089	202
口腔医院	Dental Hospitals	101	6
眼科医院	Eye Hospitals	94	7
耳鼻喉科医院	ENT Hospitals		
肿瘤医院	Cancer Hospitals	342	25
心血管病医院	Cardiovascular Hospitals	41	4
胸科医院	Chest Hospitals		
血液病医院	Blood Disease Hospitals		
妇产（科）医院	Obstetrics and Gynecologist Hospitals	61	3
儿童医院	Children□s Hospitals	733	66
精神病医院	Psychiatric Hospitals	260	24
传染病医院	Hospitals for Infectious Diseases	124	15
皮肤病医院	Skin Hospitals		
结核病医院	Tuberculosis Hospitals	165	22
麻风病医院	Leprosy Hospitals		
职业病医院	Occupational Diseases Hospitals		
骨科医院	Orthopedic Hospitals	54	8
康复医院	Rehabilitation Hospitals	11	
整形外科医院	Plastic Surgery Hospitals		
美容医院	Beauty Hospitals		
其他专科医院	Other Specialized Hospitals	103	22
护理院	Nursing Centets		
二、基层医疗卫生机构	**Commuting health care service centre**	**4131**	**703**
社区卫生服务中心(站)	Community Health Care Center(Station)	1274	286
社区卫生服务中心	Community Health Care Center	1089	252
社区卫生服务站	Community Health Care Station	185	34

continued 1

（人） Total Number of Employed Persons (person)				
Among:Medical Technical Personnel		其他技术人员 Other Technical Personnel	管理人员 Administrative Personnel	工勤技能人员 Logistics Technical Workers
技师（士） Technicians	#检验师 Laboratory Technicians			
3622	**2622**	**895**	**6769**	**6789**
2638	**1845**	**644**	**5158**	**5386**
2137	1525	507	3981	4347
224	119	99	392	326
2	2		4	5
275	199	38	781	708
11	6		61	25
2	2	2	31	29
39	22	9	111	142
8	5		12	6
8	4	2	12	9
80	66		156	117
25	17	8	145	139
18	18	3	93	71
41	27	2	77	30
13	7	2	16	28
11	11		10	31
19	14	10	57	81
575	**400**	**63**	**791**	**832**
251	183	29	356	398
231	164	29	329	377
20	19		27	21

19-11 续表2

卫生机构	Health Care Institutions	机构数(个) Number of Institutions (unit)	床位数(张) Number of Beds (unit)
卫生院	Health Center	100	1288
街道卫生院	Urban Health-center		
乡镇卫生院	Rural Health-center	100	1288
中心卫院	Center Health-center	23	667
乡卫生院	Country Health-center	77	621
村卫生室	Village clinics	3117	
门诊部	Outpatient department	167	56
综合门诊部	Comprehensive out-patient department	125	26
中医门诊部	Chinese medicine out-patient department	21	
中西医结合门诊部	Integrative Medicine outpatient department	3	
民族医门诊部	The national medicine out-patient department		
专科门诊部	Specialist out-patient department	18	30
诊所、卫生所、医务室	Clinic, health center, Infirmary	1627	
诊所	Clinic	1307	
卫生所、医务室	Clinic, Infirmary	320	
护理站	Nurses' station		
三、专科公共卫生机构	**College of public health institutions**	**53**	**1302**
疾病预防控制中心	Center for Disease Control and Prevention	17	
专科疾病防治院（所、站）	Specialized disease prevention and cure center (place, station)	1	450
1.专科疾病防治院（所）	Specialist for Disease Control and Prevention center (place)	1	450
2.专科疾病防治所（站、中心）	Specialized disease prevention (station, center)		
健康教育所（站、中心）	Health Education Institute (station, center)	2	
妇幼保健院（所、站）	Maternal and Child Health Hospital (Station)	15	852
1.妇幼保健院	Maternal and Child Health Hospital	9	852
2.妇幼保健所	Maternal and Child Health	2	
3.妇幼保健站	Maternal and Child Health Station	4	
4.生殖保健中心	Center for Reproductive Health		
急救中心（站）	Emergency Center	1	
采供血机构	Blood Collection Agencies	1	
卫生监督所（中心）	Health Supervision Agencies （Center）	15	
计划生育技术服务机构	Familiy Planning Technical Serverice Institution	1	
四、其他卫生机构	**Other Health Institution**	**20**	**482**
医学科学研究机构	Medical scientific research institutions	4	
医学在职培训机构	Medical training institutions	5	
临床检验中心（所、站）	Clinical testing center (place, station)	1	

continued 2

人员合计（人） Total Number of Employed Persons (person)	卫生技术人员 Medical Technical Personnel	执业(助理)医师数 Licensed（Assistant） Doctors	#执业医师 Chartered Doctors
2482	1997	575	334
2482	1997	575	334
1089	880	261	169
1393	1117	314	165
5245	980	802	275
2198	1871	862	731
1732	1494	655	566
230	194	118	103
54	37	18	17
182	146	71	45
5026	4935	2807	2446
3713	3672	2157	1880
1313	1263	650	566
4261	**3029**	**860**	**777**
1011	727	224	209
296	203	63	60
296	203	63	60
63	21	5	5
1981	1565	510	447
1844	1458	463	406
38	27	12	10
99	80	35	31
123	49	38	38
156	97	17	16
599	348		
32	19	3	2
680	**333**	**117**	**109**
172	90	45	44
203	76	10	9
29	26	13	13

19-11 续表3

卫生机构	Health Care Institutions	人员合计 卫生技术人员中 注册护士 Registered Nurses	药师（士） Junior Paramedics
卫生院	Health Center	413	117
街道卫生院	Urban Health-center		
乡镇卫生院	Rural Health-center	413	117
中心卫院	Center Health-center	212	46
乡卫生院	Country Health-center	201	71
村卫生室	Village clinics	178	
门诊部	Outpatient department	588	150
综合门诊部	Comprehensive out-patient department	505	116
中医门诊部	Chinese medicine out-patient department	29	25
中西医结合门诊部	Integrative Medicine outpatient department	9	4
民族医门诊部	The national medicine out-patient department		
专科门诊部	Specialist out-patient department	45	5
诊所、卫生所、医务室	Clinic, health center, Infirmary	1678	150
诊所	Clinic	1201	87
卫生所、医务室	Clinic, Infirmary	477	63
护理站	Nurses' station		
三、专科公共卫生机构	**College of public health institutions**	**846**	**98**
疾病预防控制中心	Center for Disease Control and Prevention	32	12
专科疾病防治院（所、站）	Specialized disease prevention and cure center (place, station)	74	11
1.专科疾病防治院（所）	Specialist for Disease Control and Prevention center (place)	74	11
2.专科疾病防治所（站、中心）	Specialized disease prevention (station, center)		
健康教育所（站、中心）	Health Education Institute (station, center)		
妇幼保健院（所、站）	Maternal and Child Health Hospital (Station)	697	66
1.妇幼保健院	Maternal and Child Health Hospital	662	59
2.妇幼保健所	Maternal and Child Health	7	3
3.妇幼保健站	Maternal and Child Health Station	28	4
4.生殖保健中心	Center for Reproductive Health		
急救中心（站）	Emergency Center	9	1
采供血机构	Blood Collection Agencies	28	8
卫生监督所（中心）	Health Supervision Agencies（Center）		
计划生育技术服务机构	Familiy Planning Technical Serverice Institution	6	
四、其他卫生机构	**Other Health Institution**	**68**	**19**
医学科学研究机构	Medical scientific research institutions	15	4
医学在职培训机构	Medical training institutions		2
临床检验中心（所、站）	Clinical testing center (place, station)	8	

continued 3

（人） Total Number of Employed Persons (person)				
Among:Medical Technical Personnel		其他技术人员	管理人员	工勤技能人员
技师（士）				
	#检验师			
Technicians	Laboratory Technicians	Other Technical Personnel	Administrative Personnel	Logistics Technical Workers
151	83	12	229	244
151	83	12	229	244
80	41	6	83	120
71	42	6	146	124
130	98	22	206	99
108	83	18	150	70
9	7		28	8
4	2	4	5	8
9	6		23	13
43	36			91
11	8			41
32	28			50
371	**343**	**95**	**675**	**462**
203	193	38	136	110
18	14	2	58	33
18	14	2	58	33
		11	27	4
116	102	18	218	180
107	94	16	201	169
1	1		7	4
8	7	2	10	7
		10	28	36
34	34	11	36	12
		5	167	79
			5	8
38	**34**	**93**	**145**	**109**
19	15	18	36	28
2	2	60	50	17
5	5		1	2

19-12 各区县卫生机构、床位及人员数（2011年）

Number of Health Care Institutions, Beds and Employed Persons in Health Care Institutions By Region（2011）

区 县	Region	机构数(个) Number of Health Care Institutions (unit)	床位数(张) Number of Beds (unit)	人员合计(人) Total Number of Employed Persons (person)	卫生技术人员 Total Number of Medical Technical Personnel
全 市	**Total**	**5554**	**41010**	**79999**	**61281**
新城区	Xincheng	302	6236	12843	9930
碑林区	Beilin	338	6250	12299	9883
莲湖区	Lianhu	337	4994	9610	7883
灞桥区	Baqiao	550	2157	4687	3773
未央区	Weiyang	274	2718	5042	4117
雁塔区	Yanta	461	7542	13979	11076
阎良区	Yanliang	155	1265	2003	1559
临潼区	Lintong	463	1756	3502	2336
长安区	Chang'an	771	2772	5305	3690
蓝田县	Lantian	632	1225	2232	1356
周至县	Zhouzhi	488	1026	3105	1837
户 县	Huxian	575	2035	3681	2610
高陵县	Gaoling	208	1034	1711	1231

19-13 主要年份卫生机构各类人员数

Number of Employed Persons in Health Care Institutions in Representative Years

单位：人 (person)

指　　标	Item	2000	2005	2006	2007	2008	2009	2010	2011
人员总数	**Total**	**53111**	**52821**	**54912**	**55551**	**59934**	**65003**	**71230**	**79999**
卫生技术人员	Medical Technical Personnel	41836	42255	43862	43707	47433	51641	56579	61281
执业（助理）医师	Licensed（Assistant） Doctors	18750	17730	18007	17266	18066	19284	18763	21551
#执业医师	Chartered Doctors	16146	15533	15778	15142	15975	17286	16613	18904
注册护士	Registered Nurses	14344	14004	15538	15337	17186	20167	22640	25043
药师（士）	Junior Paramedics	3475	3084	2987	2707	2721	2814	3030	3127
技　师（士）	Technicians	2179	2252	2242	3046	3168	3350	4589	3622
#检验师	Laboratory Technicians	2179	2252	2242	2150	2204	2290	2439	2622
其　他	Other	3088	5185	5088	5351	6292	6026	7557	7938
其他技术人员	Other Technical Personnel	855	1425	1601	1399	1051	1325	1156	895
管理人员	Administrative Personnel	5647	5199	5309	5532	6007	6067	6416	6769
工勤技能人员	Logistics Technical Workers	4773	3942	4140	4913	5443	5970	7079	6789

19–14 医疗卫生机构门诊、住院及病床使用情况（2011年）

指　　标	Item	诊疗人次数总计 总 计 Total
总　计	**Total**	**42916048**
一、医院	**Hospitals**	**21117010**
综合医院	General Hospitals	17290344
中医医院	Hospitals Specialized in Traditional Chinese Medicine	1678909
中西医结合医院	Hospitals Integrating Traditional Chinese Medicine with Western Therapeutics in Practice	8838
民族医院	Nationalities Hospitals	
专科医院	Specialized Hospitals	2138919
口腔医院	Dental Hospitals	228307
眼科医院	Eye Hospitals	89720
耳鼻喉科医院	ENT Hospitals	
肿瘤医院	Cancer Hospitals	21012
心血管病医院	Cardiovascular Hospitals	21525
胸科医院	Chest Hospitals	
血液病医院	Blood Disease Hospitals	
妇产（科）医院	Obstetrics and Gynecologist Hospitals	63019
儿童医院	Children's Hospitals	1324161
精神病医院	Psychiatric Hospitals	97742
传染病医院	Hospitals for Infectious Diseases	31946
皮肤病医院	Skin Hospitals	
结核病医院	Tuberculosis Hospitals	60117
麻风病医院	Leprosy Hospitals	
职业病医院	Occupational Diseases Hospitals	
骨科医院	Orthopedic Hospitals	95667
康复医院	Rehabilitation Hospitals	19960
整形外科医院	Plastic Surgery Hospitals	
美容医院	Beauty Hospitals	
其他专科医院	Other Specialized Hospitals	85743
护理院	Nursing Centets	

Medical and Health Institutions Outpatient, Inpatient and Utilization of Beds

Total Number of Clinics			观察室 Observation Room		急诊抢救总人次 The Total Number of Emergency Rescue	急诊抢救成功总人次 Emergency Rescue Success the Total Number of Attendances
其中:门、急诊人次数 Number of Outpatient and Emergency			留观病例数（人）Number of Patients Receiving (person)	死亡人数(人) Number of Deaths (person)		
门诊人次数 Number of Outpatients	急诊人次数 Number of Emergency					
	小计 Subtotal	死亡人数 Number of Deaths				
39664773	**2083601**	**1982**	**21648**	**175**	**85810**	**83558**
19108637	**1871625**	**1957**	**14165**	**173**	**85078**	**82888**
15583866	1581628	1930	13616	161	76172	74045
1622644	46249	7	460	10	850	807
8780	58					
1893347	243690	20	89	2	8056	8036
225629	2678					
88449	1271					
21010	2					
18515	3010		30		6	6
48487	14532		5	2	5	5
1118349	205812	16			8016	8000
95845	1507		3		7	7
28515	3331	3	26		10	7
59627	490					
84734	9805					
19760	200				3	3
84427	1052	1	25		9	8

19-14 续表1

指　　标	Item	入院人数合计（人）Total Number of Admissions (person)	出院人数合计（人）Total Number of Discharge Patients (person)
总　计	**Total**	**1075316**	**1068803**
一、医院	**Hospitals**	**975287**	**969799**
综合医院	General Hospitals	821065	816446
中医医院	Hospitals Specialized in Traditional Chinese Medicine	64770	64548
中西医结合医院	Hospitals Integrating Traditional Chinese Medicine with Western Therapeutics in Practice		
民族医院	Nationalities Hospitals		
专科医院	Specialized Hospitals	89452	88805
口腔医院	Dental Hospitals	1482	1478
眼科医院	Eye Hospitals	4945	4970
耳鼻喉科医院	ENT Hospitals		
肿瘤医院	Cancer Hospitals	16385	16245
心血管病医院	Cardiovascular Hospitals	1833	1656
胸科医院	Chest Hospitals		
血液病医院	Blood Disease Hospitals		
妇产（科）医院	Obstetrics and Gynecologist Hospitals	2102	2104
儿童医院	Children□s Hospitals	34381	34343
精神病医院	Psychiatric Hospitals	6277	6225
传染病医院	Hospitals for Infectious Diseases	5030	4925
皮肤病医院	Skin Hospitals		
结核病医院	Tuberculosis Hospitals	8554	8532
麻风病医院	Leprosy Hospitals		
职业病医院	Occupational Diseases Hospitals		
骨科医院	Orthopedic Hospitals	3120	2995
康复医院	Rehabilitation Hospitals	564	564
整形外科医院	Plastic Surgery Hospitals		
美容医院	Beauty Hospitals		
其他专科医院	Other Specialized Hospitals	4779	4768
护理院	Nursing Centets		

continued 1

治愈率（%） Curative Ratio (%)	好转率（%） Improvement Rate (%)	死亡率（%） Mortality Rate (%)	病床周转次数（次） Nnumber of Bed Rurnover (time)	病床使用率（%） Bed occupancy rate (%)	出院者平均住院日（天） Average Stay Days in Hospital (day)
59	**39**	**1**	**25**	**78**	**11**
57	**41**	**1**	**26**	**81**	**11**
58	40	1	27	81	11
41	56		20	76	13
			1	1	7
61	37		20	91	17
86	14		15	57	13
89	11		25	58	8
68	28	1	24	110	17
31	69				
83	15		28	48	6
78	21		42	110	10
33	64		8	88	42
40	55	1	22	99	16
3	92	1	13	109	31
59	37		13	34	10
59	30		22	90	15
38	61		7	51	25

19-14 续表2

指　标	Item	诊疗人次数总计 总 计 Total
二、基层医疗卫生机构	**Commuting health care service centre**	**20635105**
社区卫生服务中心(站)	Community Health Care Center(Station)	3261090
社区卫生服务中心	Community Health Care Center	2581848
社区卫生服务站	Community Health Care Station	679242
卫生院	Health Center	855348
街道卫生院	Urban Health-center	
乡镇卫生院	Rural Health-center	855348
中心卫院	Center Health-center	339238
乡卫生院	Country Health-center	516110
村卫生室	Village clinics	9668286
门诊部	Outpatient department	1686688
诊所、卫生所、医务室	Clinic, health center, Infirmary	5163693
诊所	Clinic	4140251
卫生所、医务室	Clinic, Infirmary	1023442
护理站	Nurses' station	
三、专业公共卫生机构	**College of public health institutions**	**1107030**
专科疾病防治院（所、站）	Specialized disease prevention and cure center (place, station)	24121
妇幼保健院（所、站）	Maternal and Child Health Hospital (Station)	1082909
（内）妇幼保健院	Maternal and Child Health Hospital	1061888
急救中心（站）	Emergency Center	
四、其他卫生机构	**Other Health Institution**	**56903**
疗养院	Sanatorium	56903
临床检验中心	Clinical testing center	

continued 2

Total Number of Clinics			观察室 Observation Room		急诊抢救总人次	急诊抢救成功总人次
其中:门、急诊人次数 Number of Outpatient and Emergency			留观病例数（人）Number of Patients Receiving (person)	死亡人数(人) Number of Deaths (person)	The Total Number of Emergency Rescue	Emergency Rescue Success the Total Number of Attendances
门诊人次数 Number of Outpatients	急诊人次数 Number of Emergency					
	小计 Subtotal	死亡人数 Number of Deaths				
19436220	**167959**	**20**	**7440**	**2**	**185**	**125**
3123169	88654	7	6359	1		
2475967	66309	6	5623	1		
647202	22345	1	736			
818897	29785	13	1021	1		
818897	29785	13	1021	1		
321998	12457	13	20	1		
496899	17328		1001			
8840480						
1632277	49520		60		185	125
5021397						
4013628						
1007769						
1063359	**43671**	**4**	**43**		**520**	**519**
24068	53					
1039291	43618	4	43		520	519
1018270	43618	4	43		520	519
56557	**346**	**1**			**27**	**26**
56557	346	1			27	26

19-14 续表3

指　标	Item	入院人数合计（人）Total Number of Admissions (person)	出院人数合计（人）Total Number of Discharge Patients (person)
二、基层医疗卫生机构	**Commuting health care service centre**	**48903**	**48002**
社区卫生服务中心(站)	Community Health Care Center(Station)	31067	30572
社区卫生服务中心	Community Health Care Center	30957	30464
社区卫生服务站	Community Health Care Station	110	108
卫生院	Health Center	17350	16944
街道卫生院	Urban Health-center		
乡镇卫生院	Rural Health-center	17350	16944
中心卫院	Center Health-center	8869	8576
乡卫生院	Country Health-center	8481	8368
村卫生室	Village clinics		
门诊部	Outpatient department	486	486
诊所、卫生所、医务室	Clinic, health center, Infirmary		
诊所	Clinic		
卫生所、医务室	Clinic, Infirmary		
护理站	Nurses' station		
三、专业公共卫生机构	**College of public health institutions**	**46209**	**46130**
专科疾病防治院（所、站）	Specialized disease prevention and cure center (place, station)	4004	3950
妇幼保健院（所、站）	Maternal and Child Health Hospital (Station)	42205	42180
（内）妇幼保健院	Maternal and Child Health Hospital	42205	42180
急救中心（站）	Emergency Center		
四、其他卫生机构	**Other Health Institution**	**4917**	**4872**
疗养院	Sanatorium	4917	4872
临床检验中心	Clinical testing center		

continued 3

治愈率（%） Curative Ratio (%)	好转率（%） Improvement Rate (%)	死亡率（%） Mortality Rate (%)	病床周转次数（次） Nnumber of Bed Rurnover (time)	病床使用率（%） Bed occupancy rate (%)	出院者平均住院日（天） Average Stay Days in Hospital (day)
75	24		11	35	11
75	24		12	37	11
74	26				
68	31		18	40	8
			18	47	9
68	31		18	39	8
60	39		19	39	8
77	23		16	37	8
97	3		16	58	10
86	**12**		**37**	**98**	**10**
11	85		10	124	47
94	6		50	86	6
94	6		50	86	6
69	**22**		**11**	**23**	**7**
69	22		11	23	7

19-15 社会福利事业单位基本情况（2011年）

Basic Statistics on Social Welfare Insititutions（2011）

单位：个、人 （unit,person）

指标	Item	福利院数 Number of Homes	工作人员 Number of Staff	床位数 Number of Beds	年末在院人数 Number of Persons Housed at the Year-end
一、社会福利院情况	**Statistics on Social Welfare**	**73**	**1608**	**10321**	**6962**
1.社会福利院	Social Welfare Homes	3	77	782	597
2.儿童福利院	Baby Welfare Homes	1	78	900	798
3.社会福利医院	Social Welfare Hospitals	1	156	500	477
4.收养性老年福利机构	Welfare Units Adopting the Elderly	68	1297	8139	5090
城镇	Urban	45	1097	5840	3858
农村	Rural	23	200	2299	1232

19-16 主要年份社会福利事业单位机构、人员数

Number of Social Welfare Institutions and Employed Persons

单位：个、人 （unit,person）

项目	Item	2000	2005	2006	2007	2008	2009	2010	2011
一、机构	**Insititutions**								
烈士纪念建筑物管理单位	Institutions Managing Memorial Buildings of Martyrs	2	2	2	2	2	2	2	2
救助类单位	Units Providing Assistance	8	8	8	8	8	8	8	8
殡仪服务单位	Funeral Service Units	18	20	22	21	20	20	22	21
殡仪馆	Funeral Homes	4	4	4	5	4	4	4	5
公墓	Cemeteries	12	13	14	13	12	12	14	12
殡葬管理单位	Funeral Management Units	2	3	4	3	4	4	4	4
二、人员	**Staff**	**0**	0	0	0	0	0	0	0
烈士纪念建筑物管理单位	Institutions Managing Memorial Buildings of Martyrs	43	43	40	37	39	39	37	38
救助类单位	Units Providing Assistance	99	112	116	113	110	118	116	119
殡仪服务单位	Funeral Service Units	613	756	765	902	1015	1046	1371	1313
殡仪馆	Funeral Homes	164	204	177	239	220	218	375	408
公墓	Cemeteries	425	516	533	624	745	776	939	838
殡葬管理单位	Funeral Management Units	24	36	55	39	50	52	57	67

19-17 各区县福利企业单位基本情况（2011年）

Basic Statistics on Social Welfare Insititutions（2011）

单位：个、人 （unit,person）

区 县	Region	单位数 Number of Enterprise	年末职工人数 Number of Staff and Workers at the end of year	年末残疾职工人数 Number of Disabled Staff and Workers at the end of year	残疾职工中女性 Number of Female Disabled Staff and Workers
全 市	**Total**	**101**	**6166**	**2415**	**950**
市本级	City Level	12	806	294	72
新城区	Xincheng	10	386	182	68
碑林区	Beilin				
莲湖区	Lianhu	13	969	385	128
灞桥区	Baqiao	20	1257	471	248
未央区	Weiyang	10	973	359	169
雁塔区	Yanta	2	119	35	25
阎良区	Yanliang	4	163	78	18
临潼区	Lintong	2	210	62	40
长安区	Chang'an	10	585	210	58
蓝田县	Lantian	2	156	64	18
周至县	Zhouzhi	2	105	34	9
户 县	Huxian	14	437	241	97
高陵县	Gaoling				

19-18 社会保险基本情况

Basic Sitiation of Social Insurance

指标名称	Item	2010	2011
城镇基本养老保险参保人数（万人）	Number of Urban Basic Old-age Insurance(10 000 people)	208.03	242.7
城镇基本医疗保险参保人数（万人）	Number of urban basic medical insurance(10 000 people)	365.49	404.27
失业保险参保人数（万人）	Number of unemployed insurance(10 000 people))	130.54	134.82
城镇基本养老保险覆盖率（%）	Coverage rate of urban basic Old-age insurance(%)		
城镇基本医疗保险覆盖率（%）	Coverage rate of urban basic medical insurance(%)		96.0
城镇基本失业保险覆盖率（%）	Coverage rate of unemployed insurance(%)		
生育保险参保人数（万人）	Number of Maternity insurance(10 000 people)	87.9	95.5
工伤保险参保人数（万人）	Number of industrial injury insurance(10 000 people)	109.52	123.07
养老、失业、医疗、工伤、生育保险基金当年支出额（万元）	Expenditures of this year's Old-age t,unempolyed,medical, industrial and Maternity insurance(10 000 yuan)	1401284	1813906

19-19 全市及各区县新型农村合作医疗情况（2011年）

Situation of the New Rural Cooperative Medical Care of the Whole City and Area County

区 县	Region	参加新型农村合作医疗人口数（万人） Participate in the new rural cooperative medical Population (million) (10 000 persons)	参加新型农村合作医疗比率（参合率）（%） Participate in the new rural cooperative medical care ration (%)
全 市	**Total**	**394.85**	**97.8**
新城区	Xincheng		
碑林区	Beilin		
莲湖区	Lianhu		
灞桥区	Baqiao	28.21	99.2
未央区	Weiyang	18.64	100.0
雁塔区	Yanta	17.07	101.9
阎良区	Yanliang	16.25	99.7
临潼区	Lintong	54.62	99.2
长安区	Chang'an	79.09	95.6
蓝田县	Lantian	55.44	95.8
周至县	Zhouzhi	57.14	97.1
户 县	Huxian	46.70	98.7
高陵县	Gaoling	21.69	99.7

19-20 各区县优抚对象人员情况（2011年）

Statistics on Persons Enjoying Favoured Treatment by Region（2011）

单位：人 （person）

指 标	Item	全市 Total	市本级 City Level	新城区 Xincheng	碑林区 Beilin	莲湖区 Lianhu
合 计	**Total**	**40022**	**86**	**928**	**958**	**1141**
1.革命伤残人员	Number of Disabled Veterans	4965	86	670	591	707
2.烈军属人员	Number of Family Members of Martyrs and Soldiers	476		27	16	29
3.在乡红军老战士	Old Red Army Men in Hometown	5			2	1
4.在乡复原军人	Demobilized Soldiers in Hometown	7165		16	13	35
5.在乡退伍军人	Veterans in Hometown	4346		1	6	5

19-20 续表1 continued 1

单位：人 （person）

指 标	Item	灞桥区 Baqiao	未央区 Weiyang	雁塔区 Yanta	阎良区 Yanliang	临潼区 Lintong
合 计	**Total**	**2412**	**1033**	**2366**	**1646**	**5251**
1.革命伤残人员	Number of Disabled Veterans	260	198	654	88	296
2.烈军属人员	Number of Family Members of Martyrs and Soldiers	32	9	15	22	63
3.在乡红军老战士	Old Red Army Men in Hometown					
4.在乡复原军人	Demobilized Soldiers in Hometown	596	138	140	299	1172
5.在乡退伍军人	Veterans in Hometown	253	5	587	55	279

19-20 续表2 continued 2

单位：人 （person）

指 标	Item	长安区 Chang'an	蓝田县 Lantian	周至县 Zhouzhi	户 县 Huxian	高陵县 Gaoling	沣东新城 Fengdongxincheng
合 计	**Total**	**6210**	**4053**	**5930**	**4571**	**2163**	**1274**
1.革命伤残人员	Number of Disabled Veterans	377	225	318	288	128	79
2.烈军属人员	Number of Family Members of Martyrs and Soldiers	36	47	129	21	24	6
3.在乡红军老战士	Old Red Army Men in Hometown			1		1	
4.在乡复原军人	Demobilized Soldiers in Hometown	1075	795	1062	935	658	231
5.在乡退伍军人	Veterans in Hometown	155	2031	209	138	167	455

19-21 各区县计划生育和婚姻情况（2011年）

Conditions of Birth Control and Marriage Registration by Region（2011）

区 县	Region	晚婚率(%) Late Marriage Rate	计划生育率(%) Family Planning Rate	综合节育率(%) Contraceptive Rate
全 市	**Total**	**67.1**	**99.3**	**91.7**
新城区	Xingcheng	96.1	100.0	88.0
碑林区	Beilin	99.6	100.0	87.6
莲湖区	Lianhu	93.6	99.9	90.4
灞桥区	Baqiao	93.6	99.5	91.3
未央区	Weiyang	63.8	99.9	90.4
雁塔区	Yanta	51.2	99.9	88.4
阎良区	Yanliang	57.6	99.9	91.1
临潼区	Lintong	70.7	99.0	93.9
长安区	Chang'an	59.8	98.3	94.2
蓝田县	Lantian	69.7	98.7	91.2
周至县	Zhouzhi	56.7	99.1	94.5
户 县	Huxian	60.9	98.4	93.6
高陵县	Gaoling	42.9	99.9	90.2
沣东新城	Fengdongxincheng			

19-21 续表 continued

区 县	Region	独生子女领证率(%) Only-child Certificate Rate	结婚对数（对） Marriages (couple)	再婚数（人） Remarriages	离婚对数（对） Divorced Couple (couple)
全 市	**Total**	**49.0**	**94398**	**23106**	**19421**
新城区	Xingcheng	56.5	5994	2004	1616
碑林区	Beilin	54.3	11708	2569	2163
莲湖区	Lianhu	67.1	5993	1809	1751
灞桥区	Baqiao	61.6	6905	1761	1253
未央区	Weiyang	65.4	5343	1404	1292
雁塔区	Yanta	57.3	10204	2979	3104
阎良区	Yanliang	63.4	2998	940	736
临潼区	Lintong	28.9	6830	1051	1124
长安区	Chang'an	39.1	11223	3102	2271
蓝田县	Lantian	22.7	11229	2371	1602
周至县	Zhouzhi	14.0	5229	829	615
户 县	Huxian	34.6	5637	1110	977
高陵县	Gaoling	29.8	4045	1008	718
沣东新城	Fengdongxincheng		1060	169	199

19-22 各区县妇幼保健卫生情况（2011年）

Care Health Conditions of Women and Child by Region

单位：% (%)

区 县	Region	死亡率 Mortality rate	新生儿死亡率 Mortality rate of newborn	婴儿死亡率 Mortality rate of baby	孕产妇死亡率 The maternal mortality rate	产妇住院分娩比例 Maternal hospitalization the proportion of deliveries
全 市	**Total**	**5.2**	**4.3**	**2.9**	**16.0**	**99.6**
新城区	Xingcheng	1.2	1.2			100.0
碑林区	Beilin	6.7	6.7	3.8		100.0
莲湖区	Lianhu	4.5	4.5	3.8		100.0
灞桥区	Baqiao	4.1	3.2	1.3	31.5	100.0
未央区	Weiyang	2.9	2.5	1.2	41.4	100.0
雁塔区	Yanta	7.1	4.4	4.4		100.0
阎良区	Yanliang	4.1	3.1	3.1	51.1	100.0
临潼区	Lintong	5.5	4.8	3.2	17.6	100.0
长安区	Chang'an	6.2	4.6	3.1	38.6	99.7
蓝田县	Lantian	4.6	3.4	2.1		100.0
周至县	Zhouzhi	5.0	4.7	3.3		96.3
户 县	Huxian	7.9	7.1	4.6		100.0
高陵县	Gaoling	7.3	5.1	3.9		100.0

19–23 主要年份律师、公证及调解情况

Basic Statistics on Lawyer, Notaries and Mediation in Representative Years

指　　标	Item	2000	2005	2006	2007	2008	2009	2010	2011
一、律师工作	**Lawyers**								
律师事务所（个）	Number of Law Offices（unit)	46	65	70	71	73	79	95	97
律师（人）	Lawyers(person)	534	866	902	864	940	1058	1202	1347
#专职	Full-time	469	825	851	808	865	1001	1139	1275
兼职	Part-time	65	41	51	56	66	55	63	68
二、公证工作	**Notarization**								
公证处（个）	Number of Notary Offices（unit)	14	14	14	14	14	14	14	14
公证人员（人）	Notarial Personnel（person）	158	192	205	243	189	194	202	233
#公证员	Notaries	96	93	102	156	100	102	112	118
办理公证件数（件）	Number of Notarized Documents Issued（case）	79199	68110	70777	70863	74440	88637	106491	108120
国内	Domestic	62060	46427	45717	42996	43640	57190	72670	68239
民事	Civil	24576	11737	13258	15466	15782	22337	24813	24356
经济	Economics	37484	34690	32459	27530	27858	34853	47857	43883
涉外	Foreign-related	16990	21451	24857	27616	30481	31082	33410	39545
涉港、澳、台	Hong Kong、Macco and Taiwan related	149	232	203	251	319	365	411	336
三、人民调解工作	**Number of People Mediations**								
已建调委会数（个）	Number of Mediation Committees（unit）	4379	3904	3952	3952	3961	3961	3911	4031
调解人员数（人）	Number of Mediators（person）	13059	16156	15930	15525	15424	17198	15717	12848
调解纠纷数（件）	Number of Civil Disputes Mediated（case）	34212	17770	17608	14986	12223	23185	22247	33851
#调解成功数	Number of Cases Successfully Mediated	31574	14084	14597	13756	11201	21373	22164	32109

19-24 主要年份共青团组织情况

Basic Facts on Communist Youth League in Representative Years

单位：个、人 (unit,person)

指 标	Item	2000	2005	2006	2007	2008	2009	2010	2011
一、基层团组织	**Grass-root Youth League Organisations**	**10323**	**7726**	**9560**	**9329**	**10985**	**9054**	**7006**	**11248**
二、共青团员	**Youth League Members**	**278165**	**344035**	**329669**	**327332**	**348141**	**324785**	**308141**	**345682**
#女团员	Female Youth League Members	134289	153493	142431	141271	145777	144027	142379	159725
三、专职团干部	**Full-time Youth League Cadre**	**845**	**537**	**524**	**576**	**601**	**387**	**311**	**270**

19-25 妇联组织情况（2011年）

Women's Organizations Status（2011）

单位：个 (unit)

项 目	Item	2011
一、妇联组织	**Women's Organizations**	
市级妇联	Municipal Women's Federation	1
街道妇联	Street Women's Federation	101
社区妇联	Community Women's Federation	650
县（区）妇联	County (district) Women's Federation	13
乡（镇)妇联	Township (town) Women's Federation	74
村妇代会	Village Women's Representative Conference	2894
二、非公有制经济组织中妇女组织	**Women's Organizations in Non-public Economic Organizations**	
个体劳动者协会中的妇女组织	Women's Organizations in Association of Individual Workers	10
专业市场中的妇女组织	Women's Organizations in the Professional Market	
私营企业中的妇女组织	Women's Organizations in the Private Sector	207
三资企业中的妇女组织	Foreign-funded Enterprises in the Women's Organizations	
三、机关事业单位妇女组织	**Women's Organizations in Government Departments and Institutions**	
直属机关妇委会（妇工委）	Women's Committee of Direct-affiliated Departments	24
部门机关妇委会（妇工委）	Women's Committee of Affiliated Departments	302
事业单位妇委会（妇工委）	Women's Committee of Government Institutions	89
四、民主党派妇女组织	**Women's Organizations of Democratic Parties**	
民主党派妇委会	Women's Committee of Democratic Parties	7
五、团体会员	**Members of Organisation**	
工会女职工委员会	Women Staff Committee of Labor Unions	4228
民政部门登记注册的妇女社团	Women's Communities Registered at Civil Administration Departments	7

19-26 妇联工作情况（2011年）

Basic Facts on Women's Federation（2011年）

单位：人、个 （person,unit）

项　　目	Item	2011
一、双学双比活动	**Double Learning and Double Competition Activities**	
(一)科技培训	Scientific and Technical Training	
接受技术培训人数	Number of People Receiving Technical Training	30190
获绿色证书人数	Number of People Gaining Green Certificates	93
妇代会主任中农民技术员数	Number of Farmer in Women's Head Technicians	262
(二)巾帼扶贫	Women Aid-the-poor Project	
脱贫户数	Households out of Poverty	627
扶贫项目数	Number of Poverty Alleviation Projects	7
二、巾帼建功活动	**Women Make Achievements**	
(一)巾帼建功	Women Make Achievements	
评选巾帼建功标兵数	Number of Pacemakes	268
巾帼建功先进工作者数	Number of Advanced Workers	49
巾帼建功先进协调单位数	Number of Advanced Supporting Units	
巾帼文明示范岗数	Number of Model Workers	244
(二)下岗失业妇女再就业	Re-employment of Laid-off and Unemployed Women	2328
妇女就业服务机构数	Number of Institutions for Women's Employment Services	
妇联主办的劳务市场	Labor Markets Sponsored by Women's Federation	10
三、三八红旗手	**Models of Women**	**165**
四、三八红旗集体	**Models of Women Group**	**63**
五、实施春蕾计划	**Carrying out of CHUNLEI Project**	
资助女童入学或返校数	Helping Women Children Enter School or Back School	277
社会捐资总额(万元)	Amount of Money That Social Attributes（10 000yuan）	16
六、来信来访情况	**Conditions of Letters and Visits**	
女职工劳动保护信访案件	Cases about Labor Protection of Employed Women through Letters and Visits	41
侵犯妇女财产权利信访案件	Cases about Encroachment of Women's Property through Letters and Visits	161

19-27 主要年份交通事故情况

Statistics on Traffic Accidents in Representative Years

指　　标	Item	2000	2005	2006	2007	2008	2009	2010	2011
次　数(起)	Number of Traffic Accidents（case）	4099	4903	3709	3643	2576	2702	2323	2264
死亡人数（人）	Number of Deaths（person）	589	617	617	597	551	531	531	531
受伤人数 （人）	Number of Injuries（person）	2884	3081	3075	3002	2464	2247	2520	2260
直接财产损失（万元）	Direct Property Loss（10000yuan）	1116.1	2024.4	1328.3	1038.0	522.8	851.7	736.6	611.9

注：2006年及以前道路交通数据不含高速公路数据,故年度数据不可比。

Note:As road data of traffic didn't include expressways, annual data were not comparable.

19-28 主要年份火灾情况

Statistics on Fires in Representative Years

指　　标	Item	2000	2005	2006	2007	2008	2009	2010	2011
次　数（起）	Number of Traffic Accidents（case）	1040	2664	2310	2009	1537	1485	1825	1920
死亡人数（人）	Number of Deaths（person）	17	13	9	13	11	17	13	8
受伤人数（人）	Number of Injuries（person）	12	15	9	11	4	3	7	3
直接财产损失(万元）	Direct Property Loss（10000yuan）	472.4	1565.5	1376.0	773.9	1907.7	1850.6	2224.2	1587.2

19-29 主要年份安全生产情况

Dato on Sasfety in Production

指　　标	Item	2006	2007	2008	2009	2010	2011
全市合计	**Sum of Entire City**						
起数（起）	Number of Cases（case）	6065	5685	4138	4225	4173	4199
死亡人数（人）	Number of Deaths（person）	676	648	591	586	568	566
受伤人数（人）	Number of Injuries（person）	3090	3013	2472	2264	2529	2271
损失（万元）	Economic Loss（10 000yuan）	3004.1	2308.4	2802.0	3128.9	3666.8	2780.5
道路交通事故	**Road Accidents**						
起数（起）	Number of Cases（case）	3709	3643	2576	2702	2323	2264
死亡人数（人）	Number of Deaths（person）	617	597	551	531	531	531
受伤人数（人）	Number of Injuries（person）	3075	3002	2464	2247	2520	2260
损失（万元）	Economic Loss（10 000yuan）	1328.3	1038.0	522.8	851.7	736.6	611.9
火灾事故	**Fire Accidents**						
起数（起）	Number of Cases（case）	2310	2009	1537	1485	1825	1920
死亡人数（人）	Number of Deaths（person）	9	13	11	17	13	8
受伤人数（人）	Number of Injuries（person）	9	11	4	3	7	3
损失（万元）	Economic Loss（10 000yuan）	1376.0	773.9	1907.7	1850.6	2224.2	1587.2
农机事故	**Farm Machinery Accidents**						
起数（起）	Number of Cases（case）	2	3	2	11	5	
死亡人数（人）	Number of Deaths（person）	1	3	1			
受伤人数（人）	Number of Injuries（person）	1		1	2	2	
损失（万元）	Economic Loss（10 000yuan）				1.1	3.1	
工矿商贸事故	**Accidents in Industry,Mine, Business and Trade**						
起数（起）	Number of Cases（case）	42	30	22	27	20	15
死亡人数（人）	Number of Deaths（person）	47	35	27	38	24	27
受伤人数（人）	Number of Injuries（person）	5		3	12		8
损失（万元）	Economic Loss（10 000yuan）	293.0	496.5	366.5	425.5	703.0	581.5
特种设备	**Special Accidents**						
起数（起）	Number of Cases（case）	2		1			
死亡人数（人）	Number of Deaths（person）	2		1			
受伤人数（人）	Number of Injuries（person）						
损失（万元）	Economic Loss（10 000yuan）	7		5			

注：1.2006年及以前道路交通数据不含高速公路数据,故年度数据不可比.

2.2007年、2009年工矿商贸事故数据含特种设备数据.

Note: 1.As statistics of roads did not include that of highway before 2006, the indexes were not comparable with those in corresponding period.

2.Data of accidents in industry , mine, business and trade include special equipment in 2007 and 2009.

19-30 主要年份刑事案件情况

Data on Criminal Cases in Representative Years

指 标	Item	2005	2006	2007	2008	2009	2010	2011
一、案件数情况	**Data on Number of Cases**							
立案数（起）	Number of Registered Cases(caes)	23537	43856	43583	41811	42321	48566	71499
破案数（起）	Number of Cleared up Cases(caes)	13145	13952	17241	19284	21921	18906	17585
破案率（%）	Percent of Cleared up Cases(%)	56	32	40	46	52	39	246
抓获作案人员（人）	Number of Criminals Caught(person)	10690	11068	12717	12364	11870	13104	14672
二、查获犯罪集团情况	**Data on Hunted down and Seized Criminal Gangs**							
查获犯罪集团个数（个）	Number of Hunted down and Seized Criminal Gangs（person）	221	203	230	211	154	186	209
查获犯罪集团人数（人）	Number of Members of Hunted down and Seized Criminal Gangs（person）	985	938	1061	916	663	939	970
涉及案件（起）	Number of Cases Involved(case)	1102	847	1225	1328	622	1172	485
三、涉枪案件情况	**Data on Cases with Guns Involved**							
立案数（起）	Number of Registered Cases(caes)	34	37	10	11	25	16	13
破案数（起）	Number of Cleared up Cases(caes)	32	35	8	9	24	11	10
破案率（%）	Percent of Cleared up Cases(%)	94.1	94.6	80.0	81.8	96.0	68.8	76.9

19-31 主要年份治安案件情况

Data on Public Order Cases in Representative Years

指 标	Item	2005	2006	2007	2008	2009	2010	2011
案件数情况	**Data on Number of Cases**							
受理数（起）	Number of Accepted Cases	45484	40550	41213	45226	45925	58968	63289
查处数（起）	Number of Investigated and Prosecuted Cases	40743	35598	38737	44202	45871	57151	62647
查处率（%）	Percent of Investigated and Prosecuted Cases(%)	89.6	87.8	94.0	97.7	99.9	96.9	99.0
查处违法犯罪人数（人）	Number of Investigated and Prosecuted Law-breakers and Crime Committer(person)	48949	37109	36739	38606	39214	45856	44199

19-32 各区县刑事、治安案件情况（2011年）

Data on Criminal Cases and Public Order Cases Grouped by Region（2011）

单位：件 (case)

区县 Region	刑事案件 Criminal cases			治安案件 Public order cases		
	立案数 Number of Registered Cases	破案数 Number of Cleared up Cases	破案率 (%) Percent of Ceared up Cases (%)	受理数 Number of Accepted Cases	查处数 Number of Investigated and Prosecuted Cases	查处率 (%) Percent of Investigated and Prosecuted Cases(%)
新城区 Xincheng	5265	1687	32.0	6571	6571	100.0
碑林区 Beilin	6055	1990	32.9	9653	9643	99.9
莲湖区 Lianhu	8909	2811	31.6	7960	7907	99.3
灞桥区 Baqiao	4825	965	20.0	6983	6481	100.0
未央区 Weiyang	6253	1159	18.5	5890	5737	97.4
雁塔区 Yanta	12067	2354	19.5	6252	6252	100.0
阎良区 Yanliang	1227	450	36.7	987	778	78.8
临潼区 Lintong	2328	589	25.7	2064	2047	99.2
长安区 Chang'an	4631	734	15.8	1904	1898	99.7
蓝田县 Lantian	2112	650	30.8	2877	2767	96.2
周至县 Zhouzhi	1508	363	24.1	830	830	100.0
户　县 Huxian	1726	314	18.2	962	927	96.4
高陵县 Gaoling	1307	437	31.9	1219	1214	99.6

19-33 主要年份西安市人民检察院案件受理情况

Data on Acceptance of Cases of Xi'an People's Procuratorate

指　　标	Item	受 案 Acceptance of Cases					
		2006	2007	2008	2009	2010	2011
总　计	**Toatl**	**7354**	**7972**	**8924**	**8462**	**8044**	**12318**
一、贪污贿赂案件（件）	**Cases about Corporation and Bribery（case）**	**425**	**383**	**431**	**316**	**327**	**166**
二、渎职、侵权案件（件）	**Cases about Misprision and Tortious（case）**	**99**	**83**	**115**	**89**	**89**	**33**
三、审查逮捕（件）	**Examination and Arresting（case)**	**3175**	**3497**	**3835**	**3656**	**3476**	**5741**
决定逮捕贪污贿赂犯罪嫌疑人（人）	Suspects of Corporation and Bribery to be Arrested（person）	101	73	104	97	51	28
决定逮捕渎职、侵权犯罪嫌疑人（人）	Suspects of Misprision and Tortious to be Arrested（person）	16	4	11	11	2	
批准逮捕刑事犯罪嫌疑人（人）	Suspects of Criminal to be Arrested（person）	4480	4935	5702	5321	6130	5077
四、刑事立案监督、侦查活动监督（件）	**Supervision of Acceptance of Criminal Cases and Investigation（case）**	**163**	**204**	**218**	**159**	**343**	**89**
五、审查起诉（件）	**EXamination and Prosecution（case)**	**3492**	**3805**	**4325**	**4242**	**3809**	**6289**
被告人（人）被告人（人）	Prosecution of Corporation and Bribery to be Defendants（person）	169	126	158	159	163	102
起诉渎职、侵权犯罪被告人（人）	Prosecution of Misprision and Tortious to be Defendants（person）	16	23	15	11	22	7
起诉刑事犯罪被告人（人）	Prosecution of Criminal to be Defendants（person）	4524	4947	5435	5444	5761	4863

19-34 西安市中级人民法院案件基本情况（2011年）

Xi'an Intermediate People's Court Basic Data of the Law Cases（2011）

单位：件、万元 (case,10 000 yuan)

指 标	Item	合计结案 Number of Total Case	诉讼标的总金额 Subject Matter of Litigation the Total Amount	中级人民法院结案 Number of the Intermediate People's Court Case	中级人民法院诉讼标底总金额 The Intermediate People's Court Litigation Total Amount
合 计	**Total**	**71102**	**1062857.4**	**8712**	**616628.3**
一、刑 事	**Criminal**	**5851**	**8358.1**	**911**	**1905.2**
二、民商事	**Civil and Commercial Matters**	**46756**	**678767.0**	**6684**	**388575.0**
三、行 政	**Administration**	**656**	**6.0**	**174**	
四、申诉、申请再审	**Appeals，Apply for Retrial**	**2927**		**252**	
五、司法赔偿	**Judicial Indemnification**	**1**		**1**	
六、执 行	**Execution**	**14911**	**375726.4**	**690**	**226148.1**
海事海商	Maritime Affairs & Business				
知识产权	Intellectual Property	188	1094.5	143	1094.5
一 审	First Instance	46598	559984.7	1258	264357.9
二 审	Second Instance	6427	123019.2	6427	123019.2
审判监督	Trial Supervision	238	4127.2	84	3103.2

19-34 续表

Continued

单位：件、万元 (case,10 000 yuan)

指 标	Item	基层人民法院结案 Number of the Basic People's Court Case	基层人民法院诉讼标的总金额 The Basic People's Court Litigation Total Amount	其中人民法庭结案 Number of the People's Tribunal Case	其中人民法庭标的总金额 Total Number of the People's Tribunal Litigation
合 计	**Total**	**62390**	**446229.1**	**13389**	**47649.2**
一、刑 事	**Criminal**	**4940**	**6452.9**		
二、民商事	**Civil and Commercial Matters**	**40072**	**290192.0**	**13314**	**47607.1**
三、行 政	**Administration**	**482**	**6.0**		
四、申诉、申请再审	**Appeals，Apply for Retrial**	**2675**			
五、司法赔偿	**Judicial Indemnification**				
六、执 行	**Execution**	**14221**	**149578.3**	**75**	**42.1**
海事海商	Maritime Affairs & Business				
知识产权	Intellectual Property	45			
一 审	First Instance	45340	295626.9	13314	47607.1
二 审	Second Instance				
审判监督	Trial Supervision	154	1024.0		

主 要 统 计 指 标 解 释

艺术表演团体 指由文化部门主办或实行行业管理（经文化市场行政部门审批或已申报登记并领取相关许可证），专门从事表演艺术等活动的各类专业艺术表演团体，含民间职业剧团。如话剧团、方言话剧团、滑稽剧团、儿童剧团、歌剧团、木偶团、皮影团等以及由若干剧种组成的综合性专业艺术表演团体。不包括群众业余文艺表演团体。

艺术表演场馆 指由文化部门主办或实行行业管理（经文化市场行政部门审批或已申报登记并领取相关许可证），有观众席、舞台、灯光设备，公开售票、专供文艺团体演出的文化活动场所。附属于文化部门机构内非独立核算的剧场、排演场，公开营业的也应单独统计。

电影放映单位 指具有放映机器设备、固定或不固定的放映场所与专职或兼职的放映技术人员，经有关部门登记批准，经常为一定的观众对象放映电影的机构。包括经批准对外开放进行营业，并与电影发行放映管理机构分帐的专用放映单位和军委系统租片单位。

广播节目综合人口覆盖率 指根据国家广电总局制定的《广播电视人口覆盖率统计技术标准和方法》进行统计调查的，在对象区内采用无线、有线、卫星等技术手段能够收听到包括中央、省、地市、县广播节目其中任意一套的人口数占全国总人口数的百分比。

电视节目综合人口覆盖率 指根据国家广电总局制定的《广播电视人口覆盖率统计技术标准和方法》进行统计调查的，在对象区内采用无线、有线、卫星等技术手段能够收看到包括中央、省、地市、县级电视节目中任意一套的人口数占全国总人口数的百分比。

有线电视入户率 通过广播电视有线传输网收看电视节目的用户数占全国总户数的百分比。

等级运动员人数 指经考核正式批准授予等级运动员称号的人数。运动员等级分为国际级运动健将、运动健将、一级运动员、二级运动员、三级运动员、少年级运动员。

等级裁判员人数 指经考核正式批准授予等级裁判员称号的人数。裁判员等级分为国际裁判、国家级裁判、一级裁判、二级裁判、三级裁判。

体育场 指有400米跑道（中心含足球场），有固定道牙，跑道6条以上，并有固定看台的室外田径场地。体育场按看台容纳观众人数分为: 甲级25000人以上，乙级15000–25000人，丙级5000–15000人，丁级5000人以下。

体育馆 指有固定看台，可供篮球、排球、羽毛球、乒乓球、体操等项目训练比赛活动用的室内运动场地。体育馆按看台容纳观众人数分为: 甲级6000人以上，乙级4000–6000人，丙级2000–4000人，丁级2000人以下。

卫生机构 指从卫生行政部门取得《医疗机构执业许可证》，或从民政、工商行政、机构编制管理部门取得法人单位登记证书，为社会提供医疗保健、疾病控制、卫生监督服务或从事医学科研和教育等工作的单位。卫生机构包括医院、疗养院、社区卫生服务中心（站）、卫生院、门诊部、诊所（卫生所、医务室）、急救中心（站）、采供血机构、妇幼保健院（所、站）、专科疾病防治院（所、站）、疾病预防控制中心（防疫站）、卫生监督所、卫生监督监测机构、医学科研机构、医学在职培训机构、健康教育所（站）等其他卫生机构。

医疗机构 指从卫生行政部门取得《医疗机构执业许可证》的机构，包括医院、疗养院、社区卫生服务中心（站）、卫生院、门诊部、诊所（卫生所、医务室）、妇幼保健院（所、站）、专科疾病防治院（所、站）、急救中心（站）和临床检验中心。

社区卫生服务中心（站） 指为本社区居民提供预防、医疗、保健、康复、健康教育、计划生育技术服务等的基层卫生机构。包括社区卫生服务中心和社区卫生服务站。

卫生人员 指在医疗、预防保健、医学科研和在职教育等卫生机构工作的职工，包括卫生技术人员、其他技术人员、管理人员和工勤人员。

卫生技术人员 包括执业（助理）医师、注册护士、药师（士）、检验和影像人员等卫生专业人员。不包括从事管理工作的卫生技术人员。

执业医师 指《医师执业证》“级别”为“执业医师”且实际从事医疗、预防保健工作的人员，不包括实际从事管理工作的执业医师。执业医师类别分为临床、中医、口腔和公共卫生四类。

执业助理医师 指《医师执业证》“级别”为“执业助理医师”且实际从事医疗、预防保健工作的人员，不包括实际从事管理工作的执业助理医师。执业助理医师类别同样分为临床、中医、口腔和公共卫生四类。

死亡率（疾病） 指在一定时期内,在一定人群中,死于某病的频率。

死亡率=某期间内（因某病）死亡总数/同期平均人口数×100%

社会福利企业 指以集中安置有一定劳动能力的残疾人员就业为目的（残疾职工占生产人员10%以上）、带有社会福利性质的企业总称。主要包括福利工厂、假肢厂和其他福利企业。

公证人员 指在国家公证机关依法办理公证事务的司法人员，包括公证员、助理公证员和在公证处工作的其他人员。

办理公证文书 指公证处在一定时期内办结的公证文书件数。公证文书按司法部规定或批准的格式制作，包括国内公证和涉外公证两部分。国内公证分为经济合同公证和民事法律关系公证两大类。

调解人员 指在人民调解委员会担负调解民间一般民事纠纷和轻微违法行为引起纠纷的工作人员，包括调解委员会的委员和调解小组的调解员。

调解民间纠纷 指调解委员会依照法律规定，根据自愿原则，用说服教育的方法调解民间发生的有关民事权利和义务的争执，促成当事双方达到协议和谅解，解决纠纷。包括婚姻家庭纠纷，财产权益纠纷等，不包括法院受理调解的民事案件数。

受理劳动争议案件数 指劳动争议仲裁委员会根据国家有关规定，对劳动争议当事人的申请予以审查，符合受理条件而正式立案、准备处理的劳动争议案件数。

立案 指检察机关对犯罪线索进行初步调查后，认为存在职务犯罪事实并需要追究刑事责任时，依法决定作为刑事案件进行侦查的诉讼活动，是追究犯罪的开始。

Explanatory Notes on Main Statistical Indicators

Arts Performance Troupes refer to the various professional performing arts groups, which sponsored by the cultural sectors or guided by the cultural society (approved by the cultural market administration, or registered and permitted with the relative certificate), including non-governmental troupes, such as drama troupes, dialect troupes, comedy troupes, children troupes, Opera troupes, puppetry troupes, Shadowgraph troupes, etc., comprehensive professional arts performance troupes. The mass sparetime arts performance troupes are not included.

Arts Performance Places refer to the various sites for cultural activities, which sponsored by the cultural sectors or guided by the cultural society (approved by the cultural market administration, or registered and permitted with the relative certificate), with the facility of auditorium, stage, and lighting, and selling tickets in public, including the opera halls and rehearse sites, etc. which are affiliated to the culture sectors without independent financial accounts and open to the public.

Film Projection Units refer to units with film projection equipment, full or part time projectionists, permanent or non permanent places, approved by related administrative departments to show films regularly for certain groups of audience, including those film projection units which have been approved to give commercial shows and run business with independent accounting system as well as those film-renting units of the military system.

Radio Coverage of Population refers to the percentage of population, which can listen to one of central, provincial, city, prefecture, and county radio programs by wireless, cable, satellite and other technical means, in the surveying area, to total population, according to Statistical Standard and Method on Television and Radio Coverage of Population established by the State Administration of Broadcasting, Film and Television.

Television Coverage of Population refers to the percentage of population, which can watch one of central, provincial, city, prefecture, and county television programs by wireless, cable, satellite and other technical means, in the surveying area, to total population, according to Statistical Standard and Method on Television and Radio Coverage of Population established by the State Administration of Broadcasting, Film and Television.

Cable Television Coverage of Household refers to the percentage of household, which can watch television by cable of radio and television network, to total household.

Number of Athletes in Grades refers to the number of athletes who have been given titles through examination. The titles of athletes include international masters of sports, masters of sports, first-grade, second-grade and third-grade sportsmen and young athletes.

Number of Referees in Grades refers to the number of referees who have been given titles after examination. They are classified as international referees, national referees and referees of the first, second and third grades.

Stadiums refer to stadiums for track and field events with six lane 400-meter tracks around soccer fields, permanent track marks and permanent bleachers. Stadiums are classified according to seating capacity. they include: class a stadiums seating 25000 people each. class b stadiums seating 15000 to 25000 people each. Class C stadiums seating 5000 to 15000 people each, and Class D stadiums seating fewer than 5000 people.

Gymnasiums refer to indoor sports grounds with permanent seats in which basketball, volleyball. badminton, table tennis and gymnastics competitions can be held. Gymnasiums are classified according to seating capacity. They include Class A gymnasiums seating over 6000 people. Class B gymnasiums seating 4000 to 6000 people. Class C gymnasiums seating 2000 to 4000 people, and Class D gymnasiums seating fewer than 2000 people.

Health Care Institutions refer to the units which have been qualified the Certification of Health Care Institution by the administration of public health, or qualified the Certification of Corporate Unit by the civil affairs, administration for industry and commerce, commission office for public sector reform, and engaging in medical care, disease prevention and control, health supervision and inspection, medicine research and health education, etc., including: hospitals, sanatoriums, community health service centers (stations), health centers, clinics (health stations and infirmaries), first-aid centres (stations), blood gathering and supplying institutions, women and children care agencies (centres and stations), special disease prevention and curing agencies (centres and stations), disease prevention and control centres (epidemic prevention stations), health supervision and inspection agencies, sanitary inspection institutions, medicinal scientific research and on-job training institutions, health education centres and so on.

Medical Organizations refer to the institutions which have been qualified the Certification of Health Care Institution by the administration of public health, including: hospitals, sanatoriums, community health service centers (stations), health centers, clinics (health stations and infirmaries), women and children care agencies (centres and stations), special disease prevention and curing agencies (centres and stations), first-aid centres (stations) and clinic inspection centers.

Community Health Service Centres (stations) refer to the primary units that provide the health care for community residents, such as disease prevention and control, medical treatment, health care, rehabilitation, health education, family planning technical services, including community health service centres and community health service stations.

Health Care Employee refer to all employee engaged in the health care institutions, such as medical organizations, disease prevention and control centres, health care agencies, medicinal scientific research and on-job training institutions, including medical technical personnel, other technical personnel, manager and labour.

Medical Technical Personnel refer to the professional staff engaged in health care, including licensed (assistant) doctors, registered nurse, pharmacists, laboratory technician, and imaging staff, excluding the medical technical personnel engaged in management job.

Licensed Doctors refer to the medical workers who have obtained the licenses of qualified doctors and are employed in medical treatment, disease prevention or healthcare institutions, excluding the licensed doctors engaged in management job. The licensed doctors are divided into 4 categories: clinician, Chinese medicine physicians, dentist and public health physicians.

Licensed Assistant Doctors refer to the medical workers who have obtained the licenses of qualified assistant doctors and are employed in medical treatment, disease prevention or healthcare institutions, excluding the licensed assistant doctors engaged in management job. The classification of licensed assistant doctors is clinician, Chinese medicine, dentist and public health.

Mortality Rate refers to the ratio of deaths caused by diseases at reference period to the certain group of population.

Mortality Rate = total deaths (caused by diseases) at reference period/average population at same period × 100%.

Social Welfare Enterprises refers to those welfare-oriented enterprises employing a significant number of handicapped people with certain labour ability (handicapped employees shall exceed 10% of the production staff), including welfare factories, artificial limb plants as well as other welfare enterprises.

Notary Personnel refers to judicial workers of the state notary offices handling notarization work according to law. They include notaries, assistant notaries, and other people working for notary offices.

Notarized Documents refer to the documents settled by notary offices in a year. The notary documents are drawn up in accordance with the regulations of the Ministry of Justice, including domestic documents and foreign-related documents. Domestic documents are divided into two major categories, documents on economic contracts and documents on civil legal relations.

Mediators refer to workers on peoples mediation committees responsible for mediating in civil disputes and cases of slight infraction of the law. They include members of the mediation committees and mediators of mediation groups.

Mediation of Civil Disputes refers to mediation committees work in mediating in civil disputes concerning civil rights and duties through persuasion and education in accordance with the provisions of law on a voluntary basis, so as to solve disputes by helping the parties involved come to an agreement and understanding. these disputes include divorce cases and disputes over property ownership, but exclude the civil cases to be handled by the court.

Number of Labour Dispute Cases Accepted refers to the number of cases of labour dispute submitted that, after being reviewed by the labour dispute arbitration committees in line with the relevant state regulations, are accepted and registered for treatment.

Acceptance of Case refers to the decision made by the procurators office to confirm the act of crime after initial investigation and to start legal proceedings of the case as criminal case.

20 企业调查

ENTERPRISES INVESTIGATION

资料整理：刘　艳

Data management:Liu Yan

第二十部分　企业调查

一、简要说明

本章资料主要包括各行业企业景气调查指数和企业家信心指数等，由国家统计局西安调查队提供。

二、主要指标

企业景气指数	127.9	比上年下降　5.2点
企业家信心指数	121.8	比上年下降　17.8点

20 ENTERPRISES INVESTIGATION

Ⅰ.Brief Introduction

Data in this chapter consists prosperity survey indices of various industries and Entrepreneur Expectation Indicator, provided by Enterprise Survey Crew of NBS Survey Office in Xi'an.

Ⅱ.Major Indicators

		Increase over Preceding Year
Business Climate Index	127.9	-5.2 points
Entrepreneur Expectation Indicator	121.8	-17.8 points

20-1 企业景气指数（2011年）

Business Climate Index（2011）

指　　标	Item	一季度 First Quarter	二季度 Second Quarter	三季度 Third Quarter	四季度 Forth Quarter
企业景气指数	**Business Climate Index**	**131.5**	**136.4**	**126.9**	**127.9**
按行业门类分	Grouped by Sector				
工业	Industry	120.4	128.9	117.5	122.1
建筑业	Construction	150.1	144.3	130.2	121.5
交通运输、仓储及邮政业	Transport, Storage and Post	150.6	146.3	146.3	144.1
批发和零售业	Wholesale and Retail Sales	133.9	131.7	126.9	132.5
房地产业	Real Estate	121.9	140.2	118.6	118.6
社会服务业	Social Services	136.8	136.6	132.9	138.2
信息传输 、计算机服务和软件业	Information Transmission, Computer Service and Safeware Service	154.6	163.6	154.6	147.7
住宿和餐饮业	Hotels and Catering Services	107.4	139.9	143.1	137.2
按企业（单位）登记注册类型分	Grouped by Registration				
国有企业	State-owned Enterprises	137.6	132.5	125.4	135.2
集体企业	Collective-owned Enterprises	122.7	130.4	122.7	130.8
股份合作企业	Share-holding Cooperative Enterprises	120.0	100.0	100.0	100.0
联营企业	Joint Ownership Enterprises				
有限责任公司	Limited Liability Corporations	116.7	127.6	111.6	115.0
股份有限公司	Share-holding Corporations Ltd.	129.1	150.3	145.5	142.2
私营企业	Privately Owned Enterprises	100.0	150.0	100.0	150.0
港、澳、台投资企业	Enterprises Invested by Foreigners or Investors from Hongkong,Macro and Taiwan	161.3	159.0	106.0	118.5
外商投资企业	Enterprises Invested by Foreigners or Investors from Hongkong,Macro and Taiwan	121.9	139.8	137.1	125.7
按企业规模分	Grouped by Size of Enterprises				
大型企业	Large-size	171.3	181.1	139.6	157.8
中型企业	Medium-size	126.4	130.7	127.7	124.7
小型企业	Small-size	97.6	105.7	108.6	106.5
特殊分组	Special-Grouped				
国家重点企业	State Key Enterprises	92.9	125.4	123.0	123.0
国家试点企业集团成员	Member of State Experimental Enterprises Group	92.9	118.7	118.7	118.7
出口企业	Town and Township Enterprises	140.7	152.4	126.7	123.8
上市公司	Listed Companies	150.7	162.7	148.4	146.3
国有控股企业	State-holding Enterprises	137.6	141.4	129.1	136.0
生产总量	Total Production	100.1	132.5	126.7	120.4
盈利（亏损）变化	Change of Profits or Losses	101.7	116.9	111.3	108.2
流动资金	Circulating Funds	91.0	82.6	77.3	77.4
货款拖欠	Delinquent Loans	104.6	90.0	96.1	96.1
劳动力需求	Demand of Labor Force	117.2	124.5	120.0	111.0
固定资产投资	Investment of fixed Assets	109.7	117.0	110.9	107.9
产品订货	Product Order	111.1	122.8	114.6	101.7
企业融资	Accommodation	76.7	72.9	72.9	71.2

20-2 企业家信心指数（2011年）

Entrepreneur Expectation Indicator（2011）

指　　标	Item	一季度 First Season	二季度 Second Season	三季度 Third Season	四季度 Fourth Season
企业家信心指数	**Entrepreneur Expectation Indicator**	**141.7**	**133.6**	**129.3**	**121.8**
按行业门类分	Grouped by Sector				
工业	Industry	134.7	127.3	127.9	122.9
建筑业	Construction	156.4	132.3	120.8	106.5
交通运输、仓储及邮政业	Transport, Storage and Post	153.1	150.6	137.6	144.1
批发和零售业	Wholesale and Retail Sales	143.5	127.8	123.1	126.0
房地产业	Real Estate	103.2	96.6	91.6	62.5
社会服务业	Social Services	166.4	170.1	162.7	153.6
信息传输、计算机服务和软件业	Information Transmission, Computer Service and Safeware Service	143.3	143.3	134.2	134.2
住宿和餐饮业	Hotels and Catering Services	126.2	148.1	151.3	120.5
按企业登记注册类型分	Grouped by Registration				
国有企业	State-owned Enterprises	147.6	131.9	130.0	127.6
集体企业	Collective-owned Enterprises	130.8	138.1	123.1	130.4
股份合作企业	Share-holding Cooperative Enterprises	140.0	125.0	100.0	100.0
联营企业	Joint Ownership Enterprises				
有限责任公司	Limited Liability Corporations	132.2	122.1	118.8	114.7
股份有限公司	Share-holding Corporations Ltd.	138.6	136.5	134.2	127.3
私营企业	Privately Owned Enterprises	150.0	150.0	150.0	150.0
港、澳、台投资企业	Enterprises Invested by Foreigners or Investors from Hongkong,Macro and Taiwan	138.6	127.5	121.2	96.6
外商投资企业	Enterprises Invested by Foreigners or Investors from Hongkong,Macro and Taiwan	121.8	142.9	145.7	125.7
按企业规模分	Grouped by Size of Enterprises				
大型企业	Large-size	171.7	143.0	144.2	143.8
中型企业	Medium-size	137.1	138.0	127.1	119.9
小型企业	Small-size	117.7	114.3	118.7	106.5
特殊分组	Special-Grouped				
国家重点企业	State Key Enterprises	132.5	120.5	107.1	102.3
国家试点企业集团成员	Member of State Experimental Enterprises Group	118.7	107.4	92.9	88.7
出口企业	Town and Township Enterprises	152.7	132.7	123.6	122.4
上市公司	Listed Companies	153.1	130.4	123.9	119.5
国有控股企业	State-holding Enterprises	148.7	135.1	132.1	129.6

主要统计指标解释

企业景气指数：是根据企业家对本企业综合生产经营情况所作的判断与预期（通常是对“良好”、“一般”、“不佳”的选择）而编制的指数，用以综合反映企业的生产经营状况。企业景气指数也称“企业综合生产经营景气指数”。

企业家信心指数：是根据企业家对企业外部市场经济环境与宏观政策的认识、看法判断和预期（通常是对“乐观”、“一般”、“不乐观”的选择）而编制的指数，用以综合反映企业家对宏观经济环境的感受与信心。企业家信心指数也称“宏观经济景气指数”。

景气指数的表示方式：景气指数的表示范围在0～200之间，其含义：100为景气指数的临界值，表明景气状况变化不大；100～200为景气区间，表明景气状况趋于上升或改善，越接近于200，状况越景气；0～100为不景气区间，表明经济状况趋于下降或恶化，越接近于0，状况越不景气。

Explanatory Notes on Main Statistical Indicators

Business Climate Index it is an index worked out according to the judgment and anticipation (normally a choice from good , ordinary , not good) of entrepreneurs made based on synthetic productive and operational situation of the enterprise. It is used to reflect synthetically the productive and operational situation of the enterprise. It is also referred to as synthetic productive and operational prosperity index of enterprise .

Confidence index of entrepreneur it is an index worked out according to the judgment and anticipation (normally a choice from optimistic , ordinary , not optimistic) of entrepreneurs made based on their understandings and views of the market and economic environment outside the enterprise and the macro policies. It is used to reflect synthetically the confidence and feelings of the entrepreneurs to the macro economic environment. It is also referred to as macro-economy prosperity index .

The way to express prosperity index the range of prosperity index is from 0 to 200; 100 is the critical value, and means economic situation didn't change largely; from 100 to 200 is the interval of prosperity; and from 0 to 100 is the interval of not prosperity, meaning economic situation is going down or worse, the closer to 0, the worse the economic situation.

中国统计出版社最新资料书简目

（仅供参考，以最后出书为准）

统计资料

中国统计年鉴-2012　中国统计摘要-2012　国际统计年鉴-2012

2012中国发展报告　中国第三产业统计年鉴-2012　中国区域经济统计年鉴-2012

中国劳动统计年鉴-2012　中国社会统计年鉴-2012　中国城市统计年鉴-2009

中国建筑业统计年鉴-2012　中国人口和就业统计年鉴-2012　中国工业经济统计年鉴-2012

中国商品交易市场统计年鉴-2012　中国房地产统计年鉴-2012　中国能源统计年鉴-2012

中国民政统计年鉴-2012　中国贸易外经统计年鉴-2012　2012中国地区经济监测报告

中国科技统计年鉴-2012　中国农村统计年鉴-2012　中国农产品价格调查年鉴-2012

中国高技术产业统计年鉴-2012　中国教育经费统计年鉴-2010　中国农村贫困监测报告-2012

全国农产品成本收益资料汇编-2012　中国科学技术协会统计年鉴-2012　工业企业科技活动资料-2012

大中型批发零售和住宿餐饮企业统计年鉴-2012　中国农村住户调查年鉴-2012（中、英文）　中国城市(镇)生活与价格年鉴-2012

中国县（市）社会经济统计年鉴-2012　第二次全国R&D资源清查资料汇编－工业企业卷　中国农村全面建设小康监测报告-2012

第二次全国R&D资源清查资料汇编－综合卷　中国民族统计年鉴2011、2012　中国零售和餐饮连锁企业统计年鉴-2012

2010年中国第六次人口普查公报

2012年省级综合统计年鉴系列

北京　天津　河北　山西　内蒙古　辽宁　吉林　黑龙江　上海　江苏　浙江　安徽　福建　江西　山东

河南　湖北　湖南　广东　广西　海南　重庆　四川　贵州　云南　西藏　陕西　甘肃　青海　宁夏

新疆　新疆生产建设兵团

2012年市（县）级综合统计年鉴系列

天津滨海新区　石家庄　唐山　邯郸　太原　大同　长治　阳泉　晋城　朔州　晋中

运城　忻州　临汾　呼和浩特　包头　沈阳　大连　长春　吉林市　四平　哈尔滨　黑龙江垦区

上海浦东新区　苏州　无锡　常州　徐州　南通　盐城　镇江　江阴　丹阳

杭州　宁波　绍兴　台州　温州　金华　嘉兴　衢州　福州　福州经济技术开发区

厦门经济特区　南昌　上饶　济南　青岛　潍坊　郑州　洛阳　三门峡　南阳　武汉　宜昌

十堰　荆州　咸宁　长沙　广州　东莞　惠州　深圳　桂林　南宁　柳州　来宾　河池　海口　成都　绵阳

贵阳　昆明　庆阳　西安　兰州　银川　乌鲁木齐

2010年人口普查资料系列

中国2010年人口普查资料　北京　天津　河北　山西　内蒙古　辽宁　吉林　黑龙江　上海　江苏

浙江　安徽　福建　江西　山东　河南　湖北　湖南　广东　广西　海南　重庆　四川　贵州　云南

西藏　陕西　甘肃　青海　宁夏　新疆　新疆生产建设兵团　河南省各市2010年人口普查资料丛书

中国分县2010年人口普查资料　中国分乡镇、街道2010年人口普查资料　中国分民族2010年人口普查资料

“十一五”规划教材

非参数统计　医学统计学　概率论与数理统计　统计学　现代金融投资统计分析

多元统计分析　经济计量学教程　应用时间序列分析　统计指数理论及应用

统计数据处理概论　质量管理统计方法　社会统计学　多元统计分析实验

企业经营管理统计　市场调查与预测　统计学原理（非统计专业使用）

统计学:从数据到结论　国民经济核算教程（国民经济统计学）　概率论与数理统计（经济、管理类专业使用）

重点图书

挑大学选专业2012—高考志愿填报指南　挑大学选专业2012—考研择校指南
